Status Bar

| 7.0000, 0.0000,0.0000 | SNAP | GRID | ORTHO | OSNAP | MODEL | TILE |

X,y,z-coordinates   Snap   Grid   Ortho   Osnap   Paper Tilemode /Model Space

Layer Icons

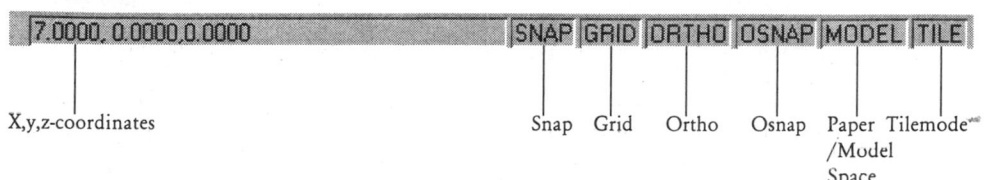

Name	On	Freeze in All Viewports	Freeze in Current Viewport	Freeze in New Viewports	Lock	Color	Linetype
0						White	Continuous
Layer1						Yellow	Hot_water_supply

Layers   On/Off   Freeze/Thaw in current viewport   Freeze/Thaw in new viewports.   Color   Linetype

Freeze/Thaw in all viewports.   Lock/Unlock

Object Properties Toolbar

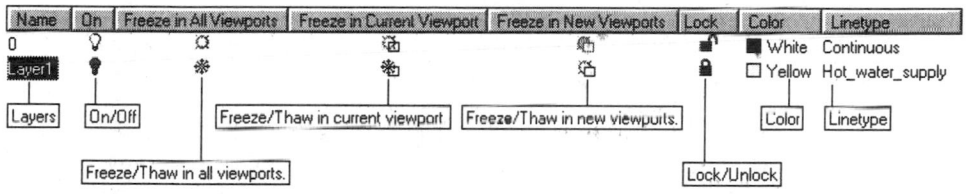

Make Object Layer Current   Display Layer Dialog Box   Layer Properties   Select Color   Display Linetype Dialog Box   Select Linetype   Object Properties

Command Line Keystrokes

Enter or ⎵	Executes the command.
←	Moves cursor back to the left.
Home	Places cursor at the beginning of the line.
End	Places cursor at the end of the line.
→	Moves cursor forward to the right.
Insert	Turns insertion mode and off.
Delete	Deletes the character to the right of the cursor.
Ctrl + H	Or Backspace: Deletes the character to the left of the cursor.
↑	Displays the previous line in the command history.
↓	Displays the next line in the command history.
Ctrl + V	Pastes text from the Clipboard.

The Illustrated

AutoCAD

Quick Reference Guide R14

RALPH GRABOWSKI

NOTICE TO THE READER

Trademarks

COPYRIGHT © 1998
Delmar Publishers Inc.
Autodesk Press imprint
an International Thomson Publishing Company

The ITP logo is a trademark under license.
Printed in the United States of America

For more information, contact

Autodesk Press
3 Columbia Circle, Box 15-015
Albany, New York USA 12212-5015

International Thomson Editores
Campos Eliseos 385, Piso 7
Colonia Polanco
11560 Mexico D. F. Mexico

International Thomson Publishing Europe
Berkshire House 168-173
High Holborn
London, WC1V 7AA
United Kingdom

International Thomson Publishing GmbH
Konigswinterer Strasse 418
53227 Bonn Germany

International Thomson Publishing France
Tour Maine-Montparnasse
33, Avenue du Maine
75755 Paris Cedex 15, France

Thomas Nelson Australia
102 Dodds Street
South Melbourne, Victoria 3205
Australia

International Thomson Publishing–Japan
Hirakawacho Kyowa Building, 3F
2-2-1 Hirakawa-cho Chiyoda-ku
Tokyo 102 Japan

Nelson Canada
1120 Birchmont Road
Scarborough, Ontario
Canada, M1K 5G4

International Thomson Publishing Asia
221 Henderson Road
#05-10 Henderson Building
Singapore 0315

International Thomson Publishing Southern Africa
Building 18, Constantia Park
240 Old Pretoria Road
P.O. Box 2459
Halfway House, 1685 South Africa

5 6 7 8 9 10 XXX 03 02 01 00 99 98

Library of Congress Cataloging-in-Publication Data
Grabowski, Ralph.
    The illustrated AutoCAD quick reference : release 14 / Ralph Grabowski.
        p.   cm.
    Includes index.
    ISBN 0-7668-0126-8
    1. Computer graphics. 2. AutoCAD (Computer file) I. Title.
T385.G692423   1998
620'.0042'02855369—dc21

97–25354
CIP

Contents

About This Book

The Illustrated AutoCAD Quick Reference R14, presents concise facts about all commands found in AutoCAD Release 14. The clear format of this reference book demonstrates each command starting on its own page, illustrated by 670 figures, plus these exclusive features:

- All variations of commands, such as **OSnap, -Osnap,** and **DdOsnap.**
- More than a dozen"Quick Start" mini-tutorials that help you get started quicker.
- Over 100 definitions of acronyms and hard-to-understand terms.
- More than 850 context-sensitive tips.
- Full coverage of the Bonus CAD Tools in Appendix A.
- All system variables, including those not listed by the **SetVar** command, in Appendix B.
- Obsolete commands that no longer work in Release 14, in Appendix C.

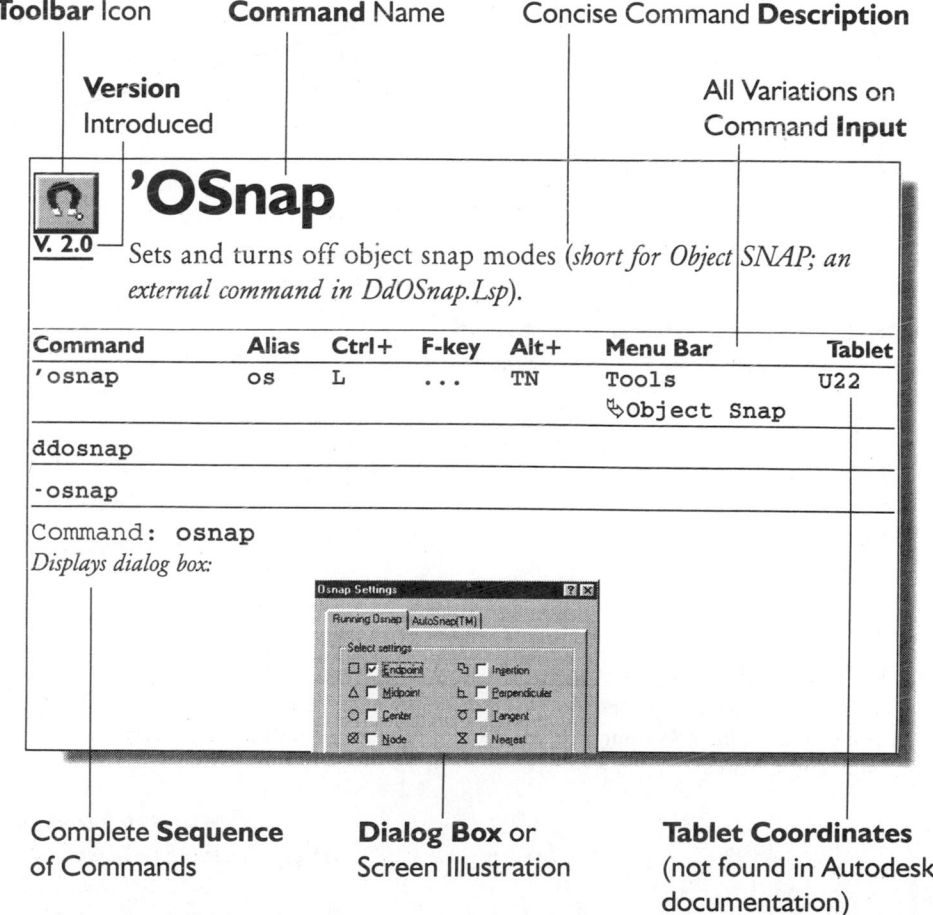

Toolbar Icon   **Command** Name   Concise Command **Description**

Version Introduced   All Variations on Command **Input**

'OSnap

V. 2.0 — Sets and turns off object snap modes (*short for Object SNAP; an external command in DdOSnap.Lsp*).

Command	Alias	Ctrl+	F-key	Alt+	Menu Bar	Tablet
'osnap	os	L	...	TN	Tools ↳Object Snap	U22
ddosnap						
-osnap						

Command: **osnap**
Displays dialog box:

Complete **Sequence** of Commands   **Dialog Box** or Screen Illustration   **Tablet Coordinates** (not found in Autodesk documentation)

COMMAND NAMES

The name of the command is in mixed upper and lower case to help you understand the source of the command name, which is often condensed. For example, DdAttDef is short for "Dynamic Dialog ATTribute DEFinition." Each command incudes all alternative methods of command input:

- Alternate command spelling, such as **Donut** and **Doughnut**.
- ' (the apostrophe prefix) indicates transparent commands, such as **'blipmode**.
- All aliases, such as **L** for the **Line** command.
- Pull-down menu picks, such as **Draw ⬎ Construction Line** for the **XLine** command.
- Control-key combinations, such as **[Ctrl]+E** for the **Isoplane** toggle.
- Function keys, such as **[F1]** for the **Help** command.
- Alt-key combinations, such as **[Alt]+TS** for the **Spell** command.
- Table menu coordinates, such as **M2** for the **Hide** command.

The brief command description notes when the command is an *external* command (defined by an AutoLISP, ADS, or ObjectARx routine), a command *renamed* from an earlier release of AutoCAD, or is *undocumented* by Autodesk.

VERSION & RELEASE NUMBERS

The version or release number indicates when the command first appeared in AutoCAD, such as **V. 1.0** or **Rel. 14**. This is useful when working with older versions of AutoCAD. See Appendix C for the list of commands removed from every release of AutoCAD.

RELATED COMMANDS & VARIABLES

Each command includes one or more of the following:

- Command line options.
- Dialog box options.
- Right-click options.
- Related commands.
- Related toolbar icons.
- Related system variables.
- Related dimension variables.
- Related files and blocks.

DEFINITIONS & TIPS

Many commands include one or more tips that help you use the command more efficiently or warn you of the command's limitations. Fifteen commands include a list of definitions of acronyms and jargon words.

Ralph Grabowski
Abbotsford, British Columbia, Canada
June 21, 1997
Contact: ralphg@xyzpress.com

'About

Rel.12 Displays the AutoCAD version, serial number, and copyright notice.

Command	Alias	Ctrl+	F-key	Alt+	Menu Bar	Tablet
'about	...	...	...	HA	Help	...
					↳About AutoCAD	

Command: **about**
Displays dialog box:

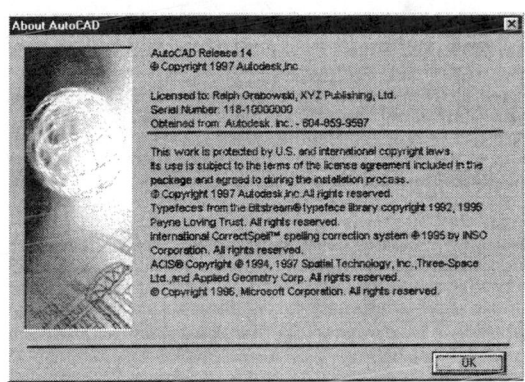

DIALOG BOX OPTION
OK   Dismisses dialog box.

RELATED COMMANDS
Status   Displays information about the drawing and environment.
Stats   Displays information about the rendering environment.

RELATED SYSTEM VARIABLES
_PkSer   The AutoCAD software serial number.
_Server   Network authorization code.

TIP
■ "Serial" is an alias for the **_PkSer** system variable.

AcisIn

Rel.13 Imports an SAT file (*short for "save as text," an ASCII-format ACIS file*) into the drawing, then creates 3D solids, 2D regions, and bodies.

Command	Alias	Ctrl+	F-key	Alt+	Menu Bar	Tablet
acisin	...	...	...	IA	Insert ⬐ACIS Solid	...

Command: **acisin**
Displays dialog box:

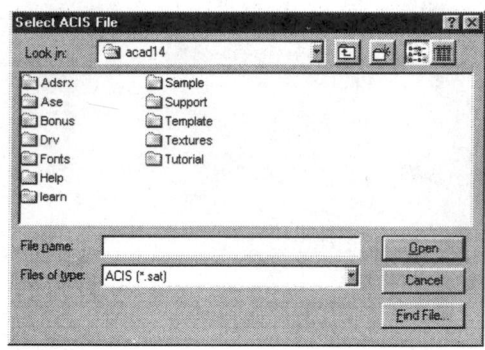

DIALOG BOX OPTIONS
Cancel   Dismisses the dialog box.
Find File   Searches the hard drive and network for the filename.
Open   Opens the SAT file.

RELATED COMMANDS
AcisOut   Exports ACIS objects (3D solids, 2D regions, and bodies) to an SAT file.
AmeConvert   Converts AME v2.0 and v2.1 solid models and regions into ACIS solids.

RELATED FILE
*.SAT   The ASCII format of ACIS model files.

TIP
- ACIS is short for the "Andy, Charles, Ian's System," the solids modeling engine from Spatial Technologies used in Release 13, 14, and Designer.

AcisOut

Rel.13 Exports AutoCAD 3D solids, 2D regions, and bodies to an SAT file.

Command	Alias	Ctrl+	F-key	Alt+	Menu Bar	Tablet
acisout	...	...	...	FE	File	...
				⌂ACIS	⌂Export	
					⌂ACIS	

```
Command: acisout
Select objects: [pick]
Select objects: [Enter]
```
Displays dialog box:

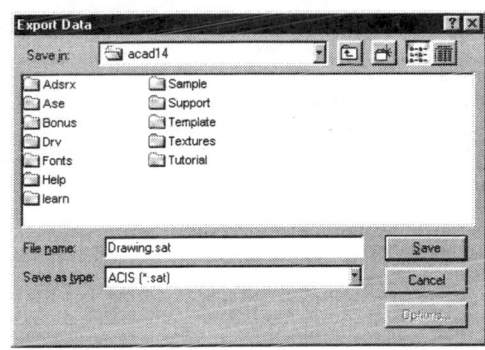

DIALOG BOX OPTIONS
Cancel	Dismisses the dialog box.
Save	Saves the selected objects as a SAT file.

RELATED COMMANDS
AcisIn	Imports an SAT file and creates 3D solids, 2D regions, and bodies.
StlOut	Exports ACIS solid model in STL format.
3dsOut	Exports ACIS solid models as 3D faces.

RELATED FILE
*.SAT	The ASCII format of ACIS model files.

TIPS
- **AcisOut** does not export objects that are not 3D solids, 2D regions, or bodies.

- SAT files can be read by other ACIS-based CAD programs.

Ai_Box *etc.*

Rel.11 Draws nine basic 3D surface wireframe objects from polygon meshes: box, pyramid, wedge, dome, dish, mesh, sphere, cone, and torus (*an external command in 3d.Lsp*).

Command	Alias	Ctrl+	F-key	Alt+	Menu Bar	Tablet
ai_box	...	...	...	...	...	...
ai_cone	...	...	...	...	...	...
ai_dish	...	...	...	...	...	...
ai_dome	...	...	...	...	...	...
ai_mesh	...	...	...	...	...	...
ai_pyramid	...	...	...	...	...	...
ai_sphere	...	...	...	...	...	...
ai_torus	...	...	...	...	...	...
ai_wedge	...	...	...	...	...	...

```
Command: ai_box
Corner of box: [pick]
Length: [pick]
Cube/<Width>: [pick]

Command: ai_cone
Base center point: [pick]
Diameter/<radius> of base: [pick]
Diameter/<radius> of top: [pick]
Height: [pick]
Number of segments <16>: [Enter]

Command: ai_dish
Center of dish: [pick]
Diameter/<radius>: [pick]
Number of longitudinal segments <16>: [Enter]
Number of latitudinal segments <16>: [Enter]

Command: ai_dome
Center of dome:[pick]
Diameter/<radius>:[pick]
Number of longitudinal segments <16>: [Enter]
Number of latitudinal segments <16>: [Enter]
```

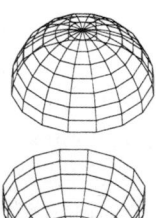

```
Command: ai_mesh
First corner:[pick]
Second corner:[pick]
Third corner:[pick]
Fourth corner:[pick]
Mesh M size:
Mesh N size:

Command: ai_pyramid
First base point: [pick]
Second base point: [pick]
Third base point: [pick]
Tetrahedron/<Fourth base point>: [pick]
Ridge/Top/<Apex point>: [pick]
```
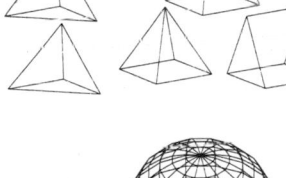
```
Command: ai_sphere
Diameter/<radius>: [pick]
Number of longitudinal segments <16>: [pick]
Number of latitudinal segments <16>: [pick]
```
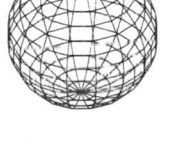
```
Command: ai_torus
Center of torus: [pick]
Diameter/<radius> of torus: [pick]
Diamter/<radius> of tube: [pick]
Segments around tube circumference <16>: [Enter]
Segments around torus circumference <16>: [Enter]
```
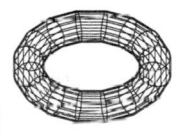
```
Command: ai_wedge
Corner of wedge: [pick]
Length: [pick]
Width: [pick]
Height: [pick]
Rotation angle about Z axis: [pick]
```

RELATED COMMANDS

3D	Displays a dialog box with all nine 3D surface objects.
Box	Draws a 3D solid box.
Cone	Draws a 3D solid cone.
Cylinder	Draws a 3D solid cylinder.
Sphere	Draws a 3D solid sphere.
Torus	Draws a 3D solid torus.
Wedge	Draws a 3D solid wedge.

RELATED SYSTEM VARIABLES

SurfU	Surface mesh density in the m-direction.
SurfV	Surface mesh density in the n-direction.

TIPS

- You *cannot* perform Boolean operations (such as intersect, subtract, and union) on 3D surface objects.

- You cannot convert 3D surface objects into 3D solid objects.

- To convert 3D solid objects into 3D surface objects, export with the **3dsOut** command, then import with the **3dsIn** command.

- Variants of 3D objects drawn by the **Ai_** series of commands:

Command	Variant
Ai_Box	Rectangular box, cube.
Ai_Cone	Pointy cone, truncated cone.
Ai_Pyramid	Pyramid, truncated pyramid, tetrahedron, truncated tetrahedron, roof shape.
Ai_Torus	Donut, football.

- Mesh m- and n-sizes are limited to values between 2 and 256.

 Align

Rel.12 Moves, transforms, and rotates objects in three dimensions (*an external command in Geom3d.Exp*).

Command	Alias	Ctrl+	F-key	Alt+	Menu Bar	Tablet
align	al	...	...	M3L	Modify ↳3D Operation ↳Align	X14

```
Command: align
Select objects: [pick]
Select objects: [Enter]
1st source point: [pick]
1st destination point: [pick]
2nd source point: [pick]
2nd destination point: [pick]
3rd source point: [pick]
3rd destination point: [pick]
```

COMMAND LINE OPTIONS

1st point	Moves object in 2D or 3D when one source and destination point are picked.
2nd point	Moves, rotates, and scales object in 2D or 3D when two source and destination points are picked.
3rd point	Moves, rotates, and scales object in 3D when three source and destination points are picked.

RELATED COMMANDS

Move	Performs a move in two dimensions.
Mirror3d	Mirrors objects in three dimensions.
Rotate3d	Rotates objects in three dimensions.

TIPS

■ Enter the first pair of points to define the move distance:

```
1st source point: [pick]
1st destination point: [pick]
2nd source point: [Enter]
```

■ Enter two pairs of points to define a 2D (or 3D) transformation, scaling, and rotation:

Points	Alignment Defined
First	Basepoint for alignment.
Second	Rotation angle.
Third	Scale based on distance between 1st and 2nd destination points.

■ The third pair defines the 3D transformation.

AmeConvert

Rel.13 Converts solid models and regions created by AME v2.0 and v2.1 (*from AutoCAD Release 12*) into ACIS solids models.

Command	Alias	Ctrl+	F-key	Alt+	Menu Bar	Tablet
ameconvert	...	...	...	...	...	...

```
Command: ameconvert
Select objects: [pick]
Processing Boolean operations.
```

COMMAND LINE OPTION

Select object   Selects AME objects to convert; ignores non-AME objects.

RELATED COMMAND

AcisIn   Imports ACIS models from an SAT file.

TIPS

- After conversion, the AME model remains in the drawing in the same location as the ACIS model. Erase, if necessary.

- AME holes may become blind holes in ACIS.

- AME fillets and chamfers may be placed higher or lower in ACIS.

- Once the **AmeConvert** command converts a Release 12 PADL drawing into Release 14 ACIS model, it cannot be converted back to PADL format.

- Old AME models are stored in Release 14 as an anonymous Block Reference.

DEFINITIONS

ACIS   The name of the solids modeling technology in AutoCAD R13 and R14.

AME   Short for "Advanced Modeling Extension," the name of the solids modeling module used by AutoCAD in Release 10 through 12.

PADL   Short for "Parts and Description Language," the solids modeling technology used in AutoCAD Release 10 through 12.

'Aperture

V. 1.3 Sets the size, in pixels, of the object snap target height (or box cursor).

Command	Alias	Ctrl+	F-key	Alt+	Menu Bar	Tablet
'aperture	...	...	...	...	...	...

```
Command: aperture
Object snap target height (1-50 pixels) <10>:
```

Aperture size = 1 (left), 10 (center), and 50 pixels (right):

RELATED COMMANDS

DdOSnap   Sets the aperture size interactively.
DdSelect   Sets the size of the object selection pickbox.
OSnap   Sets the object snap modes.

RELATED SYSTEM VARIABLE

Aperture   Contains the current target height, in pixels:

Aperture	Meaning
1	Minimum size.
10	Default size, in pixels.
50	Maximum size.

TIPS

- This box cursor only appears during object snap selection; to change the size of the pick cursor, use the **Pickbox** command.

- Use the **DdOsnap** command to visually change the size of the aperture.

'AppLoad

Rel.12 Creates a list of AutoLISP, ADS, and ObjectARx applications to load (*an external file in Acadapp.Exp; short for APPlication LOADer*).

Command	Alias	Ctrl+	F-key	Alt+	Menu Bar	Tablet
'appload	ap	...	...	TL	Tools ⌖Load Applications	V10

Command: **appload**
Displays dialog box:

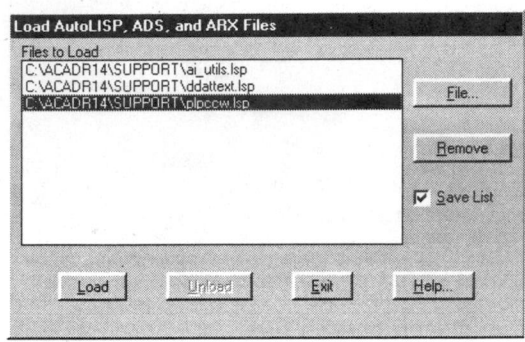

DIALOG BOX OPTIONS

File	Displays file dialog box to select LSP (AutoLISP), EXE (ADS), and ARX (ObjectARx) files.
Remove	Removes selected filenames from the list.
Save List	Saves the list to file AppLoad.Dfs.
Load	Loads all or selected files into AutoCAD.
Unload	Unloads all or selected files out of AutoCAD.
Exit	Exits the dialog box.

RELATED COMMAND

Arx   Lists ObjectARx programs currently loaded in AutoCAD.

RELATED AUTOLISP FUNCTIONS

(load)	Loads an AutoLISP program.
(xload)	Loads an ADS program.
(autoload)	Predefines commands to load AutoLISP program.
(autoxload)	Predefines commands to load ADS program.

RELATED FILES

AppLoad.Dfs   Contains list of programs to load.
.Lsp,.Exe,*.Arx   AutoLISP, ADS, and ObjectARx programs loaded by **AppLoad**.

TIP

- Use the **AppLoad** command when AutoCAD does not automatically load a command or external application for you.

 # Arc

V. 1.0 Draws a 2D arc of less than 360 degrees, by eleven methods.

Command	Alias	Ctrl+	F-key	Alt+	Menu Bar	Tablet
arc	a	...	...	DA	Draw ⮑Arc	R10

```
Command: arc
Center/<Start point>: [pick]
Center/End/<Second point>: [pick]
Endpoint: [pick]
```

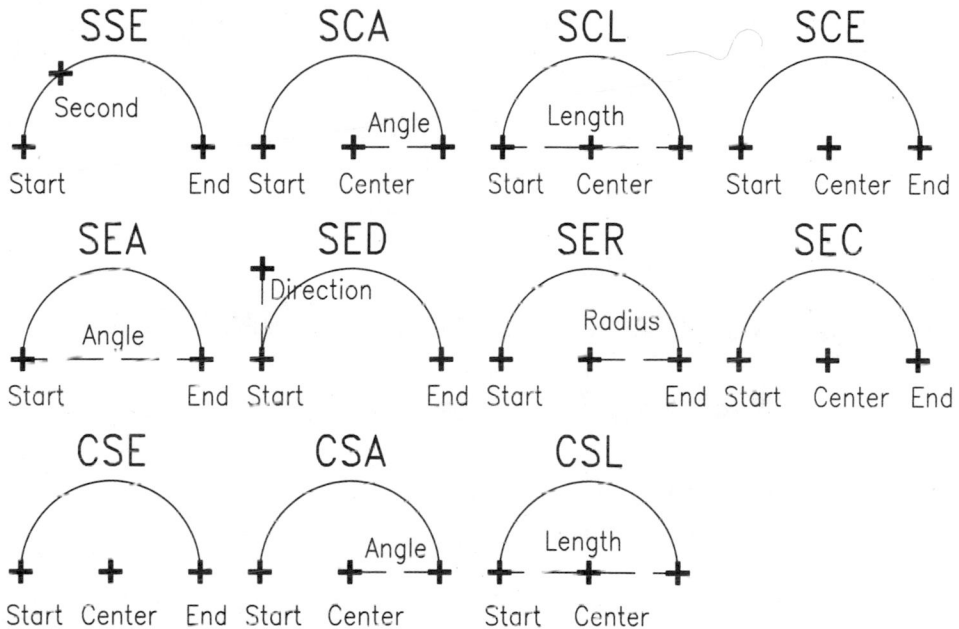

COMMAND LINE OPTIONS

SSE arc options:

Start point   Indicates the start point of a three-point arc (*see figure above*).
Second point   Indicates a second point anywhere along the arc.
Endpoint   Indicates the endpoint of the arc.

SCE, SCA, and SCL arc options:

Start point   Indicates the start point of a two-point arc.
Center   Indicates the center point of the arc.
Angle   Indicates the arc's included angle.
Length of chord Indicates the length of the arc's chord.
Endpoint   Indicate the endpoint of the arc.

SEA, SED, SER, and SEC arc options:

Start point   Indicates the start point of a two-point arc.
End   Indicates the endpoint of the arc.
Center point Indicates the arc's center point.
Angle   Indicates the arc's included angle.
Direction   Indicates the tangent direction from the arc's start point.
Radius   Indicates the arc's radius.

CSE, CSA, and CSL arc options:

Center   Indicates the center point of a two-point arc.
Start point   Indicates the arc's start point.
Endpoint   Indicates the arc's endpoint.
Angle   Indicates the arc's included angle.
Length of chord
                  Indicates the length of the arc's chord.

Continued arc option:

[Enter]   Continues arc from endpoint of last-drawn line or arc.

RELATED TOOLBAR ICONS

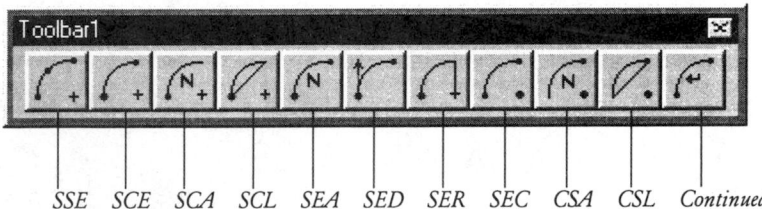

SSE   SCE   SCA   SCL   SEA   SED   SER   SEC   CSA   CSL   *Continued*

RELATED COMMANDS

Circle   Draws an "arc" of 360 degrees.
Ellipse   Draws elliptical arcs.
Polyline Draws connected polyline arcs.
ViewRes   Controls the roundness of arcs.

RELATED SYSTEM VARIABLE

LastAngle Saves the included angle of the last-drawn arc (*read-only*).

TIPS

- To precisely start an arc from the endpoint of the last line or arc, press **[Enter]** at the 'Enter/<Start point>' prompt.

- You can only drag the arc with during the last-entered option.

- Specifying an x,y,z-coordinate as the starting point of the arc draws the arc at the z-elevation.

- In some cases, it may be easier to draw a circle and use the **Break** and **Trim** commands to convert the circle into an arc.
- The components of an AutoCAD arc:

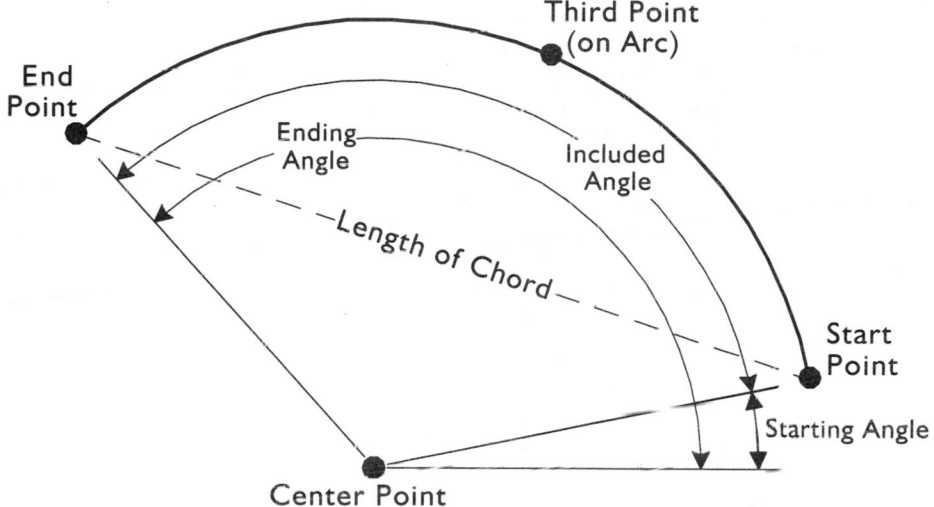

 # Area

V. 1.0   Calculates the area and perimeter of areas, closed objects, or polylines.

Command	Alias	Ctrl+	F-key	Alt+	Menu Bar	Tablet
area	aa	...	...	TQA	Tools ⓈInquiry ⓈArea	T7

```
Command: area
<First point>/Object/Add/Subtract: [pick]
Next point: [pick]
Next point: [pick]
Next point: [pick]
Next point: [Enter]
Area = 1.8398, Perimeter = 6.5245
```

COMMAND LINE OPTIONS

First point	Indicates the first point to begin measurement.
Object	Indicates the object to be measured.
Add	Switches to add-area mode.
Subtract	Switches to subtract-area mode.
Enter	Indicates the end of the area outline.

RELATED COMMANDS

Dist	Returns the distance between two points.
Id	Lists the x,y,z-coordinates of a selected point.

RELATED SYSTEM VARIABLES

Area	Contains the most recently calculated area.
Perimeter	Contains the most recently calculated perimeter.

TIPS

- At least three points must be picked to create an area.

- AutoCAD automatically "closes the polygon" before measuring the area.

- You can specify 2D x,y-coordinates or 3D x,y,z-coordinates.

- The **Object** option returns the following information:

Object	Measurement Returned
Circle, ellipse	Area and circumference.
Planar closed spline	Area and circumference.
Closed polyline, polygon	Area and perimeter.
Open objects	Area and length.
Region	Area of all objects in region.
Solid	Surface area.

- The area of a wide polyline is measured along its centerline; closed polylines must have only one closed area.

⊞ Array

Creates a 2D rectangular or polar array of objects.

Command	Alias	Ctrl+	F-key	Alt+	Menu Bar	Tablet
array	ar	...	...	MA	Modify ⤷Array	V18

```
Command: array
Select objects: [pick]
Select objects: [Enter]
```

Rectangular array options:
```
Rectangular or Polar array (R/P): r
Number of rows (—) <1>: [type number]
Number of columns (|||) <1>: [type number]
Unit cell or distance between rows (—): [show distance]
Distance between columns (|||): [show distance]
```

A 3-row by 5-column rectangular array:

Polar array options:
```
Rectangular or Polar array (R/P): p
Center point of array: [pick]
Number of items:
Angle to fill (+=ccw, -=cw) <360>:
Rotate objects as they are copied? <Y>
```

Nine-item polar arrays — rotated (left) and unrotated (right):

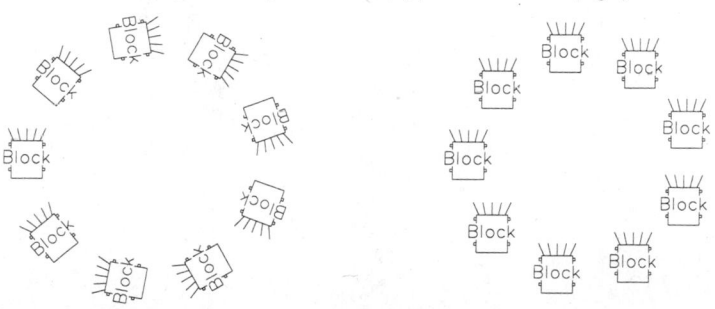

COMMAND LINE OPTIONS

R	Creates a rectangular array of the selected object.
P	Creates a polar array of the selected object.
Rows	Specifies number of horizontal rows.
Columns	Specifies number of vertical columns.
Unit cell	Specifies the vertical and horizontal spacing between objects.

RELATED TOOLBAR ICONS

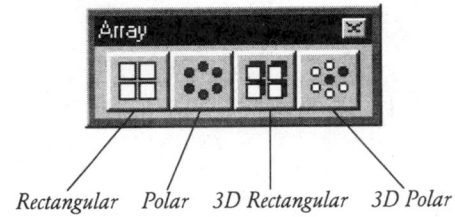

Rectangular   Polar   3D Rectangular   3D Polar

RELATED COMMANDS

3dArray	Creates rectangular or polar array in 3D space.
Copy	Creates one or more copies of the selected object.
MInsert	Creates a rectangular block array of blocks.

RELATED SYSTEM VARIABLE

SnapAng	Determines the angle of a rectangular array.

TIPS

■ To create a rectangular array at an angle, use the **Rotation** option of the **Snap** command to set the angle of rotation.

■ Rectangular array draws up in the positive x-direction; right in the positive y-direction; to draw the array in the opposite directions, specify negative row and column distances.

■ Polar arrays are drawn in the counterclockwise direction; to draw the array in the opposite direction, specify a negative angle.

■ In polar arrays, you can choose to have the objects rotated as they are copied.

■ Use the **Divide** or **Measure** command to create a linear array along a path.

Arx

Rel.13 Displays information regarding currently loaded ObjectARx programs.

Command	Alias	Ctrl+	F-key	Alt+	Menu Bar	Tablet
arx	. . .	. . .	. . .	. . .	. . .	. . .

```
Command: arx
Enter an option (?/Load/Unload/Commands/Options): o
Options: Groups/CLasses/Services:
```

COMMAND LINE OPTIONS

?	Lists names of currently loaded ObjectARx programs.
Load	Loads the ObjectARx program into AutoCAD.
Unload	Unloads the ObjectARx program out of memory.
Commands	Lists the names of command associated with each ObjectARx program.

Options options:

CLasses	Lists the class hierarchy for ObjectARx objects.
Groups	Lists the names of objects entered into the "system registry."
Services	Lists names of services entered in the ObjectARx "service dictionary."

RELATED AUTOCAD COMMAND

AppLoad	Loads AutoLISP, ADS, and ARx programs via dialog box.

RELATED AUTOLISP FUNCTIONS

(arx)	Lists currently load ARx programs.
(arxload)	Loads an ARx application.
(autorxload)	Predefines commands that load the ARx program.
(arxunload)	Unloads an ARx application.
(load)	Loads an AutoLISP program.
(xload)	Loads an ADS program.
(ads)	Lists the ADS programs currently loaded.

RELATED FILE

*.ARX	ARx program files.

TIPS

- Use the **Load** option to load external commands that don't seem to work.

- Use the **Unload** option of the **Arx** command to remove ObjectARx programs from AutoCAD to free up additional memory. These are the largest programs (250KB or more):

ObjectArx	Meaning
Acmted.Arx	MText text editor.
Ase.Arx	AutoCAD SQL extension.
Asilisp.Arx	AutoCAD SQL interface LISP functions.
Ism.Arx	The **Image**-related commands.
Render.Arx	The rendering commands.

AseAdmin

Rel.12 Administers links between the drawing and an external database (*short for AutoCAD Sql Extension ADMINistration; an external command in Ase.Arx*).

Command	Alias	Ctrl+	F-key	Alt+	Menu Bar	Tablet
aseadmin	aad	...	...	TEA	Tools ↳External Database ↳Administration	W12

Command: **aseadmin**
Displays dialog box:

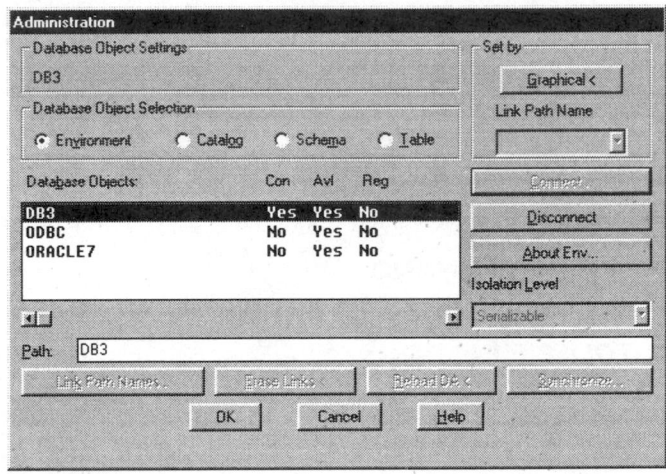

DIALOG BOX OPTIONS

Database Object Selection options:

Environment	Displays list of environments.
Catalog	Displays list of catalogues after connection with DBMS driver.
Schema	Displays list of schemas; not supported by all databases.
Table	Displays list of tables in current schema.

Database Objects options:

Yes	Available.
No	Not available.
?	Not detected by AutoCAD.
Path	Names the database object or logical path name.

Set By options:

Graphical	Selects objects in the drawing.
Link Path Name	Specifies the database object hierarchy with key column definitions.
Connect	Loads database driver and connects it with AutoCAD; displays dialog box:

Connect to Environment dialog box:

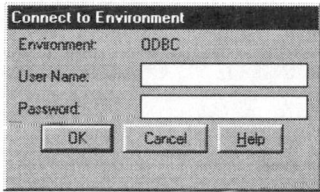

User name	Specifies the user's login name.
Password	Specifies the password.
Disconnect	Disconnects the database driver from AutoCAD.

Isolation Level *options:*

Serializable	Concurrent SQL transactions have same result as sequential transactions.
Uncommitted	Does not lock records in use.
Committed	Locks out in-use records.
Repeatable	Does not lock out selection sets being changed.
Erase Links	Removes all links with selected database objects.
Reload DA	Updates **Displayable Attributes**; deleted rows show ****.
Synchronize	Resynchronizes link info between drawing and database; displays dialog box:

Synchronize Links dialog box:

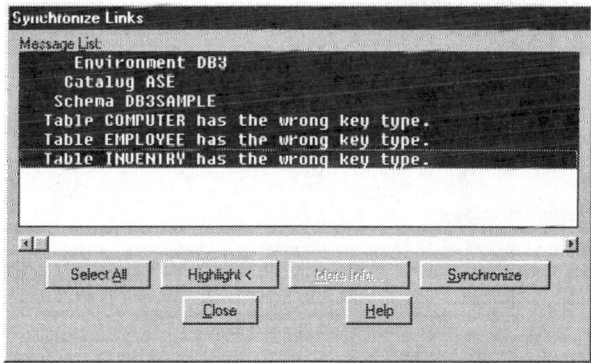

Select All	Selects all links.
Highlight	Highlight all objects with links.
More Info	Displays more info about selected links.
Synchronize	Synchronize links with database.

Link Path Names Displays dialog box.

Link Path Names dialog box:

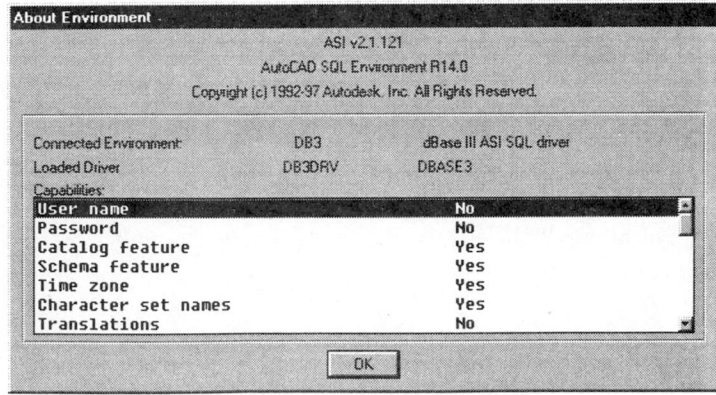

Key Selection options:
On	Makes the selected column a key column.
Off	Turns off key column status.

Link Path options:
New	Specify a new link path.
Existing	The current link path.
Erase	Erase links to current database object.
Erase All	Erases all link paths and links to database objects.
Rename	Changes the link path.

About Env Displays information about the ASE environment; displays dialog box.

About Environment dialog box:

OK   Dismisses dialog box.

RELATED FILES

Asi*.Exe	ASI SQL drivers for database programs.
Asi*.Xmx	Database driver message files.
*.Dbf	Sample database files.
AseSmp.Dwg	Sample ASE drawing file.
*.Xmx	International language message files.
*.H, *.Lib	ASI programming support files.

RELATED TOOLBAR ICONS

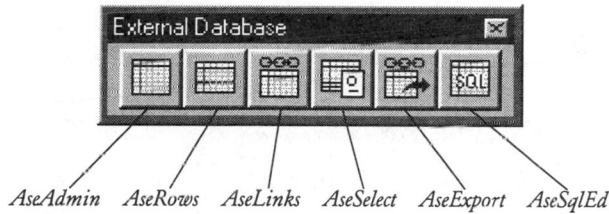

AseAdmin   AseRows   AseLinks   AseSelect   AseExport   AseSqlEd

RELATED PROGRAMS

AsiConfig.Exe ASI configuration utility program.

TIP

■ The **Undo** command does not work reliably with ASE commands.

AseExport

Rel.12 Exports link information to an external database file (*an external command in Ase.Arx*).

Command	Alias	Ctrl+	F-key	Alt+	Menu Bar	Tablet
aseexport	aex	...	...	TEE	Tools ⌐External Database ⌐Export Links	Y12

```
Command: aseexport
All/Environment/Catalog/Schema/<Table>/Lpn: [Enter]
Sdf/Cdf/<Native>/sKip:
Name of file:
```

When system variable CmdDia is turned on (= 1), the AseExport command displays the following dialog box:

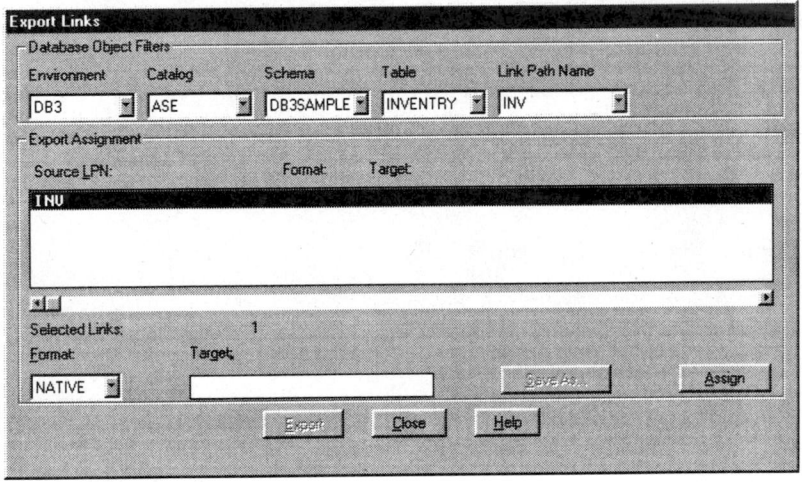

COMMAND LINE OPTIONS

All	Exports all link information.
Environment	Exports environment-related link information.
Catalog	Exports a catalog with links to selected objects.
Schema	Exports a schema with links to selected objects.
Table	Exports a table with links to selected objects:
Lpn	Exports links for a single table registration (*LPN is short for Link Path Name*).
Sdf	Specifies a space-delimited file, 1 line per link, space-padded to 16 characters.
Cdf	Specifies a comma-delimited file, one line per link.
Native	Specifies a native database file format, one file per source LPN and one record per link.
sKip	Exits the command.

TIP

■ Enter * to export all link information.

 # AseLinks

Rel.12 Lists, edits, and displays link information between drawing and database.

Command	Alias	Ctrl+	F-key	Alt+	Menu Bar	Tablet
aselinks	ali	...	...	TEL	Tools ↳External Database ↳Links	X12

```
Command: aselinks
All/Environment/Catalog/Schema/Table/Lpn/Object/<eXit>: A
Browse/Next/Prior/First/Del/delAll/Update/Rows/<eXit>: R
Cursor-state/Textual/Keys/<eXit>: C
Scrollable/Updatable/<Read-only>: K
Enter value for key-column-name-n: [enter value]
Browse/Next/Prior/First/Last/<eXit>:
```

*When system variable CmdDia is turned on (= 1), the **AseLinks** command displays the following dialog box:*

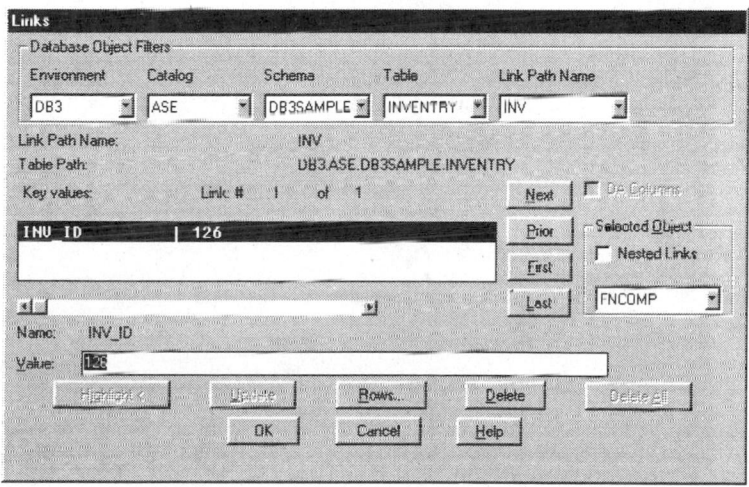

COMMAND LINE OPTIONS

All	Select all links and displays the following options:
Browse	Displays all links.
Next	Displays next link.
Prior	Displays prior link.
First	Displays first link.
Last	Displays last link.
Del	Deletes current link.
delAll	Deletes all links to the selected object.
Update	Updates key values to the current link.
Rows	Edits the current link; if a read-only cursor cannot be opened.
Textual	Selects a row or rows matching an SQL search condition.
Keys	Selects a row that matches the key values.

Cursor-state	Displays the following options:
Scrollable	Makes a row the current row.
Updatable	Allows a row to be edited but not scrolled.
Read-only	Prevents rows from being edited and deleted.
Environment	Selects all links within the current environment.
Catalog	Selects all links in the current catalogue.
Schema	Selects all links in the current schema.
Table	Selects all links in the current table.
Lpn	Selects all links in the current link path name.
Object	Filters out nested links in blocks and xrefs.
eXit	Exits the command.

RELATED COMMANDS
All ASE commands.

TIPS
■ Press **[Enter]** to the 'Enter text condition' prompt to select all rows in the table.

■ A read-only cursor is nonscrollable.

AseRows

Rel.12 Creates links and selection sets; displays and edits table data (*an external command in Ase.Arx*).

Command	Alias	Ctrl+	F-key	Alt+	Menu Bar	Tablet
aserows	aro	...	...	TER	Tools ⤷External Database ⤷Rows	W13

```
Command: aserows
Settings/Insert/Cursor-state/Textual/Keys/<eXit>/Select
object: [pick]
Browse/Next/Prior/First/Last/Select/Unselect/Edit/Insert/Del/
Mlink/MDA/linKs/<eXit>: M
Enter a column name or ? for list:
Justify/Style/<Start point>:
```

When system variable CmdDia is turned on (= 1), the AseRows command displays the following dialog box:

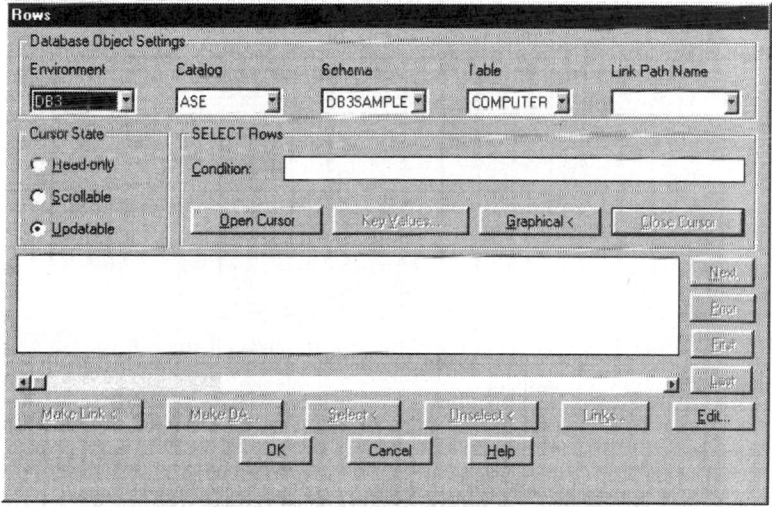

COMMAND LINE OPTIONS

Settings	Displays the following options:
Environment	Sets up an environment or selects a different one.
Catalog	Changes the catalogue.
Schema	Changes the current schema.
Table	Changes the current table.
Lpn	Sets the current link path name.
Insert	Inserts a new row in the current table.

Cursor-state	Displays the following options:
Scrollable	Makes a row the current row.
Updatable	Allows a row to be edited but not scrolled.
Read-only	Prevents a rows from being edited or deleted.
Textual	Selects a row or rows from a table.
Keys	Selects a new row that matches key values.
Select object	After selecting an object, displays the following options:
Browse	Displays all links.
Next	Displays next link.
Prior	Displays prior link.
First	Displays first link.
Last	Displays last link.
Select	Highlights linked objects and adds them to selection set.
Unselect	Removes objects from selection set.
Edit	Changes the current row.
Insert	Inserts row into table.
Del	Deletes current link.
Mlink	Make link between row and selected object.
MDA	Make displayable attribute.
linKs	Displays link information.
eXit	Exits the command.

RELATED COMMANDS
All ASE commands.

TIPS
■ Press **[Enter]** to the 'Enter text condition' prompt to select all rows in the table.

■ A read-only cursor is nonscrollable.

AseSelect

Rel.12 Creates a selection set from rows linked to graphic and text selection sets (*an external command in Ase.Arx*).

Command	Alias	Ctrl+	F-key	Alt+	Menu Bar	Tablet
aseselect	ase	...	...	TES	Tools ↳External Database ↳Select Objects	X13

```
Command: aseselect
Graphical/Textual/<eXit>: T
All/Environment/Catalog/Schema/<Table>/Lpn: L
Union/Intersect/subtractA/SubtractB/<eXit>:
```

When system variable CmdDia is turned on (= 1), the AseSelect command displays the following dialog box:

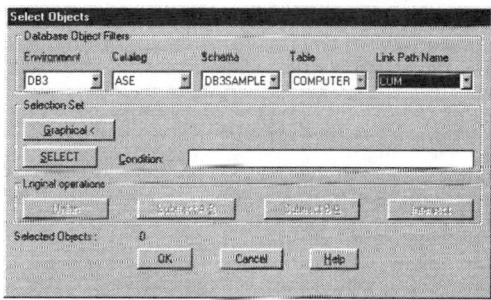

COMMAND LINE OPTIONS

Graphical	Selects objects from screen.
Textual	Makes an SQL selection.
All	Selects all objects linked to rows matching SQL condition.
Environment	Selects all objects within the current environment.
Catalog	Selects all objects in the current catalog.
Schema	Selects all objects in the current schema.
Table	Selects all objects in the current table.
Lpn	Selects all objects in the current link path name.
Union	Creates a selection set containing all linked objects meeting criteria and selected graphic objects.
Intersect	Creates a selection set containing objects in both sets.
subtractA	Subtracts first selection set from second set.
SubtractB	Subtracts second selection set from first set.
eXit	Exits the command.

RELATED COMMANDS

All ASE commands.

TIP

■ By default, all external database objects are selected.

AseSqlEd

Rel.12 Executes SQL statements (*short for SQL EDitor; an external command in Ase.Arx*).

Command	Alias	Ctrl+	F-key	Alt+	Menu Bar	Tablet
asesqled	asq	...	...	TEQ	Tools ⮡External Database ⮡SQL Editor	Y13

```
Command: asesqled
Settings/Options/Isolation/Autocommit/File/<SQL>/Native/
Commit/Rollback/eXit: I
Uncommitted/Committed/Repeatable/<Serializable>:
```

When system variable CmdDia is turned on (= 1), the AseSqlEd command displays the following dialog box:

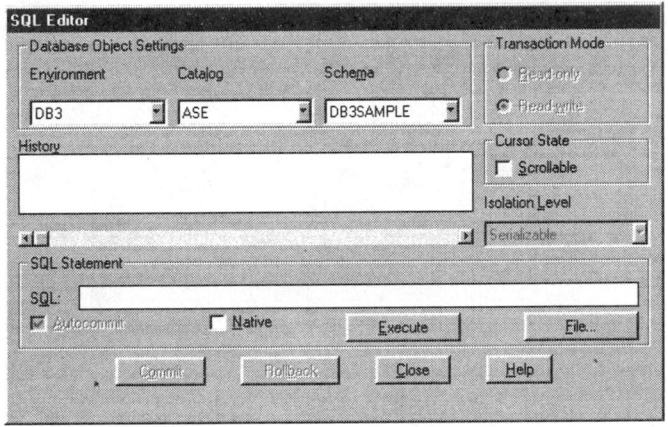

COMMAND LINE OPTIONS:

Settings	Changes database object settings:
Environment	Sets up an environment or selects a different one.
Catalog	Changes the catalogue.
Schema	Changes the current schema.
Options	Specifies transaction mode and cursor type.
Scrollable	Makes a row the current row.
read-Write	Allows rows to be edited and deleted.
Read-only	Prevents rows from being edited and deleted.
Isolation	Selects level of SQL isolation.
Uncommitted	Allows other users to access any record.
Committed	Allows other users to access completed records.
Repeatable	Allows other users to access the current selection set.
Serializable	Specifies that concurrent transactions have same result as consecutive ones.

Autocommit	Automatically makes multiple changes to the database.
File	Runs SQL statements from a file in batch mode; displays the **Open SQL File** dialog box.
SQL	Executes an SQL statement at the **'SQL>'** prompt.
Native	Allows use of non-SQL database commands.
Commit	Save changes made to database.
Rollback	Cancels changes made to database.
eXit	Exits the command.

RELATED COMMANDS

All ASE commands.

RELATED FILE

- ***.Txt**   File containing SQL statements to be executed in batch mode.

TIPS

- Database column values (except column names) are case-sensitive.

- Search string character values are enclosed by ' ' (single quotes)

- Use a pair of single quotes (") to create an apostrophe.

- Use the following metacharacters when entering column data at the 'Command' prompt:

Metacharacter	Meaning
Period (.)	Represents a null.
Pair of periods (..)	Represents a single period.
Press [Enter]	Leaves column data unchanged.

- The SQL batch file can use the following metacharacters:

Prefix or Suffix	Meaning
; (semi-colon) prefix	Comment line.
$ (dollar) prefix	Comment echoed to the command line.
& (ampersand) suffix	Continues SQL command on next line.

AttachURL

Rel.14 Attaches a URL to an object or an area (*an external command in DwfIu.Arx*).

Command	Alias	Ctrl+	F-key	Alt+	Menu Bar	Tablet
attachurl	...	...	...	...	...	...

```
Command: attachurl
URL by (Area/<Objects>): [Enter]
Select objects: [pick]
1 found Select objects: [Enter]
Enter URL: http://users.uniserve.com/~ralphg/
```

COMMAND LINE OPTIONS

Area   Creates a 2D hyperlink by specifying two corners of a rectangle.
Object   Creates a 1D hyperlink by selecting one or more objects.
Enter URL   Allows you to type a valid URL.

RELATED COMMANDS

DetachUrl   Removes the URL from an object.
DwfOut   Exports the drawing in DWF format.
ListUrl   Lists URLs embedded in the drawing.
SelectUrl   Selects all objects with attached URLs.

TIPS

■ The URLs placed in the drawing become links *after* the drawing is exported as a DWF file with the **DwfOut** command; the hyperlinks cannot be used while in DWG format.

■ Examples of URLs include:

http://www.autodesk.com	Autodesk primary Web site.
http://data.autodesk.com	Autodesk Data Publishing Web site.
http://www.autodeskpress.com	Autodesk Press Web site.
http://users.uniserve.com/~ralphg/	Author Ralph Grabowski's Web site.
news://adesknews.autodesk.com	Autodesk news server.
ftp://ftp.autodesk.com	Autodesk FTP server.

■ Autodesk recommends that you use the following URL formats:

File Location	Example URL
Web Site	**http:**//*servername*/*pathname*/*filename*.**dwg**
FTP Site	**ftp:**//*servername*/*pathname*/*filename*.**dwg**
Local File	**file:**///*drive:*/*pathname*/*filename*.**dwg**
or	**file:**///*drive*/*pathname*/*filename*.**dwg**
or	**file:**//*localPC\pathname\filename*.**dwg**
or	**file:**////*localPC*/*pathname*/*filename*.**dwg**
Network File	**file:**//*localhost*/*drive:*/*pathname*/*filename*.**dwg**
or	**file:**//*localhost*/*drive*/*pathname*/*filename*.**dwg**

- The **Area** option: (1) creates a layer named URLLAYER with the default color of red; and (2) places a rectangle object on that layer.
- Don't delete layer URLLAYER.
- The URL is stored as follows:

Attachment	URL
One object	Stored as xdata (extended entity data).
Multiple objects	Stored as xdata in each object.
Area	Stored as xdata in a rectangle object on layer URLLAYER.

DEFINITIONS

DWF   Short for "drawing Web format," Autodesk's file format for displaying drawings on the Internet.

URL   Short for "uniform resource locator," the universal file naming convention for the Internet.

URLs take the following generalized format:

scheme://netloc

The *scheme* lets your Web browser access a specific resource on the Internet:

Scheme	Meaning
file://	Files on your computer's hard drive or local area network.
ftp://	File Transfer Protocol.
http://	Hyper Text Transfer Protocol.
mailto://	Electronic mail.
news://	Usenet news.
telnet://	Telenet protocol.
gopher://	Gopher protocol.

How to use a URL.

The **AttachURL** command places URLs in the drawing for later use by a Web browser. URLs cannot be used while in AutoCAD; they become active links only after the drawing is exported in DWF format. To help make the process clearer, here are the steps that you go through to make use of URLs:

Step 1: ATTACHURL COMMAND

Place URLs in the drawing with the **AttachURL** command.

Step 2: DWFOUT COMMAND

Export the drawing in DWF format with the **DwfOut** command.

Step 3: DRAG'N DROP

Drag the DWF file from Windows Explorer or (File Manager) into your Web browser. This step assumes your Web browser has the DWF plug-in installed. The plug-in — called Whip! — is available from the Autodesk Web site at http://www.autodesk.com . (AutoCAD itself neither displays nor translates DWF files.)

Step 4: <EMBED> TAG

Include the DWF file in your Web page with the HTML **<embed>** tag:

```
<embed src=filename.dwf>
```

Step 5: HYPERLINK!

While viewing the DWF file, press the **[Shift]** key. This causes all hyperlink zones (areas with a URL) to highlight. Pass the cursor over a hyperlink zone to display the name of the URL on the status line of the Web browser.

Click on a hyperlink zone to jump to that URL.

AttDef

V. 2.0 Defines attribute modes and prompts (*short for ATTribute DEFinition*).

Command	Alias	Ctrl+	F-key	Alt+	Menu Bar	Tablet
attdef	-at	...	...	...	...	...

```
Command: attdef
Attribute modes — Invisible:N  Constant:N  Verify:N  Preset:N
Enter (ICVP) to change, RETURN when done: [Enter]
Attribute tag:
Attribute prompt:
Default attribute value:
Justify/Style/<Start point>: [pick]
```

Block with attribute value (left) and attribute tags (right):

COMMAND LINE OPTIONS

Attribute mode	Selects the modes for the attribute:
I	Toggles visibility of attribute text in drawing (*short for Invisible*).
C	Toggles fixed or variable value of attribute (*short for Constant*).
V	Toggles confirmation prompt during input (*short for Verify*).
P	Toggles automatic insertion of default values (*short for Preset*).
Justify	Selects the justification mode for the attribute text.
Style	Selects the text style for the attribute text.
Start point	Indicates the start point of the attribute text.

RELATED TOOLBAR ICONS

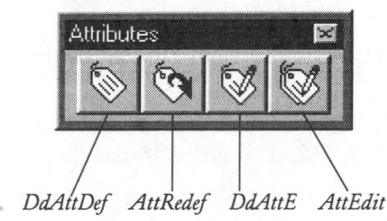

DdAttDef   AttRedef   DdAttE   AttEdit

RELATED COMMANDS

AttDisp	Controls the visibility of attributes.
AttEdit	Edits the values of attributes.
AttExt	Extracts attributes to disk.
AttRedef	Redefines an attribute or block.
Block	Binds attributes to objects.
DdAttDef	Defines attributes via a dialog box.
DdAttE	Extracts the values of attributes via a dialog box.
DdEdit	Edits the values of attribute definitions via a dialog box.
Insert	Inserts a block and prompts for attribute values.

RELATED SYSTEM VARIABLES

AFlags   Contains the value of modes in bit form:

AFlags	Meaning
0	No attribute mode selected.
1	Invisible.
2	Constant.
4	Verify.
8	Preset.

AttDia   Toggles use of dialog box during **Insert** command:

AttDia	Meaning
0	Uses command-line prompts.
1	Uses dialog box.

AttReq   Toggles use of defaults or user prompts during **Insert** command:

AttReq	Meaning
0	Assumes default values of all attributes.
1	Prompts for attributes.

TIPS

- Constant attributes cannot be edited.

- Attribute tags cannot be null (have no value); attribute values may be null.

- You can type any characters for the attribute tag, except a space or an exclamation mark. All characters are converted to uppercase.

- When you press **[Enter]** at 'Attribute Prompt,' AutoCAD uses the attribute *tag* as the prompt.

- 'Attribute Prompt' and 'Default Attribute Value' are not when displayed when constant mode is turned on. Instead, AutoCAD prompts 'Attribute Value.'

- When you press **[Enter]** at the 'Starting point:' prompt, **AttDef** automatically places the next attribute below the previous one.

'AttDisp

V. 2.0 Controls the display of all attributes in the drawing (*short for ATTribute DISPlay*).

Command	Alias	Ctrl+	F-key	Alt+	Menu Bar	Tablet
'attdisp	...	...	...	VLA	View ⤷Display ⤷Attribute Display	L1

```
Command: attdisp
Normal/ON/OFF <Normal>:
Regen queued.
```

*Attribute display **Normal** (left), **Off** (center), and **On** (right):*

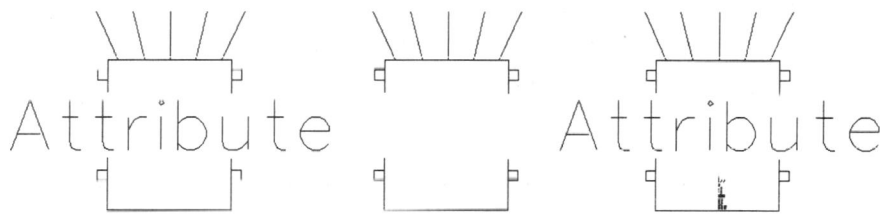

COMMAND LINE OPTIONS

Normal	Displays attributes according to **AttDef** setting.
ON	Displays all attributes, regardless of **AttDef** setting.
OFF	Displays no attributes, regardless of **AttDef** setting.

RELATED COMMANDS
- **AttDef**   Defines new attributes, including their default visibility.
- **DdAttDef** Defines new attributes via dialog box.

RELATED SYSTEM VARIABLE
- **AttMode**   Contains current setting of **AttDisp**:

AttMode	Meaning
0	Off: no attributes are displayed.
1	Normal: invisible attributes are not displayed.
2	On: all attributes are displayed.

TIPS
- Use the **Regen** command after **AttDisp** to see change to attribute display.

- When you define invisible attributes, use the **AttDisp** command to view them.

- Use the **AttDisp** command to turn off the display of attributes, which helps increase display speed and reduce drawing clutter.

AttEdit

V. 2.0 Edits attributes in a drawing (*short for ATTribute EDIT*).

Command	Alias	Ctrl+	F-key	Alt+	Menu Bar	Tablet
attedit	-ate	...	...	MOAG	Modify	...
					↳Object	
					↳Attribute	
					↳Global	

Command: **attedit**

One-at-time attribute editing options:
Edit attributes one at a time? <Y> **[Enter]**
Block name specification <*>: **[Enter]**
Attribute tag specification <*>: **[Enter]**
Attribute value specification <*>: **[Enter]**
Select Attributes: **[pick]**
1 attributes selected.
Value/Position/Height/Angle/Style/Layer/Color/Next <N>:

*During single attribute editing, **AttEdit** marks the current attribute with an 'X':*

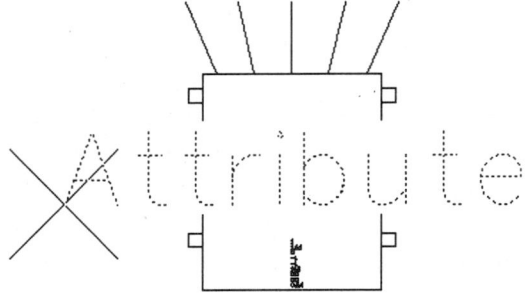

Global attribute editing options:
Edit attributes one at a time? <Y> **n**
Global edit of attribute values.
Edit only attributes visible on screen? <Y> **[Enter]**
Block name specification <*>: **[Enter]**
Attribute tag specification <*>: **[Enter]**
Attribute value specification <*>: **[Enter]**
Select Attributes: **[pick]**
Select Attributes: **[Enter]**
1 attributes selected.
String to change: **[type string]**
New string: **[type string]**

COMMAND LINE OPTIONS

Value	Changes or replaces the value of the attribute:
Change	Changes some or all of the attribute's values.
Replace	Replaces attribute with a new value.
Position	Moves the text insertion point of the attribute.
Height	Changes the attribute text height.
Angle	Changes the attribute text angle.
Style	Changes the text style of the attribute text.
Layer	Moves the attribute to a different layer.
Color	Changes the color of the attribute text.
Next	Edits the next attribute.

RELATED COMMANDS

AttDef	Defines an attribute's original value and parameter.
AttDisp	Toggles an attribute's visibility.
AttEdit	Edits the values of attributes.
AttRedef	Redefines attributes and blocks.
DdAttDef	Defines attributes via a dialog box.
DdAttE	Edits all attribute values.
DdEdit	Edits a single attribute's value.
Explode	Reduces an attribute to its tag.

TIPS

- Constant attributes cannot be edited with **AttEdit**.

- You can only edit attributes parallel to the current UCS.

- Unlike other text input to AutoCAD, attribute values are case-sensitive.

- To edit null attribute values, use **AttEdit**'s global edit option and enter \ (backslash) at the 'Attribute value specification' prompt.

- The wildcard characters ? and * are interpreted literally at the 'String to change' and 'New String' prompts.

AttExt

V. 2.0 Extracts attribute data from the drawing to a file on disk (*short for ATTribute EXTract*).

Command	Alias	Ctrl+	F-key	Alt+	Menu Bar	Tablet
attext	...	...	...	FE	File	...
				⇘DXX	⇘Export	
					⇘DXX Extract	

Command: **attext**
CDF, SDF or DXF Attribute extract (or Objects)? <C>:
*Displays the **Select Template File** and **Create Extract File** dialog boxes:*

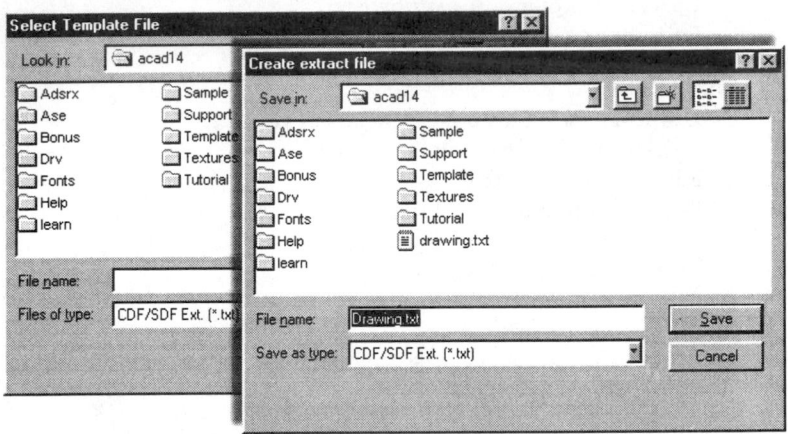

COMMAND LINE OPTIONS

CDF	Outputs attributes in comma-delimited format.
SDF	Outputs attributes in space-delimited format.
DXF	Outputs attributes in DXF format.
Objects	Selects objects to extract attributes from.

RELATED COMMANDS

AttDef	Defines attributes.
DdAttExt	Defines attribute extraction via a dialog box.

RELATED FILES

*.TXT	Required extension for the template file.
*.TXT	Extension for CDF and SDF extraction files.
*.DXX	Extension for DXF extraction files.

TIPS

- To output the attributes to the printer, specify:

Logical Filename	Meaning
CON	Text screen
PRN *or* LPT1	Print to parallel port 1
LPT2 *or* LPT3	Print to parallel port 2 or 3

- Before you can specify the SDF or CDF option, you must create the template file.

- The DXF option does not require a template file.

- CDF files use the following conventions:

  - Specified field widths are the maximum width.
  - Positive number fields have a leading blank.
  - Character fields are enclosed in ' ' (single quote marks).
  - Trailing blanks are deleted.
  - Null strings are '' (two single quote marks).
  - Uses spaces; do not uses tabs.
  - Use the C:DELIM and C:QUOTE records to change the field and string delimiters to another character.

Exporting attributes.

How to extract attribute data from a drawing:

Step 1: CREATE A TEMPLATE FILE

When you want the attribute extracted in CDF or SDF format, you must first create a template file. The DXF format does not use a template file.

The *template file* is used by the **AttExt** (or **DdAttExt**) command to:

1. Determine which attributes to extract.

2. Format the extracted information.

Field Name	Type, Width, Precision	Description
BL:NAME	Cwww000	Name of block
BL:NUMBER	Nwww000	Number of occurrences
CHAR_ATTRIBUTE_TAG	Cwww000	Character attribute tag
NUMERIC_ATTR_TAG	Nwwwddd	Numeric attribute tag
BL:LAYER	Cwww000	Block's layer name
BL:ORIENT	Nwwwddd	Block rotation angle
BL:LEVEL	Nwww000	Block's nesting level
BL:X	Nwwwddd	Block insertion x-coordinate
BL:Y	Nwwwddd	Block insertion y-coordinate
BL:Z	Nwwwddd	Block insertion z-coordinate
BL:XSCALE	Nwwwddd	Block's x-scale factor
BL:YSCALE	Nwwwddd	Block's y-scale factor
BL:ZSCALE	Nwwwddd	Block's z-scale factor
BL:XEXTRUDE	Nwwwddd	Block's x-extrusion
BL:YEXTRUDE	Nwwwddd	Block's y-extrusion
BL:ZEXTRUDE	Nwwwddd	Block's z-extrusion
BL:HANDLE	Cwwwddd	Block's handle hex-number.

The template file uses the following format codes:

- **Type** describes the type of attribute data:
  - C   Alpha-numeric characters.
  - N   Numbers only.

- **Width** (*www*) describes the field width from 001 to 999 characters wide, padded with leading zeros.

- **Precision** (*ddd*) describes the number of decimal places from 001 to 999 (ie, .1 to .00000...001), padded with leading zeros.

Use a text editor, such as Notepad, to create a template file. Here is an example:

Field	Template	Description
BL:NAME	C008000	*8-character block name.*
BL:NUMBER	N004000	*Number of occurrences.*
VENDOR	C016000	*Vendor attribute (16 chars).*
MODELNO	N012000	*Model # attr (12 digits).*

Save the file as ASCII text with the .TXT extension and return to AutoCAD.

Step 2: SELECT OUTPUT FORMAT

Use either the **AttExt** or **DdAttExt** command to extract attribute data. Decide on the output format:

- CDF Comma-delimited format (the default), best for importing into a spreadsheet; sample output:
  ```
  'Desk',55,'Steelcase',2248599597
  ```

- DXF Drawing interchange format, similar to an objects-only DXF file.

- SDF Space-delimited format, best for importing into a database program; sample output:
  ```
  Desk       55               Steelcase  2248599597
  ```

Step 3: SELECT THE OBJECTS

Either select the blocks you want to extract attributes from, or select all objects in the drawing. AutoCAD ignores all non-block objects and blocks with no attributes.

Step 4: SPECIFY THE TEMPLATE FILE

Enter the name of the template file you created earlier.

Step 5: SPECIFY OUTPUT FILENAME (Optional)

If you do not specify an output filename, AutoCAD uses the drawing's name, appending a .TXT to CDF and SDF files, or DXX to DXF files. Otherwise, specify any name except the template file's name.

Step 6: CLICK OK

Click the **OK** button and AutoCAD places extracted attribute data into the output file. AutoCAD stops if it finds any errors in the format of the template file, or if the selection set contains no attributes.

'AttRedef

Rel.13 Redefines blocks and attributes (*short for ATTribute REDEFinition; an external command in AttRedef.Lsp*).

Command	Alias	Ctrl+	F-key	Alt+	Menu Bar	Tablet
'attredef	at	...	...	...	...	...

```
Command: redefine
Name of Block you wish to redefine: [type name]
Select objects for new Block...
Select objects: [pick]
Select objects: [Enter]
Insertion base point of new block: [pick]
```

RELATED COMMANDS

AttDef	Defines an attribute's original value and parameter.
AttDisp	Toggles an attributes visibility.
AttEdit	Edits the values of attributes.
DdAttDef	Defines attributes via a dialog box.
DdAttE	Edits all attribute values.
DdEdit	Edits a single attribute's value.
Explode	Reduces an attribute to its tag.

TIPS

■ Existing attributes retain their values.

■ Existing attributes not included in the new block are erased.

■ New attributes added to an existing block take on default values.

Audit

Rel.11 Examines a drawing file for structural errors.

Command	Alias	Ctrl+	F-key	Alt+	Menu Bar	Tablet
audit	...	...	...	FMA	File ⤷Management ⤷Audit	Y24

```
Command: audit
Fix any errors detected? <N> y
```

Sample output:
```
0 Blocks audited
Pass 1 132 objects audited
Pass 2 132 objects audited
Total errors found 0 fixed 0
```

COMMAND LINE OPTIONS
N   Reports errors found; does not fix errors.
Y   Reports and fixes errors found in drawing file.

RELATED COMMANDS
Save   Saves a recovered drawing to disk.
Recover   Recovers a damaged drawing file.

RELATED SYSTEM VARIABLE
AuditCtl   Controls the creation of the ADT audit log file:

AuditCtl	Meaning
0	No log file written.
1	ADT log file is written to drawing directory.

RELATED FILE
*.ADT   Audit log file reports the progress of the auditing process.

TIPS
- The **Audit** command is a diagnostic tool for validating and repairing the contents of a DWG file.

- Objects with errors are placed in the Previous selection set. Use an editing command, such as **Copy**, to view the objects.

- If **Audit** cannot fix a drawing file, use the **Recover** command.

Background

Rel.14 Places a solid color, linear gradient, raster image, or the current view in the background of a rendering (*an external command in LsObj.Arx*).

Command	Alias	Ctrl+	F-key	Alt+	Menu Bar	Tablet
background	...	...	...	VEB	View	Q2
					⅏Render	
					⅏Background	

Command: **background**
Displays dialog box:

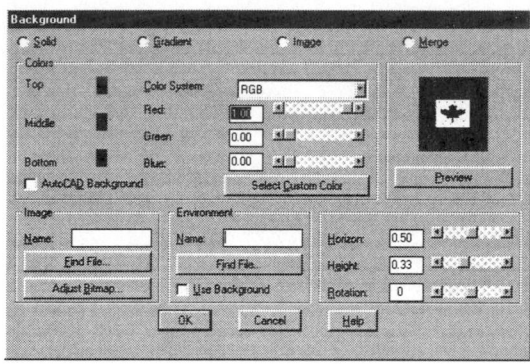

DIALOG BOX OPTIONS

Solid options:

Colors
: Specifies a color from the RGB (red-green-blue) or HLS (hue-lightness-saturation) slider bars; **Select Custom Color** displays the Windows **Color** dialog box.

AutoCAD Background
: Uses the current AutoCAD background color (*default = white*).

Gradient options:

Top
: Specifies a color for the top of the 2- and 3-color gradient.

Middle
: Specifies a color for the middle of the 3-color gradient.

Bottom
: Specifies a color for the bottom of the 2- and 3 color gradient.

Horizon
: Determines the center of a gradient; percent of viewport height.

Height
: Determines the second color's start of a 3-color gradient; set to 0 for a 2-color gradient.

Rotation
: Rotates the angle of the gradient.

Image options:

Image Name
: Specifies the name of the raster file to use as the background image

Find File
: Displays file dialog box; allows selections of a BMP (Windows bitmap), GIF, JPG (JPEG), PCX (PC Paintbrush), TGA (Targa), or TIFF file.

Adjust Bitmap
: Adjust the position of a raster image; displays dialog box.

Adjust Background Bitmap Placement dialog box:

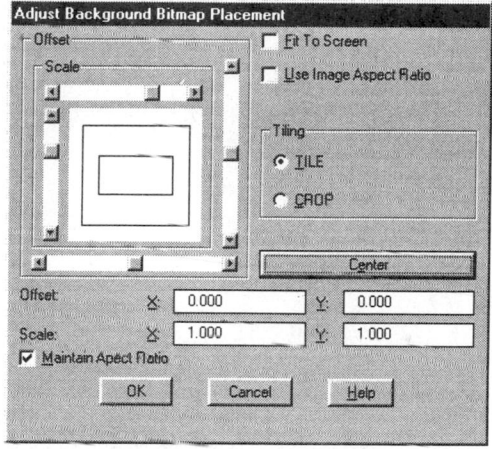

Offset   Use the slider bars to position the image in the viewport.

Fit to Screen Stretches the image to fit the viewport.

Use Image Aspect Ratio

           Ensures the image is not distorted.

Tiling   When the image does not fit the viewport, Render either (1) *tiles* the too-small image to repeat it; or (2) *crops* the too-large image to make it smaller.

Center   Centers the image in the viewport.

X,Y Offset   Changes the position of the image.

X,Y scale   Changes the size of the image.

Environment options:

Environment Allows reflection and refraction effects on objects: (1) mirror effect with the Photo Real renderer; (2) raytracing with the Photo Raytrace renderer.

Use Background

           Specifies that objects reflect the background, whether a color, gradient, image, or merged image.

Merge options:
None.

RELATED COMMANDS

Fog   Creates a fog-like effect.

ImageAttach Loads a raster image as an xref file.

Render   Renders 3D objects in the drawing.

Replay   Displays a raster image in the current viewport.

TIPS

- Gradient backgrounds are useful for simulating a sunset (cyan-pink-orange) or underwater view (green-blue-black).

- To create a 2-color gradient, set **Height** to 0.

- Image backgrounds are useful for placing the 3D rendered model in its environment, such as a rendered house on its building site.

- AutoCAD includes some background images in \acadr14\textures.

- The four types of background:

*The **Solid** option displays a uniform color (left); **Gradient** option displays a 2- or 3-color linear gradient (right).*

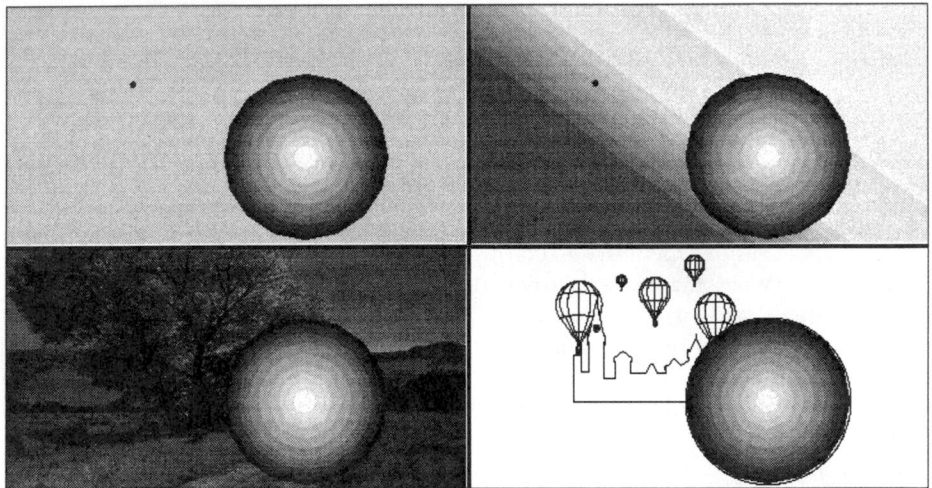

***Image** option displays a raster image (left); **Merge** option displays the current AutoCAD viewport (right).*

'Base

V. 1.0 Changes the 2D or 3D insertion point of the current drawing, located by default at (0,0,0).

Command	Alias	Ctrl+	F-key	Alt+	Menu Bar	Tablet
'base	...	...	...	DKB	Draw	...
					⮩Block	
					⮩Base	

```
Command: base
Base point <0.0000,0.0000,0.0000>:
```

COMMAND LINE OPTION
Base point   The x,y,z-coordinates of the new insertion point.

RELATED COMMANDS
Block   Allows you to specify the insertion point of a new block.
Insert   Inserts another drawing into the current drawing.
Xref   References another drawing.

RELATED SYSTEM VARIABLE
InsBase   Contains the current setting of the drawing insertion point.

TIPS
■ Use this command to shift the insertion point of the current drawing.

■ This command does not affect the current drawing. Instead, it comes into effect when you insert it or xref it into another drawing.

BHatch

Rel.12 Automatically applies an associative hatch pattern within a boundary (*short for Boundary HATCH*).

Command	Alias	Ctrl+	F-key	Alt+	Menu Bar	Tablet
bhatch	bh	...	...	DH	Draw ⌖Hatch	P9
-bhatch	h					

```
Command: -bhatch
Properties/Select/Remove islands/Advanced/<Internal point>:
```

COMMAND LINE OPTION

Property options:

Enter pattern name

　　　　　　Allows you to type the name of the hatch pattern.

?　　　　Lists the names of available hatch patterns.

Solid　　Floods the area with a solid fill in the current color.

User defined　Creates a simple, user-defined hatch pattern.

Select option:

Select options Selects objects to fill with hatch pattern.

Remove islands option:

Select island to remove

　　　　　　Selects island to remove, which are not filled with the hatch pattern.

Advanced options:

Boundary set Defines the objects **BHatch** analyzes when defining a boundary from a specified pick point: (1) a new set of objects; or (2) all objects visible in the current viewport.

Retain boundary

　　　　　　Yes: The boundary created during the hatching process is kept after the **BHatch** command finishes.

　　　　　　No: The boundary is discarded.

Island detection

　　　　　　Yes: Objects within the outermost boundary are used as boundary objects.

　　　　　　No: All object withing outermost boundary are filled.

Style　　Selects the hatching style: ignore, outer, or normal.

Associativity　*Yes*: Hatch pattern is associative.

　　　　　　No: Hatch pattern is not associative.

eXit　　Exits this submenu of choices.

Internal point option:

[pick]　　Creates a boundary based on the point you pick.

Command: **bhatch**
Displays dialog box:

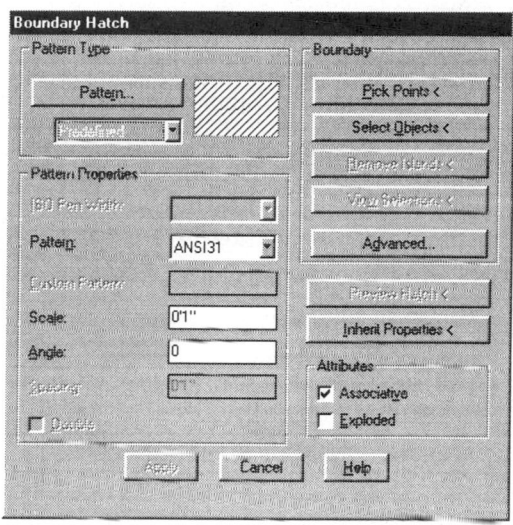

`DIALOG BOX OPTIONS

Pattern   Selects hatch pattern; displays dialog box.

Hatch Pattern Palette dialog box:

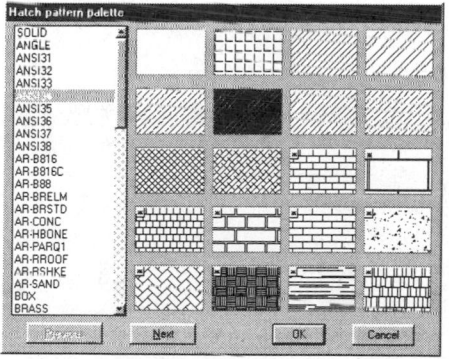

Previous   Displays previous 20 hatch pattern samples.
Next   Displays next 20 hatch pattern samples.
OK   Selects highlighted pattern and dismisses dialog box.
Cancel   Dismisses dialog box with no changes.

Pattern Properties options:
ISO Pen Width When an ISO hatch pattern is selected, scales pattern according to pen
             width.

Pattern   Name of hatch pattern, as defined in Acad.Pat.

Custom Pattern Specify name of a user-defined pattern.

Scale   Hatch pattern scale (*default: = 1.0*).

Angle   Hatch pattern angle (*default = 0 degrees*).

Spacing   Spacing between lines of a user-defined hatch pattern.

Double   *Yes*: Hatch is applied a second time at 90 degrees to the first pattern.
       No: Hatch is applied once.

Preview Hatch Preview the hatch pattern before it is applied.

Inherit Properties
     Select the hatch pattern parameters from an existing hatch pattern.

Default Properties
     Change pattern parameters back to default values.

Attributes options:

Associative   *Yes*: Hatch is associative.
       No: Hatch is non-associative.

Exploded   *Yes*: Hatch pattern is places as lines and points.
       No: Hatch pattern is places as a hatch object.

Boundary options:

Pick Points   Allows you to pick points that define the hatch pattern boundary.

Select Objects Selects objects to be hatched.

Remove Islands
     Removvse islands from the hatch pattern selection set.

View Selections Views hatch pattern selection set.

Advanced   Allows you to specifiy additional hatching options; displays dialog box.

Advanced Options dialog box:

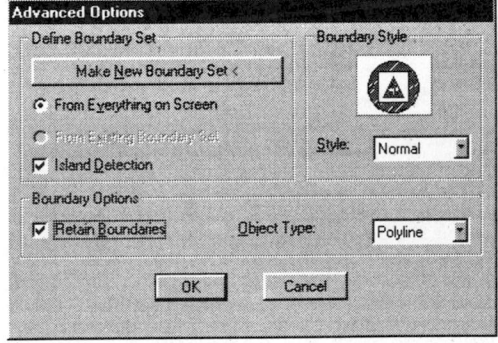

Define Boundary Set options:

Make New Boundary Set
     Allow you to select the boundary from the drawing.

From Everything on Screen
     Selects all objects visible in current view for hatching.

From Existing Boundary Set
> Selects the current boundary selection set for hatching.

Island Detection
> *Yes*: Objects within the outermost boundary are used as boundary objects.
> *No*: All object withing outermost boundary are filled.

Boundary Style options:

Normal	Alternate areas are hatched.
Outer	Only the outermost areas are hatched.
Ignore	Everything within boundary is hatch.

Boundary options:

Retain Boundaries
> *Yes*: The boundary created during the hatching process is kept after the
> **BHatch** command finishes.
> *No*: The boundary is discarded.

Object Type
> Boundary is constructed from either: (1) a polyline object; or (2) a region
> object

RELATED COMMANDS

Boundary	Automatically traces a polyline around a closed boundary.
Convert	Converts R13 hatch patterns into R14 format.
HatchEdit	Edits the hatch pattern.
PsFill	Floods a closed polyline with a PostScript fill pattern.

RELATED SYSTEM VARIABLES

DelObj
> Toggles whether boundary is erased after hatch is place:

DelObj	Meaning
0	Boundary is deleted (*default*).
1	Boundary is retained.

HpAng
> Indicates the current hatch pattern angle (*default* = 0).

HpBound
> Indicates the hatch boundary object:

HpBound	Meaning
0	Polyline object.
1	Region object (*default*).

HpDouble
> Indicates single or double hatching:

HpDouble	Meaning
0	Single hatch (*default*).
1	Double hatch.

| HpName | Indicates the current hatch pattern name (*up to 31 characters long*): |

HpName	Meaning
ANSI31	Default hatch pattern.
""	No current hatch pattern name.
"."	Eliminate current name.

HpScale	Indicates the current hatch pattern scale factor (*default = 1*).
HpSpace	Indicates the current hatch pattern spacing factor (*default = 1*).
PickStyle	Controls the selection of hatch patterns:

PickStyle	Meaning
0	Neither groups nor hatches selected.
1	Groups selected (*default*).
2	Associative hatches selected.
3	Both selected

SnapBase   Starting coordinates of hatch pattern (*default = 0,0*).

RELATED FILE
Acad.Pat   Hatch pattern definition file.

TIPS
- The **BHatch** command first generates a boundary, then hatches the inside area.
- Use the **Boundary** command to create just the boundary.
- **BHatch** stores hatching parameters in the pattern's extended object data.
- See the **Hatch** command for a list of all hatch patterns supplied with AutoCAD.

'Blipmode

V. 2.1 Turns the display of pick-point markers, known as "blips," off and on.

Command	Alias	Ctrl+	F-key	Alt+	Menu Bar	Tablet
'blipmode	...	...	...	...	...	...

```
Command: blipmode
ON/OFF <On>: off
```

A blipmark at the center of the screen:

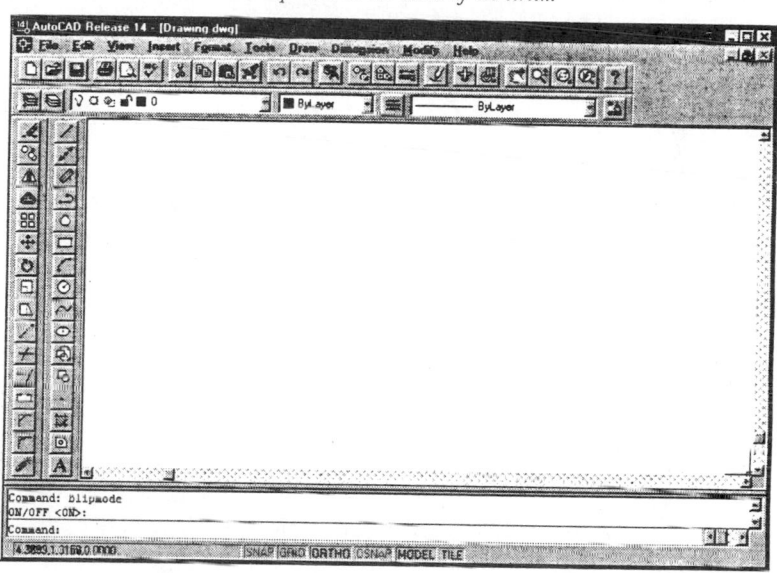

COMMAND LINE OPTIONS
ON	Turns on display of pick point markers.
OFF	Turns off display of pick point markers.

RELATED COMMANDS
DdRModes	Allows blipmode toggling via a dialog box.
Redraw	Cleans blips off the screen.

RELATED SYSTEM VARIABLE
Blipmode	Contains the current setting of blipmode.

TIPS
- You cannot change the size of the blipmark.
- Blipmarks are erased by any command that redraws the view, such as **Redraw**, **Regen**, **Zoom**, and **Vports**.

Block

V. 1.0 Defines a group of objects as a single named object; creates symbols.

Command	Alias	Ctrl+	F-key	Alt+	Menu Bar	Tablet
block	-b	...	...	...	...	N9

```
Command: block
Block name (or ?): [type name]
Insertion base point: [pick]
Select objects: [pick]
Select objects: [Enter]
```

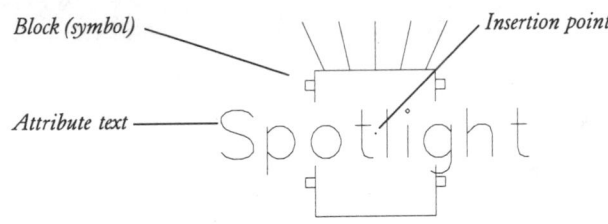

Block (symbol) — Insertion point

Attribute text — Spotlight

COMMAND LINE OPTIONS

Block name Allows you to type the name of the block.
? Lists the blocks stored in the drawing.
Insertion base point
  Specifies the x,y-coordinates of the block's insertion point.
Select objects Selects the objects and attributes that make up the block.

RELATED COMMANDS

Explode Reduces a block into its original objects.
Insert Adds a block or another drawing to the current drawing.
Oops Returns objects to the screen after creating the block.
WBlock Writes a block to a file on disk as a drawing.
XRef Displays another drawing in the current drawing.

RELATED FILE

*.DWG All drawing files are insertable as blocks.

TIPS

■ A block name has up to 31 alphanumeric characters, including $, -, and _.

■ Use the **INSertion** object snap to select the block's insertion point.

■ A block created on a layer other than layer 0 is always inserted on that other layer.

■ A block created on layer 0 is inserted on the current layer.

BMake

Rel.12 Creates a block via dialog box (*short for Block MAKE; an external command in BMake.Lsp*).

Command	Alias	Ctrl+	F-key	Alt+	Menu Bar	Tablet
bmake	b	. . .	. . .	DKM	Draw	. . .
					⇘Block	
					⇘Make	

Command: **bmake**
Displays dialog box:

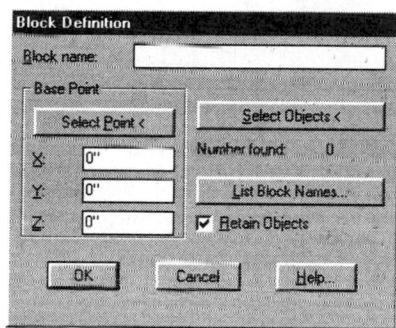

DIALOG BOX OPTIONS

Block Name   Names the block (*maximum = 31 characters*).

Base Point options:
Select Point   Picks the block's insertion point from the drawing.
X,Y,Z   Specify the x,y,z-coordinates of the insertion point.

Select Objects Picks the objects that make up the block from the drawing.
Number Found
   Displays the number of objects selected.
Retain Objects *Yes*: AutoCAD leaves objects in place after block is created.
   No: AutoCAD erases objects after block is created.
List Block Names
   Lists the names of blocks already defined in the current drawing; displays
   dialog box.

Block Names In This Drawing dialog box:

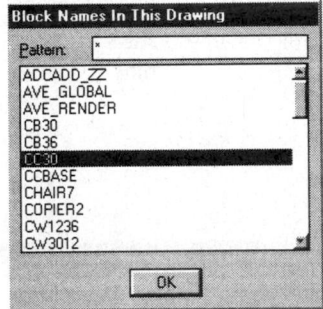

Pattern Allows the use of wildcard characters (* and ?) to shorten the list of names.
OK Selects the name of the highlighted block and dismisses the dialog box.

RELATED COMMANDS

Block Creates a block via the command line.
DdInsert Inserts blocks via dialog box.
XAttach Attaches a drawing as an external reference.

TIPS

■ A block name has up to 31 alphanumeric characters, including $, -, and _.

■ Use the **INSertion** object snap to select the block's insertion point.

■ A block created on a layer other than layer 0 is always inserted on that other layer.

■ A block created on layer 0 is inserted on the current layer.

■ Release 14 has five types of blocks:

Block	Meaning
User block	A named block created by the user.
Nested block	A block inside of another block.
Unnamed block	A block created by AutoCAD.
Xref	An externally-referenced drawing.
Dependend block	A block in an externally referenced drawing.

■ AutoCAD creates these unnamed blocks (also called "anonymous blocks"):

Name	Meaning
*An	Group.
*Dn	Associative dimension.
*Un	Created by AutoLISP or ObjectARx app.
*Xn	Hatch pattern.

■ AutoCAD automatically purges unreferenced anonymous blocks when the drawing is first loaded.

■ You cannot place an anonymous block with the **Insert** command.

BmpOut

<u>Rel.13</u> Exports selected objects in the current viewport to a BMP file.

Command	Alias	Ctrl+	F-key	Alt+	Menu Bar	Tablet
bmpout	...	...	...	FE	File	...
				⇘BMP	⇘Export	
					⇘BMP	

```
Command: bmpout
Select objects: [pick]
Select objects: [Enter]
```

Displays Create BMP File dialog box.

COMMAND LINE OPTION
Select objects Selects the objects to export in BMP format.

RELATED COMMANDS
CopyClip   Copies selected objects to the Windows Clipboard in several formats.
WmfOut   Exports selected objects to a WMF file.

RELATED WINDOWS COMMANDS
[Prt Scr]   Saves screen to Windows Clipboard.
[Alt]+[Prt Scr] Saves the topmost window to the Clipboard.

TIPS
■ BMP is short for "bitmap," the raster file standard for Windows.

■ When responding All to the 'Select objects:' prompt, the **BmpOut** command does not select all objects in the drawing; rather, it selects all objects visible in the current viewport.

■ By default, the **BmpOut** command creates a compressed BMP file, which is not read by most Windows programs. To create an uncompressed file that can be read by most applications, add the following line to the [General] section of the **Acad.Ini** file:

```
BmpOutCompression=0
```

Boundary

Rel.12 Creates a boundary as a polyline or 2D region.

Command	Alias	Ctrl+	F-key	Alt+	Menu Bar	Tablet
boundary	bo	...	...	DB	Draw	Q9
					⸂Boundary	
-boundary	-bo					
bpoly						

Command: **boundary** *or* **bpoly**
Displays dialog box:

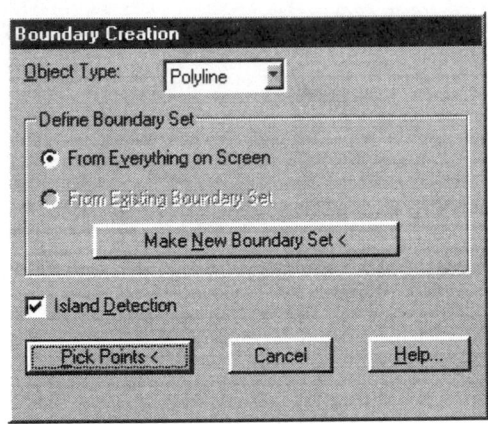

DIALOG BOX OPTIONS

Object Type   Creates boundary from a polyline or a region.

Define Boundary Set options:

From Everything on Screen
>   Selects all objects visible in current view.

From Existing Boundary Set
>   Selects all object in the current boundary selection set.

Make New Boundary Set
>   Allows you to select the boundary from the drawings.

Island detection
>   *Yes*: Objects within the outermost boundary are used as boundary objects.
>   *No*: All object withing outermost boundary are filled.

Pick Points   Picks point inside of closed area.

```
Command: -boundary
Advanced options/<Internal point>: A
Boundary set/Island detection/Object type/<eXit>: O
Region/Polyline: R
Boolean subtract inner islands?
```

COMMAND LINE OPTIONS

Advanced Options options:

Boundary set Defines the objects **BHatch** analyzes when defining a boundary from a specified pick point: (1) a new set of objects; or (2) all objects visible in the current viewport.

Island detection

 Yes: Objects within the outermost boundary are used as boundary objects.
 No: All object withing outermost boundary are filled.

Object type Selects polyline or region as the boundary object.

eXit Exits this submenu of choices.

Internal Point option:

[pick] Creates a boundary based on the point you pick.

RELATED COMMANDS

PLine Draws a polyline.

PEdit Edits a polyline.

Region Creates a 2D region from a collection of objects.

RELATED SYSTEM VARIABLE

HpBound Object used to create boundary:

HpBound	Meaning
0	Draw as polyline.
1	Draw as region (*default*)

TIPS

- Use the **Boundary** command together with the **Offset** command to help create poching.

- Although the **Boundary Creation** dialog box looks similar to the **BHatch** command's **Advanced Options** dialog box, be aware of some differences.

Box

Rel.13 Draws a 3D box as a solid model (*an external command in Acis.Dll*).

Command	Alias	Ctrl+	F-key	Alt+	Menu Bar	Tablet
box	...	...	...	DIB	Draw	J7
					⤷Solids	
					⤷Box	

```
Command: box
Center/<Corner of box> <0,0,0>: [pick]
Cube/Length/<other corner>: [pick]
Height:
```

Cube:

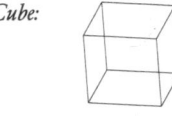

Box:

COMMAND LINE OPTION

Center	Draws the box about a center point.
Corner of box	Specify one corner for the base of box.
Cube	Draws a cube box — all sides are the same length.
Length	Specify the x, y, z-lengths.
Height	Specify the height of the box.

RELATED COMMANDS

Ai_Box	Draws a 3D wireframe box.
Cone	Draws a 3D solid cone.
Cylinder	Draws a 3D solid tube.
Sphere	Draws a 3D solid ball.
Torus	Draws a 3D solid donut.
Wedge	Draws a 3D solid wedge.

RELATED SYSTEM VARIABLES

DispSilh   Display of 3D objects as silhouettes after hidden-line removal and shading.
IsoLines   Number of isolines on solid surfaces:

IsoLines	Meaning
0	No isolines; minimum.
4	Default value.
12 *or* 16	Reasonable values.
2047	Maximum.

 # Break

V. 1.4 Removes a portion of an object.

Command	Alias	Ctrl+	F-key	Alt+	Menu Bar	Tablet
break	br	...	...	MK	Modify	W17
					⇖Break	

```
Command: break
Select object: [pick]
Enter second point (or F for first point): f
Enter first point: [pick]
Enter second point: [pick]
```

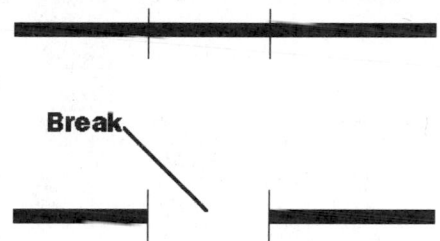

COMMAND LINE OPTIONS

Select object Selects one object to break; pick point becomes first break point, unless the F option is used at the next prompt.

Enter second point
  Selects the second break point.

F Specify the first break point.

@ Use the first break point's coordinates for the second break point.

RELATED COMMANDS

Change Changes the length lines.

PEdit Removes and relocates vertices of polylines.

Trim Shortens the lengths of open objects.

TIPS

- Use the **Break** command to convert a circle into an arc.

- The **Break** command can erase a portion of an object, as shown in the figure, above, or remove the end of an open object.

- The second point does not need to be on the object; AutoCAD breaks the object nearest to the pick point.

- The **Break** command works on the following objects: line, arc, circle, polyline, ellipse, and spline, as well as objects made from polylines, such as donuts and polygons.

Browser

Rel.14   Launches a Web browser (*an external command in Browser.Arx*).

Command	Alias	Ctrl+	F-key	Alt+	Menu Bar	Tablet
browser	...	...	...	HC	Help	Y8
					⅏Connect to the Internet	

```
Command: browser
Default Browser: C:\NETSCAPE\PROGRAM\NETSCAPE.EXE
Location  <www.autodesk.com>: [Enter]
```
Launches browser:

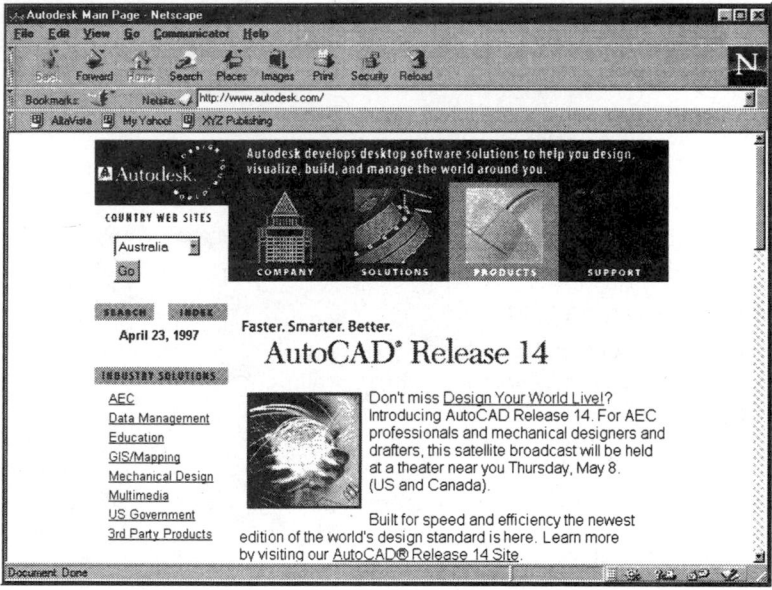

COMMAND LINE OPTION
Location   Specifies the URL; see **AttachURL** command for info about URLs.

RELATED COMMAND
InetCfg   Configures AutoCAD for access to the Internet.

TIPS
■ **URL** is short for "uniform resource locator," the universal file-naming system used on the Internet.

■ Examples of URLs include:

http://www.autodeskpress.com	Autodesk Press Web site.
http://www.autodesk.com	Autodesk primary Web site.
http://data.autodesk.com	Autodesk Data Publishing Web site.
news://adesknews.autodesk.com	Autodesk news server.
ftp://ftp.autodesk.com	Autodesk FTP server.
http://users.uniserve.com/~ralphg/	Author Ralph Grabowski's Web site.

'Cal

Rel.12 Command-line algebraic and vector geometry calculator (*an external command in GeomCal.Exp*).

Command	Alias	Ctrl+	F-key	Alt+	Menu Bar	Tablet
'cal	. . .	. . .	. . .	. . .	. . .	. . .

```
Command: cal
>>Expression:
```

COMMAND LINE OPTIONS

( )	Grouping of expressions.
[ ]	Vector expressions.
+	Addition.
-	Subtraction.
*	Multiplication.
/	Division.
^	Exponentiation.
&	Vector product of vectors.

sin	Sine.
cos	Cosine.
tang	Tangent.
asin	Arc sine.
acos	Arc cosine.
atan	Arc tangent.
ln	Natural logarithm.
log	Logarithm.
exp	Natural exponent.
exp10	Exponent.
sqr	Square.
sqrt	Square root.
abs	Absolute value.
round	Round off.
trunc	Truncate.

cvunit	Converts units using Acad.Unt.
w2u	WCS to UCS conversion.
u2w	UCS to WCS conversion.

r2d	Radians-to-degrees conversion.
d2r	Degrees-to-radians conversion.
pi	The value PI.

xyof	x- and y-coordinates of a point.
xzof	x- and z-coordinates of a point.
yzof	y- and z-coordinates of a point.
xof	x-coordinate of a point.
yof	y-coordinate of a point.
zof	z-coordinate of a point.

rxof	Real x-coordinate of a point.
ryof	Real y-coordinate of a point.
rzof	Real z-coordinate of a point.
cur	x,y,z-coordinates of picked point.
rad	Radius of object

pld	Point on line, distance from.
plt	Point on line, using parameter *t*.
rot	Rotate point through angle about origin.
ill	Intersection of two lines.
ilp	Intersection of line and plane.
dist	Distance between two points.
dpl	Distance between point and line.
dpp	Distance between point and plane.
ang	Angle between lines.
nor	Unit vector normal.

RELATED COMMANDS
All.

RELATED SYSTEM VARIABLES
UserI1 — UserI5   User-definable integer variables.
UserR1 — UserR5   User-definable real variables.

TIPS
- Since '**Cal** is a transparent command, it can be used to perform a calculation in the middle of another command.

- **Cal** understands the following prefixes:
    - *   Scalar product of vectors.
    - &   Vector product of vectors

- And the following suffixes:
    - r   Radian (*degrees is the default*)
    - g   Grad
    - '   Feet (*unitless distance is the default*)
    - "   Inches

Chamfer

V. 2.1 Bevels the intersection of two lines, all vertices of a 2D polyline, and the faces of a 3D solid model.

Command	Alias	Ctrl+	F-key	Alt+	Menu Bar	Tablet
chamfer	cha	...	...	MC	Modify ⤷Chamfer	W18

```
Command: chamfer
Polyline/Distances/Angle/Trim/Method<Select first line>: D
Enter first chamfer distance: [pick]
Enter second chamfer distance: [pick]
Polyline/Distances/Angle/Trim/Method<Select first line>: [pick]
Select second line: [pick]
```

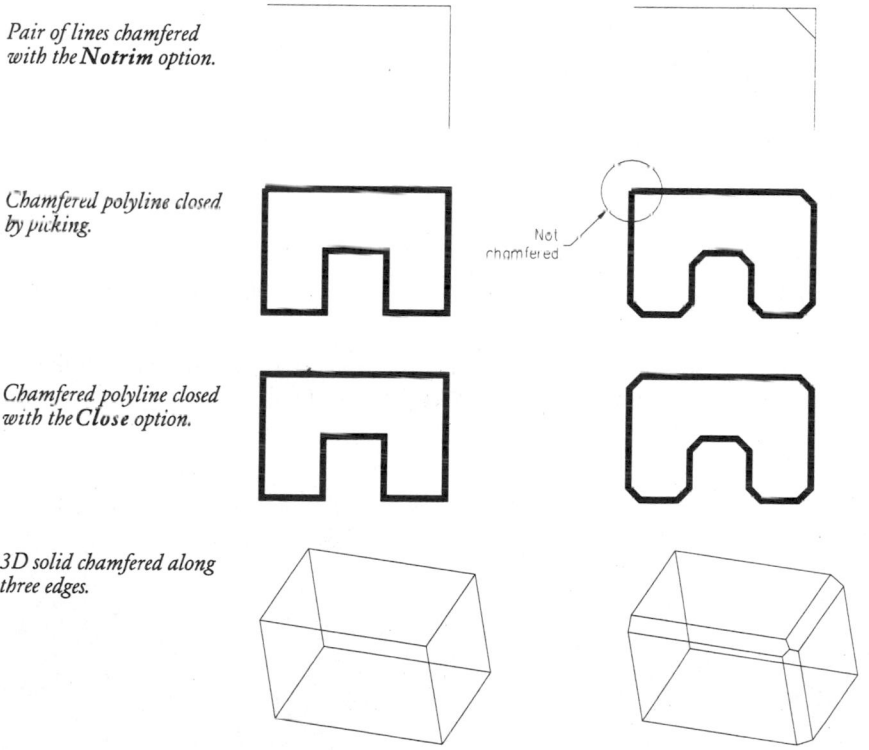

*Pair of lines chamfered with the **Notrim** option.*

Chamfered polyline closed by picking.

Not chamfered

*Chamfered polyline closed with the **Close** option.*

3D solid chamfered along three edges.

COMMAND LINE OPTIONS

PLine   Chamfers all vertices of a polyline.
Distances Specifies the chamfer distances.
Angle   Specifies the chamfer by a distance and an angle.
Trim   Toggles whether lines/edges are trimmed after chamfer.
Method   Toggles whether distance or angle are used.

RELATED COMMAND

Fillet   Rounds the intersection with a radius.

RELATED SYSTEM VARIABLES

ChamferA   First chamfer distance (*default = 0.5*).
ChamferB   Second chamfer distance (*default = 0.5*).
ChamferC   Length of chamfer (*default = 0*).
ChamferD   Chamfer angle (*default = 0*).
ChamMode   Toggles chamfer measurement:

ChamMode	Meaning
0	Chamfer by two distances (*default*).
1	Chamfer by distance and angle.

TrimMode   Determines whether lines/edges are trimmed after chamfer:

TrimMode	Meaning
0	Do not trim selected edges.
1	Trim selected edges (*default*).

TIPS

- *Caution*: The associativity of a hatch pattern is only maintained when the pattern boundary is a polyline; when the pattern boundary consists of lines, associativity is lost.

- When **TrimMode** is set to 1 and when lines do not intersect, **Chamfer** extends or trims the lines to intersect.

- When the two objects are not on the same layer, **Chamfer** places the chamfer line on the current layer; the chamfer lines takes on the layer or current color and linetype.

Change

V. 1.0 Modifies the color, elevation, layer, linetype, linetype scale, and thickness of any object, and certain other properties of lines, circles, blocks, text, and attributes.

Command	Alias	Ctrl+	F-key	Alt+	Menu Bar	Tablet
change	-ch	...	...	...	...	...

```
Command: change
Select objects: [pick]
Select objects: [Enter]
Properties/<Change point>: p
Change what property (Color/Elev/LAyer/LType/ltScale/Thickness)?
```

COMMAND LINE OPTIONS

Change point	Selects an object to change:
[pick line]	Indicates the new length of line.
[pick circle]	Indicates the new radius of circle.
[pick block]	Indicates the new insertion point or rotation angle of a block.
[pick text]	Indicates the new location of text.
[pick block]	Indicates an attribute's new text insertion point, text style, height, rotation angle, text, tag, prompt, or default value.
[Enter]	Changes the insertion point, style, height, rotation angle, and text string.

Properties options:

Color	Changes the color of the object.
Elev	Changes the elevation of the object.
LAyer	Moves the object to a different layer.
LType	Changes the linetype of the object.
ltScale	Changes the scale of the linetype.
Thickness	Changes the thickness of any object, except blocks.

RELATED COMMANDS

AttRedef	Changes a block or attribute.
ChProp	Contains the properties portion of the **Change** command.
Color	Changes the current color setting.
Colour	Changes the current colour setting.
DdChProp	Displays dialog box for changing object properties.
DdModify	Displays dialog box for changing one object at a time.
Elev	Changes the working elevation and thickness.
Modify	Changes most aspects of all objects.

RELATED SYSTEM VARIABLES

CeColor	The current color setting.
CeLType	The current linetype setting.
CircleRad	The current circle radius.
CLayer	The name of the current layer.
Elevation	The current elevation setting.
LtScale	The current linetype scale.
TextSize	The current height of text.
TextStyle	The current text style.
Thickness	The current thickness setting.

TIPS

■ The **Change** command cannot change the size of donuts, the radius or length of arcs, the length of polylines, or the justification of text.

■ Use the **Change** command to change the endpoints of a group of lines to a common vertex:

Change with Ortho mode turned off.

Change point

Change wiht Ortho mode turned on.

■ Turn ortho mode on to extend or trim a group of lines, without needing a cutting edge (as do the **Extend** and **Trim** commands).

ChProp

Rel.10 Modifies the color, layer, linetype, linetype scale, and thickness of most objects.

Command	Alias	Ctrl+	F-key	Alt+	Menu Bar	Tablet
chprop	...	...	...	...	...	...

```
Command: chprop
Select objects: [pick]
Select objects: [Enter]
Change what property (Color/LAyer/LType/ltScale/Thickness)?
```

COMMAND LINE OPTIONS

Color	Changes the color of the object.
LAyer	Moves the object to a different layer.
LType	Changes the linetype of the object.
ltScale	Changes the linetype scale.
Thickness	Changes the thickness of any object, except blocks.

RELATED COMMANDS

Change	Allows changes to lines, circles, blocks, text and attributes.
Color	Changes the current color setting.
Colour	Changes the current colour setting.
DdChProp	Displays dialog box version of the ChProp command.
DdModify	Changes most aspects of a single object.
Elev	Changes the working elevation.
LtScale	Sets the linetype scale.

RELATED SYSTEM VARIABLES

CeColor	Indicates the current color setting.
CeLtype	Indicates the current linetype name.
CLayer	Indicates the name of the current layer.
LtScale	Indicates the current linetype scale.
Thickness	Indicates the current thickness setting.

TIP

- Use the **Change** command to change the elevation of an object.

Circle

V. 1.0 Draws 2D circles by five different methods.

Command	Alias	Ctrl+	F-key	Alt+	Menu Bar	Tablet
circle	c	...	...	DC	Draw ⌖Circle	J9

```
Command: circle
3P/2P/TTR/<Center point>: [pick]
Diameter/<Radius>: [pick]
```

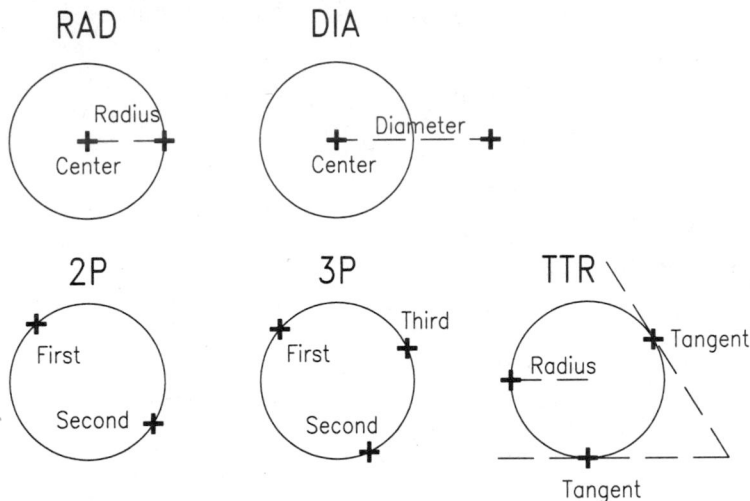

COMMAND LINE OPTIONS

Center and Radius or Diameter circle options:
Center point   Indicates the circle's center point.
Radius   Indicates the circle's radius.
Diameter   Indicates the circle's diameter.

3P (three-point) circle options:
3P   Draws a three-point circle.
First point   Indicates first point on circle.
Second point   Indicates second point on circle.
Third point   Indicates third point on circle.

2P (two-point) circle options:
2P   Draws a two-point circle.
First point on diameter
                Indicates first point on circle.
Second point on diameter
                Indicates second point on circle.

Tangent-tangent-radius circle options:

TTR   Draw a circle tangent to two lines.
Enter Tangent spec
                   Indicate first point of tangency.
Enter second Tangent spec
                   Indicate second point of tangency.
Radius   Indicate first point of radius.
Second point   Indicate second point of radius.

RELATED TOOLBAR ICONS

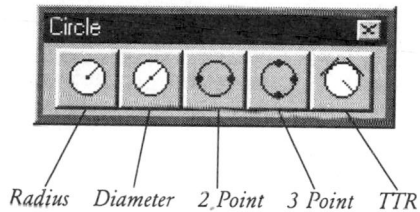

Radius   Diameter   2 Point   3 Point   TTR

RELATED COMMANDS

Arc   Draws an arc.
Donut   Draws a solid-filled circle or donut.
Ellipse   Draws an elliptical circle or arc.
Sphere   Draws a 3D solid ball.
ViewRes   Controls the visual roundness of circles.

RELATED SYSTEM VARIABLE

CircleRad   The current circle radius.

TIPS

- Sometimes it is easier to create an arc by drawing a circle, then using the **Break** or **Trim** command to convert the circle into an arc.

- The 3P (three-point) circle defines three points on the circle's circumference.

- When drawing a TTR (tangent, tangent, radius) circle, AutoCAD draws the circle with tangent points closest to the pick points; note that more than one circle placement is possible.

- Selecting **Draw | Circle | Tan, Tan, Radius** from the menu bar automatically turns on the TANgent object snap.

- Giving a circle thickness turns it into a cylinder.

'Color *or* 'Colour

V. 2.5 Sets the new working color.

Command	Alias	Ctrl+	F-key	Alt+	Menu Bar	Tablet
'color	...	...	...	...	...	...
'colour						

```
Command: color
New object color <BYLAYER>:
```

COMMAND LINE OPTIONS

BYLAYER	Sets working color to color of current layer.
BYBLOCK	Sets working color of inserted blocks.
Color Number	Sets working color using number (1 to 255), name, or abbreviation:

Color Number	Color Name	Abbreviation
1	Red	R
2	Yellow	Y
3	Green	G
4	Cyan	C
5	Blue	B
6	Magenta	M
7	White	W
8 - 249	Other colors	
250 - 255	Greys	

RELATED COMMANDS

DdColor	Displays the Select Color dialog box.
Change	Changes the color of objects.
ChProp	Changes the color of objects.
DdChProp	Changes the color of objects via a dialog box.
Preferences	The **Monochrome Vectors** option displays the drawing in black-white.

RELATED SYSTEM VARIABLES

CeColor	The current object color setting:

CeColor	Meaning
1	Red; minimum value.
7	White; default value.
255	Maximum value.

TIPS

- 'BYLAYER' means that objects take on the color assigned to that layer.

- 'BYBLOCK' means objects take on the color in effect at the time the block is inserted.

- White objects display as black when the background color is white.

- When more than one method is used to assign color to objects in a block , unpredictable results occur when the block is inserted or has its color changed.

Compile

Rel.12 Compiles SHP shape and SHP font files into SHX format.

Command	Alias	Ctrl+	F-key	Alt+	Menu Bar	Tablet
compile	...	...	...	...	...	...

Command: **compile**
Displays Select Shape or Font File dialog box.

COMMAND LINE OPTIONS
None.

RELATED COMMANDS
Load	Loads a compiled SHX shape file into the current drawing.
Style	Loads SHX and TTF font files into the current drawing.

RELATED SYSTEM VARIABLE
ShpName	The current SHP filename.

TIPS
- As of Release 12, the **Style** command converts SHP font files on-the-fly; it is only necessary to use the **Compile** command to obtain an SHX font file.

- As of Release 14, AutoCAD no longer supports PostScript font files.

- TrueType fonts are not compiled.

Cone

Rel.11 Draws a 3D ACIS cone with a circular or elliptical base (*an external command in Acis.Dll*).

Command	Alias	Ctrl+	F-key	Alt+	Menu Bar	Tablet
cone	...	...	...	DIO	Draw ↳Solids ↳Cone	M7

```
Command: cone
```

Cone with circular base:
```
Elliptical/<center point> <0,0,0>:[pick center point]
Diameter/<Radius>: [specify radius or type D]
Apex/<Height>: [specify height]
```

Cone with elliptical base and apex:
```
Elliptical/<center point> <0,0,0>: E
<Axis endpoint>/Center: C
Center of ellipse <0,0,0>: [pick]
Axis endpoint: [pick]
Other axis endpoint: [pick]
Apex/<Height>: A
Apex: [pick]
```

Cone: ——————————————

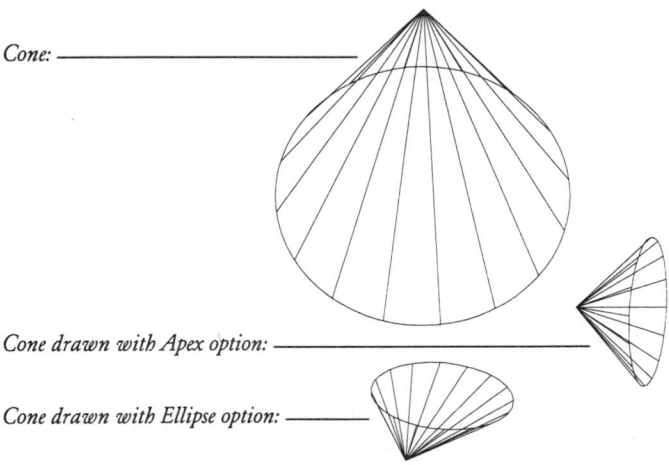

Cone drawn with Apex option: ——————————————

Cone drawn with Ellipse option: ————————

COMMAND LINE OPTIONS

Elliptical   Draws a cone with an elliptical base.
Center point   Specifies the center point of the cone's base.
Axis endpoint Picks the endpoint of the axis defining the elliptical base.
Center of ellipse
          Picks the center of the elliptical base.

| Height | Specifies the height of the cone. |
| Apex | Determines height and orientation of the cone's tip. |

RELATED COMMANDS

Ai_Cone	Draws a 3D wireframe cone.
Box	Draws a 3D solid box.
Cylinder	Draws a 3D solid tube.
Sphere	Draws a 3D solid ball.
Torus	Draws a 3D solid donut.
Wedge	Draws a 3D solid wedge.

RELATED SYSTEM VARIABLES

| DispSilh | Toggles display of 3D objects as silhouettes after hidden-line removal and shading. |
| IsoLines | Number of isolines on solid surfaces: |

IsoLines	Meaning
0	Minimum; no isolines.
4	Default.
12 or 16	A reasonable value.
2047	Maximum value.

TIPS

■ You define the elliptical base in two ways: (1) by the length of the major and minor axes; or (2) by the center point and two radii.

■ To draw a cone at an angle, use the **Apex** option.

REMOVED COMMAND

The **Config** command now executes the **Preferences** command.

Convert

Converts 2D polylines and associative hatches to their R14 formats.

Command	Alias	Ctrl+	F-key	Alt+	Menu Bar	Tablet
convert	...	...	...	...	...	...

```
Command: convert
Hatch/Polyline/<All>: [Enter]
Select/<All>: [Enter]
10 hatch objects converted.
203 2d polyline objects converted.
```

COMMAND LINE OPTIONS

Hatch	Converts associative hatch patterns from anonymous block to R14 format.
Polyline	Converts 2D polylines to R14's Lwpolyline object.
All	Converts all polylines and hatch patterns.
Select	Selects the hatch patterns and polylines to convert.

RELATED COMMANDS

BHatch	Creates associative hatch patterns.
PLine	Draws 2D polylines.

RELATED SYSTEM VARIABLE

PLineType   Determines whether pre-R14 polylines are converted in Release 14.

PlineType	Meaning
0	Not converted; **PLine** creates old-format polylines.
1	Not converted; **PLine** creates new-format polylines.
2 (*default*)	Converted; **PLine** creates new-format polylines.

TIPS

■ When an R13 — or earlier — drawing is opened in Release 14, AutoCAD automatically converts most (not all) 2D polylines to the new Lwpolyline (short for "light weight polyline") object; hatch patterns are not automatically updated.

■ A hatch pattern is automatically updated the first time the **HatchEdit** command is applied, or when its boundary is changed.

■ Autodesk warns that "hatch pattern rotation information may not update properly if the UCS has changed since the hatch was created." For this reason, Autodesk recommends using the **Select** option of the **Convert** command to check the effect of the conversion on an individual basis.

■ You need only use the **Convert** command when polylines are: (1) created in Release 14 by a non-R14 third-party application; or (2) in a pre-R14 block that was exploded after being inserted in R14.

■ Polylines are not converted when they contain: (1) curve fit segments; (2) splined segments; (3) extended object data in their vertices; or (4) 3D polylines.

■ System variable **PLineType** affects: **Boundary** (*when a polyline*), **Donut**, **Ellipse** (*PEllipse = 1*), **PEdit** (*converting a line or arc*), **Polygon**, and **Sketch** (*SkPoly = 1*).

 # Copy

V. 1.0 Creates one or more copies of an object.

Command	Alias	Ctrl+	F-key	Alt+	Menu Bar	Tablet
copy	co	...	...	MC	Modify ⤷Copy	V15
	cp					

```
Command: copy
Select objects: [pick]
Select objects: [Enter]
<Base point or displacement>/Multiple: [pick]
Second point of displacement: [pick]
```

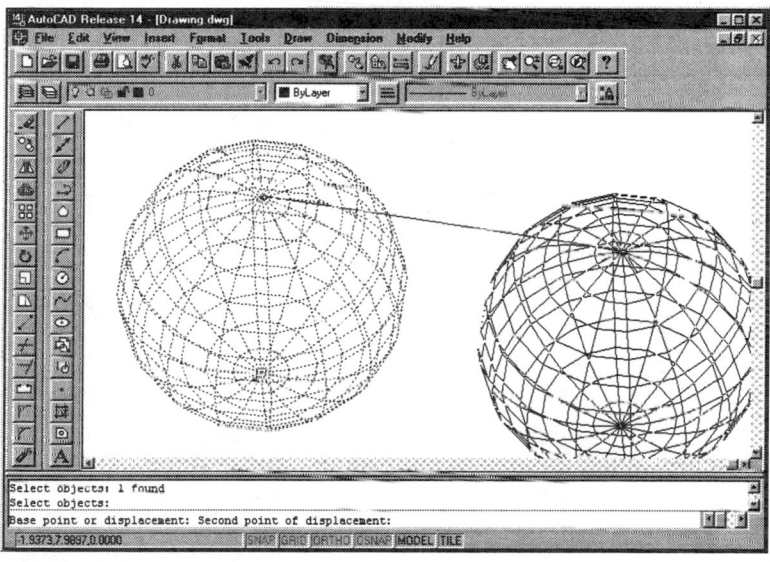

COMMAND LINE OPTIONS

Base point or displacement
    Indicates the starting point, or the distance to move.
Second point Indicates the point to move.
Multiple   Allows the object to be copied more than once.
[Esc]   Cancels multiple object copying.

RELATED COMMANDS

Array   Draws a rectangular or polar array of objects.
MInsert   Places an array of blocks.
Move   Moves an object to a new location.
Offset   Draws parallel lines, polylines, circles, and arcs.

TIPS

- Use the **M** (*multiple*) option to quickly place several copies of the original object.

- Inserting a block multiple times is more efficient than placing multiple copies.

- Turn ortho mode on to copy objects in a precise horizontal and vertical direction.

- Turn snap mode on to copy objects in precise increments.

- Use object snap modes to precisely copy objects from one geometric feature to another.

- To copy an object by a known distance, enter 0,0 as the 'Base point.' Then enter the known distance as the 'Second point.'

- **Copy** works in 2D (supply coordinate pairs) and 3D (supply coordinate triplets). In 2D, the current elevation is used as the z-coordinate.

CopyClip

Rel.12 Copies selected objects to the Windows Clipboard (*short for COPY to CLIPboard*).

Command	Alias	Ctrl+	F-key	Alt+	Menu Bar	Tablet
copyclip	...	C	...	EC	Edit ⤷Copy	T14

```
Command: copyclip
Select objects: [pick]
Select objects: [Enter]
```

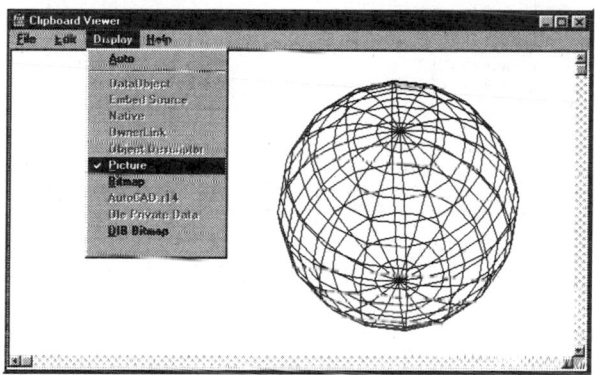

COMMAND LINE OPTION
Select objects   Selects the objects to copy to Clipboard.

RELATED COMMANDS
BmpOut   Exports selected objects in the current view to a BMP file.
CopyHist   Copies Text window text to the Windows Clipboard.
CopyLink   Copies current viewport to the Clipboard.
CutClip   Cuts selected objects to the Clipboard.
PasteClip   Pastes from the Clipboard into the drawing.
WmfOut   Exports selected objects to a WMF file.

RELATED WINDOWS COMMANDS
[Prt Scr]   Copies the entire screen to the Windows Clipboard
[Alt]+[Prt Scr] Copies the topmost window to the Clipboard.

TIPS
■ Contrary to the AutoCAD *Command Reference*, text objects are *not* copied to the Clipboard in text format.

■ When specifying the **All** option to the 'Select objects' prompt, the **CopyClip** command only selects all objects visible in the current viewport.

CopyHist

Rel.13 Copies Text window text to the Windows Clipboard (*short for COPY HISTory*).

Command	Alias	Ctrl+	F-key	Alt+	Menu Bar	Tablet
copyhist	...	...	...	EH	Edit ↳Copy History	...

Command: **copyhist**

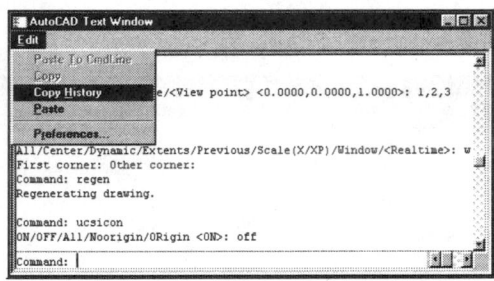

COMMAND LINE OPTIONS
None.

RELATED COMMANDS
CopyClip — Copies selected text from the drawing to the Clipboard in text format.
CopyLink — Copies current viewport to the Clipboard.
CutClip — Cuts selected objects to the Clipboard.

RELATED WINDOWS COMMAND
[Alt]+[Prt Scr] Copies the Text window to the Clipboard in graphics format.

TIPS
- To copy a selected portion of Text window text to the Clipboard, highlight the text first, then select **Edit | Copy** from the Text window's menu bar.

- To paste text to the command line, select **Edit | Paste to Cmdline** from the menu bar. However, this only works when the Windows Clipboard contains text — not graphics.

- As an alternative, you can right-click in the Text window to bring up the cursor menu:

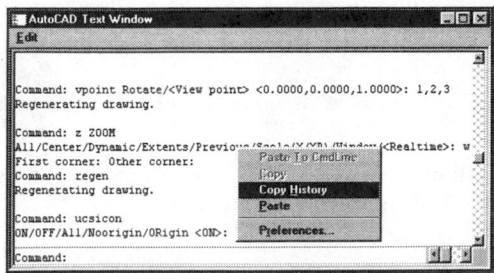

CopyLink

Rel.13 Copies the current viewport to the Windows Clipboard.

Command	Alias	Ctrl+	F-key	Alt+	Menu Bar	Tablet
copylink	...	...		CL	Edit	...
					⮡Copy Link	

Command: **copyclip**

COMMAND LINE OPTIONS
None.

RELATED COMMANDS
BmpOut	Exports selected objects in the current view to a BMP file.
CopyClip	Copies selected objects to the Windows Clipboard.
CopyHist	Copies Text window text to the Clipboard.
CutClip	Cuts selected objects to the Clipboard.
PasteClip	Pastes from the Clipboard into the drawing.
WmfOut	Exports selected objects to a WMF file.

RELATED WINDOWS COMMANDS
[Prt Scr]	Copies the entire screen to the Windows Clipboard
[Alt]+[Prt Scr]	Copies the topmost window to the Clipboard.

TIPS
- In the other application, use the **Edit | Paste** or **Edit | Paste Special** commands to paste the AutoCAD image into the document; the **Paste Special** command lets you specify the pasted format.

- AutoCAD does not let you link a drawing to itself.

CutClip

Rel.12 Cuts the selected objects to the Windows Clipboard (*short for CUT to CLIPboard*).

Command	Alias	Ctrl+	F-key	Alt+	Menu Bar	Tablet
cutclip	...	X	...	ET	Edit ⤷Cut	T13

```
Command: cutclip
Select objects: [pick]
Select objects: [Enter]
```

COMMAND LINE OPTION

Select objects   Selects the objects to cut to Clipboard.

RELATED COMMANDS

BmpOut	Exports selected objects in the current view to a BMP file.
CopyClip	Copies selected objects to the Clipboard.
CopyHist	Copies Text window text to the Windows Clipboard.
CopyLink	Copies current viewport to the Clipboard.
PasteClip	Pastes from the Clipboard into the drawing.
WmfOut	Exports selected objects to a WMF file.

RELATED WINDOWS COMMANDS

[Prt Scr]   Copies the entire screen to the Windows Clipboard
[Alt]+[Prt Scr]   Copies the topmost window to the Clipboard.

TIPS

- Contrary to the AutoCAD *Command Reference*, text objects are *not* copied to the Clipboard in text format.

- In the other application, use the **Edit | Paste** or **Edit | Paste Special** commands to paste the AutoCAD image into the document; the **Paste Special** command lets you specify the pasted format.

- When specifying the **All** option to the 'Select objects:' prompt, the **CutClip** command only selects all objects visible in the current viewport.

Cylinder

Rel.12 Draws a 3D ACIS cylinder with a circular or elliptical cross section (*an external command in Acis.Dll*).

Command	Alias	Ctrl+	F-key	Alt+	Menu Bar	Tablet
cylinder	...	...	...	DIC	Draw ⮑Solids ⮑Cylinder	L7

```
Command: cylinder
Elliptical/<center point> <0,0,0>: [pick]
Diameter/<Radius>: [pick]
Center of other end/<Height>: [pick]
```

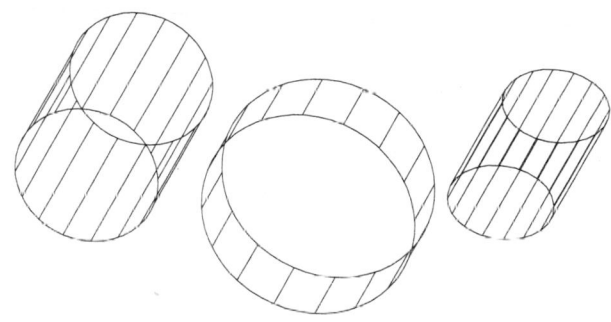

RELATED COMMANDS

Box	Draws a 3D solid box.
Cone	Draws a 3D solid cone.
Elevation	Turns a circle into a wireframe cylinder.
Extrude	Creates a cylinder with an arbitrary cross-section and sloped walls.
Sphere	Draws a 3D solid ball.
Torus	Draws a 3D solid donut.
Wedge	Draws a 3D solid wedge.

RELATED SYSTEM VARIABLES

DispSilh   Displays 3D objects as silhouettes after hidden-line removal and shading.
IsoLines   Number of isolines on solid surfaces:

IsoLines	Meaning
0	Minimum (no isolines).
4	Default.
12 *or* 16	A reasonable value.
2047	Maximum value.

TIP

■ The **Ellipse** option draws a cylinder with an elliptical cross-section.

DbList

<u>V. 1.0</u> Lists information on all objects in the drawing (*short for Data Base LISTing*).

Command	Alias	Ctrl+	F-key	Alt+	Menu Bar	Tablet
dblist	...	...	...	...	...	...

Command: **dblist**

Sample listing:

```
        LINE        Layer: 1
                    Space: Model space
      from point, X=   3.7840  Y=   4.7169  Z=   0.0000
        to point, X=   4.1440  Y=   4.7169  Z=   0.0000
   Length =   0.3600,  Angle in X-Y Plane =        0
  Delta X =   0.3600, Delta Y = 0.0000, Delta Z = 0.0000

        ARC         Layer: 2
                    Space: Model space
    center point, X=   2.1000  Y=   7.0000  Z=   0.0000
    radius     1.2000
    start angle      0
      end angle    180
```

COMMAND LINE OPTIONS
[Enter]	Continues display after pause.
[Esc]	Cancels database listing.

RELATED COMMANDS
Area	Lists the area and perimeter of objects.
Dist	Lists the 3D distance and angle between two points.
Id	Lists the 3D coordinates of a point.
List	Lists information about selected objects in the drawing.

DdAttDef

Rel.12 Defines an attribute definition via a dialog box (*short for Dynamic Dialog ATTribute DEFinition; an external file in DdAttDef.Lsp*).

Command	Alias	Ctrl+	F-key	Alt+	Menu Bar	Tablet
ddattdef	at	...	...	DKD	Draw	...
					↳Block	
					↳Define Attribute	

Command: **ddattdef**
Displays dialog box:

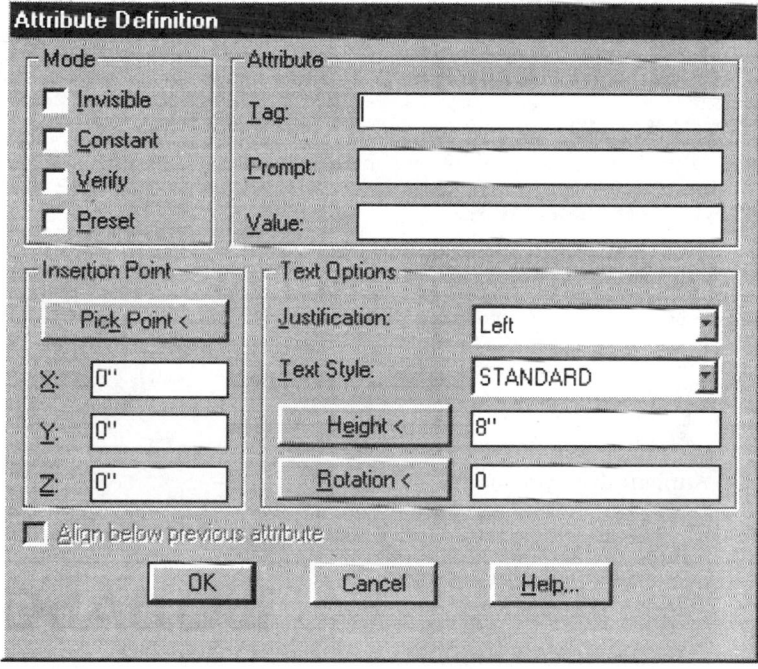

DIALOG BOX OPTIONS

Mode options:

Invisible	Makes the attribute text invisible.
Constant	Uses constant values for the attributes.
Verify	Verifies the text after input.
Preset	Presets the variable attribute text.

Attribute options:

Tag	Identifies the attribute.
Prompt	Prompts the user for input.
Value	Sets the default value for the attribute.

Insertion Point *options:*

Pick point	Picks insertion point with cursor.
X	Specifies the x-coordinate insertion point.
Y	Specifies the y-coordinate insertion point.
Z	Specifies the z-coordinate insertion point.

Text *options:*

Justification	Sets the justification.
Text style	Selects a style.
Height	Specifies the height.
Rotation	Sets the rotation angle.
Align	Automatically places the text below the previous attribute.

RELATED COMMAND

AttDef   Defines attribute definitions via the command line.

RELATED SYSTEM VARIABLES

■ **AFlags**   Attribute mode:

AFlags	Meaning
0	No mode specified (*default*).
1	Invisible.
2	Constant.
4	Verify.
8	Preset.

■ **AttMode**   Attribute display modes:

AFlags	Meaning
0	Off.
1	Normal (*default*).
2	On.

■ **AttReq**   Toggles prompt for attributes:

AFlags	Meaning
0	Assumes the default values.
1	Prompts for attributes (*default*).

DdAttE

Rel.9 Edits attribute data via a dialog box (*short for Dynamic Dialog ATTribute Editor*).

Command	Alias	Ctrl+	F-key	Alt+	Menu Bar	Tablet
ddatte	ate	...	...	MOAS	Modify ↳Object ↳Attribute ↳Single	Y20

Command: **ddatte**
Select block: **[pick]**
Displays dialog box:

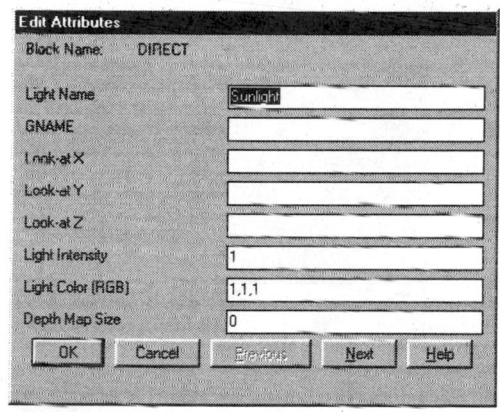

DIALOG BOX OPTIONS
Block Name Names the selected block.
Attribute prompt Allows you to change the attribute value.

RELATED COMMANDS
AttEdit	Globally edits attributes.
AttReDef	Changes the definition of attributes.
DdEdit	Edits attribute definitions.

RELATED SYSTEM VARIABLE
AttDia   Toggles use of **DdAttE** during **Insert** command.

TIP
■ To edit the different parts of an attribute, use the following commands:

Command	Edit Attribute
DdEdit	Attribute *definitions*.
DdAttE	Non-constant attribute *values* in one block.
AttEdit	Attribute *values* and *properties* (such as position, height, and style) in one block or in all attributes.

DdAttExt

Rel.12 Extracts attribute information to a file (*short for Dynamic Dialog ATTribute EXTraction; an external command in Ddattext.Lsp*).

Command	Alias	Ctrl+	F-key	Alt+	Menu Bar	Tablet
ddattext	...	...	...	FE	File	...
				⭢DXX	⭢Export	
					⭢DXX Extract	

Command: **ddattext**
Displays dialog box:

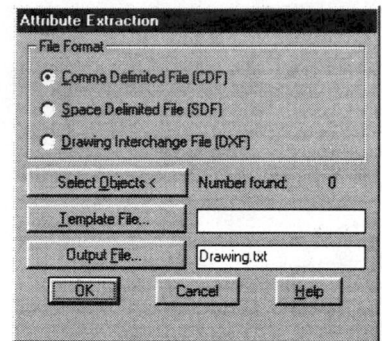

DIALOG BOX OPTIONS

Comma delimited
> Creates a CDF text file, where commas separate fields.

Space delimited
> Creates an SDF text file, where spaces separate fields.

Drawing interchange
> Creates an ASCII DXF file.

Select Objects Returns to the graphics screen to select attributes for export.

Template file Specifies the name of the TXT template file for CDF and SDF files.

Output File Specifies the name of the attribute output file: **TXT** for CDF and SDF formats; **DXX** for DXF format.

RELATED COMMAND

AttExt Extracts attributes via command line interface.

TIPS

■ See **AttExt** for a Quick Start Tutorial on extracting attributes from a drawing.

■ **CDF** (short for "Comma Delimited File") format has one record for each block reference; a comma separates each field; single quote marks delimit text strings.

■ **SDF** (short for "Space Delimited File") format has one record for each block reference; fields have fixed width padded with spaces; string delimiters are not used.

■ **DXF** (short for "Drawing Interchange File") format contains only block reference, attribute, and end-of-sequence DXF objects; no template file is required.

DdChProp

Rel.12 Modifies the color, layer, linetype, linetype scale, and thickness of most objects via a dialog box (*short for Dynamic Dialog CHange PROPerties; an external command in DdChProp.Lsp*).

Command	Alias	Ctrl+	F-key	Alt+	Menu Bar	Tablet
ddchprop	ch	...	...	MP	Modify ⬎Properties	...

```
Command: ddchprop
Select objects: [pick]
Select objects: [Enter]
```
Displays dialog box:

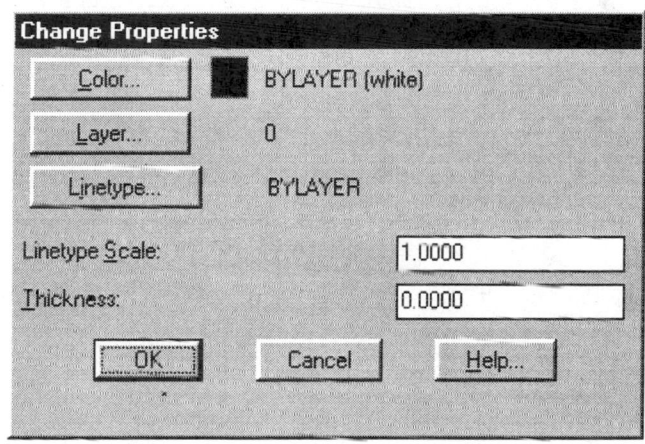

DIALOG BOX OPTIONS

Color   Changes color of the selected objects; displays the **Select Color** dialog box.
Layer name   Moves selected objects to another layer; displays the **Select Layer** dialog box.
Linetype   Changes the linetype of the selected objects; displays the **Select Linetype** dialog box.
Linetype Scale   Changes the linetype scale of the selected objects.
Thickness   Changes the thickness of the selected objects.

RELATED COMMANDS

ChProp   Changes properties via command line.
Change   Allows changes to lines, circles, blocks, text, and attributes.
DdModify   Changes the properties of a single object.

RELATED SYSTEM VARIABLES

CeColor   Indicates the current object color setting.
CeLtype   Indicates the current object linetype setting.
CLayer   Indicates the name of the current layer.
Thickness   Indicates the current thickness setting.

TIPS

■ The **Select Color** dialog box:

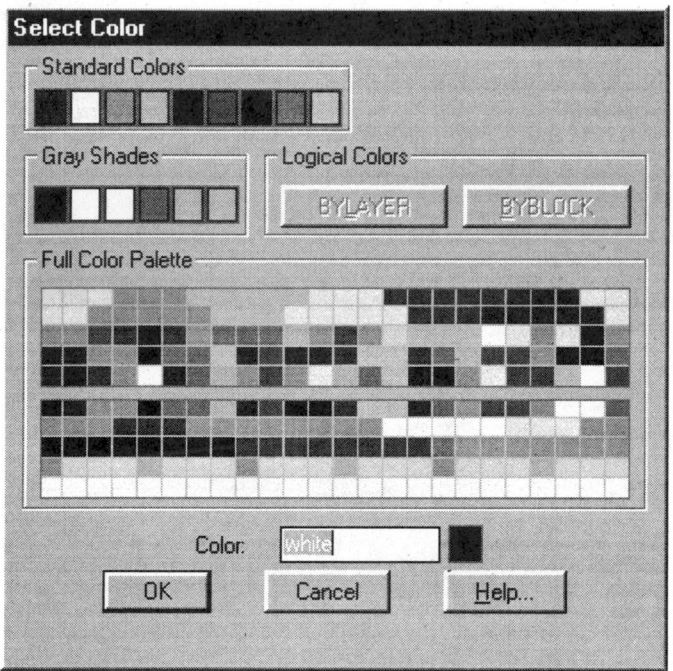

■ The **Select Linetype** dialog box:

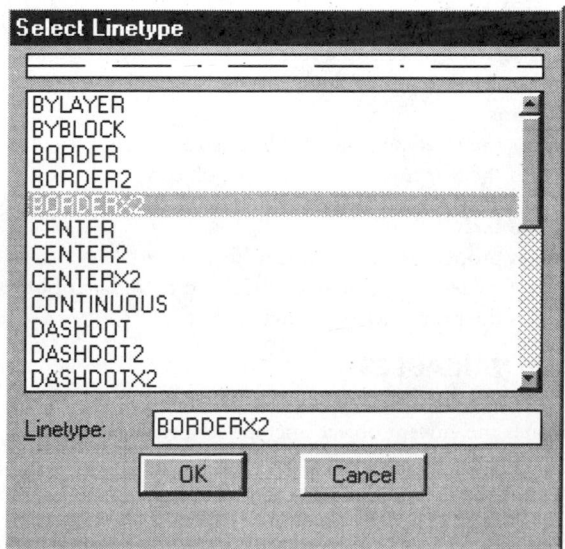

■ The **Select Layer** dialog box:

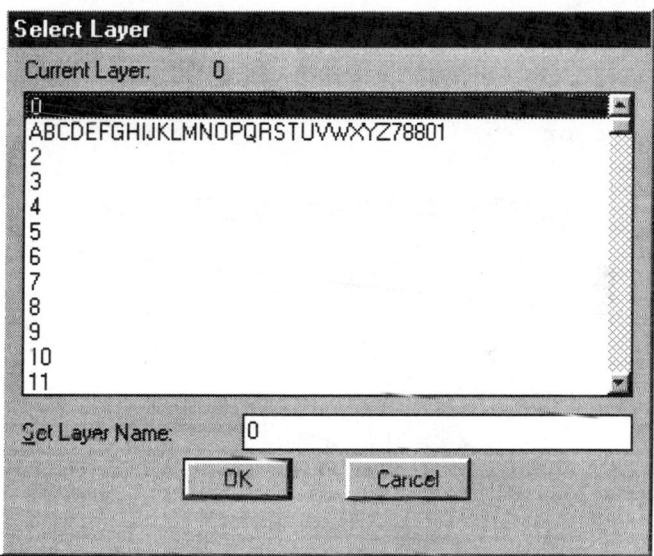

■ Before you can select a linetype or a layer from the **Select** dialog boxes, the linetype or layer must have been already loaded by the **Layer** command.

'DdColor

Rel.13 Set thes current working color by dialog box (*an external command in DdColor.Lsp*).

Command	Alias	Ctrl+	F-key	Alt+	Menu Bar	Tablet
'ddcolor	col	...	...	OC	Format ⌵Color	U4

Command: **ddcolor**
Displays dialog box:

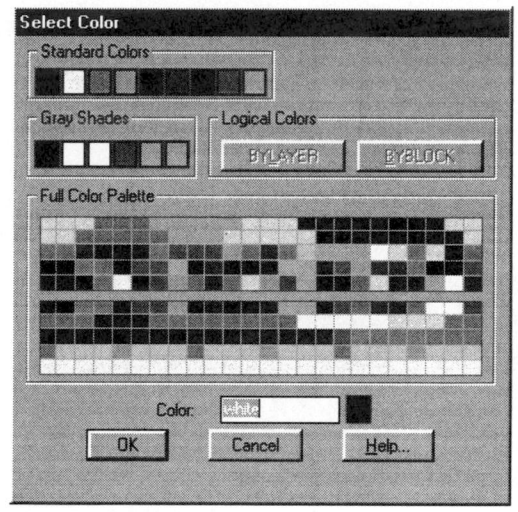

DIALOG BOX OPTIONS

Standard Colors options:
>   Selects one of the first nine colors, #1 through #9.

Gray Shades options:
>   Selects one of the six last colors, #250 through #255.

Logical Colors options:
Bylayer   Sets color to BYLAYER.
Byblock   Sets color to BYBLOCK.

Full Color Palette options:
>   Selects one of the other 240 other colors, #10 through #249.

Color   Sets the color number or name.

RELATED COMMANDS
Color   Changes the color from the 'Command' prompt.
DdChProp   Changes the color of selected objects.

RELATED SYSTEM VARIABLE
CeColor   Contains the number for the current working color.

DdEdit

Rel.11 Edits a single line of text or a single attribute using a dialog box; launches the text editor for editing multiline text (*short for Dynamic Dialog EDITor*).

Command	Alias	Ctrl+	F-key	Alt+	Menu Bar	Tablet
ddedit	ed	. . .	. . .	MOT	Modify	Y21
					↳Object	
					↳Text	

```
Command: ddedit
<Select a TEXT or ATTDEF object>/Undo: [pick text]
```

For single-line text (placed by the DText or Text command), displays dialog box:

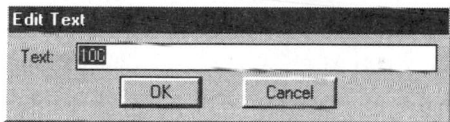

For paragraph text (placed by MText command), displays dialog box:

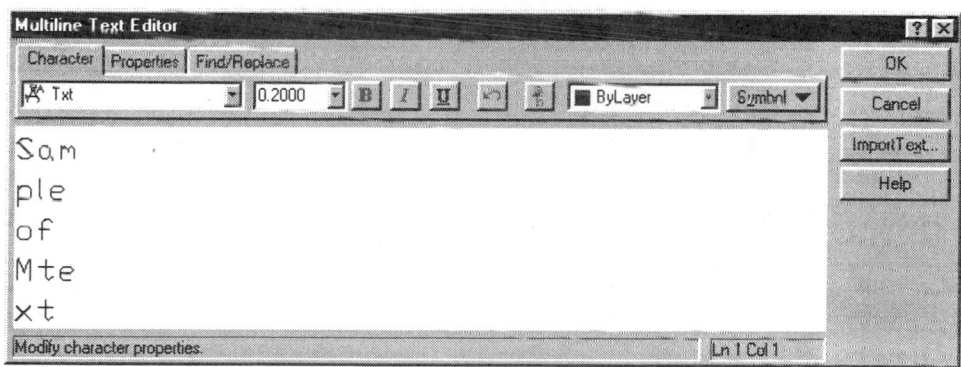

For attribute text (placed by the Block command), displays dialog box:

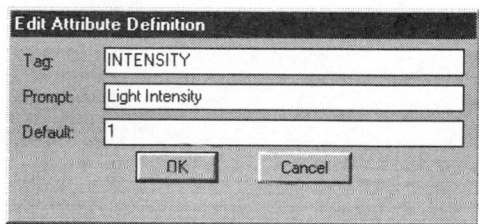

COMMAND LINE OPTIONS

U	Undoes editing operation.
[Esc]	Ends the command.

RELATED COMMANDS

DdAttE   Edits all text attributes connected with a block.
Change   Edits some text *properties*, not the text itself.
MtEdit   Edits paragraph text.

RELATED SYSTEM VARIABLE

MTextEd   Name of the text editor used for editing multiline text.

TIPS

- The **DdEdit** command automatically repeats; press **[Esc]** to cancel the command.

- Use the **DdAttE** command to edit attribute values.

- Start a text string with a backslash (\) to prefix with a space.

- Start a text string with two backslashes (\\) to prefix with a backslash.

- To edit the different parts of an attribute, use the following commands:

Command	Edit Attribute
DdEdit	Attribute *definitions*.
DdAttE	Non-constant attribute *values* in one block.
AttEdit	Attribute *values* and *properties* (such as position, height, and style) in one block or in all attributes.

REMOVED COMMAND

The **DdEModes** command has been removed from Release 14. In its place, use the **Object Properties** toolbar.

'DdGrips

Rel.12 Turns object grips on and off; defines the size and color of grips (*an external command in DdGrips.lsp*).

Command	Alias	Ctrl+	F-key	Alt+	Menu Bar	Tablet
'ddgrips	gr	A	...	TG	Tools ↳Grips	X10

Command: **ddgrips**
Displays dialog box:

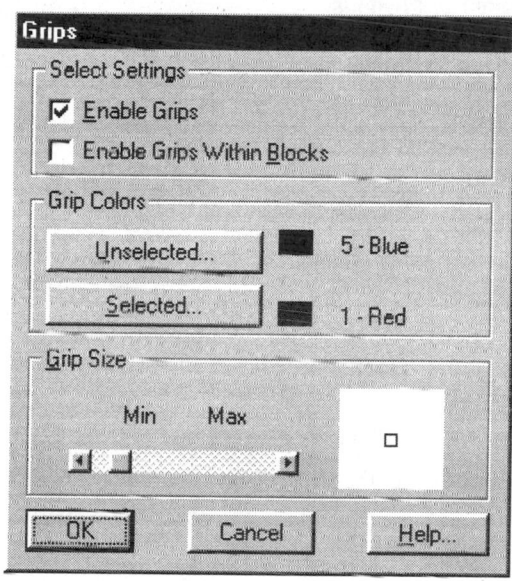

DIALOG BOX OPTIONS

Select Settings options:

Enable Grips   *Yes*: Grips are displayed when an object is picked.
    No: Grips are not displayed.

Enable Grips Within Blocks
    Displays grips on objects within blocks.

Grip Colors options:

Unselected   Defines the color of unselected grips; displays **Select Color** dialog box.
Selected   Defines the color of selected grips; displays **Select Color** dialog box.

Grip Size   Changes the size of the grip box.

RELATED COMMAND

Select   Creates a selection set of objects.

RELATED SYSTEM VARIABLES

Grips	Toggles use of grips:

Grips	Meaning
0	Disable grips.
1	Enable grips (*default*).

GripBlock Toggles display of grips inside blocks:

GripBlock	Meaning
0	Display grip at insertion point (*default*).
1	Display grips on all objects in block.

GripColor Color of unselected grips (*default = 5, blue*).
GripHot Color of selected grip (*default = 1, red*).
GripSize Size of grip in pixels:

GripSize	Meaning
1	Minimum size, in pixels.
3	Default size.
255	Maximum size.

TIPS

- *Grips* are small squares that appear on an object when the object is selected at the 'Command' prompt. In other Windows applications, grips are known as *handles*.

- When an object is first selected, the grips are blue squares; these are called *unselected* or *cold* grips.

- When a grip is selected, it turns into a solid red square; this is called a *hot* grip.

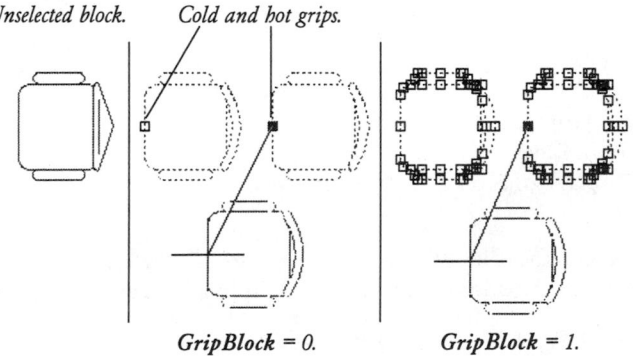

Unselected block. *Cold and hot grips.*

GripBlock = 0. *GripBlock = 1.*

- Press [Esc] twice to turn off unselected grips.
- Press [Esc] three times to turn off hot grips.

DDim

Rel.12 Sets dimension styles and variables via a dialog box (*short for Dialog DIMension*).

Command	Alias	Ctrl+	F-key	Alt+	Menu Bar	Tablet
ddim	d	...	...	OD	Format	Y5
					⤷Dimension Style	

Command: **ddim**
Displays dialog box:

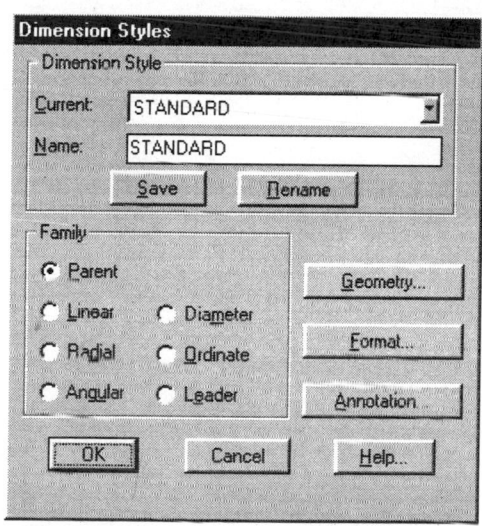

DIALOG BOX OPTIONS

Dimension Style options:

Current	Selects a dimstyle (short for "dimension style") name.
Name	Creates a new named dimstyle.
Save	Saves the dimstyle.
Rename	Renames the dimstyle.

Family options:

Parent	Makes changes to all aspects of a dimension style.
Linear	Makes changes to variables relating to linear dimensions.
Radial	Makes changes to variables relating to radial dimensions.
Angular	Makes changes to variables relating to angular dimensions.
Diameter	Makes changes to variables relating to diameter dimensions.
Ordinate	Makes changes to variables relating to ordinates.
Leader	Makes changes to variables relating to leaders.
Geometry	Specify the dimension geometry variables: dimension, extension, and center lines; center marks; arrowheads; and overall scale; displays dialog box.

Geometry dialog box:

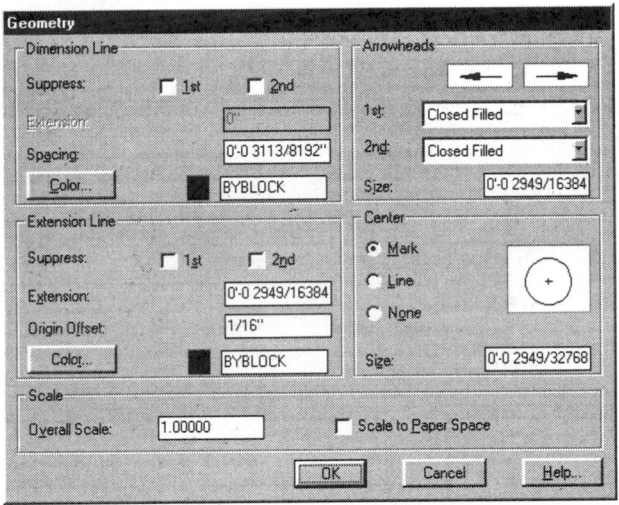

Dimension Line options:

Suppress Suppresses display of first and/or second dimension line when outside extension lines; stored in **DimSD1** and **DimSD2**.

Extension Specifies distance the dimension line extends past the extension line (when oblique strokes are used for arrowheads); stored in **DimDLE**.

Spacing Sets the spacing between dimension lines of a baseline dimension; stored in system variable **DimDLi**.

Color Specifies color of the dimension line; stored in **DimClrD**.

Extension Line options:

Suppress Suppresses display of first and/or second extension line; stored in **DimSE1** and **DimSE2**.

Extension Specifies the distance that the extension line extends above dimension line; stored in **DimExe**.

Origin Offset Specifies the offset distance of extension line from origin point; stored in **DimExO**.

Color Color of extension lines; stored in **DimClrE**.

Arrowheads options (when a different arrowhead is selected, DimSAh is turned on):

1st Selects first (lefthand) arrowhead; stored in **DimBlk1**.

2nd Selects second (righthand) arrowhead; stored in **DimBlks**.

Size Sizes the arrowheads; stored in **DimASz**.

Center options:
Mark, Line, None

Specifies the size and style of a center mark drawn in radial and diameter dimensions; stored in **DimCen**:

DimCen	Meaning
0	Draws no center mark.
positive	Draws the center mark only (*default = 0.09*).
negative	Draws the center mark and extension lines.

Size
Sizes the center mark; stored in **DimCen**.

Scale options:
Overall Scale Specifies the scale factor for all dimensions; stored in **DimScale**.
Scale to Paper Space

Specifies the scale factor between model space and paper space; usually stored as 0 in **DimScale**; when **TileMode** = 1, then **DimScale** = 1.0.

Format
Specifies the dimension format variables: location of dimension text; arrowheads; and leader and dimension lines; displays dialog box.

Format dialog box:

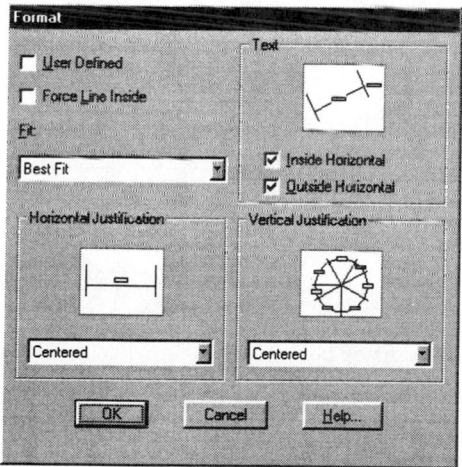

Format options:
User Defined Places text at the position specified by you at the 'Dimension Line Location' prompt; stored in **DimUpT**.
Force Line Inside

Specifies how dimension lines are drawn between extension lines; stored in **DimTOFL**.

| Fit | Specifies the placement of text and/or arrowheads inside or outside extension lines; stored in **DimFit**: |

DimFit	Meaning
0 (Text and Arrows)	Place between extension lines if possible.
1 (Text Only)	Text has priority over arrowheads.
2 (Arrows Only)	Whichever fits between extension lines.
3 (Best Fit)	Whatever fits (*default*).
4 (Leader)	Place text at end of leader line.
5 (No Leader)	Don't draw a leader line.

Horizontal Justification

Specifies the horizontal justification of dimension text along dimension line and extension line; stored in **DimJust**:

DimJust	Meaning
0	Center justify (*default*)
1	Next to first extension line.
2	Next to second extension line.
3	Above first extension line.
4	Above second extension line.

| Text | Specifies the orientation of dimension text inside or outside extension lines; stored in **DimTIH** and **DimTOH**. |

Vertical Justification

Specifies the vertical justification of dimension text along dimension line; stored in **DimTAD**:

DimTAD	Meaning
0	Center justify (*default*)
1	Above dimension line.
2	Outside of dimension line.
3	Conform to JIS standard.

| Annotation | Specify the dimension annotation variables: controls the look of dimension text; displays dialog box. |

Annotation dialog box:

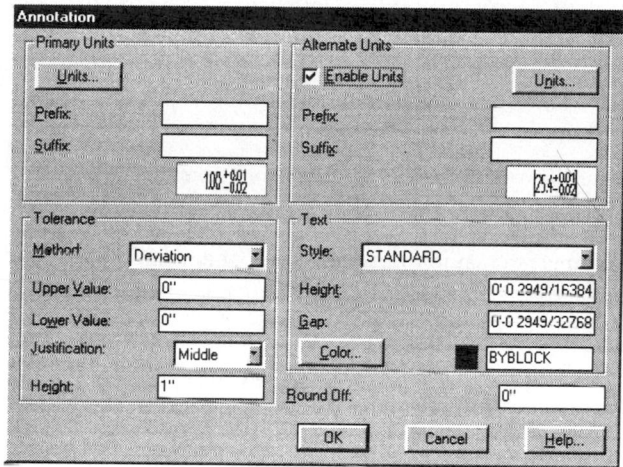

Primary Units options:

Units	Specifies the units in linear, angle, and tolerance dimensions.
Prefix	Specifies the prefix for dimension text.
Suffix	Specifies the suffix for dimension text; stored in **DimPost**.

Tolerance options:

Method   Determines the type of tolerance; stored in **DimTol** and **DimLim**:

DimTol	DimLim	Meaning
0	0	No tolerance (*default*).
1	0	Symmetrical tolerance value.
1	0	Deviation.
0	1	Limits.

Upper Value	Specifies the maximum (upper or plus) tolerance value; stored in **DimTP**.
Lower Value	Specifies the minimum (lower or minus) tolerance value; stored in **DimTM**.
Justification	Controls text justification for symmetrical and deviation tolerances; stored in **DimTolJ**:

DimTolJ	Meaning
0	Bottom.
1	Middle (*default*).
2	Top.

Height   Specifies the scaled height of tolerance text; stored in **DIMTFac**.

Alternate Units options:

Enable Units	Turns on alternate units; **DimAlt** set to 1.
Units	Specifies the units in linear, angle, and tolerance dimensions.
Prefix	Specifies the prefix for dimension text.
Suffix	Specifies the suffix for dimension text; stored in **DimAPost**.

Text options:

Style	Selects the text style for dimension text; stored in **DimTxSty**.
Height	Specifies the height of dimension text; stored in **DimTxt**.
Gap	Specifies the text gap, the distance the dimension line is broken to fit dimension text; stored in **DimGap**.
Color	Selects the color of dimension text; stored in **DimClrT**.
Round Off	Sets the rounding rule for dimension; stored in **DimRnd**.

RELATED COMMANDS

DimStyle   Changes dimension variables at the 'Command' prompt..
All commands beginning with Dim.

RELATED SYSTEM VARIABLES

DimStyle   Contains the name of the current dimension style.
All system variables beginning with Dim.

TIPS

- An overridden dimstyle has a + (plus) prefix to the dimstyle name, as in +STANDARD.

- You cannot rename the default dimstyle named "Standard."

- You access dimstyles stored in externally referenced drawings via the **XBind** command.

- The rounding value does not apply to angular dimensions.

- *Rounding* works like this: a value of 0.5 rounds all dimension distances to the nearest 0.5 unit; a value of 0.3 rounds all dimensioning to the nearest 0.3.

- The number of digits displayed after the decimal point is set in the **Primary Units** or **Alternate Units** dialog boxes.

- Use the **Style** command to create and modify text styles for dimension text.

- When **Overall Scale (DimScale)** sets a scale factor dimensions, it does not affect tolerances, measured lengths, coordinates, or angles.

DdInsert

Rel.12 Insert blocks (symbols) via dialog box (*short for Dialog Dynamic INSERT; an external command in DdInsert.Lsp*).

Command	Alias	Ctrl+	F-key	Alt+	Menu Bar	Tablet
ddinsert	i	...	...	...	Insert ⌐Block	T5

Command: **ddinsert**
Displays dialog box:

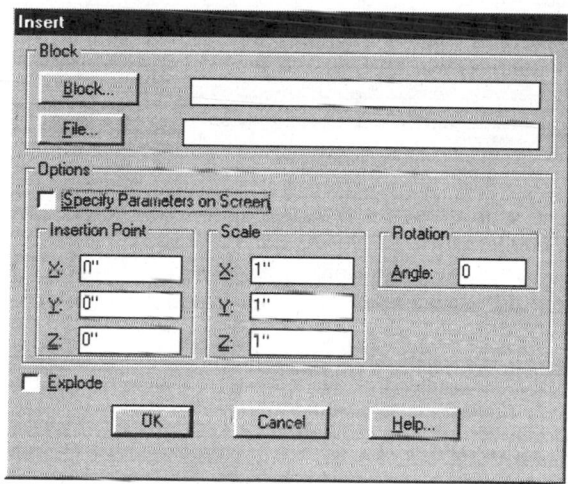

DIALOG BOX OPTIONS

Block options:

Block   Selects the block name from a dialog box.

Defined Blocks dialog box:

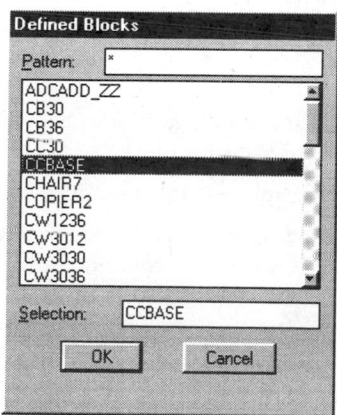

Pattern   Shortens list of block names via wildcards ? and *.
Selection   Displays name of the selected block.

File   Selects the drawing name from dialog box.

Select Drawing File dialog box:

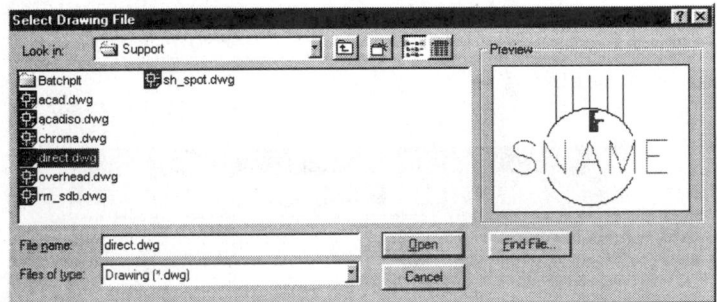

Options options:
Specify parameters on screen
        Uses the cursor to position the block.
Insertion point Specifies the block's insertion point coordinates.
Scale   Specifies the block's scale.
Rotation   Specifies the block's angle of rotation.

Explode   Inserts the block as individual objects.

RELATED COMMANDS

Block   Creates a block from a group of objects.
BMake   Creates block with a dialog box.
Explode   Explodes a block after insertion.
Insert   Inserts blocks via the command line.
MInsert   Inserts an array as a block.

RELATED SYSTEM VARIABLE

InsName   Specifies the name of the most-recently inserted block.

TIPS

- When you select a filename, that becomes the block's name. However, you can change the block name by typing a different name for **Block**.

- When the block is to be placed exploded, only the x-scale factor can be specified.

- When the block is placed exploded, objects with color BYBLOCK become the white color and objects with linetype BYBLOCK get the continuous linetype.

REMOVED COMMANDS

The **DdLModes** and **DdLtype** commands will be removed in Release 15. While they still work in Release 14, they have been replaced by the **Layer** and **Linetype** commands.

DdModify

Rel.12 Views and edits properties of all objects via a dialog box (*an external command in DdModify.Lsp*).

Command	Alias	Ctrl+	F-key	Alt+	Menu Bar	Tablet
ddmodify	mo	...	...	MP	Modify ⤷Properties	Y14

Command: **ddmodify**
Select object to list: **[pick object]**
*A different dialog box appears for object. However, all **Modify** dialog boxes have an area in common:*

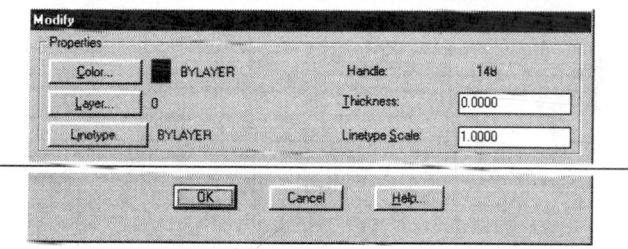

IN-COMMON DIALOG BOX OPTIONS

Color   Changes the object's color via a dialog box.
Layer   Moves the object to a different layer.
Linetype   Changes the object's linetype via dialog box.
Handle   Displays the object's handle in hexadecimal notation; cannot be changed.
Thickness   Changes the object's thickness.
Linetype Scale   Changes the object's linetype scale.

[pick arc]   Displays the **Modify Arc** dialog box:

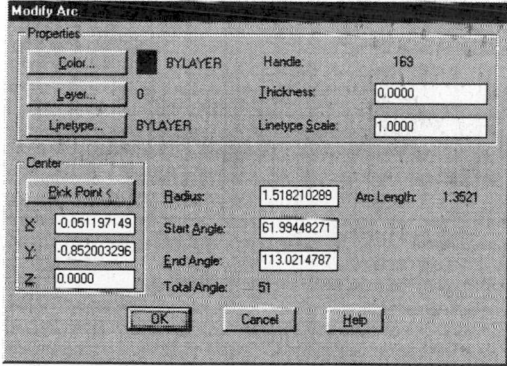

[pick associative hatch pattern]   Displays the **Modify Hatch** dialog box:

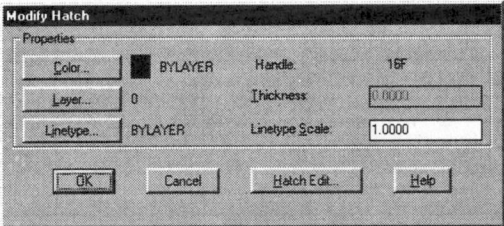

[pick attribute] Displays the **Modify Attribute Definition** dialog box:

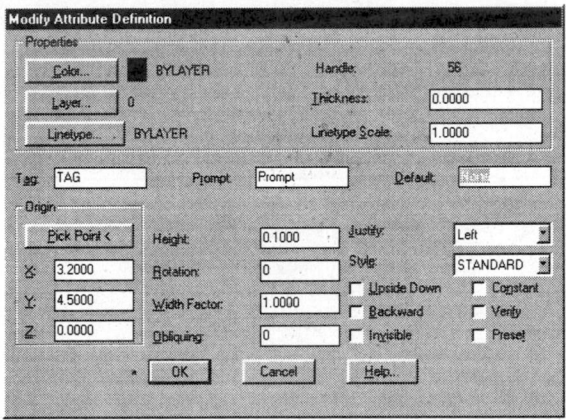

[pick block or minsert or non-associative hatch]
Displays the **Modify Block Insertion** dialog box:

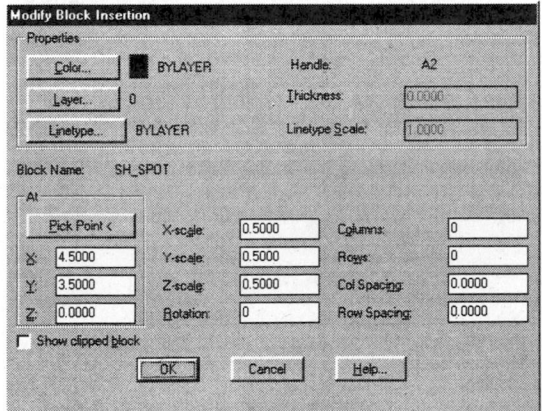

[pick body]   Displays the **Modify Body** dialog box:

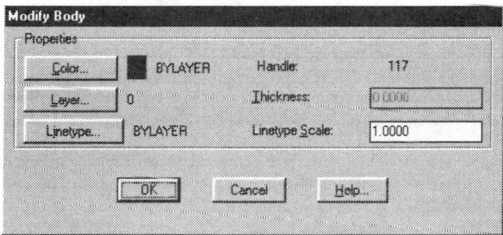

[pick circle]   Displays the **Modify Circle** dialog box:

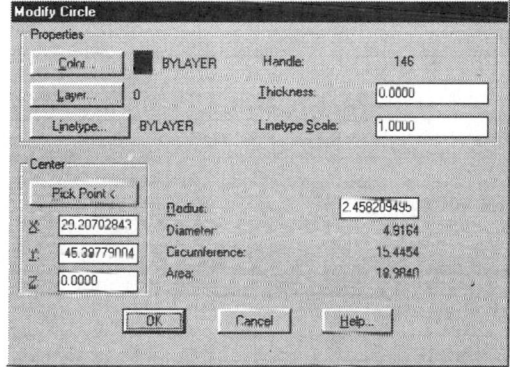

[pick associative dimension]   Displays the **Modify Dimension** dialog box:

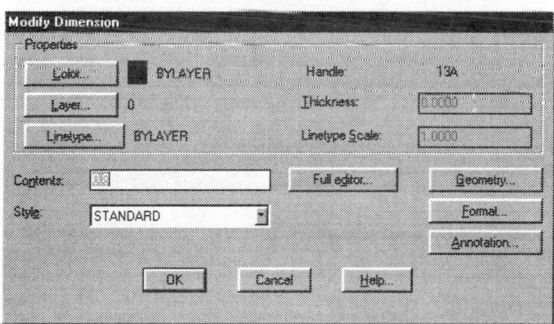

[pick ellipse or elliptical arc] Displays the **Modify Ellipse** dialog box:

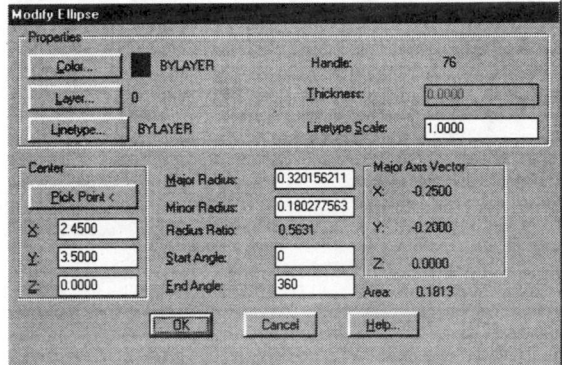

[pick raster image] Displays the **Modify Image** dialog box:

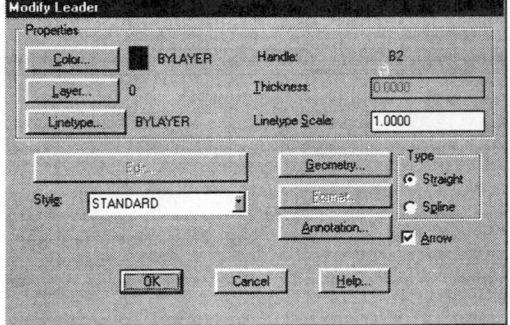

[pick leader] Displays the **Modify Leader** dialog box:

[pick line]   Displays the **Modify Line** dialog box:

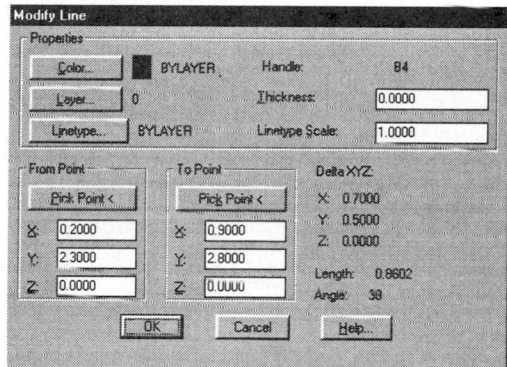

[pick multiline]   Displays the **Modify Multiline** dialog box:

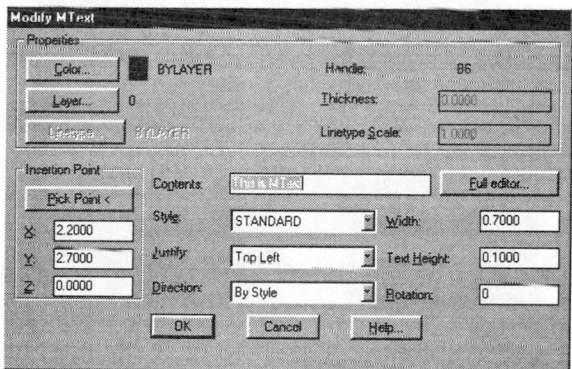

[pick multi-line text]   Displays the **Modify MText** dialog box:

[pick point]   Displays the **Modify Point** dialog box:

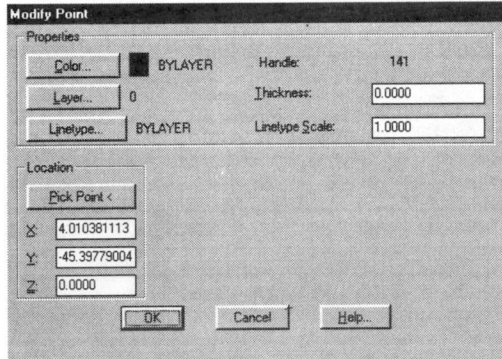

[pick polyline, 3D polyline, or polymesh]   Displays the **Modify Polyline** dialog box:

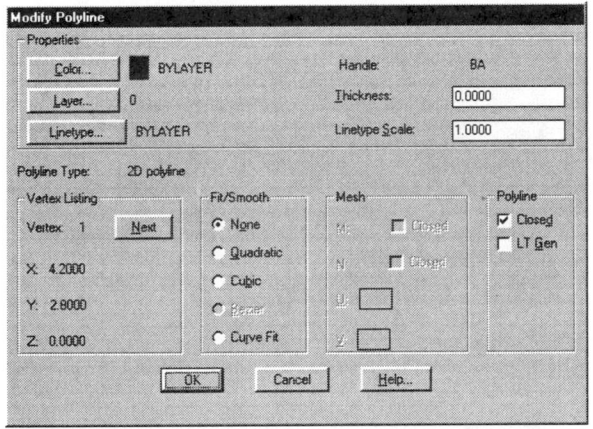

[pick ray]   Displays the **Modify Ray** dialog box:

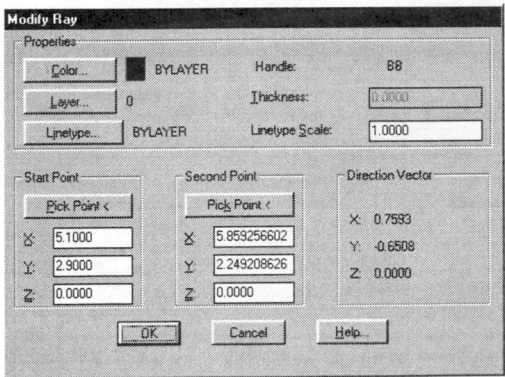

[pick region]   Displays the **Modify Region** dialog box:

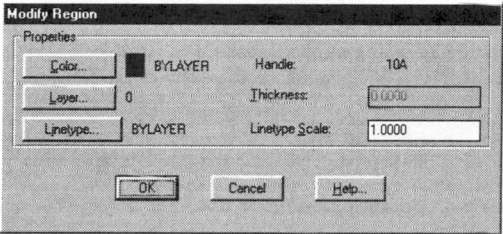

[pick shape]   Displays the **Modify Shape** dialog box:

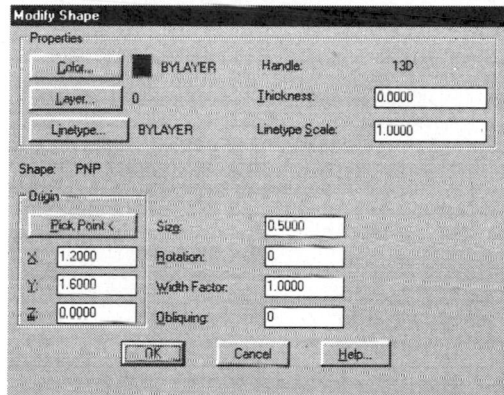

[pick 2D solid] Displays the **Modify Solid** dialog box:

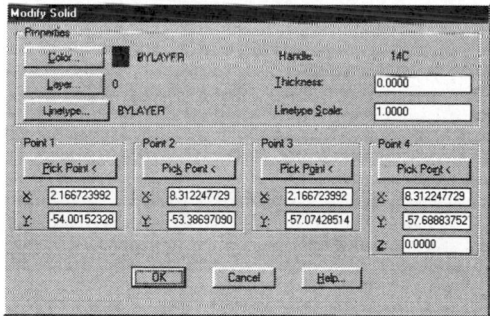

[pick spline]   Displays the **Modify Spline** dialog box:

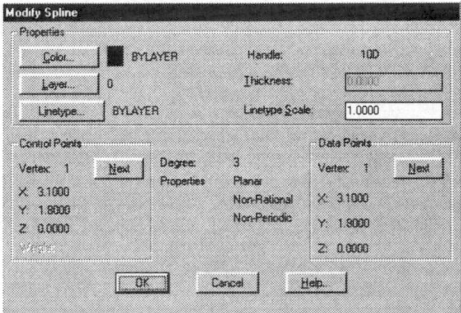

[pick single-line text]   Displays the **Modify Text** dialog box:

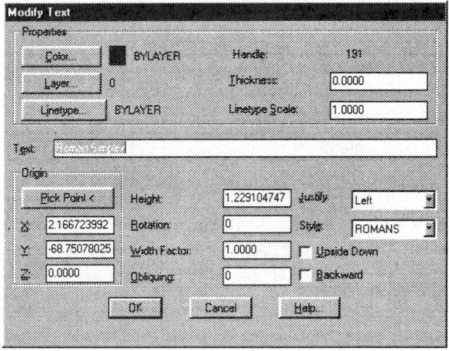

[pick tolerance]   Displays the **Modify Tolerance** dialog box:

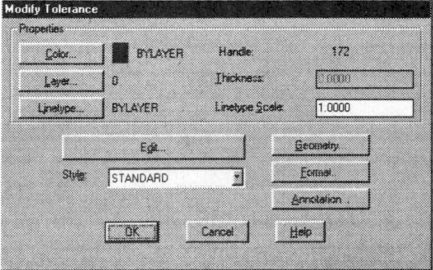

[pick trace]   Displays the **Modify Trace** dialog box:

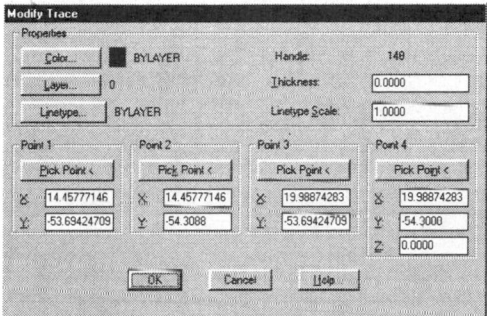

[pick viewport] Displays the **Modify Viewport** dialog box:

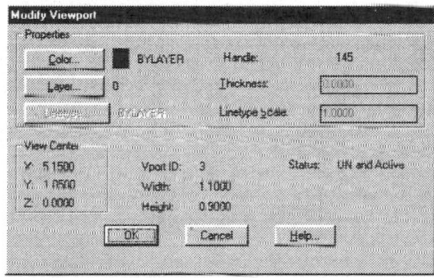

[pick xline]   Displays the **Modify Xline** dialog box:

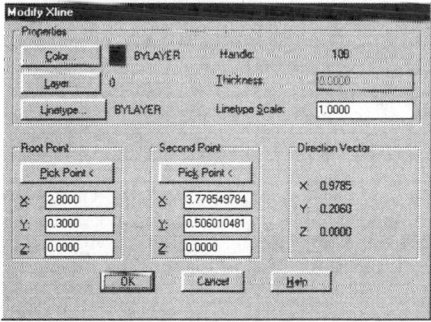

[pick xref]   Displays the **Modify External Reference** dialog box:

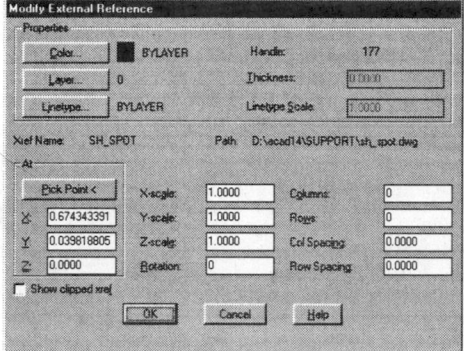

[pick 3D face]   Displays the **Modify 3D Face** dialog box:

[pick 3D solid] Displays the **Modify 3D Solid** dialog box:

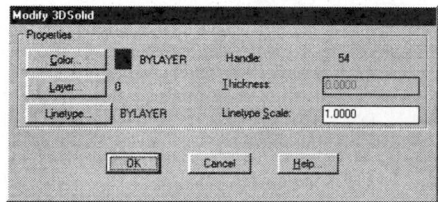

RELATED COMMANDS

Change	Changes most properties of objects.
ChProp	Changes some properties of objects.
Color	Changes color of objects.
DdChProp	Edits properties via dialog box.
DdColor	Changes color via dialog box.
DdEdit	Edits text via dialog box.
Layer	Changes layer and linetype via dialog box.
LtScale	Changes the linetype scale.
PEdit	Edits polylines and meshes.
Thickness	Changes the thickness of an object.

TIPS

■ All edges of a 3D face are visible when **SplFrame** = 1, regardless of the edge visibility setting in the **Modify 3D Face** dialog box.

■ The **Modify Text** dialog box lets you change the linetype of text from Continuous but the linetype pattern does not display or plot.

■ When you change the height, rotation, width, and obliquing angle of text, the **Modify Text** dialog box affects only the selected text and not the associated text style.

■ Select the **Modify Text** dialog box's **Style** list to reset the height, rotation, width, and obliquing angle of text to its style's defaults.

■ The **Modify Block** dialog box lets you change the columns, rows, and spacing of blocks when you create the array with the **MInsert** command.

'DdPtype

Rel.12 Sets the type and size of points via dialog box (*short for Dynamic Dialog Point TYPE; an external command in DdPtype.Lsp*).

Command	Alias	Ctrl+	F-key	Alt+	Menu Bar	Tablet
'ddptype	...	...	...	OP	Format	U1
					⌐Point Style	

Command: **ddptype**
Displays dialog box:

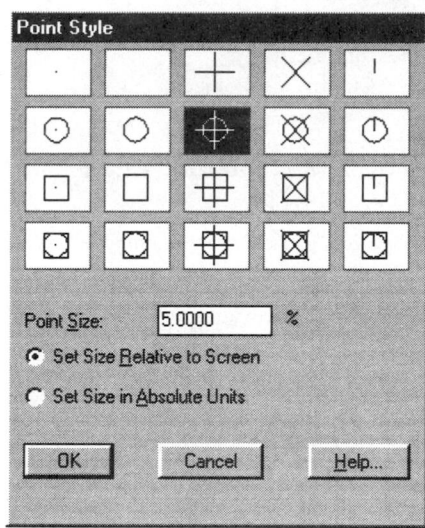

DIALOG BOX OPTIONS
Point size Set size in percent or pixels.
Set Size Relative to Screen
Set size in percent of total viewport height.
Set Size in Absolute Units
Set size in pixels.

RELATED COMMANDS
Point Draws points.
Regen New point format does not appear until the next regeneration.

RELATED SYSTEM VARIABLES
PdMode Determines the look of a point.
PdSize Contains the size of the point:

PdSize	Meaning
0	Point is 5% of viewport height (*default*).
positive	Absolute size in pixels.
negative	Percentage of the viewport size.

DdRename

Rel.12 Changes the names of blocks, dimension styles, layers, linetypes, text styles, UCS names, views, and viewports via dialog box (*an external command in DdRename.Lsp*).

Command	Alias	Ctrl+	F-key	Alt+	Menu Bar	Tablet
ddrename	ren	...	...	OR	Format	V1
					⇘Rename	

Command: **ddrename**
Displays dialog box:

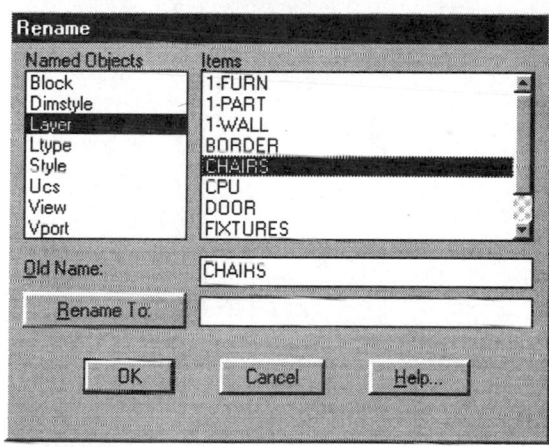

DIALOG BOX OPTIONS

Named Objects

        Objects that can be changed.

Items   Names associated with objects.

Old Name   Specifies the name – or group of names – to change.

Rename To   Indicates the new name.

RELATED COMMANDS

DdModify   Changes names and many other properties of objects.

Rename   Changes the names of objects via the command line.

TIPS

■ You cannot rename layer "0", dimstyle "Standard", anonymous blocks, groups, nor linetype "Continuous."

■ To rename a group of similar names, use * (the wildcard for "all") and ? (the wildcard for a single character).

■ Names can be up to 31 characters in length, including the $, -, and _ characters.

'DdRModes

Rel. 9 Controls the current settings of snap, snap angle, grid, axes, ortho, blip marks, and isometric modes (*short for Dynamic Dialog dRawing MODES*).

Command	Alias	Ctrl+	F-key	Alt+	Menu Bar	Tablet
`'ddrmodes`	`rm`	...	...	`TD`	`Tools` ↳`Drawing Aids`	`W10`

`Command:` **`ddrmodes`**

Displays dialog box:

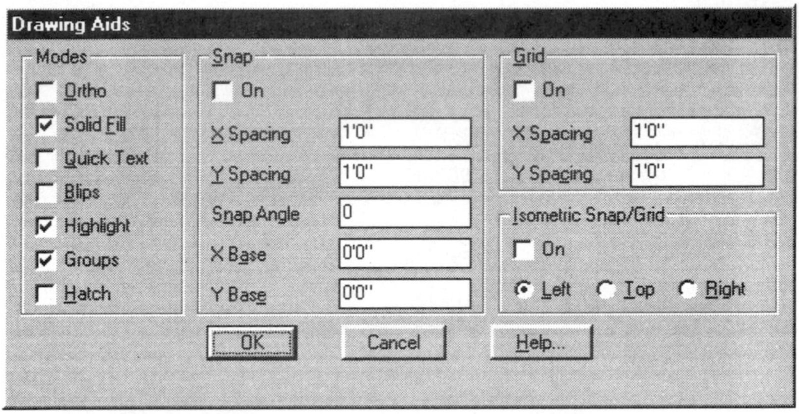

DIALOG BOX OPTIONS

***Modes** options:*

Ortho Turns orthographic mode on and off.
Solid Fill Turns solid fill on and off.
Quick Text Turns quick text on and off.
Blips Turns blipmarks on and off.
Highlight Turns object highlighting on and off.
Groups *Yes*: Selecting a group member selects the entire group.
No: Selecting a member of a group selects only the member.
Hatch *Yes*: Hatch pattern boundary is also selected.
No: Hatch pattern boundary is not selected.

***Snap** options:*

On Turns on snap mode.
X Spacing Sets x-spacing for snap.
Y Spacing Sets y-spacing for snap.
Snap Angle Sets angle for snap and grid; also affects ortho and hatch pattern angle.
X Base Sets snap, grid hatch x-basepoint; also affects grid and hatch pattern origin.
Y Base Sets snap, grid hatch y-basepoint; also affects grid and hatch pattern origin.

***Grid** options:*

On Turns on grid marks.
X spacing Sets grid x-spacing; when set to 0, grid = snap spacing.
Y spacing Sets grid y-spacing; when set to 0, grid = snap spacing.

Isometric Snap/Grid options:
On   Turns on isometric mode.
Left,Top,Right Sets the left, top, or right isometric plane.

RELATED COMMANDS
BHatch	Creates hatch patterns.
Blipmode	Toggles visibility of blip markers.
Fill	Toggles fill mode.
Grid	Sets the grid spacing and toggles visibility.
Group	Creates named groups.
Highlight	Toggles highlight mode.
Isoplane	Selects the working isometric plane.
Ortho	Toggles orthographic mode.
QText	Toggles quick text mode.
Snap	Sets the snap spacing and isometric mode.

RELATED SYSTEM VARIABLES
BlipMode   Indicates the current blip marker visibility:

BlipMode	Meaning
0	Off.
1	On (*default*).

FillMode   Indicates the current fill mode:

FillMode	Meaning
0	Off.
1	On (*default*).

GridMode   Indicates the current grid visibility:

GridMode	Meaning
0	Off (*default*).
1	On.

GridUnit   Indicates the current grid spacing (*default = 0.0*).
Highlight   Indicates the current highlight mode:

Highlight	Meaning
0	Off.
1	On (*default*).

OrthoMode   Indicates the current orthographic mode setting:

OrthoMode	Meaning
0	Off (*default*).
1	On.

| QTextMode | Indicates the current quick text mode setting: |

QTextMode	Meaning
0	Off (*default*).
1	On.

| PickStyle | Controls group selection: |

PickStyle	Meaning
0	Groups and associative hatches not selected.
1	Groups selected.
2	Associative hatches selected.
3	Both selected.

SnapAng	Current snap rotation angle (*default* = 0).
SnapBase	Base point of snap rotation angle (*default* = 0,0).
SnapIsoPair	Current isoplane:

SnapIsoPair	Meaning
0	Left isoplane (*default*)
1	Top isoplane.
2	Right isoplane.

| SnapMode | Current snap mode setting: |

SnapMode	Meaning
0	Off (*default*).
1	On.

| SnapStyl | Snap style setting: |

SnapStyl	Meaning
0	Standard (*default*).
1	Isometric (*default*).

| SnapUnit | Current snap spacing (*default* = 1,1). |

TIPS

■ **DdRModes** is an alternative to the **SetVar** command for the above system variables.

■ Use the function keys to change modes during a command:.

Mode	Ctrl Key	Function Key
Grid	Ctrl+G	F7
Group	Ctrl+A	...
Ortho	Ctrl+O	F8
Snap	Ctrl+B	F9

'DdSelect

Rel.12 Defines the type of object selection mode and pickbox size via a dialog box (*an external command in DdSelect.Lsp*).

Command	Alias	Ctrl+	F-key	Alt+	Menu Bar	Tablet
'ddselect	se	...	...	TC	Tools ⤷Selection	X9

Command: **ddselect**
Displays dialog box:

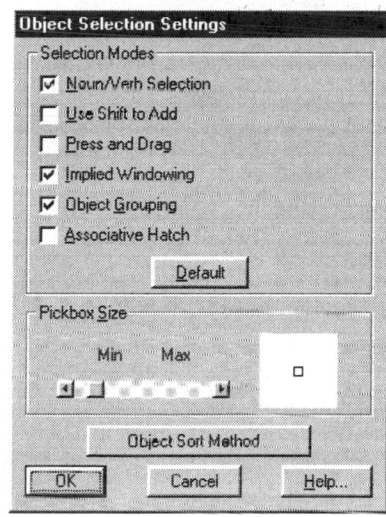

DIALOG BOX OPTIONS

Selection Modes options:

Noun/Verb Selection
Selects objects first, then enter the command.

Use Shift to Add
The **[Shift]** key adds objects to selection set.

Press and Drag Creates a windowed selection set by pressing mouse key and dragging window, rather than specifying two points.

Implied Windowing
Automatically creates a windowed selection box.

Object Grouping
Selecting one object in a group selects the entire group.

Associative Hatch
Selecting a hatch pattern also selects its boundary.

Default   Resets modes to turn on **Noun/Verb** and **Implied Windowing**.

Pickbox Size   Interactively change the size of the pickbox.

Object Sort Method
> Specifies the commands that sort objects by drawing database order; displays dialog box.

Object Sort Method dialog box:

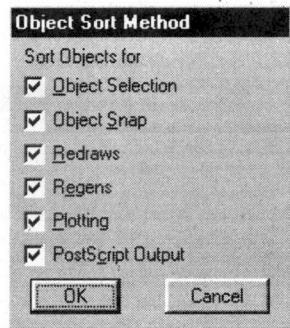

Object Selection
> Objects are added to the selection in database order.

Object Snap   Object snap modes find objects in database order.
Redraws   Redraws objects in database order.
Slide Creation **MSlide** command draws objects in database order.
Regens   Regenerates objects in database order.
Plotting   **Plot** command processes objects in database order.
PostScript Output
> **PsOut** command processes objects in database order.

RELATED COMMANDS
DrawOrder   Change the display order of objects.
MSlide   Creates an SLD slide file of the current viewport.
Plot   Plots the drawing.
PsOut   Creates an EPS encapsulated PostScript file of the drawing.
Select   Creates a selection set before executing an editing commands.

RELATED SYSTEM VARIABLES
PickAdd   Determines effect of **[Shift]** key on creating selection set:

PickAdd	Meaning
0	[Shift] key adds to selection set.
1	[Shift] key removes from selection set (*default*).

PickAuto   Determines automatic windowing:

PickAuto	Meaning
0	Disabled.
1	Enabled (*default*).

| PickBox | Specifies the size of the pickbox (*default = 3*). |
| PickDrag | Method of creating selection window: |

PickDrag	Meaning
0	Click at both corners (*default*).
1	Click first corner, drag to second corner.

PickFirst   Object selection:

PickFirst	Meaning
0	Enter command first.
1	Select objects first (*default*).

SortEnts   Objects are displayed in database order during:

SortEnts	Meaning
0	Off.
1	Object selection.
2	Object snap.
4	Redraw.
8	Slide generation.
16	Regeneration.
32	Plots.
64	PostScript output.

TIPS

■ These commands work with noun-verb selection: **Array, Block, Change, ChProp, Copy, DdChProp, DView, Erase, Explode, Hatch, List, Mirror, Move, Rotate, Scale, Stretch,** and **WBlock.**

■ A larger pickbox makes it easier to select objects, but also makes it easier to accidently select unintended objects.

■ Use **Object Sort Method** if the drawing requires that objects be processed in the order they appear in the drawing, such as for NC applications.

■ **Plotting** and **PostScript Output** are turned on, by default; setting more sort methods increases processing time.

■ The first time you use the **DrawOrder** command, it turns on all object sort method options.

DdUcs

Rel.10 Creates and controls UCS planes via a dialog box (*short for Dynamic Dialog User Coordinate System*).

Command	Alias	Ctrl+	F-key	Alt+	Menu Bar	Tablet
dducs	uc	...	...	TUC	Tools	W8
					⟍UCS	
					⟍Named UCS	

Command: **dducs**
Displays dialog box:

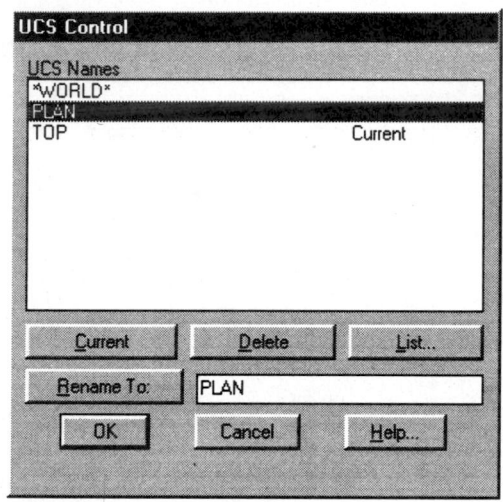

DIALOG BOX OPTIONS

Current	Makes the selected name the current UCS.
Delete	Deletes a named UCS.
Rename to	Renames a UCS.
List	Lists information about the selected UCS; displays dialog box.

UCS dialog box:

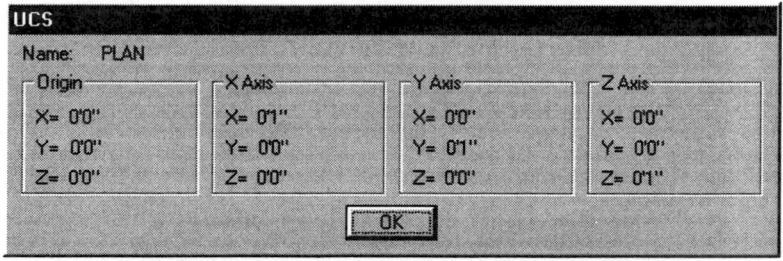

OK   Dismisses dialog box.

RELATED COMMANDS

DdUcsP   Selects a predefined UCS from a dialog box.
Ucs   Creates and save user-defined coordinate systems.

RELATED SYSTEM VARIABLES

UcsFollow   Controls how a new UCS is displayed:

UcsFollow	Meaning
0	No change (*default*).
1	Automatically displays plan view in a new UCS view.

UcsName   Current name of UCS (*default = ""*).
UcsOrg   WCS origin of the current UCS in x,y,z-coordinates (*default = 0,0,0*).
UcsXdir   X-direction of the current UCS in x,y,z-vector (*default = 1,0,0*).
UcsYdir   Y-direction of the current UCS in x,y,z-vector (*default = 0,1,0*).
ViewMode   Current clipped viewing mode:

ViewMode	Meaning
0	Off (*default*).
1	Perspective view.
2	Front clipping on.
4	Back clipping on.
8	**UcsFollow** mode on.
16	Front clip not at eye.

WorldUcs   UCS=WCS toggle:

WorldUcs	Meaning
0	Current UCS is not WCS.
1	UCS is WCS (*default*).

WorldView   Display during the **DView** and **VPoint** commands:

WorldUcs	Meaning
0	Display UCS (*default*).
1	Display WCS.

TIPS

- AutoCAD automatically names the following UCSs:

UCS Name	Meaning
WORLD	The WCS (*world coordinate system*).
PREVIOUS	The previous UCS view.
NO NAME	An unnamed UCS.

- You step through all the previous UCS views (independend of the U and **Zoom Previous** commands) by repeatedly clicking on *PREVIOUS*.

- You cannot delete or rename the *WORLD* and *PREVIOUS* named UCSs.

DdUcsP

Rel.12 Selects one of seven predefined user coordinate systems (*short for Dynamic Dialog UCS Preset; an external command in DdUcsP.Lsp*).

Command	Alias	Ctrl+	F-key	Alt+	Menu Bar	Tablet
dducsp	ucp	...	...	TUU	Tools	W9
					⌖UCS	
					⌖Preset	

Command: **dducsp**
Displays dialog box:

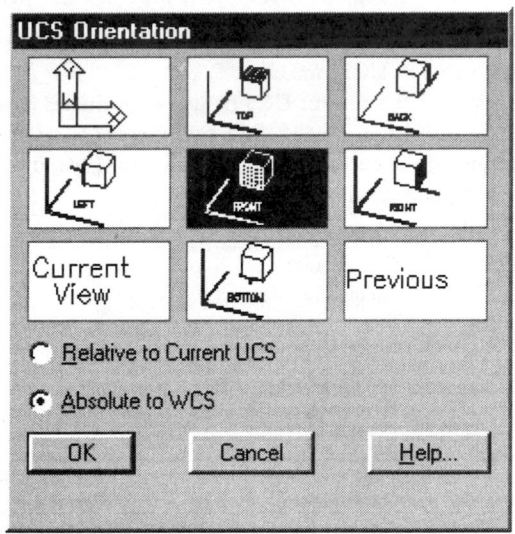

DIALOG BOX OPTIONS
Relative to current UCS
Absolute to WCS

RELATED COMMANDS
DdUcs	Creates and selects named UCS.
Ucs	Sets the current UCS via the command line.

RELATED SYSTEM VARIABLES
UcsFollow	Controls how a new UCS is displayed: 0 = no change; 1 = automatically display plan view in a new UCS view.
UcsName	Current name of UCS.
UcsOrg	WCS origin of the current UCS in x,y,z-coordinates.
UcsXdir	X-direction of the current UCS in x,y,z-vector.
UcsYdir	Y-direction of the current UCS in x,y,z-vector.
WorldUcs	UCS=WCS toggle: 0 = current UCS is not WCS; 1 = UCS is WCS.
WorldView	Display during the **DView** and **VPoint** commands: 0 = display UCS; 1 = display WCS.

'DdUnits

Rel.12 Select the display of units and angles via a dialog box (*an external command in DdUnits.Lsp*).

Command	Alias	Ctrl+	F-key	Alt+	Menu Bar	Tablet
'ddunits	un	...	...	OU	Format ↳Units	V4

Command: **ddunits**
Displays dialog box:

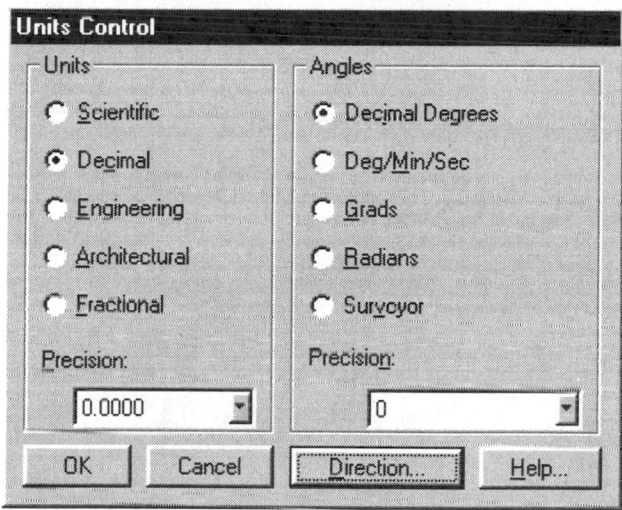

DIALOG BOX OPTIONS

Units options:

Scientific	0.0000E+01
Decimal	0.0000 (*default*)
Engineering	0'-0.0000" (*feet and decimal inches*)
Architectural	0'-0/64" (*feet and fractional inches*)
Fractional	0 0/64 (*unitless fractional*)
Precision	Display precision of units.

Angles options:

Decimal degrees	0.0000 (*default*)
Deg/Min/Sec	0d0'0.0000" (*degrees, minutes, decimal seconds*)
Grads	0.0000g
Radians	0.0000r
Surveyor	N0d'0.0000"E
Precision	Display precision of angles.

Direction   Specifies the direction of 0 degrees; displays dialog box.

Direction Control dialog box:

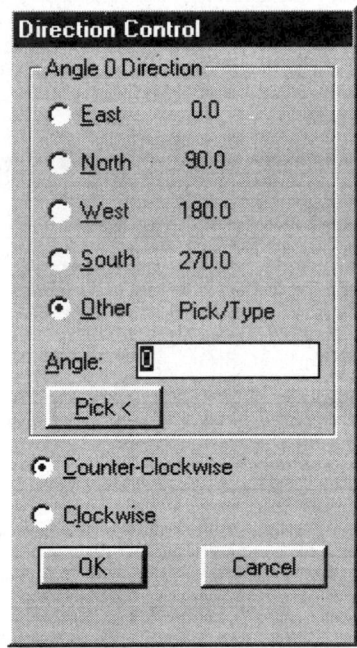

Angle 0 Direction options:

East   Specifies that 0 degrees points East (default).
North   Specifies that 0 degrees points North.
West   Specifies that 0 degrees points West.
South   Specifies that 0 degrees points South.
Other   Specifies that 0 degrees is not in one of the four cardinal directions.
Angle   Specifies the angle for 0 degrees.
Pick   Picks the direction of 0 degrees from the drawing.

Counter-clockwise
             Measures angle in counter-clockwise direction from 0 degrees (*default*).
Clockwise   Measures angle in clockwise direction from 0 degrees.

RELATED COMMANDS

New   Sets up a new drawing with a **Set Up** wizard.
Units   Sets units and angles via the command line

RELATED SYSTEM VARIABLES

AngBase	Direction of zero degrees relative to the current UCS (*default = East*).
AngDir	Direction of angle measurement:

AngDir	Meaning
0	Clockwise.
1	Counter-clockwise (*default*).

AUnits   Style of angle units:

AUnits	Meaning
0	Decimal degrees (*default*).
1	Degree/minutes/seconds.
2	Grads.
3	Radians.
4	Surveyor's units.

AuPrec	Decimal places of angle units (*default = 0*).
LUnits	Style of linear units:

LUnits	Meaning
0	Scientific.
1	Decimal (*default*).
2	Engineering.
3	Architectural.
4	Fractional.

LuPrec	Decimal places of linear units (*default = 4*).
UnitMode	Displays input units:

UnitMode	Meaning
0	As set by **DdUnits** (*default*).
1	As input by the user.

DdView

Rel.12 Select named views via dialog box (*external command in DdView.Lsp*).

Command	Alias	Ctrl+	F-key	Alt+	Menu Bar	Tablet
ddview	v	...	...	VN	View	M5
					⤷Named Views	

Command: **ddview**
Displays dialog box:

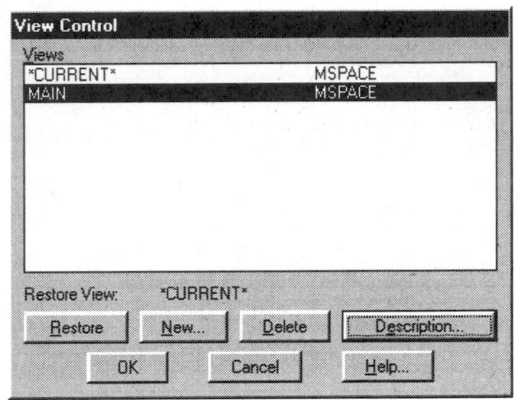

DIALOG BOX OPTIONS

Views   Lists names of the currently defined views.
Restore   Restores a named view.
Delete   Deletes a named view.
Description   Lists the parameters of the selected view; displays dialog box.

View Description dialog box:

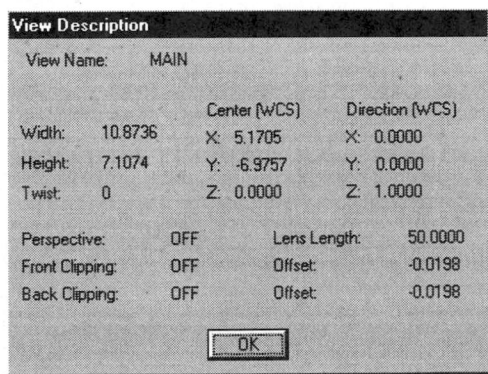

OK   Dismisses dialog box.

New   Define a new view; displays dialog box.

Define New View dialog box:

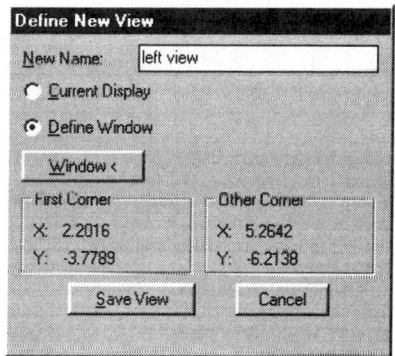

New Name   Specifies the name of the new view.
Current Display Creates new view from the current view.
Define Window Defines a view using window selection mode.
Window   Removes dialog box, enabling you to pick two corners of view window.
Save View   Saves the newly name view; returns to **View Control** dialog box.

RELATED COMMAND
View   Defines and displays named views via the command line.

RELATED SYSTEM VARIABLES
ViewCtr   Coordinates of the view's centerpoint (*default = 5,6,0*).
ViewDir   View direction relative to UCS (*default = 0,0,1*)
ViewMode   Current clipped viewing mode:

ViewMode	Meaning
0	Off (*default*).
1	Perspective view.
2	Front clipping on.
4	Back clipping on.
8	**UcsFollow** mode on.
16	Front clip not at eye.

ViewSize   View height (*default = 9*).
ViewTwist   Twist angle of current view (*default = 0*).

TIPS
■ Use named views to quickly move from one view to another.

■ The **Zoom Previous** command keeps named views in its stack.

■ The **Plot** command recognized named views.

DdVPoint

Rel.12 Changes the viewpoint of drawings via a dialog box (*short for Dynamic Dialog ViewPOINT; an external command in DdVpoint.Lsp*).

Command	Alias	Ctrl+	F-key	Alt+	Menu Bar	Tablet
ddvpoint	vp	...	...	V3C	View	N5
					↳3D Viewpoint	
					↳Select	

Command: **ddvpoint**
Displays dialog box:

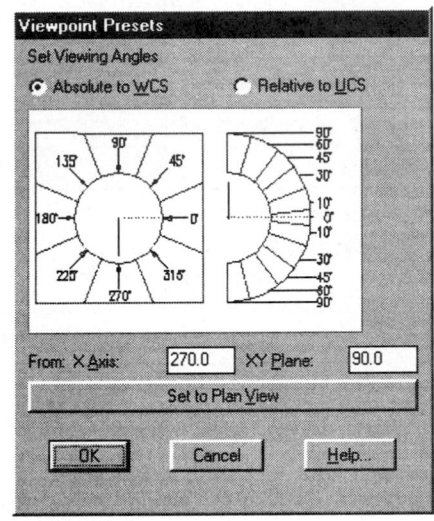

DIALOG BOX OPTIONS

Set Viewing Angles options:
Absolute to WCS
        Sets the view direction relative to the WCS.
Relative to UCS Sets the view direction relative to the current UCS.
From X Axis Measures view angle from the x-axis.
From XY Plane Measures view angle from the x,y-plane
Set to Plan View
        Changes view to plan view.

RELATED COMMANDS

DView	Interactively changes the viewpoint.
VPoint	Adjusts the viewpoint from the command line.

RELATED SYSTEM VARIABLE

WorldView   Determines whether viewpoint coordinates are in WCS or UCS.

TIPS

- After changing the viewpoint, AutoCAD performs an automatic **Zoom** extents.

- In the image tile, the black arm indicates the new angle.

- In the image tile, the red arm indicates the current angle.

- To select an angle with your mouse:

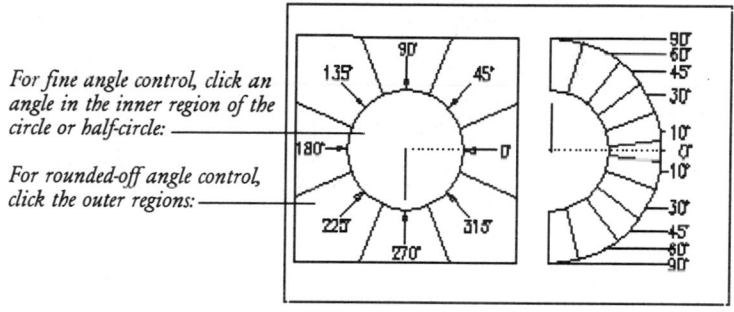

For fine angle control, click an angle in the inner region of the circle or half-circle:

For rounded-off angle control, click the outer regions:

'Delay

V. 1.4 Delays the next command, in milliseconds.

Command	Alias	Ctrl+	F-key	Alt+	Menu Bar	Tablet
'delay	...	...	...	...	...	...

```
Command: delay
Delay time in milliseconds: [type a number]
```

COMMAND LINE OPTION
Delay time Number of milliseconds to delay the next command.

RELATED COMMAND
Script Initiates a script

TIPS
- Use the **Delay** command to slow down the execution of a script file.

- The maximum delay is 32767, just over 32 seconds.

DetachURL

Rel.14 Removes a URL from an object or an area.

Command	Alias	Ctrl+	F-key	Alt+	Menu Bar	Tablet
detachurl	...	...	...	...	...	...

```
Command: detachurl
Select objects: [pick]
Select objects: [Enter]
```

COMMAND LINE OPTION

Select objects Pick the objects that should have their URLs removed.

RELATED COMMANDS

AttachUrl	Attaches a URL to an object or an area.
DwfOut	Exports the drawing in DWF format.
ListUrl	Lists URLs embedded in the drawing.
SelectUrl	Selects all objects with attached URLs.

TIPS

■ When you select a URL area to detach, AutoCAD reports, "DetachURL, deleting the Area."

■ When you select an object with no URL, AutoCAD reports, "1 was filtered out."

■ A URL (*short for "uniform resource locator"*) is the universal file naming convention of the Internet.

Dim

<u>V. 1.2</u> Changes the prompt from 'Command' to 'Dim'; allows access to AutoCAD's old dimensioning commands (*short for DIMensions*).

Command	Alias	Ctrl+	F-key	Alt+	Menu Bar	Tablet
dim	. . .	. . .	. . .	. . .	. . .	. . .

Command: **dim**
Dim:

COMMAND LINE OPTIONS

Aliases for the dimension commands are shown in uppercase (version or release introduced in parentheses):

ALigned — Draws linear dimension aligned with object (*ver. 2.0*); replaced by the **DimAligned** command.

ANgular — Draws angular dimension that measures an angle (*ver. 2.0*); replaced by the **DimAngular** command.

Baseline — Continues a dimension from a basepoint (*ver. 1.2*); replaced by the **DimBaseline** command.

CEnter — Draws a centermark on circle and arc centers (*ver. 2.0*); replaced by the **DimCenter** command.

COntinue — Continues dimension from the previous dimension's extension line (*ver. 1.2*); replaced by the **DimContinue** command.

Diameter — Draws diameter dimension on circles, arcs, and polyarcs (*ver. 2.0*); replaced by the **DimDiameter** command.

Exit — Returns to 'Command' prompt from 'Dim' prompt (*ver. 1.2*).

HOMetext — Returns associative dimension text to its original position (*ver. 2.6*); replaced by the **DimEdit** command.

HORizontal — Draws a horizontal dimension (*ver. 1.2*); replaced by the **DimLinear** command.

LEAder — Draws a leader (*ver. 2.0*); replaced by the **Leader** command.

Newtext — Edits text in associative dimensions (*ver. 2.6*); replaced by the **DimEdit** command.

OBlique — Changes angle of extension lines in associative dimensions (*rel. 11*); replaced by the **DimEdit** command.

ORdinate — Draws x- and y-ordinate dimensions (*rel. 11*); replaced by the **DimOrdinate** command.

OVerride — Overrides the current set of dimension variables (*rel. 11*); replaced by the **DimOverride** command.

RAdius — Draws radial dimension on circles, arcs, and polyline arcs (*ver. 2.0*); replaced by the **DimRadius** command.

REDraw — Redraws the current viewport (*same as 'Redraw; ver. 2.0*).

REStore — Restores a dimension to the current dimension style (*rel. 11*); replaced by the **DDim** command.

ROtated — Draws a linear dimension at any angle (*ver. 2.0*); replaced by the **DimLinear** command.

SAve	Saves the current setting of dimension styles as a dimstyle (*rel. 11*); replaced by the **DDim** command.
STAtus	Lists the current settings of dimension variables (*ver. 2.0*).
STYle	Sets a style for the dimensions (*ver. 2.5*); replaced by the **DimStyle** command.
TEdit	Changes location and orientation of text in associative dimensions (*rel. 11*); replaced by the **DimTEdit** command.
TRotate	Changes the rotation of text in associative dimensions (*rel. 11*); replaced by the **DimEdit** command.
Undo	Undo the last dimension action (*ver. 2.0*); replaced by the **Undo** command.
UPdate	Update selected associative dimensions to the current dimvar setting (*ver. 2.6*); replaced by the **DDim** command.
VAriables	Lists value of variables associated with a dimension style, *not* dimvars (*rel. 11*).
VErtical	Draws vertical linear dimensions (*ver. 1.2*); replaced by **DimLinear** command.

RELATED COMMANDS

DDim	Dialog box for setting dimension variables.
Dim1	Executes a single R12-style dimension command.
DimAligned	Places aligned linear dimensions.
DimAngular	Places angular dimensions.
DimBaseline	Continues a dimension from the baseline of the previous dimension.
DimCenter	Places the center mark on circles and arcs.
DimContinue	Continues dimension from second extension line of the previous dimension.
DimDiameter	Places diameter dimensions for circles and arcs.
DimEdit	Edits dimensions.
DimLinear	Places linear dimensions.
DimOrdinate	Places ordinate point dimensions.
DimOverride	Overrides dimension system variables.
DimRadius	Places radial dimensions.
DimStyle	Modifies dimension styles at the command line.
DimTEdit	Moves and rotates dimension text.
Style	Determines the text style of the dimensioning text.

RELATED DIM VARIABLES

DimAso	Determines whether dimensions are drawn associatively.
DimScale	Determines the dimension scale.
Dimxxx	All system variables beginning with Dim.

RELATED DIM BLOCK

Dot	Dim uses a dot in place of the arrowhead.

TIPS

- The 'Dim' prompt dimension commands are included for compatibility with Release 12 and earlier.

- Only transparent commands and dimension commands work at the 'Dim' prompt. To use other commands, you must exit the 'Dim' prompt back to the 'Command' prompt with the **Exit** command.

- Most dimensions consists of four basic components: dimension line, extension lines, arrowheads, and text, as shown below:

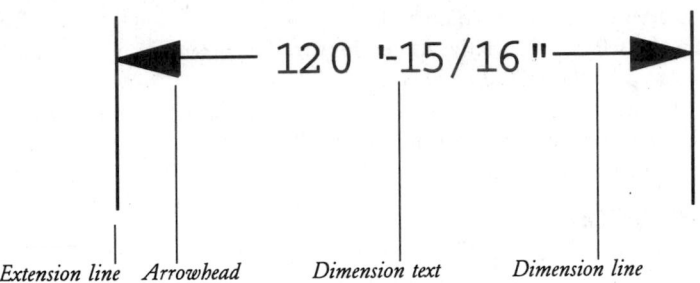

Extension line   Arrowhead   Dimension text   Dimension line

- All the components of an *associative dimension* are treated as a single object; components of a nonassociative dimension are treated as individual objects.

Dim1

V. 2.5 Executes a single dimensioning command, returns to the 'Command' prompt (*short for DIMension once; an undocumented command in Release 14*).

Command	Alias	Ctrl+	F-key	Alt+	Menu Bar	Tablet
dim1	. . .	. . .	. . .	. . .	. . .	. . .

```
Command: dim1
Dim:
```

COMMAND LINE OPTIONS
All "old" dimension commands; see **Dim** *command for complete list.*

RELATED COMMANDS
DDim   Dialog box for setting dimension variables.
Dim   Switches to "old" dimensioning mode and remains there.

RELATED DIM VARIABLES
DimAso   Determines whether dimensions are drawn associatively.
DimTxt   Determines the height of text.
DimScale   Determines the dimension scale.

RELATED DIM BLOCK
Dot   Dim uses a dot in place of the arrowhead.

TIP
■ Use the **Dim1** command when you need to use just a single "old" dimension command.

DimAligned

Rel 13 Draws linear dimensions aligned with an object.

Command	Alias	Ctrl+	F-key	Alt+	Menu Bar	Tablet
dimaligned	dal	...	...	NG	Dimension ⤷Aligned	W4
	dimali					

```
Command: dimaligned
First extension line origin or RETURN to select: [Enter]
Select object to dimension: [pick]
Dimension line location (Text/Angle): T
Dimension text <>: [Enter]
```

*A circle, line, arc, and polyline segments dimensioned with the **DimAligned** command:*

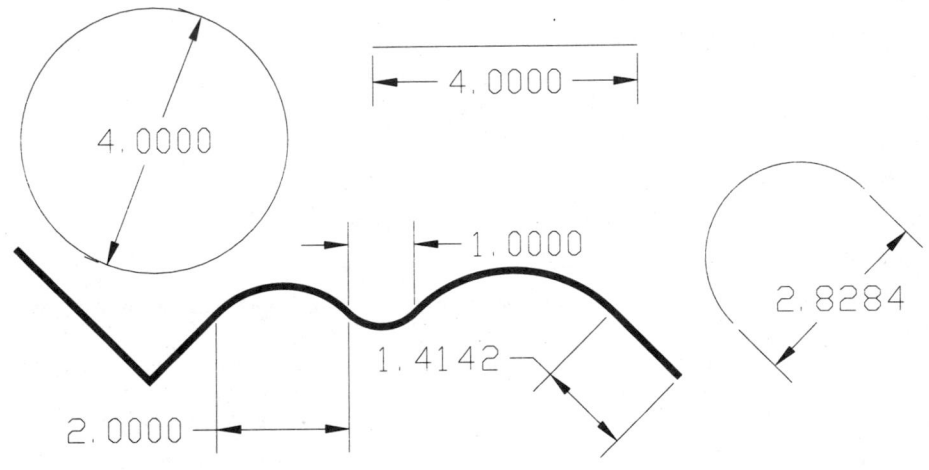

COMMAND LINE OPTIONS

[Enter]	Displays the submenu for selecting objects:
[pick line]	Dimensions a line.
[pick arc]	Dimensions an arc.
[pick circle]	Dimensions circle.
[pick pline]	Dimensions an individual segment of a polyline.

Dimension line location options:
Text   Positions the text.
Angle   Changes the angle of dimension text.

Dimension text Allows you to change the dimension text.

RELATED DIM COMMAND
DimRotated   Draws angular dimension line with perpendicular extension line.

RELATED DIM VARIABLE
DimExo   Dimension line offset distance.

DimAngular

__Rel 13__ Draws a dimension that measures an angle.

Command	Alias	Ctrl+	F-key	Alt+	Menu Bar	Tablet
dimangular	dan	...	...	NA	Dimension ↳Angular	X3
	dimang					

```
Command: dimangular
Select arc, circle, line, or RETURN: [pick]
Second angle endpoint: [pick]
Dimension line arc location (Text/Angle): T
Dimension text <>: [Enter]
```

Line, arc, and circle dimensioned with the ***DimAngular*** *command:*

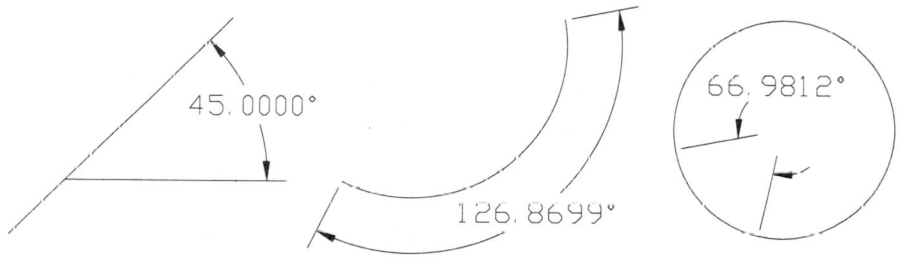

COMMAND LINE OPTIONS

[Enter]	Displays the sub'menu for selecting objects:
[pick arc]	Measures the angle of the arc.
[pick circle]	Prompts you to pick two points on the circle.
[pick line]	Prompts you to pick two lines.
[Enter]	Prompts you to pick points to make an angle.

Second angle endpoint
Positions the secondendpoint of the angle.

Dimension line location options:

Text Positions the text.

Angle Changes the angle of dimension text.

Dimension text
Allows you to change the dimension text.

DimBaseline

Rel 13 Draws linear dimension from the previous starting point.

Command	Alias	Ctrl+	F-key	Alt+	Menu Bar	Tablet
dimbaseline	dba	...	...	NB	Dimension ⮑Baseline	W2
	dimbase					

```
Command: dimbaseline
Second extension line origin or RETURN to select: [pick]
Dimension text:
```

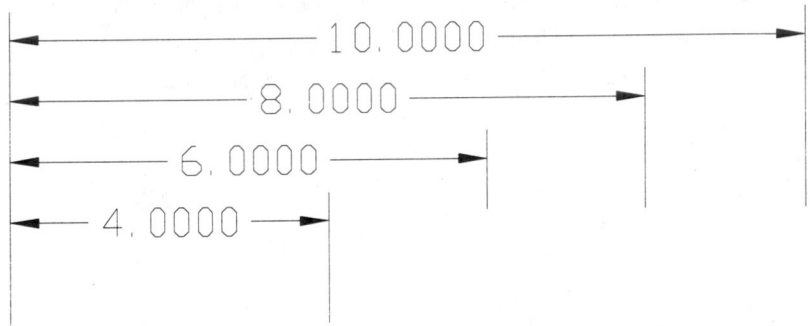

Horizontal dimension (leftmost) and baseline dimensions (right).

COMMAND LINE OPTIONS

Second extension line origin or RETURN to select
        Positions the extension line of the next baseline dimension.
[Enter]   Prompts you to selected the originating dimension.
Dimension text Allows you to change the dimension text.

RELATED DIM COMMAND

Continue   Continues linear dimensioning from last extension point.

RELATED DIM VARIABLES

DimDli   Specifies the distance between baseline dimension lines.
DimSe1   Suppresses first extension line.

DimCenter

__Rel 13__ Draws center mark and lines on arcs and circles.

Command	Alias	Ctrl+	F-key	Alt+	Menu Bar	Tablet
dimcenter	dce	...	...	NM	Dimension ⮑Center Mark	X2

```
Command: dimcenter
Select arc or circle: [pick]
```

Center marks on a circle, arc, and polyline arcs.

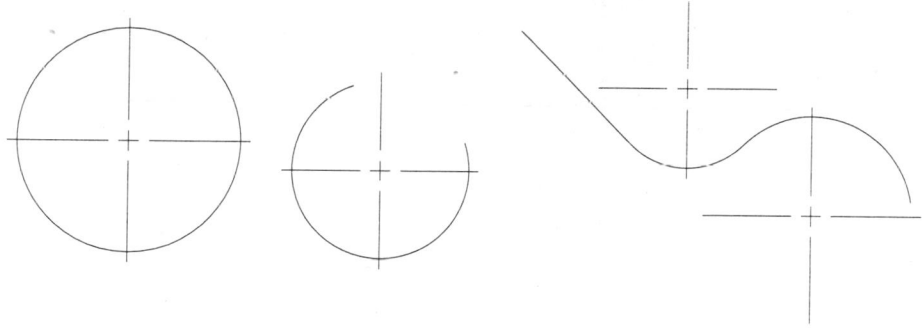

COMMAND LINE OPTION
Select arc or circle
> Places the center mark on the selected arc, circle, or polyarc.

RELATED DIM COMMANDS
DimAligned   Dimensions arcs and circles.
DimDiameter Dimensions arcs and circles by diameter value.
DimRadius   Dimensions arcs and circles by radius value.

RELATED DIM VARIABLE
DimCen   Size of the center mark.

DimContinue

Rel 13 Continues a dimension from the second extension line of the previous dimension.

Command	Alias	Ctrl+	F-key	Alt+	Menu Bar	Tablet
dimcontinue	dco	...	...	NC	Dimension ⇘Continue	W1
	dimcont					

```
Command: dimcontinue
Select continued dimension: [pick]
Second extension line origin or RETURN to select: [pick]
Dimension text:
```

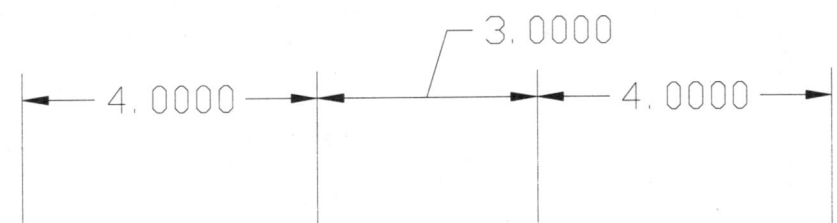

Horizontal dimension (left) and continued dimensions (right).

COMMAND LINE OPTIONS
Second extension line origin
>Positions the extension line of the next coninued dimension.

RETURN to select
>Pressing **[Enter]** prompts you to selected the originating dimension.

Dimension text Allows you to change the dimension text.

RELATED DIM COMMAND
DimBaseline   Continues dimensioning from first extension point.

RELATED DIM VARIABLES
DimDli   Distance between continuous dimension lines.
DimSe1   Suppresses first extension line.

DimDiameter

<u>Rel 13</u> Draws a diameter dimension on arcs, circles, and polyline arcs (*formerly the Dim:Diameter command*).

Command	Alias	Ctrl+	F-key	Alt+	Menu Bar	Tablet
dimdiameter	ddi	...	...	ND	Dimension ⤷Diameter	X4
	dimdia					

Dim: **diameter**
Select arc or circle: **[pick]**
Dimension text: **[Enter]**
Enter leader length for text: **[pick]**

Diameter dimensioning on a circle, arc, and polyarc segment.

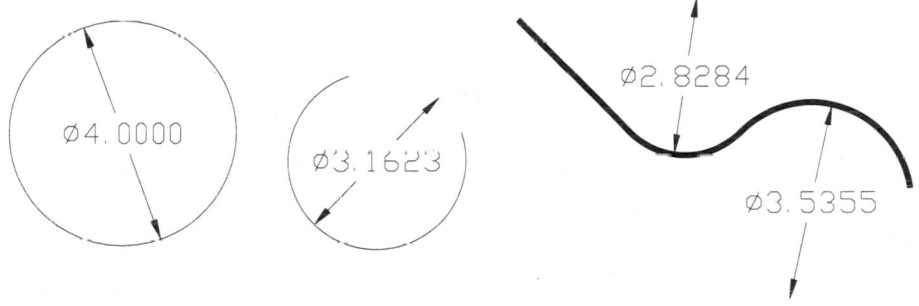

COMMAND LINE OPTIONS
Select arc or circle
        Selects an arc, circle, or polyarc.
Dimension text Specifies the text for the diameter.
Enter leader length for text
        When a leader is used, specifies the length and position.

RELATED DIM COMMANDS
DimCenter   Marks the center point of arcs and circles.
DimRadius   Draws the radius dimension of arcs and circles.

DimEdit

__Rel 13__ Applies editing changes to text in one or more dimensions.

Command	Alias	Ctrl+	F-key	Alt+	Menu Bar	Tablet
dimedit	ded	...	...	NQ	Dimension ⮡Oblique	Y1
	dimed					

```
Command: dimedit
Dimension Edit (Home/New/Rotate/Oblique) <Home>:
```

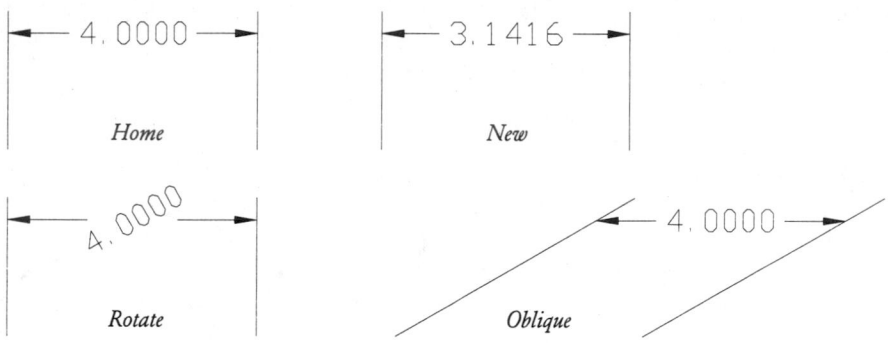

Home   *New*

Rotate   *Oblique*

COMMAND LINE OPTIONS

Angle   Rotates the dimension text.
Home   Returns dimension text to original position.
Left   Moves dimension text to the left.
Right   Moves dimension text to the right.

RELATED DIM COMMANDS
All.

RELATED DIM VARIABLES
Most.

TIPS

■ When entering dimension text with the **DimEdit** command's **New** option, AutoCAD recognizes the following metacharacters:

[Square brackets]   Alternate units format string.
< Angle brackets >   Prefix and suffix text format string.

■ Use the **Oblique** option to angle dimension lines by 30 degrees, suitable for isometric drawings. Use the **Style** command to oblique text by 30 degrees.

Creating isometric dimensions.

AutoCAD's dimensions must be modified for isometric drawings so that the dimension text looks "correct" in isometric mode. This involves two steps — (1) create isometric text styles and (2) change dimension variables — done three times, once for each isoplane.

Step 1: CREATE ISO TEXT STYLES

1. From the menu bar, select **Format | Text Style**.

2. When the **Text Style** dialog box appears, click **New**.

3. Type **isotop** for the name of the new text style, which is used for text in the top isoplane.

4. Click **OK**.

5. When the **Text Style** dialog box reappears, select **Simplex.Shx** from **Font Name**.

6. Change the **Oblique Angle** to **-30**.

7. Click **Apply**.

8. Create text styles for the other two isoplanes:

Style Name	Font Name	Oblique Angle
IsoTop	Simplex.Shx	-30
IsoRight	Simplex.Shx	30
IsoLeft	Simpelx.Shx	30

Enter these values into the **Text Style** dialog box and click **Apply**, then **Close**.

Step 2: CREATE ISO DIMSTYLES

1. Create the dimension styles for the three isoplanes by selecting **Format | Dimension Styles** from the menu bar. Three dimension variables must be changed:

2. Force dimension text to align with the dimension line:

   - Click **Format**.
   - Click **Inside Horizontal** and **Outside Horizontal**.
   - Click **OK**.

3. Specify text style for dimension text:

   - Click **Annotation**.
   - Select **ISOLEFT** from the text **Style** list box.
   - Click **OK**.

4. Save the dimension style by name:

   - In the **Name** text box, type **isoleft**.
   - Click **Save**.

5. One of the three needed dimension styles has been created. Create dimstyles for the other two isoplanes using these parameters:

Dimstyle Name	Text Style
Isotop	IsoTop
Isoright	IsoRight
Isoleft	IsoLeft

6. Save each. Click **OK** to exit the **Dimension Styles** dialog box.

Step 3: PLACE ISO DIMENSIONS

To place linear dimensions in a isometric drawing, use the **DimAligned** command, because it aligns the dimension along the iso axes. Place all dimensioning in one isoplane, then switch to the next isoplane.

1. Press **[F5]** to switch to the appropriate isoplane, such as Top.

2. Use the **DDim** command to select the **associated** dimension style, such as IsoTop.

3. Place the dimension with the **DimAligned** command. It is helpful to use INTersection object snaps.

4. Use the **DimEdit** command's **Oblique** option to skew the dimension by 30 or -30 degrees:

IsoPlane	DimStyle	Oblique Angle
Top	IsoTop	30
Left	IsoLeft	30
Right	IsoRight	-30

*Aligned dimension text before (left) and after applying **DimEdit**'s **Oblique** option (right).*

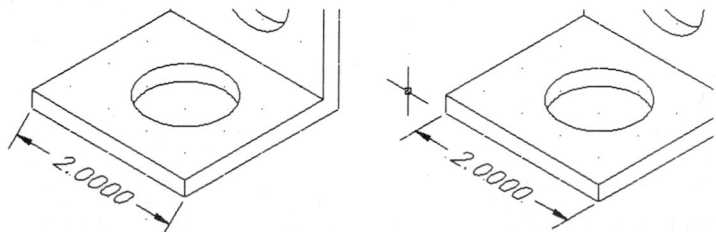

5. To place a leader, use the **Standard** dimstyle and **Standard** text style.

DimLinear

Rel 13 Draws horizontal dimensions.

Command	Alias	Ctrl+	F-key	Alt+	Menu Bar	Tablet
dimlinear	dli	...	...	NL	Dimension ⍦Linear	W5
	dimlin					

```
Command: dimlinear
First extension line origin or RETURN to select: [Enter]
Select line, arc or circle: [pick]
Dimension line location(Text/Angle/Horizontal/Vertical/
Rotated): T
Dimension text <>: [Enter]
```

*Objects with vertical and horizontal dimensions created by the **DimLinear** command.*

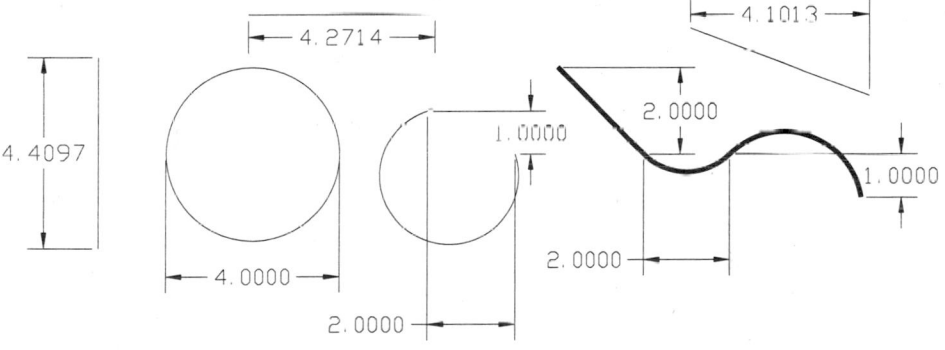

COMMAND LINE OPTIONS

[Enter]   Displays the submenu for dimensioning objects:
Select line, arc or circle
        Automatically dimensions a line, arc, and circle.

*Dimension line location **options:***
Text   Allows you to change the position of the dimension text.
Angle   Specifies the angle of the text.
Horizontal Forces dimension to be horizontal.
Vertical   Forces dimension to be vertical.
Rotated   Force dimension to be rotated.

Dimension text Allows you to change thedimension text.

RELATED DIM COMMAND

DimAligned   Draws linear dimensions aligned with objects.

DimOrdinate

Rel 13 Draws an x- or y-ordinate dimension.

Command	Alias	Ctrl+	F-key	Alt+	Menu Bar	Tablet
dimordinate	dor	...	...	NO	Dimension ↳Ordinate	W3
	dimord					

```
Command: dimordinate
Select Feature: [pick]
Leader endpoint (Xdatum/Ydatum/Text): [pick]
Leader endpoint: [pick]
```

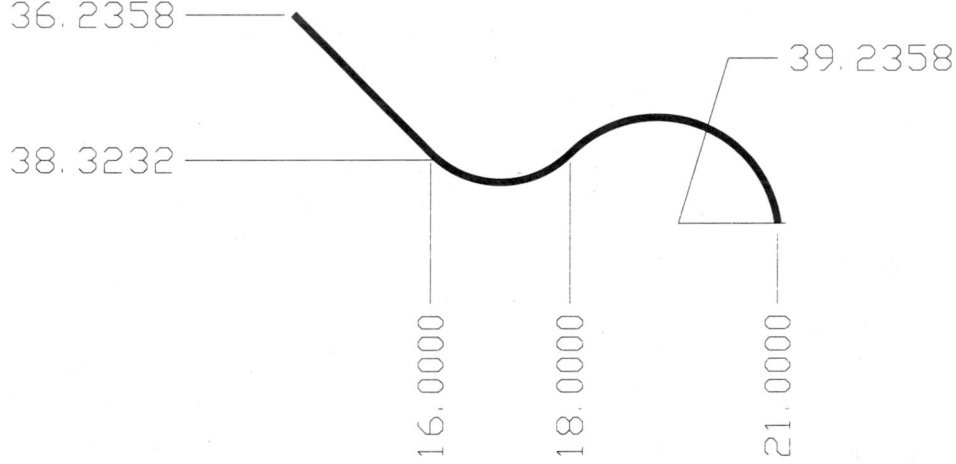

Horizontal (x datum) and vertical (y datum) ordinate dimensions.

COMMAND LINE OPTIONS

Text	Places text, rather than dimension.
Xdatum	Forces x-ordinate dimension.
Ydatum	Forces y-ordinate dimension.

RELATED DIM COMMANDS

DimLinear	Draws regular horizontal and vertical dimensions.
Leader	Draws leader dimensions.

RELATED TOOLBAR ICONS

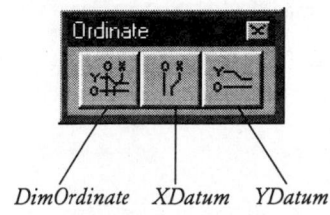

DimOrdinate XDatum YDatum

DimOverride

Rel 13 Overrides the currently set dimension variables.

Command	Alias	Ctrl+	F-key	Alt+	Menu Bar	Tablet
dimoverride	dov	...	...	NV	Dimension ⤷Override	Y4
	dimover					

```
Command: dimoverride
Dimension variable to override:
Current value xxx New Value:
Select objects: [pick]
```

COMMAND LINE OPTIONS

Dimension variable to override
> Requires you to type the name of the dimension variable.

Current value Displays the current value of the dimvar.
New Value Specifies the new value of the dimvar.
Select objects Selects the dimension objects that the change should apply to.

RELATED DIM COMMAND

DimStyle Creates and modifies dimension styles.

RELATED DIM VARIABLES

All dimension variables.

DimRadius

Rel 13 Draws radial dimensions on circles, arcs, and polyline arcs.

Command	Alias	Ctrl+	F-key	Alt+	Menu Bar	Tablet
dimradius	dra	...	...	NR	Dimension ⮡Radius	X5
	dimrad					

```
Command: dimradius
Select arc or circle: [pick]
Dimension line location (Text/Angle): T
Dimension text <>:
```

Circle, radius, and polyarc segments dimensioned by DimRadius.

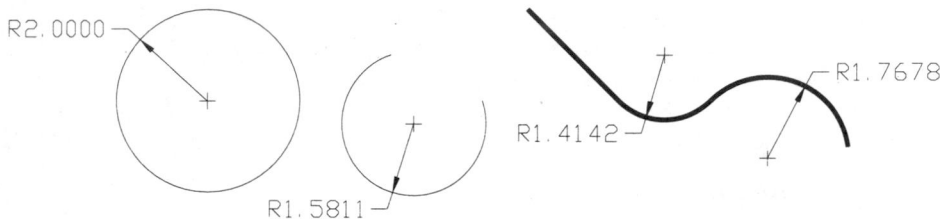

COMMAND LINE OPTIONS

Select arc or circle

Selects the arc, circle, or polyarc to dimension.

Dimension line location options:

Text   Positions the text.
Angle   Changes the angle of dimension text.

Dimension text Allows you to change the dimension text.

RELATED DIM COMMANDS

DimCenter   Draws center mark on arcs and circles.
DimDiameter Draws diameter dimensions on arcs and circles.

RELATED DIM VARIABLE

DimCen   Determines the size of the center mark.

TIP

■ To include the diameter symbol, use the **%%d** code or the Unicode **\U+2205** .

DimStyle

Rel 13 Creates and edits dimstyles (*short for dimension styles; formerly the Dim:REStore, Dim:SAve, Dim:STAtus, and Dim:VAriables commands*).

Command	Alias	Ctrl+	F-key	Alt+	Menu Bar	Tablet
dimstyle	dst	...	...	NS	Dimension ⤷Style	Y3

```
Command: dimstyle
Dimension style STANDARD
Dimension style overrides: dimvar list
Dimension Style Edit (Save/Restore/STatus/Variables/Apply/?):
```

COMMAND LINE OPTIONS

Save	Saves current dimvar settings as a named dimstyle.
Restore	Sets dimvar settings from a named dimstyle.
STatus	Lists dimvars and current settings, then exits the DimStyle command.
Variables	Lists dimvars and their current settings.
Apply	Updates selected dimension objects with current dimstyle settings.
?	Lists names of dimstyles stored in drawing.

INPUT OPTIONS

~*dimvar*	(*Tilde*) Lists the differences between current and selected dimstyle.
[Enter]	Lists the dimvar settings for selected dimension object.

RELATED DIM COMMANDS

DDim	Changes dimvar settings.
DimScale	Determines the scale of dimension text.

RELATED DIM VARIABLES

All
DimStyle   Name of the current dimstyle.

TIPS

■ At the 'Dim' prompt, the **Style** command sets the text style for dimension text and does *not* select a dimension style.

■ Dimstyles cannot be stored to disk, except in a drawing.

■ Read dimstyles from other drawings with the **XBind Dimstyle** command.

■ Dimstyles stored in prototype drawings:

Dimension Style	Drawing File
AutoCAD default	Acad.Dwg
American architectural	Us_Arch.Dwg
American mechanical	Us_Mech.Dwg
ISO	AcadIso.Dwg
JIS architectural	Jis_Arch.Dwg
JIS mechanical	Jis_Mech.Dwg

DimTEdit

Rel 13 Dynamically changes location and orientation of text in dimensions.

Command	Alias	Ctrl+	F-key	Alt+	Menu Bar	Tablet
dimtedit	...	...	...	NX	Dimension ⤷Align Text	Y2

```
Command: dimtedit
Select dimension: [pick]
Enter text location (Left/Right/Home/Angle):
```

Original dimension (left); DimTEdit applied left, right, and angle.

COMMAND LINE OPTIONS

Select   Selects the dimension to edit.

Enter text location otpions:
Angle   Rotates the dimension text.
Home   Returns dimension text to original position.
Left   Moves dimension text to the left.
Right   Moves dimension text to the right.

RELATED DIM COMMANDS

DDim   Changes dimvar values.
DimEdit   Edits associative dimension text.

RELATED DIM VARIABLES

DimSho   Dimension text dynamically updates while dragged.
DimTih   Dimension text is drawn horizontally or aligned with dimension line.
DimToh   Dimension text is forces inside dimension lines.

RELATED TOOLBAR ICONS

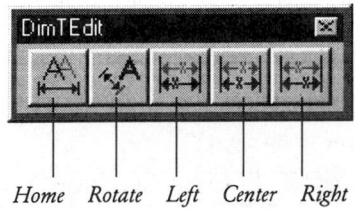

Home   Rotate   Left   Center   Right

TIPS

■ The **DimTEdit** command works only with associative dimension. Use the **DdEdit** command to edit text in non-associative dimensions.

■ An angle of 0 returns dimension text to its default orientation.

 # 'Dist

V. 1.0 Lists the 3D distances and angles between two points (*short for DISTance*).

Command	Alias	Ctrl+	F-key	Alt+	Menu Bar	Tablet
'dist	di	...	...	TQD	Tools ↳Inquiry ↳Dist	T8

```
Command: dist
First point: [pick]
Second point: [pick]
```

Example result:
```
Distance=17.38, Angle in X-Y Plane=358, Angle from X-Y Plane=0
Delta X = 16.3000, Delta Y = -7.3000,  Delta Z = 0.0000
```

COMMAND LINE OPTIONS

First point   Determines starting point of distance measurement.
Second point Determines ending point.

RELATED COMMANDS

Area   Calculates the area and perimeter of objects.
Id   Lists the 3D coordinates of a point.
List   Lists information about selected objects.

RELATED SYSTEM VARIABLE

Distance   Last calculated distance.

TIPS

■ Use object snaps to precisely measure between two geometric features.

■ When the z-coordinate is left out, the **Dist** command assumes the current elevation for z.

Divide

V. 2.5 Places points or blocks at equally-divided distances along an object.

Command	Alias	Ctrl+	F-key	Alt+	Menu Bar	Tablet
divide	div	...	...	DOD	Draw ⓈPoint ⓈDivide	V13

```
Command: divide
Select object to divide: [pick]
<Number of segments>/Block: B
Block name to insert: [type name]
Align block with object? <Y>: [Enter]
Number of segments: 10
```

Polyline (left) divided by ten points (right).

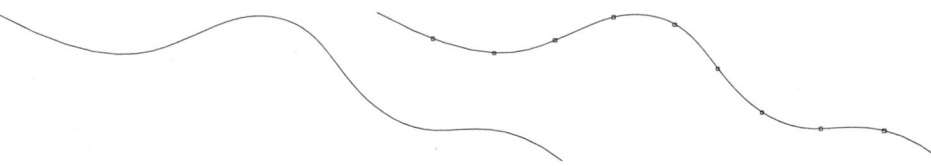

COMMAND LINE OPTIONS

Select object to divide
> Selects a single open or closed object.

Number of segments
> Types a number between 2 and 32767.

Block   Specifies the name of the block to insert along the object.

Align block with object
> Aligns the block's x-axis with the object.

RELATED COMMANDS

Block	Creates the block to use with the **Divide** command.
Insert	Places a single block in the drawing.
MInsert	Places an array of blocks in the drawing.
Measure	Divides an entity into measured distances.

RELATED SYSTEM VARIABLES

PdMode	Sets the style of point drawn.
PdSize	Sets the size of the point, in pixels.

TIPS

- Use **PdSize** and **PdMode** to make points visible along object.

- On closed polylines, the first dividing point is its initial vertex.

- On circles, the first dividing point is in the 0-degree direction from the center.

- The points or blocks are placed in the **Previous** selection set so that you can select them with the next 'Select Objects' prompt.

Donut *or* Doughnut

V. 2.5 Draws solid circles with a pair of wide polyline arcs.

Command	Alias	Ctrl+	F-key	Alt+	Menu Bar	Tablet
donut	do	...	...	DD	Draw ⍦Donut	K9
doughnut						

```
Command: donut
Inside diameter <0.5000>: [type number]
Outside diameter <1.0000>: [type number]
Center of doughnut: [pick]
Center of doughnut: [Enter]
```

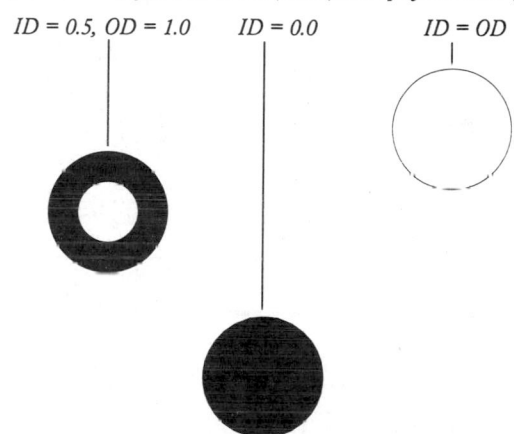

Default donut (left), solid donut (center), and polyline circle (right).

ID = 0.5, OD = 1.0   ID = 0.0   ID = OD

COMMAND LINE OPTIONS

Inside diameter Indicates the inner diameter by typing a number or picking two points.
Outside diameter
        Indicates the outer diameter.
Center of donut
        Indicates the donut's centerpoint by typing coordinates by picking a point.
[Enter]   Exits the **Donut** command.

RELATED COMMAND

Circle   Draws a circle.

RELATED SYSTEM VARIABLES

DonutId   The current donut internal diameter.
DonutOd   The current donut outside diameter.
Fill   Toggles the filling of the donut.

TIP

■ Command automatically repeats itself until cancelled.

'Dragmode

V. 2.0 Controls the display of objects during dragging operations.

Command	Alias	Ctrl+	F-key	Alt+	Menu Bar	Tablet
dragmode	...	...	...	...	...	...

```
Command: dragmode
ON/OFF/Auto <Auto>:
```

Highlight image (left) and drag image (right).

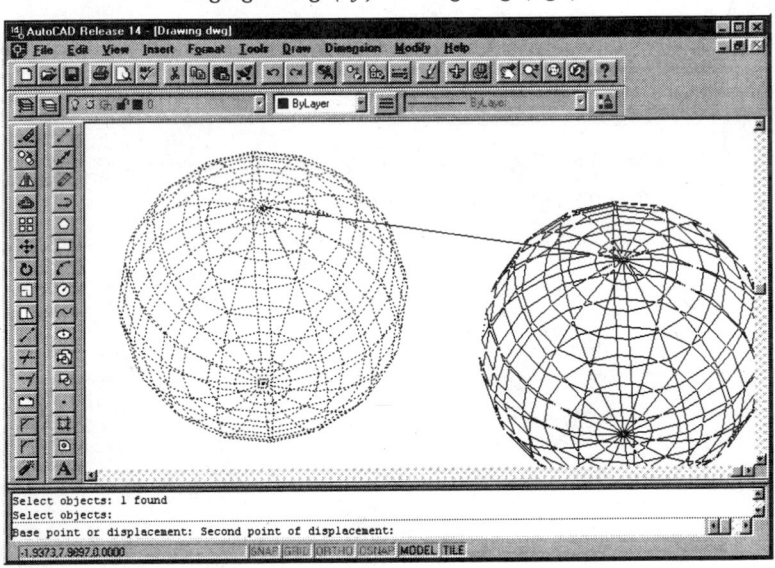

COMMAND LINE OPTIONS

ON	Enables dragging display only with the **Drag** option.
OFF	Turns off all dragging displays.
Auto	AutoCAD determines when to display dragging.

COMMAND MODIFIER

Drag	Displays drag image when **DragMode** = on.

RELATED SYSTEM VARIABLES

DragMode   Current drag setting:

DragMode	Meaning
0	No drag image.
1	On if required.
2	Automatic.

Drag1	Drag regeneration rate (*default = 10*).
Drag2	Drag redraw rate (*default = 25*)

TIP

- Turn off **DragMode** and **Highlight** in very large drawings to help speed up editing.

DrawOrder

Rel. 14 Controls the display of overlapping objects.

Command	Alias	Ctrl+	F-key	Alt+	Menu Bar	Tablet
draworder	dr	...	...	TO	Tools ↳Display Order	T9

```
Command: draworder
Select objects: [pick]
Above object/Under object/Top/<Bottom>: A
Select reference object: [pick]
```

*Text **under** solid (left) and text **above** solid (right).*

Illus...nce   **Illustrated Quick Reference**

COMMAND LINE OPTIONS

Select objects	Picks the objects you want moved.
Above object	The selected objects will appear above the reference object.
Under object	The selected objects will appear below the reference object.
Top	The selected objects are brought to the top of the display order.
Bottom	The selected objects are moved to the bottom of the display order.

Select reference object
Selects the object to bring objects above or below.

TIPS

- When you pick more than one object for reordering, AutoCAD maintains the relative display order of the selected objects.

- The order in which you select objects has no effect on drawing order.

- The first time you use the **DrawOrder** command, AutoCAD turns on all object sort method options found in the **DdSelect** command.

 # DsViewer

Rel.13 Displays the bird's-eye view window; provides real-time pan and zoom (*short for "DiSplay VIEWer"*).

Command	Alias	Ctrl+	F-key	Alt+	Menu Bar	Tablet
dsviewer	av	...	...	VW	View	K2
					⮡Aerial View	

Command: **dsviewer**
Displays Aerial View window:

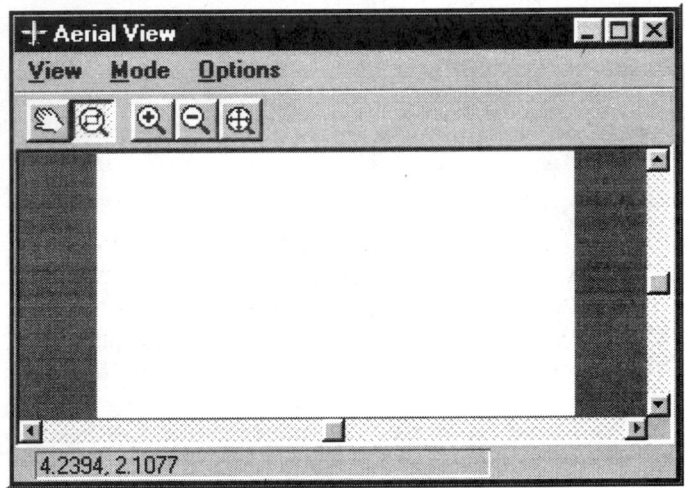

DIALOG BOX OPTIONS

View options:
Zoom In	Increases centered zoom by factor of 2.
Zoom Out	Decreases centered zoom a factor of 2.
Global	Displays entire drawing in Aerial View window.

Mode options:
Pan	Switches Aerial View to pan mode.
Zoom	Switches Aerial View to zoom mode.

Options options:
Auto Viewport Automatically updates the **Aerial View** with the current viewport.
Dynamic Update
Automatically updates the **Aerial View** with editing changes in the current viewport.

TOOLBAR ICONS

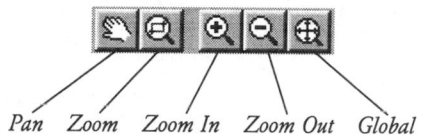

Pan   Zoom   Zoom In   Zoom Out   Global

RELATED COMMANDS

Pan	Moves the drawing view.
View	Creates and displays named views.
Zoom	Makes the view larger or smaller.

TIPS

- The purposes of the **Aerial View** are to let you: (1) see the entire drawing at all times; and (2) zoom and pan without typing the **Zoom** and **Pan** commands, nor selecting items from the menu.

- To quickly switch between **Pan** (*the default*) and **Zoom** modes, right-click the **Aerial View** window.

- *Warning*: When in paper space, the **Aerial View** window shows only paper space objects and real-time update of the AutoCAD window from the Aerial View window is not available.

- When the view fills the **Aerial View** window, some of the toolbar icons might be grayed out (*unavailable*).

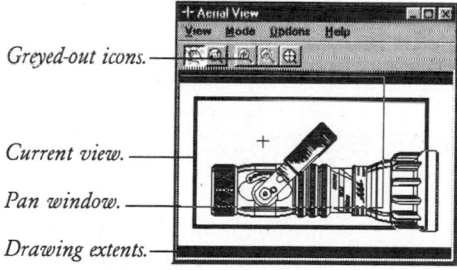

Greyed-out icons.

Current view.

Pan window.

Drawing extents.

 # DText

V. 2.5 Enters text in the drawing in a visual mode (*short for Dynamic TEXT*).

Command	Alias	Ctrl+	F-key	Alt+	Menu Bar	Tablet
dtext	dt	...	...	TXS	Draw ↳Text ↳Single Line Text	K8

```
Command: dtext
Justify/Style/<Start point>: J
Align/Fit/Center/Middle/Right/TL/TC/TR/ML/MC/MR/BL/BC/BR:
Height:
Rotation Angle:
Text:
```

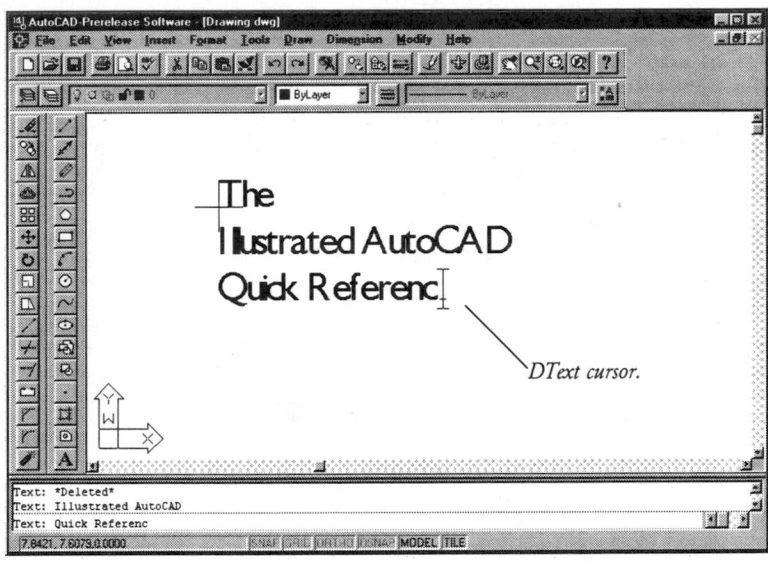

COMMAND LINE OPTIONS

Justify options:

Align	Aligns the text between two points with adjusted text height.
Fit	Fits the text between two points with fixed text height.
Center	Centers the text along the baseline.
Middle	Centers the text horizontally and vertically.
Right	Right-justifies the text.
TL	Applies top-left justification.
TC	Applies top-center justification.
TR	Applies top-right justification.
ML	Applies middle-left justification.
MC	Applies middle-center justification.
MR	Applies middle-right justification.
BL	Applies bottom-left justification.
BC	Applies bottom-center justification.

| **BR** | Applies bottom-right justification. |
| **Start point** | Left-justifies the text. |

Style options:

| **Style name** | Indicates a different style name. |
| **?** | Lists the currently loaded styles. |

| **[Enter]** | Exits the **DText** command. |

TEXT MODIFIERS

%%c	Draws diameter symbol: Ø.
%%d	Draws degree symbol: °.
%%o	Starts and stops overlinning.
%%p	Draws the plus-minus symbol: ±.
%%u	Starts and stops underlining.
%%%	Draws the percent symbol: %.

RELATED COMMANDS

DdEdit	Edits the text.
Change	Change the text height, rotation, style, and content.
DdModify	Changes all aspects of text.
Style	Creates new text styles.
Text	Adds new text to the drawing.
MText	Places paragraph text in drawings.

RELATED SYSTEM VARIABLES

TextSize	The current height of text.
TextStyle	The current style.
ShpName	The default shape name

TIPS

■ Use the **DText** command to easily place text in many locations on the drawing. It displays text on screen as you type.

■ You can erase text by pressing the **[Backspace]** key while at the 'Text' prompt.

■ *Warning:* the spacing between lines of text does not match the current snap spacing.

■ The menus are not available during the **DText** command.

■ Transparent commands do not work during the **DText** command.

■ You can enter any justification mode at the 'Start point' prompt.

■ The command automatically repeats until cancelled with **[Enter]**.

DView

Rel.10 Dynamically zooms and pans 3D drawings, and turns on perspective mode (*short for Dynamic VIEW*).

Command	Alias	Ctrl+	F-key	Alt+	Menu Bar	Tablet
dview	dv	...	...	VY	View	R5
					↳3D Dynamic View	

```
Command: dview
Select objects: [Enter]
CAmera/TArget/Distance/POints/PAn/Zoom/TWist/CLip/Hide/Off/
    Undo/<eXit>:
```

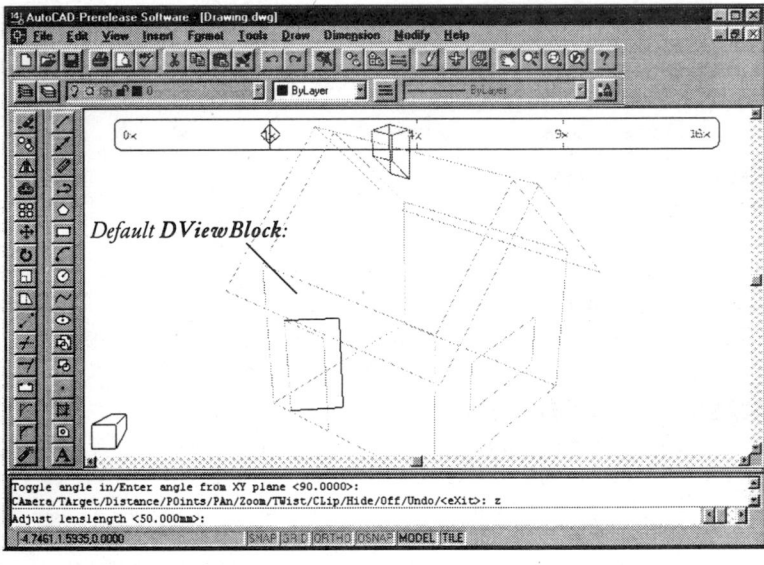

COMMAND LINE OPTIONS

CAmera	Indicates the camera angle relative to the target:
Toggle	Switches between input angles.
TArget	Indicates the target angle relative to the camera.
Distance	Indicates the camera-to-target distance; turns on perspective mode.
POints	Indicates both the camera and target points.
PAn	Dynamically pans the view.
Zoom	Dynamically zooms the view.
TWist	Rotates the camera.

CLip options:
  Back *clip options:*
ON	Turns on the back clipping plane.
OFF	Turns off the back clipping plane.

  Distance from target
        Indicates the location of the back clipping plane.

Front clip options:
- **Eye** — Positions the front clipping plane at the camera.
- **Distance from target** — Indicates the location of the front clipping plane.
- **Off** — Turns off view clipping.

- **Hide** — Performs hidden-line removal.
- **Off** — Turns off the perspective view.
- **Undo** — Undoes the most recent **DView** action.
- **eXit** — Exits the **DView** command.

RELATED COMMANDS
- **Hide** — Removes hidden-lines from a non-perspective view.
- **Pan** — Pans a non-perspective view.
- **VPoint** — Selects a non-perspective viewpoint of a 3D drawing.
- **Zoom** — Zooms a non-perspective view.

RELATED SYSTEM VARIABLES
- **BackZ** — Back clipping plane offset.
- **FrontZ** — Front clipping plane offset.
- **LensLength** — Perspective view lens length, in millimeters.
- **Target** — UCS 3D coordinates of target point.
- **ViewCtr** — 2D coordinates of current view center.
- **ViewDir** — WCS 3D coordinates of camera offset from target.
- **ViewMode** — Perspective and clipping settings.
- **ViewSize** — Height of view.
- **ViewTwist** — Rotation angle of current view.

RELATED SYSTEM BLOCK
- **DViewBlock** — Alternate viewing object during **DView**.

TIPS
- The view direction is from camera to target.
- Press **[Enter]** at the 'Select objects' prompt to display the house.
- You can replace the house block with your own by redefining the **DVIewBlock** block.
- To view a 3D drawing in one-point perspective, use the **DView Zoom** command.
- Menus and transparent zoom and pan are not available during **DView**.
- Once the view is in perspective mode, you cannot use the **Sketch, Zoom**, and **Pan** commands.

Two- and 3-point perspective.

In 2-point perspective, the camera and the target are at the same height. Vertical lines remain vertical. In 3-point perspective, the camera and target are at different heights.

Step 1: TWO-POINT PERSPECTIVE

1. Start the **DView** command and select all objects:

```
Command: dview
Select objects: all
1 found Select objects: [Enter]
```

Step 2: PLACE CAMERA AND TARGET

1. The **POints** option combines the **TArget** and **CAmera** options into one step:

```
CAmera/TArget/Distance/POints/.../Undo/<eXit>: po
```

2. Use the **.xy** filter to pick the target point on the floorplan:

```
Enter target point <0.4997, 0.4999, 0.4997>: .xy
of [pick target point]
```

3. Type a number for your eye height, such as 5'10" or 180cm:

```
(need Z): [type height]
```

4. Use the .xy filter to pick the camera point:

```
Enter camera point <0.4997, 0.4999, 1.4997>: .xy
of [pick camera point]
```

5. Type the same z-coordinate for the camera height:

```
(need Z): [type same height]
```

Step 3: TURN ON PERSPECTIVE MODE

1. The **Distance** option turns on perspective mode:

```
CAmera/TArget/Distance/POints/.../Undo/<eXit>: d
```

2. In perspective mode, the UCS icon becomes a perspective icon. While in **Distance** mode, use the slider bar to set the distance:

```
New camera/target distance <1.0943>: [move slider bar]
```

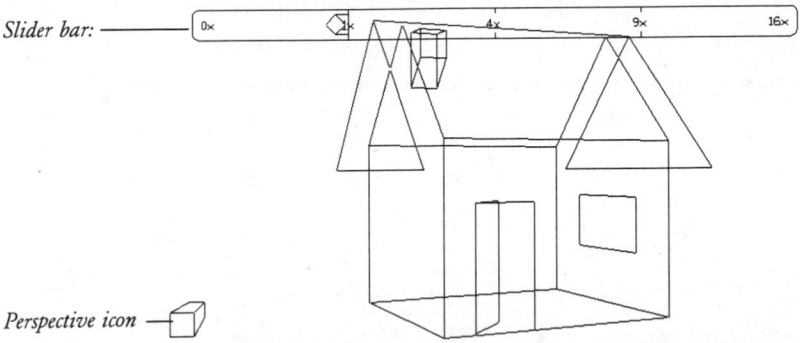

Slider bar: ——

Perspective icon ——

Step 4: THREE-POINT PERSPECTIVE

- In 3-point perspective, the target and camera heights differ. Most commonly, the camera is higher than the target, so that you look down on the 3D scene.

1. Follow the earlier steps but change the camera and target heights, as follows:

```
Command: dview
Select objects: all
1 found Select objects: [Enter]
CAmera/TArget/Distance/POints/.../Undo/<eXit>: po
```

2. For target height, type the height of an object you are looking at, such as a window or table:

```
Enter target point <0.4997, 0.4999, 0.4997>: .xy
of [pick target point]
(need Z): [type a height]
```

3. For the camera height, type your eye height or a larger number for a bird's-eye view:

```
Enter camera point <0.4997, 0.4999, 1.4997>: .xy
of [pick camera point]
(need Z): [type a taller height]
CAmera/TArget/Distance/POints/.../Undo/<eXit>: d
New camera/target distance <1.0943>: [adjust distance]
```

4. Use the **Hide** option to create a hidden-line view:

```
CAmera/TArget/Distance/POints/.../Hide/Off/Undo/<eXit>: h
```

Hidden-line view in three-point perspective mode.

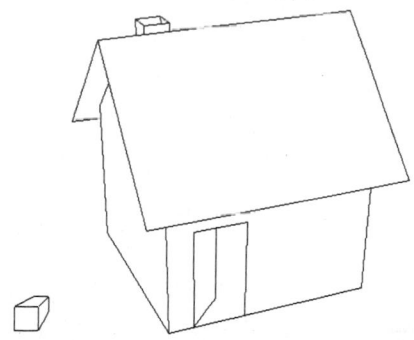

Step 5: EXIT DVIEW

1. Exit the **DView** command:

```
CAmera/TArget/Distance/POints/.../Undo/<eXit>: [Enter]
```

- The view remains in perspective mode. While in perspective mode, the **Zoom**, **Pan**, and **DsViewer** commands and scroll bars do not work.

2. To exit perspective mode, use the **Plan** command.

DwfOut

<u>Rel.14</u> Exports the current drawing in DWF format (*short for Draw Web Format OUTput; an external command in DwfOut.Arx*).

Command	Alias	Ctrl+	F-key	Alt+	Menu Bar	Tablet
dwfout	...	...	...	FE	File	...
				⌷DWF	⌷Export	
					⌷Drawing Web Format	

dwfoutd

Command: **dwfout**
Displays dialog box:

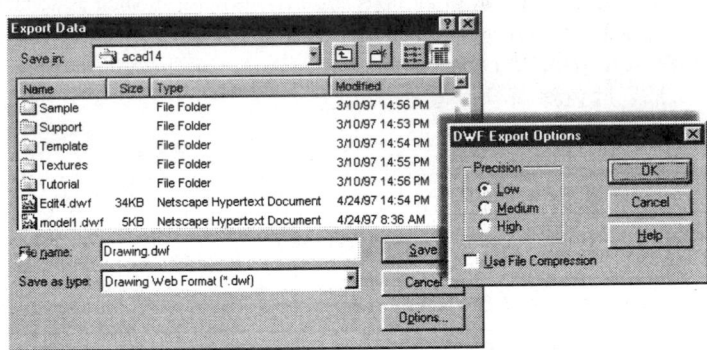

Command: **dwgfoutd**
Enter file name <default>:

DIALOG BOX OPTIONS

Options options:

Precision   Higher precision results in larger DWF file:

Precision	Meaning
Low	16-bit precision: low precision creates a smaller file.
Medium	20-bit precision: the default.
High	24-bit precision: for drawings with small details.

Use File Compression
Makes DWF file smaller but may make it less compatible.

COMMAND LINE OPTION

Enter file name Type a filename or press **[Enter]** to accept the default.

TIPS

■ The DWF file is created from the Whip display driver and is resolution-dependent. For a better image, zoom in. Also, consider the effect of the **ViewRes, FaceTRes, DispSilh,** and **Hide** commands on image quality.

■ DWF is strictly 2D; set the 3D viewpoint before making a DWF file of 3D objects.

■ The DWF file uses the same background color as the current AutoCAD setting.

Adding DWF to your Web site.

To let others view your DWF file over the Internet, you need to *embed* the DWF file in a Web page.

Step 1: EMBEDDING A DWF FILE

1. This HTML (short for "hyper text markup language") code places a DWF file in your Web page:

   ```
   <embed src="filename.dwf">
   ```

2. The code has the following meaning:

   - **<embed>** embeds an object in a Web page.
   - **scr** is short for "source."
   - Replace **"filename.dwf"** with the URL of the DWF file. Remember to keep the quotation marks in place. The URL can have the following formats:

URL	Meaning
filename.dwf	The DWF file is in same directory as HTML file.
subdir/filename.dwf	DWF file is in a subdirectory below the HTML file.
http://www.nnn.com/filename.dwf	DWF is located at another Web site.
ftp://ftp.nnn.com/filename.dwf	Located at an FTP site.
file:///C|filename.dwf	On a local hard drive.

Step 2: SIZING THE IMAGE

1. HTML normally displays an image as large as possible. To size of the DWF file, add the **Width** and **Height** options.

   ```
   <embed width=800 height=600 src="filename.dwf">
   ```

2. The **Width** and Height **values** are measured in pixels. Replace 800 and 600 with any appropriate numbers, such as:

   - 100 and 75 for a "thumbnail" image
   - 300 and 200 for a small image
   - 640 and 480 for a medium-size image.

Step 3: IDENTIFYING THE IMAGE

1. To speed up a Web page's display speed, some users turn off the display of images. For this reason, it is useful to include a description, which is displayed in place of the image:

   ```
   <embed width=800 height=600 name=description src="filename.dwf">
   ```

2. The **Name** option displays a textual description of the image when the browser does not load images. You might replace "description" with the DWF filename.

Step 4: SPECIFYING VIEWS

1. When the original drawing contains named views created by the **View** command, these are transferred to the DWF file. Specify the initial view for the DWF file:

```
<embed width=800 height=600 name=description namedview="viewname"
src="filename.dwf">
```

2. The **NamedView** option specifies the name of the view to display upon loading. Replace "viewname" with the name of a valid view name.

3. When the drawing contains named views, the user can right-click on the DWF image to get a list of all named views.

4. As an alternative, you can specify the 2D coordinates of the initial view:

```
<embed width=800 height=600 name=description view="0,0 9,12"
src="filename.dwf">
```

5. The **View** option specifies the x,y-coordinates of the lower-left and upper-right corners of the initial view. Replace **"0,0 9,12"** with other coordinates. Since DWF is 2D-only, you cannot specify a 3D viewpoint. You can use **View** or **Namedview** but not both.

Step 5: AUTO-LOADING THE PLUG-IN

1. Before a DWF image can be displayed, the Web browser must have the DWF plug-in called "Whip!". For users of Netscape Navigator, you include a description of where to get the Whip plug-in when the Web browser is lacking it.

```
<embed pluginspage=http://www.autodesk.com/products/autocad/whip/
whip.htm width=800 height=600 name=description view="0,0 9,12"
src="filename.dwf">
```

2. The **pluginspage** option describes the page on the Autodesk Web site where the Whip-DWF plug-in can be downloaded.

Step 6: ADAPTING FOR EXPLORER

1. The code listed above works for Netscape Navigator. To provide for those users who might be using Internet Explorer, the following HTML code must be added:

```
<object classid ="clsid:B2BE75F3-9197-11CF-ABF4-08000996E931"
codebase = "ftp://ftp.autodesk.com/pub/autocad/plugin/
whip.cab#version=2,0,0,0" width=800 height=600>
<param name="Filename" value="filename.dwf">
<param name="View" value="0,0 9,12">
<param name="Namedview" value="viewname">
<embed pluginspage=http://www.autodesk.com/products/autocad/whip/
whip.htm width=800 height=600 name=description view="0,0 9,12"
src="filename.dwf">
</object>
```

2. The two **<object>** and three **<param>** tags are ignored by Netscape Navigator; they is required for compatibility with Internet Explorer. The **classid** and **codebase** options tell Explorer where to find the plug-in. Remember that you can use **View** or **Namedview** but not both.

Step 7: REGISTERING THE MIME TYPE

1. To publish DWF files from your Web site, ask your Internet server provider to add the following MIME (short for "multipurpose Internet mail extensions") type:

   `"drawing/x-dwf"`

2. When the original DWG drawing file is located in the same directory as the DWF file, the user will be able to drag the image from their Web browser into AutoCAD.

3. As an alternative to DWF, you can display thumbnail raster image of drawing (in either GIF or JPEG format) and allow downloading of the DWG file via FTP, as follows:

   ```
   <img src="thumbnail.gif" alt="thumbnail" height=75 width=100>
   Click here to download the drawing file in DWG format:
   <a href="filename.dwg">
   Filename.Dwg
   </a>
   ```

4. To display the original DWG file, download the DWG-DXF plug-in from either of these two sites:

   - SoftSource: http://www.softsource.com/
   - California Software Labs: http://www.cswl.com

Dxbin

V. 2.1 Imports a DXB-format file into the current drawing (*short for Drawing Exchange Binary INput*).

Command	Alias	Ctrl+	F-key	Alt+	Menu Bar	Tablet
dxbin	...	...	...	IE	Insert	...
					↳Drawing Exchange Binary	

Command: **dxbin**
Displays Select DXB File dialog box.

COMMAND LINE OPTIONS
None.

RELATED COMMANDS
DxfIn	Reads DXF-format files.
Plot	Writes DXB-format files when configured for ADI plotter.

TIP
■ Configure AutoCAD with the ADI plotter driver to produce a DXB file.

Dxfin

V. 2.0 Reads a DXF-format file into a drawing (*short for Drawing interchange Format INput*).

Command	Alias	Ctrl+	F-key	Alt+	Menu Bar	Tablet
dxfin	...	...	...	FO ↳DXF	File ↳Open ↳DXF	...

Command: **dxfin**

Displays ***Open*** *dialog box.*

COMMAND LINE OPTIONS

None.

RELATED COMMANDS

DxbIn Reads a DXB-format file.

DxfOut Writes a DXF-format file.

TIPS

- DXF files come in two styles: (1) *complete*; and (2) *partial.*
- To load a complete DXF file, AutoCAD requires the current drawing be empty.
- To create an empty drawing, use the **New** command with the **Start from Scratch** option.
- When you try to import a complete DXF file but the drawing is not new, AutoCAD complains, "DXFIN requires a new drawing."
- If you need to import the complete DXF file into a non-empty drawing (called, say, "First.Dwg"), take these steps:

  Step 1. Use the **DxfIn** command to import the complete DXF file into an empty drawing.

  Step 2. Save the drawing with the **SaveAs** command, with the name of, say, "Second.Dwg."

  Step 3. Open the non-empty First.Dwg drawing and use the **Insert** command with the * option to place the contents of the Second.Dwg.
- A partial DXF file can be imported into any drawing, empty or not.

DxfOut

<u>**V. 2.0**</u> Writes a DXF-format file of part or all of the current drawing (*short for Drawing interchange Format OUTput*).

Command	Alias	Ctrl+	F-key	Alt+	Menu Bar	Tablet
dxfout	...	...	...	FE ⤷DXF	File ⤷Export ⤷DXF	...

Command: **dxfout**
Displays dialog box:

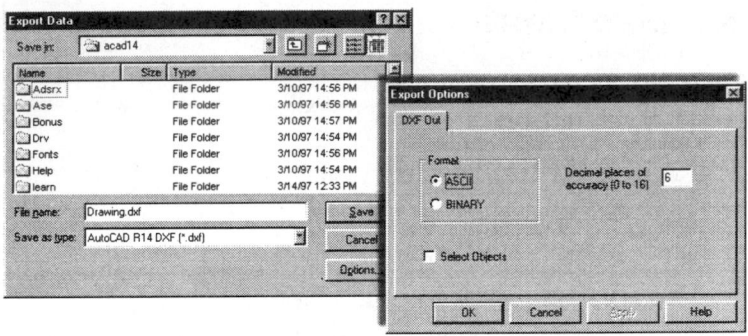

*When **CmdDia** is set to 0:*
Command: **dxfout**
File name: **[type filename]**
Enter decimal places of accuracy (0 to 16)/Objects/
  Binary <6>: **o**
Select objects: **[pick]**
Select objects: **[Enter]**
Enter decimal places of accuracy (0 to 16)/Binary <6>: **[Enter]**

DIALOG BOX OPTIONS
Format options:
ASCII   Text format is human-readable and importable by most applications.
Binary   Creates a smaller filesize but cannot be read by all applications.

Decimal Places of Accuracy
          Type a number between 0 and 16.
Select Objects Select objects to export, instead of the entire drawing.

COMMAND LINE OPTIONS
Filename   Type a filename; AutoCAD adds the .DXF extension.
Enter decimal places of accuracy
          For ASCII files, indicate decimal places of accuracy between 0 and 16.
Objects   Select objects to export in DXF format.
Binary   Create a binary DXF file.

RELATED COMMANDS

DxfIn Reads a DXF-format file.
Save Writes the drawing in DWG format.

TIPS

- Use the ASCII DXF format to exchange drawings with other CAD and graphics programs.

- A binary DXF file is much smaller and is created much faster than an ASCII binary file; however, few applications read a binary DXF file.

- You can save the DXF file compatible with six versions of AutoCAD:

    AutoCAD Release 14 and LT Release 4.
    AutoCAD Release 13 and LT for Windows 95.
    AutoCAD Release 12 and LT Release 2.

- The R12 dialect of DXF is the most compatible with other applications; however, AutoCAD erases or converts R13- and R14-specific objects into simpler objects. See the **SaveAs** command for more information.

 # Edge

Rel.12 Toggles the visibility of 3D faces (*an external command in Edge.Lsp*).

Command	Alias	Ctrl+	F-key	Alt+	Menu Bar	Tablet
edge	...	...	...	DFE	Draw ↳Surfaces ↳Edge	...

```
Command: edge
Display/<Select edge>: D
Select/<All>: S
Select objects: [pick]
Display/<Select edge>: [Enter]
```

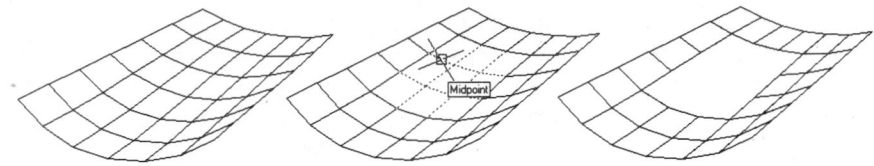

*3d faces (left), edges selected with **Edge** command (center), and invisible edges (right).*

Command Line Options

Select edge	Selected edge is no longer visible.
Display	Highlights invisible edges.
Select	Regenerates selected hidden edges.
All	Selects all hidden edges and regenerates them

RELATED COMMAND

3dFace Creates 3D faces.

RELATED SYSTEM VARIABLE

SplFrame Toggles visibility of 3D face edges.

TIPS

- Make edges invisible to make 3D objects look nicer.

- The **Edge** command applies only to objects made of 3d faces; it does not work with polyface meshes or solid models.

- Use the **Explode** command to convert meshed objects into 3d faces.

- Command repeats itself until you press **[Enter]** at the 'Display/<Select Edge>' prompt.

EdgeSurf

Rel.10 Draws a 3D polygon mesh as a Coons surface patch between four boundaries (*short for EDGE-defined SURFace*).

Command	Alias	Ctrl+	F-key	Alt+	Menu Bar	Tablet
edgesurf	...	...	...	DF	Draw	R8
					⬑Surfaces	
					⬑Edge	

```
Command: edgesurf
Select edge 1: [pick]
Select edge 2: [pick]
Select edge 3: [pick]
Select edge 4: [pick]
```

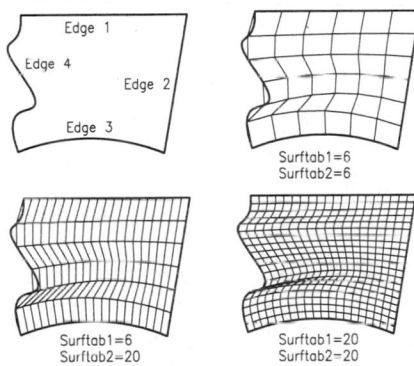

COMMAND LINE OPTION
Select edge   Picks an edge.

RELATED COMMANDS
3dMesh   Creates a 3D mesh by specifying every vertex.
3dFace   Creates a 3D mesh of irregular vertices.
PEdit   Edits the mesh created by Edgesurf.
TabSurf   Creates a tabulated 3D surface.
RuleSurf   Creates a ruled 3D surface.
RevSurf   Creates a 3D surface of revolution.

RELATED SYSTEM VARIABLES
SurfTab1   The current m-density of meshing.
SurfTab2   The current n-density of meshing.

TIPS
- The Coons surface created by the **EdgeSurf** command is an interpolated bi-cubic surface.
- The four boundary edges can be made from lines, arcs, and open 2D and 3D polylines; the edges must meet at their endpoints.
- The maximum mesh density is 32767.

'Elev

Sets elevation and thickness of extruded 3D objects (*short for ELEVation*).

Command	Alias	Ctrl+	F-key	Alt+	Menu Bar	Tablet
'elev	...	...	...	...	...	...

```
Command: elev
New current elevation <0.0000>:
New current thickness <0.0000>:
```

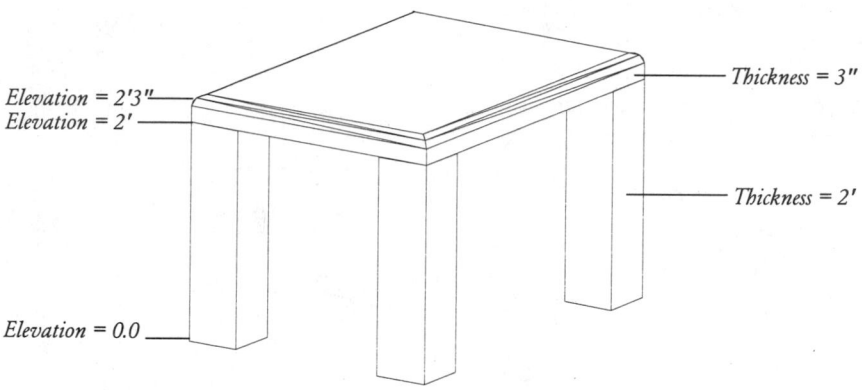

Elevation = 2'3"
Elevation = 2'
Elevation = 0.0
Thickness = 3"
Thickness = 2'

COMMAND LINE OPTIONS

Elevation — Changes the base elevation from z = 0.
Thickness — Extrudes 2D objects in the z-direction.

RELATED COMMANDS

Change — Changes the thickness and z-coordinate of objects.
DdModify — Changes the thickness of objects.
Move — Moves objects, including in the z-direction.

RELATED SYSTEM VARIABLES

Elevation — Stores the current elevation setting.
Thickness — Stores the current thickness setting.

TIPS

■ The current value of elevation is used whenever a z-coordinate is not supplied.

■ Thickness is measured up from the current elevation in the positive z-direction.

Ellipse

V. 25 Draws an ellipse — by four different methods — and elliptical arcs and isometric circles.

Command	Alias	Ctrl+	F-key	Alt+	Menu Bar	Tablet
ellipse	el	...	...	DE	Draw ⮡Ellipse	M9

Command: **ellipse**
Arc/Center/Isocircle/<Axis endpoint 1>: **[pick]**
Axis endpoint 2: **[pick]**
<Other axis distance>/Rotation: **[pick]**

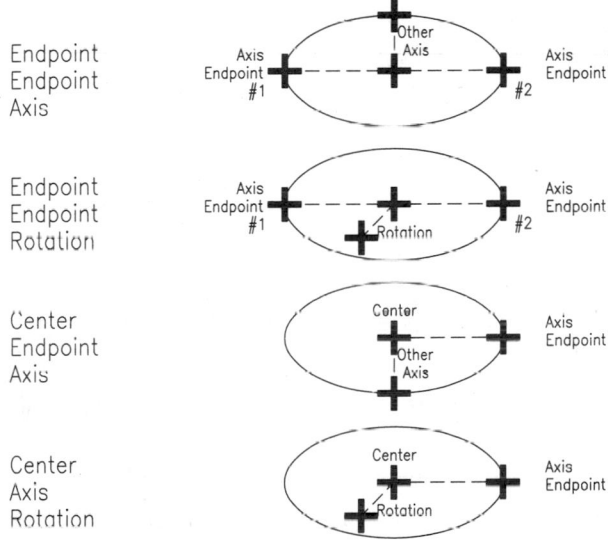

COMMAND LINE OPTIONS

Axis endpoint 1 Indicates the first endpoint of the major axis.
Axis endpoint 2 Indicates the second endpoint of the major axis.
Center Indicates the center point of the ellipse.
Arc Draws an elliptical arc.
Rotation Indicates a rotation angle around the major axis.
Isocircle Draws isometric circles; this option only appears when the **Snap** command's isometric mode is turned on.

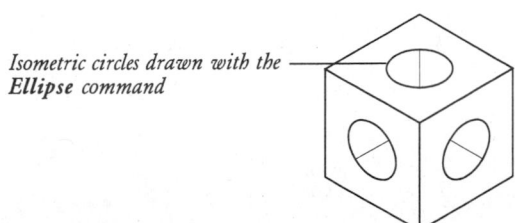

Isometric circles drawn with the **Ellipse** *command*

RELATED COMMANDS

IsoPlane	Sets the current isometric plane.
PEdit	Edits ellipses (when drawn with a polyline).
Snap	Controls the setting of isometric mode.

RELATED SYSTEM VARIABLES

PEllispe   Determines how the ellipse is drawn:

PEllipse	Meaning
0	Draw ellipse with the ellipse object (*default*).
1	Draw ellipse as series of polyline arcs.

SnapIsoPair   Current isometric plane:

SnapIsoPair	Meaning
0	Left (*default*).
1	Top.
2	Right.

SnapStyl   Regular or isometric drawing mode:

SnapStyl	Meaning
0	Standard (*default*).
1	Isometric.

TIPS

- Previous to Release 13, the **Ellipse** command constructed the ellipse as a series of short polyline arcs.

- When **PEllipse** = 1, the **Arc** option is not available.

- Use ellipses to draw circles in isometric mode. When **Snap** is set to isometric mode, the **Ellipse** command's isocircle option projects a circle into the working isometric drawing plane. Use **[Ctrl]+E** to toggle isoplanes.

End

V. 1.0 Saves the drawing and exits AutoCAD to the operating system.

Command	Alias	Ctrl+	F-key	Alt+	Menu Bar	Tablet
end	...	...	...	...	...	...

Command: **end**
If the drawing has not been saved, displays the Save Drawing As dialog box.

COMMAND LINE OPTIONS
None.

RELATED COMMANDS
SaveAs   Saves read-only drawings by another name.
Quit   Leaves AutoCAD without saving the drawing

RELATED SYSTEM VARIABLE
DbMod   Determines whether the drawing has been modified since it was loaded.

TIPS
■ AutoCAD renames the drawing file to .BAK before saving the contents of the drawing editor.

■ The End command does not work with drawings set to read-only; use the **SaveAs** command instead.

Erase

V. 1.0 Erases objects from the drawing.

Command	Alias	Ctrl+	F-key	Alt+	Menu Bar	Tablet
erase	e	...	...	ME	Modify	U14
					⤷Erase	V14

```
Command: erase
Select objects: [pick]
Select objects: [Enter]
```

COMMAND LINE OPTION

Select objects   Selects the objects to erase.

RELATED COMMANDS

Break	Erases a portion of a line, circle, arc, or polyline.
Oops	Returns the most-recently erased objects to the drawing.
Undo	Returns the erased objects to the drawing.

TIPS

- The **Erase L** command combination erases the last-drawn item visible on the screen.

- The **Oops** command brings back the most-recently erased objects; use the **U** command to bring back other erased objects.

- *Warning:* The **Erase All** command erases all objects in the drawing, except on locked, frozen, and off layers.

Explode

V. 2.5 Explodes a polyline, block, associative dimension, hatch, multiline, 3D solid, region, body, or polyface mesh into its constituent objects.

Command	Alias	Ctrl+	F-key	Alt+	Menu Bar	Tablet
explode	x	...	...	MX	Modify ⇘Explode	Y22

```
Command: explode
Select objects: [pick]
Select objects: [Enter]
```

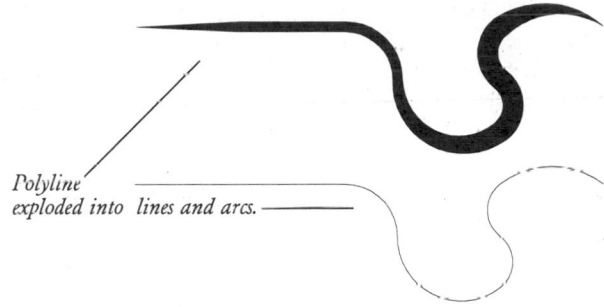

Polyline exploded into lines and arcs.

COMMAND LINE OPTION

Select objects   Selects the objects to explode.

RELATED COMMANDS

Block	Recreates a block after an explode.
PEdit	Converts a line into a polyline.
Region	Converts 2D objects into a region.
Undo	Reverses the effects of explode.

RELATED SYSTEM VARIABLE

ExplMode   Toggles whether non-uniformly scaled blocks can be exploded:

ExplMode	Meaning
0	Does not explode (*R12-compatible*).
1	Does explode (*default*).

TIPS

■ As of Release 13, you *can* explode blocks inserted with unequal scale factors, mirrored blocks, and blocks created by the **MInsert** command.

■ You cannot explode xrefs and dependent blocks (blocks from an xref drawing).

- Parts making up exploded blocks and associative dimensions may change their color and linetype, most commonly to color White (or Black when the background color is white) and linetype Continuous.
- Resulting objects become the previous selection set.
- The **Explode** command reduces:

Object	Exploded
Block	Constituent parts.
Circle within a non-uniform scaled block	Ellipse.
Arc within a non-uniform scaled block	Elliptical arc.
Associative dimension	Lines, solids, and text.
2D polyline	Lines and arcs; width and tangency information is lost.
3D polyline	Lines.
Multiline	Lines.
Polygon mesh	3D faces.
Polyface mesh	3D faces, lines, and points.
3D solid	Regions and bodies.
Region	Lines, arcs, ellipses, and splines.
Body	Single bodies, regions, and curves.

Export

<u>Rel.13</u> Save the drawing in formats other than DWG.

Command	Alias	Ctrl+	F-key	Alt+	Menu Bar	Tablet
export	exp	...	...	FE	File ⮑Export	W24

Command: **export**
Displays dialog box:

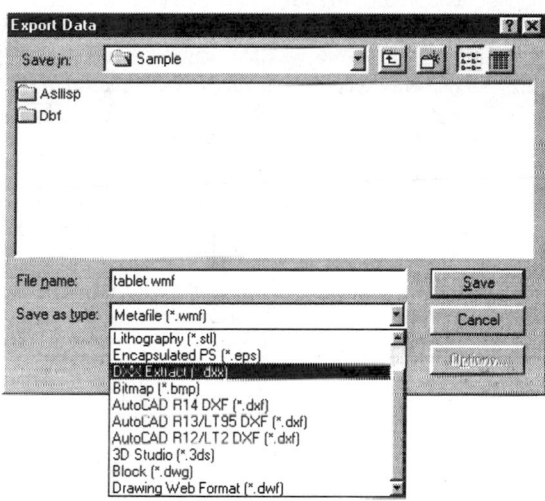

DIALOG BOX OPTIONS

Cancel	Dismisses the dialog box and return to AutoCAD.
Options	Displays the **Options** dialog box; varies with filetype.
Save	Saves the drawing.

RELATED COMMANDS

AseExport	Exports external database data in drawing.
AttExt	Exports attribute data in drawing as CDF, SDF, or DXF formats.
CopyClip	Exports drawing to Clipboard.
CopyHist	Exports text screen to Clipboard.
CopyLink	Exports drawing to Clipboard.
CutClip	Exports drawing as to Clipboard.
DdAttExt	Exports attribute data in drawing as CDF, SDF, or DXF formats.
Import	Imports several vector and raster formats.
LogFileOn	Saves command line text to ASCII file Acad.Log.
MassProp	Exports mass property data in drawing as ASCII text in MPR file.
MSlide	Exports current viewport as an SLD slide file.
Plot	Exports drawing in a couple of dozen vector and raster formats.
Save	Saves drawing as AutoCAD Release 14 DWG format.
SaveAs	Exports drawing as AutoCAD Release 12 or 13 DWG format.
SaveImg	Exports rendering as TIFF, Targa, or BMP format.

TIPS

■ The **Export** command acts as a "shell" command; it launches other AutoCAD commands that perform the actual export function, as noted below.

■ The Export command exports the current drawing in the following formats:

Extension	Meaning
3DS	3D Studio file: **3dsOut** command.
BMP	Device-independent bitmap file: **BmpOut** command.
DWG	AutoCAD drawing file : **WBlock** command.
DWF	Drawing Web format file: **DwfOut** command.
DXF	Release 14 drawing interchange file: **DxfOut** command.
or	R13 & LT95 drawing interchange file.
or	R12 & LT2 drawing interchange file.
DXX	Attribute extract DXF file: **AttExt** command.
EPS	Encapsulated PostScript file: **PsOut** command.
SAT	ACIS solid object file: **AcisOut** command.
STL	Solid object stereo-lithography file: **StlOut** command.
WMF	Windows metafile: **WmfOut** command

Extend

V. 2.5 Extends the length of a line, open polyline, or arc to a boundary.

Command	Alias	Ctrl+	F-key	Alt+	Menu Bar	Tablet
extend	ext	...	...	MD	Modify ⮑Extend	W16

```
Command: extend
Select boundary edges:(Projmode=UCS,Edgemode=No extend)
Select objects: [pick]
Select objects: [Enter]
<Select object to extend>/Project/Edge/Undo: P
None/Ucs/View:
```

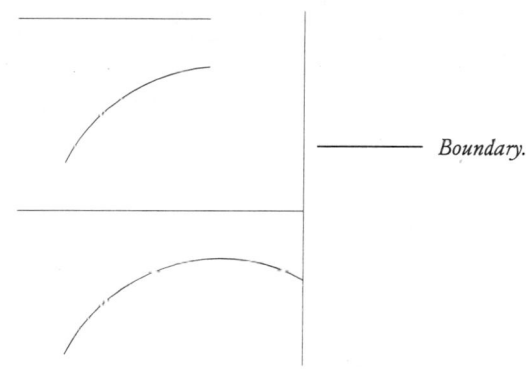

Boundary.

COMMAND LINE OPTIONS

Select objects Selects the objects used for the extension boundary.
Select objects to extend
    Selects the objects that will be extended.

Project options:
None	Extends objects to boundary (*Release 12 compatible*).
Ucs	Boundaries is x,y-plane of current UCS.
View	Boundaries is current view plane.

Edge options:
Extend	Extends to implied boundary.
No extend	Extends only to actual boundaries (*Release 12 compatible*).
Undo	Undoes the most recent extend operation.

RELATED COMMANDS

Change	Changes the length of lines.
Lengthen	Changes the length of open objects.
Stretch	Stretches objects wider or narrower.
Trim	Reduces the length of lines, polylines and arcs.

RELATED SYSTEM VARIABLES

EdgeMode   Toggles boundary mode for **Extend** and **Trim** commands:

EdgeMode	Meaning
0	Use actual edges; Release 12 compatible (*default*).
1	Use implied edge.

ProjMode   Toggles projection mode for **Extend** and **Trim** commands:

ProjMode	Meaning
0	None; Release 12 compatible.
1	Current UCS (*default*)
2	Current view plane.

TIPS

■ The following objects can be used as a boundary:

2D polyline.	Line.
3D polyline.	Ray.
Arc.	Region.
Circle.	Spline.
Ellipse.	Text.
Floating viewport.	Xline.

■ When a wide polyline is the edge, **Extend** extends to the polyline's centerline.

■ Pick the object a second time to extend it to a second boundary line.

■ Circles and other closed objects are valid edges: the object is extended in direction nearest to the pick point.

■ Extending a variable-width polyline widens it proportionately; extending a splined poyline adds a vertex.

Extrude

Rel. 11 Creates a 3D solid by extruding a 2D object, with optional tapered sides (*an external command in Acis.Dll*).

Command	Alias	Ctrl+	F-key	Alt+	Menu Bar	Tablet
extrude	ext	...	...	DIX	Draw	P7
					↳Solids	
					↳Extrude	

```
Command: extrude
Select objects: [pick]
Path/<Height of extrusion>:
Extrusion taper angle <0>:
```

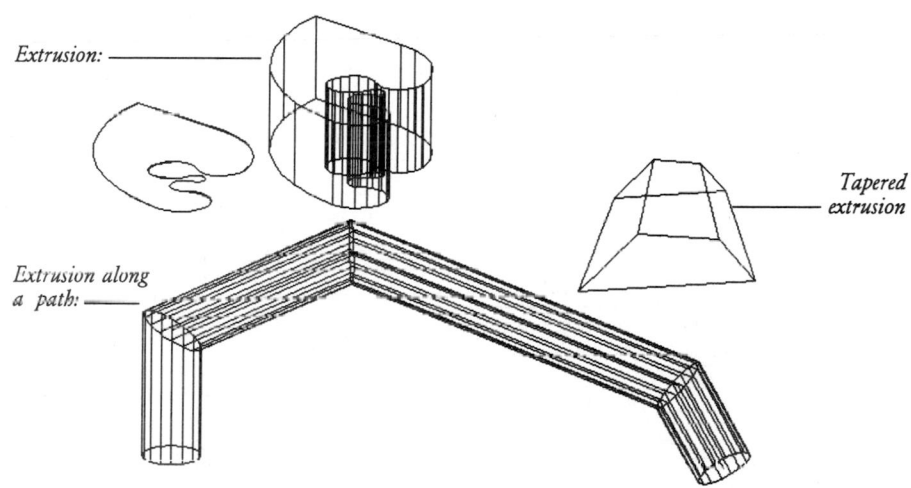

Extrusion:

Extrusion along a path:

Tapered extrusion

COMMAND LINE OPTIONS

Path   Selects an open object for the extusion path.
Height   Specifies the extrusion height.
Extrusion taper angle
     Specifies the taper angle, -90 to +90 degrees.

RELATED COMMANDS

Revolve   Creates a 3D solid by revolving a 2D object.
DdModify   Gives thickness to non-solid objects to extrude them.

TIPS

■ You can extrude the following objects:

Circle.	Ellipse.
Donut.	Closed polyline.
Polygon.	Closed spline.
Region.	

- You *cannot* extrude polylines with less than 3 or more than 500 vertices; crossing nor self-intersecting polylines.
- Objects within a block cannot be extruded; the the **Explode** command first.
- The taper angle must between 0 (*default*) and 90 degrees.
- Positive angle tapers in from base; negative angle taper out.
- The **Extrude** command does not work when a taper angle is less than -90 degrees or more than +90 degrees.
- **Extrude** also does not work if the combination of angle and height makes the object's extrusion walls intersect.
- You can use the following objects as extrusion paths:

Line.	Polyline.
Arc.	Elliptical arc.
Circle.	Ellipse.

FileOpen

<u>Rel.12</u> Opens a drawing file without displaying a dialog box.

Command	Alias	Ctrl+	F-key	Alt+	Menu Bar	Tablet
fileopen	...	...	...	...	...	...

Command: **fileopen**
Enter name of drawing: **[type filename]**

COMMAND LINE OPTION
Enter name of drawings
> Specifies the DWG drawing filename to open.

RELATED COMMANDS
Open   Opens a drawing file via a dialog box.
OpenUrl Opens a drawing using a URL for the filename.

TIPS
■ The filename cannot be blank.

■ Use the **FileOpen** command to open a drawing in toolbar, Diesel, and menu macros.

REMOVED COMMAND

The **Files** command was removed from Release 14. In its place, use Windows Explorer or File Manager.

'Fill

V. 1.4 Toggles wide objects — traces, multilines, solids, and polylines — to be displayed and plotted as solid-filled or as outlines.

Command	Alias	Ctrl+	F-key	Alt+	Menu Bar	Tablet
'fill	...	...	...	...	...	...

```
Command: fill
ON/OFF <On>:
```

Fill on (left) and off (right) of a 2D solid, wide polyline, and donut.

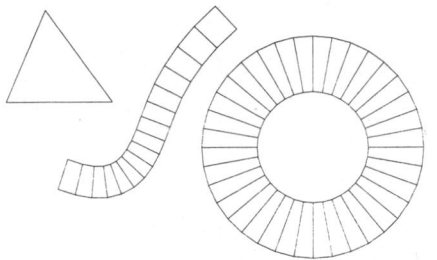

COMMAND LINE OPTIONS

ON   Turns on fill after the next regeneration.

OFF   Turns off fill after the next regeneration.

RELATED SYSTEM VARIABLES

FillMode   Current setting of fill status:

FillMode	Meaning
0	Fill mode is off.
1	Fill mode is on (*default*).

TextFill   Toggles whether TrueType fonts are filled:

TextFill	Meaning
0	Fonts not filled.
1	Fonts filled (*default*).

RELATED COMMAND

Regen   Adjusts display to reflect fill-nofill status.

TIPS

■ The state of fill (or no fill) does not come into effect until the next regeneration.

■ Traces, solids, and polylines are not filled when the view is *not* in plan view, regardless of the setting of the **Fill** command.

■ Since filled objects take longer to regenerate, redraw, and plot, consider leaving fill off during editing and plotting. During plotting, use a wide pen for filled areas.

■ **Fill** affects objects derived from polylines including donut, polygon, rectangle, and ellipse (when created with **PEllipse** = 1).

Fillet

<u>**V. 1.4**</u> Joins two intersecting lines, polylines, arcs, circles, or 3D solids with a radius.

Command	Alias	Ctrl+	F-key	Alt+	Menu Bar	Tablet
fillet	f	...	...	MF	Modify ⮑Fillet	W19

```
Command: fillet
Polyline/Radius/Trim/<Select first object>: [pick]
Select second object: [pick]
```

*Lines before (top) and after (bottom) applying the **Fillet** command:*
1. Crossing lines.   2. Touching lines.   3. Non-intersecting lines.   4. Parallel lines.

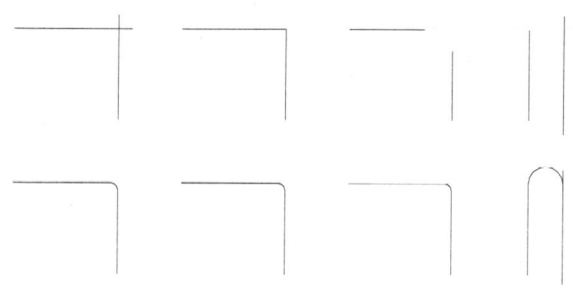

When a 3D solid is selected:
```
Enter radius:
Chain/Radius <Select edge>: [pick]
```

*Box before (left) and after (right) applying the **Fillet** and **Render** commands to a 3D solid.*

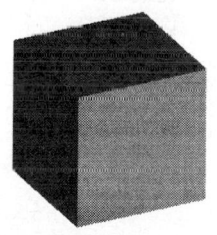 

COMMAND LINE OPTIONS

2D fillet options:

Polyline	Fillets all vertices of a polyline.
Radius	Indicates the filleting radius.
Trim	Toggles whether objects are trimmed.

3D fillet options:

Chain	Switches to selecting a chain of edges.
Edge	Switches to selecting a single edge.
Edge chain	Selects all tangental edges.
Radius	Specifies the fillet radius.
Select edge	Selects a single edge.

RELATED COMMAND

Chamfer   Beveld intersecting lines or polyline vertices.

RELATED SYSTEM VARIABLES

FilletRad   The current filleting radius.
TrimMode   Toggles whether objects are trimmed.

TIPS

■ Pick the end of the object you want filleted; the other end will remain untouched.

■ The lines, arcs, or circles need not touch.

■ As a faster substitute for the **Extend** and **Trim** commands, use the **Fillet** command with the radius of zero.

■ If the lines to be filleted are on two different layers, the fillet is drawn on the current layer.

■ The fillet radius must be smaller than the length of the lines. For example, if the lines to be filleted are 1.0m long, the fillet radius can be no more than 0.9999m.

■ Use the **Close** option of the **PLine** command to ensure a polyline is filleted at all vertices.

*Polyline closed with **Close** option (left) and without (right).*

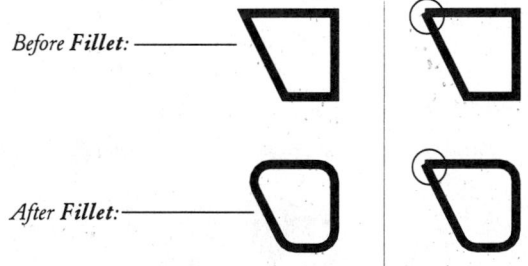

*Before **Fillet**:* ——————

*After **Fillet**:*——————

■ You cannot fillet polyline segments from different polylines.

■ Filleting a pair of circles does not trim them.

■ As of Release 13, the **Fillet** command fillets a pair of parallel lines; the radius of fillet is automatically determined as half the offset distance.

'Filter

Rel.12 Creates a filter list applied to selection sets (*an external command in Filter.Lsp*).

Command	Alias	Ctrl+	F-key	Alt+	Menu Bar	Tablet
'filter	fi	...	...	...	...	...

Command: **filter**
Displays dialog box:

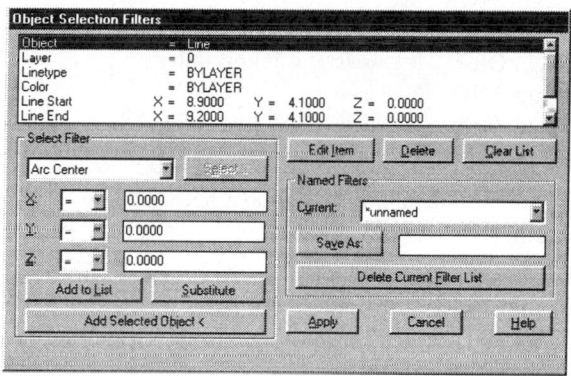

DIALOG BOX OPTIONS

Select Filter	Selects filter based on object properties.
Select	Displays all items of specified type in drawing.
X, Y, Z	Specifies object coordinates.
Add to List	Adds current select-filter option to filter list.
Substitute	Replaces a highlighted filter with selected filter.
Add Selected Object	
	Selects object to be added from drawing.
Edit Item	Lets you edit highlighted filter item.
Delete	Deletes highlighted filter item.
Clear list	Clears entire filter list.
Current Named Filter	
	Selects named filter from list.
Save As	Saves filter list with name and .NFL extension.
Delete Current Filter List	
	Deletes named filter.
Apply	Applies filter operation.

RELATED COMMANDS
Any AutoCAD command with a 'Select objects' prompt.

RELATED FILE
*.NFL — Named filter list.

TIPS

■ The selection set created by the **Filter** command is accessed via the **P** (previous) selection option; alternatively, **'Filter** is used transparently at the 'Select objects' prompt.

■ **Filter** cannot find objects when color is set to BYLAYER and linetype is set to BYLAYER.

■ Save selection sets by name to an NFL (short for *named filter*) file on disk for use in other drawings or editing sessions.

■ The **Filter** command uses the following grouping operators:

**Begin OR	*with*	**End OR
**Begin AND	*with*	**End AND
**Begin XOR	*with*	**End XOR
**Begin NOT	*with*	**End NOT

■ The **Filter** command uses the following relational operators:

Operator	Meaning
<	Less than.
<=	Less than or equal to.
=	Equal.
!=	Not equal to.
>	Greater than.
>=	Greater than or equal to.
*	All values.

Fog

Creates a fog-like effect in renderings (*an external command in Render.Arx*).

Command	Alias	Ctrl+	F-key	Alt+	Menu Bar	Tablet
fog	...	...	...	VEF	View	P2
					⬦Render	
					⬦Fog	

Command: **fog**
Displays dialog box:

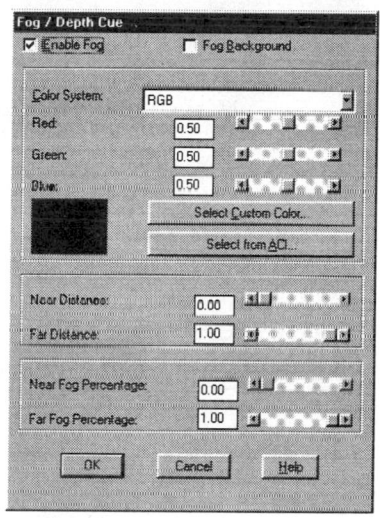

DIALOG BOX OPTIONS

Enable Fog Turns fog effect on; allows turning fog off without affecting parameters.
Fog Background Applies fog effect to background; see **Background** command.
Colors Selects the color of the fog.
Near Distance Defines where the fog effect begins; value is the percent distance between camera and the back clipping plane.
Far Distance Defines where the fog effect ends.
Near Fog Specifies percentage of fog effect at near distance; ranges between 0 and 100%.
Far Fog Specifies percentage of fog effect at the far distance.

RELATED COMMAND

Render Creates a rendering with optional fog effect.

TIPS

■ The fog can be any color:

Color	RGB	HLS	Effect
White	1,1,1	0,1,0	Fog.
Black	0,0,0	0,0,0	Distance.
Green	0,1,0	0.33,0.5,0	Alien mist.

- The effect of using White as the fog color:

- The effect of using Black as the fog color:

- It can be tricky getting the fog effect to work. Use the **DView** command to set the back clipping plane at the back of the model or where you want the fog to have its full effect. Then use the **Fog** command to set up the following parameters:

  Near distance: 0.70
  Far distance: 1.00
  Near fog percentage: 0.00
  Far fog percentage: 1.00

REMOVED COMMAND

The **GiffIn** command was removed from Release 14. In its place, use the **Image** command.

'GraphScr

V. 2.1 Switches the text window back to the graphics window.

Command	Alias	Ctrl+	F-key	Alt+	Menu Bar	Tablet
'graphscr	...	...	[F2]	...	...	...

Command: **graphscr**

Text window (left) and graphics windows (right).

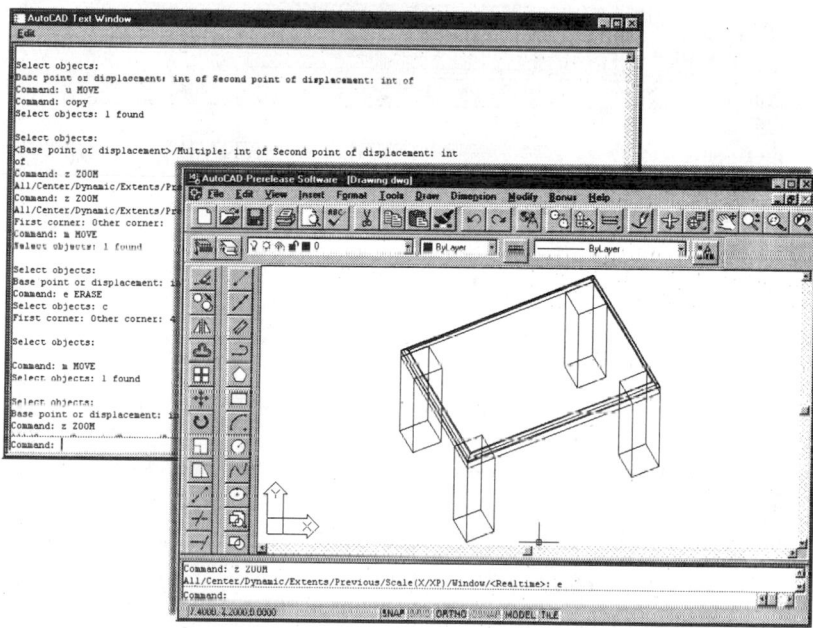

COMMAND LINE OPTIONS
None.

RELATED COMMANDS
Copy Hist   Copies text from the Text window to the Clipboard.
TextScr   Switches from graphics window to Text window.

RELATED SYSTEM VARIABLE
ScreenMode   Indicates whether current screen is text or graphics mode:

ScreenMode	Meaning
0	Text window.
1	Graphics window (*default*).
2	Dual screen displaying both text and graphics.

TIP
- The Text window appears to be frozen when a dialog box is active. Click the dialog box's **OK** or **Cancel** buttons to regain access to the Text window.

'Grid

V. 1.0   Displays a grid of reference dots within the currently set limits.

Command	Alias	Ctrl+	F-key	Alt+	Menu Bar	Tablet
'grid	. . .	G	F7	. . .	. . .	V20

```
Command: grid
Grid spacing(X) or ON/OFF/Snap/Aspect <1.0000>:
```

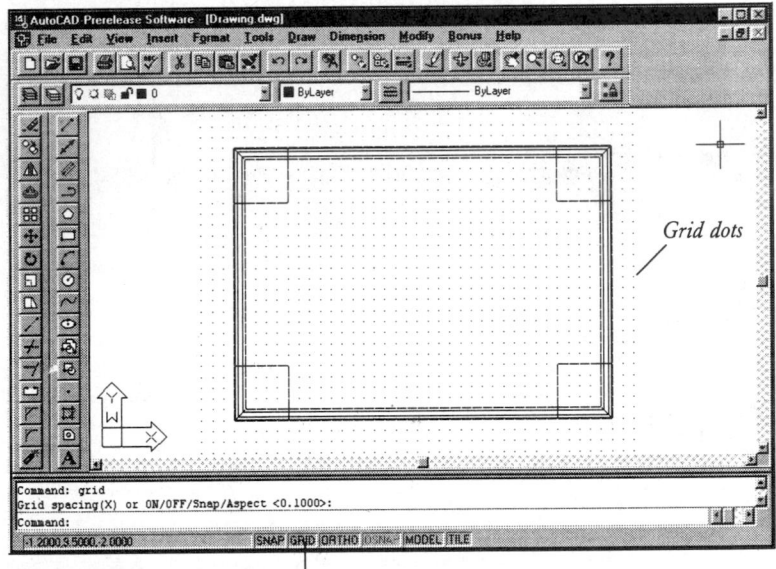

Double-click GRID to turn the grid display on (black) and off (gray).

COMMAND LINE OPTIONS

Aspect options:

Horizontal	Ssets the spacing in the x-direction.
Vertical	Sets the spacing in the y-direction.

Grid spacing(X)	Sets the x- and y-direction spacing; an *X* following the value sets the grid spacing a multiple of the current snap setting.
OFF	Turns off grid markings.
ON	Turns on grid markings.
Snap	Makes the grid spacing the same as the snap spacing.

RELATED COMMANDS

DdRModes	Sets the grid via a dialog box.
Limits	Sets the limits of the grid in WCS.
Snap	Sets the snap spacing.

RELATED SYSTEM VARIABLES

GridMode   Current grid visibility:

GridMode	Meaning
0	Grid is off (*default*).
1	Grid is on.

GridUnit   Current grid x,y-spacing.

LimMin   X,y-coordinates of the lower-left corner of the grid display.

LimMax   X,y-coordinates of the upper-right corner of the grid display.

SnapStyl   Displays a normal or isometric grid:

SnapStyl	Meaning
0	Normal (*default*)
1	Isometric grid.

TIPS

- The grid is most useful when set to the snap spacing, or to a multiple of the snap spacing.

- When the grid spacing is set to 0, it matches the snap spacing.

- You can set a different grid spacing in each viewport and a different grid spacing in the x- and y-directions.

- Rotate the grid with the **Snap** command's Rotate option; **Snap**'s Isometric option creates an isometric grid.

- If a very dense grid spacing is selected, the grid will take a long time to display; press **[Esc]** to cancel the display.

- AutoCAD will not display a grid that is too dense and displays the message, "Grid too dense to display."

- Grid markings are not plotted; to create a plotted grid, use the **Array** command to place an array of points.

 # Group

Rel.13 Creates a named selection set of objects.

Command	Alias	Ctrl+	F-key	Alt+	Menu Bar	Tablet
group	g	A	...	TB	Tools ⤷Object Group	X8
-group	-g					

Command: **group**
Displays dialog box:

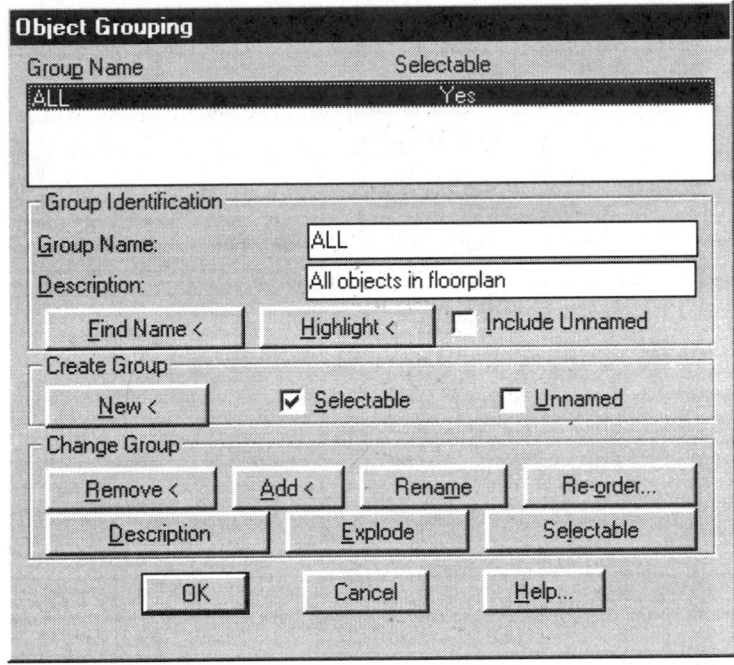

DIALOG BOX OPTIONS

Group Identification options:

Group Name	Displays the name of the current group.
Description	Describes the group with a 64-character-long description.
Find Name	Lists the name(s) of group(s) that a selected object belongs to.
Highlight	Highlights the objects included in the current group.
Include Unnamed	Lists unnamed groups in dialog box.

Create Group options:

New	Selects objects for the new group.
Selectable	Toggles selectability: picking one object picks the entire group.
Unnamed	Creates an unnamed group; AutoCAD gives the name *A*n.

Change Group options:

Remove	Removes objects from the current group.
Add	Adds objects to the current group.
Rename	Renames the group.
Description	Changes the description of the group.
Explode	Removes the group description; does not erase group members.
Selectable	Toggles selectability.
Re-order	Changes the order of objects in the group; displays dialog box:

Order Group dialog box:

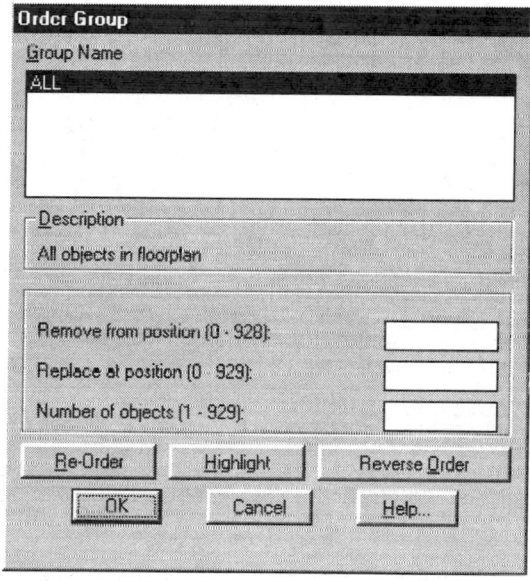

Remove from position (0-n)
> Selects the object to move.

Replace at position (0-n)
> Moves to new position.

Number of objects (1-n)
> The number of objects to reorder.

Re-Order	Applies the order changes.
Highlight	Highlights the objects in the current group.
Reverse Order	Reverses the order of the groups.

```
Command: -group
?/Order/Add/Remove/Explode/REName/Selectable/<Create>:
```

COMMAND LINE OPTIONS

?	Lists names and descriptions of currently defined groups.
Add	Adds objects to group.
Remove	Removes objects from group.
Explode	Remove sgroup definition from drawing.
REName	Renames the group.
Selectable	Toggles whether group is selectable.
Create	Creates a new named group from objects selected.
Order	Changes the order of objects within the group:

RELATED COMMANDS

Block	Creates a named symbol from a group of objects.
Select	Creates a selection set.

RELATED SYSTEM VARIABLE

PickStyle   Toggles whether groups are selected by the usual selection process:

PickStyle	Meaning
0	Groups and associative hatches are not selected.
1	Groups are included in selection sets.
2	Associate hatches included in selection sets.
3	Both are selected (*default*).

TIPS

- Toggle groups on and off with the **[Ctrl]+A** keys.

- Consider a group as a named selection set; unlike a regular selection set, a group is not "lost" when the next group is created.

- Group names are up to 31 characters long, including $, _ , and - .

- Group descriptions are up to 64 characters long.

- Anonymous groups are unnamed; AutoCAD refers to them as *A*n.

Hatch

<u>V. 1.4</u> Draws a non-associative crosshatch pattern within a closed boundary.

Command	Alias	Ctrl+	F-key	Alt+	Menu Bar	Tablet
hatch	-h	...	...	...	...	...

```
Command: hatch
Pattern (? or name/U,style): [type pattern name]
Scale for pattern <1.0000>: [Enter]
Angle for pattern <0>: [Enter]
Select hatch boundaries or RETURN for direct hatch option,
Select objects: [Enter]
Retain polyline <N>: [Enter]
From point: [pick]
Arc/Close/Length/Undo/<Next Point>: [pick]
From point or RETURN to apply hatch: [Enter]
```

COMMAND LINE OPTIONS

Pattern options:

?	Lists the hatch pattern names.
Name	Types the valid name of a hatch pattern.
U	Creates a user-defined hatch pattern.
Style	Determines how hatch crosses boundaries:

Style	Meaning
N	Hatch alternate boundaries (*Normal*).
O	Hatch only outermost boundaries (*Outermost*).
I	Hatch everything within boundary (*Ignore*).

Scale	Hatches pattern scale.
Angle	Hatches pattern angle.
Select	Selects objects that make up the hatch pattern boundary.

Direct Hatch options:

Retain polyline	*Yes*: leaves boundary in place after hatch is complete.
	No: erases boundary after hatching.
From point	Begins drawing the hatch boundary.
Next point	Draws straight line.
Arc	Draws an arc hatch boundary.
Close	Closes the hatch boundary.
Length	Continues the boundary by specified distance.
Undo	Undoes last-drawn segment

RELATED COMMANDS

BHatch	Automatic, associative hatching.
Boundary	Automatically creates polyline or region boundary.
Explode	Reduces hatch pattern to its constituent lines.
PsFill	Fills closed polyline with a PostScript pattern.
Snap	Changes the hatch pattern's origin.

RELATED SYSTEM VARIABLES

HpAng	Hatch pattern angle.
HpDouble	Doubled hatch pattern.
HpName	Hatch pattern name.
HpScale	Hatch pattern scale.
HpSpace	Hatch pattern spacing.
SnapBase	Controls the origin of the hatch pattern.
SnapAng	Controls the angle of the hatch pattern.

RELATED FILE

Acad.Pat	Hatch pattern definition file.

TIPS

- The **Hatch** command draws non-associative hatch patterns; the pattern remains in place when its boundary is edited.

- For complex hatch areas, you may find it easier to outline the area with a polyline (using object snap) or to use the **BHatch** command.

- The hatch is created as a block; the name begins with the letter "X" followed by a consecutive number. To create the hatch as lines, precede the pattern name with * (*asterisk*).

- AutoCAD includes the following hatch patterns in the file Acad.Pat:

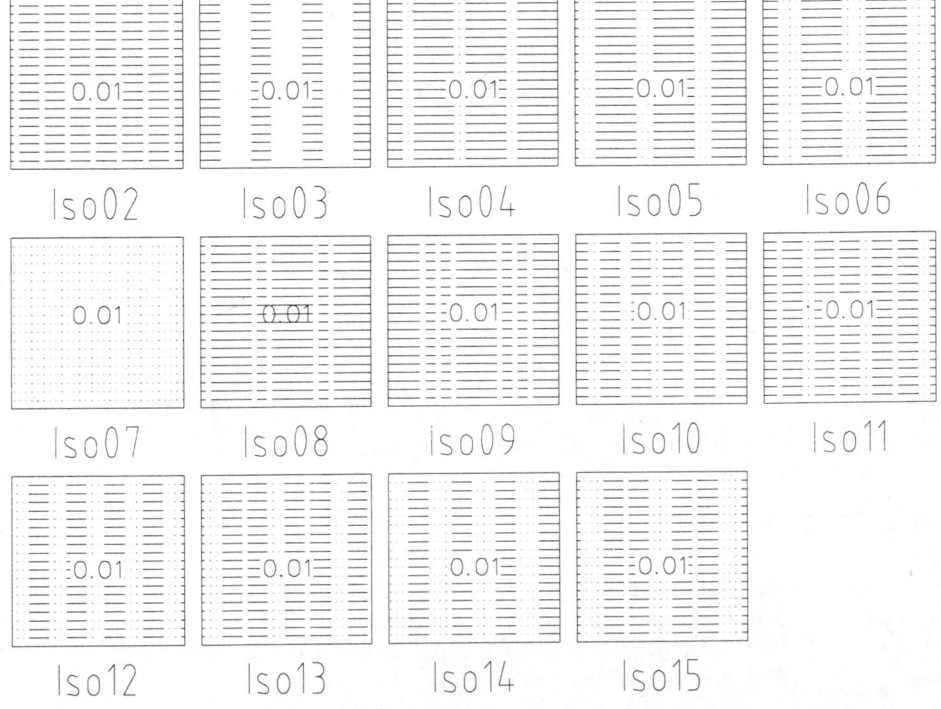

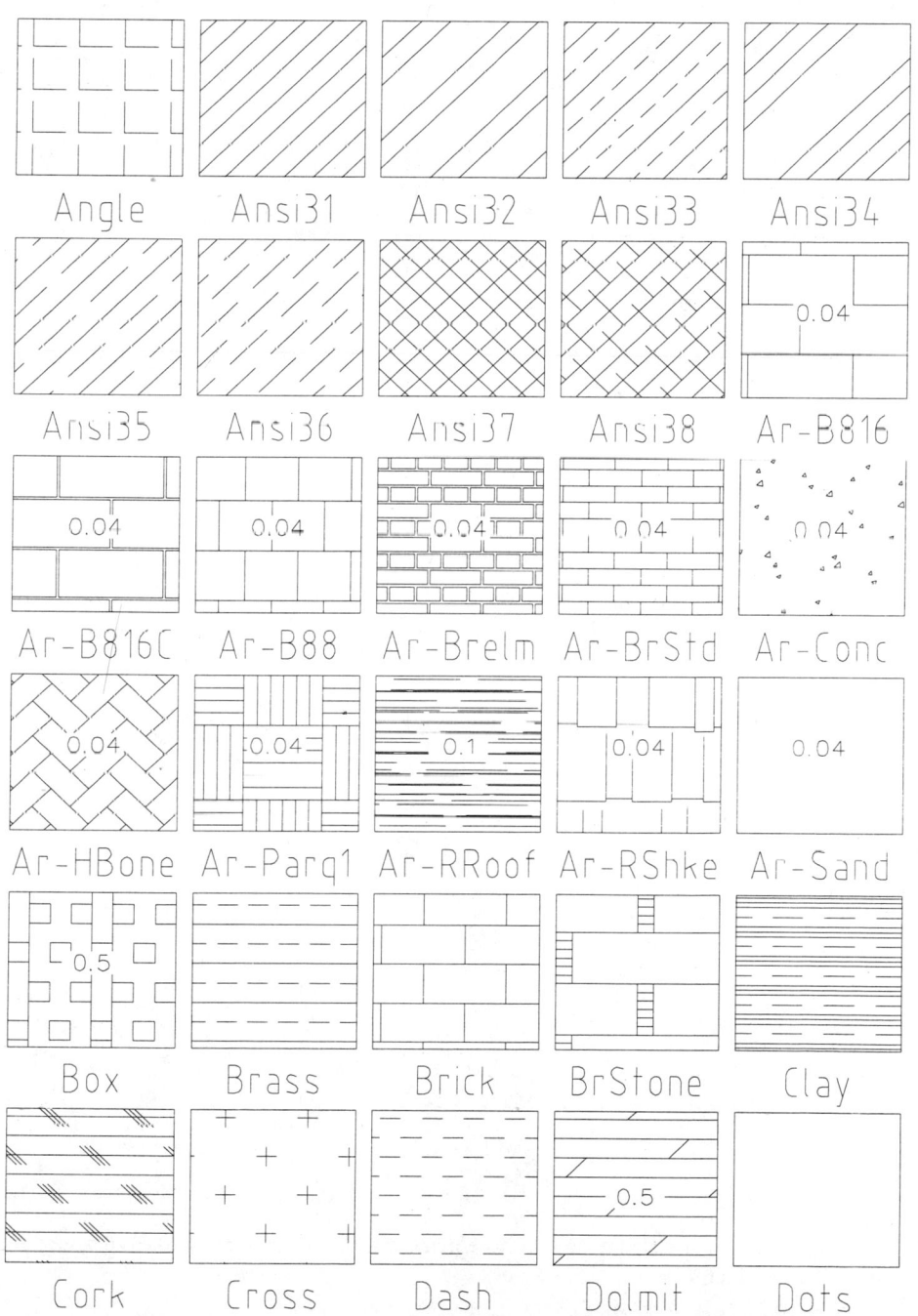

Angle Ansi31 Ansi32 Ansi33 Ansi34

Ansi35 Ansi36 Ansi37 Ansi38 Ar-B816

Ar-B816C Ar-B88 Ar-Brelm Ar-BrStd Ar-Conc

Ar-HBone Ar-Parq1 Ar-RRoof Ar-RShke Ar-Sand

Box Brass Brick BrStone Clay

Cork Cross Dash Dolmit Dots

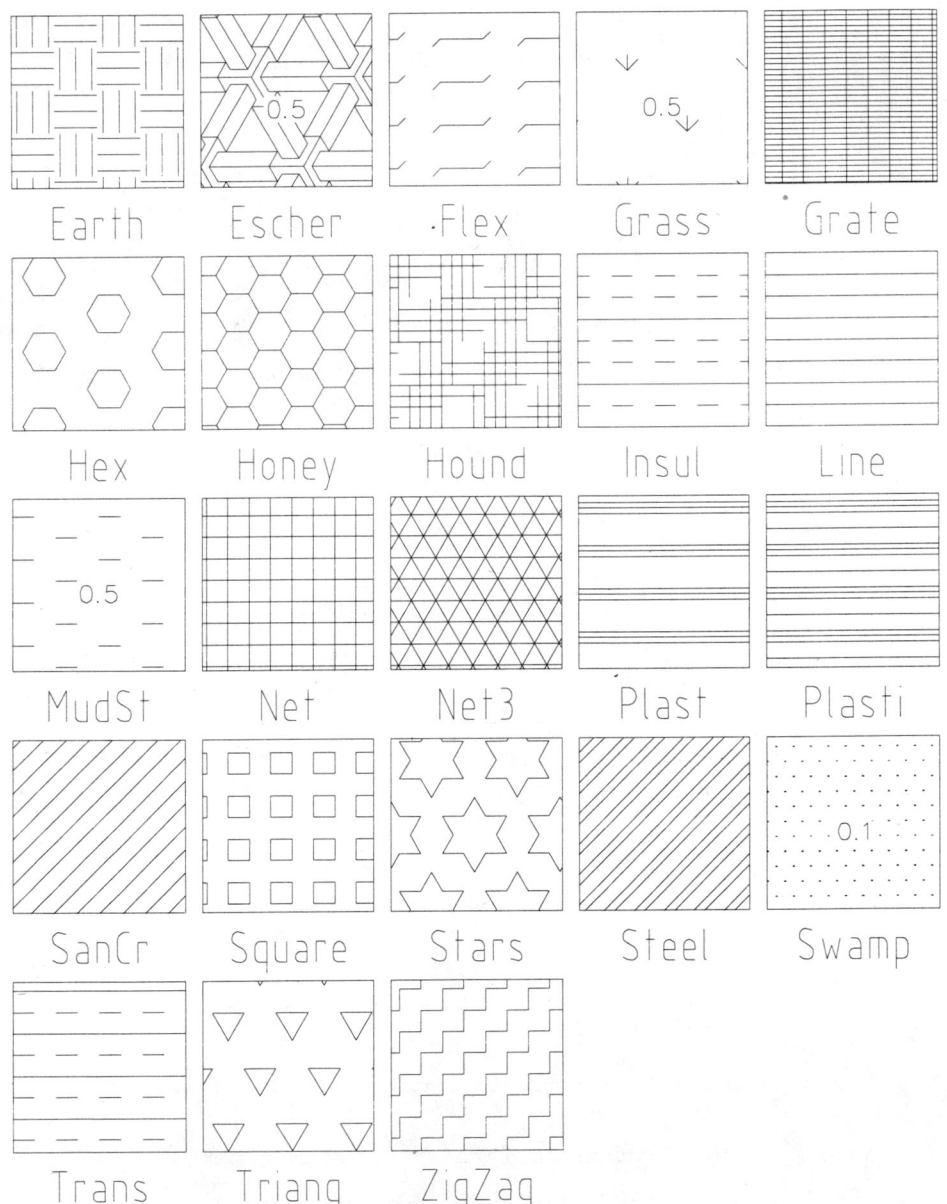

Earth　Escher　·Flex　Grass　Grate

Hex　Honey　Hound　Insul　Line

MudSt　Net　Net3　Plast　Plasti

SanCr　Square　Stars　Steel　Swamp

Trans　Triang　ZigZag

■ Patterns are drawn at scale factor 1.0; those marked with a scale number (0.01, 0.5, etc) are shown at a smaller scale.

HatchEdit

Rel.13   Edits associative hatch patterns.

Command	Alias	Ctrl+	F-key	Alt+	Menu Bar	Tablet
hatchedit	he	...	...	MOH	Modify	Y16
					⮡Object	
					⮡Hatch	

`-hatchedit`

Command: **hatchedit**
Displays dialog box:

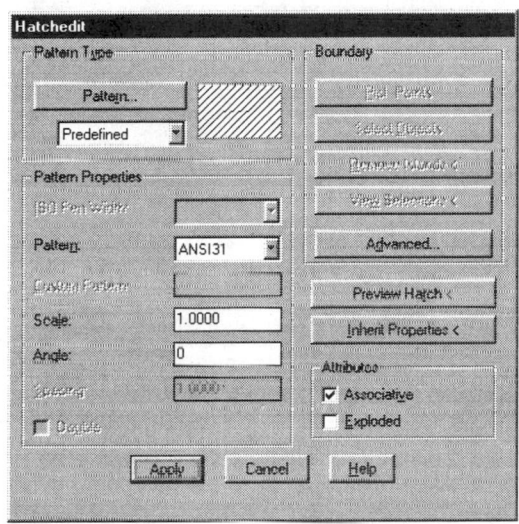

DIALOG BOX OPTIONS

Pattern Type options:

Pattern	Selects the pattern from an icon menu.
Pattern Type	Selects the source of the hatch pattern:

Source	Meaning
Predefined	Acad.Pat (*default*).
User-defined	Create hatch pattern on the fly.
Custom	Select hatch from another PAT file.

Pattern Properties options:

ISO Pen Width	Specifies plotting width for ISO hatch patterns.
Pattern	Names the hatch pattern from Acad.Pat.
Custom Pattern	Names the custom hatch pattern.
Scale	Specifies the hatch pattern scale.
Angle	Specifies the hatch pattern angle.
Spacing	Specifies the spacing between pattern lines.
Double	Double hatches; second pattern isapplied at 90 degrees.

Inherit Properties

Selects another hatch pattern to match parameters.

Exploded   Places hatch pattern as dot and lines, rather than as a hatch object.

Associative   Toggles associativity of hatch pattern.

Boundary option:

Advanced   Advanced hatch boundary options; displays dialog box:

Advanced Options dialog box:

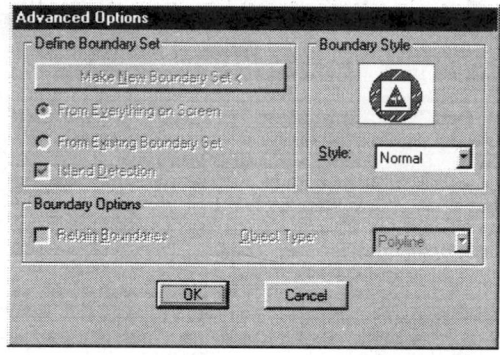

Boundary Style option:

Style   Determines how hatch crosses boundaries:

Style	Meaning
N	Hatches alternate boundaries (*Normal*).
O	Hatches only outermost boundaries (*Outermost*).
I	Hatches everything within boundary (*Ignore*).

```
Command: -hatchedit
Select hatch object: [pick]
Disassociate/Style/<Properties>: p
Enter pattern name or [?/Solid/User defined] <ANSI31>: [Enter]
Scale for pattern <1.0000>: [Enter]
Angle for pattern <0>: [Enter]
```

COMMAND LINE OPTIONS

Select   Selects a single associative hatch pattern.
Disassociate   Removes associativity from hatch pattern.

Style options:
Style   Determines how hatch crosses boundaries:

Style	Meaning
N	Hatches alternate boundaries (*Normal*).
O	Hatches only outermost boundaries (*Outermost*).
I	Hatch everything within boundary (*Ignore*).

Properties options:
Pattern name   Types name of a valid hatch pattern.
?   Lists available hatch pattern names.
Solid   Replaces hatch pattern with solid fill.
User defined   Creates new on-the-fly hatch pattern.
Scale   Changes hatch pattern scale.
Angle   Changes hatch pattern angle.

RELATED COMMANDS

BHatch   Applies associative hatch pattern.
Hatch   Applies non-associative hatch pattern.
Explode   Explodes a hatch pattern block into lines.

RELATED SYSTEM VARIABLES

HpAng   Hatch pattern angle.
HpDouble   Doubled hatch pattern.
HpName   Hatch pattern name.
HpScale   Hatch pattern scale.
HpSpace   Hatch pattern spacing.

TIPS

- **HatchEdit** only works with associative hatch objects.

- To select a solid fill, click the outer edge of the hatch pattern or use a crossing window selection overtop of the solid fill.

- Even though the **HatchEdit** dialog box looks identical to the **BHatch** dialog box, the **Pick Points, Select Objects, Remove Islands,** and **View Selection** options are not available.

'Help *or* **'?**

V. 1.0 Lists text screens of information for using AutoCAD's commands.

Command	Alias	Ctrl+	F-key	Alt+	Menu Bar	Tablet
'help	'?	...	F1	HH	Help	Y7
					⤷AutoCAD Help Topics	

Command: **help**
Displays dialog box:

RELATED COMMANDS
All.

RELATED FILES
Acad.Hlp   AutoCAD help file.
Asicfg.Hlp   AutoCAD SQL Interface help file.
History.Hlp   Changes from previous releases of AutoCAD.
Hpr14win.Hlp Help file for HP plotters.
Inet.Hlp   Internet commands help file.
Ocehelp.Hlp   Help file for Oce plotters.
Plpccw.Hlp   Help file for CalComp plotters.

TIPS
■ Since **Help**, **?**, and **[F1]** are transparent commands, you can use them during another command to get help on the command's options.

■ The text of the Windows help file is stored in the file Acad.Hlp — this file is not ASCII and cannot be edited; it can be customized with the **Edit | Annotate** command.

Hide

V. 2.1 Removes hidden lines from 3D drawings.

Command	Alias	Ctrl+	F-key	Alt+	Menu Bar	Tablet
help	hi	...	...	VH	View ⟜Hide	M2

```
Command: hide
Regenerating drawing.
Removing hidden lines: 25
```

3D object without (left) and with hidden-lines removed (right).

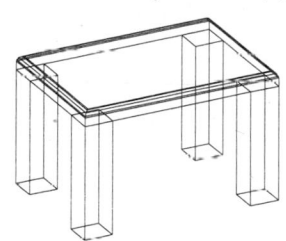   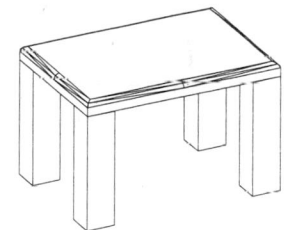

COMMAND LINE OPTIONS
None.

RELATED COMMANDS.
DView	Removes hidden lines of perspective 3D views.
MView	Removes hidden lines during plots of paper space drawings.
Plot	Removes hidden lines during plots of 3D drawings.
Regen	Returns the view to wireframe.
Render	Performs realistic renderings of 3D models.
Shade	Performs quick renderings and quick hides of 3D models.
VPoint	Select the 3D viewpoint.

TIPS
- The **Hide** command considers the following objects as opaque:

Circle.	2D solid.
Trace.	Wide 2D polyline.
3D face.	Polygon mesh.
Any object with thickness.	

- Use the **MSlide** (or **SaveImg**) to save the hidden-line view as an SLD (or TIFF, TGA, or GIF) file. View the saved image with the **VSlide** (or **Replay**) command.

- The **Shade** command simulates hidden-line removal when **ShadEdge** is set to 2.

- Freezing layers speeds up the hide process since **Hide** ignores those objects.

- **Hide** does not consider the visibility of text and attributes.

- To create a hidden-line view when plotting in paper space, select the **HidePlot** option of the **MView** command.

 **'Id**

V. 1.0   Identifies the 3D coordinates of a picked point (*short for IDentify*).

Command	Alias	Ctrl+	F-key	Alt+	Menu Bar	Tablet
'id	...	...	...	TQI	Tools ⮑Inquiry ⮑Id Pint	U9

```
Command: id
Point: [pick]
```

Example output:
```
X = 1278.0018     Y = 1541.5993     Z = 0.0000
```

COMMAND LINE OPTION
Point   Pick a point.

RELATED COMMANDS
List   Lists information about a picked object.
Point   Draws a point.

RELATED SYSTEM VARIABLE
LastPoint   The 3D coordinates of the last picked point.

TIPS
- The **Id** command stores the picked point in the **LastPoint** system variable. Access that value by entering @ at the next prompt for a point value.

- Use the **Id** command to set the value of the **LastPoint** system variable, which can be used as relative coordinates in another command.

- The z-coordinate displayed by the **Id** command is the current elevation setting; if you use the **Id** command with an object snap, then the z-coordinate is the osnap'ed value.

- The **Id** command, when used in a menu macro or AutoLISP routine, quickly labels 3D points on the drawing, such as:

```
(defun c:label (/ xyz)
  (setq xyz (getpoint "Pick point: "))
  (command "text" xyz 200 0 xyz)
)
```

 # Image

Rel.14 Controls the attachment of raster images (*an external command in Ism.Arx*).

Command	Alias	Ctrl+	F-key	Alt+	Menu Bar	Tablet
image	im	...	...	II	Insert ⮡Raster Image	T3
-image	-im					

Command: **image**
Displays dialog box:

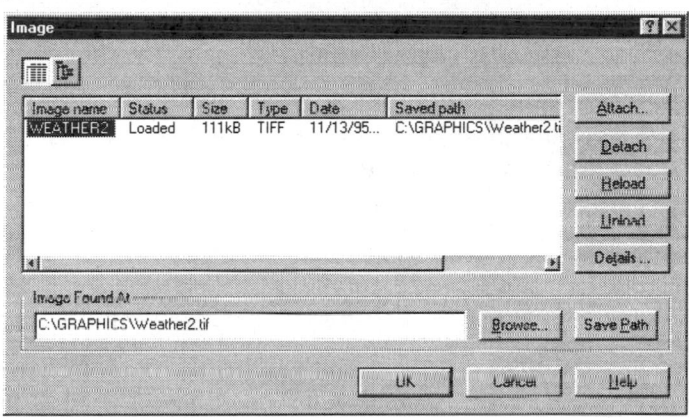

DIALOG BOX OPTIONS

Attach	Displays the **Attach Image File** dialog box; see **ImageAttach** command.
Detach	Erases the image from the drawing.
Reload	Reloads the image file into the drawing.
Unload	Removes the image from memory without erasing the image.
Save Path	Describes the drive and subdirectory location of the file.
Browse	Searches for file; displays the **Attach Image File** dialog box.
Details	Describes the technical details of the images; displays dialog box.

Image File Details dialog box:

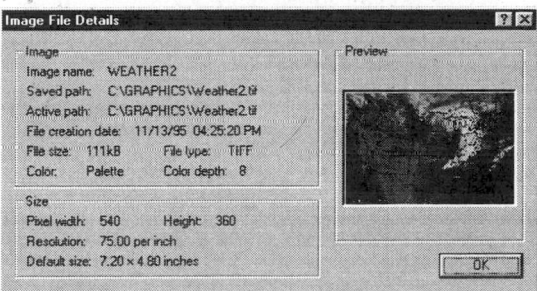

```
Command: -image
?/Detach/Path/Reload/Unload/<Attach>:
```

COMMAND LINE OPTIONS

?	Lists currently attached image files.
Detach	Erases the image from the drawing.
Path	Displays the drive and subdirectory location of the file.
Reload	Reloads the image file into the drawing.
Unload	Removes the image from memory without erasing the image.
Attach	Displays the **Attach Image File** dialog box; see **ImageAttach** command.

RELATED COMMANDS

ImageAdjust	Controls brightness, contrast, and fading of the image.
ImageAttach	Attaches an image in the current drawing.
ImageClip	Creates a clipping boundary on an image.
ImageFrame	Toggles display of the image's frame.
ImageQuality	Toggles display between draft and high-quality mode.
Transparency	Changes the transparency of the image.
Xref	Attaches a DWG drawing as an externally referenced file.

TIPS

■ The **Image** command handles raster images of these color depths:

Depth	Colors
Bitonal	Black and white.
8-bit gray	256 shades of gray.
8-bit color	256 colors.
24-bit color	16.7 million colors.

■ The **Image** command can handle the following formats:

Format	Meaning
BMP	Windows bitmap.
TIF	TIFF: tagged image file format.
RLE	Run-length encoding.
JPG	JPEG: joint photographic expert group.
GIF	Graphic interchange format.
TGA	Targa.

■ AutoCAD can display one or more images in any viewport.

■ There is no theoretical limit to the number and size of images.

ImageAdjust

Rel.14 Controls brightness, contrast, and fading of the attached raster image (*an external command in Ism.Arx*).

Command	Alias	Ctrl+	F-key	Alt+	Menu Bar	Tablet
imageadjust	iad	...	...	MOIA	Modify	X20
					⮑Object	
					⮑Image	
					⮑Adjust	

-imageadjust

Command: **imageadjust**
Select objects: **[pick]**
Select objects: **[Enter]**
Displays dialog box:

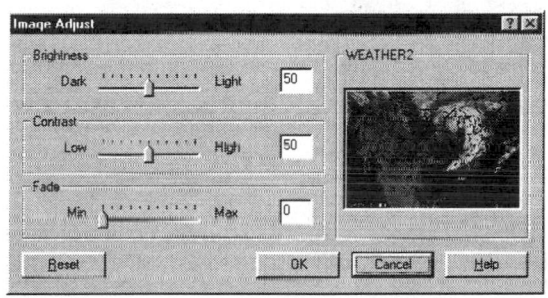

DIALOG BOX OPTIONS

Brightness options:
Dark   Darken the image — values closer to 0.
Light   Lighten the image — values closer to 100.

Contrast options:
Low   Reduce the image contrast — values closer to 0.
High   Increase the image contrast — values closer to 100.

Fade options:
Min   Less fading — values closer to 0.
Max   More fading — values closer to 100.

Command: **-imageadjust**
Select objects: **[pick]**
Select objects: **[Enter]**
Contrast/Fade/<Brightness>:

COMMAND LINE OPTIONS

Contrast   Adjusts the contrast between 0 and 100 (*default = 50*).
Fade   Adjusts the fading 0 and 100 (*default = 0*).
Brightness Adjusts the brightness between 0 and 100 (*default = 50*).

RELATED COMMANDS

Fog	Fades the image of a rendering.
Image	Controls the loading of raster image files in the drawing.
ImageAttach	Attaches an image in the current drawing.
ImageClip	Creates a clipping boundary on an image.
ImageFrame	Toggles display of the image's frame.
ImageQuality	Toggles display between draft and high-quality mode.
Transparency	Changes the transparency of the image.

TIPS

■ **Brightness** ranges from 0 (*left*) to 50 (*default*) and 100 (*right*).

■ **Contrast** ranges from 0 (*left*) to 50 (*default*) and 100 (*right*).

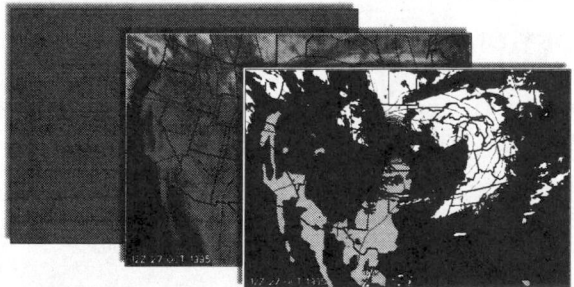

■ **Fade** ranges from 0 (*default*) to 50 (*center*) and 100 (*right*).

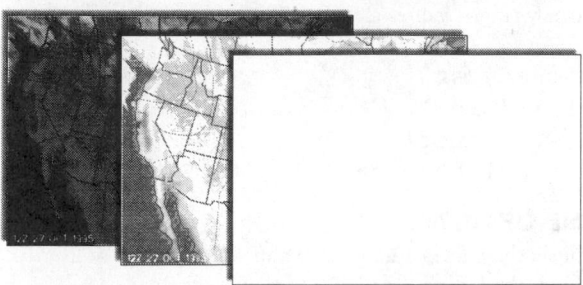

ImageAttach

Rel.14 Selects a raster file to attach to the current drawing (*an external command in Ism.Arx*).

Command	Alias	Ctrl+	F-key	Alt+	Menu Bar	Tablet
imageattach	iat	...	...	...	...	...

Command: **imageattach**
Displays dialog box:

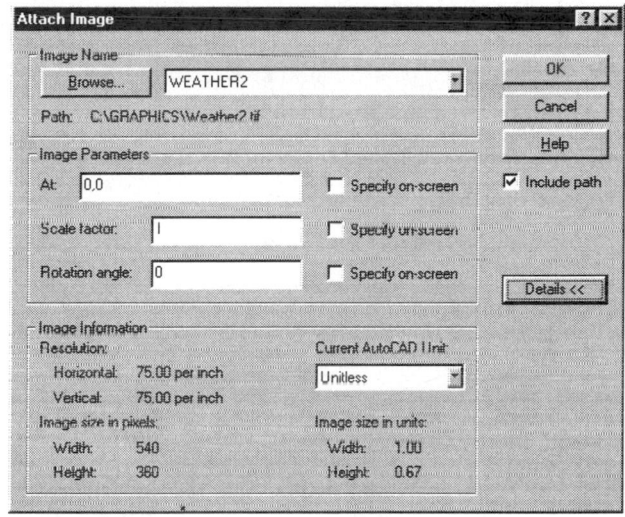

DIALOG BOX OPTIONS
Image Name options:
Image Name Selects from a list of previously attached image names.
Browse Selects file; displays dialog box.

Attach Image File dialog box:

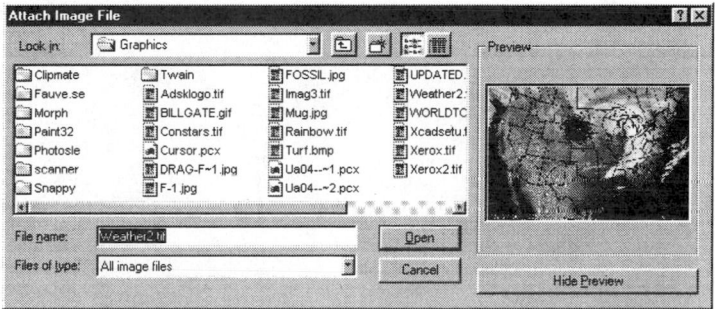

Image Parameters options:

At   X,y-coordinates of image's insertion point, which is at lower-left corner.

Scale Factor   Specifies scale factor; 1.0 = width of image is one drawing unit.

Rotation Angle Specifies angle of rotation; positive values rotate image counterclockwise.

Specify On-Screen

        Selects insertion point, scale factor, and/or rotation angle on the screen.

Details   Displays information about the image.

Current AutoCAD Unit

        Set units to unitless (*default*), millimeters, centimeters, meters, kilometers, inches, feet, yards, or miles; this option is only available when the image file contains resolution data.

ImageClip

Rel.14 Clips a raster image (*an external command in Ism.Arx*).

Command	Alias	Ctrl+	F-key	Alt+	Menu Bar	Tablet
imageclip	icl	...	...	MOG	Modify	X22
					↳Object	
					↳Image Clip	

```
Command: imageclip
Select image to clip: [pick]
ON/OFF/Delete/<New boundary>: [Enter]
Polygonal/<Rectangular>: p
First point: [pick]
Undo/<Next point>: [pick]
Undo/<Next point>: [pick]
Close/Undo/<Next point>: c
```

COMMAND LINE OPTIONS

Select image	Selects one image to clip.
ON	Turns on a previous clipping boundary.
OFF	Turns off the clipping.
Delete	Erases the clipping.

New Boundary options:

Polygonal	Creates a polygonal clipping path.
Rectangular	Creates a rectangular clipping boundary.
Undo	Undoes the last vertex.
Close	Closse the polygon clipping path.

RELATED COMMANDS

Image	Controls the loading of raster image files in the drawing.
ImageAdjust	Controls brightness, contrast, and fading of the image.
ImageAttach	Attaches an image in the current drawing.
ImageFrame	Toggles display of the image's frame.
ImageQuality	Toggles display between draft and high-quality mode.
Transparency	Changes the transparency of the image.
XrefClip	Clips a DWG drawing an attached external reference file.

TIPS

■ You can use object snap modes on the image's frame but not on the image itself.

■ To clip a hole in the image, create the hole, then double back on the same path:

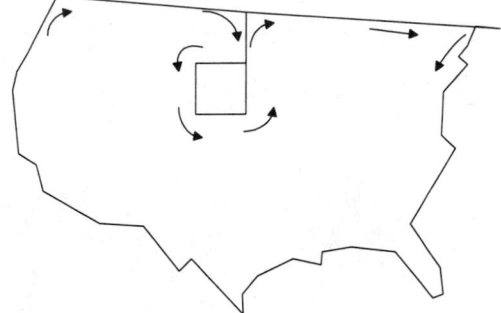

ImageFrame

Rel.14 Toggles the display of the frame around the image (*an external command in Ism.Arx*).

Command	Alias	Ctrl+	F-key	Alt+	Menu Bar	Tablet
imageframe	...	...	...	MOIF	Modify ⤷Object ⤷Image ⤷Frame	...

```
Command: imageframe
ON/OFF/<on>:
```

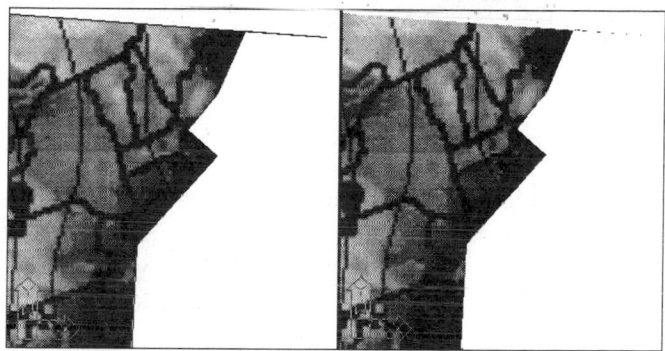

Image frame turned on (left) and turned off (right).

COMMAND LINE OPTIONS

ON	Turn on image frame (*default*).
OFF	Turn off display of image frame.

RELATED COMMANDS

Image	Controls the loading of raster image files in the drawing.
ImageAdjust	Controls brightness, contrast, and fading of the image.
ImageAttach	Attaches an image in the current drawing.
ImageClip	Creates a clipping boundary on an image.
ImageQuality	Toggles display between draft and high-quality mode.
Transparency	Changes the transparency of the image.

TIPS

- *Warning!* When **ImageFrame** is turned off, you cannot select the image.

- The frame is turned on (or off) in all viewports.

ImageQuality

<u>Rel.14</u> Toggles the quality of the image between draft and quality (*an external command in Ism.Arx*).

Command	Alias	Ctrl+	F-key	Alt+	Menu Bar	Tablet
imagequality	...	...	...	MOIQ	Image ⇖Object ⇖Image ⇖Quality	...

Command: **imagequality**
High/Draft <High>: **d**

COMMAND LINE OPTIONS

High   Displays image at its full quality.
Draft   Displays image at a lower quality.

RELATED COMMANDS

Image   Controls the loading of raster image files in the drawing.
ImageAdjust   Controls brightness, contrast, and fading of the image.
ImageAttach   Attaches an image in the current drawing.
ImageClip   Creates a clipping boundary on an image.
ImageFrame   Toggles display of the image's frame.
Transparency   Changes the transparency of the image.

TIP

■ High quality displays the image more slowly; draft displays the image more quickly.

Import

Rel.13 Imports vector and raster files into the current drawing.

Command	Alias	Ctrl+	F-key	Alt+	Menu Bar	Tablet
import	im	...	...	...	...	T2

Command: **import**
Displays dialog box:

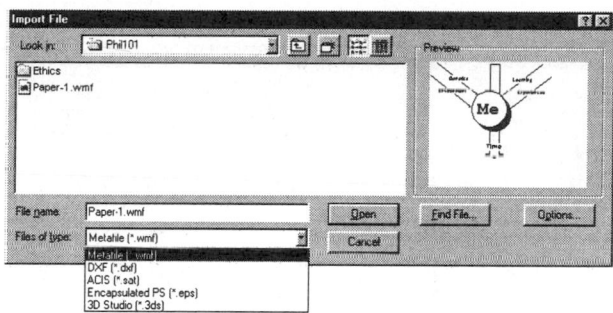

DIALOG BOX OPTIONS

Metafile	Windows metafile WMF; executes the **WmfIn** command.
DXF	Drawing interchange format; executes the **DxfIn** command.
ACIS	ASCII SAT (Save As Text); executes the **AcisIn** command.
Encapsulated PS	Encapsulated PostScript; executes the **PsIn** command.
3D Studio	3D Studio 3DS format; executes the **3dsIn** command.

RELATED COMMANDS

AppLoad	Loads AutoLISP, ADS, and ARx routines.
DxbIn	Imports DXB file.
Export	Exports drawing in several vector and raster formats.
Load	Imports SHX shape objects.
Insert	Places another DWG drawing in the current drawing.
InsertObj	Places OLE object in drawing via Clipboard.
MatLib	Imports rendering material definitions.
MenuLoad	Loads menu file into AutoCAD.
Open	Opens AutoCAD (any version) DWG file.
PasteClip	Pastes object from the Clipboard.
PasteSpec	Pastes or links object from the Clipboard.
Replay	Displays rendering in TIFF, Targa, or GIF format.
VSlide	Displays an SLD slide file.
XBind	Imports named objects from another DWG file.
XRef	Displays another DWG file in the current drawing.

TIP

- The **Import** command acts as a "shell" command; it launches other AutoCAD commands that perform the actual import function.

InetCfg

Rel.14 Configures AutoCAD for Internet access (*short for InterNET ConFiGuration; an external command in Internet.Arx*).

Command	Alias	Ctrl+	F-key	Alt+	Menu Bar	Tablet
inetcfg	...	...	...	...	...	...

Command: **inetcfg**
Displays dialog box:

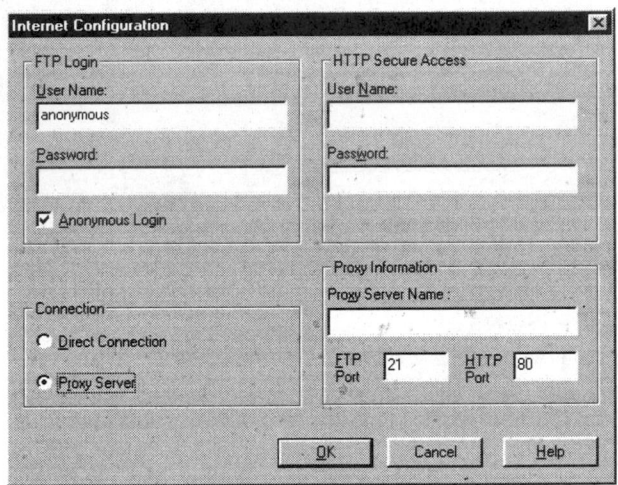

DIALOG BOX OPTIONS

FTP Login options:
User Name   Types your user name.
Password   Types the password.
Anonymous Login
            Yes: username = anonymous; password = blank (nothing).
            No: requires you to enter a username and password.

HTTP Secure Access options:
User Name   Types your user name.
Password   Types the password.

Connection options:
Direct Connection
            Select this option when your computer accesses the Internet via an Internet
            service provider (ISP).
Proxy Server   Select this option when your computer accesses another computer serving as a
            gateway (sometimes called a "firewall") between your internal network
            (sometimes called an "intranet") and the Internet.

Proxy Information options:

Proxy Server   Types the name of the proxy server.

FTP Port   Although the FTP port number is set automatically, you can type a different port number here.

HTTP Port   Although the HTTP port number is set automatically, you can type a different port number here.

RELATED COMMANDS

Browser   Launches a Web browser, which provides HTTP and FTP services.

InetHelp   Provides help on Internet-related commands.

RELATED SYSTEM VARIABLE

INetLocation   The most-recently accessed URL.

DEFINITIONS

FTP   File transfer protocol.

HTTP   Hyper text transfer protocol.

URL.   Uniform resource locator.

TIPS

- The **InctCfg** command configures AutoCAD for FTP login, HTTP access, Internet connection, and proxy information.

- When you log in to an FTP site as an anonymous user, no password is required.

- When you leave the username and password blank in the HTTP area, AutoCAD displays the **User Authentication** dialog box, allowing you to enter a username and password.

- The FTP and HTTP passwords are not remembered between AutoCAD sessions.

- The **InetCfg** command is available from the **InsertURL, OpenURL,** and **SaveURL** commands via the **Options** button.

- If you don't know proxy server settings, ask your network manager or check for proxy settings in your Web browser.

InetHelp

Rel.14 Provides help in using AutoCAD's Internet commands (*short for InterNET HELP; an external command in Internet.Arx*).

Command	Alias	Ctrl+	F-key	Alt+	Menu Bar	Tablet
inethelp	...	...	...	...	...	...

Command: **inethelp**
Displays dialog box:

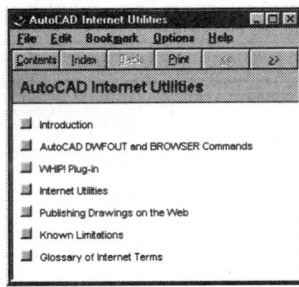

DIALOG BOX OPTIONS
None.

RELATED COMMANDS
Help	Displays general help for AutoCAD.
AttachURL	Attaches a URL to an object or rectangular area in a drawing.
Browser	Launches a Web browser.
DetachURL	Removes a URL from an object.
DwfOut	Exports drawing in DWF format via dialog box.
DwfOutD	Exports drawing in DWF format via command line.
InetCfg	Configures AutoCAD for accessing the Internet.
InsertURL	Inserts a DWG file as a block from a URL location.
ListURL	Lists URLs embedded in the current drawing.
OpenURL	Opens a DWG file from a URL location.
SaveURL	Saves the current drawing to the URL location.
SelectURL	Selects all objects with an attached URL.

DEFINITIONS
DWF	Drawing Web Format; a format for displaying vector images on the Internet.
FTP	File Transfer Protocol; a method of transferring files between computers over the Internet.
HTML	Hyper Text Markup Language; the format for displaying text and graphics on the World Wide Web.
ISP	Internet Service Provider; an independent company that provides users access to the Internet, usually by modem.
TCP/IP	Transmission Control Protocol/Internet Protocol; the standard for communicating on the Internet.
URL	Uniform Resource Locator; the universal file naming system for the Internet.
WWW	World Wide Web.

Insert

V. 1.0 Inserts a previously defined block into the drawing.

Command	Alias	Ctrl+	F-key	Alt+	Menu Bar	Tablet
insert	-i	...	...	...	...	...

```
Command: insert
Block name (or ?): [type block name]
Insertion point: [pick]
X scale factor <1> / Corner / XYZ: [Enter]
Y scale factor (default=X): [Enter]
Rotation angle <0>: [Enter]
```

COMMAND LINE OPTIONS

Block name	Indicates the name of the block to be inserted.
?	Lists the names of blocks stored in the drawing.
X scale factor	Indicates the x-scale factor.
Corner	Indicates the x- and y-scale factors by pointing on the screen.
XYZ	Displays the x-, y- and z-scale submenu.
P	Supplies predefined block name, scale, and rotation values.

INPUT OPTIONS

In response to the 'Block Name' prompt, you can enter:

Option	Meaning
~	Display a dialog box of blocks stored on disk: `Block name: ~`
*	Insert block exploded: `Block name: *filename`
=	Redefine existing block with a new block: `Block name: oldname=newname`

In response to the 'Insertion point' prompt, you can enter:

Option	Meaning
Scale	Specify x-, y-, z-scale factors.
PScale	Preset the x-, y-, and z-scale factors.
XScale	Specify x-scale factor.
PxScale	Preset x-scale factor.
YScale	Specify y-scale factor.
PyScale	Preset y-scale factor.
ZScale	Specify z-scale factor.
PzScale	Preset the z-scale factor.
Rotate	Specify the rotation angle.
PRotate	Preset the rotation angle.

RELATED COMMANDS

Block	Creates a block of a group of objects.
DdInsert	Dialog box for inserting blocks.
Explode	Reduces an inserted block to its constituent objects.
InsertUrl	Inserts a block from the Internet using a URL.
MInsert	Inserts blocks as a blocked rectangular array.
Rename	Renames blocks.
WBlock	Writes blocks to disk.
XRef	Displays drawings stored on disk in the drawing.

RELATED SYSTEM VARIABLES

ExplMode   Toggles whether non-uniformly scaled blocks can be exploded:

ExplMode	Meaning
0	Cannot explode; Release 12 compatible.
1	Can be exploded (*default*).

InsBase   Name of most-recently inserted block.

TIPS

■ You can insert any other AutoCAD drawing into the current drawing.

■ A *preset* scale factor or rotation means the dragged image is shown at that factor.

■ Drawings are normally inserted as a block; prefix the filename with an * (asterisk) to insert the drawing as separate objects.

■ Redefine all blocks (of the same name) in the current drawing by adding the = (equal) suffix after its name at the 'Block name' prompt.

■ Insert a mirrored block by supplying a negative x- or y-scale factor, such as:

```
X scale factor: -1
```

■ AutoCAD converts a negative z-scale factor into its absolute value, which makes it always positive.

■ As of Release 13, you can explode a mirrored block and a block inserted with different scale factors when system variable **ExplMode** is turned on.

InsertObj

Rel.13 Places an OLE object as a linked or embedded object (*short for INSERT OBJect; an external command in OleProt.Arx*).

Command	Alias	Ctrl+	F-key	Alt+	Menu Bar	Tablet
insertobj	io	...	...	IO	Insert ⮡OLE Object	T1

Command: **insertobj**
Displays dialog box:

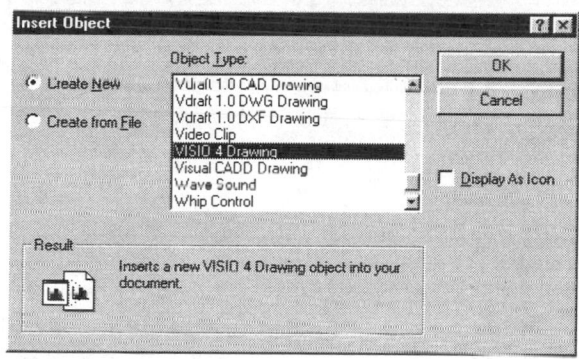

DIALOG BOX OPTIONS
Create New Creates a new OLE object in another application, then embeds the object in the current drawing.
Create from File Selects a file to embed in the current drawing.
Object Type Selects an object type from the list; the related application automatically launches.
Display As Icon Displays the object as an icon, rather than the object itself.

RELATED COMMANDS
OleLinks   Controls the OLE links.
PasteSpec   Places an object from the Clipboard in the drawing as a linked object.

RELATED WINDOWS COMMANDS
Edit | Copy   Copies an object to the Clipboard in another Windows application.
File | Update Updates an OLE object.

InsertURL

Rel.14 Inserts a DWG drawing as a block from a URL (*an external command in Internet.Arx*).

Command	Alias	Ctrl+	F-key	Alt+	Menu Bar	Tablet
inserturl	...	...	...	...	...	...

Command: **inserturl**
Displays dialog box:

DIALOG BOX OPTIONS

Options   Displays the **Internet Configuration** dialog box; see **InetCfg** command.
Insert DWG from URL
              Types a URL or select a previous URL from the drop list.
Insert   Displays the **Remote Transfer in Progress** dialog box, then inserts the
              drawing as a block in the current drawing.
Cancel   Dismiss the dialog box without inserting a drawing.

Remote Transfer in Progress dialog box:

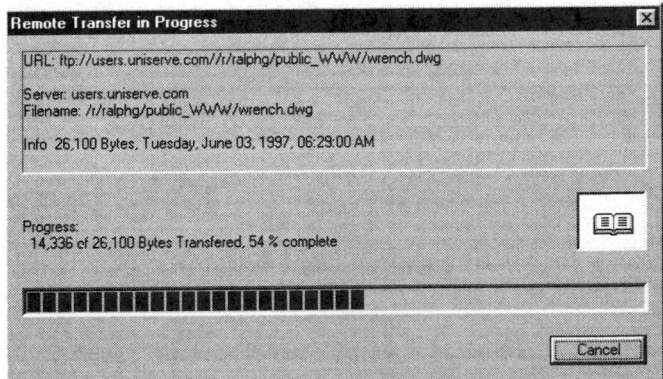

TIPS

■ URL is short for "uniform resource locator," the universal filename convention for the Internet. A typical URL looks like **http://www.autodeskpress.com**

■ AutoCAD does not check whether an Internet connection exists.

■ As an alternative to the **InsertURL** command, you can hold down the **[Ctrl]** key while dragging a DWF file from the Web browser into AutoCAD.

■ For drag'n drop to operate, the DWG file that created the DWF file must be in the same directory as the DWF file.

Interfere

Rel.11 Determines the interference of two or more 3D solid objects; creates a 3D solid body of the volumes in common (*an external command in Acis.Dll*).

Command	Alias	Ctrl+	F-key	Alt+	Menu Bar	Tablet
interfere	in	...	...	DII	Draw	...
					⌖Solids	
					⌖Interference	

```
Command: interfere
Select the first set of solids:
Select objects: [pick]
Select objects: [Enter]
Select the second set of solids:
Select objects: [pick]
Select objects: [Enter]
Comparing 1 solid against 1 solid.
Interfering solids (first  set): 1
                (second set): 1
Interfering pairs            : 1
Create interference solids ? <N>: y
```

A pair of interfering solids (left) and the interference (right).

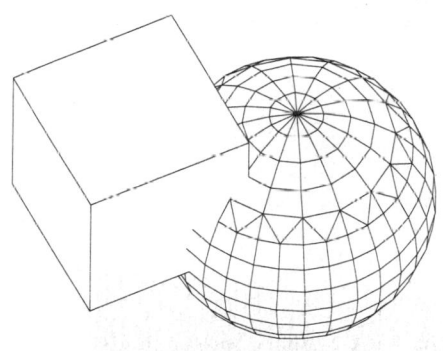

COMMAND LINE OPTIONS

Select objects   Checks all solids in a single selection set for interference against each other.
Create interference solids
          Creates a solid representing the volume of interference.

RELATED COMMANDS

- **Intersect**   Creates a new volume from the intersection of two volumes.
- **Section**   Creates a 2D region from a 3D solid.
- **Slice**   Slices a 3D solid with a plane.

Intersect

Rel.11 Creates a 3D solid of 2D region via Boolean intersection of two or more solids or regions (*an external command in Acis.Dll*).

Command	Alias	Ctrl+	F-key	Alt+	Menu Bar	Tablet
intersect	int	...	...	MBI	Modify	X17
					⌐Boolean	
					⌐Intersection	

```
Command: intersect
Select objects: [pick]
Select objects: [pick]
Select objects: [Enter]
```

Two intersecting solids (left) and the resulting intersection (right).

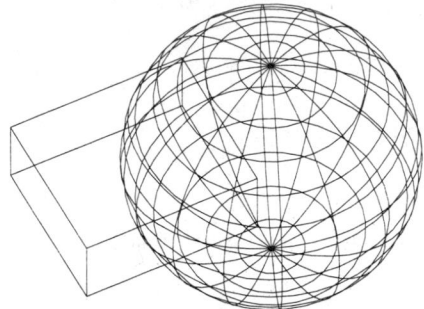 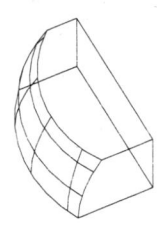

COMMAND LINE OPTION

Select objects   Selects two or more objects to intersect.

RELATED COMMANDS

Interfere   Creates a new volume from the interference of two or more volumes.
Subtract   Subtracts one 3D solid from another.
Union   Joins 3D solids into a single body.

TIPS

- You can use the **Intersect** command on 2D regions and 3D solids.

- The **Interference** and **Intersect** command may seem similar. Here is the difference between the two:

  Intersect *erases* all of the 3D solid parts that do not intersect.
  Interfere *creates a new object* that results from the intersection; it does not erase the original objects.

'Isoplane

V. 2.0 Switches the crosshairs and grid pattern among the three isometric drawing planes.

Command	Alias	Ctrl+	F-key	Alt+	Menu Bar	Tablet
'isoplane	...	E	F5	...	...	...

```
Command: isoplane
Left/Top/Right/<Toggle>: [Enter]
Current Isometric plane is: Left
```

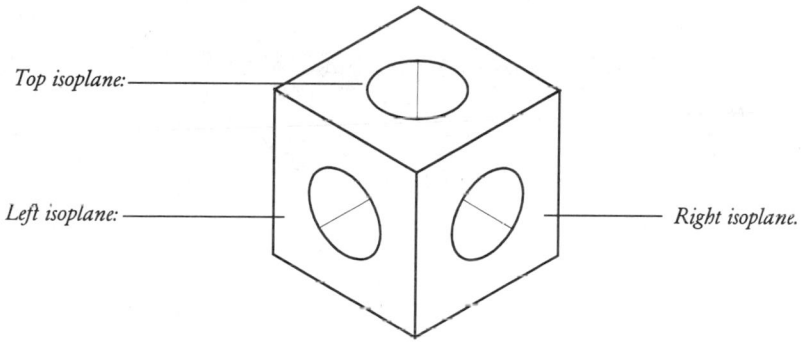

Top isoplane: ———

Left isoplane: ———   ——— Right isoplane.

COMMAND LINE OPTIONS

Left   Switches to the left isometric plane.
Top   Switchs to the top isometric plane.
Right   Switches to the right isometric plane.
Toggle   Switches to the next isometric plane in the order of: left, top, right.

RELATED COMMANDS

DdRModes   Dialog box for setting isometric mode and planes.
Ellipse   Draws isocircles.
Snap   Turns on isometric drawing mode.

RELATED SYSTEM VARIABLE

SnapIsoPair   Contains the current isometric plane.
GridMode   Current grid visibility:

GridMode	Meaning
0	Grid is off (*default*).
1	Grid is on.

GridUnit   Current grid x,y-spacing.
LimMin   X,y-coordinates of the lower-left corner of the grid display.
LimMax   X,y-coordinates of the upper-right corner of the grid display.
SnapStyl   Displays a normal or isometric grid:

SnapStyl	Meaning
0	Normal (*default*)
1	Isometric grid.

'Layer

V. 1.0 Controls the creation and visibility of layers.

Command	Alias	Ctrl+	F-key	Alt+	Menu Bar	Tablet
'layer	la	...	...	OL	Format ⌖Layer	U5

ddlmodes

-layer	-la

Command: **layer** *or* **ddlmodes**
Displays tabbed dialog box:

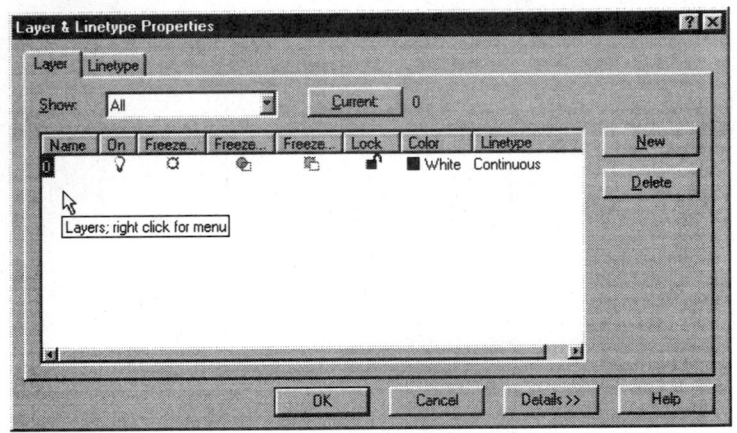

DIALOG BOX OPTIONS

Show   Displays the following groups of layers:

Show	Meaning
All	Displays all layers defined in the current drawing.
All in use	Displays all layers with at least one object.
All unused	Display any layer with no content.
All xref dependent	Displays layers in externally referenced drawings.
All not xref dependent	Displays all non-xref layers.
All that pass filter	Displays layers that match filter specs.
Set Filter dialog	Displays **Set Layer Filter** dialog box.

Current   Sets the selected layer as the current layer.

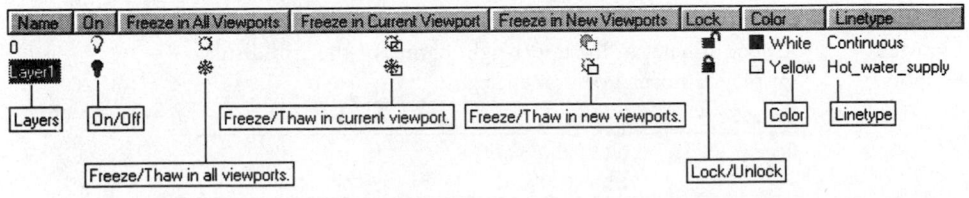

New	Creates a new layer.
Delete	Purges the selected layer(s).
Details	Displays the **Details** portion of the **Layer & Linetype Properties** dialog box:

Set Layer Filters dialog box:

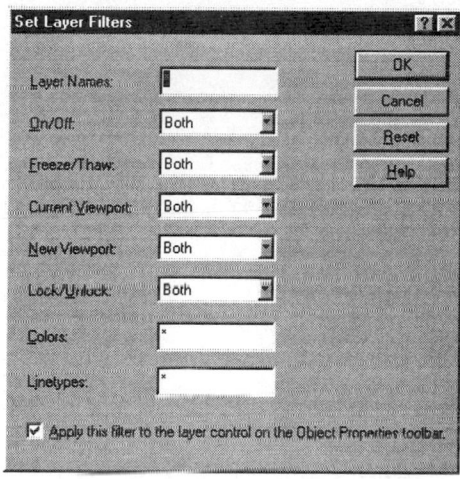

Layer Names	Specifies names of layers to filter.
On/Off	Selects layers that are on, off, or both.
Freeze/Thaw	Selects layers that are frozen, thawed, or both.
Current Viewport	
	Selects layers that are frozen, thawed, or both in the current viewport.
New Viewport	Selects layers that are frozen, thawed, or both in the new viewport.
Lock/Unlock	Selects layers that are locked, unlocked, or both.
Colors	Selects layers of a specific color.
Linetypes	Selects layers with a specific linetype.
Apply	Displays layers that match the filter spec.
Reset	Resets filters to default values.

Details dialog box:

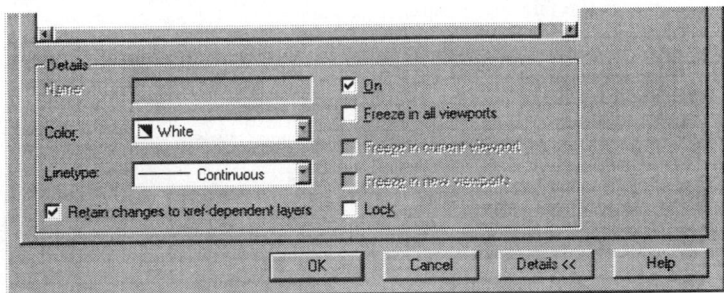

Details options:

Name	Names the seelcted layer.
Color	Selects the color.
Linetype	Selects the linetype.
Retain changes	Forces xref'ed layers to retain the changes made to them.
On	Turns on layer.
Freeze in all viewports	
	Freezes layer.
Freeze in current viewport	
	Freezse layer when **TileMode** = 0, off.
Freeze in new viewport	
	Freeze this layer when a new viewport is created and when **TileMode** = 0.
Lock	Locks this layer; is seen but cannot be edited.

```
Command: -layer
?/Make/Set/New/ON/OFF/Color/Ltype/Freeze/Thaw/LOck/Unlock:
```

COMMAND LINE OPTIONS

Color	Indicates the color for all objects drawn on the layer.
Freeze	Disables the display of the layer.
LOck	Locks the layer.
Ltype	Indicates the linetype for all objects drawn on the layer.
Make	Creates a new layer and make it the working layer.
New	Creates a new layer.
OFF	Turns off the layer.
ON	Turns on the layer.
Set	Makes the layer the working layer.
Thaw	Un-freezes the layer.
Unlock	Unlocks the layer.
?	Lists the names of layers created in the drawing.

OBJECT PROPERTIES TOOLBAR

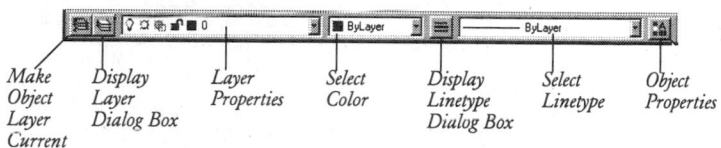

Make Object Layer Current | Display Layer Dialog Box | Layer Properties | Select Color | Display Linetype Dialog Box | Select Linetype | Object Properties

RELATED COMMANDS

Change	Moves objects to a different layer.
ChProp	Moves objects to a different layer.
Purge	Removes unused layers from the drawing.
Rename	Renames layer names.
VpLayer	Controls the visibility of layers in paper space viewports.

RELATED SYSTEM VARIABLE

CLayer	Contains the name of the current layer.

TIPS

- The **DdLModes** command will be removed in Release 15.

- Layer **DimPts** is a non-plotting layer.

- To sort layers alphabetically by name, color, linetype, or status (such On, Lock, Freeze, etc.), click on the title bar. Click a second time to sort in reverse order:

Layers sorted in alphabetical order:

Layers sorted in reverse alphabetical order:

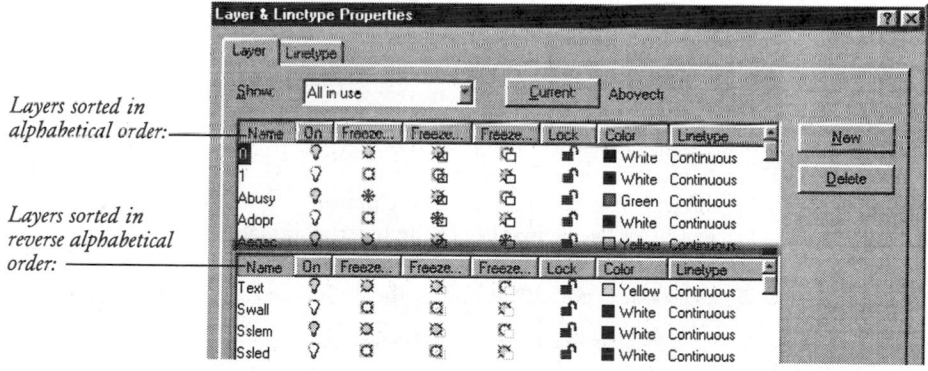

 # Leader

Rel.13 Draws a leader line with one or more lines of text.

Command	Alias	Ctrl+	F-key	Alt+	Menu Bar	Tablet
leader	le	...	...	NE	Dimension ↳Leader	R7
	lead					

```
Command: leader
From point: [pick]
To point: [pick]
To point (Format/Annotation/Undo) <Annotation>: F
Spline/STraight/Arrow/None/<eXit>: [Enter]
Tolerance/Copy/Block/None/<MText>: [Enter]
```

COMMAND LINE OPTIONS

From point	Specifies the location of arrowhead.
To point	Positions the leader's vertex.

Format options:

Spline	Draws leader line as a NURBS ("non uniform rational Bezier spline") curve.
STraight	Draws straight leader line (*default*).
Arrow	Draws leader with arrowhead (*default*).
None	Draws leader with no arrowhead.

Annotation options:

Tolerance	Places one or more tolerance symbols.
Copy	Copies text from another part of the drawing.
Block	Places a block in the manner of the **Insert** command.
None	No annotation.
MText	Places an mtext note at the end of the leader line.
Undo	Undo the leader line to the previous vertex.

RELATED DIM VARIABLES

DimAsz	Arrowhead and hookline size.
DimBlk	Type of arrowhead.
DimClrd	Color of leader line and arrowhead.
DimGap	Gap between hookline and annotation; gap between box and text.
DimScale	Overall scale of leader.

TIPS

- The text in a leader is an mtext (multiline text) object.
- Use the \P metacharacter to create line breaks in leader text.

Lengthen

Rel.13 Lengthens and shortens open objects by four methods.

Command	Alias	Ctrl+	F-key	Alt+	Menu Bar	Tablet
lengthen	len	...	...	MG	Modify ⮡Lengthen	W14

```
Command: lengthen
DElta/Percent/Total/DYnamic/<Select object>: [pick]
Current length: <>, included angle: <>
```
DElta option:
```
Angle/<Enter delta length>: A
Enter delta angle:
<Select angle to change>/Undo:
```
Percent option:
```
Enter percent length:
<Select angle to change>/Undo:
```
Total option:
```
Angle/<Enter total length>: A
Enter delta angle:
<Select angle to change>/Undo:
```
DYnamic option:
```
<Select angle to change>/Undo:
```

COMMAND LINE OPTIONS

Select object	Displays length and included angle; does not change object.
DElta	Changes length by incremental length.
Percent	Changes length by a percentage of the original length.
Total	Changes by absolute value.
DYnamic	Dynamically changes length by dragging.
Angle	Sets the angle of the selected arc.
Undo	Undo the most-recent lengthening operation.

RELATED COMMANDS

Extend	Lengths an open object to a cutting edge.
Trim	Trims open and closed objects back to a cutting edge.

TIPS

- Unlike the **Extend** and **Trim** commands, the **Lengthen** command does not require an object to work as a cutting edge.

- **Lengthen** command only works with open objects, such as lines, arcs, and polylines; it does not work with closed objects, such as circles, polygons, and regions.

- **DElta** option changes the length or angle using the following measurements: (1) distance from endpoint of the selected object to the pick point; or (2) for arc angles, changed by the incremental length measured from the endpoint of the arc.

- **Percent** option works relative to 100%: less than 100% shortens the object; for example, 50% shortens object by half; 100%: length does not change; more than 100% lengthens.

Light

Rel.12 Places four types of lights for use by the **Render** command (*an external command in Render.Arx*).

Command	Alias	Ctrl+	F-key	Alt+	Menu Bar	Tablet
`light`	...	...	...	VEL	View ↳Render ↳Light	O1

`Command: `**`light`**

Displays dialog box:

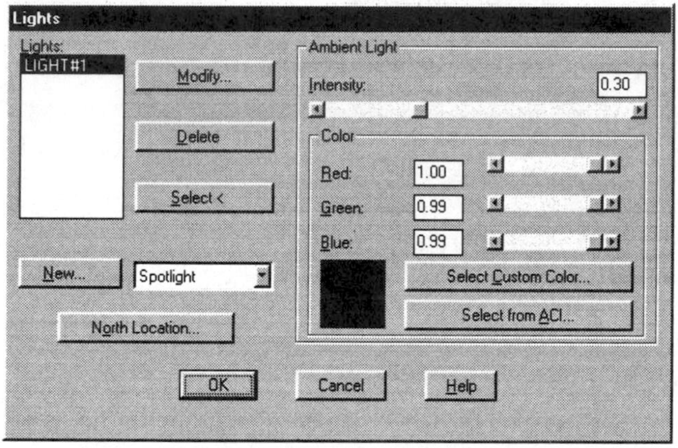

DIALOG BOX OPTIONS

Lights Lists currently defined lights in the drawing.

Modify Modifyies an existing light in the drawing; displays **Modify Light** dialog box.

Delete Deletes the selected light.

Select Selects a light from the drawing.

New Creates a new point, spot, or direct light; displays **New Light** dialog box.

North Location Selects the direction for North; displays **North Location** dialog box.

Ambient Light *option:*

Ambient Light Intensity
Adjusts intensity of ambient light from 0 (*dark*) to 1.0 (*bright*).

Color *options:*

Red Adjust the level of red from 0 (*black*) to 1.0 (*full red*).

Green Adjust the level of green from 0 (*black*) to 1.0 (*full green*).

Blue Adjust the level of blue from 0 (*black*) to 1.0 (*full blue*).

Select Custom Color
Displays Windows' **Color** dialog box.

Select from ACI
Displays AutoCAD's **Select Color** dialog box.

North Location dialog box:

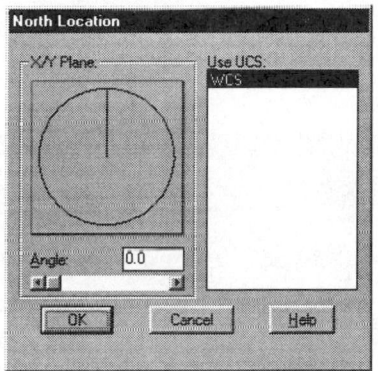

XY Plane options:

Angle   Selects angle from icon, type a number, or drag the slider bar.
Use UCS   Selects a named UCS (user-defined coordinate system).

New Point Light dialog box:

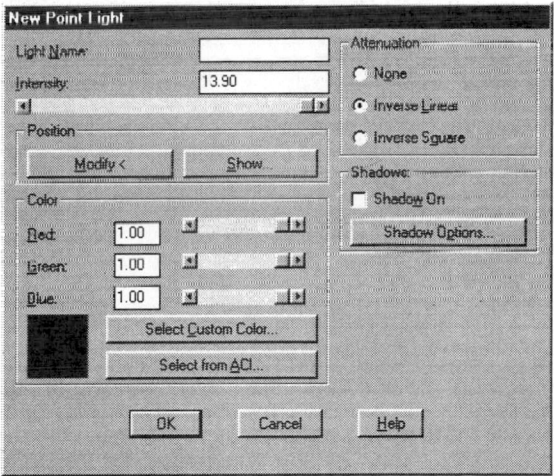

Light Name   Names the light; maximum = 8 characters, no spaces.
Intensity   Intensity of the light, from 0 (*turned off*) to 10.0.

Attenuation options:
None   Light does not diminish in intensity with distance.
Inverse Linear   Light intensity decreases with distance.
Inverse Square   Light intensity decreases with the square of the distance.

Position options:
Modify   Changes the location of the light.
Show   Displays **Show** dialog box.

Shadows options:

Shadows On   Turns on shadow casting.

Shadow Options Displays dialog box.

Shadow Options dialog box:

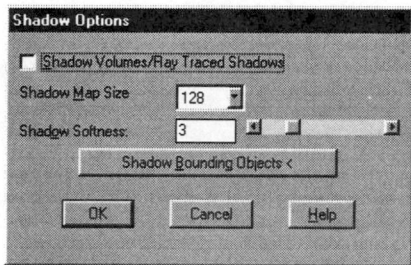

Shadow Volumes/Raytrace Shadows

Creates volumetric shadows; raytracer creates ray-traced shadows; disables shadow map.

Shadow Map Size

Specifies the size of one side of the shadow map; ranges from 64 to 4096 pixels; larger values give more accurate the shadows.

Shadow Softness

Specifies the number of pixels at shadow's edge blended with underlying image; ranges from 1 to 10.

Shadow Bounding Objects

Selects objects to clip the shadow maps.

Color   Selects a color for the light.

Show Light Position dialog box:

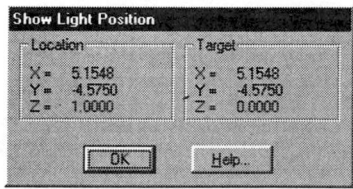

New Distant Light dialog box:

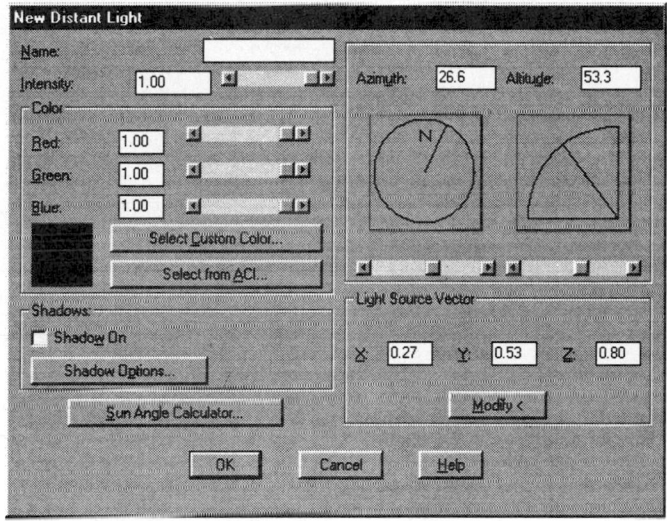

Name	Names the light; maximum = 8 characters.
Intensity	Specifies the intensity of the light; set to 0 to turn off.
Color	Specifies the color of the light.
Shadows	Creates shadows.
Azimuth	Sets light's potion between -180 and 180 degrees.
Altitude	Sets an angle for the light between 0 and 90 degrees.

Light Source Vector options:

X	Specifies the vector x-coordinate ranges from 0.0 to 1.0.
Y	Specifies the vector y-coordinate ranges from 0.0 to 1.0.
Z	Specifies the vector z-coordinate ranges from 0.0 to 1.0.
Modify	Changes the position of the light.

Sun Angle Calculator
Displays dialog box.

Sun Angle Calculator dialog box:

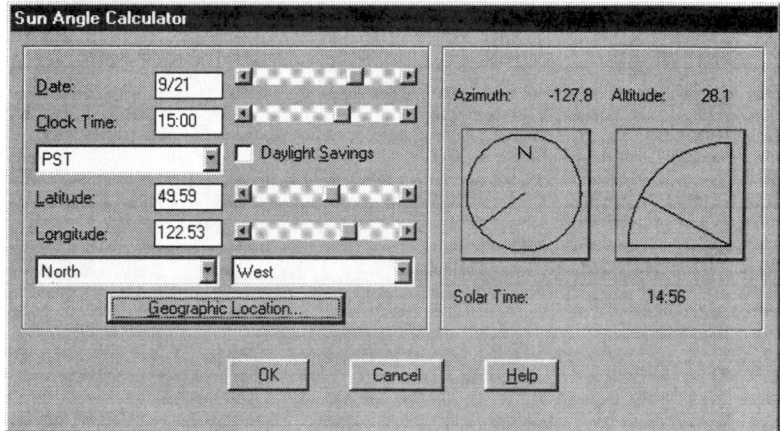

Date	Displays today's date or any date of the year.
Clock Time	Displays the current time or any time of day.
Latitude	Displays the latitude position on earth.
Longitude	Displays the longitude position.
Geographic Locator	
	Displays dialog box.

Geographic Locator dialog box:

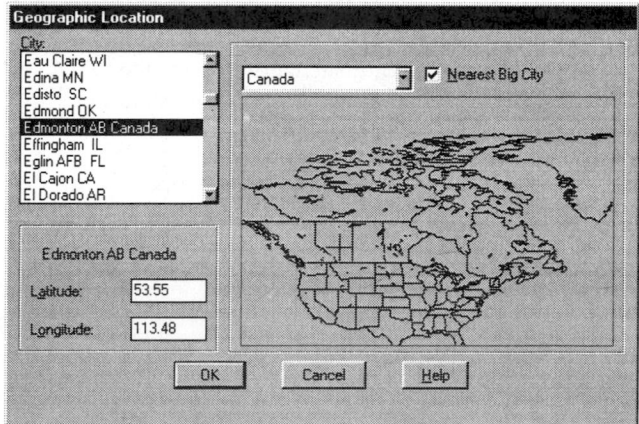

City	Selects the name of a city.
Latitude	Displays the latitude position on earth of the city.
Longitude	Displays the longitude position.
Nearest Big City	Selects a city from its list closest to your pick point.

New Spotlight dialog box:

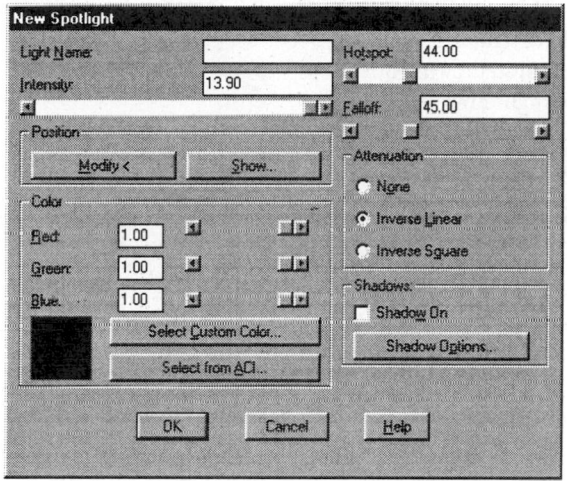

Light Name	Names the light; maximum = 8 characters, no spaces.
Intensity	Specifies the intensity of the light, from 0 (*turned off*) to 10.0.

Attenuation options:

None	Light does not diminish in intensity with distance.
Inverse Linear	Light intensity decreases with distance.
Inverse Square	Light intensity decreases with the square of the distance.

Position options:

Modify	Changes the location of the light.
Show	Displays **Show Light Position** dialog box.

Shadows options:

Shadows On	Turn on shadow casting.
Shadow Options	Displays **Shadows Options** dialog box
Color	Selects the color of the light.

RELATED COMMANDS

Render	Renders the drawing.
Scene	Specifies lights and view to use in rendering.

RELATED SYSTEM VARIABLE

Target	Coordinates of light's target point.

RELATED FILES
In \Acad14\Support subdirectory:
Direct.Dwg   Direct light block
Overhead.Dwg Overhead drawing block.
Sh_Spot.Dwg Spotlight drawing block.

Direct (left), Overhead (center), and Spotlight (right).

TIPS

- When you use the **Render** command with no lights defined, AutoCAD assumes a single light source located at your eye.

- While it is not necessary to define any lights to use the **Render** command, a light must be included in a **Scene** definition for the **Render** command to make use of the light.

- The light beam travels from the *light location* (light block placement) to the *light target*.

- Ambient light ensures every object in the scene has illumination; ambient light is an omnipresent light source.

- Set ambient light to 0 to turn off for night scenes.

- Place one distant light to simulate the Sun; distant lights have parallel light beams with constant intensity.

- Place several point lights as light bulbs (lamps); a point light beams light in all directions, with inverse linear, inverse square, or constant intensity.

- Spot lights beam light in a cone.

- Intensity of 0 turns light off.

DEFINITIONS

Constant light	Attenuation is 0; default intensity is 1.0.
Inverse linear light	Light strength decreases to ½-strength two units of distance away, and ¼-strength four units away; default intensity is ½ extents distance.
Inverse square light	Light strength decreases to ¼-strength two units away, and 1/8-strength four units away; default intensity is ½ the square of the extents distance.
Extents distance	Distance from minimum lower-left coordinate to the maximum upper-right coordinate.
RGB color	The three primary colors — red, green, blue — shaded from black to white.
HLS color:	Changes each color by hue (color), lightness (more white or more black), and saturation (less grey).
Hotspot	The brightest cone of light; beam angle ranges from 0 to 160 degrees (default: 45 degrees).
Falloff	The angle of the full light cone; field angle ranges from 0 to 160 degrees (default: 45 degrees).

'Limits

V. 1.0 Defines the 2D limits in the WCS for the grid markings and the **Zoom All** command; optionally prevents drawing outside of limits.

Command	Alias	Ctrl+	F-key	Alt+	Menu Bar	Tablet
'limits	...	...	...	OA	Format ⮡Drawing Limits	V2

```
Command: limits
Reset Model space limits:
ON/OFF/<Lower left corner> <0.0000,0.0000>: [pick]
Upper right corner <12.0000,9.0000>: [pick]
```

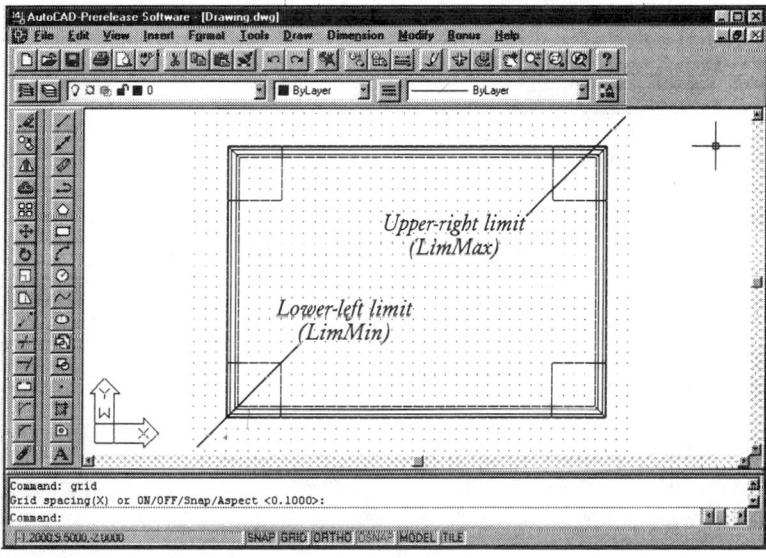

COMMAND LINE OPTIONS
OFF	Turns off limits checking.
ON	Turns on limits checking.
[Enter]	Retains limits values.

RELATED COMMANDS
Grid	Grid dots are bounded by limits.
Status	Lists the current drawing limits.
Zoom	**Zoom All** displays the drawing's extents or limits.

RELATED SYSTEM VARIABLES

LimCheck   Toggle for limit's drawing check:

LimCheck	Meaning
0	Off (*default*).
1	On.

LimMin	Lower-right 2D coordinates of current limits.
LimMax	Upper-left 2D coordinates of current limits.

Line

V. 1.0 Draws straight 2D and 3D lines.

Command	Alias	Ctrl+	F-key	Alt+	Menu Bar	Tablet
line	1	...	...	DL	Draw ↳Line	J10

```
Command: line
From point: [pick]
To point: [pick]
To point: [Enter]
```

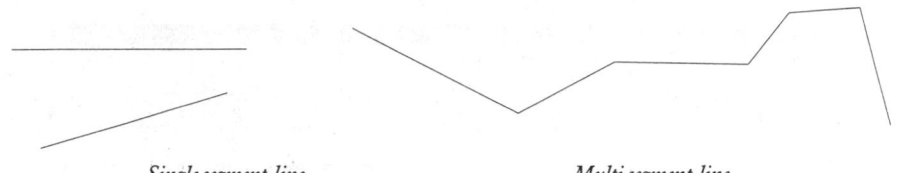

Single-segment line   *Multi-segment line*

COMMAND LINE OPTIONS

C	Closes the line from the current point to the starting point.
U	Undoes the last line drawn.
[Enter]	At the 'From point' prompt, continues the line from the last endpoint; at the 'To point' prompt, terminates the **Line** command.

RELATED COMMANDS

MLine	Draws up to 16 parallel lines.
PLine	Draws polylines and polyline arcs.
Trace	Draws lines with width.
Ray	Creates a semi-infinite construction line.
XLine	Creates an infinite construction line.

RELATED SYSTEM VARIABLES

Elevation	Distance above (or below) the x,y-plane a line is drawn.
Lastpoint	Last-entered coordinate triple.
Thickness	Determines thickness of the line.

TIPS

- To draw a 2D line, enter x,y-coordinate pairs; the z-coordinate takes on the value of the **Elevation** system variable.

- To draw a 3D line, enter x,y,z-coordinate triples.

- When system variable **Thickness** is not zero, the line has thickness, which makes it a plane.

'Linetype

V. 2.0 Loads linetype definitions into the drawing, creates new linetypes, and sets the working linetype.

Command	Alias	Ctrl+	F-key	Alt+	Menu Bar	Tablet
'linetype	lt	...	...	..	...	U3
ddltype						
-linetype	-lt					

Command: **linetype** *or* **ddltype**
Displays tabbed dialog box:

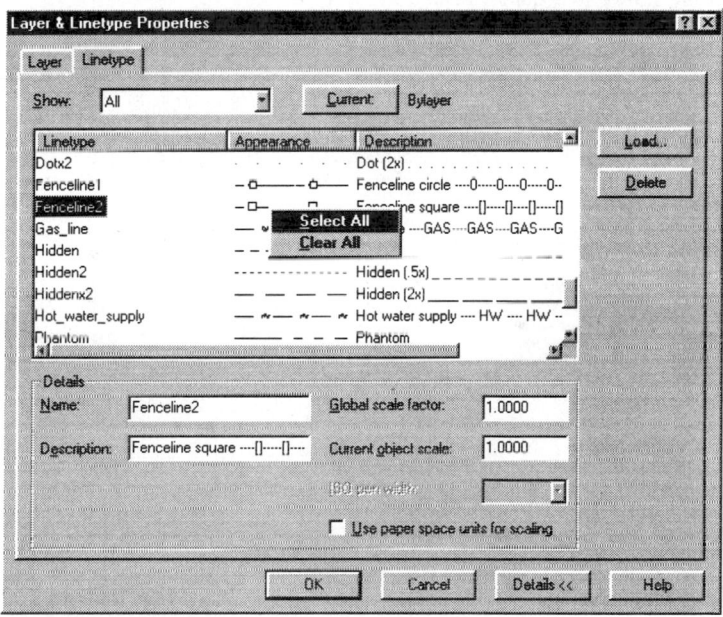

DIALOG BOX OPTIONS

Show   Display the following linetypes:

Show	Meaning
All	Displays all loaded linetypes.
All in use	Displays all linetypes used by at least one object in the current drawing.
All unused	Diaplays unused linetypes.
All xef dependent	Displays linetypes in xref drawings.
All not xref dependent	Displays all non-xref linetypes.

Current   Makes linetype current.
Load   Loads linetype definitions into drawing; displays dialog box.
Delete   Purges one or more linetypes from the drawing.

Details options:
Global Scale Factor
>Specifies the scale factor for all linetypes in the drawing.

Current Object Scale
>Specifies the scale factor for all subsequently-drawn linetypes.

ISO pen width Standard scale factors for ISO-only linetypes.

Use Paper Space Units for Scaling
>Paper space linetype scale is used, even in model space.

Load or Reload Linetypes dialog box:

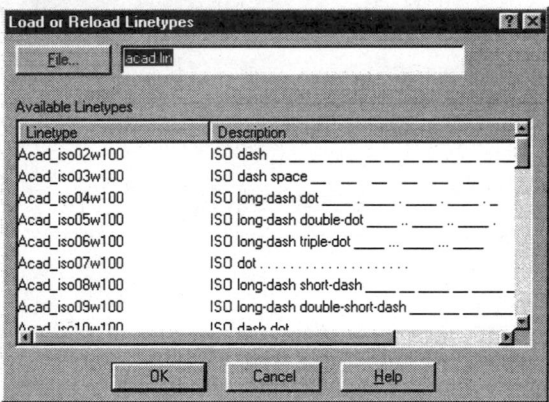

File   Names the LIN linetype definition file.

```
Command: -linetype
?/Create/Load/Set:
```

COMMAND LINE OPTIONS

Create	Create a new user-defined linetype; see Quick Start Tutorial.
Load	Load a linetype from an LIN linetype definition file.
Set	Set the working linetype.
?	List the linetypes loaded into the drawing.

RELATED COMMANDS

Change	Changes objects to a new linetype; changes linetype scale.
ChProp	Changes objects to a new linetype.
LtScale	Sets the scale of the linetype.
Rename	Changes the name of the linetype.

OBJECT PROPERTIES TOOLBAR

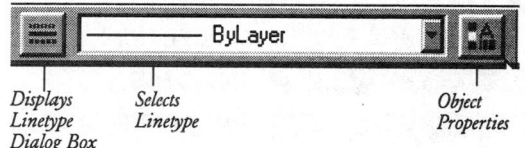

Displays   *Selects*   *Object*
Linetype   *Linetype*   *Properties*
Dialog Box

RELATED SYSTEM VARIABLES

CeLtype	The current linetype setting.
LtScale	The current linetype scale.
PsLtScale	Linetype scale relative to paper scale.
PlineGen	Controls how linetypes are generated for polylines.

TIPS

- The only linetype initially defined in an AutoCAD drawing is the CONTINUOUS linetype.

- Linetypes must be loaded from LIN definition files before being used in a drawing.

- When loading one or more linetypes, it's faster to load all linetypes, then use the **Purge** command to remove linetype definitions the drawing hasn't used.

- As of Release 13, objects can have independent linetype scales.

RELATED FILES

- The following ISO-standard linetypes are in \Acad14\Support\AcadIso.Lin:

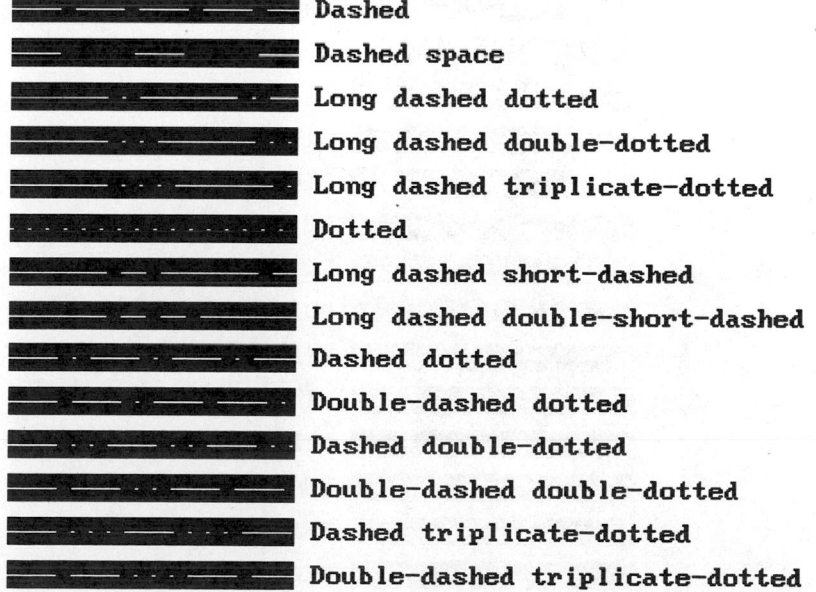

	Dashed
	Dashed space
	Long dashed dotted
	Long dashed double-dotted
	Long dashed triplicate-dotted
	Dotted
	Long dashed short-dashed
	Long dashed double-short-dashed
	Dashed dotted
	Double-dashed dotted
	Dashed double-dotted
	Double-dashed double-dotted
	Dashed triplicate-dotted
	Double-dashed triplicate-dotted

■ Linetypes stored in \Acad14\Suppport\Acad.Lin:

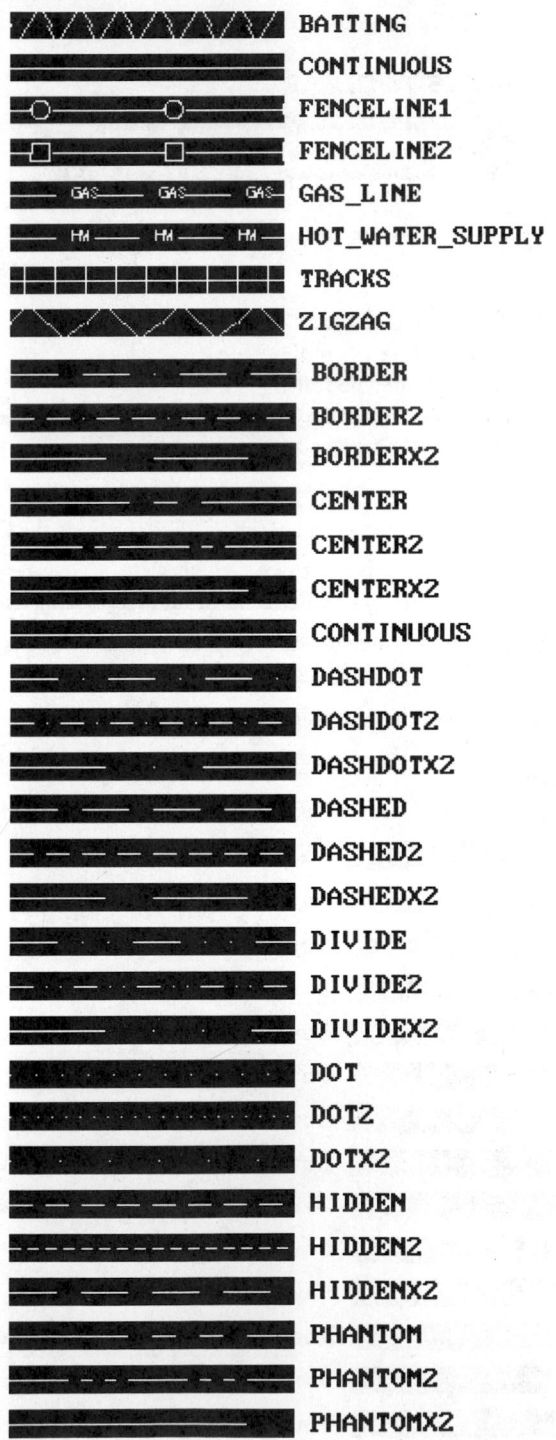

Create a custom linetype.

To create a custom linetype on-the-fly:

1. Type the **-Linetype Create** command:

```
Command: -linetype
?/Create/Load/Set: C
```

2. Name the linetype in three steps:

- First, the linetype name:

```
Name of linetype to create: [enter up to 31 characters]
```

- Second, the LIN filename. If you select Acad.Lin, AutoCAD appends your new linetype description to Acad.Lin; if you type a new filename, AutoCAD creates a new LIN file.

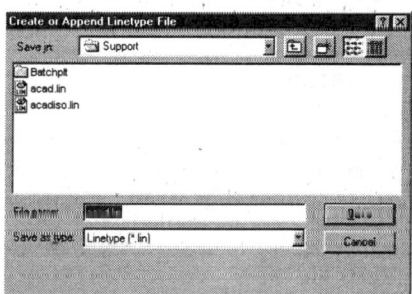

- Third, describe the linetype:

```
Descriptive text: [enter up to 47 characters]
```

3. Define the linetype pattern by using five codes:

- Positive number for dashes; for example, **0.5** is a dash 0.5 units long.
- Negative number for gaps; for example, **-0.25** is a gap 0.25 units long.
- Zero is for dots: **0** is a single dot.
- An **A** forces linetype to align between two endpoints; linetypes always start and stop with a dash.
- Commas (,) separate values.

Example:

```
*DASHDOT,__ . __ . __ . __ . __ . __ . __ . __ .
A,.5,-.25,0,-.25 [Enter]
```

4. Press **[Enter]** to end linetype definition.

5. Use the **-Linetype Load** command to load the pattern into the drawing.

```
Linetype to load: [type name]
```

6. Use the **Set** option to set the linetype.

```
New object linetype (or ?) <>: [type name]
```

Alternatively, use the **DdModify** command to change objects to the new linetype.

 # List

V. 1.0   List information about selected objects in the drawing.

Command	Alias	Ctrl+	F-key	Alt+	Menu Bar	Tablet
list	li	...	...	TQL	Tools ↳Inquiry ↳List	U8
	ls					

```
Command: list
Select objects: [pick]
Select objects: [Enter]
```

Example output:
```
        LINE       Layer: 36
                   Space: Model space
          Color: BYLAYER     Linetype: CONTINUOUS
          Handle = 24A6
    from point, X=  10.0000   Y=   6.0000   Z=   0.0000
      to point, X=   9.0000   Y=   4.0000   Z=   0.0000
 Length =   2.2361,   Angle in X-Y Plane =     243
 Delta X =  -1.0000, Delta Y =   -2.0000, Delta Z =   0.0000
```

COMMAND LINE OPTIONS

[Enter]	Continues the display.
[Esc]	Cancels the display.
[F2]	Returns to graphics screen.

RELATED COMMANDS

Area	Calculates the area and perimeter of some objects.
DbList	Lists information about all objects in the drawing.
Dist	Calculates the 3D distance and angle between two points.
MassProp	Calculates the properties of 2D regions and 3D solids.

TIPS

- Use the **List** command as a faster alternative to using the **Dist** and **Area** commands for finding lengths and areas of objects.

- The **List** command does *not* list *all* information about the selected objects. The following information is only listed under certain conditions:

Information	Condition
Object color	When not set BYLAYER.
Linetype	When not set BYLAYER.
Thickness	When not 0.
Elevation	Must read from the z-coordinate.
Extrusion direction	When z-axis differs from current UCS.

- Object handles are described by hexadecimal numbers.

ListURL

Rel.14 Lists the URL(s) attached to selected objects in the drawing (*an external command in DwfIu.Arx*).

Command	Alias	Ctrl+	F-key	Alt+	Menu Bar	Tablet
listurl	...	...	...	...	...	...

```
Command: listurl
Select objects: all
16 found 14 were filtered out.
Select objects: [Enter]
```

Example output:
```
URL for selected object is: http://www.autodeskpress.com
URL for selected object is: http://users.uniserve.com/~ralphg
```

COMMAND LINE OPTION

Select Objects Selects any object in the drawing; AutoCAD filters out those without a URL.

RELATED COMMANDS

AttachURL	Attaches a URL to an object or to an area.
DetachURL	Removes a URL from an object or an area.
SelectURL	Highlights all objects and areas with a URL.

TIPS

■ A URL (short for "uniform resource locator") is the universal file naming system used by the Internet.

■ See the **AttachURL** command for more information.

Load

V. 1.0 Loads SHX-format shape files into the drawing via a dialog box.

Command	Alias	Ctrl+	F-key	Alt+	Menu Bar	Tablet
load	. . .	. . .	. . .	. . .	. . .	. . .

Command: **load**
*Displays **Load Shape File** dialog box.*

COMMAND LINE OPTIONS
None.

RELATED AUTOCAD COMMAND
Shape   Inserts shapes into the current drawing.

TIPS
- Shapes are more efficient than blocks but are harder to create.

- The **Load** command cannot load SHX files that are meant for fonts. AutoCAD complains, "D:\ACAD14\support\gdt.shx is a normal text font file, not a shape file."

RELATED FILES
*.SHP   Source code for shape files.
*.SHX   Compile shape files.

In \Acad14\Bonus\Fonts subdirectory:
Es.Shx, Es.Shp Electronic component shapes.
Pc.Shx, Pc.Shp Printed circuit board shapes.
St.Shx, St.Shp Surface texture shapes for mechanical parts drawings.

In \Acad14\Support subdirectory:
Gdt.Shx, Gdt.Shp
         Geometric tolerance shapes (used by the **Tolerance** command).
LtypeShp.Shx, LtypeShp.Shp
         Linetype shapes (used by the **Linetype** command).

Using shapes in your drawing.

Step 1. COMPILE SHP FILE
(*If required*) Use the **Compile** command to compile the source code SHP file into an SHX file.

Step 2. LOAD SHX FILE
Use the **Load** command to load the SHX shape file into the drawing.

Step 3. USE SHAPE COMMAND
Use the **Shape** command to place shapes.
The ? option lists the names of shapes defined by the SHX file.

LogFileOff

Rel.13 Closes the Acad.Log file.

Command	Alias	Ctrl+	F-key	Alt+	Menu Bar	Tablet
logfileoff	...	Q	...	...	...	...

Command: **logfileoff**

COMMAND LINE OPTIONS
None.

RELATED AUTOCAD COMMAND
LogFileOn   Turns on recording 'Command' prompt text to file Acad.Log.

RELATED SYSTEM VARIABLE
LogFileMode   Text window written to log file:

LogFileMode	Meaning
0	Text not written to file (*default*).
1	Text recorded to file.

TIP
■ AutoCAD places a dashed line at the end of each log file session.

LogFileOn

Rel.13 Opens Acad.Log file and records 'Command' prompt text to the file.

Command	Alias	Ctrl+	F-key	Alt+	Menu Bar	Tablet
logfileon	...	Q	...	...	...	...

Command: **logfileon**

COMMAND LINE OPTIONS
None.

RELATED AUTOCAD COMMANDS
CopyHist   Copies all command text from the Text window to the Windows Clipboard.
LogFileOff   Turns off recording 'Command' prompt text to file Acad.Log.

RELATED SYSTEM VARIABLES
LogFileMode   Text window written to log file:

LogFileMode	Meaning
0	Text not written to file (*default*).
1	Text recorded to file.

LogFileName   Name of the log file (*default = acad.log*).

RELATED FILE
■ **Acad.Log**   Default filename for log file.

TIPS
■ If log file recording is left on, it resumes when AutoCAD is next loaded.

■ AutoCAD places a dashed line at the end of each log file session.

■ Press **Ctrl+Q** to quickly turn log file recording on and off. (*Historical note*: In some early versions of AutoCAD, Ctrl+Q meant "quick screen print" and output the current screen display to the printer. In Release 14, Ctrl+Q reappeared to record command text to a file.)

■ You give the log file a different name with the **Preferences** command's **Files** tab or with system variable **LogFileName**.

LsEdit

Rel.14 Edits the properties of a landscape object (*short for LandScape EDIT; an external command in LsObj.Arx*).

Command	Alias	Ctrl+	F-key	Alt+	Menu Bar	Tablet
lsedit	...	...	...	VEE	View	...
					ⓈRender	
					ⓈLandscape Edit	

```
Command: lsedit
Select a Landscape Object: [pick]
```
Displays dialog box:

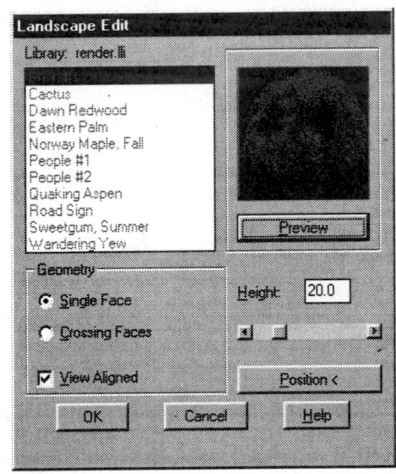

DIALOG BOX OPTIONS

Height	Changes height of the object, by typing a new value or moving the slider bar.
Position	Moves the object to another position in the drawing.

Geometry options:

Single Face	Renders faster but is less realistic.
Crossing Face	Produces more realistic ray-traced shadows.
View Aligned	Forces object to always face the camera.

RELATED COMMANDS

LsLib	Lets you add and remove raster images from the Render.Lli file.
LsNew	Places a landscape object in the drawing.
Render	Renders the landscape object.

LsLib

Rel.14 Maintains a library of landscape objects (*short for LandScape LIBrary; an external command in LsObj.Arx*).

Command	Alias	Ctrl+	F-key	Alt+	Menu Bar	Tablet
lsedit	...	...	...	VEC	View	...
					⇘Render	
					⇘Landscape Library	

Command: **lsedit**
Select a Landscape Object: **[pick]**
Displays dialog box:

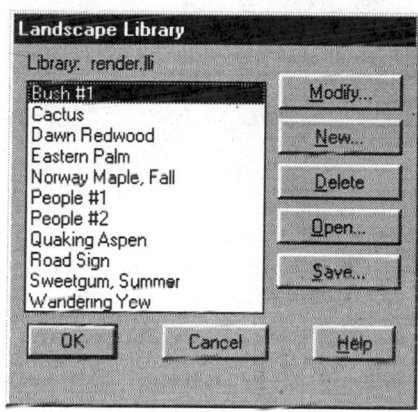

DIALOG BOX OPTIONS

Modify	Changes the properties of a landscape object; displays **Landscape Library Edit** dialog box.
New	Assigns defaults values to a landscape object; displays **Landsacpe Library New** dialog box.
Delete	Removes landscape object from library.
Open	Opens a landscape library file; displays **Open Landscape Library** dialog box.
Save	Saves landscape objects to LLI file; displays dialog box:

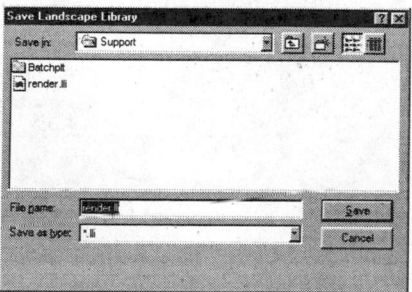

Landscape Library Edit dialog box:

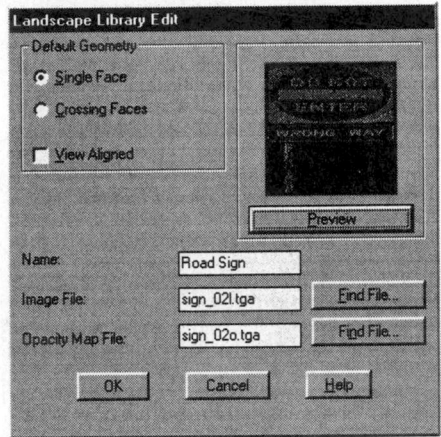

Default Geometry options:

Single Face	Renders faster but is less realistic.
Crossing Face	Produces more realistic ray-traced shadows.
View Aligned	Forces the object always faces the camera.

Preview	Previews the landscape image.

Name	Names the landscape object.
Image File	Specifies the type of raster image file: BMP, GIF, JPG, PCX, TGA, or TIF.
Opacity Map File	
	Names the raster file that provides opacity.
Find File	Finds the file; displays the **Find Image File** dialog box.

Landscape Library New dialog box:

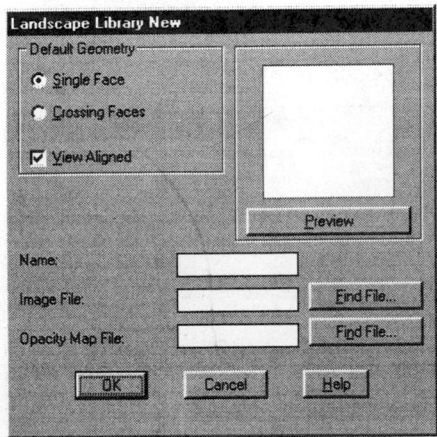

Default Geometry options:

Single Face   Renders faster but is less realistic.
Crossing Face Produces more realistic ray-traced shadows.
View Aligned Forces the object always faces the camera.

Preview   Previews the landscape image.

Name   Names the landscape object.
Image File   Specifies the type of raster image file: BMP, GIF, JPG, PCX, TGA, or TIF.
Opacity Map File
                  Names the raster file that provides opacity.
Find File   Finds the file; displays the **Find Image File** dialog box.

RELATED COMMANDS

LsEdit   Edits the properties of a landscape object.
LsNew   Places a landscape object in the drawing.
MatLib   Library of surface textures.

TIP

■ An *opacity map* determines which part of a raster image is opaque and which is transparent.

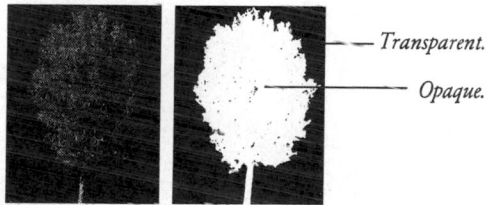

— *Transparent.*

— *Opaque.*

LsNew

Rel.14 Places a landscape object in the drawing (*short for LandScape NEW; an external command in LsObj.Arx*).

Command	Alias	Ctrl+	F-key	Alt+	Menu Bar	Tablet
lsnew	...	...	...	VEN	View ⮡Render ⮡Landscape New	...

```
Command: lsnew
Select a Landscape Object: [pick]
```
Displays dialog box:

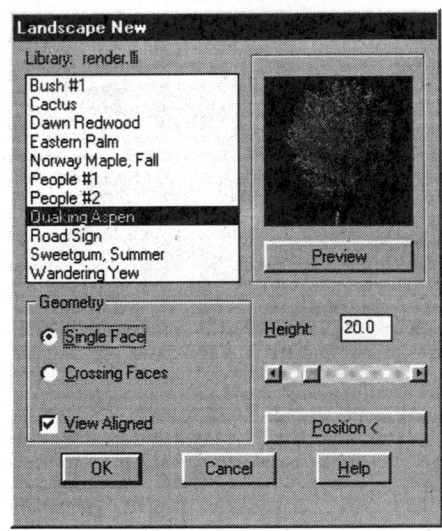

DIALOG BOX OPTIONS

Preview   Views the raster image.

Height   Changes height of the object, by typing a new value or moving the slider bar.
Position   Moves the object to another position in the drawing.

Geometry options:
Single Face   Renders faster but is less realistic.
Crossing Face   Produces more realistic ray-traced shadows.
View Aligned   Forces the object to always face the camera.

RELATED COMMANDS

LsLib   Lets you add and remove raster images from the Render.Lli file.
LsEdit   Edits the properties of a landscape object.
Render   Renders the landscape object.

TIPS

- A *landscape object* is defined as a **Plant** object in the AutoCAD database.

- Turn on **View Aligned** when you want the landscape object — such as a tree — to always faces the camera.

- Turn off **View Aligned** when you want the landscape object — such as a store front — to keep its orientation fixed.

*A landscape object with **crossing faces** (left) and **single face** (right).*

- Although AutoCAD's standard grip commands — stretch, move, scale, and rotate — work on landscape objects, the grips at the base, top, and corners have special meaning:

Grip	Meaning
Top	Change the object's height.
Bottom corner	Rotate (if not view aligned) and scale.
Base	Move the object.

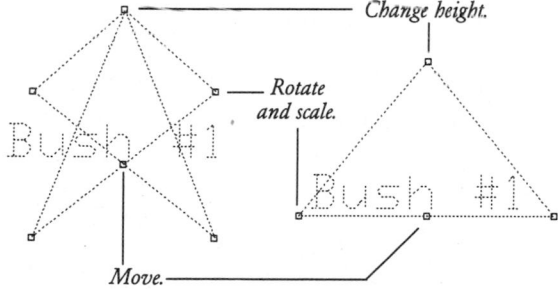

'LtScale

V. 2.0 Sets the scale factor of linetypes (*short for Line Type SCALE*).

Command	Alias	Ctrl+	F-key	Alt+	Menu Bar	Tablet
'ltscale	lts	...	...	...	...	Y19

```
Command: ltscale
New scale factor <1.0000>:
Regenerating drawing.
```

    Dashed (1x)   *Dashed2 (0.5x)*   *DashedX2 (2x)*

COMMAND LINE OPTION
New scale factor Change the global scale factor of all linetypes in the drawing.

RELATED COMMANDS
DdModify   Changes linetype scale of individual objects.
Linetype   Loads, creates, and sets the working linetype.

RELATED SYSTEM VARIABLES
LtScale   Contains the current linetype scale factor.
PlineGen   Controls how linetypes are generated for polylines.
PsLtScale   Linetype scale relative to paper space.

TIPS
- If the linetype scale is too large, the linetype appears solid.

- If the linetype scale is too small, the linetype appears as a solid line that redraws very slowly.

- In addition to setting the scale with the **LtScale** command, the Acad.Lin contains each linetype in three scales: normal, half-size, and double-size.

REMOVED COMMAND
The **MakePreview** command has been removed from Release 14.

MassProp

Rel.11

Reports the mass properties of a 3D solid model, body, or 2D region (*short for MASS PROPerties; an external command in Acis.Dll*).

Command	Alias	Ctrl+	F-key	Alt+	Menu Bar	Tablet
masprop	...	...	...	TQM	Tools	P1
					⌖Inquiry	
					⌖MassProp	

```
Command: massprop
Select objects: [pick]
Select objects: [Enter]
```

Example output of a solid sphere:

```
————————— SOLIDS ——————————
Mass:                  112.6241
Volume:                12.6241
Bounding box:          X: 4.7910  —  10.7826
                       Y: -1.0540  —  4.9376
                       Z: -2.9958  —  2.9958
Centroid:              X: 7.7868
                       Y: 1.9418
                       Z: 0.0000
Moments of inertia:    X: 828.9818
                       Y: 7233.2389
                       Z: 7657.9057
Products of inertia:   XY: 1702.9437
                       YZ: 0.0000
                       ZX: 0.0000
Radii of gyration:     X: 2.7130
                       Y: 8.0140
                       Z: 8.2459
Principal moments and X-Y-Z directions about centroid:
                       I: 404.3150 along [1.0000 0.0000 0.0000]
                       J: 404.3150 along [0.0000 1.0000 0.0000]
                       K: 404.3150 along [0.0000 0.0000 1.0000]
Write to a file <N>? y
```

COMMAND LINE OPTIONS

Select objects   Selects the ACIS objects — 2D regions, 3D solids, and bodies — to analyze.
Write to a file   *Yes*: write mass property report to an MPR file.
                      No: don't write report to file.

RELATED COMMAND

Area   Calculates area of non-ACIS objects.

RELATED FILE

*.MPR   **MassProp** writes its results to an MPR mass properties report file.

TIPS

- As of Release 13, AutoCAD's solid modeling no longer allows you to apply a material density to a solid model. All solids and bodies have a density of 10.

- AutoCAD only analyzes regions coplanar to the first region selected.

DEFINITIONS

Area Total surface area of selected 3D solids, bodies, or 2D regions.

Bounding Box The lower-right and upper-left coordinates of a rectangle enclosing the 2D region; the x,y,z-coordinate pair of a 3D box enclosing the 3D solid or body.

Centroid The x,y,z-coordinates of the center of the 2D region; the center of mass for 3D solids and bodies.

Mass Equal to the volume, since density = 1; not calculated for regions.

Moment of Inertia
For 2D regions = **Area** * **Radius**^{2}
For 3D solids and bodies = **Mass** * **Radius**^{2}

Perimeter Total length of inside and outside loops of 2D regions; not calculated for 3D solids and bodies.

Product of Inertia
For 2D regions = **Mass** * **Distance** (of centroid to y,z-axis) * **Distance** (of centroid to x,z-axis)
For 3D solids and bodies = **Mass** * **Distance** (of centroid to y,z-axis) * **Distance** (of centroid to x,z-axis)

Radius of Gyration
For 2D regions and 3D solids = (**MomentOfInertia** / **Mass**)$^{1/2}$

Volume 3D space occupied by a 3D solid or body; not calculated for regions.

MatchProp

Rel.14 Matches the properties between selected objects (*an external command in Match.Arx*).

Command	Alias	Ctrl+	F-key	Alt+	Menu Bar	Tablet
matchprop	ma	...	...	MM	Modify ⤷Match Properties	Y15

painter

```
Command: matchprop or painter
Select Source Object: [pick]
Current active settings = color layer ltype ltscale thickness
    text dim hatch
Settings/<Select Destination Object(s)>: [pick]
Settings/<Select Destination Object(s)>: [Enter]
```

COMMAND LINE OPTIONS

Select Source Object

> Gets property settings from the source object.

Select Destination Objects

> Passes property settings to the destination objects.

Settings   Displays dialog box:

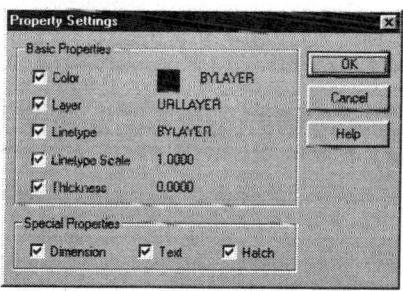

DIALOG BOX OPTIONS

Basic Properties options:

Color	Specifies the color for the destination object.
Layer	Specifies the layer name for the destination object.
Linetype	Specifies the linetype for the destination object.
Linetype Scale	Specifies the linetype scale for the destination objectn.
Thickness	Specifies the thickness for the destination object; available only for objects that can have a thickness.

Special Properties options:

Text	Changes the text style of text and paragraph text objects.
Dimension	Changes the dimension style of dimension, leader, and tolerance objects.
Hatch	Changes the hatch pattern of hatched objects.

RELATED COMMAND

DdModify   Changes most aspects of one selected object.

MatLib

Rel.13 Imports and exports material-look definitions for use by the **RMat** command (*short for MATerial LIBrary; an external command in Render.Arx*).

Command	Alias	Ctrl+	F-key	Alt+	Menu Bar	Tablet
matlib	...	...	...	VEB	View	Q1
					⬍Render	
					⬍MatLib	

Command: **matlib**
Displays dialog box:

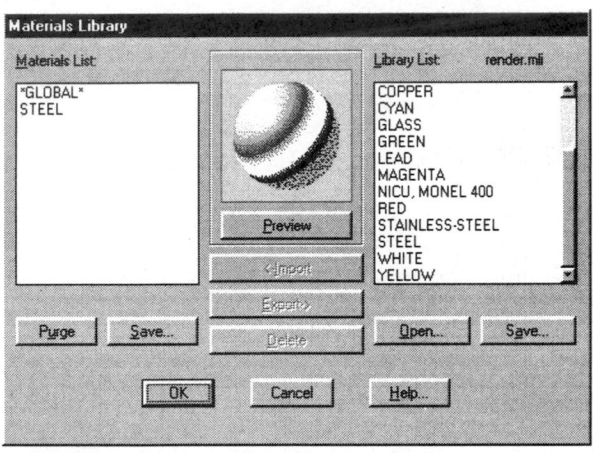

DIALOG BOX OPTIONS

Import	Brings a material definition into the drawing; when there is a conflict, displays **Reconcile Imported Material Names** dialog box.
Preview	Previews the selected material mapped to a sphere object.
Export	Adds material definition to MLI library file; if there is a conflict, displays the **Reconcile Exported Material Names** dialog box, which is identical to **Reconcile Imported Material Names** dialog box.
Purge	Deletes unattached material definitions from the **Materials** list.
Save	Saves to an MLI file.
Delete	Deletes selected material definitions from the **Materials** or **Library** lists.
Open	Loads material definitions from an MLI file; displays file dialog box.

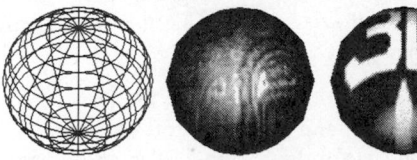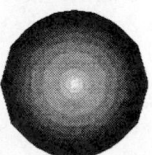

Reconcile Imported Material Names dialog box:

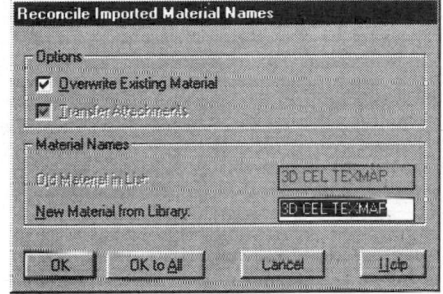

Options *options:*
Overwrite Existing Material
> Selected material definition overwrites existing material definition.

Transfer Attachments
> Keeps objects attached to material definition.

Material Names *options:*
Old Material in List
> Allows you to edit the name of the material.

New Material from Library
> Allows you to edit the name of the material.

RELATED COMMAND
RMat   Attaches a material definition to objects, colors, and layers.

RELATED FILE
Render.Mli   Material library; contains the material definitions.

TIPS
- **MatLib** only loads and purges material definitions; use **RMat** to attach the definitions to objects.

- A *material* defines the look of a rendered object: coloring, reflection (shininess), roughness, and ambience reflection.

- Materials do not define the density of 3D solids and bodies.

- By default, a drawing contains a single material definition, called *GLOBAL*, with the default parameters for color, roughness, ambience, and reflection.

Measure

V. 2.5 Divides lines, arcs, circles, and polylines into equidistant segments, placing a point or a block at each segment.

Command	Alias	Ctrl+	F-key	Alt+	Menu Bar	Tablet
measure	me	...	...	DOM	Draw	V12
					⮑Point	
					⮑Measure	

```
Command: measure
Select object to measure: [pick]
<Segment length>/Block: B
Block name to insert: [type name]
Align block with object? <Y> [Enter]
Segment length:
```

Polyline (left) and measured with ten points (right):

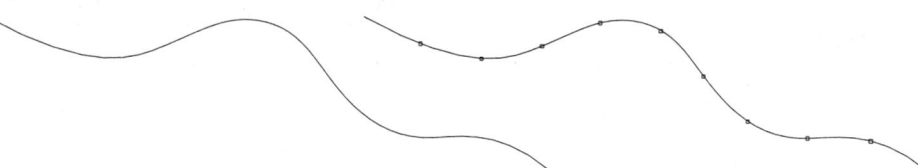

COMMAND LINE OPTIONS

Block   Indicates the name of the block to use as a marker.
Align block with object?
     Aligns the block's x-axis with object.
Segment length
     Indicates the distance between markers.

RELATED COMMANDS

Block   Creates blocks that can be used with **Measure**.
Divide   Divides an object into a number of segments.

RELATED SYSTEM VARIABLES

PdMode   Controls the shape of a point.
PdSize   Controls the size of a point.

TIPS

- You must define the block before it can be used with the **Measure** command.

- The **Measure** distance does not place a point or block at the beginning of the measured object.

Menu

V. 1.0 Loads MNS and MNU menu files.

Command	Alias	Ctrl+	F-key	Alt+	Menu Bar	Tablet
menu	...	...	...	...	...	...

```
Command: menu
```
Displays Select Menu File dialog box.

When FileDia = 0:
```
Command: menu
Menu file name or . for none <D:\ACAD14\support\acad>: [Enter]
Menu loaded successfully. MENUGROUP: ACAD
AutoCAD menu utilities loaded.
```

COMMAND LINE OPTIONS
Menu file name
　　　　　　Specifies the name of the menu file to load.
. for none　　(*Dot*) Removes current menu from AutoCAD.
[Enter]　　Reloads current menu.

RELATED COMMANDS
MenuLoad　　Loads a partial menu file.
Tablet　　Configures digitizing tablet for use with overlay menus.

RELATED SYSTEM VARIABLES
MenuName　　The currently loaded menu file.
MenuEcho　　Suppresses menu echoing.
ScreenBoxes　　Specifies the number of menu lines displayed on the side menu.

TIPS
- AutoCAD automatically compiles MNS files into MNC files for faster loading.

- The MNU file defines the function of the screen menu, menu bar, cursor menu, icon menus, digitizing tablet menus, pointing device buttons, and the AUX: device.

MenuLoad

Rel.13 Loads a part of a menu file.

Command	Alias	Ctrl+	F-key	Alt+	Menu Bar	Tablet
menuload	...	...	...	TM	Tools] ↳Customize Menus	Y9

Command: **menuload**
Displays tabbed dialog box:

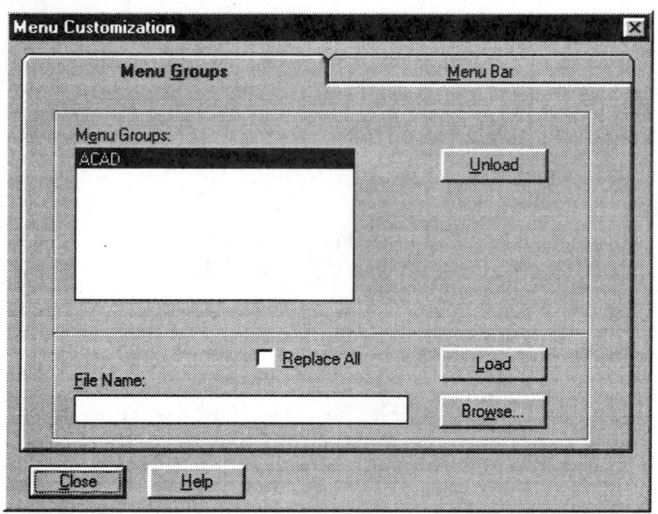

When FileDia = 0:
Command: **menuload**
Enter name of menu file to load: **acad**
Menu loaded successfully. MENUGROUP: ACAD

DIALOG BOX OPTIONS

Menu Groups Lists the names of loaded menu groups and files.
Unload Unloads selected menu group.

Replace All Replaces all currently loaded menus with the newly loaded menu.
Load Loads selected menu group into AutoCAD.
File Name Displays the name of the menu file.
Browse Displays the **Select Menu File** dialog box.

Close Closes the dialog box.
Help Provides context-sensitive help.

Menu Bar tab:

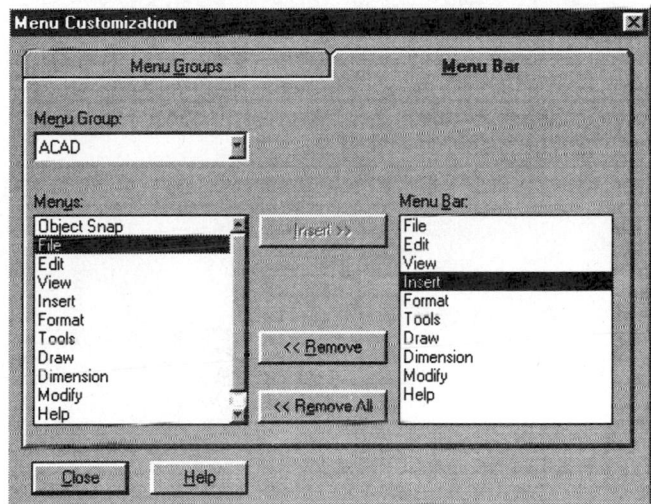

Menu Group	Selects a menu group or file.
Menus	Names of menu items in selected menu group.
Insert	Inserst a menu item on the menu bar.
Remove	Removes a menu item from the menu bar.
Remove All	Removes all menu items from the menu bar.
Menu Bar	Names of menu items on the menu bar.

RELATED COMMANDS

Menu	Loads a full menu file.
MenuUnload	Unloads part of the menu file.
Tablet	Configures digitizing tablet for use with overlay menus.

RELATED SYSTEM VARIABLES

MenuName	The currently loaded menu file.
MenuEcho	Suppresses menu echoing.
ScreenBoxes	Specifies the number of menu lines displayed on the side menu.

TIP

- The **MenuLoad** allows you to add *partial* menu files, such as Ac_Bonus.Mns and INet.Mns.

MenuUnLoad

Rel.13   Unloads a partial menu file.

Command	Alias	Ctrl+	F-key	Alt+	Menu Bar	Tablet
menuunload	...	...	...	TM	Tools ⤷Customize Menus	...

Command: **menuunload**
Displays tabbed dialog box:

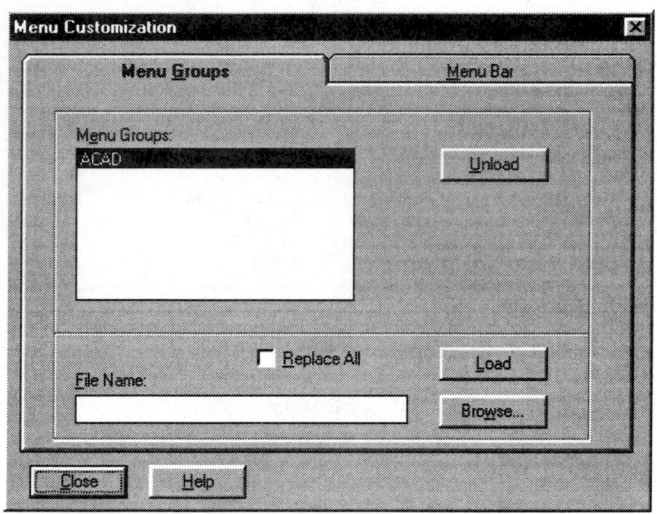

When FileDia = 0:
Command: **menuunload**
Enter the name of the MENUGROUP to unload: **acad**
Menu unloaded successfully. MENUGROUP: acad

DIALOG BOX OPTIONS

Menu Groups   Lists the names of loaded menu groups and files.
Unload   Unloads selected menu group.

Replace All   Replaces all currently loaded menus with the newly loaded menu.
Load   Loads selected menu group into AutoCAD.
File Name   Displays the name of the menu file.
Browse   Displays the **Select Menu File** dialog box.

Close   Closes the dialog box.
Help   Provides context-sensitive help.

Menu Bar tab:

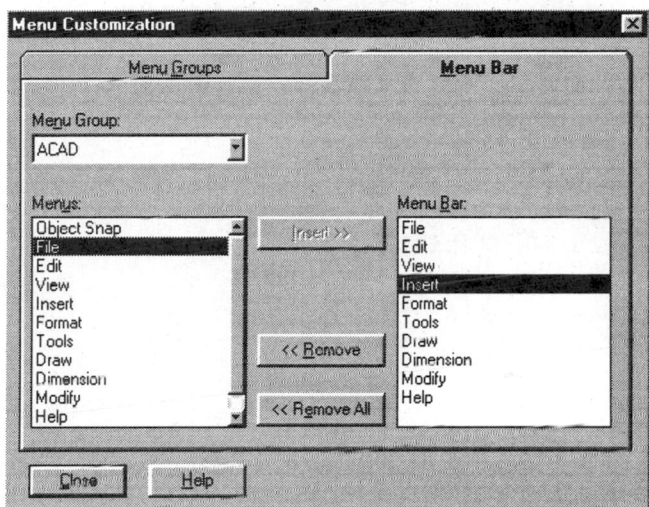

Menu Group	Selects a menu group or file.
Menus	Names of menu items in selected menu group.
Insert	Inserst a menu item on the menu bar.
Remove	Removes a menu item from the menu bar.
Remove All	Removes all menu items from the menu bar.
Menu Bar	Names of menu items on the menu bar.

RELATED COMMANDS

Menu	Loads a full menu file.
MenuLoad	Loads part of the menu file.
Tablet	Configures digitizing tablet for use with overlay menus.

RELATED SYSTEM VARIABLES

McnuName	The currently loaded menu file.
McnuEcho	Suppresses menu echoing.
ScreenBoxes	Specifies the number of menu lines displayed on the side menu.

TIP

- The **MenuUnload** allows you to remove *partial* menu files, such as Ac_Bonus.Mns and INet.Mns.

MInsert

V. 2.5 Inserts an array of blocks as a single block (*short for Multiple INSERT*).

Command	Alias	Ctrl+	F-key	Alt+	Menu Bar	Tablet
minsert	...	...	...	...	...	...

```
Command: minsert
Block name (or ?) <>: [type name]
Insertion point: [pick]
X scale factor <1> / Corner / XYZ: [pick]
Y scale factor (default=X): [pick]
Rotation angle <0>: [pick]
Number of rows (—) <1>:
Number of columns (|||) <1>:
Unit cell or distance between rows (—):
Distance between columns (|||):
```

COMMAND LINE OPTIONS

Block name Indicates the name of the block to be inserted.

? Lists the names of blocks stored in the drawing.

X scale factor Indicates the x-scale factor.

Corner Indicates the x- and y-scale factors by pointing on the screen.

XYZ Specifies x-, y-, and z-scaling.

P Supplies predefined block name, scale, and rotation values.

Number of rows
Specifies the number of horizontal rows.

Number of columns
Specifies the number of vertical columns.

Unit cell or distance between rows
Shows the cell distance on the screen or type the row distance.

Distance between columns
Specifies the distance between columns.

RELATED COMMANDS

3dArray Creates 3D rectangular and polar arrays.

Array Creates 2D rectangular and polar arrays.

Block Creates a block.

TIP

■ The array placed by the **MInsert** command is a single block.

Mirror

V. 2.0   Creates a mirror copy of a group of objects in 2D space.

Command	Alias	Ctrl+	F-key	Alt+	Menu Bar	Tablet
mirror	mi	...	...	MI	Modify ⮡Mirror	V16

```
Command: mirror
Select objects: [pick]
Select objects: [Enter]
First point of mirror line: [pick]
Second point: [pick]
Delete old objects? <N> [Enter]
```

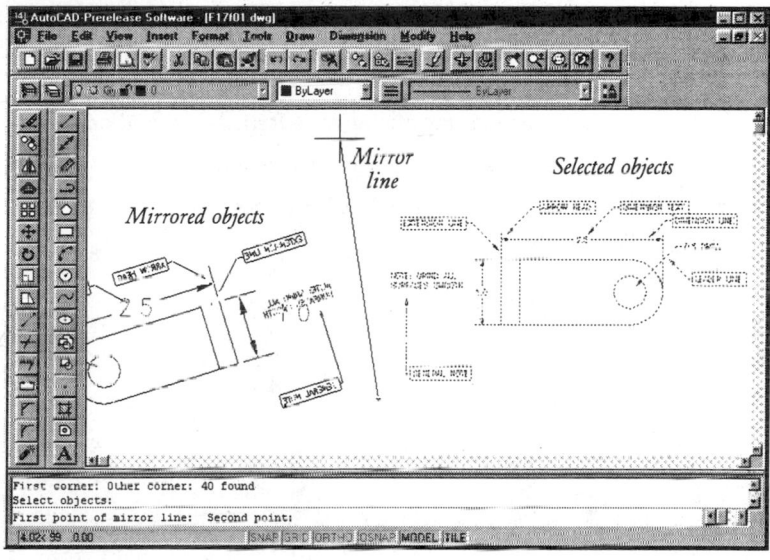

COMMAND LINE OPTIONS

Select objects   Selects the objects to mirror.
First point of mirror line
    Specifies the starting point of the mirror line.
Second point   Specifies the ending point of the mirror line.
Delete old objects
    No: Does not delete selected objects.
    Yes: Deletes selected objects.

RELATED COMMANDS

Array	Mirrors object around a circle.
Copy	Creates a non-mirrored copy of a group of objects.
Mirror3d	Mirrors objects in 3D-space.

RELATED SYSTEM VARIABLE

MirrText   Determines whether text is mirrored by the **Mirror** command:

MirrText	Meaning
0	Text is not mirrored about horizontal axis (*default*).
1	Text is mirrored.

TIPS

- The **Mirror** command is excellent for cutting your drawing work in half for symmetrical objects. For double-symmetric objects, use the Mirror command twice.

- To "mirror" around a circle, use the **Array** command with the **Polar** option.

- Although you can mirror a viewport in paper space, that does not mirror the model space objects inside the viewport.

- Turn on **Ortho** mode to ensure that the mirror is perfectly horizontal or vertical.

- The **MirrText** system variable determines whether text is mirrored.

- The mirror line become a mirror plane in 3D; it is perpendicular to the XY plane of the UCS containing the mirror line.

Mirror3d

Rel.11 Mirrors objects about a plane in 3D space (*an external command in Geom3d.Exp*).

Command	Alias	Ctrl+	F-key	Alt+	Menu Bar	Tablet
mirror3d	...	...	...	M3M	Modify	W21
					↳3D	
					↳Mirror 3D	

```
Command: mirror3d
Select objects: [pick]
Select objects: [Enter]
Plane by Object/Last/Zaxis/View/XY/YZ/ZX/<3 points>:
Delete old objects? <N> [Enter]
```

COMMAND LINE OPTIONS

Object	Selects a circle, arc or 2D polyline segment.
Last	Selects last-picked mirroring plane.
View	Specifies that the current view plane is the mirror plane.
XY	Specifies that the x,y-plane is the mirror plane.
YZ	Specifies that the y☐Y,z-plane is the mirror plane.
ZX	Specifies that the z,x-plane is the mirror plane.
Zaxis	Defines mirroring plane by a point on the plane and on the normal to the plane (*z-axis*).
3 points	Defines three points on mirroring plane.

RELATED COMMANDS

Mirror	Mirrors objects in 2D space.
Rotate3d	Rotates objects in 3D space.

RELATED SYSTEM VARIABLE

MirrText — Determines whether text is mirrored by the **Mirror** command:

MirrText	Meaning
0	Text is not mirrored about horizontal axis (*default*).
1	Text is mirrored.

MIEdit

Rel.13 Edits multiline vertices (*short for MultiLine EDITor*).

Command	Alias	Ctrl+	F-key	Alt+	Menu Bar	Tablet
mledit	...	...	...		Modify	Y19
					↳Object	
					↳Multiline	

-mledit

Command: **mledit**
Displays dialog box:

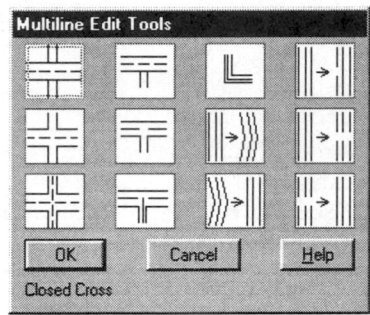

DIALOG BOX OPTIONS

	U	Undoes the most-recent multiline edit.
	Closed Cross	Closes the intersection of two multilines.
	Open Cross	Opens the intersection of two multilines.
	Merged Cross	Merges a pair of multilines: opens exterior lines; closes interior lines.
	Closed Tee	Closes a T-intersection.
	Open Tee	Opens a T-intersection.
	Merged Tee	Merges a T-intersection: opens exterior lines; closes interior lines.
	Corner Joint	Creates a corner joint of a pair of intersecting multilines.
	Add Vertex	Adds a vertex (*joint*) to a multiline segment.
	Delete Vertex	Removes a vertex from a multiline segment.
	Cut Single	Places a gap in a single line of a multiline.
	Cut All	Places a gap in all lines of a multiline.
	Weld All	Removes a gap in a multiline.

```
Command: -mledit
Mline editing option AV/DV/CC/OC/MC/CT/OT/MT/CJ/CS/CA/WA:
```

COMMAND LINE OPTIONS

AV	Adds a vertex.
DV	Deletes a vertex.
CC	Closes a cross.
OC	Opens a cross.
MC	Merges a cross.
CT	Closes a tee.
OT	Opens a tee.
MT	Merged tee
CJ	Creates a corner joint.
CS	Cuts a single line.
CA	Cuts all lines.
WA	Welds all lines.
U	Undoes the most-recent multiline edit.

RELATED COMMANDS

MLine	Draws up to 16 parallel lines.
MlProp	Defines the properties of a multiline.

RELATED SYSTEM VARIABLES

CMlJust   Current multiline justification:

CMlJust	Meaning
0	Top (*default*).
1	Middle.
2	Bottom.

CMlScale	Current multiline scale factor (*default = 1.0*).
CMlStyle	Current multiline style name (*default = " "*).

RELATED FILE

*.MLN   Multiline style definition file in \Acad14\Support.

TIPS

■ Use the **Cut All** option to open up a gap before placing door and window symbols in a multiline wall.

■ Use the **Weld All** option to close up a gap after removing the door or window symbol in a multiline.

■ Use the **Stretch** command to move a door or window symbol in a multiline wall.

 # MLine

Rel.13 Draws up to 16 parallel lines (*short for Multiple LINE*).

Command	Alias	Ctrl+	F-key	Alt+	Menu Bar	Tablet
mline	ml	...	...	DM	Draw ↳Multiline	M10

```
Command: mline
Justification=Top, Scale=1.0000, Style=STANDARD
Justification/Scale/STyle/<From point>: [pick]
Undo/<To point>: [pick]
Close/Undo/<To point>: [pick]
Close/Undo/<To point>: C
```

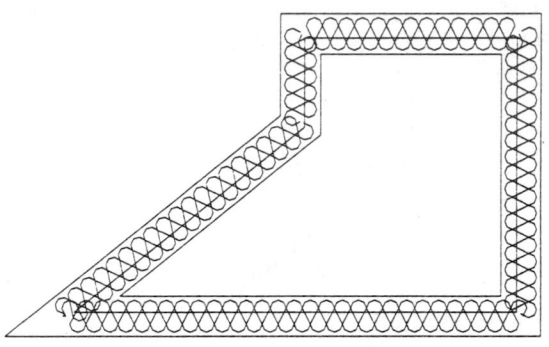

COMMAND LINE OPTIONS

To point Specify the end point.
Undo Backs up by one segment.
Close Closes the multiline to its start point.

Justification options:

Top Draws top line of multiline at cursor; remainder of multiline is "below" cursor.
Zero Draws center (*zero offset point*) of multiline at cursor.
Bottom Draws bottom line of multiline at cursor; remainder of multiline is "above" cursor.

Scale option examples:

1.0 Default scale factor.
2.0 Draws multiline twice as wide
-1.0 Flips multiline.
0 Collapses multiline to a single line.

STyle options:

Multiline style name

  Specifies the name of multiline style.
? Lists names of multiline styles defined in drawing.

RELATED COMMANDS

MlEdit	Edits multilines.
MlProp	Defines the properties of a multiline.

RELATED SYSTEM VARIABLES

CMlJust   Current multiline justification:

CMlJust	Meaning
0	Top (*default*).
1	Middle.
2	Bottom.

CMlScale	Current multiline scale factor (*default = 1.0*).
CMlStyle	Current multiline style name (*default = ""*).

RELATED FILE

*.MLN   Multiline style definition file in \Acad13\Common\Support.

TIP

- Multiline styles are stored in MLN files in DXF-like format.

 # MIStyle

Rel.13 Defines the characteristics of multilines (*short for MultiLine STYLE*).

Command	Alias	Ctrl+	F-key	Alt+	Menu Bar	Tablet
mlstyle	...	...	...	OM	Format ⵌMultiline Style	V5

Command: **mlstyle**
Displays dialog box:

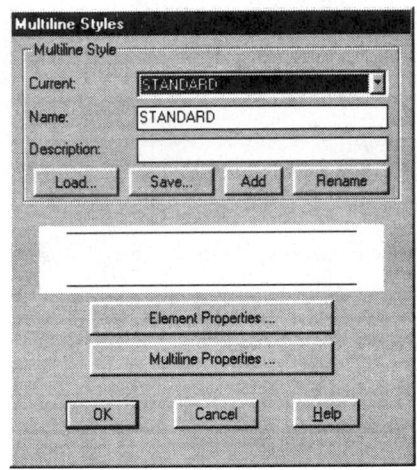

DIALOG BOX OPTIONS

Multiline Style options:

Current	Lists currently loaded multiline style names (*default = STANDARD*)
Name	Gives a new multiline style a name, or rename an existing style.
Description	Describes multiline style, with up to 255 characters.
Load	Loads style from the multiline library file Acad.Mln; displays **Load Multiline Styles** dialog box.
Save	Saves a multiline style or rename a style; displays dialog box.
Add	Adds the multiline style fromthe **Name** box to the **Current** list.
Remove	Removes the multiline style from the **Current** list.

Element Properties
  Specifies the properteis of multiline elements; displays the **Element Properties** dialog box.

Multiline Properties
  Specifies additional properties for multilines; displays **Multiline Properties** dialog box.

Load Multiline Styles dialog box:

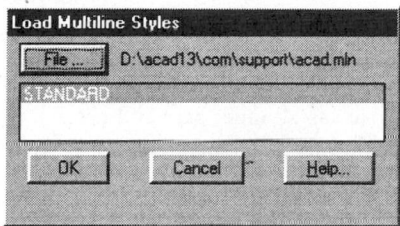

File   Selects an MLN multiline definition file.

Element Properties dialog box:

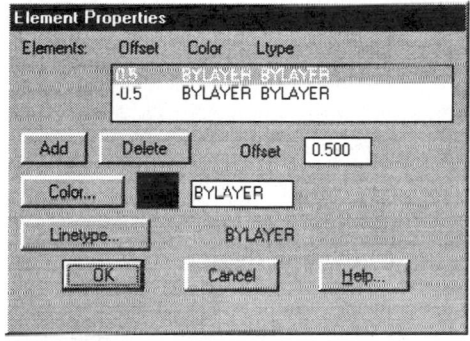

Add   Adds an element (*line*).
Delete   Deletes an element.
Offset   Specifies the distance from origin to element.
Color   Specifies the element color; displays **Select Color** dialog box.
Linetype   Specifies the element linetype; displays **Select Linetype** dialog box.

Multiline Properties dialog box:

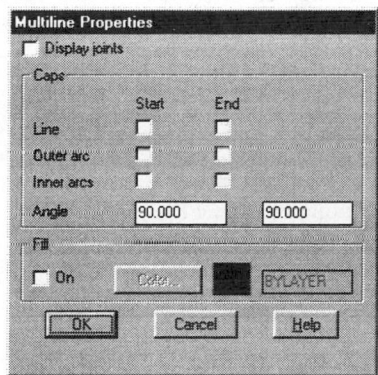

Display Joints Toggles the display of joints (*miters*) at vertices; affects all multiline segments.

Caps options:
Line	Draws a straight line start and/or end cap.
Outer Arc	Draws an arc to cap the outermost pair of lines.
Inner Arcs	Draws an arc to cap all inner pairs of lines.
Angle	Draws a straight line cap at an angle.

Fill options:
On	Specifies the fill color.
Color	Displays the **Select Color** dialog box.

RELATED COMMANDS
MlEdit	Edits multilines.
MLine	Draws up to 16 parallel lines.

RELATED SYSTEM VARIABLES
CMlJust Current multiline justification:

CMlJust	Meaning
0	Top (*default*).
1	Middle.
2	Bottom.

CMlScale	Current multiline scale factor (*default = 1.0*).
CMlStyle	Current multiline style name (*default = " "*).

RELATED FILE
Acad.Mln Multiline style definition file in \Acad14\Support.

TIPS
■ Use the **MlEdit** command to create (or close up) gaps to place door and window symbols in multiline walls.

■ The multiline scale factor has the following effect on the look of a multiline:

Scale	Meaning
1.0	Default scale factor.
2.0	Draw multiline twice as wide, not twice as long.
-1.0	Flip multiline about its origin.
0.0	Collapse multiline to a single line.

■ The MLN file describes multiline styles in a DXF-like format.

 # Move

V. 1.0 Moves a group of objects to a new location.

Command	Alias	Ctrl+	F-key	Alt+	Menu Bar	Tablet
move	m	...	...	MV	Modify	V19
					ⓑMove	

```
Command: move
Select objects: [pick]
Select objects: [Enter]
Base point or displacement: [pick]
Second point of displacement: [pick]
```

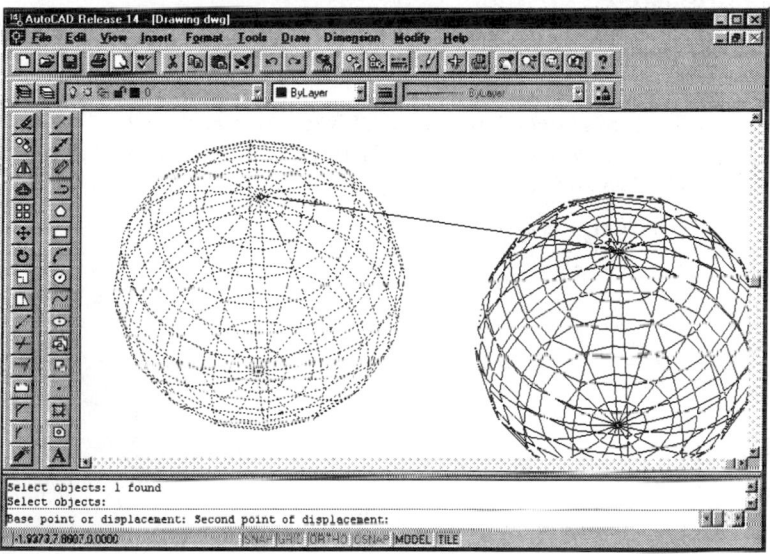

COMMAND LINE OPTIONS

Select options Selects the objects to copy.
Base point Indicates the starting point for the move.
Displacement Indicates the distance to move.

RELATED COMMANDS

Copy Makes a copy of selected objects.
MlEdit Moves the vertices of a multiline.
PEdit Moves the vertices of a polyline.

MSlide

<u>**V. 2.0**</u> Saves the current viewport as an SLD slide file on disk (*short for Make SLIDE*).

Command	Alias	Ctrl+	F-key	Alt+	Menu Bar	Tablet
mslide	...	...	...	TDS	Tools ⬐Display Image ⬐Save	...

Command: **mslide**
Displays Create Slide File dialog box.

COMMAND LINE OPTIONS
None.

RELATED COMMANDS
Save   Saves the current drawing as a DWG-format drawing file.
SaveImg   Saves the current view as a TIFF, Targa, or GIF-format raster file.
VSlide   Displays an SLD-format slide file in AutoCAD.

RELATED AUTODESK PROGRAM
Slidelib.Exe   Compiles a group of slides into an SLB-format slide library file.

MSpace

Rel.11 Switches the drawing from paper space to model space (*short for Model SPACE*).

Command	Alias	Ctrl+	F-key	Alt+	Menu Bar	Tablet
mspace	ms	...	...	VT	View ⮑Model Space (Tiled)	L4
				VF	View ⮑Model Space (Floating)	

Command: **mspace**

| -0.5701,6.6333,0.0000 | | SNAP GRID ORTHO OSNAP MODEL TILE |

Double-click MODEL to switch between Model Space and Paper Space modes.

COMMAND LINE OPTIONS
None.

RELATED COMMAND
PSpace   Switches from model space to paper space.

RELATED SYSTEM VARIABLES
MaxActVp   Maximum number of viewports with visible objects (*default = 48*).
TileMode   The current setting of tiled viewport:

TileMode	Meaning
0	Off (*default*): floating viewports.
1	On: tiled viewports.

TIPS
■ **TileMode** must be set to zero before you can switch to paper space and use the **MSpace** command:

Double-click TILE to turn TileMode off (gray).

| -0.5701,6.6333,0.0000 | | SNAP GRID ORTHO OSNAP MODEL TILE |

■ To switch from paper space back to model space, at least one viewport must be active; create the viewport with the **MView** command.

■ Objects in the current selection set are ignored if they were not collected in the current space.

■ AutoCAD clears the selection set when moving between paper and model space.

MTEdit

Rel.13 Edits an mtext object (*short for Multiline Text EDITor; an undocumented, external command in AcMTEd.Arx*).

Command	Alias	Ctrl+	F-key	Alt+	Menu Bar	Tablet
mtedit	...	...	...	...	...	...

Command: **mtedit**
Select an MTEXT object: **[pick]**
Display Mutiline Text Editor dialog box; see MText command.

COMMAND LINE OPTION
Select an MTEXT object
> Selects one paragraph text object for editing.

RELATED COMMANDS
DdEdit   Displays text editor appropriate for the text object.
DdModify   Changes the properties of an mtext object.

RELATED SYSTEM VARIABLE
MTextEd   Name of external text editor to place and edit multiline text.

MText

Rel.13 Places paragraph text in a boundary box (*short for Multline TEXT; an external command in AcMTEd.Arx*).

Command	Alias	Ctrl+	F-key	Alt+	Menu Bar	Tablet

mtext	t	...	...	DXM	Draw
					  ↳Text
					  ↳Multiline Text
						J8

	mt					
-mtext	-t					

```
Command: mtext
Current text style: STANDARD. Text height: 0.2000
Specify first corner: [pick]
```

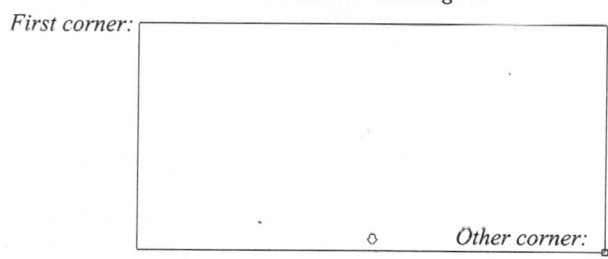

The MText bounding box:

First corner:

Other corner:

```
Specify opposite corner or [Height/Justify/Rotation/Style/
   Width]: [pick]
```
Displays tabbed dialog box.

DIALOG BOX OPTIONS
Character tab:

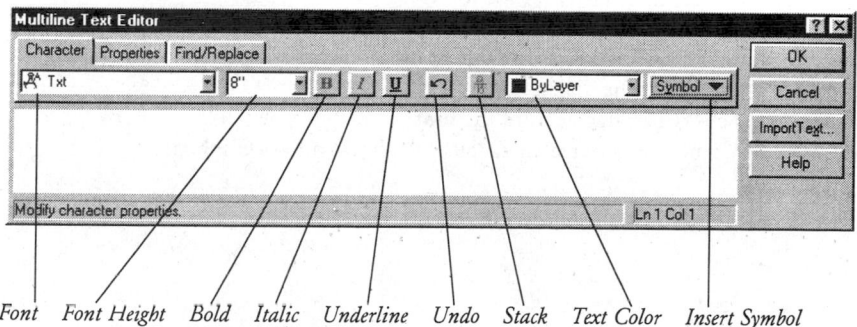

Font   Font Height   Bold   Italic   Underline   Undo   Stack   Text Color   Insert Symbol

Font	Selects a TrueType (TTF) or AutoCAD (SHX) font name (*default = TXT*).
Font Height	Specifies the height of the text (*default = 0.2 units*).
Bold	Boldfaces the text, if the font allows.
Italic	Italicizes the text, if the font allows.

Underline	Underlines the text, if the font allows.
Undo	Undoes the last action.
Stack	Stacks a pair of characters to create a fraction.
Text Color	Selects color for text; click **Other Color** to display **Select Color** dialog box.
Insert Symbol	Inserts three common symbols and a non-breaking space:

Symbol	Meaning
%%d	Degree — °
%%p	Plus-minus — ±
%%c	Diameter — ∅

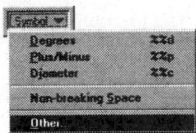

Click **Other** for **Character Map** dialog box.

Character Map dialog box:

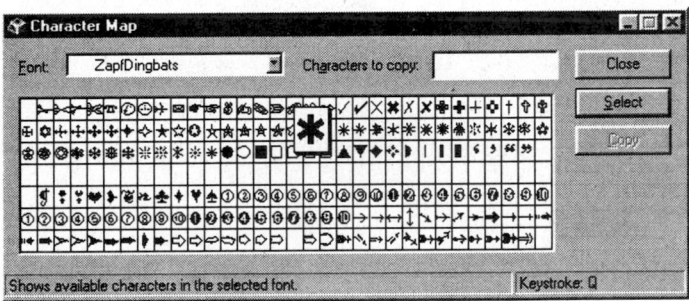

Font	Selects the TTF TrueType font.
Characters to copy	
	Lists the characters that will be copied to the Clipboard.
Close	Dismisses the dialog box.
Select	Selects a character from the font.
Copy	Copies the selected character(s) to the Windows Clipboard.

Properties tab:

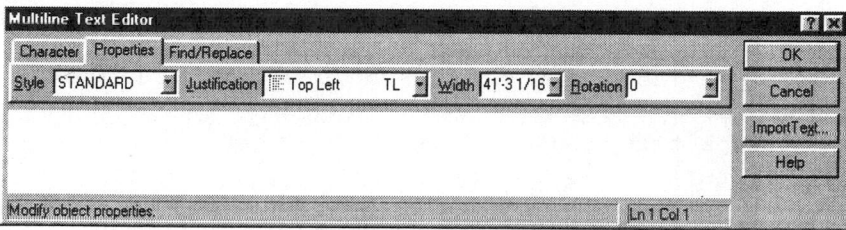

Style	Selects text style (*default = STANDARD*).
Justification	Selects bounding box justification (*default = Top Left*).
Width	Selects width of bounding box.
Rotation	Sets the rotation angle of bounding box (*default = 0 degrees*).

Find/Replace tab:

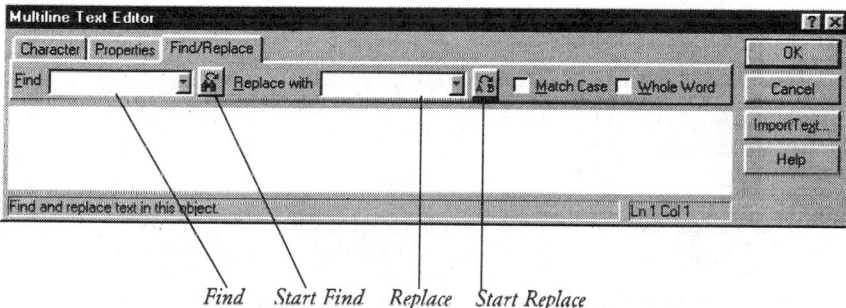

Find Start Find Replace Start Replace

Find	Type text to search for; click **Find** icon to start finding.
Replace With	Type text to replace; click **Replace** icon to start replacing.
Match Case	Match the case of the text.
Whole Word	Look for whole words, not partial words.
Import Text	Import text from an ASCII file; displays **Open** dialog box. *Careful!* The maximum size of text file is limited to 16KB.

```
Command: -mtext
Current text style: STANDARD. Text height: 0.2000
Specify first corner: [pick]
Specify opposite corner or [Height/Justify/Rotation/Style/
 Width]: [pick]
MText: [type text]
MText: [Enter]
```

COMMAND LINE OPTIONS

Height   Specifies the height of UPPERCASE text (*default = 0.2 units*).

Justify options:
TL   Top left (*default*).
TC   Top center.
TR   Top right.
ML   Middle left.
MC   Middle center.
MR   Middle right.
BL   Bottom left.
BC   Bottom center.
BR   Bottom right.

Rotation   Specifies the rotation angle of boundary box.
Style   Selects the text style for multiline text (*default = STANDARD*).
Width   Sets the width of boundary box; width of 0 eliminates bounding box.

RELATED COMMANDS

DdEdit   Edits multiline text and other kinds of text.
DdModify   Changes all aspects of mtext.
MtProp   Changes properties of multiline text.
MtEdit   Edits mtext.
PasteSpec   Pastes formatted text from the Windows Clipboard into the drawing.
Style   Creates a named text style from a font file.

RELATED SYSTEM VARIABLE

MTextEd   Name of external text editor to place and edit multiline text.

TIPS

■ Use the **MTextEd** system variable to define a different text editor.

■ The **Import Text** option is limited to ASCII (*unformatted*) text files no more than 16KB in size.

■ To import formatted text, copy text from the word processor to the Windows Clipboard, then use AutoCAD's **PasteSpec** command.

■ To link text in the drawing with a word processor, use the **InsertObj** command. When the word processor updates, the linked text is updated in the drawing.

MtProp

Rel.13 Changes the properties of multiline text (*short for Multline Text PROPerties; an external command in AcMTEd.Arx*).

Command	Alias	Ctrl+	F-key	Alt+	Menu Bar	Tablet
mtprop	...	...	...	...	...	...

Command: **mtprop**
Select an MText object: **[pick]**
Displays **Edit Multiline Text** *dialog box; see* **MText** *command.*

COMMAND LINE OPTIONS
See **MText** *command.*

RELATED COMMANDS
DdEdit	Edits multiline text.
MText	Places multiline text.
Style	Creates a named text style from a font file.

Multiple

V. 2.5　A command modifier that automatically repeats the command.

Command	Alias	Ctrl+	F-key	Alt+	Menu Bar	Tablet
multiple	...	...	...	...	...	...

Example usage:
```
Command: multiple circle
3P/2P/TTR/<Center point>: [pick]
Diameter/<Radius>: [pick]
circle 3P3P/2P/TTR/<Center point>: [pick]
Diameter/<Radius>: [pick]
circle 3P3P/2P/TTR/<Center point>: [Esc]
```

COMMAND LINE OPTION
[Esc]　　　　　Stops the command from automatically repeating itself.

COMMAND INPUT OPTIONS
[Space]　　　　Repeats the previous command.
[Click]　　　　Click on any blank spot on the tablet menu to repeat a command.

RELATED COMMANDS
Redo　　　　　Undos a undo
U　　　　　　Undoes the previous command; undoes one multiple command at a time.

RELATED COMMAND MODIFIERS
’　　　　　　(*Apostrophe*) Allows use of some commands within another command.
.　　　　　　(*Period*) Forces use of undefined command.
-　　　　　　(*Dash*) Forces display of prompts on command line for some commands.
_　　　　　　(*Underscore*) Uses English command in international version of AutoCAD.
(　　　　　　(*Open parenthesis*) Executes AutoLISP function on command line.
$(　　　　　(*Dollar, parenthesis*) Executes Diesel function on command.

TIPS
- **Multiple** is *not* a command but a command modifier; it does nothing on its own.

- **Multiple** only repeats the command name; it does not repeat command options.

- Some commands automatically repeat, including **Point** and **Donut**.

MView

Rel.11 Creates and manipulates overlapping viewports (*short for Make VIEWports*).

Command	Alias	Ctrl+	F-key	Alt+	Menu Bar	Tablet
mview	mv	R	...	VV	View ⤷Floating Viewports	M4

```
Command: mview
ON/OFF/Hideplot/Fit/2/3/4/Restore/<First Point>: [pick]
Other corner: [pick]
Regenerating drawing.
```

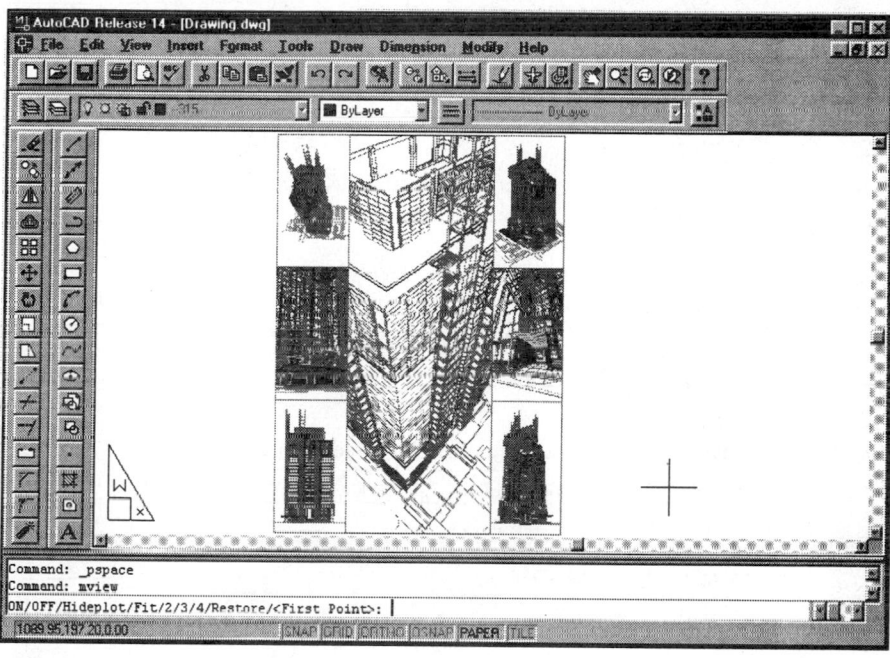

COMMAND LINE OPTIONS

First Point	Indicates the first point of a single viewport (*default*).
Fit	Creates a single viewport that fits the screen.
Hideplot	Creates a hidden-line view during plotting and printing.
OFF	Turns off a viewport.
ON	Turns on a viewportn.
Restore	Restores a saved viewport configuration.

2 options:

Horizontal	Stacks two viewports.
Vertical	Places two viewports side-by-side viewports (*default*).

3 options:

Horizontal	Stack the three viewports.
Vertical	Side-by-side viewports.
Above	Two viewports above the third.
Below	Two viewports below the third.
Left	Two viewports to the left of the third.
Right	Two viewports to the right of the third (*default*).

4 options:

Fit	Creates four same-size viewports to fit the screen.
First Point	Indicate the area for the four viewports (*default*).

RELATED COMMANDS

[Ctrl]+R	Switches to the next viewport.
MSpace	Switches to model space.
PSpace	Switches to paper space before creating viewports.
RedrawAll	Redraws all viewports.
RegenAll	Regenerates all viewports.
VpLayer	Controls the visibility of layers in each viewport.
VPorts	Creates tiled viewports in model space.
Zoom	The **XP** option zooms a viewport relative to paper space.

RELATED SYSTEM VARIABLES

CvPort	Current viewport.
MaxActVp	Controls the maximum number of visible viewports:

MaxActVP	Meaning
1	Minimum.
48	Default.
32767	Maximum.

TileMode	Controls the availability of overlapping viewports.

TIPS

- Although system variable **MaxActVp** limits the number of simultaneously visible viewports, the **Plot** command plots all viewports.

- **TileMode** must be set to zero to switch to paper space and use the **MSpace** command.

- **Snap, Grid, Hide, Shade,** et cetera, can be set separately in each viewport.

MvSetup

Rel. 11 Inserts predefined title blocks, creates a set of viewports, sets a global scale factor (*short for Model View SETUP; an external command in MvSetup.Lsp*).

Command	Alias	Ctrl+	F-key	Alt+	Menu Bar	Tablet
mvsetup	mvs	. . .	. . .	. . .	. . .	. . .

Command: **mvsetup**

Command prompt when TileMode = 1:
Enable paper space? (No/<Yes>): **N**
Units type (Scientific/Decimal/Engineering/Architectural/
 Metric):
Enter the scale factor:
Enter the paper width:
Enter the paper height:

Command prompt when TileMode = 0:
Align/Create/Scale viewports/Options/Title block/Undo: **A**
Angles/Horizontal/Vertical alignment/Rotate view/Undo: **A**
Base point: **[pick]**
Other point: **[pick]**
Distance from basepoint:
Angle from basepoint:

COMMAND LINE OPTIONS

Align   Aligns new viewport with base point of existing viewport
Create   Creates viewports in four layouts:

Layout	Meaning
0	No layout.
1	Single viewport.
2	Standard engineering layout.
3	Array viewports along x- and y-axes.

Scale viewports Scales border with respect to drawing objects.

Options options:
Set layer   Specifies layer for title block.
Limits   Specifies whether to reset limits after title block insertion.
Units   Specifeis inch or millimeter paper units.
Xref   Specifies whether title is inserted as a block or as an xref.

Title block   Specifies title block style.
Undo   Undoes **MvSetup** operations in reverse order.

RELATED SYSTEM VARIABLE

TileMode   The current setting of TileMode.

RELATED FILES

MvSetup.Dfs   The **MvSetup** default settings file.
AcadIso.Dwg   Prototype drawing with ISO defaults.

TIPS

- When option 2 (Std. Engineering) is selected at the **Create** option, the following views are created (counterclockwise from upper left):

  Top view.
  Isometric view.
  Front view.
  Right view.

- To create the title block, **MvSetup** searches the path specified by the **AcadPrefix** variable. If the appropriate drawing cannot be found, **MvSetup** creates the default border.

- **MvSetup** makes use the following predefined title blocks:

  None
  ISO A0 through A4 (mm, metric)
  ANSI A through E, ANSI V (in, imperial)
  Architectural and engineering D-size
  Generic D-size.

- The metric A0 size is similar to the imperial E-size, while the metric A4 is similar to A-size.

- You can add your own title block with the **Add** option. Before doing so, create the title block as an AutoCAD drawing.

Using MvSetup.

MvSetup has many options but does not present them in a logical fashion. To set up a drawing with **MvSetup**, follow these basic steps:

Step 1: MVSETUP COMMAND
Start the **MvSetup** command:

    Command: **mvsetup**

Step 2: TITLE BLOCK
1. Place the title block with the **Title** option.

Step 3: VIEWPORTS
1. Set up the viewports with the **Create** option.

2. For standard drawings, select option #2, Std. Engineering.

Step 4: SCALE OBJECT
1. Make the object the same size in all four viewports with the **Scale** option.

2. When you are prompted to 'Select objects', select the four viewports, not the objects in the drawing.

3. You can interrupt the **MvSetup** command at any time with the **[Esc]** key, then resume the command complete the setup.

New

Rel.12 Starts a new drawing from scratch, from a template drawing, or via step-by-step drawing setup assistance.

Command	Alias	Ctrl+	F-key	Alt+	Menu Bar	Tablet
new	...	N	...	FN	File ⇲New	T24

Command: **new**
Displays dialog box:

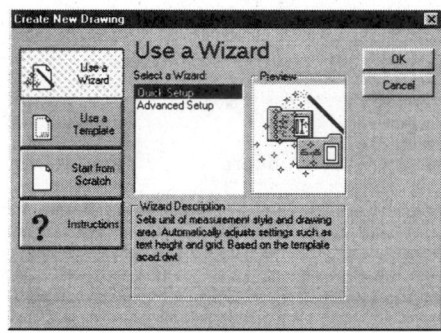

When FileDia = 0:
Command: **new**
Enter template file (or . for none) <D:\ACAD14\template\acad.dwt>:

DAILOG BOX OPTIONS

Use a Wizard   *Quick Setup:* sets up a new drawing in two steps.
                           Advanced Setup: sets up a new drawing in seven steps.
Use a Template Creates a new drawing based on a DWT template file.
Start from Scratch
                      Creates a new drawing based on the Acad.Dwt (English units) or AcadIso.Dwt (metric units) template drawings.
Instructions   Provides help in using the **New** command.
OK   Proceds to the next dialog box.
Cancel   Cancels the **New** command.

IN-COMMON DIALOG BOX OPTIONS

Cancel   Cancels the wizard and return to the previous drawing.
More Info   Displays brief help about the current step, such as:

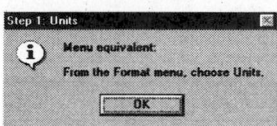

Help   Brings up Help window.
Back   Moves back one step.
Next   Moves forward to next step.
Done   Skips ahead to the end of the wizard.

Use a Wizard, Quick Setup dialog box:

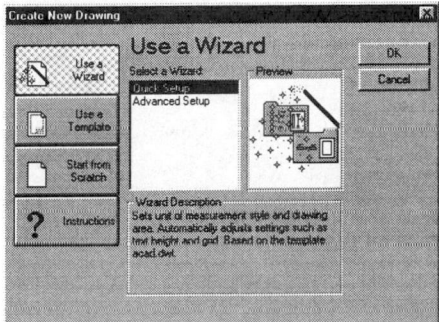

Step 1: Units dialog box:

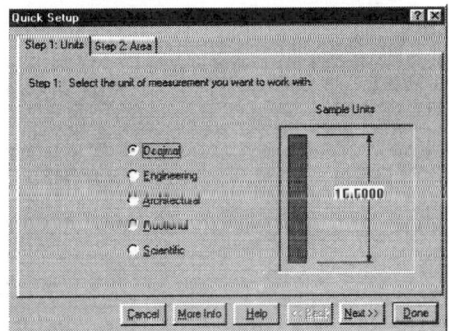

Decimal	Displays units in decimal — or metric — notation (*default*): 123.5000
Engineering	Displayed in feet and decimal inches: 10'-3.5000"
Architectural	Displays units in feet, inches, and fractional inches: 10' 3-1/2"
Fractional	Displays units in inches and fractions: 123 1/2
Scientific	Displays units in scientific notation: 1.235E+02

Step 2: Area dialog box:

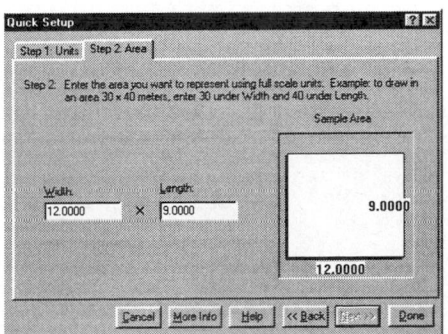

Width	Width of drawing in real-world — not scaled — units (*default = 12 units*).
Length	Length (or depth) of drawing in real-world units (*default = 9 units*).

Use a Wizard, Advanced Setup dialog box:

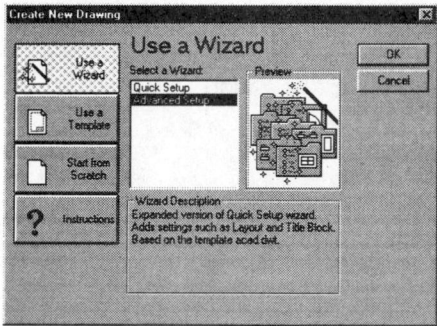

Step 1: Units dialog box:

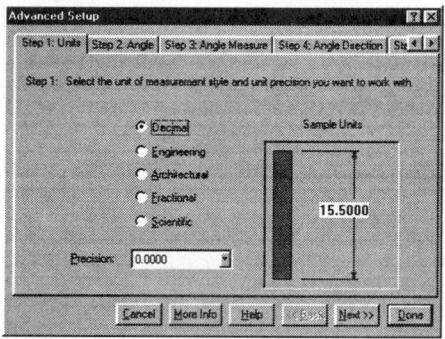

Decimal	Displays units in decimal — or metric — notation (*default*): 123.5000
Engineering	Displays units in feet and decimal inches: 10'-3.5000"
Architectural	Displays units in feet, inches, and fractional inches: 10' 3-1/2"
Fractional	Displays units in inches and fractions: 123 1/2
Scientific	Displays units in scientific notation: 1.235E+02
Precision	Selects a precision of display.

Step 2: Angle dialog box:

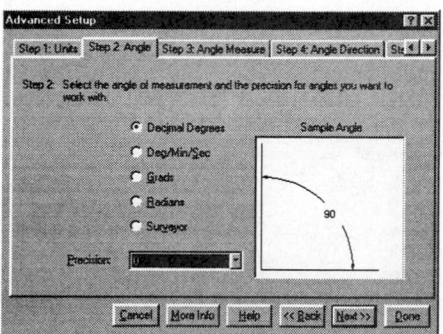

Decimal Degrees	Displays decimal degrees (*default*): 22.5000
Deg/Min/Sec	Displays degrees, minutes, and seconds: 22 30
Grads	Displays grads: 25g.
Radians	Displays radians: 25r
Surveyor	Displays surveyor units: N 25d0'0" E
Precision	Selects a precision.

Step 3: Angle Measure dialog box:

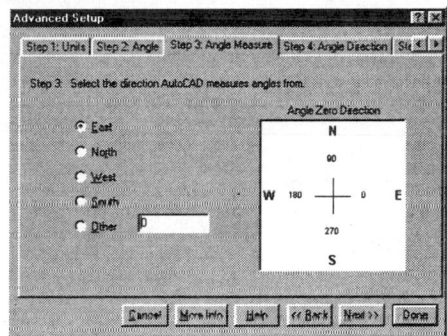

East	Zero degrees points to East (*default*).
North	Zero degrees points North.
West	Zero degrees points West.
South	Zero degrees points South.
Other	Zero degrees points any in of the 360 degrees.

Step 4: Angle Direction dialog box:

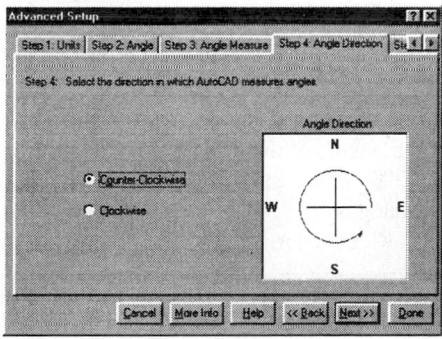

Counter-Clockwise	
	Measures positive angles counterclockwise from 0 degrees (*default*).
Clockwise	Measures positive angles clockwise from 0 degrees.

Step 5: Area dialog box:

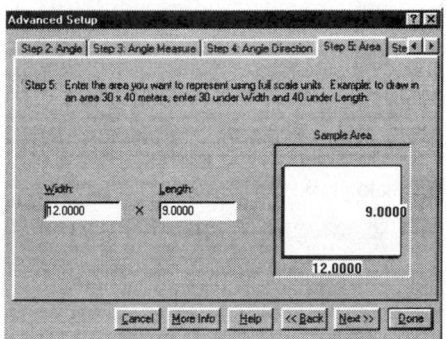

Width | Width of drawing in real-world — not scaled — units (*default = 12 units*).
Length | Length (or depth) of drawing in real-world units (*default = 9 units*).

Step 6: Title Block dialog box:

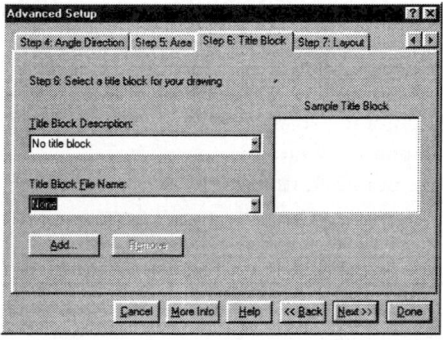

Title Block Description
Briefly describes the title block format; stored in file Wizard.Ini.

Title BLock File Name
Specifies the filename of the DWT template (*default = none*).

Add | Adds a new DWT file to the template file collection; displays **Select Title Block File** dialog box.

Remove | Removes a DWT file from the \Acad14\Template subdirectory.

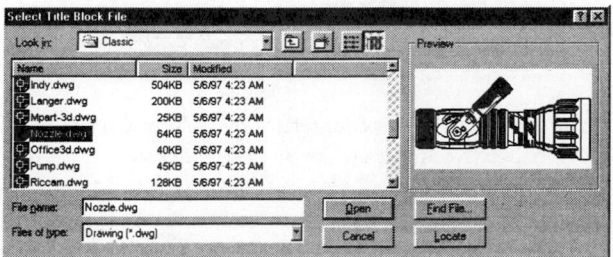

Step 7: Layout dialog box:

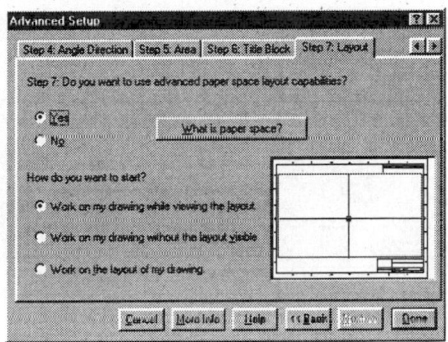

Yes	Sets up drawing in paper space (*default*).
No	Sets up drawing in model space.

What Is Paper Space?

Provides help in explaining paper space and model space, as shown below:

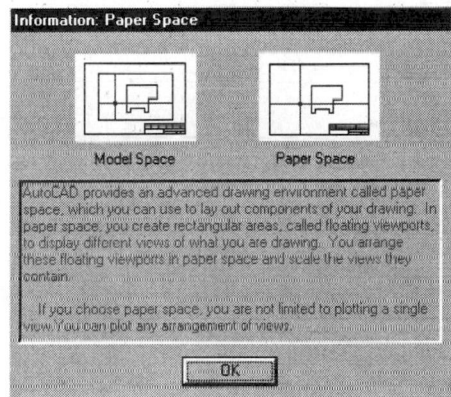

Work on my drawing while viewing the layout.

Allows you to work in model space with TileMode set to 0 (*default*).

Work on my drawing without the layout visible.

Allows you to work in model space with TileMode set to 1.

Work on the layout of my drawing.

Allows you to work in paper space.

Use a Template dialog box:

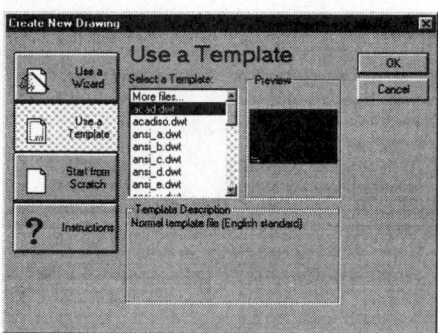

Select a Template

Selects a DWT template file:

Filename	Meaning	Units
acad.dwt	Generic AutoCAD	English
acadiso.dwt	Generic AutoCAD	Metric
archeng.dwt	Arch/Eng	English
gs24x36.dwt	Generic D	English
ansi_a.dwt	ANSI A	English
ansi_b.dwt	ANSI B	English
ansi_c.dwt	ANSI C	English
ansi_d.dwt	ANSI D	English
ansi_e.dwt	ANSI E	English
ansi_v.dwt	ANSI V	English
din_a0.dwt	DIN A0	Metric
din_a1.dwt	DIN A1	Metric
din_a2.dwt	DIN A2	Metric
din_a3.dwt	DIN A3	Metric
din_a4.dwt	DIN A4	Metric
iso_a0.dwt	ISO A0	Metric
iso_a1.dwt	ISO A1	Metric
iso_a2.dwt	ISO A2	Metric
iso_a3.dwt	ISO A3	Metric
iso_a4.dwt	ISO A4	Metric
jis_a0.dwt	JIS A0	Metric
jis_a1.dwt	JIS A1	Metric
jis_a2.dwt	JIS A2	Metric
jis_a3.dwt	JIS A3	Metric
jis_a4l.dwt	JIS A4 - landscape	Metric
jis_a4r.dwt	JIS A4 - portrait	Metric

Start from Scratch dialog box:

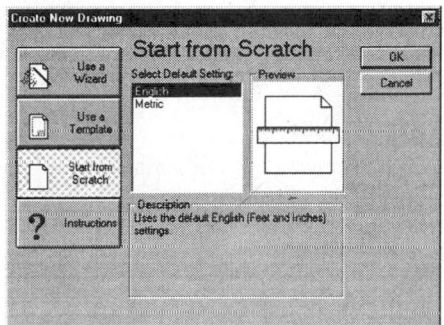

English	Starts a new blank drawing using Acad.Dwt and default English units (*default*).
Metric	Starts a new blank drawing using AcadIso.Dwt and default metric units.

Instructions dialog box:

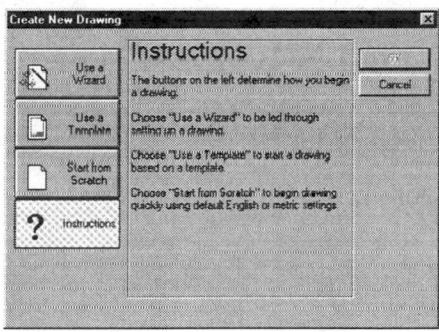

RELATED COMMAND

SaveAs	Saves drawing in DWG or DWT formats; allows the saving of template files.

RELATED SYSTEM VARIABLES

DbMod	Indicates whether drawing has changed since being loaded.
DwgName	Name of current drawing.
FileDia	Displays prompts at the 'Command' prompt.

RELATED FILES

Wizard.Ini	Names and descriptions of template files.
*.DWT	Template file.

TIPS

- AutoCAD allows you to save your work before using the **New** command.

- Until you give the drawing a name, AutoCAD names it Drawing.Dwg.

- The default prototype drawing is Acad.Dwg; edit and save DWT template drawings to change the defaults in new drawings.

- The /t switch creates a new drawing based on a template drawing:

  acad /t filename

- Upon starting AutoCAD, it displays an additional option, **Open a Drawing**:

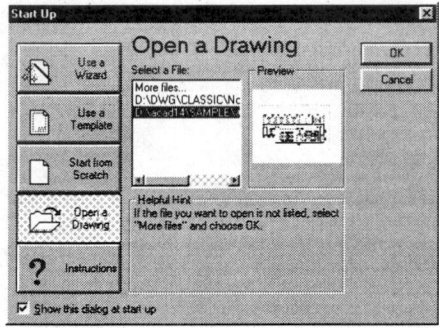

Offset

V. 2.5 Draws parallel lines, arcs, circles and polylines; repeats automatically until cancelled.

Command	Alias	Ctrl+	F-key	Alt+	Menu Bar	Tablet
offset	o	...	...	MS	Modify ⤷Offset	V17

```
Command: offset
Offset distance or Through <Through>: t
Select object to offset: [pick]
Through point: [pick]
Select object to offset: [Esc]
```

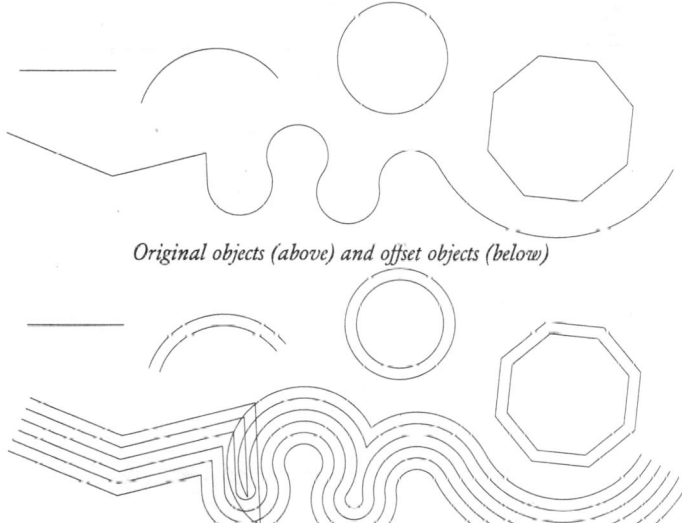

Original objects (above) and offset objects (below)

COMMAND LINE OPTIONS

Offset distance Specifies the perpendicular distance to offset.
Through   Indicates the offset distance.
[Esc]   Exits the **Offset** command.

RELATED COMMANDS

Copy   Creates one of more copies of a group of objects.
Mirror   Creates a mirror copy of a group of objects.
MLine   Draws up to 16 parallel lines.

RELATED SYSTEM VARIABLE

OffsetDist   Current offset distance.

OleLinks

Rel.13 Changes, updates, and cancels OLE links between the drawing and other Windows applications (*short for Object Linking and Embedding LINKS; an external command in OleAProt.Arx*).

Command	Alias	Ctrl+	F-key	Alt+	Menu Bar	Tablet
olelinks	...	...	...	EL	Edit	...
					⌁OLE Links	

Command: **olelinks**
Displays dialog box:

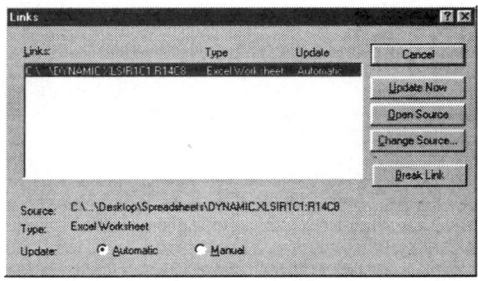

DIALOG BOX OPTIONS

Links   Displays a list of linked objects: (1) source filename; (2) portion of file; and (3) update mode — automatic or manual.

Update   Automatic or manual updates.

Update Now Updats selected links.

Open Source Starts the source application program.

Change Source Specifies a new object:

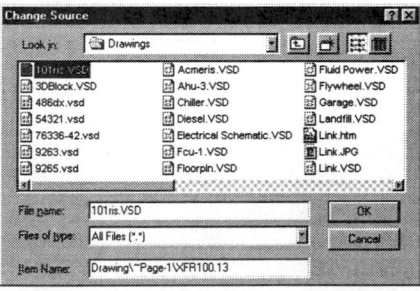

Break Link   Cancels the OLE link; keeps the object in place.

RELATED COMMANDS

InsertObj   Places an OLE object in the drawing.

PasteSpec   Places objects from Clipboard as linked objects in drawing.

RELATED WINDOWS COMMANDS

Copy   Copies object from source application to the Windows Clipboard.

Update   Updates the linked object in the source application.

Oops

V. 1.0 Unerases the last-erased group of objects; returns the group of objects after the **Block** command.

Command	Alias	Ctrl+	F-key	Alt+	Menu Bar	Tablet
oops	...	...	...	...	...	W18

Command: **oops**

COMMAND LINE OPTIONS
None.

RELATED COMMANDS

Block	Use the **Oops** command after the **Block** command to return erased objects.
Erase	Use the **Oops** command after the **Erase** command to return erased objects.
Undo	Undoes the most-recent command.

TIPS

■ **Oops** only unerases the most-recently erased object; use the **Undo** command to unerase earlier objects.

■ Use **Oops** to bring back objects after turning them into a block with the **Block** and **WBlock** commands.

 # Open

Rel.12 Loads a drawing into AutoCAD.

Command	Alias	Ctrl+	F-key	Alt+	Menu Bar	Tablet
open	...	O	...	FO	File ⬐Open	U25

Command: **open**
Displays dialog box:

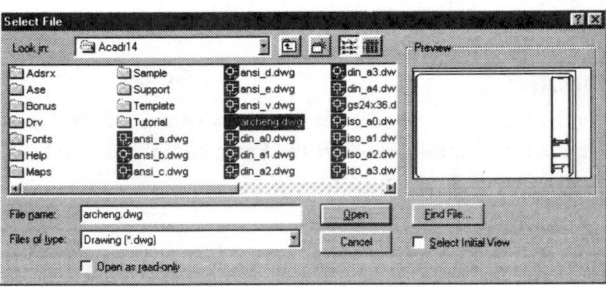

DIALOG BOX OPTIONS

Look in	Selects network drive, hard drive, or folder (*subdirectory*).
Preview	Displayes preview of Release 13 and 14 drawings.
File name	Names the drawing.
Files of type	Selects DWG (AutoCAD), DXF (interchange), or DWT (template) drawings.
Open as read-only	
	Displays drawing but you cannot edit it.
Open	Opens the drawing file.
Cancel	Returns to previous drawing.
Select initial view	
	Selects a named view from a dialog box, if the drawing has saved views.
Find File	Searches or browses for a file; displays tabbed dialog box:

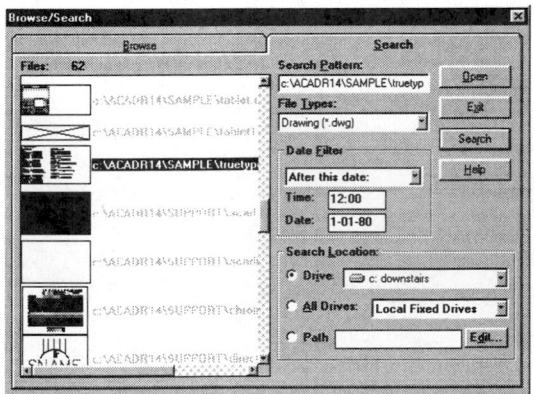

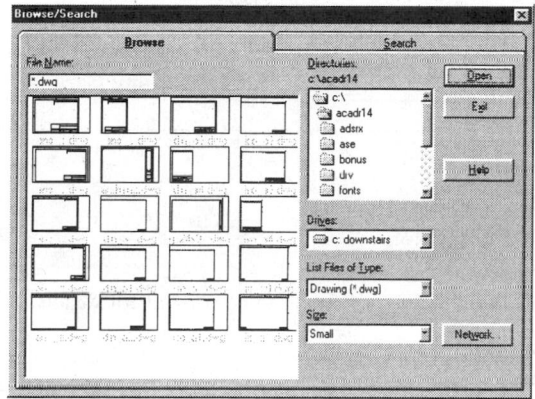

RELATED COMMANDS

FileOpen	Opens a drawing without a dialog box.
New	Starts a new drawing.
SaveAs	Saves drawing with a new name.

TIPS

■ The **Open** command loads DWG drawing files for Release 14 and earlier.

■ When a pre-Release 14 drawing is loaded, it is converted with the message, "Converting old drawing."

■ To retain a drawing in a pre-Release 14 DWG format, use the **SaveAs** command to rename the file or store it in another subdirectory. As an alternative, use the **SaveAs** command to save the drawing in Release 13 or 12 format.

■ The **Open** command does not load other file formats into AutoCAD. Instead, use these commands:

Command	Meaning
DxfIn	ASCII and binary DXF file format.
DxbIn	DXB file format.
PsIn	EPS (encapsulated PostScript).
Replay	TIFF, GIF, and TGA (Targa).
AcisIn	ASCII-format SAT (save as text) ACIS.
3dsIn	3D Studio files.
VSlide	SLD (slide) files.

OpenURL

Rel.14 Opens a drawing from a URL (*short for OPEN Uniform Resource Locator; an external command in Internet.Arx*).

Command	Alias	Ctrl+	F-key	Alt+	Menu Bar	Tablet
openurl	...	...	...	...	...	...

Command: **openurl**
Displays Open From URL dialog boc.

COMMAND LINE OPTIONS

Open	Load DWG file.
Options	Displays dialog box; see **InetCfg** command for details.

RELATED COMMANDS

AttachUrl	Attaches a URL to an object or an area.
DwfOut	Exports the drawing in DWF format.
InsertUrl	Inserts a drawing as a block from a URL in the current drawing.
SaveUrl	Saves drawing to the URL.

TIPS

- A URL (short for "uniform resource locator") is the universal file naming standard for the Internet. See the **AttachURL** command for more details.

- **OpenURL** cannot transfer files using FTP (short for "file transfer protocol") when your computer is connected to the Internet via a password-protected proxy server.

- You can drag a DWG file from your Web browser into AutoCAD. If your browser is displaying a DWF file, the source DWG file must be in the same subdirectory as the DWF file.

- Files download by the **OpenURL** command are placed in your computer's temporary directory (*default = C:\temp*). Since AutoCAD does not these temporary files, you may erase them.

'Ortho

V. 1.0 Constrains drawing and editing commands to the vertical and horizontal directions only (*short for ORTHOgraphic*).

Command	Alias	Ctrl+	F-key	Alt+	Menu Bar	Tablet
'ortho	...	L	F8	...	...	V15

```
Command: ortho
ON/OFF <Off>:
```

COMMAND LINE OPTIONS
OFF   Turns off ortho mode.
ON   Turns on ortho mode.

RELATED COMMANDS
DdRModes   Toggles ortho mode via a dialog box.
Snap   Rotates the ortho angle.

RELATED SYSTEM VARIABLES
OrthoMode   The current state of ortho mode.
SnapAng   Rotation angle of ortho mode.

TIPS
■ Use ortho mode when you want to constrain your drawing and editing to right angles.

■ Rotate the angle of ortho with the **Snap** command's **Rotate** option

■ In isoplane mode, ortho mode constraints the cursor to the current isoplane.

■ Ortho mode is ignored when entering coordinates by keyboard and in perspective mode.

'OSnap

V. 2.0 Sets and turns off object snap modes (*short for Object Snap; an external command in DdOSnap.Lsp*).

Command	Alias	Ctrl+	F-key	Alt+	Menu Bar	Tablet
'osnap	os	L	F3	TN	Tools ⮑Object Snap Settings	
ddosnap						U22
-osnap	-os					T15 - U21

Command: **osnap** *or* **ddosnap**
Displays dialog box:

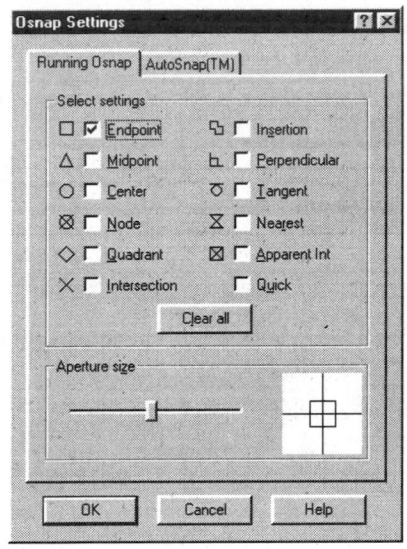

DIALOG BOX OPTIONS

Endpoint	Snaps to the endpoint of an open object, such as a line or arc.
Midpoint	Snaps to the midpoint of an open object.
Center	Snaps to the center of a circle, arc, ellipse, or other circular object.
Node	Snaps to a point object.
Quadrant	Snaps to the 90-degree points on a circle and arc.
Intersection	Snaps to the intersection of two objects or a self-crossing object.
Insertion	Snaps to text or a block insertion point.
Perpendicular	Snaps to the oerpendicular to an object.
Tangent	Snaps to the tangent to an object.
Nearest	Snaps to the nearest point on an object.
Apparent Int	Snaps to the the intersection of two objects that don't physically cross.
Quick	Picks the first snap found.
Aperture Size	Changes the size of the object snap cursor.

AutoSnap tab:

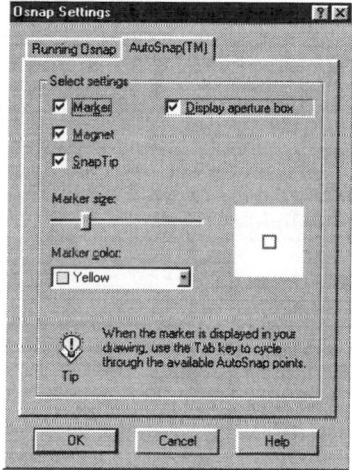

Marker   Toggles display of icon that indicates object snap location.
Magnet   Automatically moves cursor to object snap location.
SnapTip   Toggles tooltip describing object snap mode.
Display Aperture Box
                Toggles display of object snap cursor.
Marker Size   Changes the size of the AutoSnap marker.
Marker Color   Changes the color of the AutoSnap marker (*default = yellow*).

```
Command: -osnap
Object snap modes:
```

COMMAND LINE OPTIONS
For an abbreviation, you need enter the first three letters only:

APParent   Snaps to the imaginary intersection of two objects.
CENter   Snaps to center point of arcs and circles.
ENDpoint   Snaps to endpoint of lines, polylines, traces, and arcs.
FROm   Extends from a point by a given distance.
INSertion   Snaps to insertion point of blocks, shapes, and text.
INTersection   Snaps to intersection of two objects.
MIDpoint   Snaps to middle point of lines and arcs.
NEArest   Snaps to object nearest to crosshairs.
NODe   Snaps to a point object.
NONe   Temporarily turns off all object snap modes.
OFF   Turns off all object snap modes.
PERpendicular   Snaps perpendicularly to objects.
QUAdrant   Snaps the quadrant points of circles and arcs.
QUIck   Snaps to the first object found in the database.
TANgent   Snaps tangent to arcs and circles.

RELATED SYSTEM VARIABLES

Aperture	Size of the object snap aperture in pixels.
AutoSnap	Controls display of AutoSnap:

AutoSnap	Meaning
0	Turns off marker, SnapTip, and magnet.
1	Turns on the marker.
2	Turns on the SnapTip.
4	Turns on the magnet.
7	All turned on (*default*).

OsMode   The current object snap mode(s):

OsMode	Meaning
0	NONe (*default*)
1	ENDpoint
2	MIDpoint
4	CENter
8	NODe
16	QUAdrant
32	INTersection
64	INSertion
128	PERpendicular
256	TANgent
512	NEArest
1024	QUIck
2048	APParent intersection

OsnapCoord   Overrides object snaps when typing coordinates at 'Command' prompt.

TIPS

- Double-click **OSNAP** on the status line to turn on (or off) all object snap modes:

  `-0.2083,2.0636,0.0000          SNAP GRID ORTHO OSNAP MODEL TILE`

- When no object snaps are on, double-clicking **OSNAP** brings up object snap dialog box.

- The **Aperture** command controls the snap area AutoCAD searches through.

- If AutoCAD finds no snap matching the current modes, the pick point is selected.

- The **APPint** and **INT** object snap modes should not be used together at the same time.

- The elements of AutoSnap:

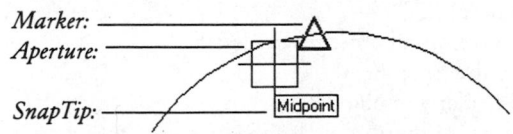

Marker:
Aperture:
SnapTip:

Midpoint

- Press **[Shift]** and right-mouse button to display a popup menu of object snap modes:

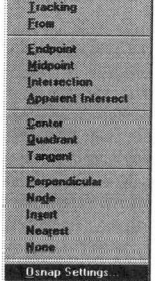

- The location of all object snaps:

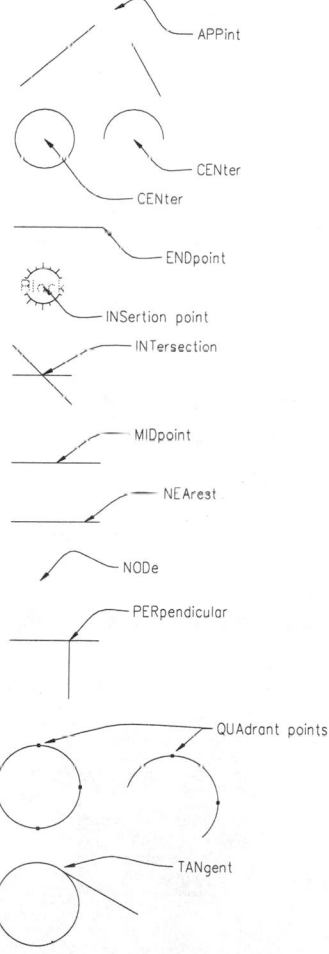

'Pan

V. 1.0 Moves the view in the current viewport to a different position.

Command	Alias	Ctrl+	F-key	Alt+	Menu Bar	Tablet
'pan	p	...	...	VP	View	N11-
					⬏ Pan	P11
-pan	-p					
rtpan						

Command: **pan** *or* **rtpan**
Press Esc or Enter to exit, or right-click to activate pop-up
   menu. [**move cursor**]
Goes into real-time panning mode; displays hand cursor:

As you move the hand cursor, the drawing pans in the viewport.
Press [Enter] or [Esc] to return to the 'Command' prompt.

Command: **-pan**
Displacement: [**pick**]
Second point: [**pick**]

Before panning to the left: *After panning to the left:*

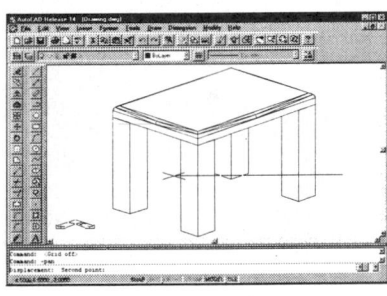   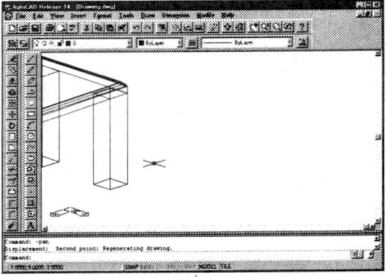

COMMAND LINE OPTIONS

[Enter] Exits real-time panning mode.
[Esc] Exits real-time panning mode.
Displacement Specifies the distance and direction to pan the view.
Second point Pans to here.

RIGHT-CLICK OPTIONS

Exit real-time pan mode: —— Exit
Real-time pan: —— ✓ Pan
Real-time zoom: —— Zoom
Zoom window: —— Zoom Window
Previous view: —— Zoom Previous
Zoom to drawing extents: —— Zoom Extents

RELATED COMMANDS

DsViewer	Aerial View pans in an independent window.
DView	Pans during perspective mode.
RegenAuto	Determines how regenerations are handled.
View	Saves and restores named views.
Zoom	The **Dynamic** option includes a pan option.

RELATED SYSTEM VARIABLES

ViewCtr	The x,y-coordinate of the view's center.
ViewDir	View direction relative to UCS.
ViewSize	Height of view in units.

TIPS

■ You pan in each viewport independently.

■ You can use the '**Pan** command transparently to start drawing an object in one area of the drawing, pan over, then continue drawing in another area of the drawing.

■ Change the **Static** button (of the Aerial View window) to **Dynamic** to perform real-time panning; the drawing pans as quickly as you move the mouse.

■ You cannot use transparent pan during:
  Paper space.
  Perspective mode.
  VPoint command.
  DView command.
  Another **Pan**, **View**, or **Zoom** command.

■ The **DView** command has its own **Pan** option.

■ When the drawing no longer moves during real-time panning, you reach the panning limit. AutoCAD changes the hand icon to show the limit:

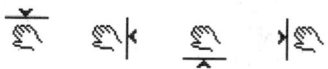

PasteClip

Rel.13 Places an object from Windows Clipboard in the drawing (*short for PASTE CLIPboard*).

Command	Alias	Ctrl+	F-key	Alt+	Menu Bar	Tablet
pasteclip	pa	V	...	EP	Edit	U13
					↳Paste	

Command: **pasteclip**

Pastes contents of the Clipboard into the upper-left corner of the current viewport:

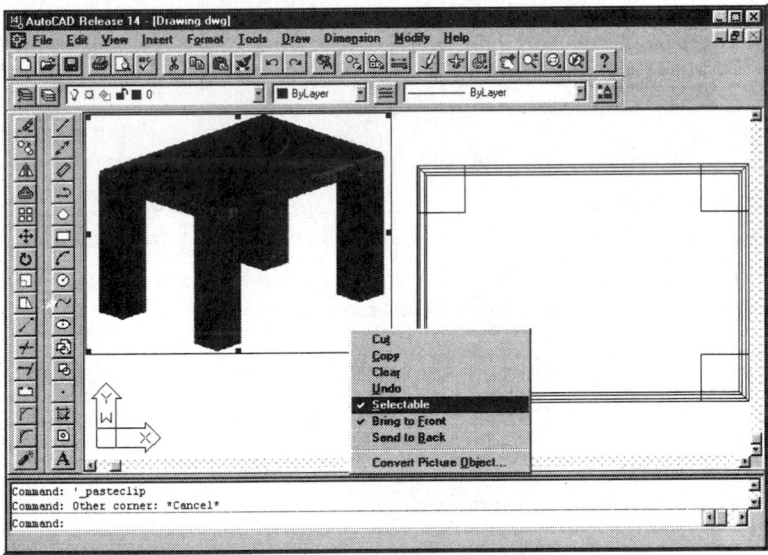

RIGHT-CLICK OPTIONS

After pasting, right-click to display cursor menu:

Cut	Cuts object from drawing to Windows Clipboard.
Copy	Copies object to Clipboard.
Clear	Erases pasted object.
Undo	Undoes last action.
Selectable	Toggles the selectability of the object; handles disappear.
Bring to Front	Displays object topmost in drawing.
Send to Back	Displays overlapping objects over top.
Edit	Edits object in originating application (*not always available*).

Convert   Converts object to AutoCAD format; displays dialog box:

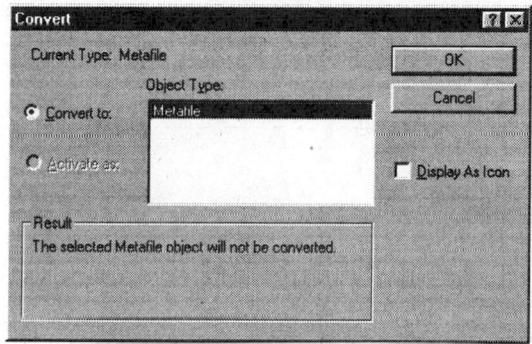

RELATED COMMANDS

CopyClip	Copies drawing to the Windows Clipboard.
DdInsert	Inserts an AutoCAD drawing in the drawing.
InsertObj	Inserts an OLE object in the drawing.
PasteSpec	Places Clipboard object as pasted or linked object.

RELATED SYSTEM VARIABLE

OleHide   Toggles the display of OLE object (*1 = off*).

TIPS

■ The **PasteClip** command places all objects in the upper-left corner of the current viewport

■ Graphical objects are placed in the drawing as an OLE object.

■ Text is placed in the drawing as an MText object.

■ Use the **PasteSpec** command to paste the object as an AutoCAD block.

■ You cannot link an AutoCAD object to AutoCAD:

REMOVED COMMAND:

The **PcxIn** command was removed from Release 14. Use the **ImageAttach** command instead.

'PasteSpec

Rel.13 Places the Clipboard object in the drawing as a linked, pasted, or converted object (*short for PASTE SPECial*).

Command	Alias	Ctrl+	F-key	Alt+	Menu Bar	Tablet
'pastespec	pa	...	...	ES	Edit ⌖Paste Special	...

Command: **pastespec**
Displays dialog box:

Paste (left) and Paste Link (right).

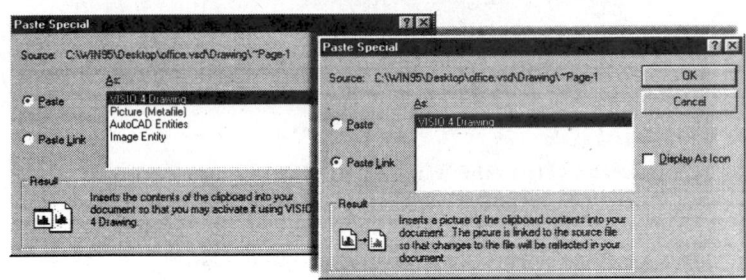

DIALOG BOX OPTIONS

Paste   Paste object as embedded object.
Paste Link   Paste object as a linked object.
Convert   Convert object into an AutoCAD block.
Display as Icon Displays the object as an icon from the originating application.
Change Icon   Allows you to select the icon; displays dialog box:

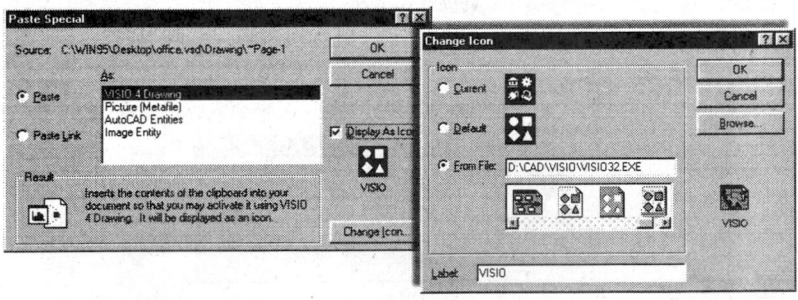

RELATED COMMANDS

CopyClip   Copies drawing to the Windows Clipboard.
InsertObj   Inserts an OLE object in the drawing.
OleLinks   Edits OLE link data.
PasteClip   Places Clipboard object as pasted object.

RELATED SYSTEM VARIABLE

OleHide   Toggles the display of OLE object (*1 = off*).

PEdit

V. 2.1 Edits a 2D polyline, 3D polyline, or 3D mesh — depending on which object is picked (*short for Polyline EDIT*).

Command	Alias	Ctrl+	F-key	Alt+	Menu Bar	Tablet
pedit	pe	...	...	MOP	Modify ↳Object ↳Polyline	Y17

Command: **pedit**

The command options vary, depending upon if a 2D polyline, 3D polyline, or polymesh is picked:

2D polyline options:

Select polyline: **[pick a 2D polyline]**
Close/Join/Width/Edit vertex/Fit/Spline/Decurve/Ltype gen
  /Undo/eXit <X>: **e**

Original polyline

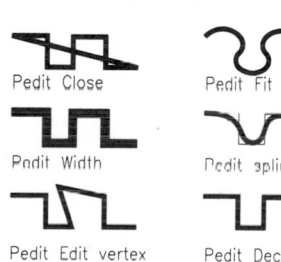

Pedit Close   Pedit Fit curve

Pedit Width   Pedit spline curve

Pedit Edit vertex   Pedit Decurve

COMMAND LINE OPTIONS

Close   Closes an open polyline by joining the two endpoints with a single segment.
Decurve   Reverses the effects of a **Fit** or **Spline** operation.

Edit vertex   Edits individual vertices and segments (*see figure below*):
  Break   Removes a segment or break the polyline at a vertex.
  Next   Moves the x-marker to the next vertex.
  Previous   Moves the x-marker to the previous vertex.

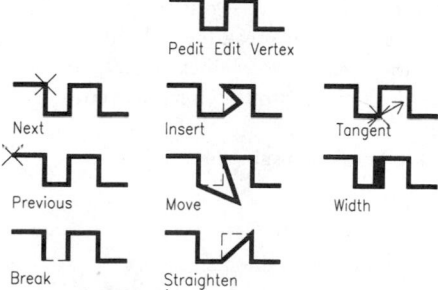

Pedit Edit Vertex

Next   Insert   Tangent

Previous   Move   Width

Break   Straighten

  Go   Performs the break.
  eXit   Exits the **Break** sub-submenu.

Insert	Inserts another vertex.
Move	Relocates a vertex.
Next	Moves the x-marker to the next vertex.
Previous	Moves the x-marker to the previous vertex.
Regen	Regenerates the screen to show effect of **PEdit** commands.
Straighten	Draws a straight segment between two vertices:
Next	Moves the x-marker to the next vertex.
Previous	Moves the x-marker to the previous vertex.
Go	Performs the straightening.
eXit	Exits the **Straighten** sub-submenu.
Tangent	Shows tangent to current vertex.
Width	Changes the width of a segment.
eXit	Exits the **Edit-vertex** submenu.
Fit	Fits a curve to the tangent points of each vertex.
Ltype gen	Specifies linetype generation style.
Join	Adds other polylines to the current polyline.
Open	Opens a closed polyline by removing the last segment.
Spline	Fits a splined curve along the polyline.
Undo	Undoes the most-recent **PEdit** operation.
Width	Changes the width of the entire polyline.
eXit	Exits the **PEdit** command.

3D polyline options:

```
Command: pedit
Select polyline: [pick a 3D polyline]
Close/Edit vertex/Spline curve/Decurve/Undo/eXit <X>: E
Next/Previous/Break/Insert/Move/Regen/Straighten/eXit <N>:
```

COMMAND LINE OPTIONS

Close	Closes an open polyline.
Decurve	Reverses the effects of a **Fit-curve** or **Spline-curve** operation.
Edit vertex	Edits individual vertices and segments:
Break	Removes a segment or break the polyline at a vertex.
Next	Moves the x-marker to the next vertex.
Previous	Moves the x-marker to the previous vertex.
Go	Performs the break.
eXit	Exits the **Break** sub-submenu.
Insert	Inserts another vertex.
Move	Relocates a vertex.
Next	Moves the x-marker to the next vertex.
Previous	Moves the x-marker to the previous vertex.
Regen	Regenerates the screen to show the effect of **PEdit** options.

Straighten	Draws a straight segment between two vertices:
Next	Moves the x-marker to the next vertex.
Previous	Moves the x-marker to the previous vertex.
Go	Performs the straightening.
eXit	Exits the **Straighten** sub-submenu.
eXit	Exits the **Edit-vertex** submenu.

Open	Removes the last segment of a closed polyline.
Spline curve	Fits a splined curve along the polyline.
Undo	Undoes the most-recent **PEdit** operation.
eXit	Exits the **PEdit** command.

3D mesh options:

```
Select polyline: [pick a 3D mesh]
Edit vertex/Smooth surface/Desmooth/Mclose/Nclose/Undo
   /eXit<X>:
```

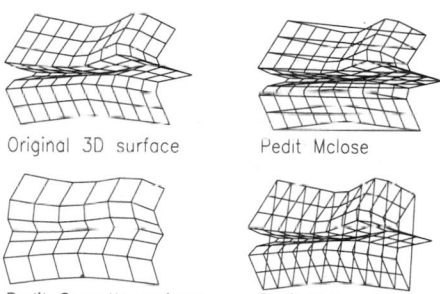

Original 3D surface Pedit Mclose

Pedit Smooth surface Pedit Nclose

COMMAND LINE OPTIONS

Desmooth	Reverses the effect of the **Smooth** surface options.
Edit vertex	Edits individual vertices with the following submenu:
Down	Moves x-marker down the mesh by one vertex.
Left	Moves x-marker along the mesh by one vertex left.
Move	Relocates the vertex to a new position.
Next	Moves x-marker along the mesh to the next vertex.
Previous	Moves x-marker along the mesh to the previous vertex.
REgen	Regenerates the drawing to show the effects of **PEdit**.
Right	Moves x-marker along the mesh by one vertex right.
Up	Moves x-marker up the mesh by one vertex.
eXit	Exits the **Edit-vertex** submenu.
Mclose	Closes the mesh in the m-direction.
Mopen	Opens the mesh in the m-direction.
Nclose	Closes the mesh in the n-direction.
Nopen	Opens the mesh in the n-direction.

Smooth surface Smooths the mesh with a Bezier-spline.
Undo Undoes the most recent **PEdit** operation.
eXit Exits the **PEdit** command.

RELATED COMMANDS
Break Breaks a 2D polyline at any position.
Chamfer Chamfers all vertices of a 2D polylines.
Convert Converts older polylines to the new LWpolyline format.
EdgeSurf Draws 3D mesh.
Fillet Fillets all vertices of a 2D polyline.
PLine Draws a 2D polyline.
RevSurf Draws a 3D surface of revolution mesh.
RuleSurf Draws a 3D ruled surface mesh.
TabSurf Draws a 3D tabulated surface mesh.
3D Draws 3D surface objects
3dPoly Draws a 3D polyline.

RELATED SYSTEM VARIABLES
SplFrame Determines visibility of a polyline spline frame:

SplFrame	Meaning
0	Do not display control frame (*default*).
1	Display control frame.

SplineSegs Number of lines used to draw a splined polyline (*default* = 8).
SplineType Determines Bezier-spline smoothing for 2D and 3D polylines:

SplineType	Meaning
5	Quadratic Bezier spline.
6	Cubic Bezier spline.

SurfType Determines the smoothing using the **Smooth** option:

SurfType	Meaning
5	Quadratic Bezier spline.
6	Cubic Bezier spline.
7	Bezier surface.

TIP
■ During vertex editing, button #2 moves the X-marker to the next vertex.

PFace

Rel.11 Draws multisided 3D meshes; meant for use by AutoLISP, ADS, and ARx programs (*short for Poly FACE*).

Command	Alias	Ctrl+	F-key	Alt+	Menu Bar	Tablet
pface	...	...	...	...	...	...

```
Command: pface
Vertex 1: [pick]
Vertex 2: [pick]
Face 1, vertex 1: 1
Face 1, vertex 2: 2
Face 2, vertex 1: 1
Face 2, vertex 2: 2
```

COMMAND LINE OPTIONS
Vertex	Defines the location of a vertex.
Face	Defines the faces, based on vertices.
Color	Gives the face a different color.
Layer	Places the face on a different layer.

RELATED COMMANDS
3dFace	Draws three- and four-sided 3D meshes.
3dMesh	Draws a 3D mesh with polyfaces.

RELATED SYSTEM VARIABLE
PFaceVMax	Maximum number of vertices per polyface (*default = 4*).
SplFrame	Controls the display of invisible faces (*0 = not displayed; default*).

TIPS

■ The difference between the **3dFace** and the **PFace** commands is that **3dFace** creates 3- and 4-sided meshes, while **PFace** creates meshes of an arbitrary number of sides.

■ Maximum number of vertices in the m- and n-direction: 256 vertices when entered from the keyboard; 32767 vertices when entered from a DXF file or created by programming.

■ **PFace** is meant for programmers; to draw 3D surface objects, use these commands instead: **3d, 3dMesh, RevSurf, RuleSurf, EdgeSurf,** or **TabSurf.**

Plan

Rel.10 Displays the plan view of the WCS or the UCS.

Command	Alias	Ctrl+	F-key	Alt+	Menu Bar	Tablet
plan	...	...	...	V3P	View ↳3D Viewpoint ↳Plan View	N3

```
Command: plan
<Current UCS>/Ucs/World: W
Regenerating drawing.
```

Example 3D view:

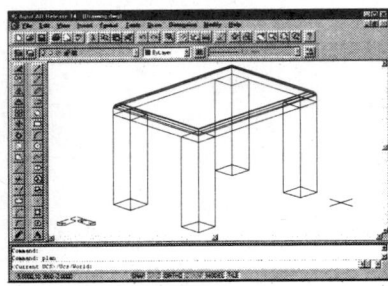

*After using **Plan World** command:*

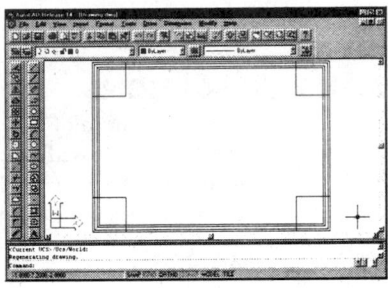

COMMAND LINE OPTIONS
Current UCS Shows the plan view of the current UCS.
Ucs Shows the plan view of a named UCS.
World Shows the plan view of the WCS.

RELATED COMMANDS
UCS Creates new UCS views.
VPoint Changes the viewpoint of 3D drawings.

RELATED SYSTEM VARIABLE
UcsFollow Automatic plan view display for UCS or WCS.

TIPS
■ Typing 'VPoint 0,0,0' is an alternative command to the **Plan** command.

■ The **Plan** command turns off perspective mode and clipping planes.

■ **Plan** does not work in paper space.

■ The **Plan** command is an excellent method for turning off perspective mode.

PLine

<u>V. 1.4</u> Draws a complex 2D line made of straight and curved sections of constant and variable width; treated as a single object (*short for Poly LINE*).

Command	Alias	Ctrl+	F-key	Alt+	Menu Bar	Tablet
pline	pl	...	...	DP	Draw	N10
					⤷Polyline	

```
Command: pline
From point: [pick]
Current line-width is 0.0
Arc/Close/Halfwidth/Length/Undo/Width/<Endpoint of line>:
```

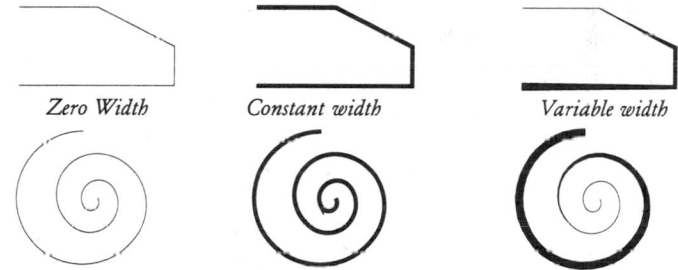

Zero Width   *Constant width*   *Variable width*

COMMAND LINE OPTIONS

Arc options:

Angle	Indicates the included angle of the arc.
CEnter	Indicates the arc's center point.
CLose	Uses an arc to close a polyline.
Direction	Indicates the arc's starting direction.
Halfwidth	Indicates the halfwidth of the arc.
Line	Switches back to the menu for drawing lines.
Radius	Indicates the arc's radius.
Second pt	Draws a three-point arc.
Undo	Erases the last drawn arc segment.
Width	Indicates the width of the arc.

Endpoint of arc
　　　　Indicates the arc's endpoint.

Close	Closes the polyline with a line segment.
Halfwidth	Indicates the half-width of the polyline.
Length	Draws a polyline tangent to the last segment.
Undo	Erases the last-drawn segment.
Width	Indicates the width of the polyline.

Endpoint of line
　　　　Indicates the polyline's endpoint.

RELATED COMMANDS

Boundary	Draws a polyline boundary.
Donut	Draws solid-filled circles as polyline arcs.
Ellipse	Draws ellipses as polyline arcs when **PEllipse** = 1.
Explode	Reduces a polyline to lines and arcs with zero width.
Fillet	Fillets polyline vertices with a radius.
PEdit	Edits the polyline's vertices, widths, and smoothness.
Polygon	Draws polygons as polylines of up to 1024 sides.
Rectang	Draws a rectangle out of a polyline.
Sketch	Draws polyline sketches, when **SkPoly** = 1.
Xplode	Explodes a group of polylines into line and arcs of zero width.
3dPoly	Draws 3D polylines.

RELATED SYSTEM VARIABLES

PLineGen   Style of linetype generation:

PlineGen	Meaning
0	Vertex to vertex (*default*).
1	End to end (*compatible with Release 12*).

PLineWid   Current width of polyline (*default = 0.0*).

TIPS

- Use the **Boundary** command to automatically outline a region; then use the **List** command to find its area.

- If you cannot see a linetype on a polyline, change system variable **PlineGen** to 1; this regenerates the linetype from one end of the polyline to the other.

- If the angle between a joined polyline and polyarc is less than 28 degrees, the transition is chamfered; at greater than 28 degrees, the transition is not chamfered.

- Use the object snap mode **INTersection** to snap to the vertices of a polyline.

Plot

V.1.0 Creates a copy of the drawing on a vector, raster, or PostScript plotter or printer via the serial or parallel ports; or plots to file on disk.

Command	Alias	Ctrl+	F-key	Alt+	Menu Bar	Tablet
plot	print P	...		FP	File ⓑPrint	W25

Command: **plot**
Displays dialog box:

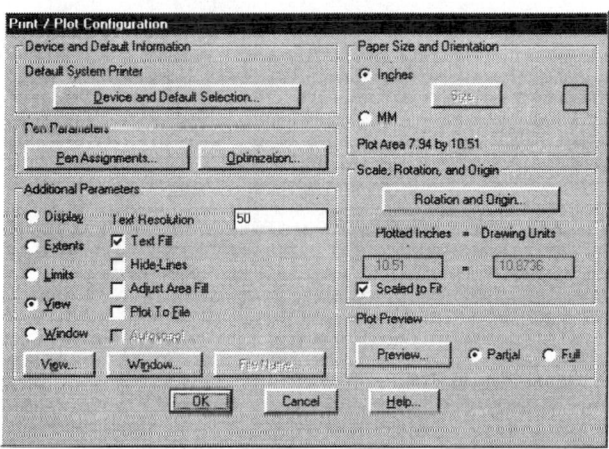

DIALOG BOX OPTIONS
Device and Default Selection options:

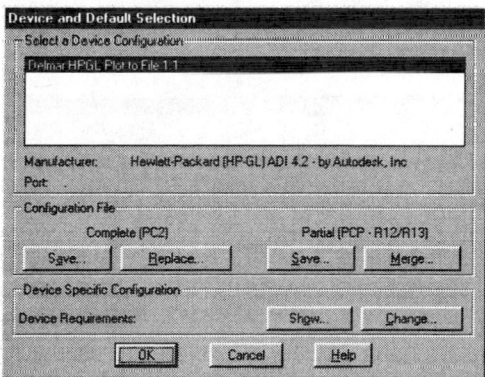

Configuration File options:

Save   Saves plotter configuration in PC2 format (*new to R14*) or PCP format; displays **Save As** dialog box.

Replace   Loads a plotter configuration file and overwrite current configuration; displays **Replace From** dialog box.

Device Specific Configuration options:

Show Displays a dialog box showing the device's current configuration; information varies according to the selected device.

Change Displays a series of dialog boxes that vary with the selected device.

Pen Parameters options:

Pen Assignments

Assign colors, etc, to pen numbers; displays dialog box:

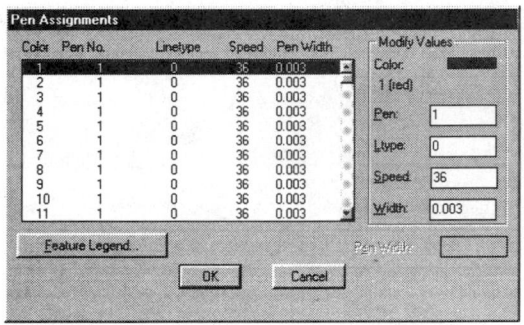

Pen Assignment options *(not all options are available for all devices):*

Color Assigns AutoCAD color number (*cannot be changed*).

Pen Usse this pen number for the AutoCAD color number.

Ltype Uses this plotter linetype for all objects with this AutoCAD color number.

Speed Plots at this plotter pen speed; usually expressed in inches per second.

Width *Raster devices*: width of line to draw.

  Pen plotters: width of pen used.

Pen Width AutoCAD uses this value to determine stroke spacing.

Feature Legend Displays dialog box:

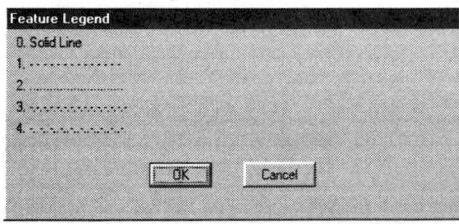

Optimization Select pen motion optimization; displays dialog box:

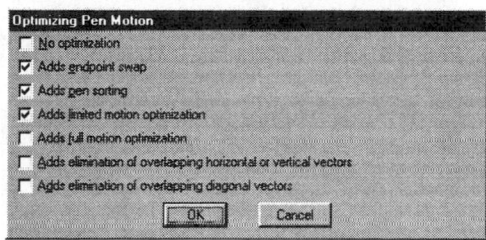

Additional Parameters options:

Display	Plot current display.
Extents	Plot drawing extents.
Limits	Plot drawing limits.
View	Plot named view.
Window	Plot windowed area.
View button	If the drawing contains named views, displays **View Name** dialog box; select a view name and click **OK**.

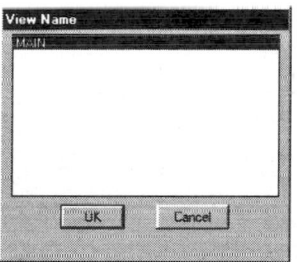

Window	Displays the **Window Selection** dialog box; type corner coordinates or select the **Pick** button to pick the window corners from the screen.

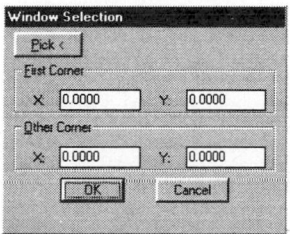

File Name	Displays the **Create Plot File** dialog box.
Text Resolution	Determines quality of TrueType text plotting; range is 0 (*fastest*) to 100 (*best*).
Text Fill	Toggles the filling of TrueType text.
Hide Lines	Remove hidden lines.
Adjust Area Fill	Adjust pen motion for filled areas.
Plot To File	Plot drawing to file.
Autospool	Buffer plot; only available with ADI devices .

Paper Size and Orientation options:

Inches	Specifies that plot parameters should be in inches.
Mm	Specifies that plot parameters should be in millimeters.
Size	Specifies the☐y size of plot; displays dialog box:

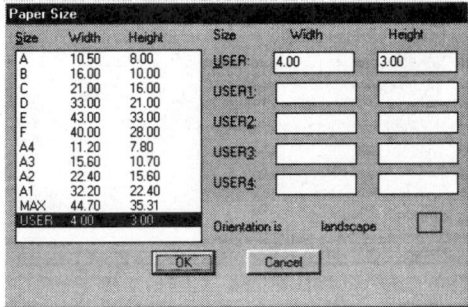

Paper Size options (sizes vary with device):

Width	Specifies the width of user-size paper.
Height	Specifies the height of user-size paper.

Scale, Rotation and Origin options:
Rotation and Origin
Displays dialog box:

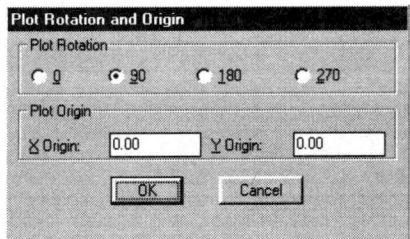

Plot Rotation	Selects a rotation angle.
Plot Origin	Enters coordinates for the plot origin.

Plotted Inches	Scaled plotter units.
Drawing Units	Drawing units.
Scaled to fit	Forces drawing to fit paper size.

Plot Preview options:

Partial   Quick plot preview; displays dialog box:

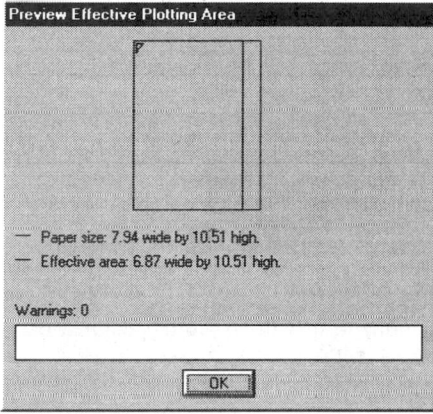

Full   Full plot preview; displays viewport.

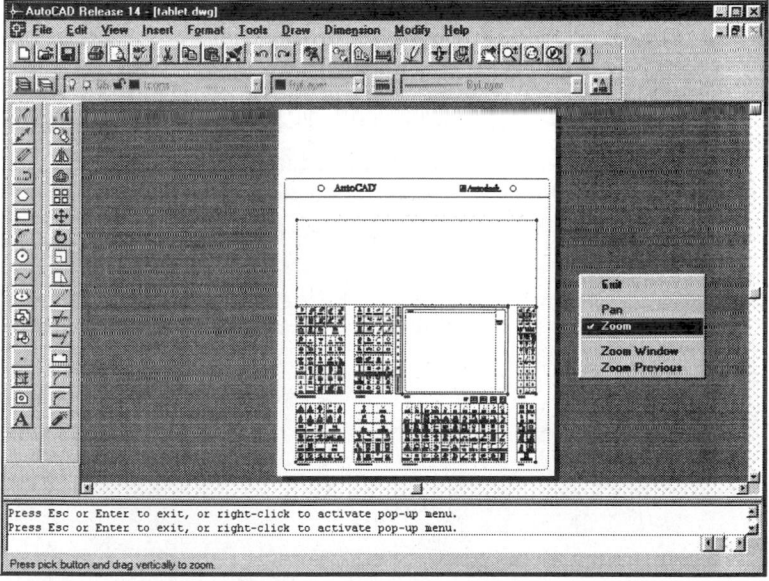

RELATED COMMANDS

Preference Selects one or more plotter devices.
PsOut   Saves a drawing in EPS format.

RELATED SYSTEM VARIABLES

CmdDia	Determines the **Plot** command's interface (*default = 1, display dialog boxes*).
PlotId	Currently selected plotter number.
Plotter	Currently selected plotter name.
TextFill	Toggles the filling of TrueType fonts.
TextQlty	Quality of TrueType fonts.

RELATED FILES

*.PC2	Plotter configuration parameter files.
*.PCP	Plotter configuration parameter files.
*.PLT	Plot files created with the **Plot** command.

RELATED UTILITY PROGRAMS

HpMPlot.Exe	Plotting command specific to plotters compatible with HPGL/2.
OceConf.Arx	Configuration utility for Oce plotters.
PlpCcw.Lsp	Configuration utility for CalComp plotters.

TIPS

- As of Release 12, the **Plot** command replaces the **PrPlot** command.

- As of Release 13, the freeplot feature (starting AutoCAD with the **-p** parameter to plot without using up a network license) is no longer available.

- Plot parameters are stored in PC2 (new to R14) or PCP (compatible with R13) files.

- Don't assume that more levels of optimization produce faster plots. In particular, the elimination of overlapping vectors can dramatically slow down the plotting process.

- AutoCAD cannot plot perspective view to scale, only to fit.

 # Point

V. 1.0 Draws a 3D point.

Command	Alias	Ctrl+	F-key	Alt+	Menu Bar	Tablet
point	po	...	...	DO	Draw ⤷Point	O9

```
Command: point
Point: [pick]
```

COMMAND LINE OPTION
Point   Picks a point or type a 2D or 3D coordinate.

RELATED COMMANDS
DdPType   Dialog box for selecting **PsMode** and **PdSize**.
Regen   A regen is required to see new point mode or size.

RELATED SYSTEM VARIABLES
PDMode   Determines the look of a point:

0	1	2	3	4
32	33	34	35	36
64	65	66	67	68
96	97	98	99	100

PDSize   Determines the size of a point:

PdSize	Meaning
0	5% of height of **ScreenSize** system variable (*default*).
1	No display.
-10	(*Negative*) Ten percent of viewport size.
10	(*Positive*) Ten pixels in size.

TIPS
■ The size and shape of the point is determined by **PdSize** and **PdMode**; changing these values changes the look and size of all points in the drawing with the next regeneration.

■ Entering only x,y-coordinate places the point at a z-coordinate of the current elevation; setting **Thickness** to a value draws the point as a line in 3D space.

■ Prefix the coordinate with * (asterisk) to place a point in the WCS, rather than the current UCS.

■ Use the object snap mode **NODe** to snap to a point.

 # Polygon

V. 2.5 Draws a 2D polygon of between three to 1024 sides.

Command	Alias	Ctrl+	F-key	Alt+	Menu Bar	Tablet
polygon	pol	...	...	Dy	Draw ⤷Polygon	P10

```
Command: polygon
Number of sides <4>:
Edge/<Center of polygon>: [pick]
Inscribed in circle/Circumscribed about circle (I/C): I
Radius of circle: [pick]
```

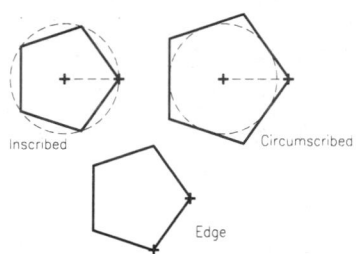

COMMAND LINE OPTIONS
Center of polygon

      Indicates the center point of the polygon; then:

C   (*Circumscribed*) Fits the polygon outside of a circle.

I   (*Inscribed*) Fits the polygon inside a circle.

Edge   Draws the polygon based on the length of one edge.

RELATED COMMANDS
Donut   Draws solid-filled circles with a polyline.
Ellipse   Draws ellipsis with a polyline, when **PEllipse** = 1.
PEdit   Edit polylines, include polygons.
PLine   Draw polylines and polyline arcs.
Rectang Draw a rectangle from a polyline.

RELATED SYSTEM VARIABLE
PolySides Most-recently specified number of sides; default is 4.

TIPS
- Polygons are drawn from polylines; use the **PEdit** command to change the polygon, such as the width of the polyline.

- The pick point determines the location of polygon's first vertex; polygons are drawn counterclockwise.

- Use the system variable **PolySides** to preset the default number of polygon sides.

- Use the **Snap** command to precisely place the polygon.

- Use object snap mode **INTersection** to snap to the polygon's vertices.

Preferences

Rel.11 Lets you set several user preferences.

Command	Alias	Ctrl+	F-key	Alt+	Menu Bar	Tablet
preferences	pr	...	...	TP	Tools ⅍Preferences	Y10

config

Command: **preferences**
Displays tabbed dialog boxes:

Files tab:

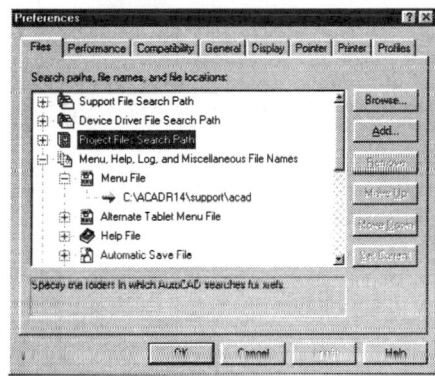

Browse	Displays **Browse for Folder** dialog box .
Add	Adds a path.
Remove	Removes the selected path.
Move Up	Moves the selected path above the preceding path.
Move Down	Moves the selected path below the following path.
Set Current	Makes the selected project or spelling dictionary current.

Performance tab:

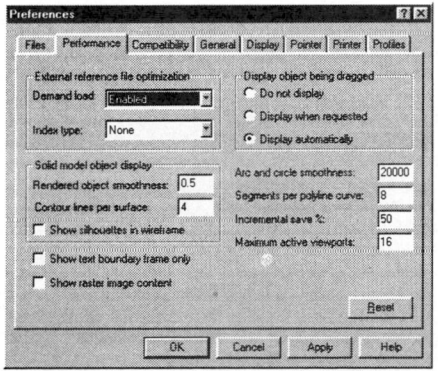

Solid model object display options:
Rendered object smoothness
> Sets the value for system variable **FaceTRes** (*default = 0.5*).

Contour lines per surface
> Sets the value for system variable **IsoLines** (*default = 4*).

Show silhouettes in wireframe
> Sets the value for system variable **DispSilh** (*default = 1*).

Display object being dragged options:
Do not display Sets system variable **DragMode** = 0 (*no drag*).

Display when requested
> Sets system variable **DragMode** = 1 (*use DRAG option modifier*).

Display automatically
> Sets system variable **DragMode** = 2 (*auto drag*).

Show text boundary frame only
> Same effect as the **QText** command; sets the **QTextMode** system variable (*default = 0, off*).

Show raster image content
> Toggles the value of system variable **RtDisplay** (*default = 0, on*).

External reference file optimization options:
Disabled   Demand loading turned off; system variable **DemandLoad** = 0.
Enabled   Demand loading turned on; file cannot be edited while referenced.
Enabled with copy
> Uses a copy of the referenced drawing so that the original can be edited.

Arc and circle smoothness
> Sets the value of the **ViewRes** command (*default = 100*).

Segments per polyline curve
> Sets the value of system variable **SplineSegs** (*default = 8*).

Incremental save %
> Sets the value of system variable **ISavePercent** (*default = 50*).

Maximum active viewports
> Sets the value of **MaxActVP** system variable (*default = 48*).

Reset   Sets preferences back to defaults.

Compatibility tab:

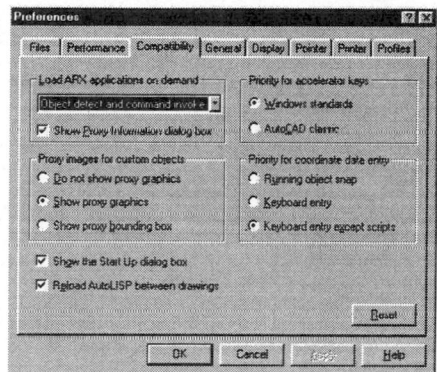

Load ARX applications on demand options (DemandLoad system variable):
Disable load on demand
Custom object detect ·
Command invoke
Object detect and command invoke
Show proxy information dialog box

Proxy images for custom objects options (ProxyGraphics system variable):
Do not show proxy graphics
Show proxy graphics
Show proxy bounding box

Priority for accelerator keys options:
Windows standards
AutoCAD classic

Priority for coordinate data entry options (OSnapCoord system variable):
Running object snap
Keyboard entry
Keyboard entry except scripts

Show the start up dialog box
       Toggles whether the **Start Up** dialog box is displayed when AutoCAD starts.
Reload AutoLISP between drawings
       Sets the **LispInit** system variable.

General tab:

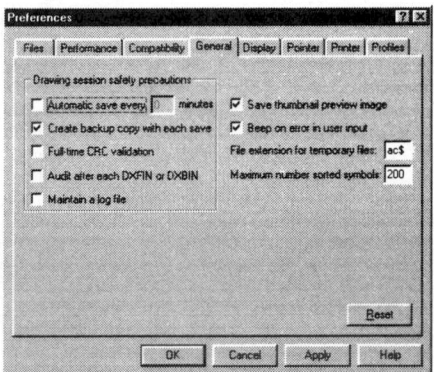

Drawing Session Safety Precautions options:
Minutes between saves
>Sets the value of the **SaveTime** system variable (*default = 15*).

Create backup copy with each save
>Creates a bak (backup) copy of the current dwg file when it is saved.

Full-time crc validation
>DWG file contains cyclic redundancy check data.

Audit after each DXFIN or DXBIN
>Runs the **Audit** command after a DXFor DXBfile is imported.

Maintain a log file
>Equivalent to the **LogFileOn** and **LogFileOff** commands.

Save thumbnail preview image
>Toggles the value of system variable **RasterPreview** system variable.

Beep on error in user input
>Sounds a beep when AutoCAD detects an error.

File extension for temporary files
>A unique network node name for temporary filename (*default = ac$*).

Maximum number sorted symbols
>Sets the value of the **MaxSort** system variable (*default = 200*).

Display tab:

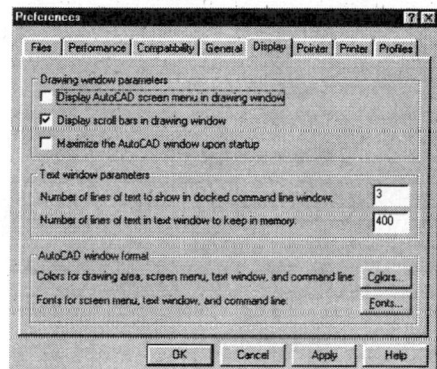

Drawing window parameters options:
Display AutoCAD screen menu in drawing window
> Default = off.

Display scroll bars in drawing window
> Default = on.

Maximize the AutoCAD window upon startup
> Default = off.

Text window parameters options:
Number of lines of text to show in docked command line window
> Default = 3 lines.

Number of lines of text in text window to keep in memory
> Default = 400 lines.

AutoCAD window format options:
Colors   Displays dialog box:

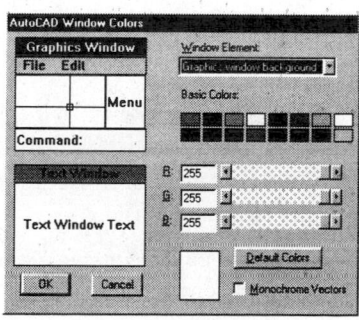

AutoCAD Window Colors options:
Window Element
> Select an element of the window or click on the graphic.

Basic Colors   Select one of 16 basic colors.
R, G, B   Or specify the exact amount of red, green, and blue in the color.

Default Colors Resets color scheme to the factory default.

Monochrome Vectors

> Displays all vectors in the drawing as black (*if background is white*) or white if background is black.

Fonts Displays dialog box:

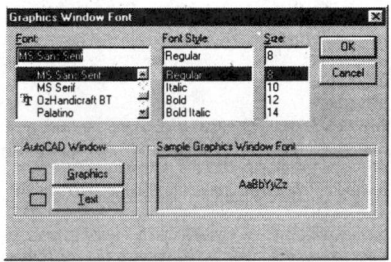

Font	Select a font name.
Font Style	Selects a font style.
Size	Selects a font size (in points).

AutoCAD Window options:

Graphics	Specify fonts for text in graphics window (not drawing).
Text	Specify fonts for text in Text window.

Pointer tab:

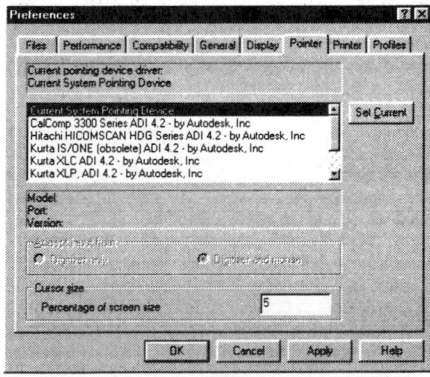

Set Current Select a pointing device from the list.

Accept Input From options (available only when a digitizer is configured):

Digitizer Only Only the digitizing tablet controls AutoCAD.

Digitizer and Mouse

> Digitizing tablet and mouse both control AutoCAD interchangeably.

Cursor Size Sizes the crosshair; range is from 1% of screen size to 99% (full screen) and 100% (invisible); default = 5%.

Printer tab:

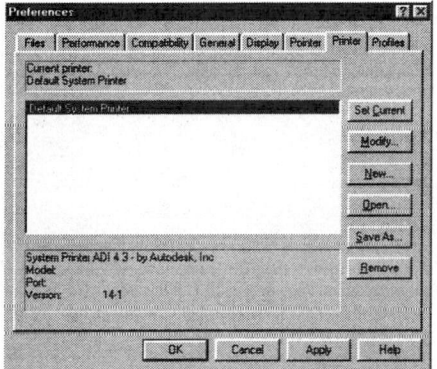

Set Current	Makes the selected printer the current printer.
Modify	Reconfigures selected printer; displays dialog box:

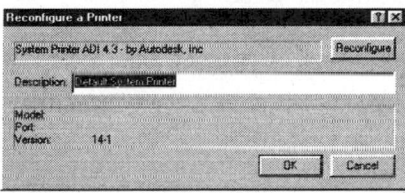

New	Displays dialog box:

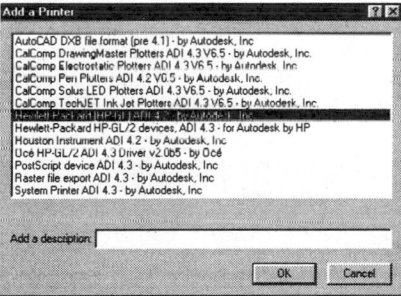

Open	Displays the **Select PC2 File** dialog box.
Save As	Displays **Save As PC2** dialog box.
Remove	Removes printer from list; does not erase device driver.

Profile tab:

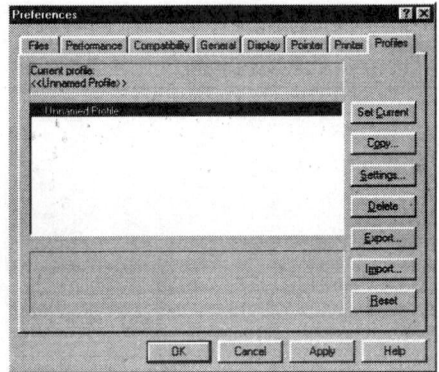

Set Current Makes the selected profile the current profile.
Copy Copies an existing profile; displays the dialog box:

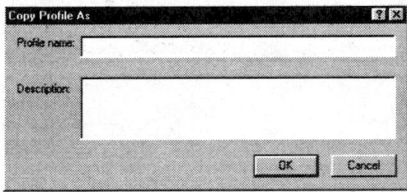

Copy Profile As options:
Profile name Type a name for the new profile.
Description Type a description for the profile to be copied.

Rename Changes the name and/or description of the selected profile; displays a dialog box:

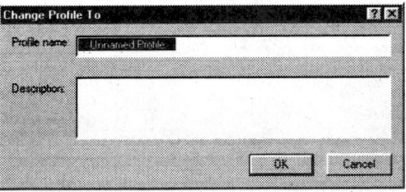

Change Profile To options:
Profile name Type a new name for the profile.
Description Type a description for the profile to be redescribed.

Delete Deletes the selected profile; displays dialog box:

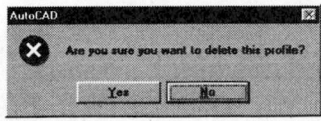

Export   Exports all profiles as a REG file; displays dialog box:

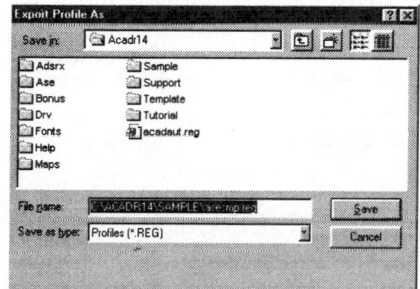

Import   Imports REG profile file; displays **Import A Profile** dialog box.
Reset   Resets values of the selected profile to their defaults.

RELATED FILES
*.DWG   Template drawing files in \Acad14\Template subdirectory.
*.REG   Stores profiles from **Preferences** command.

TIPS
- Use the **Profiles** tab to create named customizations of AutoCAD. You can create profiles for different users or different projects.

- You export REG files for use on other different computers.

Preview

Rel.13   Displays plot preview; bypasses the **Plot** command.

Command	Alias	Ctrl+	F-key	Alt+	Menu Bar	Tablet
preview	pre	...	...	FV	File ↳Print Preview	X24

Command: **preview**
Press Esc or Enter to exit, or right-click to activate pop-up menu.
Displays preview screen:

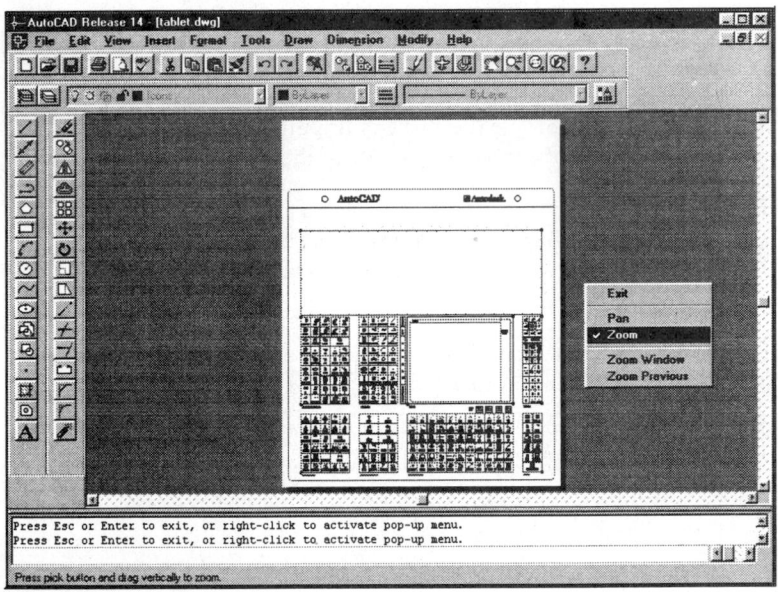

COMMAND LINE OPTIONS
[Esc]	Returns to drawing window.
[Enter]	Returns to drawing window.

RIGHT-CLICK OPTIONS

Exit preview: —— Exit
Plot drawing: —— Plot
Pan view: —— Pan
Zoom view: —— ✓ Zoom
Zoom window: —— Zoom Window
Previous view: —— Zoom Previous

RELATED AUTOCAD COMMAND
Plot	Plots drawing.

PsDrag

Rel.12 Controls the appearance of the PostScript image during the **PsIn** command (*short for PostScript DRAG; an external command in AcadPs.Arx*).

Command	Alias	Ctrl+	F-key	Alt+	Menu Bar	Tablet
psdrag	. . .	. . .	. . .	. . .	. . .		. . .

```
Command: psdrag
PSIN drag mode <0>:1
```

PsDrag set to 0:

PsDrag set to 1:

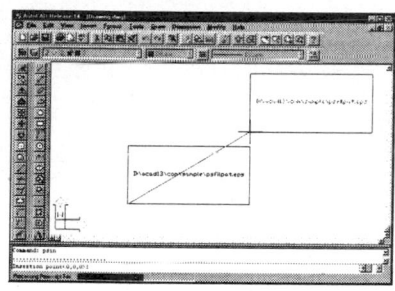
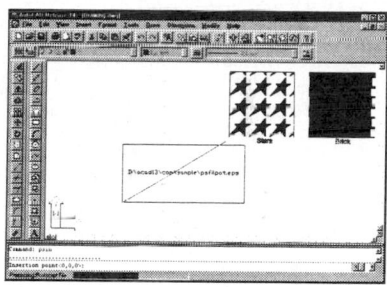

COMMAND LINE OPTIONS

0	Turns off **PsDrag**.
1	Turns on **PsDrag**.

RELATED AUTOCAD COMMAND

PsIn	Imports a PostScript file.

RELATED SYSTEM VARIABLE

PSQuality   Display options for placing an EPS file:

PsQuality	Meaning
75	(*Positive*) Display filled at 75dpi (*default*)
0	Display bounding box and filename; no image.
-75	(*Negative*) Display image outline at 75dpi; no fill.

TIP

■ The **PsDrag** command has no effect when the system variable **PsQuality** is set to zero.

PsFill

Rel.12 Fills a 2D polyline outline with a raster PostScript pattern (*short for PostScript FILL; an external command in AcadPs.Arx*).

Command	Alias	Ctrl+	F-key	Alt+	Menu Bar	Tablet
psfill	...	...	...	...	...	...

```
Command: psfill
Select polyline: [pick]
PostScript pattern (. = none) <.>/?
```

COMMAND LINE OPTIONS

Select polyline Selects the closed polyline to fill.
PostScript pattern

Specifies the name of the fill pattern.

.   Selects no fill pattern.

?   Lists available fill patterns.

*   Don't outline pattern with polyline.

RELATED COMMAND

BHatch   Fills an area with a vector hatch pattern.

RELATED SYSTEM VARIABLE

PSQuality   Display options for placing an EPS file:

PsQuality	Meaning
75	(*Positive*) Display filled at 75dpi (*default*)
0	Display bounding box and filename; no image.
-75	(*Negative*) Display image outline at 75dpi; no fill.

Psin

Rel.12 Imports an EPS (encapsulated PostScript) file into the drawing (*short for PostScript INput; an external command in AcadPs.Arx*).

Command	Alias	Ctrl+	F-key	Alt+	Menu Bar	Tablet
psin	...	...	...	IP	Insert ↳Encapsulated PostScript	...

Command: **psin**
Select filename from dialog box.
Insertion point <0,0,0>: **[pick]**
Scale factor:

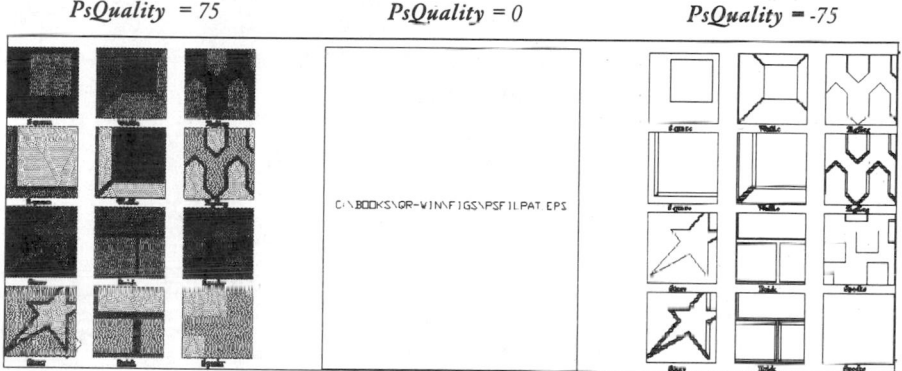

PsQuality = 75 *PsQuality = 0* *PsQuality = -75*

COMMAND LINE OPTIONS
Insertion point Location of the EPS image's lower-left corner.
Scale factor Size of the image.

RELATED COMMANDS
PsDrag Toggles display of bounding box during placement.
PsOut Exports an EPS file.

RELATED SYSTEM VARIABLE
PsQuality Display options for placing an EPS file:

PsQuality	Meaning
75	(*Positive*) Display filled at 75dpi (*default*)
0	Display bounding box and filename; no image.
-75	(*Negative*) Display image outline at 75dpi; no fill.

TIPS
- AutoCAD uses an in-house modified version of GhostScript, a freeware PostScript clone.
- **Psin** places the PostScript as an anonymous block ***U** in the drawing.
- When the EPS block is first placed in the drawing, it is of unit size.

PsOut

Rel.12 Exports the current drawing as an encapsulated PostScript file (*an external command in Acadps.Arx*).

Command	Alias	Ctrl+	F-key	Alt+	Menu Bar	Tablet
psout	...	...	...	FE	File	...
				⇔EPS	⇔Export	
					⇔Encapsulated PostScript	

Command: **psout**
Specify filename in dialog box.
Select Options to display dialog box:

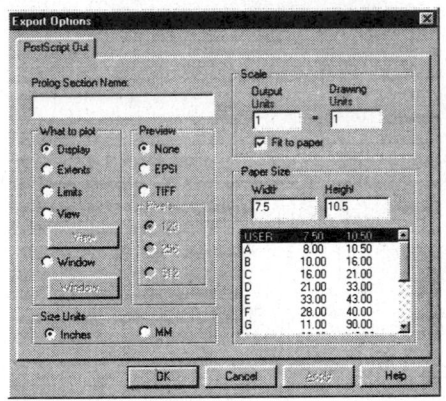

DIALOG BOX OPTIONS

Prolog Section Name

(*Optional*) The name of the prolog section read from the Acad.Psf file; customizes PostScript output.

What to plot options:

Display	Current display in the current viewport.
Extents	Drawing extents.
Limits	Drawing limits.
View	Select a named view.
Window	Pick two corners of a window.

Preview options

None	No preview image (*default*).
EPSI	Macintosh preview image format.
TIFF	Tagged Image File Format.

Pixels options:

128	128x128 pixels (*default*).
256	256x256 pixels.
512	512x512 pixels.

Size Units *options:*

Inches   Specifies plot parameters in inches.
MM   Specifies plot parameters in millimeters.

Scale *options:*
Output Units Scales plotter units.
Drawing Units Specifies drawing units.
Fit to Paper   Forces drawing to fit paper size.

Paper Size *options:*
Width   Types a width for the output size.
Height   Types a height for the output size.

RELATED COMMANDS
Plot   Exports drawing in a variety of formats, including raster EPS.
PsIn   Imports EPS files.

RELATED SYSTEM VARIABLE
PSProlog   Specifies the PostScript prologue information.

RELATED FILE
*.EPS   Extension of file produced by **PsOut**.

TIPS
■ The "screen preview image" is only used for screen display purposes since graphics software generally cannot display PostScript graphic files.

■ When you select the **Window** option, AutoCAD prompts you for the window corners *after* you finish selecting options:

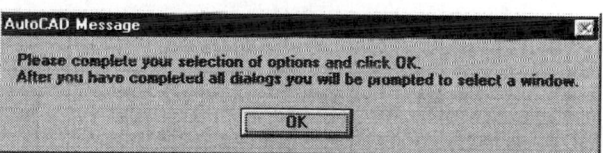

■ Although Autodesk recommends using the smallest screen preview image size (128x128), even the largest preview image (512x512) has a minimal effect on file size and screen display time.

■ Some software programs, such as those from Microsoft, might reject an EPS file when the preview image is larger than 128x128.

■ The screen preview image size has no effect on the quality of the PostScript output.

■ If you're not sure which screen preview format to use, select TIFF.

PSpace

Rel.11 Switches from model space to paper space (*short for Paper SPACE*).

Command	Alias	Ctrl+	F-key	Alt+	Menu Bar	Tablet
pspace	ps	...	...	VC	View ↳Paper Space	L5

Command: **pspace**

COMMAND LINE OPTIONS
None.

RELATED COMMANDS
MSpace	Switches from paper space to model space.
MView	Creates viewports in paper space.
UcsIcon	Toggles display of paper space icon.
Zoom	The **XP** option scales paper space relative to model space.

RELATED SYSTEM VARIABLES
MaxActVP	Maximum number of viewports displaying an image.
PsLtScale	Linetype scale relative to paper space.
TileMode	Must equal 0 for paper space to work.

TIPS
■ Use paper space to lay out multiple views of a single drawing.

■ Paper space is known as "drawing composition" in other CAD packages.

■ When a drawing is in paper space, AutoCAD displays **PAPER** on the status line and the paper space icon:

Enabling paper space.

Entering paper space for the first time can be a mystifying experience, since your drawing literally disappears. Here are the steps:

Step 1: TURN OFF TILEMODE
Command: `tilemode 0`

Step 2: ENTER PAPER SPACE
Command: `pspace`

Step 3: CREATE A VIEWPORT
Although the drawing area goes blank, don't worry: your drawing has not been erased. To see your drawing, you need to create at least one viewport:

Command: `mview fit`

Your drawing reappears!

Step 4: RETURN TO MODEL SPACE
Command: `mspace`

Step 5: ADJUST VIEW SIZE
Use the **Zoom** and **Pan** commands to make the drawing smaller or larger within the paper space viewport.

Step 6: CREATE MORE VIEWPORTS
Switch back to paper space with **PS**.

Create a few more viewports by picking points with the **MView** command.

Try overlapping several viewports.

Switch back to model space with **MS** and set different zoom levels for each viewport.

Step 7: RESIZE VIEWPORTS
Switch back to paper space with **PS**.

Now use the **Move** and **Stretch** commands to change the position and size of the paper space viewports.

Draw a title border around all the viewports.

Other paper space-related command to experiment with: **VpLayer**, **Zoom XP**, and **PsLtScale**.

Purge

V. 2.1 Removes unused named objects from the drawing: blocks, dimension styles, layers, linetypes, shapes, text styles, application ID tables, and multiline styles.

Command	Alias	Ctrl+	F-key	Alt+	Menu Bar	Tablet
purge	pu	...	...	FUP	File ⤷Drawing Utilities ⤷Purge	X25

Command: **purge**
Purge unused Blocks/Dimstyles/LAyers/LTypes/SHapes/STyles/
    Mlinestyles/All: **A**

Sample response:
No unreferenced blocks found.
Purge layer DOORWINS? <N> **y**
Purge layer TEXT? <N> **y**
Purge linetype CENTER? <N> **y**
Purge linetype CENTER2? <N> **y**
No unreferenced text styles found.
No unreferenced shape files found.
No unreferenced dimension styles found.

COMMAND LINE OPTIONS
Blocks	Purges named but unused blocks.
Dimstyles	Purges unused dimension styles.
LAyers	Purges unused layers.
LTypes	Purges unused linetypes.
SHapes	Purges unused shape files.
STyles	Purges unused text styles.
APpids	Purges unused application ID table of ADS and AutoLISP apps.
Mlinestyles	Purges unused multiline styles.
All	Purges drawing of all eight named objects, if necessary.

RELATED COMMANDS
End	Two **End** commands in a row remove spurious information from a drawing.
WBlock	Writes the current drawing to disk (with the * option) and removes spurious information from the drawing.

TIPS
- As of Release 13, **Purge** can be used at any time; it no longer must be used as the first command used after a drawing is loaded.

- It may be necessary to use the **Purge** command several times; follow each purge with the **End** command, then **Open** the drawing and **Purge** again. Repeat until **Purge** reports nothing to purge.

QSave

Rel.12   Saves the current drawing without requesting a filename (*short for Quick SAVE*).

Command	Alias	Ctrl+	F-key	Alt+	Menu Bar	Tablet
qsave	. . .	S	. . .	FS	File	U24 -
					↳Save	U25

Command: **qsave**

COMMAND LINE OPTIONS
None.

RELATED COMMANDS
End	Saves the drawing, without requesting a filename, and ends AutoCAD.
Save	Saves the drawing, after requesting the filename.
SaveAs	Saves the drawing with a different filename.

RELATED SYSTEM VARIABLES
DBMod	Indicates whether the drawing has changed since it was loaded.
DwgName	Current drawing filename (*default* = "*Drawing*").
DwgTitled	Status of drawing's filename:

DwgTiled	Meaning
0	Name is "Drawing" (*default*).
1	Name has been given another name.

TIPS
■ When the drawing is unnamed, then the **QSave** command displays the **Save Drawing As** dialog box to request a file name.

■ When the drawing file, its subdirectory, or drive (such as a CD-ROM drive) are marked read-only, use the **SaveAs** command to save the drawing to another filename, subdirectory, or drive.

QText

V. 2.0 Displays each line of text as a rectangular box (*short for Quick TEXT*).

Command	Alias	Ctrl+	F-key	Alt+	Menu Bar	Tablet
qtext	...	...	...	...	...	...

```
Command: qtext
ON/OFF <Off>: on
Command: regen
```
A regeneration is required before AutoCAD displays text in quick outline form.

Normal text.   *Quick text, after a regen.*

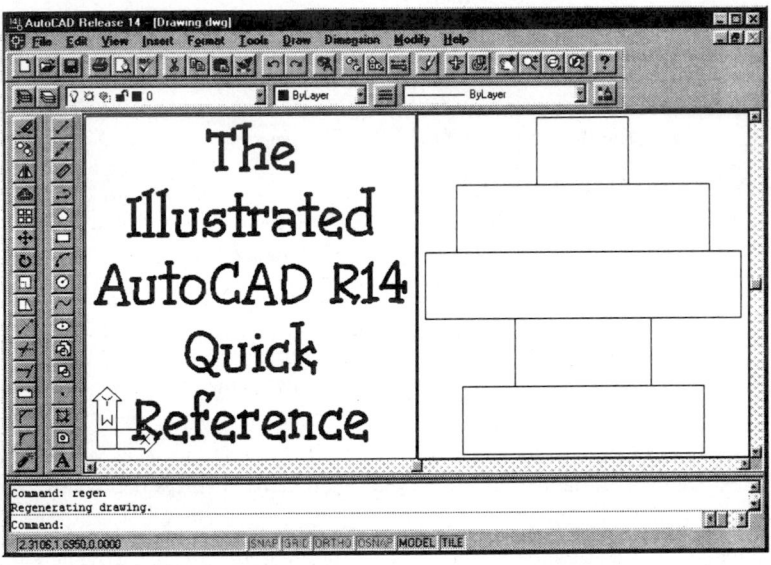

COMMAND LINE OPTIONS
ON   Turns on quick text, after the next **Regen** command.
OFF   Turns off quick text, after the next **Regen** command.

RELATED COMMANDS
DdRModes   Toggles **QText** via dialog box.
Regen   Regenerates the screen; makes quick text take effect.

RELATED SYSTEM VARIABLE
QTextMode   Holds the current state of quick text mode.

TIPS
- To reduce regen time, use **QText** to turn lines of text into rectangles, which redraw faster.

- The length of a **QText** box does not necessarily match the actual length of text.

- Turning on **QText** does not affect text during plotting; qtext blocks are plotted as text.

- To find invisible text (such as text made of spaces), turn on **QText**, thaw all layers, **Zoom** to extents, and use the **Regen** command.

Quit

V. 1.0 Exits AutoCAD without saving changes to the drawing from the most recent **Save** or **End** command.

Command	Alias	Ctrl+	F-key	Alt+	Menu Bar	Tablet
quit	exit	...	...	FX	File ⮡Exit	Y25

Command: **quit**
Displays dialog box:

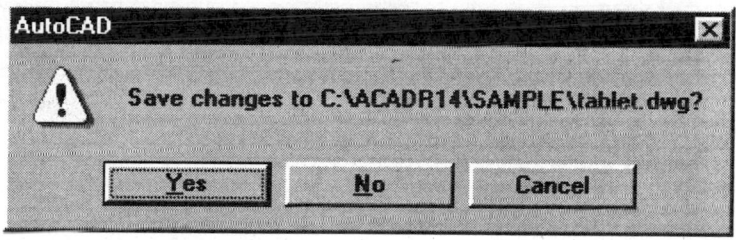

DIALOG BOX OPTIONS
Yes	Saves changes before leaving AutoCAD.
No	Doesn't save changes.
Cancel	Doesn't quit AutoCAD.

RELATED COMMANDS
End	Saves the drawing and exits AutoCAD.
SaveAs	Saves the drawing by another name or to another subdirectory or drive.

RELATED SYSTEM VARIABLE
DBMod	Indicates whether the drawing has changed since it was loaded.

RELATED FILES
*.DWG	AutoCAD drawing files.
*.BAK	Backup file.
*.BK1	Additional backup files.

TIPS
- You can make changes to a drawing, yet preserve its original format: (1) use the **SaveAs** command to save the drawing by another name; and (2) use the **Quit** command to preserve the drawing in its original state.

- Even if you accidently save over a drawing, you can recover the previous version: (1) use the Windows Explorer to rename the DWG file; and (2) use Explorer to rename the backup BAK file to DWG.

- You cannot save changes to a read-only drawing with the **Quit** command; use the **SaveAs** command instead.

 # Ray

Rel.13 Creates a semi-infinite construction line.

Command	Alias	Ctrl+	F-key	Alt+	Menu Bar	Tablet
ray	...	...	...	DR	Draw ⮫Ray	K10

```
Command: ray
From point: [pick]
Through point: [pick]
```

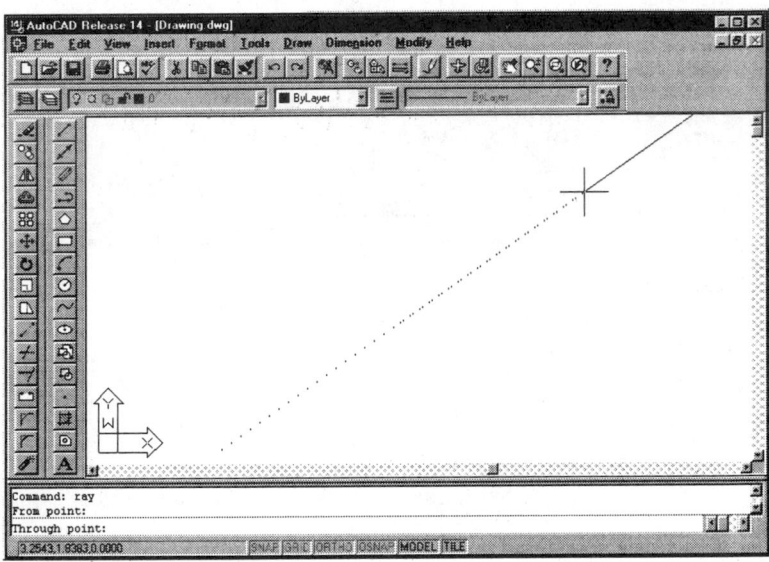

COMMAND LINE OPTIONS

From point Starting point of the ray.
Through point Point through which ray passes.

RELATED COMMANDS

DdModify Modifies a ray.
Line Draws a finite line.
XLine Creates an infinite construction line.

TIPS

- The *ray* object is semi-infinite in length.

- A ray is a "construction line"; it displays but does not plot.

- Ray has all the properties of a line: color, layer, linetype, be used as a cutting edge, etc.

REMOVED COMMAND

RConfig (Render Configuration) was removed from Release 14. It is no longer required.

Recover

Rel.12 Recovers a damaged drawing without user intervention.

Command	Alias	Ctrl+	F-key	Alt+	Menu Bar	Tablet
recover	. . .	. . .	. . .	FUR	File ↳Drawing Utilities ↳Recover	. . .

Command: **recover**
Displays Select File dialog box.

Sample output:
```
Drawing recovery.
Drawing recovery log.
Scanning completed.
Validating objects in the handle table.
Valid objects 8034    Invalid objects 0
Validating objects completed.
Used contingency data.
Salvaged database from drawing.
 8        Blocks audited
Pass 1 7589    objects audited
Pass 2 7589    objects audited
Pass 3 8000    objects audited
Total errors found 0 fixed 0
Regenerating drawing.
```

COMMAND LINE OPTIONS
None.

RELATED COMMAND
Audit   Check a drawing for integrity.

TIPS

- The **Open** command automatically invokes the **Recover** command if AutoCAD detects that the drawing is damaged.

- **Recover** does not ask permission to repair damaged parts of the drawing file; use the **Audit** command if you want control over the repair process.

- The **Quit** command discards changes made by the **Recover** command.

- If the **Recover** and **Audit** commands don't fix the problem, try using the **DxfOut** command, followed by the **DxfIn** command.

◻ Rectangle

Rel.12 Draws a rectangle out of a polyline.

Command	Alias	Ctrl+	F-key	Alt+	Menu Bar	Tablet
rectangle	rec	...	...	DG	Draw ↳Rectangle	...
	rectang					

```
Command: rectangle
Chamfer/Elevation/Fillet/Thickness/Width/<First corner>: [pick]
Other corner: [pick]
```

*Square (left) and rectangle (right) with width drawn with **Rectang** command.*

COMMAND LINE OPTIONS

First corner   Picks the first corner of the rectangle.
Other corner   Picks the opposite corner of the rectangle.

Chamfer options:
First chamfer distance for rectangles
> Sets the first chamfer distance for all four corners; same as setting system variable **ChamferA**.

Second chamfer distance for rectangles
> Sets the second chamfer distance for all four corners; same as setting system variable **ChamferB**.

Elevation option:
Elevation for rectangles
> Sets the elevation, height of the rectangle in the z-direction; same as setting system variable **Elevation** or using the **Elev** command.

Fillet option:
Fillet radius for rectangles
> Sets the fillet radius for all four corners of the rectangle; same as setting system variable **FilletRad**.

Thickness option:
Thickness for rectangles
> Sets the thickness of the rectangle's sides in the z-direction; same as setting system variable **Thickness** or using the **Elev** command.

Width option:
Width for rectangles
> Sets the width of the rectangles four sides; same as setting system variable **PLineWid**.

RELATED COMMANDS

Donut	Draws solid-filled circles with a polyline.
Ellipse	Draws ellipsis with a polyline, when **PEllipse** = 1.
PEdit	Edits polylines, include rectangles.
PLine	Draws polylines and polyline arcs.
Polygon	Draws a polygon — 3 to 1,024 sides — from a polyline.

RELATED SYSTEM VARIABLES

ChamferA	First chamfer distance.
ChamferB	Second chamfer distance.
Elevation	Current elevation.
FilletRad	Fillet radius
PLineWid	Current width of polyline.
Thickness	Current thickness.

TIPS

- Rectangles are drawn from polylines; use the **PEdit** command to change the rectangle, such as the width of the polyline.

- The values you set for the **Chamfer, Elevation, Fillet, Thickness, and Width** become the default for **Rectangle** command.

- The pick point determines the location of rectangle's first vertex; rectangles are drawn counterclockwise.

- Use the **Snap** command and object snap modes to precisely place the rectangle.

- Use object snap mode **INTersection** to snap to the rectangle's vertices.

Redefine

<u>Rel. 9</u> Restores the meaning of an AutoCAD command after being disabled by the **Undefine** command.

Command	Alias	Ctrl+	F-key	Alt+	Menu Bar	Tablet
redefine	...	...	...	...	...	...

Command: **redefine**
Command name:

COMMAND LINE OPTION
Command name
> Names the AutoCAD command to redefine.

RELATED COMMANDS
All commands All AutoCAD commands can be redefined.
Undefine Disables the meaning of an AutoCAD command.

TIPS
■ Prefix any command with a . (*period*) to temporarily redefine the undefinition, as in:

> Command: **.line**

■ Prefix any command with an _ (underscore) to make an English-language command work in any lingual version of AutoCAD, as in:

> Command: **_line**

 # Redo

V. 2.5 Reverses the effect of the most-recent **U** and **Undo** commands.

Command	Alias	Ctrl+	F-key	Alt+	Menu Bar	Tablet
redo	...	Y	...	ER	Edit ↳Redo	U12

Command: **redo**

COMMAND LINE OPTIONS
None.

RELATED COMMANDS
Oops	Un-erases the most-recently erased objects.
U	Undoes the most-recent AutoCAD command.
Undo	Undoes the most-recent series of AutoCAD commands.

TIP
■ The **Redo** command is limited to undoing a single undo, while the **Undo** and **U** commands undo operations all the way back to the beginning of the editing session.

'Redraw

V. 1.0 Redraws the current viewport to clean up the screen.

Command	Alias	Ctrl+	F-key	Alt+	Menu Bar	Tablet
'redraw	r	...	...	...	...	...

Command: **redraw**

Before redraw: *After redraw:*

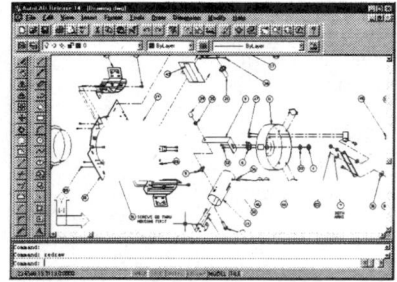   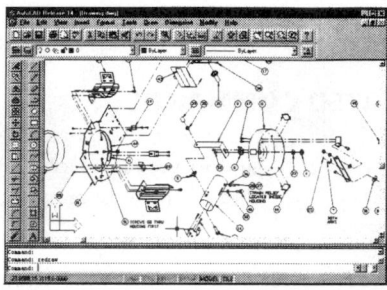

COMMAND LINE OPTION
[Esc]   Cancels the redraw.

RELATED COMMANDS
RedrawAll   Redraws all viewports.
Regen   Regenerates the current viewport.
Zoom   As of Release 14, most operations of the **Zoom** command no longer cause a regeneration.

RELATED SYSTEM VARIABLE
SortEnts   Controls the order of redrawing objects:

SortEnts	Meaning
0	Sorted by order in the drawing database.
1	Sorted for object selection.
2	Sorted for object snap.
4	Sorted for redraw.
8	Sorted for creating slides.
16	Sorted for regenerations.
32	Sorted for plotting.
64	Sorted for PostScript plotting.

TIPS
■ Use **Redraw** to clean up the screen after a lot of editing; some commands automatically redraw the screen when they are done.

■ **Redraw** does not affect objects on frozen layers.

■ Use the **RedrawAll** command to redraw all viewports.

'RedrawAll

Rel.10 Redraws all viewports to clean up the screen.

Command	Alias	Ctrl+	F-key	Alt+	Menu Bar	Tablet
'redrawall	ra	...	...	VR	View	Q11-
					↳Redraw	R11

Command: **redrawall**

COMMAND LINE OPTION
[Esc]   Cancels the redraw.

RELATED COMMANDS
Redraw   Redraws only the current viewport.
RegenAll Regenerates all viewports.

RELATED SYSTEM VARIABLE
SortEnts Controls the order of redrawing objects:

SortEnts	Meaning
0	Sorted by order in the drawing database.
1	Sorted for object selection.
2	Sorted for object snap.
4	Sorted for redraw.
8	Sorted for creating slides.
16	Sorted for regeneration.
32	Sorted for plotting.
64	Sorted for PostScript plotting.

TIPS
- **RedrawAll** does not affect objects on frozen layers.
- Use the **Redraw** command to redraw a single viewport.

Regen

<u>V. 1.0</u> Regenerates the current viewport to update the drawing.

Command	Alias	Ctrl+	F-key	Alt+	Menu Bar	Tablet
regen	re	...	...	VG	View ↳Regen	J1

```
Command: regen
Regenerating drawing.
```

COMMAND LINE OPTION
[Esc]   Cancels the regeneration.

RELATED COMMANDS
Redraw   Quickly cleans up the current viewport.
RegenAll   Regenerates all viewports.
RegenAuto   Checks with you before doing most regenerations.
ViewRes   Controls whether zooms and pans are regens or redraws.

RELATED SYSTEM VARIABLE
RegenMode   Current setting of automatic regeneration:

RegenMode	Meaning
0	Off.
1	On (*default*).

TIPS
- Some commands automatically force a regeneration of the screen; other commands queue the regen.

- The **Regen** command reindexes the drawing database for better display and object selection performance.

- To save on regeneration time, freeze layers you are not working with, apply **QText** to turn text into rectangles, and place hatching last on its own layer.

- Use the **RegenAll** command to regenerate all viewports.

RegenAll

Rel.10   Regenerates all viewports.

Command	Alias	Ctrl+	F-key	Alt+	Menu Bar	Tablet
regenall	rea	...	...	VA	View ↳Regen All	K1

Command: **regenall**
Regenerating drawing.

COMMAND LINE OPTION
[Esc]   Cancels the regeneration process.

RELATED COMMANDS
RedrawAll   Redraws all viewports.
Regen   Regenerates the current viewport.
RegenAuto   Checks with you before doing most regenerations.
ViewRes   Controls whether zooms and pans are regens or redraws.

RELATED SYSTEM VARIABLE
RegenMode   Current setting of automatic regeneration:

RegenMode	Meaning
0	Off.
1	On (*default*).

TIPS
■ **RegenAll** does not regenerate objects on frozen layers.

■ Use the **Regen** command to regenerate a single viewport.

'RegenAuto

V. 1.2 AutoCAD asks you before performing a regeneration, when turned off (*short for REGENeration AUTOmatic*).

Command	Alias	Ctrl+	F-key	Alt+	Menu Bar	Tablet
'regenauto	...	...	...	...	...	...

```
Command: regenauto
ON/OFF <On>: off
```

Example:
```
Command: regen
About to regen, proceed? <Y>:
```

COMMAND LINE OPTIONS
OFF   Turns on "About to regen, proceed?" message.
ON   Turns off "About to regen, proceed?" message.

RELATED COMMANDS
Regen   Forces a regeneration in the current viewport.
RegenAll   Forces a regeneration in all viewports.

RELATED SYSTEM VARIABLES
Expert   Suppresses "About to regen, proceed?" message when value is greater than 0
RegenMode Current setting of automatic regeneration:

RegenMode	Meaning
0	Off.
1	On (*default*).

TIPS
- If a regeneration is caused by a transparent command, AutoCAD delays it with the message, "Regen queued."
- Release 12 reduces the number of regenerations by expanding the virtual screen from 16 bits to 32 bits.

Region

Rel.11 Creates a 2D region from closed objects (*an external command in Acis.Dll*).

Command	Alias	Ctrl+	F-key	Alt+	Menu Bar	Tablet
region	reg	...	...	DN	Draw	R9
					↳Region	

```
Command: region
Select objects: [pick]
Select objects: [Enter]
1 loop extracted.
1 region created.
```

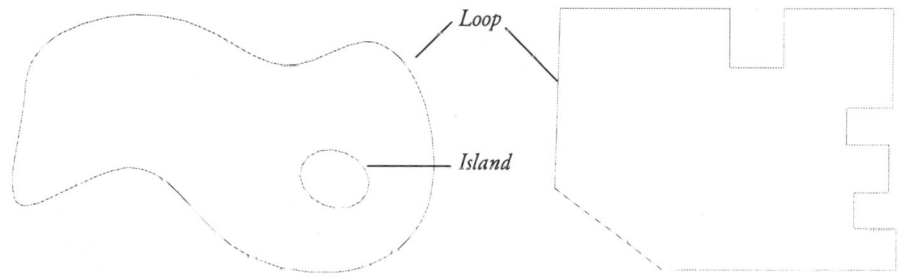

COMMAND LINE OPTION

Select objects   Selects objects to convert to a region; AutoCAD discards unsuitable objects.

RELATED COMMANDS

All.

RELATED SYSTEM VARIABLE.

DelObj   Toggles whether objects are deleted during the conversion by **Region**.

TIPS

- The **Region** command converts closed line sets, closed 2D and planar 3D polylines, and closed curves.

- The **Region** command rejects open objects, intersections, and self-intersecting curves.

- Splined and curve-fitted polylines are not converted into spline objects.

- The resulting region is unpredictable when more than two curves share an endpoint.

- Polylines with width lose their width when converted to a region.

DEFINITIONS

Curve   An object made of circles, ellipses, splines, and joined circular and elliptical arcs.

Island   A closed shape fully within (not touching or intersecting) another closed shape.

Loop   A closed shape made of closed polylines, closed lines, and curves.

Region   A 2D closed area defined as an ACIS object.

Reinit

Rel.12 Reinitializes the digitizer, display, plotter and input-output ports, and reloads the Acad.Pgp file (*short for REINITialize*).

Command	Alias	Ctrl+	F-key	Alt+	Menu Bar	Tablet
reinit	...	...	...	...	...	...

Command: **reinit**
Displays dialog box:

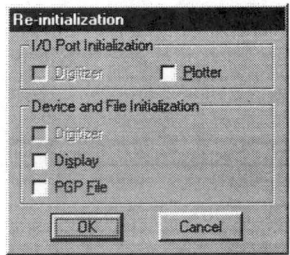

DIALOG BOX OPTIONS
I/O Port Initialization options:
Digitizer   Reinitialize sport connected to digitizer; grayed out if no digitizer configured.
Plotter   Reinitializes port connected to plotter.

Device and File Initialization options:
Digitizer   Reinitializes digitizer driver; grayed out if no digitizer configured.
Display   Reinitialize sdisplay driver.
PGP File   Reloads Acad.Pgp file.

RELATED COMMAND
Menu   Reloads menu file.

RELATED SYSTEM VARIABLE
Re-Init   Reinitializes via system variable settings.

RELATED FILES
Acad.Pgp   The program parameters file in \Acad14\Support subdir.
*.DLL   Device drivers in \Acad14\Drv subdirectory.

TIPS
- AutoCAD allows you to connect both the digitizer and the plotter to the same port since you don't need the digitizer during plotting; use the **Reinit** command to reinitialize the digitizer after plotting.

- AutoCAD reinitializes all ports and reloads the Acad.Pgp file each time another drawing is loaded.

Rename

V.2.1 Changes the names of blocks, dimension styles, layer, linetypes, text styles, UCS names, views, and viewports — via the command line.

Command	Alias	Ctrl+	F-key	Alt+	Menu Bar	Tablet
rename	-ren	...	...	...	...	...

Command: **rename**
Block/Dimstyle/LAyer/LType/Style/Ucs/VIew/VPort:

Example usage:
Command: **rename**
Block/Dimstyle/LAyer/LType/Style/Ucs/VIew/VPort: **B**
Old block name: **diode-20**
New block name: **diode-02**

COMMAND LINE OPTIONS

Block   Changes the name of a block.
Dimstyle   Changes the name of a dimension style.
LAyer   Changes the name of a layer.
LType   Changes the name of a linetype.
Style   Changes the name of a text style.
Ucs   Changes the name of a UCS configuration.
VIew   Changes the name of a view configuration.
VPort   Change sthe name of a viewport configuration.

RELATED COMMANDS

DdLModes   Changes layer names via a dialog box.
DdRename   Dialog box for renaming.
DdUcs   Changes UCS configuration names via a dialog box.

RELATED SYSTEM VARIABLES

CeLType   Name of current linetype.
CLayer   Name of current layer.
DimStyle   Name of current dimension style.
InsName   Name of current block.
TextStyle   Name of current text style.
UcsName   Name of current UCS view.

Render

Rel.12 Creates a rendering of 3D objects (*an external command in Render.Arx*).

Command	Alias	Ctrl+	F-key	Alt+	Menu Bar	Tablet
render	rr	...	...	VER	View ⌐Render ⌐Render	M1

Command: **render**
Displays dialog box:

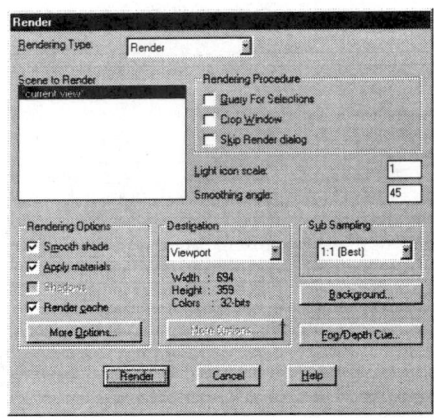

DIALOG BOX OPTIONS

Rendering Type

> Selects between basic **Render, Photo Real**, or **Photo Raytrace**; also lists third-party renderers installed.

Scene to Render

> Lists names of scenes defined by **Scene** command; default = ***Current view***.

Rendering Procedure options:

Query For Selections

> *On*: Prompts you to select the objects to render; unselected objects appear in wireframe in the rendering only when you select the **Merge** options from the **Background** options.
>
> *Off*: Renders all objects in the current viewport.

Crop Window *On*: Prompts you to select a windowed area to render.

> *Off*: Renders the entire current viewport.

Skip Render Dialog

> Does not display the **Render** dialog box the next time you use the **Render** command.

Light icon scale Sizes light blocks Overhead, Direct, and Sh_Spot.

Smoothing angle

> Converts edges to smooth curves. For example, when the angle between two surfaces is greater than the default of 45 degrees, AutoCAD renders an edge; when less than 45 degrees, the edge is smoothed to a curve.

Rendering Options options:

Smooth shade Smooths the edges of multifaced surfaces.

Apply materials Applies surface materials defined by the **RMat** command.

Shadows Generates shadows when Photo Real and Photo Raytrace rendering are selected.

Render cache Caches the objects to help speed rendering.

More options Displays dialog box, which varies according to rendering selected:

Render options:

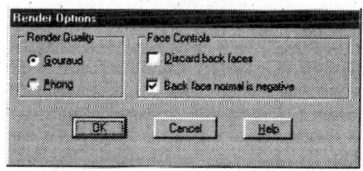

Render Quality options:

Gouraud Calculates light intensity at each vertex; faster.

Phong Calculates light intensity at each pixel; higher quality.

Face Controls options:

Discard back faces

Speeds up rendering by ignoring the backs of objects.

Back face normal is negative

Turn this option off if the rendering creates odd looking objects.

Photo Real Render options:

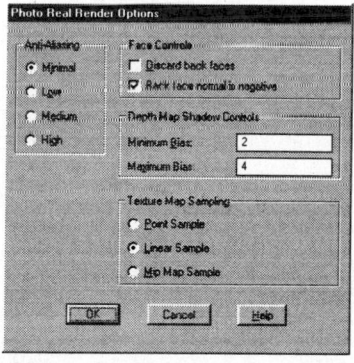

Anti-Aliasing options:

Minimal Renders with analytical horizontal anti-aliasing; fastest.

Low Renders with four samples per pixel.

Medium Renders with nine samples per pixel.

High Renders with 16 samples per pixel; best.

Face Controls options:

Discard back faces
> Speeds up rendering by ignoring the backs of objects.

Back face normal is negative
> Turn this option off if the rendering creates odd-looking objects.

Depth Map Shadow Controls options:

Minimum bias Adjusts shadow map bias to prevent self-shadows and detached shadows (*default = 2.0; ranges from 2.0 to 20.0*).

Maximum bias Limit to 10 more than minimum bias (*default = 4.0*).

Texture Map Sampling options:

Point sample Renders the nearest pixel within a bitmap.

Linear sample Averages the four neighbor pixel pyramidically (*default*).

Mip map sample
> Averages pixels with the *mip* method, which pyramidally averages a square sample area.

Raytrace Render options:

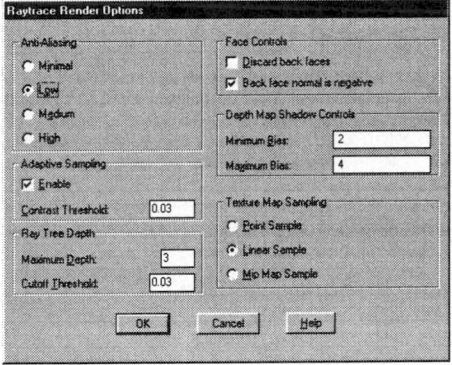

Anti-Aliasing options:

Minimal Renders with analytical horizontal anti-aliasing; fastest.

Low Renders with four samples per pixel.

Medium Renders with nine samples per pixel.

High Renders with 16 samples per pixel; best.

Adaptive Sampling options:

Enable Toggles adaptive sampling; available when minimal anti-aliasing turned off.

Contrast Threshold
> Specifies sensitivity of adaptive sampling; larger values increase rendering speed but might reduce image quality (*default = 0.03; range from 0.0 to 1.0*).

Ray Tree Depth options:

Maximum Depth Limits the ray tree depth to track reflected and refracted rays (*default = 3*).

Cutoff Threshold
> Defines percentage bounce cutoff (*default = 0.03 means 3%*).

Face Controls options:

Discard back faces

> Speeds up rendering by ignoring the backs of objects.

Back face normal is negative

> Turn this option off if the rendering creates odd looking objects.

Depth Map Shadow Controls options:

Minimum bias Adjusts shadow map bias to prevent self-shadows and detached shadows (*default = 2.0; ranges from 2.0 to 20.0*).

Maximum bias Limit to 10 more than minimum bias (*default = 4.0*).

Texture Map Sampling options:

Point sample Renders the nearest pixel within a bitmap.

Linear sample Averages the four neighbor pixel (*default*).

Mip map sample

> Averages pixels with the *mip* method, which pyramically averages a square sample area.

Destination options:

Viewport Displays the rendering in the current viewport.

Render Window

> Displays the rendering in a separate window.

File Saves the rendering to a file on disk; does not display the rendering on-screen.

More Options When **File** selected, displays dialog box:

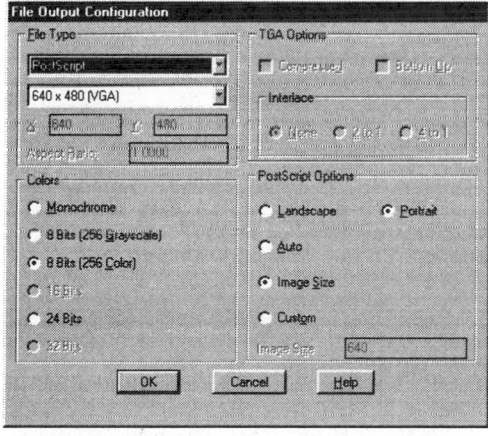

Sub Sampling Renders a fraction of pixels; ranges from 1:1 for best quality (default) to 8:1 for fastest.

Background Displays the **Background** dialog box; see **Background** command.

Fog/Depth Cue

> Displays the **Fog** dialog box; see **Fog** command.

Render Renders the scene.

RELATED COMMANDS

All rendering-related commands.

DView	Creates perspective view.
Hide	Removes hidden lines from wireframe view.
Shade	Simples shadings of 3D objects.

TIPS

- If you do not place a light or define a scene, **Render** uses the current view and places a single light at your eye.

- If you do not select a light or scene, **Render** renders all objects using all lights and the current view.

- To run a quick check rendering, use the **Render Objects** option.

- When outputting to a file, you have the following file format options: GIF, X11, PBM, BMP, TGA, PCX, Sun, FITS, PostScript, TIFF, Fax Group III, and IFF.

REMOVED COMMANDS

The **RenderUnload** command was removed from Release 14. Use the **Arx** command to unload Render.Arx, instead.

The **RendScr** command — which redisplays the most-recent rendering — does not work in Release 14. Use the **Render** command again, instead.

Your first rendering.

■ *Basic rendering:*

Step 1: 3D DRAWING

Create a 3D drawing or select a 3D sample drawing.

Step 2: RENDER

Start the **Render** command, click the **Render** button, and wait a few seconds.

■ *Advanced Rendering:*

Step 1: 3D DRAWING

Create a 3D drawing or select a 3D sample drawing.

Step 2: MATLIB

Use **MatLib** to load material definitions into drawing.

Step 3: RMAT

With the **RMat** command, assign materials to colors, layers, and/or objects.

Step 4: LIGHT

Use the **Light** command to place and aim lights: point, spot, and distant lights.

Step 5: SCENE

The **Scene** command collects lights and a viewpoint into a named object.

Step 6: RENDER

Render the named scene with the **Render** command.

Step 7: SAVEIMG

Use the **SaveImg** command to save the rendering to a TIFF, Targa, or GIF file on disk.

Step 8: REPLAY

View the save rendering file with the **Replay** command.

RENDERING EFFECTS

Wireframe drawing:

Basic rendering; most options turned off:

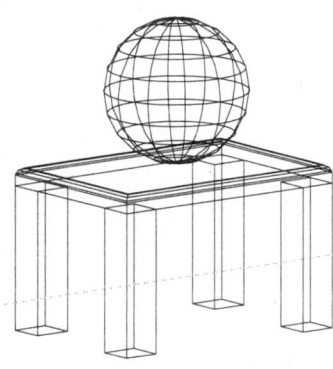

Smooth Shading on:

Attach Materials on; requires Photo Real or Raytrace mode:

Background set to **Gradient**:

And **Background** set to **Image**:

Fog set to white:

And set to black:

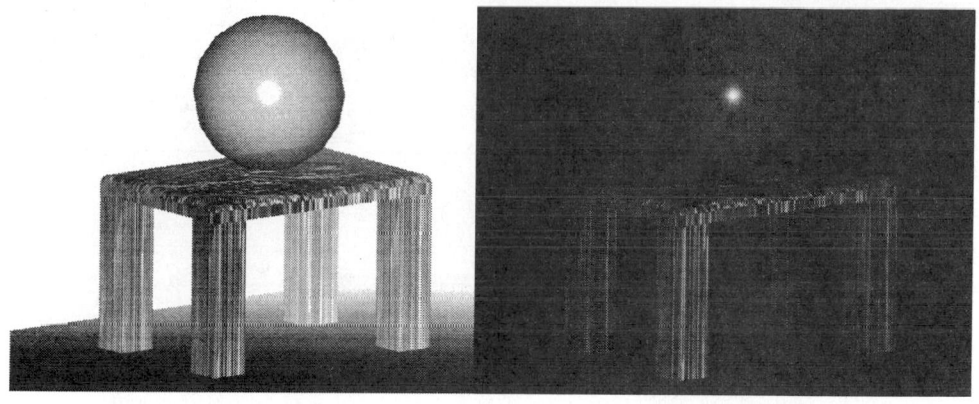

Shadows turned on:

And **Shadow Volumes** turned off:

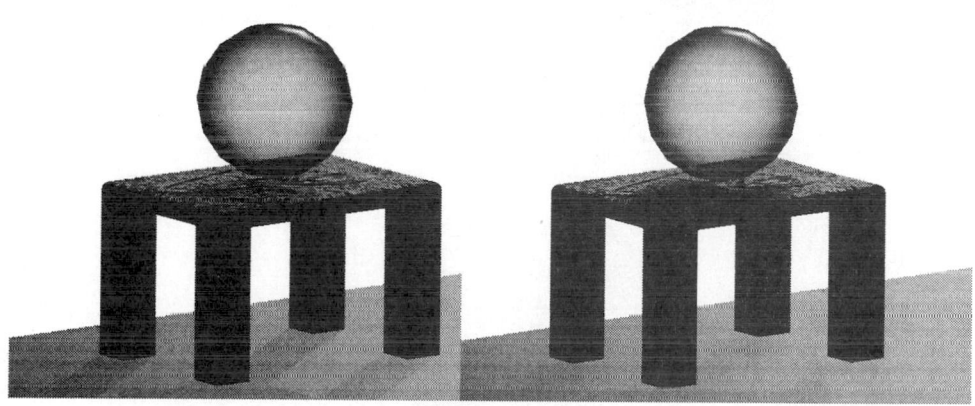

Sub Sampling set to **4:1**:

Replay

Rel.12 Displays a BMP, TIFF, or Targa file as a bitmap (*an external command in Render.Arx*).

Command	Alias	Ctrl+	F-key	Alt+	Menu Bar	Tablet
replay	...	...	...	TDV	Tools	V8
					⤷Display Image	
					⤷View	

Command: **replay**
*Displays **Select File** dialog box; select file.*
Displays dialog box:

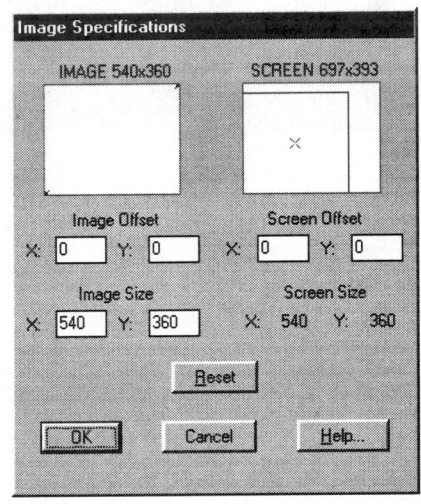

DIALOG BOX OPTIONS

Image	Selects displayed area by clicking on image tile.
Image Offset	Specifies the x,y-coordinates of the image's lower-left corner.
Image Size	Sizes of image in pixels.
Screen	Filsl entire viewport with image.
Screen Offset	Specifies the x,y-coordinates of the image's lower-left corner.
Reset	Restores values.

RELATED COMMANDS

Import	Dialog-box frontend to loading some raster and vector files.
SaveImg	Saves a rendering as a GIF, TIFF, or Targa raster file.

RELATED FILES

*.BMP	Any Windows bitmap file.
*.TIF	Any RGBA TIFF file, up to 32-bits in color depth.
*.TGA	Any RGBA Targa v2.0 file, up to 32-bits in color depth.

In subdirectory \Acad14\Textures:
*.TGA	140 Targa-format images.

'Resume

V. 2.0 Resumes a script file after pausing it by pressing the **[Backspace]** key.

Command	Alias	Ctrl+	F-key	Alt+	Menu Bar	Tablet
'resume	...	...	...	...	...	...

Command: **resume**

COMMAND LINE OPTIONS
[Backspace]   Pauses the script file.
[Esc]   Stops the script file.

RELATED COMMANDS
RScript   Reruns the current script file.
Script   Loads and runs a script file.

Revolve

Rel. I I   Creates a 3D solid object by revolving a closed object about an axis
(formerly the SolRev command; an external command in Acis.Dll).

Command	Alias	Ctrl+	F-key	Alt+	Menu Bar	Tablet
revolve	rev	...	...	DIR	Draw	Q7
					↳Solids	
					↳Revolve	

```
Command: revolve
Select objects: [pick]
Select objects: [Enter]
Axis of revolution - Object/X/Y/<Start point of axis>: [pick]
Angle of revolution <full circle>: [Enter]
```

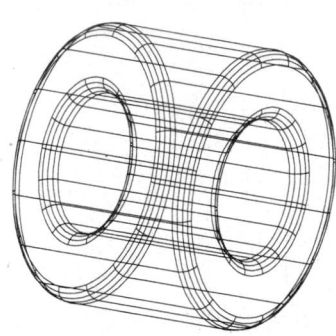

COMMAND LINE OPTIONS

Axis of revolution options:

Object	Selectes object, which determines the axis of revolution
Start point	Indicates the axis of revolution
X	Uses positive x-axis as axis of revolution
Y	Uses positive y-axis as axis of revolution

Angle of rotation
Specifies the smount of rotation; full circle = 360 degrees.

RELATED COMMANDS

Extrude	Extrude a 2D object into a 3D solid model.
Rotate	Rotates open and closed objects, forming a 3D surface.

TIP

- **Revolve** works with just one object at a time.

- **Revolve** works with closed polylines, circles, ellipses, donuts, and polygons, closed splines, and regions.

- **Revolve** will not work with open objects, crossing, or self-intersecting polylines.

RevSurf

Rel.10 Generates a 3D surface of revolution defined by a path curve and an axis (*short for REVolved SURFace*).

Command	Alias	Ctrl+	F-key	Alt+	Menu Bar	Tablet
revsurf	...	...	...	DFS	Draw	O8
					↳Surfaces	
					↳Revolved Surface	

```
Command: revsurf
Select path curve: [pick]
Select axis of revolution: [pick]
Start angle <0>: [Enter]
Included angle (+=ccw, -=cw) <Full circle>: [Enter]
```

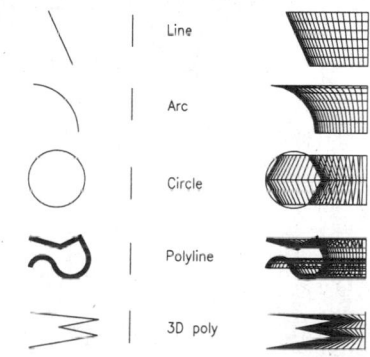

Path Curve + Axis = Resulting Revolved Surface

Line

Arc

Circle

Polyline

3D poly

COMMAND LINE OPTIONS
Full circle Revolves object through 360 degrees.
Included angle Specifies angle of revolution.

RELATED COMMANDS
EdgeSurf Creates a 3D surface bounded by four edges.
PEdit Edits revolved surfaces.
Revolve Revolves a 2D closed object into a 3D solid.
RuleSurf Creates a 3D ruled surface.
TabSurf Creates a 3D tabulated surface.

RELATED SYSTEM VARIABLES
SurfTab1 Mesh density in m-direction (*default = 6*).
SurfTab2 Mesh density in n-direction (*default = 6*).

TIPS
■ Unlike the **Revolve** command, **RevSurf** works with open and closed objects.

■ If a multi-segment polyline is the axis of revolution, the rotation axis is defined as the vector pointing from the first vertex to the last vertex, ignoring the intermediate vertices.

RMat

Rel.13 Applies material definitions to colors, layers, and objects; used by the **Render** command (*short for Render MATerials; an external command in Render.Arx*).

Command	Alias	Ctrl+	F-key	Alt+	Menu Bar	Tablet
rmat	...	...	...	VEM	View ↳Render ↳Materials	P1

Command: **rmat**
Displays dialog box:

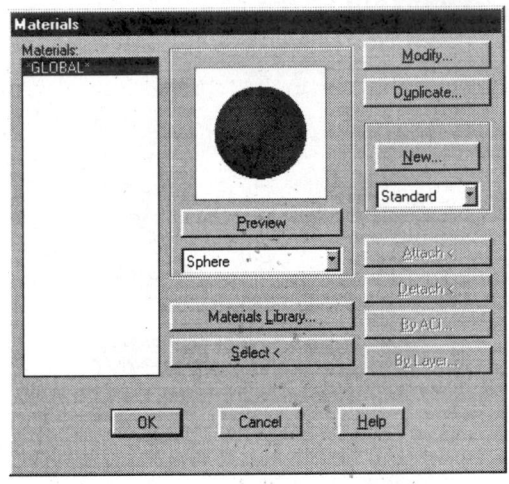

DIALOG BOX OPTIONS

Materials   Lists the names of materials loaded into drawing, by the **MatLib** command.

Preview   Previews the material mapped to a sphere.

Materials Library
    Displays the **Materials Library** dialog box; see **MatLib** command.

Select   Selects the objects to attach the material definition.

Modify   Edits a material definition; displays a different **Modify Material** dialog box for each of standard, granite, marble and wood-based materials (see **New** option).

Duplicate   Duplicates a material definition so that you can edit it; displays different **Modify Material** dialog box for each of standard, granite, marble and wood-based materials (see **New** option).

New   Creates a new material definition; displays a different dialog box for the four types of materials: standard, granite, marble, wood:

New Standard Material dialog box:

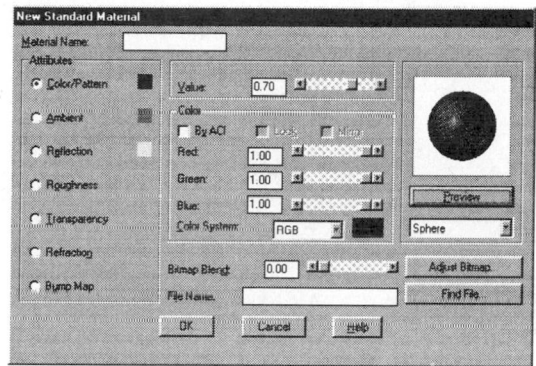

Material Name Names the material.

Attributes *options:*

Color/Pattern Sets the base color of the material.

Ambient Sets the ambient color shown in shadowed areas.

Reflection Sets the highlight color of the material.

Roughness Sets the size of the highlighted area; the higher the value of the roughness, the larger the highlight area.

Transparency Sets the amount of transparency of the material:

Transparency	Meaning
0.0	No transparency
0.1 *through* 9.9	Increasing transparency with edge fall-off.
1.0	Perfectly transparent.

Refraction Controls refraction of the material; Photo Raytrace rendering only.

Bump Map Attach a bitmap to the material.

Value Adjusts the value of some **Attributes** between 0 and a larger number.

Color *options:*

By ACI Material's base color is the same as the object's color.

Lock Locks the ambient and reflective colors to the base color.

Mirror Allows mirrored reflection.

Color System Selects RGB or HLS color system:

Color	Meaning
HLS	Hue, Luminescence, Saturation; 16.7 million colors.
RGB	Red, Green, Blue; 16.7 million colors.

Bitmap Blend Determines the degree the bitmap is rendered.

File Name Bitmap's filename.

Adjust Bitmap Displays the **Adjust Material Bitmap Placement** dialog box.

Find File Selects the bitmap file; displays the **Bitmap File** dialog box.

New Granite Material dialog box:

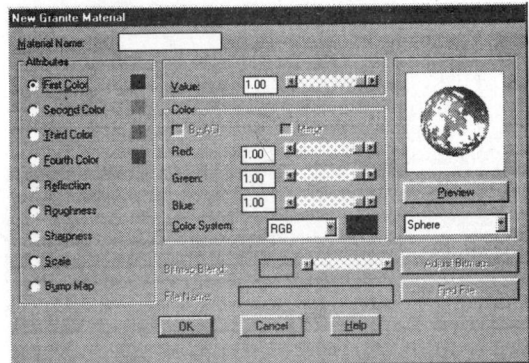

Material Name Names the granite-like material.

Attributes options:

First Color Sets the base color of the granite material.
Second Color Sets the second color of the granite material.
Third Color Sets the third color of the granite material.
Fourth Color Sets the fourth color of the granite material.
Reflection Sets the highlight color of the material.
Roughness Sets the size of the highlighted area; the higher the value of the roughness, the larger the highlight area.
Sharpness Sets the amount of sharpness among the four colors of the material:

Sharpness	Meaning
0.0	Complete blurring of colors.
0.1 *through* 9.9	Increasing sharpness of colors
1.0	All four colors are perfectly distinct.

Scale Sizes the material relative to its attached object.
Bump Map Attaches a bitmap to the material.

Value Adjusts the value of some **Attributes** between 0 and a larger number.

Color options:

By ACI Specifies that the material's base color is the same of the object's color.
Lock Locks the ambient and reflective colors to the base color.
Mirror Allows mirrored reflection.
Color System Selects RGB or HLS color system.

Bitmap Blend Determines the degree the bitmap is rendered.
File Name Bitmap's filename.
Adjust Bitmap Displays the **Adjust Material Bitmap Placement** dialog box.
Find File Selects the bitmap file; displays the **Bitmap File** dialog box.

New Marble Material dialog box:

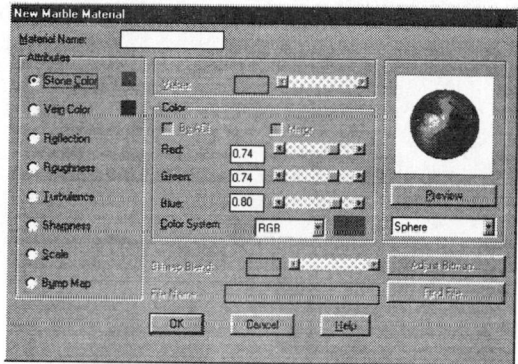

Material Name Names the marble-like material.

Attributes options:
Stone Color Sets the base color of the marble material.
Vein Color Sets the secondary color of the marble material.
Reflection Sets the highlight color of the material.
Roughness Sets the size of the highlighted area; the higher the value of the roughness, the larger the highlight area.
Turbulence Higher values create more swirling of the vein color.
Sharpness Sets the amount of sharpness among the four colors of the material:

Sharpness	Meaning
0.0	Complete blurring of colors.
0.1 *through* 9.9	Increasing sharpness of colors
1.0	Both colors are perfectly distinct.

Scale Sizes the material relative to its attached object.
Bump Map Attach a bitmap to the material.

Value Adjusts the value of some **Attributes** between 0 and a larger number.

Color options:
By ACI Material's base color is the same of the object's color.
Lock Locks the ambient and reflective colors to the base color.
Mirror Allows mirrored reflection.
Color System Selects RGB or HLS color system.

Bitmap Blend Determines the degree the bitmap is rendered.
File Name Bitmap's filename.
Adjust Bitmap Displays the **Adjust Material Bitmap Placement** dialog box.
Find File Selects the bitmap file; displays the **Bitmap File** dialog box.

New Wood Material dialog box:

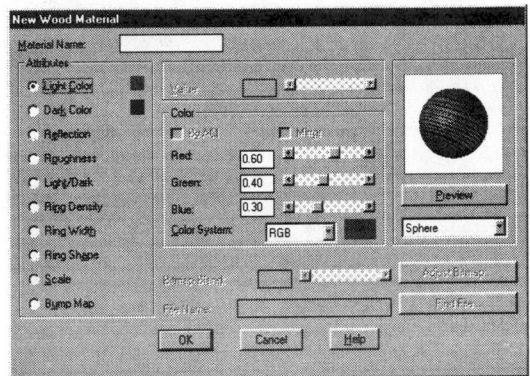

Material Name Names the wood-like material.

Attributes options:

Light Color	Sets the base color of the wood material.
Dark Color	Sets the secondary color of the wood material.
Reflection	Sets the highlight color of the material.
Roughness	Sets the size of the highlighted area; the higher the value of the roughness, the larger the highlight area.
Light/Dark	Sets the amount of contrast between the two colors of the material:

Light/Dark	Meaning
0.0	Dark color.
0.1 *through* 9.9	Increasing lightness of color.
1.0	Light color.

Ring Density	Specifies the number of rings in the material definition.
Ring Width	Variation in ring width; 0 = narrow rings; 1.0 = wide rings.
Ring Shape	0 = circular rings; 1.0 = irregular rings.
Scale	Sizes the material relative to its attached object.
Bump Map	Attaches a bitmap to the material.
Value	Adjusts the value of some **Attributes** between 0 and a larger number.

Color options:

By ACI	Specifies that the material's base color is the same of the object's color.
Lock	Locks the ambient and reflective colors to the base color.
Mirror	Allows mirrored reflection.
Color System	Selects RGB or HLS color system.
Bitmap Blend	Determines the degree the bitmap is rendered.
File Name	Bitmap's filename.
Adjust Bitmap	Displays the **Adjust Material Bitmap Placement** dialog box.
Find File	Selects the bitmap file; displays the **Bitmap File** dialog box.

Attach	Selects the objects to attach the material definition.
Detach	Selects the objects to detach the material definition.
By ACI	Attaches material via ACI number; displays dialog box:

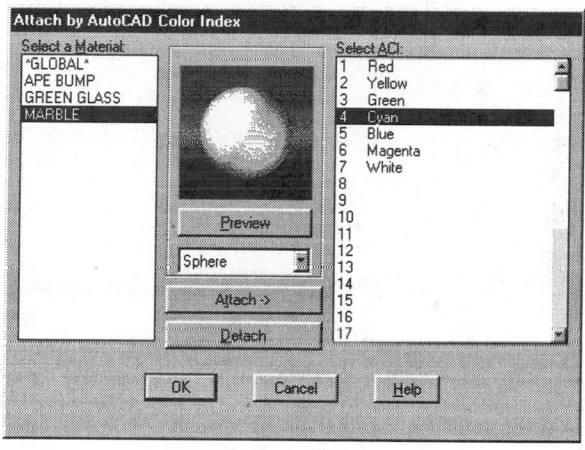

By Layer	Attaches material to layer name; displays dialog box:

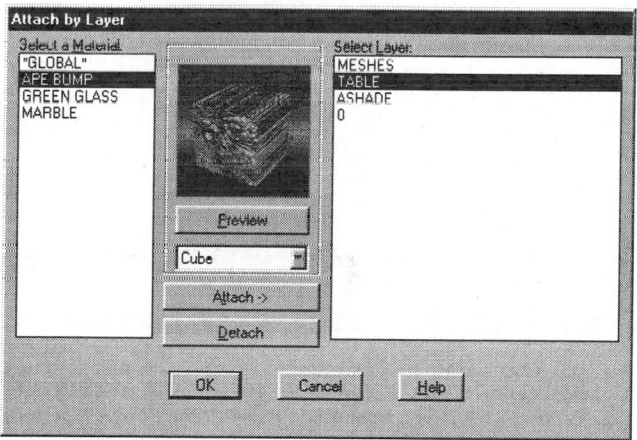

RELATED COMMANDS

MatLib	Load material definitions into drawing.
Render	Render drawing using material definitions.

TIPS

- The **By ACI** option lets you attach a material definition to all objects of one color.

- The **By Layer** option lets you attach a material definition to all objects on one layer.

Rotate

V. 2.5 Rotates objects about a base point in the 2D plane.

Command	Alias	Ctrl+	F-key	Alt+	Menu Bar	Tablet
rotate	ro	...	...	MR	Modify ⤷Rotate	V20

```
Command: rotate
Select objects: [pick]
Select objects: [Enter]
Base point: [pick]
<Rotation angle>/Reference: R
Reference angle <0>:
New angle:
```

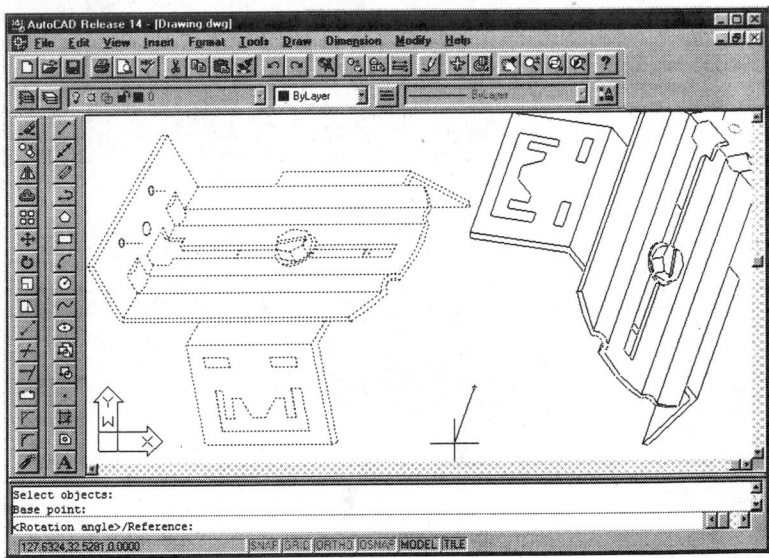

COMMAND LINE OPTIONS

Rotation angle Specifies the angle of rotation; rotation by a relative angle.
Reference Indicates starting angle and ending angle; rotation by absolute angles.

RELATED COMMANDS

Rotate3D Rotate objects in 3D space.
UCS Rotate the coordinate system.

TIPS

■ AutoCAD rotates the selected object(s) about the base point.

■ At the 'Rotation angle' prompt, you can show the rotation by moving the cursor. AutoCAD dynamically displays the new rotated position as you move the cursor.

■ Use object snap modes, such as INTersection, to accurately position the base point, as well as the rotation angle(s).

Rotate3D

Rel.11 Rotates objects about an axis in 3D space (*an external command in Geom3d.Arx*).

Command	Alias	Ctrl+	F-key	Alt+	Menu Bar	Tablet
rotate3d	...	...	...	M3R	Modify ↳3D Operation ↳Rotate 3D	W22

```
Command: rotate3d
Select objects: [pick]
Select objects: [Enter]
Axis by Object/Last/View/Xaxis/Yaxis/Zaxis/<2 points>:
<Rotation angle>/Reference: R
Reference angle <0>:
New angle:
```

COMMAND LINE OPTIONS

Axis by options:

Object	Selects object to specify rotation axis.
Last	Selects last-picked axis.
View	Specifies that the current view direction is the rotation axis.
Xaxis	Specifies that the x–axis is the rotation axis.
Yaxis	Specifies that the y-axis is the rotation axis.
Zaxis	Specifies that the z-axis is the rotation axis.
2 points	Defines two points on rotation axis.

Rotation angle	Rotates objects by specify angle; relative rotation.
Reference	Specifies starting and ending angle; absolute rotation.

RELATED COMMANDS

Align	Rotates, moves, and scales objects in 3D space.
Mirror3d	Mirrors objects in 3D space.
Rotate	Rotates objects in 2D space.

RPref

Rel.12 Specify options for the **Render** command (*short for Render PREFerences; an external command in Render.Arx*).

Command	Alias	Ctrl+	F-key	Alt+	Menu Bar	Tablet
rpref	rpr	...	...	VEP	View ⬦Render ⬦Preferences	R2

Command: **rpref**
Displays dialog box:

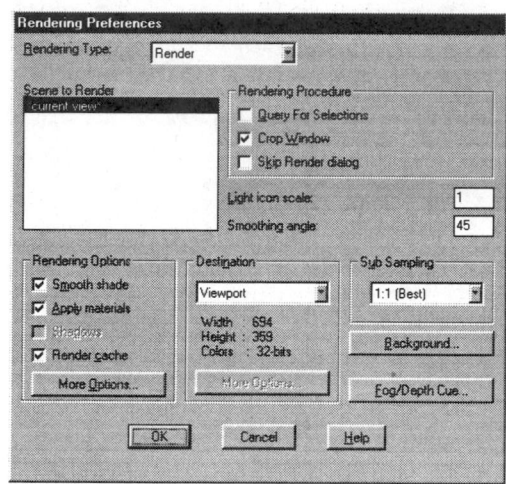

DIALOG BOX OPTIONS

Rendering Type
> Selects between basic **Render, Photo Real,** or **Photo Raytrace**; also lists third-party renderers installed.

Scene to Render
> Lists the names of scenes defined by the **Scene** command; ***Current view*** is the default.

Rendering Procedure options:

Query for Selections
> *On:* Prompts you to select the objects to render; unselected objects appear in wireframe in the rendering only when you select the **Merge** options from the **Background** options.
>
> *Off:* Renders all objects in the current viewport.

Crop Window *On:* Prompts you to select a windowed area to render.
> *Off:* Renders the entire current viewport.

Skip Render dialog
> Does not display the **Render** dialog box the next time you use the **Render** command.

Light icon scale Sizes light blocks Overhead, Direct, and Sh_Spot.
Smoothing angle

> Converts edges to smooth curves. For example, when the angle between two surfaces is greater than the default of 45 degrees, AutoCAD renders an edge; when less than 45 degrees, the edge is smoothed to a curve.

Rendering Options options:
Smooth shade Smoothes the edges of multifaced surfaces.
Apply materials Applies surface materials defined by the **RMat** command.
Shadows Generates shadows when Photo Real and Photo Raytrace rendering are selected.
Render cache Caches the objects to help speed rendering.
More options Displays dialog box, which varies according to rendering selected:

Render options:

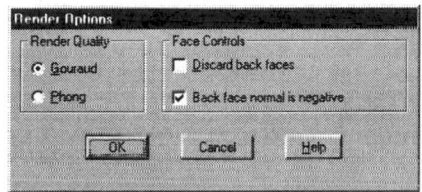

Render Quality options:
Gouraud Calculates light intensity at each vertex; faster.
Phong Calculates light intensity at each pixel; higher quality.

Face Controls options:
Discard back faces

> Speeds up rendering by ignoring the backs of objects.

Back face normal is negative

> Turn this option off if the rendering creates odd-looking objects.

Photo Real Render options:

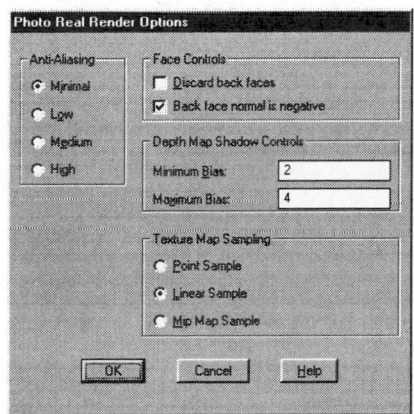

Anti-Aliasing options:

Minimal	Renders with analytical horizontal anti-aliasing; fastest.
Low	Renders with four samples per pixel.
Medium	Renders with nine samples per pixel.
High	Renders with 16 samples per pixel; best.

Depth Map Shadow Controls options:

Minimum bias Adjusts shadow map bias to prevent self-shadows and detached shadows (*default = 2.0; ranges from 2.0 to 20.0*).

Maximum bias Limit to 10 more than minimum bias (*default = 4.0*).

Texture Map Sampling options:

Point sample Renders the nearest pixel within a bitmap.

Linear sample Averages the four neighbor pixels (*default*).

Mip map sample
Averages pixels with the *mip* method, which pyramically averages a square sample area.

Raytrace Render options:

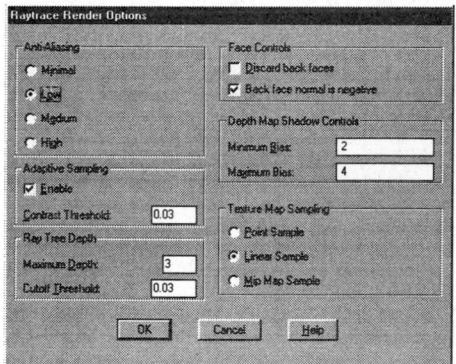

Adaptive Sampling options:

Enable Toggles adaptive sampling; available when minimal anti-aliasing turned off.

Contrast Threshold
Specifies sensitivity of adaptive sampling; larger values increase rendering speed but might reduce image quality (*default = 0.03; range from 0.0 to 1.0*).

Ray Tree Depth options:

Maximum Depth
Limits the ray tree depth to track reflected and refracted rays (*default = 3*).

Cutoff Threshold
Defines percentage bounce cutoff (*default = 0.03 means 3%*).

Destination options:

Viewport Displays the rendering in the current viewport.

Render Window
Displays the rendering in a separate window.

File   Saves the rendering to a file on disk; does not display the rendering on-screen.
More Options When **File** selected, displays dialog box.

File Output Configuration dialog box:

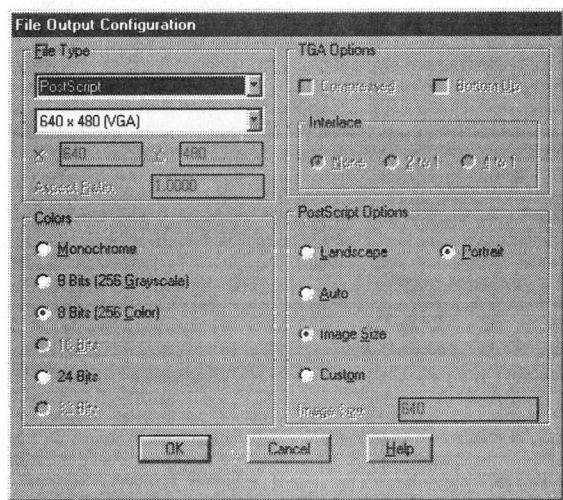

Sub Sampling Renders a fraction of pixels; ranges from 1:1 for best quality (default) to 8:1 for fastest.
Background   Displays the **Background** dialog box; see **Background** command.
Fog/Depth Cue
                  Displays the **Fog** dialog box; see **Fog** command.
Render   Renders the scene.

RELATED COMMANDS

All rendering-related commands.

DView   Creates perspective view.
Hide   Removes hidden lines from wireframe view.
Shade   Produces simples shadings of 3D objects.

'RScript

V. 2.0 Repeats the script file (*short for Repeat SCRIPT*).

Command	Alias	Ctrl+	F-key	Alt+	Menu Bar	Tablet
'rscript	...	...	...	...	...	...

Command: **rscript**

COMMAND LINE OPTIONS
None.

RELATED COMMANDS
Resume   Resumes a script file after being interrupted.
Script   Loads and runs a script file.

RuleSurf

Rel.10 Draws a 3D ruled surface between two objects (*short for RULEd SURFace*).

Command	Alias	Ctrl+	F-key	Alt+	Menu Bar	Tablet
rulesurf	...	...	...	DFR	Draw ↳Surfaces ↳Ruled Surface	Q8

```
Command: rulesurf
Select first defining curve: [pick]
Select second defining curve: [pick]
```

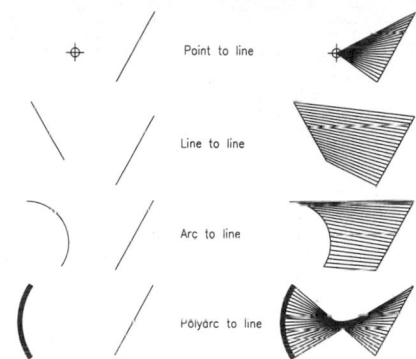

COMMAND LINE OPTIONS

Select first defining curve
> Selects the first object for the ruled surface.

Select second defining curve
> Selects the second object.

RELATED COMMANDS

Edgesurf	Draws a 3D surface bounded by four edges.
Revsurf	Draws a 3D surface of revolution
Tabsurf	Draws a 3D tabulated surface

RELATED SYSTEM VARIABLE

SurfTab1   Determines the number of rules drawn

TIPS

■ **RuleSurf** uses these objects as boundary curve: point, line, arc, circle, polyline, 3D polyline.

■ Both boundaries must be either closed or open; the exception is using the point object.

■ The **RuleSurf** command begins drawing its mesh as follows:

Object	RuleSurf
Open object	From the object's endpoint closest to your pick.
Circle	From the zero-degree quadrant.
Closed polyline	From the last vertex.

■ **RuleSurf** draws with a circle in the opposite direction of a closed polyline.

Save *and* SaveAs

V. 2.0 Saves the drawing to disk, after always prompting for a filename.

Command	Alias	Ctrl+	F-key	Alt+	Menu Bar	Tablet
save	...	...	...	...	...	...
saveas	...	...	...	FA	File ↳Save As	V24

Command: **save** *or* **saveas**
Displays dialog box.

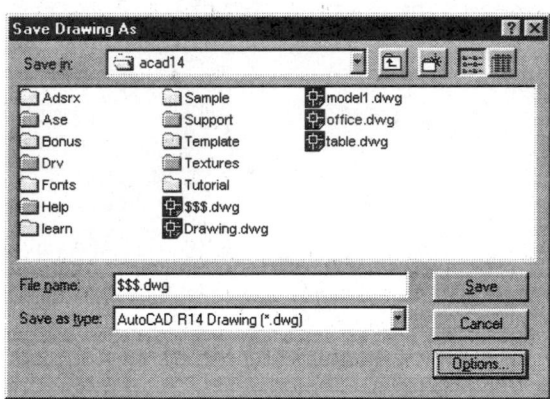

DIALOG BOX OPTIONS

Save in	Selects the subdirectory (folder), hard drive, or network drive.
File name	Names the drawing; maximum = 255 characters (*default = Drawing.Dwg*).
Save as type	Saves the drawing in different DWG versions:

Save as Type	Meaning
R14 DWG	Saves drawing in native format.
R13, LT 95 DWG	Exports drawing in R13 DWG format.
R12, LT 2 DWG	Exports drawing in R12 DWG format.
Template DWT	Saves drawing in \Template subdirectory.

Template DWT displays dialog box:

Template Description dialog box:

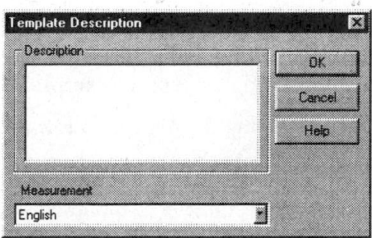

Description	Describes the template file; stored in **Wizard.Ini**.
Measurement	Selects English or metric as the default measurement system.

Save Saves the drawing and returns to AutoCAD. If a drawing of the same name already exists in the same subdirectory, displays dialog box:

Cancel Dismisses the dialog box without saving the drawing.
Options Displays dialog box:

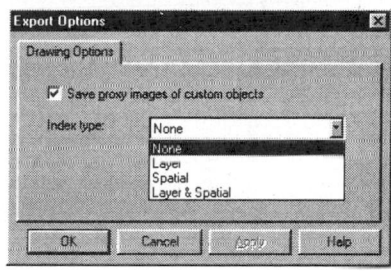

Drawing Options options:
Save proxy images of custom objects

Save	Meaning
On	Saves image of custom object in drawing file.
Off	Saves a frame around each custom object.

Index type Saves indices with drawing

Index type	Meaning
None	No indices created (*default*).
Layer	Loads only on and thawed layers.
Spatial	Loads only visible portion of clipped xrefs.
Layer and Spatial	Loads only on and thawed layers of visible clipped xref drawings.

RELATED COMMANDS

DxfOut	Saves the drawing in DXF format.
End	Saves the drawing and exits AutoCAD.
Export	Saves the drawing in a variety of raster and vector formats.
Plot	Saves the drawing in even more raster and vector formats.
Quit	Exits AutoCAD without saving the drawing.
QSave	Saves drawing without prompting for name.
SaveAs	Saves the drawing.

RELATED SYSTEM VARIABLES

DBMod	Indicates that drawing modification.
DwgName	Name of the drawing; Drawing.Dwg when unnamed.

Saving DWG as Release 13.

The **SaveAs** command translates the drawing to a DWG file format compatible with Release 13. R13 does not display some objects specific to R14; objects are not erased and display again when brought back to R14.

R14 Object	R13 Conversion
Hatch pattern	Solid-filled hatch pattern not displayed.
Drawing order	Not maintained.
Raster image	Empty rectangle.
TrueType font	Path not saved.
ASE links	Must be resynchronized.
Attached xref	Not displayed.
Xclip xref	Clipping is lost.
LwPolyline	Converted to standard 2D polyline.

TIPS

■ The **Save** command always displays the **Save Drawing As** dialog box, unlike other software applications. To avoid the dialog box, use the **QSave** command.

■ Spatial and layer indices improve performance during demand loading but increase the time to save a drawing.

■ To convert these objects to 3D polyfaces, use the **3dsOut** command, re-import with the **3dsIn** command, and then use the **SaveAs** command with the R12/LT2 option.

■ Exert some control over **SaveAs** with the **Explode** and **Xplode** commands, which convert complex objects (such as multilines and 3D solids) into polylines, arcs, and other simpler objects.

■ During conversion, the **SaveAs** command displays a list of changed and deleted objects (called the drawing log); unfortunately, AutoCAD doesn't save the log to disk, unless you first type the **LogFileOn** command to capture the text screen to the Acad.Log file.

■ When an R13 drawing with associative hatching is brought into Release 14 and modified, AutoCAD attempts to upgrade the block hatching to the R14 hatch object. If the conversion does not work, R14 removes the associative information.

■ Release 13 displays PostScript text in the drawing; Release 14 does not create or display PostScript fonts. TrueType font equivalents are provided for the PostScript fonts found in R13.

■ Use the **DxfOut** command to create DXF files compatible with Release 13 and Release 12.

Saving DWG as Release 12.

The **SaveAs** command translates the drawing to a DWG file compatible with Release 12 by: (1) converting R14-specific objects to R12 equivalents; and (2) stripping out objects that cannot be translated into R12 format.

■ These R14 objects are converted (*this list is more accurate than Autodesk's documentation*):

R14 Object	R12 Conversion
Ellipse	Polyarc.
Multiline	Parallel polylines, arcs, filled arcs, filled polygons.
Spline	Splined polyline.
Ray, Xline	Lines cut off at the drawing extents.
Hatch	Pattern associativity is dropped.
Dimension	Remains an associative dimension with text intact.
Leader	Leader line becomes a polyline; arrowhead becomes a solid; MText becomes text.
Tolerance	Polylines and text.
MText	Paragraph text becomes lines of text.
Text styles	TrueType fonts converted to the TXT font.
Bodies, regions and 3D solids	Loose collection of polylines and arcs.

■ These R14 objects are deleted (*this list is more accurate than Autodesk's documentation*):

Text formatting codes specific to MText.
Shapes in linetypes and the global linetype scale in CeLtScale.
Rays and Xlines outside of the drawing extents.
User-defined objects.
Groups and multiline styles.
OLE objects.
Xref overlays and ASE link information.
Preview BMP image.
Render's material assignments.
Dictionary group codes, ADE lock bit, and object visibility flag.
All R14-specific system variables.

REMOVED COMMAND
The **SaveAsR12** command has been removed from Release 14. Use the **SaveAs** command instead; this saves R14 drawings in R13 and R12 formats.

SaveImg

Rel.12   Saves the current viewport image — raster or vector — as a BMP, TIFF, or Targa file on disk (*an external command in Render.Arx*).

Command	Alias	Ctrl+	F-key	Alt+	Menu Bar	Tablet
saveimg	...	...	...	TDS	Tools ⤷Display Image ⤷Save	V7

Command: **saveimg**
Displays dialog box:

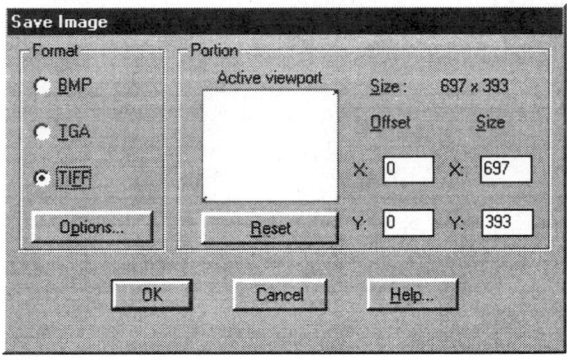

DIALOG BOX OPTIONS

Format options:

BMP	Windows bitmap format.
TGA	Targa format.
TIFF	Tagged image file format.
Options	Displays dialog box:

TGA Options options:

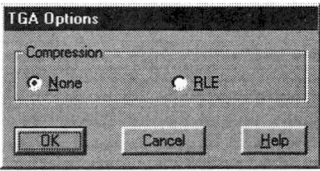

None	No file compression.
RLE	Run length encoded compression.

TIFF Options options:

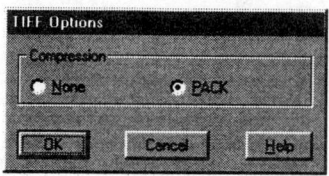

| None | No file compression. |
| PACK | Pack bits compression. |

Portion options:

Active viewport	Selects the area of the current viewport to save.
Offset	Specifies the lower-left x,y-coordinates of the image area (*default = 0,0*).
Size	Specifies the upper-right x,y-coordinates of the image area.

RELATED COMMANDS

| SaveImage | Saves a thumbnail image of the drawing to BMP file. |
| [Prt Scr] | Saves entire screen to the Windows clipboard. |

TIPS

- The **SaveImg** command saves TGA files in 32-bit RGBA TrueVision v2.0 format and TIFF in 32-bit RGBA tagged image file format.

- The GIF format (found in R12 and R13) was replaced by the BMP format in R14.

SaveURL

Rel.14   Saves the current drawing to a URL (*an external command in Internet.Arx*).

Command	Alias	Ctrl+	F-key	Alt+	Menu Bar	Tablet
saveurl	...	...	...	...	...	...

Command: **saveurl**
Displays dialog box:

DIALOG BOX OPTIONS

Options   Displays **Internet Configuration** dialog box; see the **InetCfg** command.
Save DWG to URL
                 Names the URL.
Save   Saves the drawing to the URL
Cancel   Dismisses the dialog box without saving the drawing.
Help   Displays a help window.

RELATED COMMANDS

DxfOut	Saves the drawing in DXF format.
Export	Saves the drawing in a variety of raster and vector formats.
Plot	Saves the drawing in even more raster and vector formats.
QSave	Saves drawing without prompting for name.
SaveAs	Saves the drawing.
DwfOut	Exports the drawing in DWF format.
OpenUrl	Opens a drawing from a URL.
InsertUrl	Inserts a drawing (as a block) from a URL.

TIPS

■ A URL (short for "uniform resource locator") is the universal file naming system used by the Internet.

■ Autodesk recommends that you use the following URL formats:

File Location	Example URL
Web Site	http://*servername/pathname/filename*.**dwg**
FTP Site	ftp://*servername/pathname/filename*.**dwg**
Local File	file:///*drive:/pathname/filename*.**dwg**
or	file:///*drive|/pathname/filename*.**dwg**
or	file://*localPC\pathname\filename*.**dwg**
or	file:////*localPC/pathname/filename*.**dwg**
Network File	file://*localhost/drive:/pathname/filename*.**dwg**
or	file://*localhost/drive|/pathname/filename*.**dwg**

Scale

V. 2.5 Changes the size of selected objects, to make them smaller or larger.

Command	Alias	Ctrl+	F-key	Alt+	Menu Bar	Tablet
scale	sc	...	...	ML	Modify ⤷Scale	V21

```
Command: scale
Select objects: [pick]
Select objects: [Enter]
Base point: [pick]
<Scale factor>/Reference: r
Reference length <1>:
```

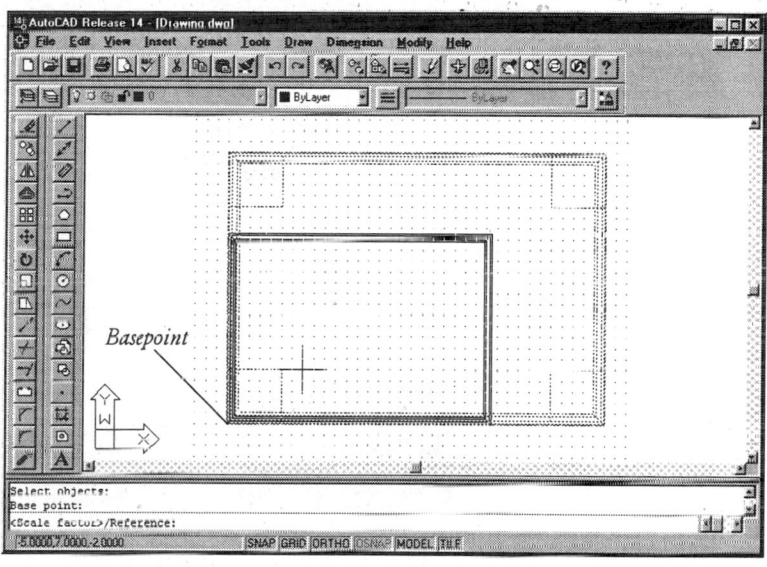

Basepoint

COMMAND LINE OPTIONS

Base point The point from which scaling takes place.
Reference Supply a reference value.
Scale factor Indicate scale factor, which applies equally in the x- and y-directions.

Scale Factor	Meaning
> 1.0	Enlarges the size of the object(s).
1.0	No change.
> 0.0 *and* < 1.0	Reduces the size of the object(s).
0.0 *or negative*	Not permitted.

RELATED COMMANDS

Align Scales an object in 3D space.
Insert Allows a block to be scaled independently in the x-, y-, and z-directions.
Plot Allows a drawing to be plotted at any scale.

Scene

Rel.12 Collects lights and a viewpoint into a named scene (*an external command in Render.Arx*).

Command	Alias	Ctrl+	F-key	Alt+	Menu Bar	Tablet
scene	...	...	...	VES	View ⇘Render ⇘Scene	N1

Command: **scene**
Displays dialog box:

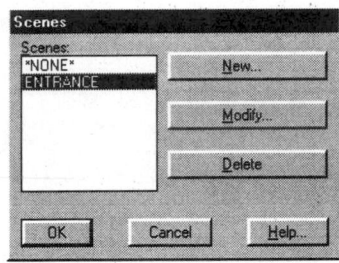

DIALOG BOX OPTIONS

New	Creates a new named scene; displays **New Scene** dialog box.
Modify	Changes an existing scene definition; displays **Modify Scene** dialog box.
Delete	Delete scene from drawing; displays dialog box:

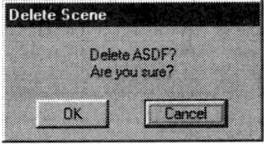

New Scene dialog box:

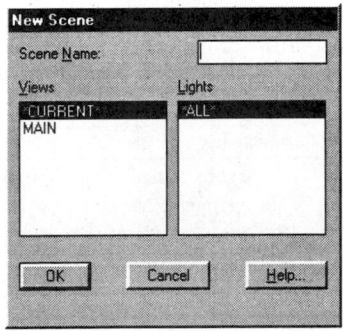

Scene Name	Enters a name for the scene; maximum = 8 characters.
Views	Selects one named view.
Lights	Selects one or more lights.

Modify Scene dialog box:

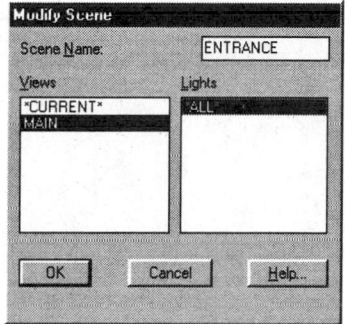

Scene name	Changes the name for the scene; maximum = 8 characters.
Views	Selects one named view.
Lights	Selects one or more lights.

RELATED COMMANDS

Light	Places lights in the drawing for the **Scene** command.
Render	Uses scenes to create renderings.
View	Creates named views for the **Scene** command.

TIPS

- Before you can use the **Scene** command, you need to create at least one named view (with the **View** command) or place at least one light (with the **Light** command). Otherwise, there is no need to use the **Scene** command.

- If you select no lights for a scene, **Render** uses ambient light.

- Scene parameters are stored as attribute definitions in a block.

'Script

V. 1.4 Runs an ASCII file containing a sequence of AutoCAD instructions to automatically execute a series of commands.

Command	Alias	Ctrl+	F-key	Alt+	Menu Bar	Tablet
'script	scr	...	...	TR	Tools ⤷Run Script	V9

Command: **script**
*Displays **Select Script File** dialog box.*
Script file begins running as soon as it is loaded.

COMMAND LINE OPTIONS
[Backspace]	Interrupts the script.
[Esc]	Stops the script.
~	Displays the file dialog box when **FileDia** is 0.

RELATED COMMANDS
Delay	Pauses, in milliseconds, before executing the next command.
Resume	Resumes a script after a script has been interrupted.
RScript	Repeats a script file.

TIPS
- Since the **Script** command is a transparent command, it can be used during another command.

- Prefix the **VSlide** command to preload it into memory; this results in a faster slide show:
    *vslide

- You can make a script file more flexible (pause for user input, branch with conditionals, and so on) by inserting AutoLISP functions.

QUICK START TUTORIAL:

Writing your first script file.

A script file consist of the exact keystrokes you type for any command.

Step 1: START TEXT EDITOR

The script file must be plain ASCII text. Write the script using a text editor, such as Notepad, not a word processor.

Step 2: WRITE SCRIPT

Here is an example script that places a door symbol in the drawing:

```
; Inserts DOOR2436 symbol at x,y = (76,100)
; x-scale = 0.5, y-scale = 1.0, rotation = 90 degrees
insert door2436 76,100 0.5 1.0 90
```

In the script, these characters have special meaning:

Character	Meaning
	(*Space or end-of-line*) Equivalent to pressing the spacebar or [Enter] key.
;	(*Semi-colon*) Include a comment in the script file.
*	(*Asterisk*) Prefix the **VSlide** command to preload the SLD file.

Step 3: SAVE FILE

Save script file with any filename and the .SCR extension. For this example, use InsertDoorBlock.Scr.

Step 4: SCRIPT COMMAND

Return to AutoCAD and run the script with the **Script** command:

```
Command: script
Script file: insertdoorblock.scr
Command: insert
Block name (or ?): door2436
Insertion point: 76,100
X scale factor <1>/Corner/XYZ: 0.5
Y scale factor (default = X):1.0
Rotation angle <0>:90
```

Step 5: RSCRIPT COMMAND

If required, you can rerun the script with the **RScript** command.

Section

Rel.11 Creates a 2D region object from the intersection of a plane and a 3D solid (*an external command in Acis.Dll*).

Command	Alias	Ctrl+	F-key	Alt+	Menu Bar	Tablet
section	sec	...	...	DLE	Draw	...
					↳Solid	
					↳Section	

```
Command: section
Select objects: [pick]
Select objects: [Enter]
Section plane by Object/Zaxis/View/XY/YZ/ZX/<3 points>:
```

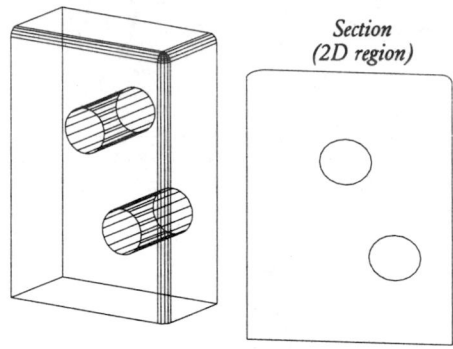

Section (2D region)

COMMAND LINE OPTIONS

Object	Aligns section plane with an object: circle, ellipse, arc, elliptical arc, 2D spline, or 2D polyline.
Zaxis	Specifies the normal (z-axis) to the section plane.
View	Uses the current view plane as the section plane.
XY	Uses the x,y-plane of the current view.
YZ	Uses the y,z-plane of the current view.
ZX	Uses the z,x-plane of the current view.
3 points	Picks three points to specify the section plane.

RELATED COMMAND

Slice   Cuts a slice out of a solid model.

TIPS

■ Section blocks are placed on the current layer, not the object's layer.

■ Regions are ignored.

■ One cutting plane is required for each selected solid.

■ The **Last** option was removed from Release 13.

Select

V. 2.5 Creates a selection set of objects before executing a command.

Command	Alias	Ctrl+	F-key	Alt+	Menu Bar	Tablet
select	...	...	...	...	...	...

```
Command: select
Select objects: [pick]
Select objects: [Enter]
```

COMMAND LINE OPTIONS

A	Continues to add objects after using the **R** option (*short for Add*).
AU	Switches from **[pick]** to **C** or **W** modes, depending on whether an object is found at the initial pick point (*short for AUtomatic*).
ALL	Select all objects in the drawing.
BOX	Goes into **C** or **W** mode, depending on how the cursor moves.
C	Selects objects in and crossing the selection box (*Crossing*).
CP	Selects all objects inside and crossing the selection polygon.
F	Selects all objects crossing a polyline (*short for Fence*).
G	Selects objects contained in a named group (*short for Group*).
L	Selects the last-drawn object still visible on the screen (*Last*).
M	Makes multiple selections before AutoCAD scans the drawing; saves time in a large drawing (*short for Multiple*).
P	Selects the previously selected objects (*short for Previous*).
R	Removes objects from the selection set (*short for Remove*).
SI	Selects only a single set of objects before terminating **Select** command (*short for SIngle*).
U	Removes the most-recently added selected objects (*short for Undo*).
W	Selects all objects inside the selection box (*short for Window*).
WP	Selects a objects inside the selection polygon (*short for Windowed Polygon*).
[pick]	Selects a single object.
[Enter]	Exits the **Select** command.
[Esc]	Aborts the **Select** command.

RELATED COMMANDS

All commands that prompt 'Select objects'.

Filter	Specifies objects that are added to the selection set.

RELATED SYSTEM VARIABLES

PickAdd	Controls how objects are added to a selection set.
PickAuto	Controls automatic windowing at the 'Select objects' prompt.
PickDrag	Controls method of creating a selection box.
PickFirst	Controls command-object selection order.

SelectURL

Rel.14 Lists the settings of system variables; allows you to change variables that are not read-only (*an external command in DwfIU.Arx*).

Command	Alias	Ctrl+	F-key	Alt+	Menu Bar	Tablet
selecturl	...	...	...	...	...	...

Command: **selecturl**
Highlights all objects and areas with a URL.

COMMAND LINE OPTIONS
None.

RELATED COMMANDS
AttachURL	Attaches a URL to an object or an area.
DetachUrl	Removes the URL from an object.
DwfOut	Exports the drawing in DWF format.
ListUrl	Lists URLs embedded in the drawing.

TIPS
■ The URL placed in the drawing becomes a hyperlink *after* the drawing is exported as a DWF file with the **DwfOut** command; the hyperlink cannot be used while in DWG format.

■ Examples of URLs include:

http://data.autodesk.com	Autodesk Data Publishing Web site.
http://www.autodesk.com	Autodesk primary Web site.
http://www.autodeskpress.com	Autodesk Press Web site.
news://adesknews.autodesk.com	Autodesk news server.
ftp://ftp.autodesk.com	Autodesk FTP server.
http://users.uniserve.com/~ralphg/	Author Ralph Grabowski's Web site.

■ Don't delete layer URLLAYER.

■ The URL is stored as follows:

Attachment	URL
One object	Stored as xdata (extended entity data).
Multiple objects	Stored as xdata in each object.
Area	Stored as xdata in a rectangle object on layer URLLAYER.

DEFINITIONS
DWF	Short for "drawing Web format," Autodesk's file format for displaying drawings on the Internet.
URL	Short for "uniform resource locator," the universal file naming convention.

 # SetUV

Rel.14 Maps materials onto objects (*an external command in Render.Arx*).

Command	Alias	Ctrl+	F-key	Alt+	Menu Bar	Tablet
setuv	...	...	...	VEA	View	R1
					⟜Render	
					⟜Mapping	

```
Command: setuv
Select objects: [pick]
Select objects: [Enter]
Updating the Render geometry database...
```
Displays dialog box:

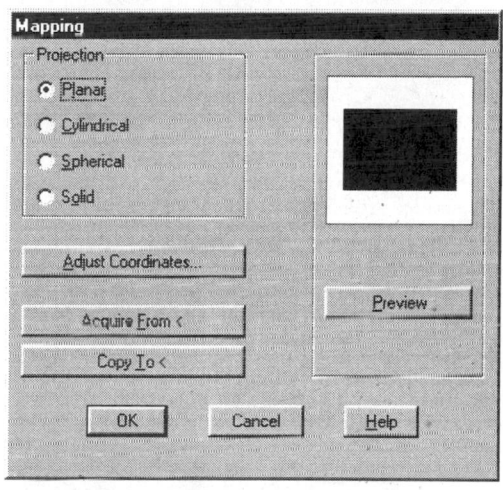

DIALOG BOX OPTIONS

Projection options:

Planar   Specifies a plane for projecting the bitmap onto the selected object.

Cylindrical   Specifies an axis of the cylindrical coordinate systemand wrap line for projecting the bitmap onto the selected object.

Spherical   Specifies the polar axis of the spherical coordinate systemand wrap line for projecting the bitmap onto the selected object.

Solid   Adjusts the coordinates to shift marble, granite, or wood materials.

Adjust Coordinates
     Displays different dialog boxes, depending on the setting of **Projection**.

Planar options:

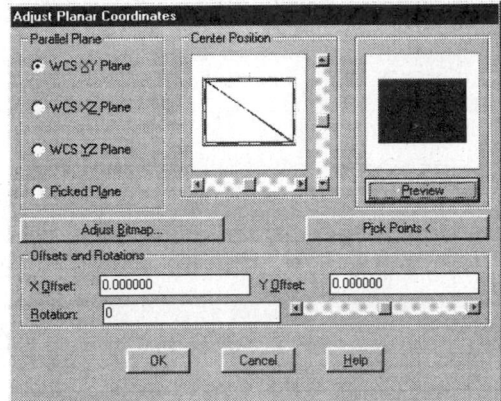

Parallel Plane   Selects a WCS reference planes of the WCS or pick a plane with the **Pick Points** radio button.

Center Position   Shows a parallel projection of the selected object's mesh onto the current parallel plane.

Position	Meaning
Blue	Current projection square.
Blue tick mark	Top of the projection square.
Green	Projection square's left edge.

Adjust Bitmap   Displays the **Adjust Object Bitmap Placement** dialog box.
Pick Points   Specifies a projection plane by picking points in the drawing.
Offset   Changes the x- and y-offset of the map.
Rotation   Changes the rotation angle of the map.

Cylindrical options:

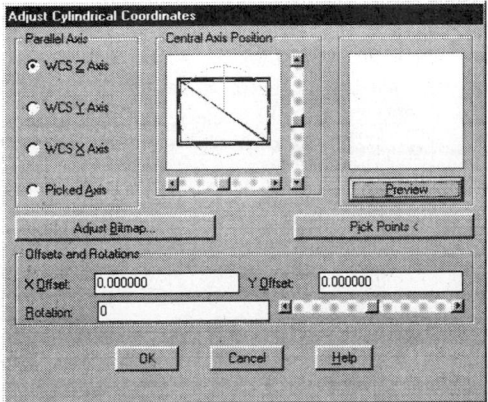

Parallel Axis   Selects a WCS reference axes of the WCS or pick an axis with the **Pick Points** radio button.
Central Axis Position

Displays a parallel projection of the object's mesh onto a plane perpendicular to the current axis.

Position	Meaning
Blue circle	Projection axis.
Green radius	Wrap line.

Adjust Bitmap   Displays the **Adjust Object Bitmap Placement** dialog box.
Pick Points   Specifies a projection axis by picking points in the drawing.
Offset   Changes the x- and y-offset of the map.
Rotation   Changes the rotation angle of the map.

Spherical options:

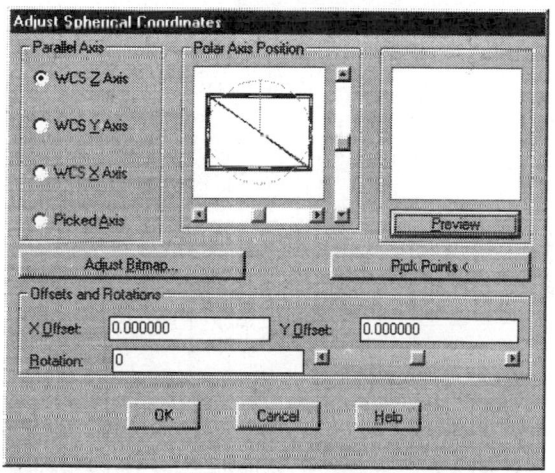

Parallel Axis   Selects one of the three perpendicular axes of the WCS or pick an axis with the **Pick Points** button.
Polar Axis Position

Displays a parallel projection of the object's mesh onto a plane perpendicular to the current axis.

Position	Meaning
Blue circle	Projection axis.
Green radius	Wrap line.

Adjust Bitmap   Displays the **Adjust Object Bitmap Placement** dialog box.
Pick Points   Specifies a projection axis by picking points in the drawing.
Offset   Changes the x- and y-offset of the map.
Rotation   Changes the rotation angle of the map.

Solid options:

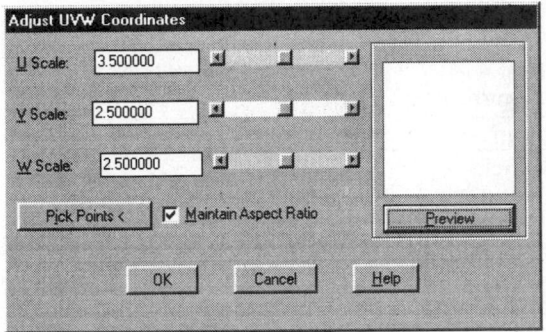

U Scale, V Scale, W Scale
> Sets 3D projection coordinates.

Pick Points   Specifies a projection axis by picking points in the drawing.

Maintain Aspect Ratio
> Maintains the aspect ratio of the material by locking the three axis values.

'SetVar

V. 2.5 Lists the settings of system variables; allows you to change variables that are not read-only (*short for SET VARiable*).

Command	Alias	Ctrl+	F-key	Alt+	Menu Bar	Tablet
'setvar	set	...	...	TQV	Tools ⭥Inquiry ⭥Set Variable	U10

```
Command: setvar
Variable name or ?: [type name]
```

Example:
```
Command: setvar
Variable name or ?: visretain
New value for VISRETAIN <0>: 1
```

COMMAND LINE OPTIONS

Variable name Indicates the system variable name you want to access.
?   Lists the names and settings of system variables.

TIPS

■ See Appendix B for the complete list of all system variables found in AutoCAD Release 14.

■ Almost all system variables can be entered without the SetVar command. For example,

```
Command: visretain
New value for VISRETAIN <0>: 1
```

Shade

Performs 16- and 256-color shaded renderings, and hidden-line removal of 3D drawings.

Command	Alias	Ctrl+	F-key	Alt+	Menu Bar	Tablet
shade	sha	...	...	VS	View ⤷Shade	N2

```
Command: shade
Regenerating drawing.
Shading 50% done.
Shading complete.
```

COMMAND LINE OPTIONS
None.

RELATED COMMANDS
DView	Does hidden-line removal of perspective views.
Hide	Does true hidden-line removal of 3D drawings.
MSlide	Saves a rendered view as an SLD-format slide file.
MView	Does a hidden-line view of individual viewports during plots and prints.
Plot	Does a hidden-line view during plotting.
Render	Performs a more realistic rendering.

RELATED SYSTEM VARIABLES
ShadEdge Determines the style of shading:

ShadEdge	Meaning
0	256-color shading.
1	256-color shading with outlined polygons.
2	Hidden-line removal.
3	16-color shading (*default*).

ShadeDif Determines the shading contrast (*default = 70*).

TIPS
- As an alternative to the **Shade** command, the **Render** module does high-quality renderings of 3D drawings but takes longer to complete the rendering.

- The smaller the viewport, the faster the rendering.

ShadEdge = 0   *ShadEdge = 1*

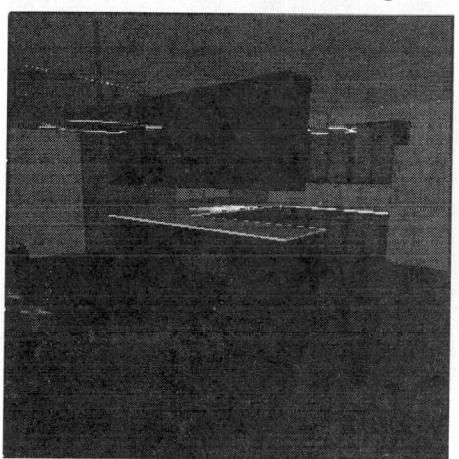 

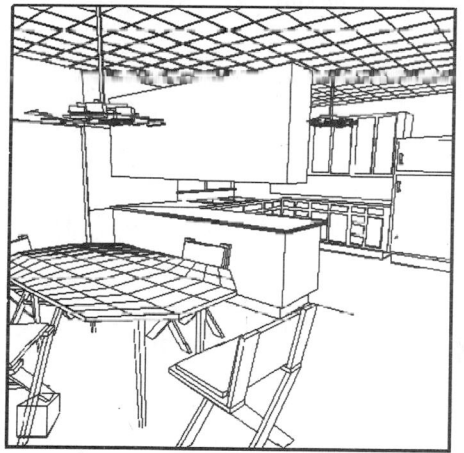

ShadEdge = 2   *ShadEdge = 3*

 # Shape

V. 1.0 Inserts a predefined shape in the current drawing.

Command	Alias	Ctrl+	F-key	Alt+	Menu Bar	Tablet
shape	...	...	...	...	...	...

```
Command: shape
Shape name (or ?): [type name]
Starting point: [pick]
Height <>: [Enter]
Rotation angle <0>: [Enter]
```

COMMAND LINE OPTIONS

Shape name	Indicates the name of the shape to insert.
?	Lists the names of currently loaded shapes.
Starting point	Indicates the insertion point of the shape.
Height	Specifies the height of the shape.
Rotation Angle	Specifies the rotation angle of the shape.

RELATED COMMANDS

Load	Loads an SHX-format shape file into the drawing.
Insert	Inserts a block into the drawing.
Style	Loads SHX font files into the drawing.

RELATED SYSTEM VARIABLE

ShpName	Current SHP filename.

TIPS

- Shapes are defined by SHP files, which must first be compiled into SHX files before they can be loaded by the **Load** command.

- Compile an SHP file into an SHX file with the **Compile** command.

- AutoCAD comes with three SHX shape files, located in the \Acad14\Bonus\Fonts subdirectory:

File	Meaning
Es.Shx	Electronic component shapes (*see figure*).
Pc.Shx	Printed circuit board shapes.
St.Shx	Surface texture shapes for mechanical parts drawings.

Some electronic shapes included in Es.Shp:

Shell

<u>V. 2.5</u> Temporarily exit AutoCAD to the DOS operating system (*an external command defined in Acad.Pgp*).

Command	Alias	Ctrl+	F-key	Alt+	Menu Bar	Tablet
shell	sh	...	...	...	...	...

```
Command: shell
OS Command:
```

Command Line Options

[Enter]	Stay in DOS for more than one command.
Exit	Return to AutoCAD from DOS.

RELATED COMMANDS

End	Exit AutoCAD back to Windows.

RELATED FILE

Acad.Pgp	The external command definition file.

Adding commands to Acad.Pgp.

Step 1:

Load the Acad.Pgp file into a text editor.

Step 2: THE PGP FILE

The PGP file uses this format to add a command:

```
CommandName, [DOS request], MemoryReserve, [*]Prompt, ReturnCode
```

Meaning of the format:

Component	Meaning
CommandName	Name typed at AutoCAD 'Command' prompt.
DOS Request	Command AutoCAD feeds to DOS.
MemoryReserve	Always 0; heldover from old AutoCAD versions.
Prompt	Phrase to prompt user action.
*Prompt	User response to prompt may contain spaces.

Meaning of the return code:

Return Code	Meaning
0	Return to AutoCAD's text screen.
1	Load $Cmd.Dxb file into drawing upon return.
2	Load $Cmd.Dxb as a block into the drawing.
4	Return to AutoCAD's previous screen mode, usually the graphics screen.

For example, add easy access to the WordPerfect word processor. Add this line anywhere in the Acad.Pgp file:

```
WP, WP, 0, File to edit: ,4
```

Step 3: SAVE FILE

Save the file and return to AutoCAD.

Step 4: REINIT COMMAND

Use the **ReInit** command to reload the Acad.Pgp file.

Step 5: TRY IT OUT

Enter **WP** at the 'Command' prompt:

```
Command: wp
```

AutoCAD shells out to the operating system and prompts you:

```
File to edit:
```

Enter the name of a text file; AutoCAD launches WordPerfect with the file. To return to AutoCAD, you must exit WordPerfect.

ShowMat

Rel.13 Lists the material attached to an object (*short for SHOW MATerial; an external command in Render.Arx*).

Command	Alias	Ctrl+	F-key	Alt+	Menu Bar	Tablet
showmat	...	...	...	...	...	...

```
Command: showmat
Select object: [pick]
```

Example output:
```
Material BRONZE is explicitly attached to the object.
```

COMMAND LINE OPTIONS
Select object   Selects the object to examine.

RELATED COMMANDS
MatLib   Loads material definitions into the drawing.
RMat   Attaches materials to objects, colors, and layers.

 # Sketch

V. 1.4   Allows freehand drawing as lines or polylines.

Command	Alias	Ctrl+	F-key	Alt+	Menu Bar	Tablet
sketch	...	...	...	...	...	...

```
Command: sketch
Record increment <0.1000>: [Enter]
Sketch.  Pen eXit Quit Record Erase Connect
```

COMMAND LINE OPTIONS

Commands can be invoked by mouse and digitizer buttons:

Connect	Connects to the last drawing segment (*button #6*).
Erase	Erases temporary segments as the cursor moves over them (*button #6*).
eXit	Records the temporary segments and exit the **Sketch** command (*button #3*).
Pen	Lifts and lowers the pen (*pick button #1*).
Quit	Discards temporary segments and exit the **Sketch** command (*button #4*).
Record	Records the temporary segments as permanent (*button #2*).
	(*Period*) Connects the last segment to the current point (*button #1*).

RELATED COMMANDS

Line	Draws line segments.
PLine	Draws polyline and polyline arc segments.

RELATED SYSTEM VARIABLES

SketchInc The current recording increment for **Sketch** (*default = 0.1*).
SKPoly Controls the type of sketches recorded:

SkPoly	Meaning
0	Record sketches as lines (*default*).
1	Record sketches as polylines.

TIPS

■ During the **Sketch** command, the definitions of the pointing device's buttons change to:

Button	Meaning	Keystroke
0	Raise and lower the *p*en	P
1	Draw line to current *point*	.
2	*R*ecord sketch	R
3	Record sketch and e*X*it	X
4	Discard sketch and *Q*uit	Q
5	*E*rase sketch	E
6	*C*onnect to last-drawn segment	C

■. Only the first three (or two) button-commands are available on three- (or two-) button mice.

■ Pull-down menus are unavailable during the **Sketch** command.

Slice

Rel.11 Cuts a 3D solid with a plane, creating two 3D solids (*an external command in Acis.Dll*).

Command	Alias	Ctrl+	F-key	Alt+	Menu Bar	Tablet
slice	sl	...	...	DIL	Draw	...
					⃗Solids	
					⃗Slice	

```
Command: slice
Select objects: [pick]
Select objects: [Enter]
Slicing plane by Object/Zaxis/View/XY/YZ/ZX/<3 points>: [Enter]
Both sides/<Point on desired side of the plane>: [pick]
```

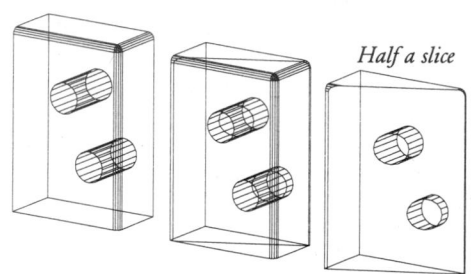

Half a slice

COMMAND LINE OPTIONS

Object	Aligns cutting plane with a circle, ellipse, arc, elliptical arc, 2D spline, or 2D polyline.
View	Aligns cutting plane with viewing plane.
XY	Aligns cutting plane with x,y-plane of current UCS.
YZ	Aligns cutting plane with y,x-plane of current UCS.
Zaxis	Aligns cutting plane with two normal points.
ZX	Aligns cutting plane with z,x-plane of current UCS.
3 points	Aligns cutting plane with three points.
Both sides	Retains both halves of cut solid model.

Point on desired side of the plane
> Retains either half of cut solid model.

'Snap

V. 1.0 Sets the drawing resolution, grid and hatch origin, isometric mode, and angle of grid, hatch, and ortho.

Command	Alias	Ctrl+	F-key	Alt+	Menu Bar	Tablet
'snap	sn	B	F9	. . .	. . .	. . .

```
Command: snap
Snap spacing or ON/OFF/Aspect/Rotate/Style <1.0000>:
```

COMMAND LINE OPTIONS

Aspect	Sets separate x- and y-increments.
OFF	Turns off snap.
ON	Turns on snap.
Rotate	Rotates the crosshairs for snap and grid.
Snap spacing	Sets the snap increment.
Style	Switches between standard and isometric style.

RELATED COMMANDS

DdRModes	Sets snap values via a dialog box.
Grid	Turns on the grid.
Isoplane	Switches to a different isometric drawing plane.

RELATED SYSTEM VARIABLES

SnapAng	Current angle of the snap rotation.
SnapBase	Base point of the snap rotation.
SnapIsoPair	Current isometric plane setting.
SnapMode	Determines whether snap is on.
SnapStyl	Determines style of snap.
SnapUnit	The current snap increment in x- and y-directions.

SolDraw

Rel.13 Creates profiles and sections in viewports (*short for SOLids DRAWing; an external command in Solids.Arx*).

Command	Alias	Ctrl+	F-key	Alt+	Menu Bar	Tablet
soldraw	...	...	...	DIUD	Draw	...
					⌐Solids	
					⌐Setup	
					⌐Drawing	

```
Command: soldraw
Viewports to draw ...
Select objects: [pick]
Select objects: [Enter]
```

COMMAND LINE OPTION

Select objects   Selects a viewport; must be a floating viewport in model space (*Tilemode = 0*).

RELATED COMMANDS

SolProf   Creates profile images of 3D solids.
SolView   Creates floating viewports

TIPS

■ The **SolView** command must be used before the **SolDraw** command.

■ **SolDraw** takes the following steps:

   1. Creates visible and hidden lines representing the silhouette and edges of solids in the viewport

   2. Projects to a plane perpendicular to the viewing direction.

   3. Silhouettes and edges are generated for all solids and portions of solids behind the cutting plane.

   4. Sectional views are crosshatched.

■ Existing profiles and sections in the selected viewport are erased.

■ All layers — except the ones needed to display the profile or section — are frozen in each viewport.

■ The following layers are used by SolDraw, SolProf, and SolView: *viewname*-**VIS**, *viewname*-**HID**, and *viewname*-**HAT**.

■ Hatching uses the values set in system variables **HpName**, **HpScale**, and **HpAng**.

Solid

<u>V. 1.0</u> Draws solid filled triangles and quadrilaterals; does *not* create a 3D solid.

Command	Alias	Ctrl+	F-key	Alt+	Menu Bar	Tablet
solid	so	...	...	DF2	Draw ↳Surfaces ↳2D Solid	L8

```
Command: solid
First point: [pick]
Second point: [pick]
Third point: [pick]
Fourth point: [pick]
Third point: [Enter]
```

Pick order makes a difference:

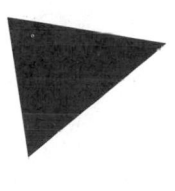

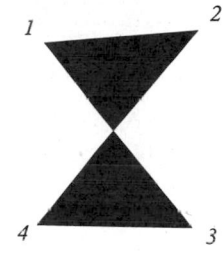

3-point solid   *4-point solids*

COMMAND LINE OPTIONS

First point	Picks the first corner.
Second point	Picks the second corner.
Third point	Picks the third corner.
Fourth point	Picks the fourth corner; or press **[Enter]** to draw triangle.
[Enter]	Draws quadilaterial; ends **Solid** command.

RELATED COMMANDS

Fill	Turns object fill off and on.
BHatch	Solid fill pattern fills any shape.
Trace	Draws lines with width.
PLine	Draws polylines and polyline arcs with width.

RELATED SYSTEM VARIABLE

FillMode	Determines whether solids are displayed filled or outlined.

SolProf

Rel.13   Creates profile images of 3D solids (*short for SOLid PROFile; an external command in Solids.Arx*).

Command	Alias	Ctrl+	F-key	Alt+	Menu Bar	Tablet
solprof	...	...	...	DIUP	Draw ⤷Solids ⤷Setup ⤷Profile	...

Command: **solprof**
Select objects: **[pick]**
Select objects: **[Enter]**
Display hidden profile lines on separate layer? <Y>: **[Enter]**
Project profile lines onto a plane? <Y>: **[Enter]**
Delete tangential edges? <Y>: **[Enter]**
4 solids selected.

COMMAND LINE OPTIONS

Select objects   Selects the objects to profile.

Display hidden profile lines on separate layer?

No: All profile lines are visible; a block is created for the profile lines for every selected solid.

Yes: Generates just two blocks: (1) one block for visible lines; and (2) one block for hidden lines.

Project profile lines onto a plane?

No: Creates profile lines with 3D objects.

Yes: Creates profile lines with 2D objects.

Delete tangential edges?

No: Does not display tangential edges (transition line between two tangent faces).

Yes: Displays tangential edges.

RELATED COMMANDS

SolDraw   Creates profiles and sections in viewports.
SolView   Creates floating viewports.

TIP

■ The **SolView** command must be used before the **SolProf** command.

 # SolView

Rel.13 Creates floating viewports in preparation for the **SolDraw** and **SolProf** commands (*an external command in Solids.Arx*).

Command	Alias	Ctrl+	F-key	Alt+	Menu Bar	Tablet
solview	...	...	...	DIUV	Draw	...
					⌇Solids	
					⌇Setup	
					⌇Views	

Command: **solview**
Ucs/Ortho/Auxiliary/Section/<eXit>:

COMMAND LINE OPTIONS

Ucs options:

Named	Creates the profile view using the x,y-plane of a named UCS.
World	Creates the profile view using the x,y-plane of the WCS
?	Lists the names of existing UCSs.
Current	Creates the profile view using the x,y-plane of the current UCS.

Ortho options:

Pick side of viewport to project

Selects the edge of one viewport.

View center	Picks the center of the view.
Clip	Pick the two corners for a clipped view.
View name	Names the view.

Auxiliary options:

Inclined plane's 1st point

Pick first point.

Inclined plane's 2nd point

Picks second point.

Side to view from

Determines the view side.

Section options:

Cutting plane 1st point

Pick first point.

Cutting plane 2nd point

Pick second pont.

Side to view from

Determines the view side.

eXit	Exit the **SolView** command.

RELATED COMMANDS

SolDraw	Creates profiles and sections in viewports.
SolProf	Creates profile images of 3D solids.

Spell

Rel.13 Checks the spelling of text in the drawing (*an external command in AcSpell.Dll*).

Command	Alias	Ctrl+	F-key	Alt+	Menu Bar	Tablet
spell	sp	...	...	TS	Tools ⏃Spelling	T10

```
Command: spell
Select objects: [pick]
Select objects: [Enter]
```

When unrecognized text is found, displays dialog box:

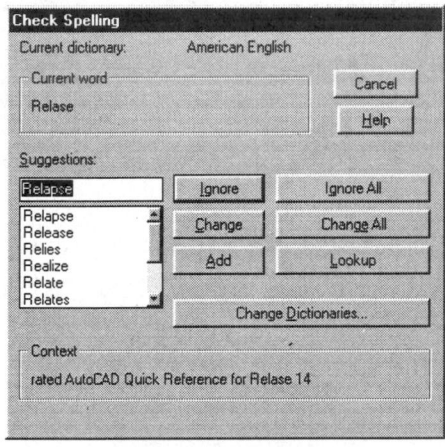

When selected text is recognized, or when spelling check is complete:

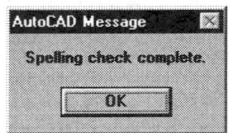

DIALOG BOX OPTIONS

Ignore	Ignores the spelling and go on to next word.
Ignore All	Ignores all words with this spelling.
Change	Changes to suggested spelling.
Change All	Changes all words with this spelling.
Add	Adds word to user dictionary.
Lookup	Checks spelling of work in **Suggestions** box.

Change dictionaries

Selects a different dictionary; displays dialog box:

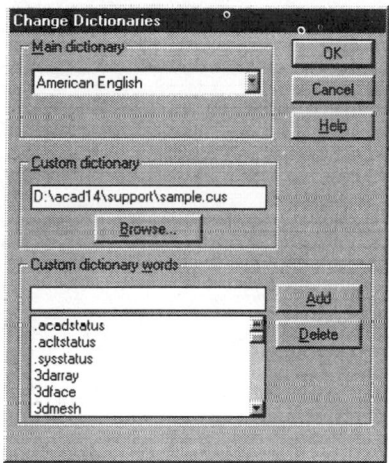

RELATED COMMAND

DdEdit   Edits text.

RELATED SYSTEM VARIABLES

DctCust   Name of custom spelling dictionary.
DctMain   Name of main spelling dictionary.

RELATED FILES

Enu.Dct   Dictionary word file.
*.Cus   Custom dictionary files.

Sphere

Rel.11 Draws a 3D sphere as a solid model (*an external command in Acis.Dll*).

Command	Alias	Ctrl+	F-key	Alt+	Menu Bar	Tablet
sphere	...	...	...	DIS	Draw ⤷Solids ⤷Sphere	K7

```
Command: sphere
Center of sphere <0,0,0>: [pick]
Diameter/<Radius> of sphere: [pick]
```

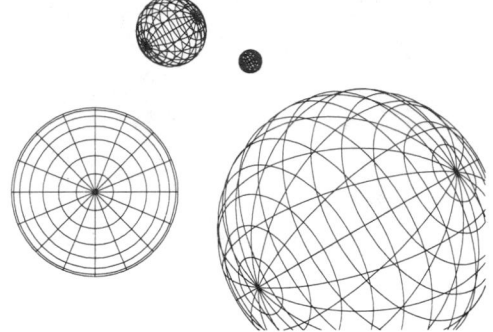

COMMAND LINE OPTIONS

Center of sphere
  Locate the center point of the sphere.
Diameter Specify diameter of the sphere.
Radius Specify radius of the sphere.

RELATED COMMANDS

Box	Draws solid boxes.
Cone	Draws solid cones.
Cylinder	Draws solid cylinders.
Torus	Draws solid tori.
Wedge	Draws solid wedges.
Ai_Sphere	Draws a surface meshed sphere.

Spline

Rel.13 Draws NURBS (non-uniform rational Bezier spline) curves (*an external command in Acis.Dll*).

Command	Alias	Ctrl+	F-key	Alt+	Menu Bar	Tablet
spline	spl	...	...	DS	Draw ⮡Spline	L9

```
Command: spline
Object/<First point>: [pick]
Enter point: [pick]
Close/Fit tolerance/<Enter point>: [pick]
Close/Fit tolerance/<Enter point>: [Enter]
Enter start tangent: [pick]
Enter end tangent: [pick]
```

Open spline   *Closed spline*

Splined polyline   *Converted to spline*

COMMAND LINE OPTIONS

Close	Closes spline at the start point.
Fit	Changes spline tolerance; 0 = curve passes through fit points.
Object	Converts 2D and 3D splined polylines into a NURBS spline.

RELATED COMMANDS

PLine	Draws splined polyline.
SplinEdit	Edits a NURBS spline.

RELATED SYSTEM VARIABLE

DelObj   Toggles whether the original polyline is deleted with the **Object** option.

SplinEdit

Rel.13 Edits a NURBS spline (*an external command in Acis.Dll*).

Command	Alias	Ctrl+	F-key	Alt+	Menu Bar	Tablet
splinedit	spe	...	...	MOS	Modify ⤷Objects ⤷Spline	W18

```
Command: splinedit
Select spline: [pick]
Fit data/Close/Move vertex/Refine/rEverse/Undo/eXit <X>: F
Add/Close/Delete/Move/Purge/Tangents/toLerance/eXit <X>: [Enter]
```

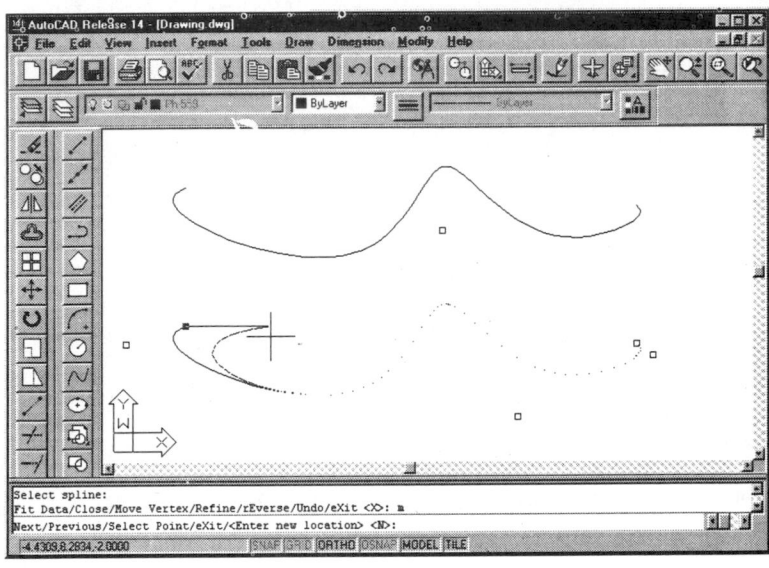

COMMAND LINE OPTIONS

Fit data options:

Add	Adds fit points.
Close	Closes the spline, if open.
Delete	Removes fit points.
Move	Moves fit points.
Open	Opens the spline, if closed.
Purge	Removes fit point data from the drawing.
Tangents	Edits the start and end tangents.
toLerance	Refits spline with new tolerance value.
eXit	Exits suboptions.

Close	Closes the spline, if open.
Move vertex	Moves a control vertex.
Open	Opens the spline, if closed.
Refine	Adds a control point, change the spline's order or weight.
rEverse	Reverses the spline's direction.
Undo	Undoes the most-recent edit change.
eXit	Exits the **SplinEdit** command.

RELATED COMMANDS

| PEdit | Edits a splined polyline. |
| Spline | Draws a NURBS spline. |

TIPS

■ The spline looses its fit data when you use the following SplinEdit command options: **Refine**; **Fit Purge**; **Fit Tolerance** followed by **Fit Move**; and **Fit Tolerance** followed by **Fit Open** or **Fit Close**.

■ The maximum order for a spline is 26; once the order has been elevated, it cannot be reduced.

■ The larger the weight, the closer the spline is to the control point.

Stats

Rel.12 Lists statistics of the most-recent rendering (*short for STATisticS; an external command in Render.Arx*).

Command	Alias	Ctrl+	F-key	Alt+	Menu Bar	Tablet
stats	. . .	. . .	. . .	VET	View ⌖Render ⌖Statistics	. . .

Command: **stats**
Displays dialog box:

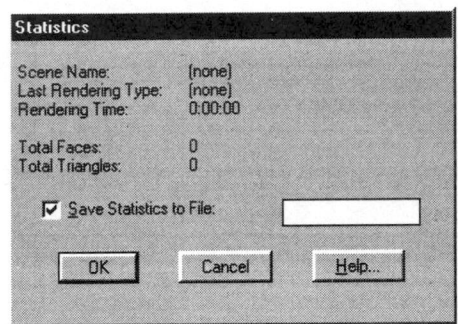

DIALOG BOX OPTION
Save Statistics to File
> Save rendering statistics to file.

RELATED AUTOCAD COMMAND
Render　　　　Creates renderings.

DEFINITIONS
Scene name　　Name of the currently selected scene; when no scene is current, displays "(none)."

Last Rendering Type
> Name of currently selected renderer; default is AutoCAD Render.

Rendering Time　Time required to create most-recent rendering; reported in HH:MM:SS (hours, minutes, seconds) format.

Total Faces　　Number of faces processed in most-recent rendering; a single 3D object consists of many faces.

Total Triangles　Number of triangles processed in most-recent rendering; a rectangular face is typically divided into two triangles.

'Status

V. 1.0 Displays information about the current drawing and environment.

Command	Alias	Ctrl+	F-key	Alt+	Menu Bar	Tablet
'status	...	...	...	TQS	Tools	...
					⬦Inquiry	
					⬦Status	

Command: **status**
Example output for the Acad.Dwg prototype drawing:

```
31 objects in D:\acad14\SUPPORT\acad.dwg
Model space limits are X:     0.0000   Y:     0.0000   (Off)
                       X:    12.0000   Y:     9.0000
Model space uses       *Nothing*
Display shows          X:     0.0000   Y:     0.0000
                       X:    17.6870   Y:     9.0000
Insertion base is      X:     0.0000   Y:     0.0000   Z:     0.0000
Snap resolution is     X:     1.0000   Y:     1.0000
Grid spacing is        X:     0.1000   Y:     0.1000

Current space:         Model space
Current layer:         0
Current color:         BYLAYER -- 7 (white)
Current linetype:      BYLAYER -- CONTINUOUS
Current elevation:     0.0000  thickness:     0.0000
Fill on  Grid off  Ortho off  Qtext off  Snap off  Tablet off
Object snap modes:     None
Free dwg disk (C:) space: 272.9 MBytes
Free temp disk (C:) space: 129.7 MBytes
Free physical memory: 0.0 Mbytes (out of 31.4M).
Free swap file space: 131.4 Mbytes (out of 172.2M).
```

COMMAND LINE OPTIONS
[Enter]   Continues the listing.
[F2]   Returns to the graphics screen.

RELATED COMMANDS
DbList   Lists information about all objects in the drawing.
List   Lists information about selected objects.
Stats   Lists information about the most-recent rendering.

DEFINITIONS

Model Space limits, Paper Space limits
> The x,y-coordinates stored in the **LimMin** and **LimMax** system variables; 'Off' indicates limits checking is turned off (**LimCheck**).

Model Space uses, Paper Space use
> The x,y-coordinates of the lower-left and upper-right extends of objects in the drawing; 'Over' indicates drawing extents exceeds the drawing limits.

Display shows
> The x,y-coordinates of the lower-left and upper-right corners of the current display.

Insertion base is
> The x,y,z-coordinates stored in system variable **InsBase**.

Snap resolution is, Grid spacing is
> The snap and grid settings, as stored in the **SnapUnit** and **GridUnit** system variables.

Current space
> Indicates whether model or paper space is current.

Current layer, Current color, Current linetype, Current elevation, Thickness
> The current values for the layer name, color, linetype name, elevation, and thickness, as stored in system variables **CLayer, CeColor, CeLType, Elevation**, and **Thickness**.

Fill, Grid, Ortho, Qtext, Snap, Tablet
> The current settings for the fill, grid, ortho, qtext, snap, and tablet modes, as stored in the system variables **FillMode, GridMode, OrthoMode, QTextMode, SnapMode**, and **TabMode**.

Object Snap modes
> The currently set object modes, as stored in system variable **OsMode**.

Free disk (dwg + temp = C)
> Amount of free disk space on the drive storing AutoCAD's temporary files, as pointed to by system variable **TempPrefix**.

Free physical memory
> Amount of free RAM.

Free swap file space
> Amount of free space in AutoCAD's swap file on disk.

StlOut

Rel.12 Exports 3D solids and bodies in binary or ASCII SLA format (*short for STereoLithography OUTput; an external command in Acis.Dll*).

Command	Alias	Ctrl+	F-key	Alt+	Menu Bar	Tablet
`stlout`	...	...	...	FE ↳STL	File ↳Export ↳Lithography	...

```
Command: stlout
Select a single solid for STL output.
Select objects: [pick]
Create binary STL file? <Y>:
```

COMMAND LINE OPTIONS

Y Creates binary-format SLA file.
N Creates ASCII-format SLA file.

RELATED COMMANDS

All solid modeling commands.

AcisOut Exports 3D solid models to an ASCII SAT-format ACIS file.
AmeConvert Converts AME v2.x solid models into ACIS models.

RELATED SYSTEM VARIABLE

FaceTRes Determines the resolution of triangulating solid models.

RELATED FILE

***.STL** Command creates SLA-compatible file with STL extension.

TIPS

- The solid model must lie in the positive x,y,z-octant of the WCS.
- The **StlOut** command exports a single 3D ACIS solid; it does not export ACIS regions or any other AutoCAD object.

DEFINITIONS

STL Stereolithography data file, which consists of a faceted representation of the ACIS model.
SLA Stereolithography Apparatus.

Stretch

V. 2.5 Stretches objects to lengthen, shorten, or distort them.

Command	Alias	Ctrl+	F-key	Alt+	Menu Bar	Tablet
stretch	s	...	...	MH	Modify ⍇Stretch	V22

```
Command: stretch
Select objects: c
First corner: [pick]
Other corner: [pick]
Select objects: [Enter]
Base point: [pick]
New point: [pick]
```

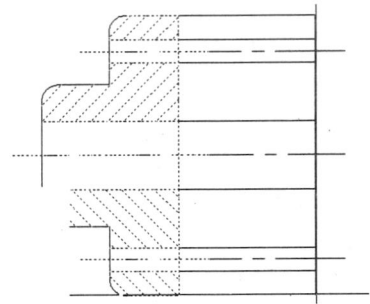

COMMAND LINE OPTIONS

First corner	First selection must be **CPolygon** or **Crossing** object selection.
Select objects	Selects other objects using any selection mode.
Base point	Indicates the starting point for stretching.
New point	Stretches the object larger or smaller.

RELATED COMMANDS

Change	Changes the size of lines, circles, text, blocks, and arcs.
Scale	Increases or decreases the size of any object.

TIPS

- The effect of the **Stretch** command is not always obvious; be prepared to use the **Undo** command.

- The first time you select objects for the **Stretch** command, you must use **Crossing** or **CPolygon** object selection.

- Objects entirely within the selection window are moved, rather than stretched.

- The **Stretch** command will not move a hatch pattern unless the hatch's origin is included in the selection set.

- Use the **Stretch** command to automatically update associative dimensions by including the dimension's endpoint in the selection set.

Style

V. 2.0 Creates and modifies a text style via dialog box (*an external command in DdStyle.Lsp*).

Command	Alias	Ctrl+	F-key	Alt+	Menu Bar	Tablet
style	st	...	...	OS	Format ⮂Text Style	U2
ddstyle						
-style						

Command: **style**
Displays dialog box:

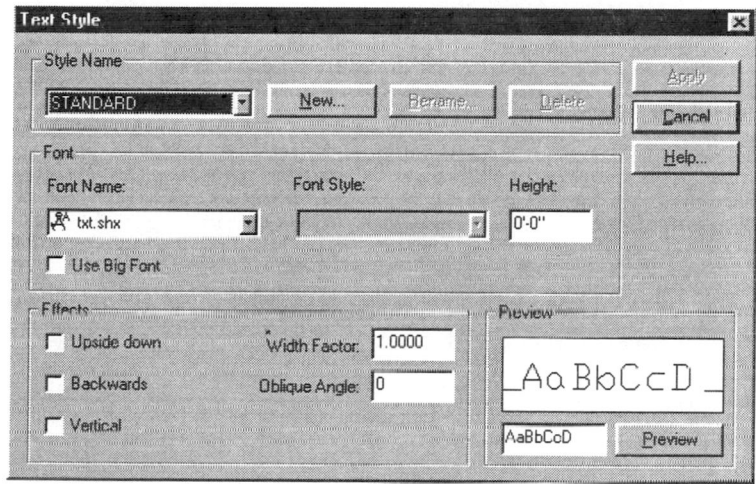

DIALOG BOX OPTIONS

Style Name options:

Style Name   Select an existing text style.
New   Create a new text style; displays dialog box:

Rename   Rename an existing text style; displays dialog box:

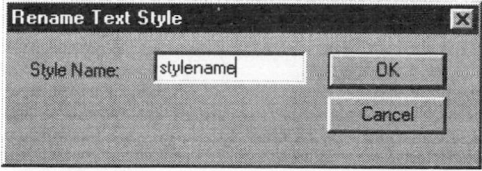

Delete	Delete a text style.

Font options:

Font Name	Name of AutoCAD SHX or Windows TrueType TTF font.
Font Style	Select from available font styles, such as Normal and Bold.
Height	Text height.
Use Big Font	Use a big font file, typically for Asian alphabets.

Effects options (not available for all fonts):

Upside Down   Draw text upside down: ⌐∀°B⍴ϽϽ D ⌐

Backwards   Draw text backwards: └ ᗡϽϽᗭoA┘

Vertical   Draw text vertically.

Width Factor   Change the width of characters.

Width factor = 0.5 (left) and 2.0 (right):

Oblique Angle   Slant characters forward or backward:

Oblique angle = 30 (left) and -30 (right):

Preview   Preview the effects on the style.

```
Command: -style
Text style name (or ?) <STANDARD>: [Enter]
Font file <ROMANS>: [Enter]
 Height <0.0000>: [Enter]
 Width factor <1.00>: [Enter]
Obliquing angle <0>: [Enter]
Backwards? <N> [Enter]
Upside-down? <N> [Enter]
Vertical? <N> [Enter]
STANDARD is now the current text style.
```

COMMAND LINE OPTIONS

Text style name	Names the text style; maximum = 31 characters (*default* = *"STANDARD"*).
?	Lists the names of styles already defined in the drawing.
Font file	Names the font file (SHX or TTF) from which the style is defined (*default* = *Txt.Shx*).
Height	Specifies the height of the text (*default* = *0 units*).
Width factor	Specifies the width factor of the text (*default* = *1.00*).

Obliquing angle

Specifies the obliquing angle or slant of the text (*default = 0 degrees*).

Backwards   *Yes*: Text is printed backwards — mirror writing.

                     No (default): Text is printed forwards.

Upside-down   *Yes*: Text is printed upside-down.

                     No (default): Text is printed rightside-up.

Vertical   *Yes*: Text is printed vertically; not available for all fonts.

                     No (default): Text is printed horizontally.

RELATED COMMANDS

Change	Changes the style assigned to selected text.
Purge	Removes unused text style definitions.
Rename	Renames a text style name.
DText	Places a single line of text.
MText	Place paragraph text.
Text	Places a single line of text.

RELATED SYSTEM VARIABLES

TextStyle	The current text style.
TextSize	The current text height.

RELATED FILES

*.SHP	Autodesk's format for vector source fonts.
*.SHX	Autodesk's format for compile vector fonts; stored in \Acad14\Fonts subdirectory.
*.TTF	TrueType font files; stored in \Windows\Fonts subdirectory.

TIPS

- A **Width Factor** of 0.85 fits in 15% more text without sacrificing legibility.

- An **Obliquing Angle** of +15% can sometimes enhance the look of a font.

- The **Obliquing Angle** can be positive (forward slanting) or negative (backward slanting).

- As of Release 14, AutoCAD no longer works with PostScript fonts.

- You can use any TrueType font with AutoCAD.

Subtract

Rel. I I Removes the volume of one 3D model or 2D region from another (*an external command in Acis.Dll*).

Command	Alias	Ctrl+	F-key	Alt+	Menu Bar	Tablet
subtract	su	...	...	MBS	Modify ⤷Boolean ⤷Subtract	X16

```
Command: subtract
Select objects: [pick]
Select objects: [Enter]
1 solid selected.
Objects to subtract from them...
Select objects: [pick]
Select objects: [Enter]
1 solid selected.
```

COMMAND LINE OPTION

Select objets   Selects the objects to be subtracted.

RELATED COMMANDS

Intersect   Removes all but the intersection of two solid volumes.
Union   Joins two solids together.

SysWindows

Rel.13 Controls multiple windows.

Command	Alias	Ctrl+	F-key	Alt+	Menu Bar	Tablet
syswindows	...	...	...	...	...	...

Command: **syswindows**
Cascade/tileHorz/tileVert/Arrangeicons:

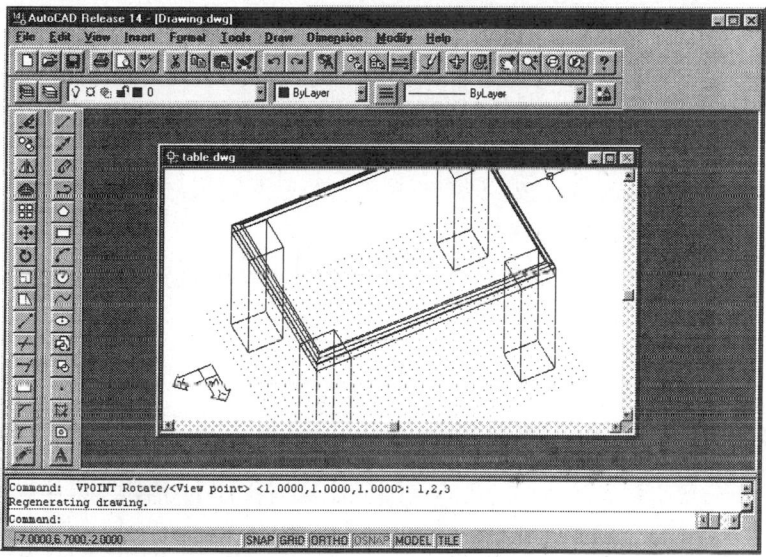

Command Line Options

Cascade	Cacades the window.
tileHorz	Tiles the window horizontally.
tileVert	Tiles the window vertically.
Arrangeicons	Arranges iconized window.

TIPS

- The **SysWindows** command has no practical effect, since AutoCAD supports only a single window.

- Window control icons:

Minimize   Maximize   Close

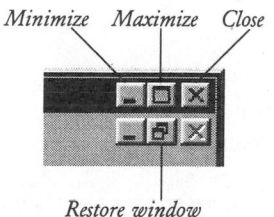

Restore window

'Tablet

V. 1.0 Configures, calibrates, and toggles the digitizing tablet.

Command	Alias	Ctrl+	F-key	Alt+	Menu Bar	Tablet
tablet	ta	T	F4	TT	Tools ⮑Tablet	X7

```
Command: tablet
Options (ON/OFF/CAL/CFG):
```

COMMAND LINE OPTIONS

CAL	Calibrates the coordinates for the tablet.
CFG	Configures the menu areas on the tablet.
OFF	Turns off the tablet's digitizing mode.
ON	Turns on the tablet's digitizing mode.

RELATED SYSTEM VARIABLE

TabMode   Toggles use of the tablet:

TabMode	Meaning
0	Tablet mode disabled.
1	Tablet mode enabled.

RELATED FILES

Acad.Mnu	Menu source code that defines functions of tablet menu areas.
Mc.Exe	Menu compiler; semi-automates the creation of a tablet menu.
Tablet14.Dwg	AutoCAD drawing of the printed template overlay.

TIPS

- AutoCAD includes a plastic tablet overlay in the package.

- To change the tablet overlay, edit the Tablet.Dwg file, then plot it out to fit your digitizer.

- **Tablet** does not work if a digitizer has not been configured with **Preferences**.

- AutoCAD supports up to four independent menu areas; macros are specified by the ***TABLET1 through ***TABLET4 sections of the Acad.Mnu menu file.

- Menu areas may be skewed but corners must form a right angle.

- Projective transformation is a limited form of "rubber sheeting": straight lines remain straight but not necessarily parallel.

DEFINITIONS

Affine transformation
   Requires three pick points; sets an arbitrary linear 2D transformation with independent x,y-scaling and skewing.

Orthogonal transformation
   Requires two pick points; sets the translation; scaling and rotation angle remain uniform.

Residual Error   Largest: where mapping is least accurate; second largest: second-least accurate.

Outcome of fit: A report on the results of transformation types (affine, orthogonal, projective:

Outcome	Meaning
Exact	Enough points to transform data.
Success	More than enough points to transform data.
Impossible	Not enough points to transform data.
Failure	Too many colinear and coincident points.
Cancelled	Fitting cancelled during projective transform.

Projective transformation

Maps a perspective projection from one plane to another plane.

RMS error Root mean square error; smaller is better: measures closeness of fit.

Standard deviation

When near zero: residual at each point is roughly the same.

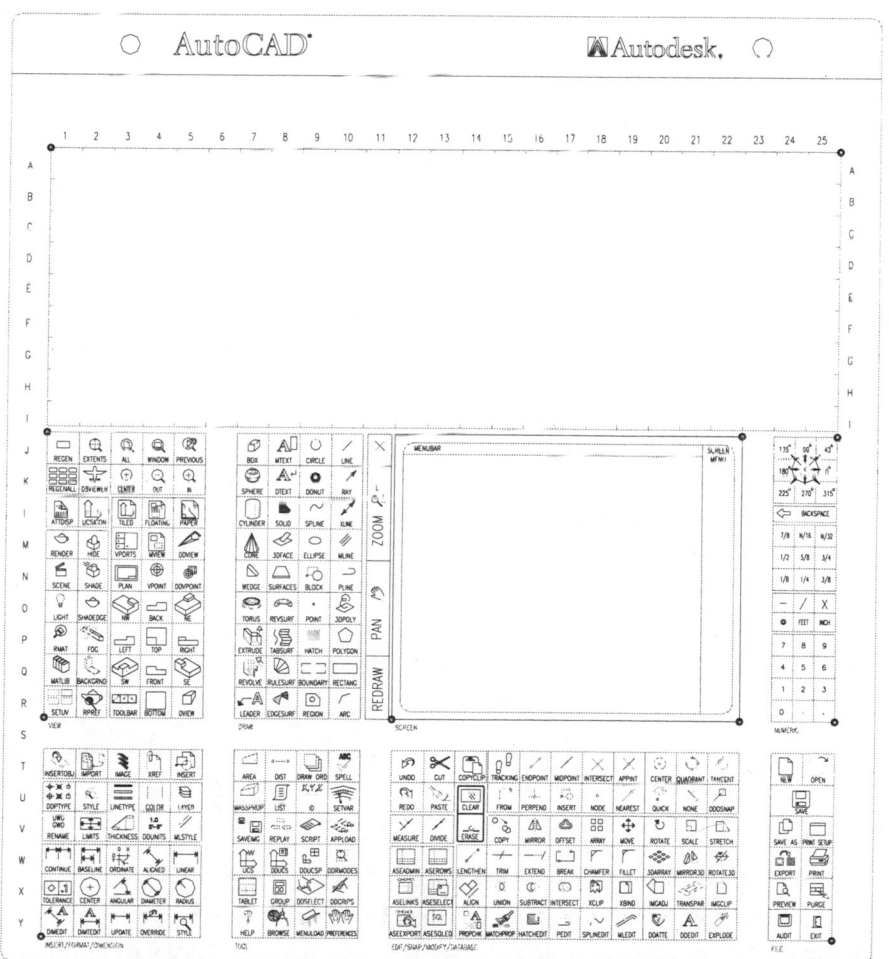

TabSurf

Rel.10 Draws a tabulated surface as a 3D mesh; defined by a path curve, and a direction vector (*short for TABulated SURFace*).

Command	Alias	Ctrl+	F-key	Alt+	Menu Bar	Tablet
tabsurf	...	...	...	DFT	Draw ⮡Surfaces ⮡Tabulated Surface	P8

```
Command: tabsurf
Select path curve: [pick]
Select direction vector: [pick]
```

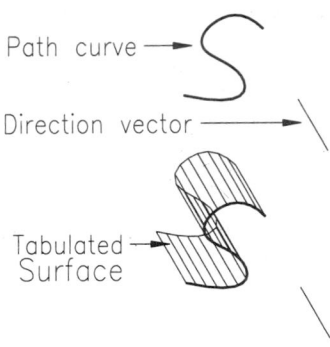

COMMAND LINE OPTIONS
Select path curve
> Selects the object that defines the tabulation path.

Select direction vector
> Selects the vector that defines the tabulation direction.

RELATED COMMANDS
Edge	Changes the visibility of 3D face edges.
Explode	Reduces a tabulated surface into 3D faces.
PEdit	Edits a 3D mesh, such as tabulated surfaces.
EdgeSurf	Draws a 3D mesh surface between boundaries.
RevSurf	Draws a revolved 3D mesh surface around an axis.
RuleSurf	Draws 3D mesh surface between open or closed boundaries.

RELATED SYSTEM VARIABLE
SurfTab1   Defines the number of tabulations drawn by **TabSurf** in n-direction.

TIPS
■ The path curve can be open or closed: line, 2D polyline, 3D polyline, arc, circle, or ellipse.

■ The direction vector defines the direction and length of extrusion.

■ The number of m-direction tabulations is always 2 and lies along direction vector.

■ The number of n-direction tabulations is determined by system variable **SurfTab1** (*default* = 6) along curves only.

 # Text

V. 1.0 Places one line of text in the drawing.

Command	Alias	Ctrl+	F-key	Alt+	Menu Bar	Tablet
text	...	...	...	...	...	...

```
Command: text
Justify/Style/<Start point>: j
Align/Fit/Center/Middle/Right/TL/TC/TR/ML/MC/MR/BL/BC/BR: r
Height <0.2000>: [Enter]
Rotation angle <0>: [Enter]
Text: [type text and press Enter]
```

COMMAND LINE OPTIONS

[Enter] Continues text one line below previously placed text line.

Justify options:

Align Aligns the text between two points with adjusted text height.
Fit Fits the text between two points with fixed text height.
Center Centers the text along the baseline.
Middle Centers the text horizontally and vertically.
Right Right-justifies the text.
TL Top-left justification.
TC Top-center justification.
TR Top-right justification.
ML Middle-left justification.
MC Middle-center justification.
MR Middle-right justification.
BL Bottom-left justification.
BC Bottom-center justification.
BR Bottom-right justification.

Start point Left-justifies the text.

Style options:

Style name Indicates a different style name.
? Lists the currently loaded styles.

RELATED COMMANDS

Change Changes the text height, rotation, style, and content.
DText Places text in the drawing interactively.
MText Places paragraph text.
Style Creates new text styles.

RELATED SYSTEM VARIABLES

TextSize The current height of the text.
TextStyle The current text style.

'TextScr

V. 2.1 Switches from the AutoCAD window to the Text window (*short for TEXT SCReen*).

Command	Alias	Ctrl+	F-key	Alt+	Menu Bar	Tablet
'textscr	...	...	[F2]	VLT	View	...
					↳Display	
					↳Text Screen	

Command: **textscr**

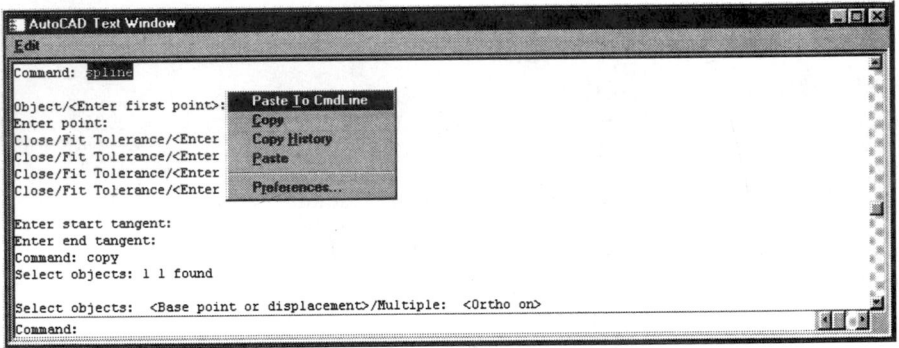

COMMAND LINE OPTIONS
None.

RIGHT-CLICK OPTIONS
Paste to CmdLine
    Pastes text from Windows Clipboard to the command line; available only when Clipboard contains text.
Copy   Copies selected text to the Clipboard.
Copy History Copies all text to the Clipboard.
Paste   Pastes text from Windows Clipboard into text window; available only when Clipboard contains text.
Preferences Displays **Preferences** dialog box.

RELATED COMMAND
GraphScr Switches from Text window to AutoCAD window.

RELATED SYSTEM VARIABLE
ScreenMode Reports whether screen is in text or graphics mode:

ScreenMode	Meaning
0	Text screen.
1	Graphics screen.
2	Dual screen displaying both text and graphics.

REMOVED COMMAND
The **TiffIn** command has been removed from Release 14. Use the **ImageAttch** command.

'Time

V. 2.5 Display time-related information about the current drawing.

Command	Alias	Ctrl+	F-key	Alt+	Menu Bar	Tablet
'time	...	...	...	TQT	Tools ↳Inquiry ↳Time	...

Command: **time**
Display/ON/OFF/Reset: **[Enter]**

Example output:

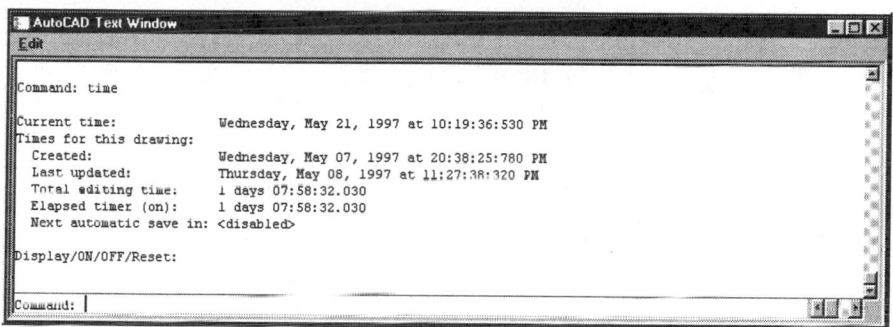

COMMAND LINE OPTIONS

Display	Displays the current time information.
OFF	Turns off the user timer.
ON	Turns on the user timer.
Reset	Resets the user timer.
[F2]	Returns to graphics screen.

RELATED COMMANDS

Status	Displays information about the current drawing and environment.
Preferences	Sets the automatic back-up time.

RELATED SYSTEM VARIABLES

CDate	The current date and time.
Date	The current date and time in Julian format.
SaveTime	The automatic drawing save interval.
TDCreate	Date and time the drawing was created.
TDInDwg	The time the drawing spent in AutoCAD.
TDUpdate	The last date and time the drawing was changed.
TDUsrTimer	The current user timer setting.

TIP

- The time displayed by the **Time** command is only as accurate as your computer's clock; unfortunately, the clock in most personal computers strays by many minutes per week.

Tolerance

Rel.13 Places geometric tolerancing symbols and text.

Command	Alias	Ctrl+	F-key	Alt+	Menu Bar	Tablet
tolerance	tol	...	...	NT	Dimension Tolerance	X1

Command: **tolerance**
Displays dialog box.

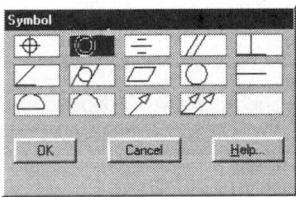

Select symbol. After clicking OK, displays dialog box:

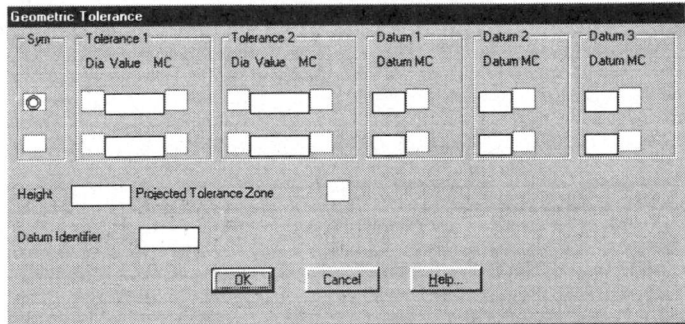

Enter tolerance location: **[pick]**

DIALOG BOX OPTIONS

Symbol options:

Orientation symbols:

$\oplus$ Position.

$\odot$ Concentricity and coaxiality.

$=$ Symmetry.

Form symbols:

⌖·   Cylindricity.

▱   Flatness.

◯   Circularity and roundness.

——   Straightness.

Orientation symbols:

//   Parallelism.

⊥   Perpendicularity.

∠   Angularity.

Profile symbols:

⌓   Profile of the surface.

⌒   Profile of the line.

↗   Circular runout.

⤯⤯   Total runout.

Geometric Tolerance options:

Sym	Geometric characteristic symbol.
Tolerance	First tolerance value.
Dia	Places optional Ø (*diameter*) symbol.
Value	Tolerance value.
Datum	Datum reference.
Height	Projected tolerance zone value.
Projected Tolerance Zone	
	Places projected tolerance zone symbol.
Datum Identifier	
	Creates datum identifier symbol, such as -A-
MC	Material Condition: modifies tolerance symbol; displays dialog box:

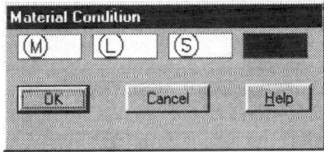

Material Condition dialog box:

(M)   Maximum material condition.

(L)   Least material condition.

(S)   Regardless of feature size.

RELATED FILES

Gdt.Shp	Tolerance symbol definition source file.
Gdt.Shx	Compiled tolerance symbol file.

DEFINITIONS

Datum	A theoretically exact geometric reference, which establishes the tolerance zone for the feature. These objects can be used as a datum: point, line, plane, cylinder, and other geometry.
Material condition	
	These symbols modify the geometric characteristics and tolerance values; modifiers for features that vary in size.
Projected tolerance zone	
	Specifies the height of the fixed perpendicular part's extended portion; changes the tolerance to positional tolerance.
Tolerance	Indicates amount of variance from perfect form.

Toolbar *or* TbConfig

Rel.13   Displays or hides one or all toolbars.

Command	Alias	Ctrl+	F-key	Alt+	Menu Bar	Tablet
toolbar	to	...	...	VO	View Toolbars	R3
-toolbar						
tbconfig						

Command: **toolbar** *or* **tbconfig**
Displays dialog box:

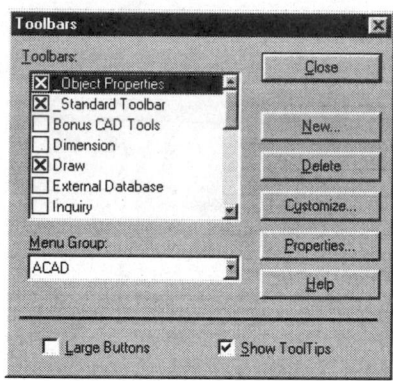

COMMAND LINE OPTIONS

Toolbars	Lists currently loaded toolbars; load other toolbars with **MenuLoad**.
Menu Group	Lists groups of toolbars.
Close	Exits the dialog box.
New	Creates a new toolbar; displays **New Toolbar** dialog box.
Delete	Deletes a toolbar definition; displays dialog box:

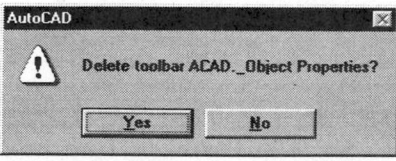

Customize	Customizes a toolbar; displays **Customize Toolbars** dialog box.
Properties	Changes the meaning and icons of a toolbar; displays **Toolbar Properties** dialog box.
Large Buttons	*Yes*: Displays large-format icons. *No*: Displays small-format icons (*default*).
Tool Tips	*Yes*: Displays tool tips (*default*). *No*: Does not display tool tips.

New Toolbar dialog box:

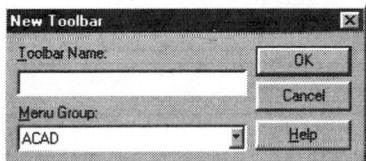

Toolbar Name Names the toolbar.
Menu Group Assigns the new toolbar to a group.

Customize Toolbars dialog box:

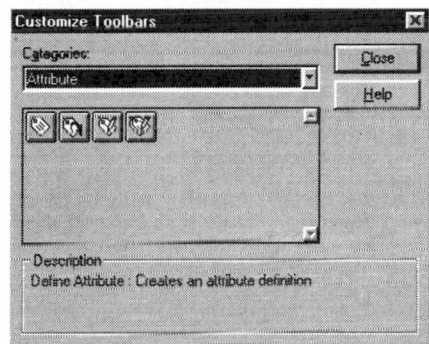

Categories	Displays groups of icons in categories.
Description	Describes the meaning of the currently selected icon.
Close	Closes the dialog box.

Toolbar Properties dialog box:

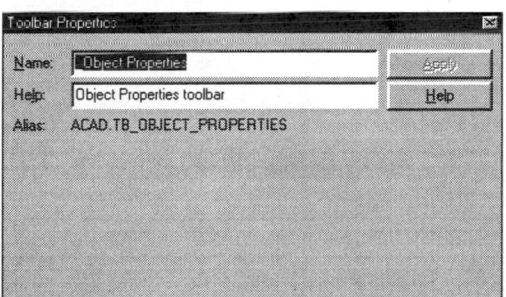

Name	Names the toolbar; appears on the toolbar's title bar.
Help	Specifies the help text displayed on the status line.
Apply	Applies the changes to the toolbar.

```
Command: -toolbar
Toolbar name (or All): all
Show/Hide: <Show>: s
```

COMMAND LINE OPTIONS

Toolbar name   Specifies the name of the toolbar.
All   Work with all toolbars.
Show   Display the toolbar.
Hide   Dismiss the toolbar.

RELATED COMMANDS

MenuLoad   Loads partial menu file, including toolbar definitions.
MenuUnload   Unloads part of the menu file.
Tablet   Configures the tablet.

RELATED SYSTEM VARIABLE

ToolTips   Toggles display of tooltips.

RELATED FILES

*.Mnc   Compiled menu file.
*.Mns   AutoCAD source menu file.
*.Bmp   BMP bitmap files define custom icon buttons.

TIP

■ Elements of a toolbar:

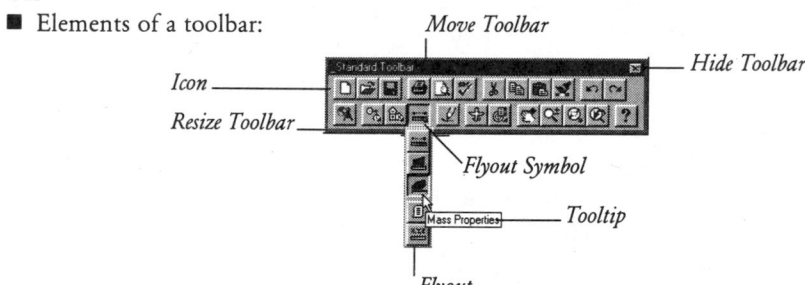

 # Torus

Rel.11 Draws a 3D torus as a solid model (*an external command in Acis.Dll*).

Command	Alias	Ctrl+	F-key	Alt+	Menu Bar	Tablet
torus	tor	...	...	DIT	Draw	O7
					Solids	
					Torus	

```
Command: torus
Center of torus <0,0,0>: [pick]
Diameter/<Radius> of torus: [pick]
Diameter/<Radius> of tube: [pick]
```

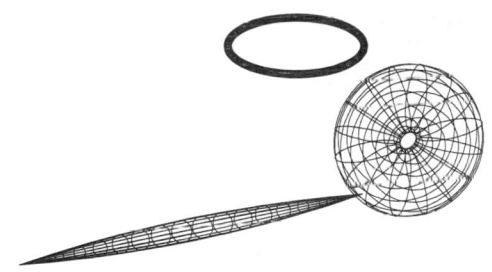

COMMAND LINE OPTIONS

Center of torus Indicates the center of the torus.
Diameter   Indicate the diameter of the torus and the tube
Radius   Indicate the radius of the torus and the tube

RELATED COMMANDS

Ai_Torus   Creates a torus made from 3D polyfaces.
Box   Draws solid boxes.
Cone   Draws solid cones.
Cylinder   Draws solid cylinders.
Sphere   Draws solid spheres.
Wedge   Draws solid wedges.

TIPS

■ **Torus** allows self-intersecting tori.

■ A negative torus radius creates the football shape.

■ When the torus radius is negative, the tube radius must be a larger positive number; for example, with torus radius of -1.99, the tube radius must be greater than +1.99.

Trace

V. 1.0 Draws lines with width.

Command	Alias	Ctrl+	F-key	Alt+	Menu Bar	Tablet
trace	...	...	...	...	...	...

```
Command: trace
Trace width <0.0500>: [Enter]
From point: [pick]
To point: [pick]
To point: [Enter]
```

COMMAND LINE OPTIONS

Trace width	Specifies the width of the trace.
From point	Picks the starting point.
To point	Picks the next vertex.
[Enter]	Exits the **Trace** command.

RELATED COMMANDS

Line	Draws lines with zero width.
MLine	Draws up to 16 parallel lines.
PLine	Draws polylines and polyline arcs with varying width.

RELATED SYSTEM VARIABLES

FillMode	Toggles display of fill or outline traces (*default = 1, on*).
TraceWid	The current width of the trace (*default = 0.05*).

TIPS

- Traces are drawn along the centerline of the pick points.

- Display of a trace segment is delayed by one pick point.

- During drawing of traces, you cannot backup since an Undo option is missing; if you require this feature, draw wide lines with the **PLine** command, setting the **Width** option.

- There is no option for controlling joints (always bevelled) or endcapping (always square); if you require these features, draw wide lines with the **MLine** command, setting the solid fill, endcap, and joint options with the **MlStyle** command.

Tracking

Rel.14 Visually locates x- or y-points; a command modifier.

Command	Alias	Ctrl+	F-key	Alt+	Menu Bar	Tablet
tacking	tk	...	...	...	...	T15
	track					

Example usage:
```
Command: line
From point: tk
First tracking point: [pick]
Next point (Press ENTER to end tracking): [pick]
Next point (Press ENTER to end tracking): [Enter]
To point: [pick]
```

COMMAND LINE OPTIONS

First tracking point
  Picks the first tracking point.
Next point Picks the next tracking point.
[Enter] Exits tracking mode.

RELATED COMMANDS

Any command that prompts for a point, such as 'From point' and 'To point.'

TIPS

- **Tracking** is not a command, but a command option modifier.

- **Tracking** can be used in conjunction with direct distance entry.

- In tracking mode, AutoCAD automatically turns on **Ortho** mode to constrain the cursor vertically and horizontally.

- If you start tracking in the x-direction, the next tracking direction is y and vice versa.

- You can use tracking as many times as you need to at 'From point' and 'To point' prompts.

Transparency

Toggles the transparency of background pixels in a raster image (*an external command in Ism_Arx*).

Command	Alias	Ctrl+	F-key	Alt+	Menu Bar	Tablet
transparency	...	...	...	MOIT	Modify ↳Object ↳Image ↳Transparency	X21

```
Command: transparency
Select objects: [pick]
Select objects: [Enter]
ON/OFF <OFF>: on
```

COMMAND LINE OPTIONS
Select objects   Selects the objects to change transparency.
ON   Makes background pixels transparent.
OFF   Makes background pixels opaque.

RELATED COMMANDS
ImageAttach   Attaches a raster image as an externally referenced file.
ImageAdjust   Changes the brightness, contrast, and fading of a raster image.
LsNew   Places a landscape object in the drawing.

'TreeStat

Rel.12 Displays the status of the drawing's spatial index, including the number and depth of nodes.

Command	Alias	Ctrl+	F-key	Alt+	Menu Bar	Tablet
'treestat	...	...	...	...	...	...

Command: **treestat**

Sample output:
```
Deleted objects: 6
Model-space branch
- - - - - - - - - - - - - - - - - - - - - -
Oct-tree, depth limit = 30
Objects on frozen layers: 73
Objects with undefined extents: 9
Subtree containing objects with defined extents:
    Nodes: 29   Objects: 10   Maximum depth: 20
    Average objects per node: 0.34
    Average node depth: 12.34  - Average object depth: 18.20
    Objects at depth 14: 1   17: 2   19: 4   20: 2
    Nodes with population 0: 23   1: 4   2: 1   4: 1
Total nodes: 32   Total objects: 92

Paper-space branch
. . . . - - - - - - - - - - - - -
Quad-tree, depth limit = 20
Subtree containing objects with defined extents:
    Nodes: 1   Objects: 0
Press RETURN to continue:
    Average objects per node: 0.00
    Average node depth: 5.00
    Nodes with population 0: 1
Total nodes: 4   Total objects: 0
```

COMMAND LINE OPTIONS
None.

RELATED SYSTEM VARIABLES

TreeDepth   Size of the tree-structured spatial index in *xxyy* format:

Depth	Meaning
xx	Number of model space nodes (*default = 30*).
yy	Number of paper space nodes (*default = 20*).
-xx	2D drawing.
+xx	3D drawing (*default*).
3020	Default value of **TreeDepth**.

TreeMax   Maximum number of nodes (*default = 10,000,000*).

TIPS

■ Better performance occurs with fewer objects per oct-tree node.

■ When redraws and object selection seem slow, increase the value of system variable **TreeDepth**.

■ Each node consumes 80 bytes of memory.

DEFINITIONS

Oct tree The model space branch of the spatial index, where all objects are either 2D or 3D. *Oct* comes from the eight volumes in x,y,z-coordinate system of 3D space.

Quad tree The paper space branch of the spatial index, where all objects are two-dimensional. *Quad* comes from the four areas in the x,y-coordinate system of 2D space.

Spatial index Objects indexed by oct-region to record their position in 3D space; has a tree structure with two primary branches: oct tree and quad tree. Objects are attached to *nodes*; each node is a branch on the *tree*.

Trim

V. 2.5 Trims lines, arcs, circles, and 2D polylines back to a real or projected cutting line or view.

Command	Alias	Ctrl+	F-key	Alt+	Menu Bar	Tablet
trim	tr	...	...	MT	Modify Trim	W15

```
Command: trim
Select cutting edges: (Projmode=UCS, Edgemode=No extend)
Select objects: [pick]
Select objects: [Enter]
<Select object to trim>/Project/Edge/Undo: [pick]
```

COMMAND LINE OPTIONS

Select objects Selets the cutting edges.
Select object to trim
        Picks the objects at the trim end.

Edge options:
Extend   Extends cutting edge to trim object.
No extend   Trims only at actual cutting edge.

Project options:
None   Uses only objects as cutting edge.
Ucs   Trims at x,y-plane of current UCS.
View   Trims at current view plane.

Undo   Untrims the last trim action.

RELATED COMMANDS

Change   Changes the size of lines, arcs and circles.
Extend   Lengthens lines, arcs and polylines.
Lengthen Lengthens open objects.
PEdit   Changes polylines.
Stretch   Lengthens or shortens lines, arcs, and polylines.

U

V. 2.5 Undoes the most recent AutoCAD command (*short for Undo*).

Command	Alias	Ctrl+	F-key	Alt+	Menu Bar	Tablet
u	...	Z	...	EU	Edit ↳Undo	T12

Command: **u**

COMMAND LINE OPTIONS
None.

RELATED COMMANDS
Oops   Unreases the most-recently erase object.
Quit   Exits the drawing, undoing all changes.
Redo   Redoes the most-recent undo.
Undo   Allows more sophisticated control over undo.

RELATED SYSTEM VARIABLE
UndoCtl   Determines the state of undo control:

UndoCtl	Meaning
0	Undo mechanism disabled.
1	Undo mechanism enabled.
2	Undo mechanism limited to one command.
4	Auto-group mode.
8	Group currently active.

TIPS
- The **U** command is convenient for stepping back through the design process, undoing one command at a time.

- The **U** command is the same as the **Undo 1** command; for greater control over the undo process, use the **Undo** command.

- The **Redo** command redoes the one most-recent undo only.

- The **Quit** command restores the drawing to its original state.

- Since the undo mechanism creates a mirror drawing file on disk, disable the **U** command with system variable **UndoCtl** (set to 0) when your computer is low on disk space.

- Commands that involve writing to file, plotting, and system variables are not undone.

 # Ucs

Rel.10 Defines a new coordinate plane (*short for User Coordinate System*).

Command	Alias	Ctrl+	F-key	Alt+	Menu Bar	Tablet
ucs	...	...	...	TU	Tools ⤷UCS	W7

```
Command: ucs
Origin/ZAxis/3point/OBject/View/X/Y/Z/Prev/Restore/Save/Del/
?/<World>: [Enter]
```

COMMAND LINE OPTIONS

Del	Deletes the name of a saved UCS.
OBject	Aligns UCS with a picked object.
Origin	Moves the UCS to a new origin point.
Prev	Restores the previous UCS orientation.
Restore	Restore a named UCS.
Save	Saves the current UCS by name.
View	Aligns the UCS with the current view.
World	Aligns the UCS with the WCS.
X	Rotates the UCS about the x-axis.
Y	Rotates the UCS about the y-axis.
Z	Rotates the UCS about the z-axis.
ZAxis	Aligns the UCS with a new origin and z-axis.
3point	Aligns the UCS with a point on the positive x-axis and positive x,y-plane.
?	Lists the names of saved UCS orientations.

RELATED COMMANDS

DdUcs	Modifies the UCS via a dialog box.
UcsIcon	Controls the visibility of the UCS icon.
Plan	Changes the view to the plan view of the current UCS.

RELATED SYSTEM VARIABLES

UcsFollow — Automatically shows the plan view in new UCS:

UcsFollow	Meaning
0	No change in view (*default*).
1	Display plan view of new UCS.

UcsIcon — Determines visibility and location of UCS icon:

UcsIcon	Meaning
0	UCS icon not displayed.
1	UCS icon displayed in lower-right corner (*default*).
2	UCS icon displayed at the UCS origin.

UcsOrg	WCS coordinates of UCS icon (*default = 0,0,0*)
UcsXDir	X-direction of current UCS (*default = 1,0,0*).

| UcsYdir | Y-direction of current UCS (*default = 0,1,0*). |
| WorldUcs | Correlation of WCS to UCS: |

WorldUcs	Meaning
0	Current UCS is WCS.
1	UCS is same as WCS (*default*).

TIPS

- Use the **UCS** command to draw objects at odd angles in 3D space.

- Although you can create a UCS in paper space, you cannot use 3D viewing commands.

- A UCS can be aligned with these objects: point, line, trace, 2D polyline, solid, arc, circle, text, shape, dimension, attribute definition, 3D face, and block reference.

- A UCS will *not* align with these objects: mline, ray, xline, 3D polyline, spline, ellipse, leader, viewport, 3D solid, 3D mesh, region.

DEFINITIONS

UCS   User-defined 2D coordinate system oriented in 3D space; sets a working plane, orients 2D objects; defines the extrusion direction and the axis of rotation.

WCS   World coordinate system is the default 3D x,y,z-coordinate system

UcsIcon

Rel.10 Controls the location and display of the UCS icon.

Command	Alias	Ctrl+	F-key	Alt+	Menu Bar	Tablet
ucsicon	. . .	. . .	. . .	VLU	View ⌲Display ⌲UCS Icon	L2

Command: **ucsicon**
ON/OFF/All/Noorigin/ORigin <ON>:

COMMAND LINE OPTIONS

All	Makes **UcsIcon** command's changes apply to all viewports.
Noorigin	Always displays UCS icon in lower-left corner.
OFF	Turns off display of UCS icon.
ON	Turns on display of UCS icon.
ORigin	Displays UCS icon at the current UCS origin.

RELATED COMMAND

UCS   Creates and controls user-defined coordinate systems.

RELATED SYSTEM VARIABLE

UcsIcon   Determines visibility and location of UCS icon:

UcsIcon	Meaning
0	UCS icon not displayed.
1	UCS icon displayed in lower-right corner (*default*).
2	UCS icon displayed at the UCS origin.

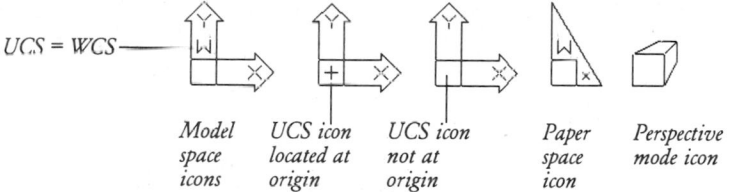

| $UCS = WCS$ | Model space icons | UCS icon located at origin | UCS icon not at origin | Paper space icon | Perspective mode icon |

Undefine

Rel. 9 Makes an AutoCAD command unavailable.

Command	Alias	Ctrl+	F-key	Alt+	Menu Bar	Tablet
undefine	...	...	...	...	...	...

```
Command: undefine
Command name:
```

Example usage:
```
Command: undefine
Command name: line
Command: line
Unknown command.  Type ? for list of commands.
Command: .line
From point:
```

COMMAND LINE OPTIONS

Command name

Specifies the command to undefine.

(*Period*) Precede undefined command with period to temporarily redefine it.

RELATED COMMAND

Redefine   Redefines an AutoCAD command.

TIPS

- The following commands cannot be undefined: AutoLISP, ADS, ObjectARx, external commands, nor aliases.

- In menu macros written with international language versions of AutoCAD, precede command names with an underscore character (_) to automatically translate the name.

Undo

V. 2.5   Undo the effect of previous commands.

Command	Alias	Ctrl+	F-key	Alt+	Menu Bar	Tablet
undo	...	...	...	...	...	...

```
Command: undo
Auto/Control/BEgin/End/Mark/Back/<number>:
```

COMMAND LINE OPTIONS

Auto	Treats a menu macro as a single command.
Back	Undo back to the marker.
BEgin	Group a sequence of operations (formerly the **Group** options).
Control	Limits the options of the **Undo** command.
All	Toggles on full undo.
None	Turns off undo feature.
One	Limits the **Undo** command to a single undo.
End	Ends the group option.
Mark	Sets a marker.
number	Indicate the number of commands to undo.

RELATED COMMANDS

Oops	Unerases the most-recently erased object.
Quit	Leave the drawing without saving changes.
Redo	Undoes the most recent undo.
U	Single-step undo.

RELATED SYSTEM VARIABLES

UndoCtl   Determines the state of undo control:

UndoCtl	Meaning
0	Undo mechanism disabled.
1	Undo mechanism enabled.
2	Undo mechanism limited to one command.
4	Auto-group mode.
8	Group currently active.

UndoMarks   Number of undo marks placed in the **Undo** control stream.

TIP

- Since the undo mechanism creates a mirror drawing file on disk, disable the **Undo** command with system variable **UndoCtl** (set it to 0) when your computer is low on disk space.

- The following commands cannot be undone: **About, Area, AttExt, CvPort, DbList, Delay, Dist, DxfIn, DxfOut, End, GraphScr, Help, Hide, Id, List, New, Open, Plot, PsOut, QSave, Quit, Recover, Redraw, RedrawAll, Regen, RegenAll, ReInit, Resume, Save, SaveAs, Shade, Shell, Status,** and **TextScr.**

Union

Rel.11 Joins solids and regions together into a single object (*an external command in Acis.Dll*).

Command	Alias	Ctrl+	F-key	Alt+	Menu Bar	Tablet
union	uni	...	...	MBU	Modify ⓥBoolean ⓥUnion	X15

```
Command: union
Select objects: [pick]
Select objects: [pick]
Select objects: [Enter]
```

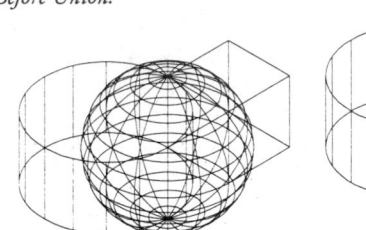
Before Union:

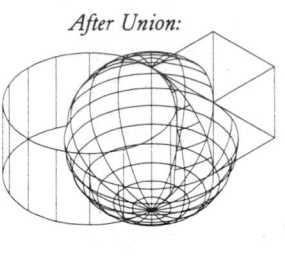
After Union:

COMMAND LINE OPTION
Select objects   Selects the objets to union.

RELATED COMMANDS
Intersect   Creates a solid model from the intersection of two objects.
Subtract   Creates a solid model by subtracting one from another.

'Units

V. 1.4   Controls the display and format of coordinates and angles.

Command	Alias	Ctrl+	F-key	Alt+	Menu Bar	Tablet
'units	...	...	...	...	...	...

```
Command: units

Report formats:        (Examples)
   1.  Scientific      1.55E+01
   2.  Decimal         15.50
   3.  Engineering     1'-3.50"
   4.  Architectural   1'-3 1/2"
   5.  Fractional      15 1/2
```

With the exception of Engineering and Architectural formats, these formats can be used with any basic unit of measurement. For example, Decimal mode is perfect for metric units as well as decimal English units.

```
Enter choice, 1 to 5 <2>: [Enter]
Number of digits to right of decimal point (0 to 8) <4>: [Enter]

Systems of angle measure:        (Examples)
   1.  Decimal degrees           45.0000
   2.  Degrees/minutes/seconds   45d0'0"
   3.  Grads                      50.0000g
   4.  Radians                    0.7854r
   5.  Surveyor's units           N 45d0'0" E

Enter choice, 1 to 5 <1>: [Enter]
Number of fractional places for display of angles (0 to 8) <0>: [Enter]

Direction for angle 0:
   East    3 o'clock  =  0
   North  12 o'clock  =  90
   West    9 o'clock  =  180
   South   6 o'clock  =  270
Enter direction for angle 0 <0>: [Enter]

Do you want angles measured clockwise? <N> [Enter]
```

COMMAND LINE OPTIONS

Report formats Selects scientific, decimal, engineering, architectural, or fractional format for length display.

Number of digits to right of decimal point
Specifies number of decimal places between 0 and 8.

Systems of angle measure
Selects decimal degrees, degrees/minutes/seconds, grads, radians, or surveyor's units for angle display.

Number of fractional places for display of angles
> Specifies number of decimal places between 0 and 8.

Direction for angle 0
> Selects direction for 0 degrees as east, north, west, or south.

Do you want angles measured clockwise?
> *Yes*: measures angles clockwise.
> *No*: measures angles counterclockwise.

[F2]   Return to graphics screen.

RELATED COMMANDS

DdUnits   Sets units via a dialog box.
New   Sets up a drawing with English or metric units.

RELATED SYSTEM VARIABLES

AngBase   Direction of zero degrees.
AngDir   Direction of angle measurement.
AUnits   Units of angles.
AUPrec   Displayed precision of angles.
LUnits   Units of measurement.
LUPrec   Displayed precision of coordinates.
UnitMode   Toggles type of display of units.

TIPS

■ Since 'Units is a transparent command, you can change units during another command.

■ The 'Direction Angle' prompt lets AutoCAD start angle measurement from any direction.

■ AutoCAD accepts the following notation for angle input:

Notation	Meaning
<	Specify an angle based on current units setting.
<<	Bypass angle translation set by **Units** command to use 0-angle-is-east direction and decimal degrees.
<<<	Bypass angle translation; use angle units set by **Units** command and 0-angle-is-east direction.

■ The system variable **UnitMode** forces AutoCAD to display units in the same manner that you enter them.

■ Do not use a suffix — such as **r** or **g** — for angles entered as radians or grads; instead, use the **Units** command to set angle measurement to radians and grads.

'View

V. 2.0 Saves and displays the view in the current viewport by name.

Command	Alias	Ctrl+	F-key	Alt+	Menu Bar	Tablet
'view	-v	. . .	. . .	. . .	. . .	. . .

```
Command: view
?/Delete/Restore/Save/Window: s
View name to save: [type name]
```

COMMAND LINE OPTIONS
Delete	Delete a named view.
Restore	Restores a named view.
Save	Saves the current view with a name.
Window	Saves a windowed view with a name.
?	Lists the names of views saved in the current drawing.

RELATED COMMANDS
DdView	Creates and display views via a dialog box.
Rename	Changes the names of views.

RELATED SYSTEM VARIABLES
ViewCtr	The coordinates of the center of the view.
ViewSize	The height of the view.

TIPS
- Name views in your drawing to quickly move from one detail to another.

- View names are up to 31 characters long and may not contain spaces.

- The **Plot** command plots named views of a drawing.

- Objects outside of the window created by the **Window** option may be displayed but are not plotted.

- You create separate views in model and paper space; when listing named views (with ?), AutoCAD indicates an **M** or **P** next to the view name.

ViewRes

Controls the roundness of curved objects; determines whether zooms and pans are performed as redraws or regens (*short for VIEW RESolution*).

Command	Alias	Ctrl+	F-key	Alt+	Menu Bar	Tablet
viewres	...	...	...	...	...	...

```
Command: viewres
Do you want fast zooms? <Y> [Enter]
Enter circle zoom percent (1-20000) <100>: 1000
Regenerating drawing.
```

ViewRes = 100 (left) and 1 (right).

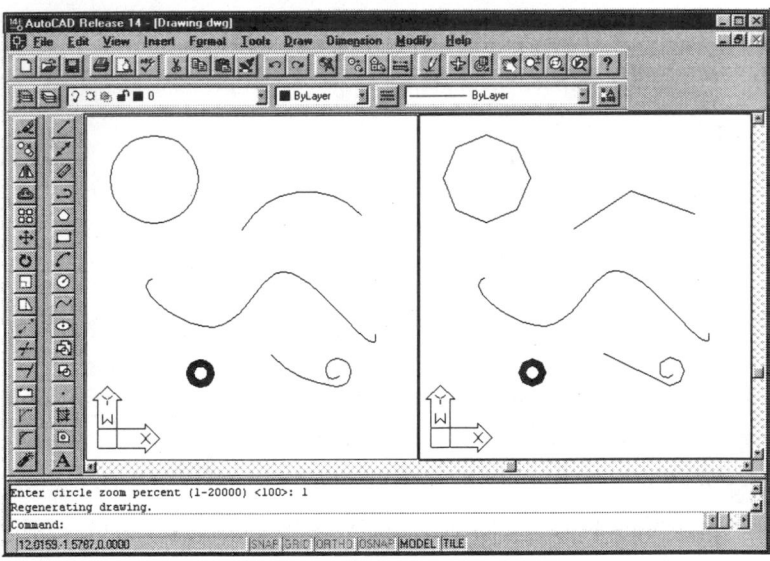

COMMAND LINE OPTIONS

Do you want fast zooms?

> *Yes*: AutoCAD tries to make every zoom and pan a redraw (*faster*).
>
> *No*: Every zoom and pan causes a regeneration (*slower*).

Enter circle zoom percent

> Smaller values display faster but make circles look less round (*see figure*).

RELATED COMMAND

RegenAuto   Determines whether AutoCAD uses redraws or regens.

REMOVED COMMAND

The **VlConv** command has been removed from Release 14. Use the **3dsIn** command instead.

VpLayer

Rel.11 Controls the visibility of layers in viewports when **TileMode** is turned off (*short for ViewPort LAYER*).

Command	Alias	Ctrl+	F-key	Alt+	Menu Bar	Tablet
vplayer	...	...	...	...	...	...

```
Command: vplayer
?/Freeze/Thaw/Reset/Newfrz/Vpvisdflt:
Select a viewport: [pick]
```

COMMAND LINE OPTIONS

Freeze	Indicates the names of layers to freeze in this viewport.
Newfrz	Creates new layers which will be frozen in newly created viewports (*short for NEW FReeZe*).
Reset	Resets the state of layers based on the Vpvisdflt settings.
Thaw	Indicates the names of layers to thaw in this viewport.
Vpvisdflt	Determines which layers will be frozen in a newly created viewport (*short for ViewPort VISibility DeFauLT*).
?	Lists the layers frozen in the current viewport.

RELATED COMMANDS

Layer	Creates and controls layers in all viewports.
MView	Creates and joins viewports when tilemode is off.

RELATED SYSTEM VARIABLE

TileMode	Controls whether viewports are tiled or overlapping.

 # VPoint

V. 2.1 Changes the viewpoint of a 3D drawing (*short for ViewPOINT*).

Command	Alias	Ctrl+	F-key	Alt+	Menu Bar	Tablet
vpoint	-vp	...	...	V3D	View	O3 -
					↳3D Viewpoint	Q5
					↳Tripod	

```
Command: vpoint
Rotate/<View point> <0.0000,0.0000,1.0000>: [Enter]
```

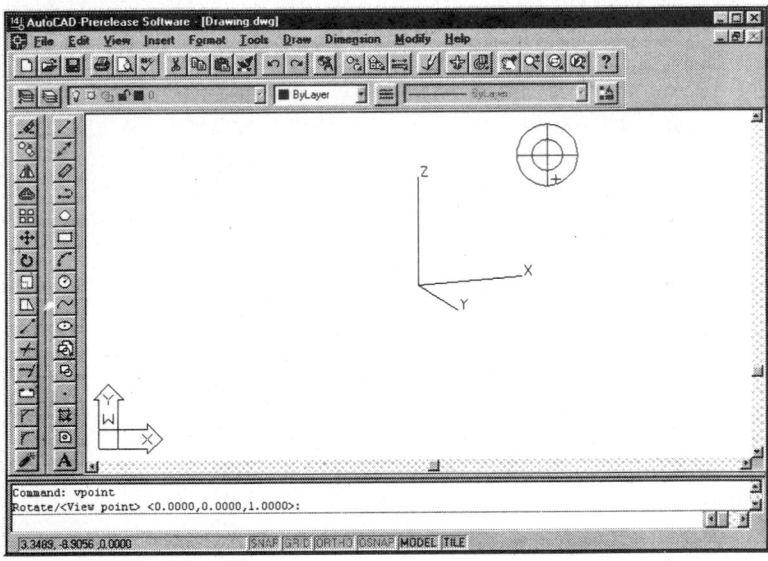

COMMAND LINE OPTIONS

[Enter]	Brings up visual guides (*see figure*).
Rotate	Indicates the new 3D viewpoint by angle.
View point	Indicates the new 3D viewpoint by coordinates.

RELATED COMMANDS

DdVpoint	Adjusts viewpoint via dialog box.
DView	Changes the viewpoint of 3D objects, plus allows perspective mode.

RELATED SYSTEM VARIABLE

WorldView   Determines whether **VPoint** coordinates are in WCS or UCS.

VPorts *or* ViewPorts

Rel.10 Creates viewports of the current drawing when **TileMode** is on.

Command	Alias	Ctrl+	F-key	Alt+	Menu Bar	Tablet
viewports	...	V	...	VD	View	M3
					⮡Tiled Viewports]	
vports						

Command: **viewports** *or* **vports**
Save/Restore/Delete/Join/SIngle/?/2/<3>/4: **[Enter]**

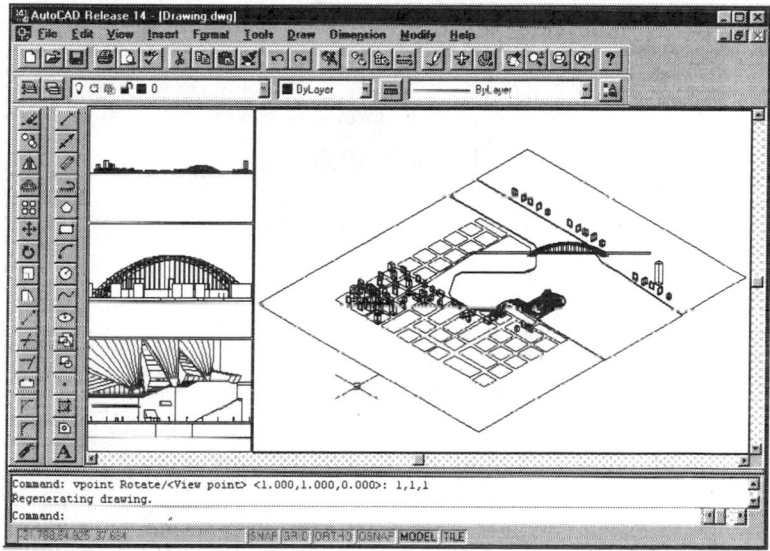

COMMAND LINE OPTIONS

Delete	Deletes a viewport definition.
Join	Joins two viewports together as one.
Restore	Restores a viewport definition.
Save	Saves the settings of a viewport by name.

SIngle Joins all viewports into a single viewport.

2 options:

Horizontal Creates one viewport over the other.

Vertical Creates one viewport beside the other (*default*).

3 options:

Horizontal Creates three viewports over each other.

Vertical Creates three viewports beside each other.

Above Creates one viewport over two viewports.

Below Creates one viewport below two viewports.

Left Creates one viewport left of two viewports.

Right Creates one viewport right of two viewports (*default*).

4 Splits the current viewport into four.

? Lists the names of saved viewport configurations.

RELATED COMMANDS
MView	Creates viewports in paper space.
RedrawAll	Redraws all viewports.
RegenAll	Regenerates all viewports.
[Ctrl]+V	Moves focus to the next viewport.

RELATED SYSTEM VARIABLES
CVPort	The current viewport.
MaxActVp	The maximum number of active viewports.
TileMode	Controls whether viewports can be overlapping or tiled.

VSlide

V. 2.0 Displays an SLD-format slide file in the current viewport (*short for View SLIDE*).

Command	Alias	Ctrl+	F-key	Alt+	Menu Bar	Tablet
vslide	...	...	...	...	...	...

Command: **vslide**
Displays Select Slide File dialog box.

COMMAND LINE OPTIONS
~   Displays file dialog box when **FileDia** = 0.

RELATED COMMANDS
MSlide   Creates an SLD-format slide file of the current viewport.
Redraw   Erases the slide from the screen.

RELATED AUTODESK PROGRAM
SlideLib.Exe   Creates an SLB-format library file of a group of slide files.

TIP
■ For faster viewing of a series of slides, an asterisk proceeding **VSlide** preloads the slide file, as in:

        Command: ***vslide filename**

WBlock

V. 1.4 Writes a block, or part, or all of the drawing to disk (*short for Write BLOCK*).

Command	Alias	Ctrl+	F-key	Alt+	Menu Bar	Tablet
wblock	w	...	...	FE	File	...
				⅋DWG	⅋Export	
					⅋Block	

Command: **wblock**
Displays Create Drawing File dialog box.
Block name: **[type name]**

COMMAND LINE OPTIONS
Block name	Types the name of a block that already exists in the drawing, or:
=	(*Equals*) Writes block to disk using block's name as filename.
*	(*Asterisk*) Writes entire drawing to disk.
[Enter]	Creates a block on disk of selected objects.
[Space]	Moves selected objects to the specified drawing.

RELATED COMMANDS
Block	Creates a block of a group of objects.
Export	Dialog-box front end for the **WBlock** command.

 # Wedge

Rel.11 Draws a 3D wedge as a solid model (*an external command in Acis.Dll*).

Command	Alias	Ctrl+	F-key	Alt+	Menu Bar	Tablet
wedge	we	...	...	DIW	Draw	N7
					ⓑSolids	
					ⓑWedge	

```
Command: wedge
Center/<Corner of wedge> <0,0,0>: [pick]
Cube/Length/<other corner>: [pick]
Height: [pick]
```

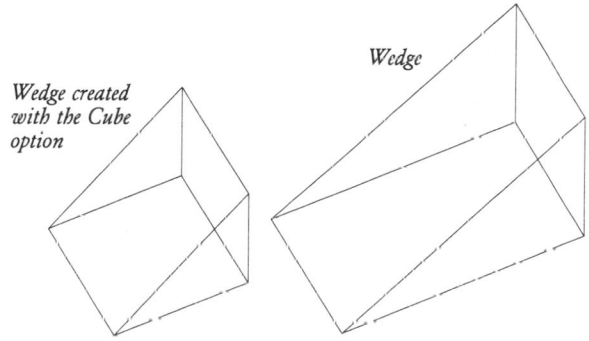

Wedge created with the Cube option

Wedge

COMMAND LINE OPTIONS

Center	Draws wedge base about a center point.
Corner	Draws wedge base between two pick points.
Cube	Draws a cubic wedge.
Length	Specify length, width, and height of wedge.

RELATED COMMANDS

Ai_Wedge	Draws wedge as a 3D surface model.
Box	Draws solid boxes.
Cone	Draws solid cones.
Cylinder	Draws solid cylinders.
Sphere	Draws solid spheres.
Torus	Draws solid tori.

Wmfln

Rel.12 Imports a WMF vector file (*short for Windows MetaFile IN*).

Command	Alias	Ctrl+	F-key	Alt+	Menu Bar	Tablet
wmfin	. . .	. . .	. . .	IW	Insert ⤷Windows Metafile	. . .

Command: **wmfin**
Displays Import WMF dialog box.
Insertion point: **[pick]**
X scale factor <1>/Corner/XYZ: **1**
Y scale factor (default=X): **[Enter]**
Rotation angle <0>: **[Enter]**

DIALOG BOX OPTIONS
Import Options options:

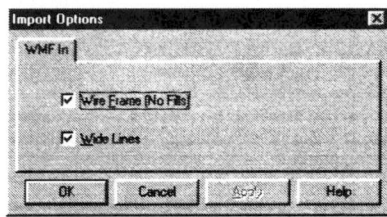

Wire Frame *On*: WMF image is displayed with lines only, no filled areas (*default*).
  Off: WMF is imported with area fills.
Wide Lines *On*: Wide lines are imported as is (*default*).
  Off: Wide lines are imported with a width of zero.

COMMAND LINE OPTIONS
Insertion point Picks the insertion point of the lower-left corner of the WMF image.
X scale factor Scales the WMF image in the x-direction (*default = 1*).
Corner Scales the WMF image in the x- and y-directions.
XYZ Scales the image in the x-, y-, and z-directions.
Y scale factor Scales the image in the y-direction (*default = x scale*).
Rotation angle Rotates the image (*default = 0*).

RELATED COMMANDS
WmfOpts Controls the importation of WMF files.
WmfOut Exports selected objects in WMF format.

TIPS
■ The WMF is placed as a block with the name **WMF0**; subsequent placements increment the digit: **WMF1, WMF2**, et cetera.

■ Exploding the WMF*n* block results in polylines; even circles, arcs, and text are converted to polylines; solid-filled areas are exploded into solid triangles.

WmfOpts

Rel.12 Controls the importation of WMF files (*short for Windows Meta File OPTionS*).

Command	Alias	Ctrl+	F-key	Alt+	Menu Bar	Tablet
wmfopts	...	...	...	IW	Import ⤷Options ⤷Windows Metafile ⤷Options	...

Command: **wmfopts**
Displays dialog box:

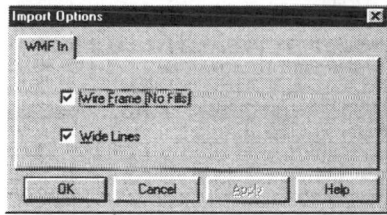

DIALOG BOX OPTIONS

Wire Frame   *On*: WMF image is displayed with lines only, no filled areas (*default*).
                 Off: WMF is imported with area fills.

Wide Lines   *On*. Wide lines are imported as is (*default*).
                 Off: Wide lines are imported with a width of zero.

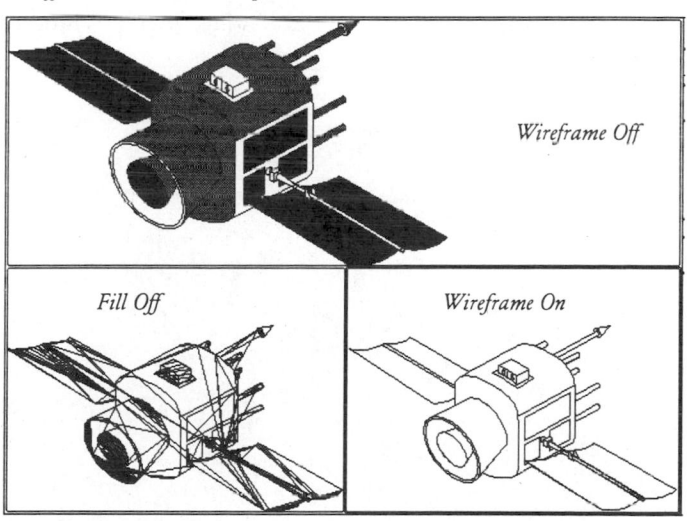

RELATED COMMANDS

WmfIn   Imports WMF files.
WmfOut   Exports selected objects in WMF format.

WmfOut

Rel.12 Exports a WMF vector file (*short for Windows MetaFile OUTput*).

Command	Alias	Ctrl+	F-key	Alt+	Menu Bar	Tablet
wmfout	...	...	...	FE	File	...
				⌐WMF	⌐Export	
					⌐Metafile	

Command: **wmfout**
Displays Create WMF File dialog box.
Select objects: **[pick]**
Select objects: **[Enter]**

COMMAND LINE OPTION
Select objects Selects objects to export.

RELATED COMMANDS
WmfOpts Controls the importation of WMF files.
WmfIn Imports files in WMF format.
CopyClip Copies selected objects to the Windows Clipboard in several formats, including WMF, also called "picture" format.

TIPS
- WMF files created by AutoCAD are resolution-dependent; small circles and arcs lose their roundness.

- The **All** selection does not select all objects in the drawing; instead, **WmfOut** selects all objects *visible* in the current viewport.

XAttach

Rel.14 Attaches an externally referenced drawing to the current drawing (*short for eXternal ATTACH*).

Command	Alias	Ctrl+	F-key	Alt+	Menu Bar	Tablet
xattach	xa	...	...	...	...	...

Command: **xattach**
Displays Select File to Attach dialog box.
After you select a DWG file, displays dialog box:

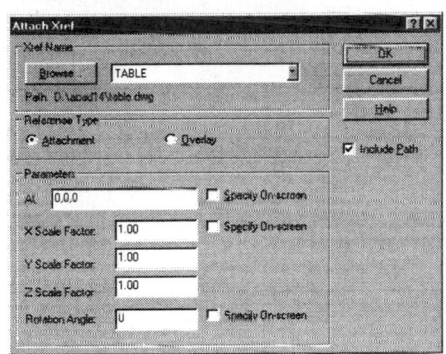

Attach Xref FILENAME: C:\acad14\filename.dwg
FILENAME loaded.

DIALOG BOX OPTIONS

Xref Name options:

Browse	Displays the **Select File To Attach** dialog box.
Xref Name	Displays the names — not necessarily the same as the filename — of currently attached xref files.

Reference Type options:

Attachment	Attaches the xref.
Overlay	Overlays the xref.

Parameters options:

Specify Onscreen
Specifies the **At, Scale Factor,** and **Rotation Angle** in the drawing.

At	Inserts the xref drawing's **Base** point (*default = 0,0*).
X Scale Factor	Scales the xref in the x-direction.
Y Scale Factor	Scales the xref in the y-direction.
Z Scale Factor	Scales the xref in the z-direction.
Rotation Angle	Rotates the xref.

Include Path	*Yes*: Saves the xref's filename and full path in the DWG file.
	No: Saves only the filename of the xref; when the xref cannot be found, AutoCAD searches the **Support File Search Path** and the **ProjectName.**

RELATED COMMANDS

XBind	Binds portions of an externally referenced drawing to the current drawing.
XClip	Inserts an externally referenced block.
XRef	Attaches another drawing to the current drawing.

RELATED SYSTEM VARIABLES

DemandLoad   Specifies if and when AutoCAD demand loads a third-party application if a drawing contains custom objects created in that application:

DemandLoad	Meaning
0	Demand loading turned off.
1	Loads app when drawing contains proxy objects.
2	Loads app when the app's command is invoked.
3 *(default)*	Loads app when drawing contains proxy. objects or when the app's command is invoked.

IdxCtl   Controls the creation of layer and spatial indices:

IndexCtl	Meaning
0	No indices created (*default*).
1	Creates layer index.
2	Creates spatial index.
3	Creates both layer and spatial indices.

ProjectName   Holds the project name for the current drawing (*default* = "").
 VisRetain   Specifies how the layer settings — on-off, freeze-thaw, color, and linetype — in xref drawings are defined by the current drawing:

VisRetain	Meaning
0	Xref layer definition in the current drawing takes precedence.
1	Settings for xref-dependent layers take precedence over xref layer definition in the current drawing.

XLoadCtl   Controls the loading of xref drawings:

XLoadCtl	Meaning
0	Loads entire xref drawing.
1	Demand loading; xref is opened.
2	Demand loading; copy of the xref is opened

XLoadPath   Stores the path of temporary copies of demand-loaded xref drawings.
 XRefCtl   Controls whether XLG external reference log files are written:

XRefCtl	Meaning
0	XLG file not written (*default*).
1	XLG log file written.

XBind

<u>Rel.11</u> Binds portions of an externally-referenced drawing to the current drawing (*short for eXternal BINDing*).

Command	Alias	Ctrl+	F-key	Alt+	Menu Bar	Tablet
xbind	xb	...	...	MOEB	Modify	X19
					⮑Object	
					⮑External Reference	
					⮑Bind	
bind	-xb					

Command: **xbind**
Displays dialog box:

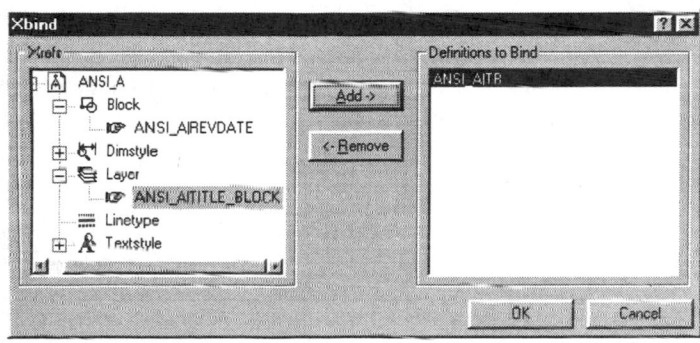

DIALOG BOX OPTIONS

Xrefs   Lists xrefs, along with their bindable objects: blocks, dimension styles, layer names, linetypes, and text styles.

Definitions to Bind
                    Lists definitions that will be bound.
Add   Adds a definition to the binding list.
Remove   Removes a definition from the binding list.

Command: **-xbind**
Block/Dimstyle/LAyer/LType/Style: **b**
Dependent Block name(s): **[type name]**

COMMAND LINE OPTIONS

Block   Binds blocks to current drawing.
Dimstyle   Binds dimension styles to current drawing.
LAyer   Binds layer names to current drawing.
LType   Binds linetype definitions to current drawing.
Style   Binds text styles to current drawing.

RELATED TOOLBAR ICONS

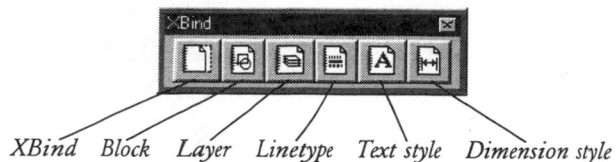

XBind   Block   Layer   Linetype   Text style   Dimension style

RELATED COMMAND

XRef   Attaches another drawing the current drawing.

TIPS

■ The **XBind** command lets you copy named objects from another drawing to the current drawing.

■ Before you can use the **XBind** command, you must first use the **XAttach** command to attach an xref to the current drawing.

■ Blocks, dimension styles, layer names, linetypes, and text styles are known as "dependent symbols."

■ When a dependent symbol is part of an xrefed drawing, AutoCAD uses a vertical bar (|) to separate the xref name from the symbol name, such as *filename|layername*. After you use the XBind command, AutoCAD replaces the vertical bar with **0**, such as *filename0layername*. The second time you bind that layer from that drawing, **XBind** increments the digit, such as *filename1layername*.

■ When **XBind** binds a layer with a linetype (other than Continuous), it automatically binds the linetype.

■ When **XBind** binds a block — with a nested block, dimension style, layer, linetype, text style, and/or reference to another xref — it automatically binds those objects as well.

XClip

Rel.12 Clips a portion of a block or an externally-referenced drawing (*short for eXternal CLIP; formerly the XRefClip command*).

Command	Alias	Ctrl+	F-key	Alt+	Menu Bar	Tablet
xclip	xc	...	...	MOC	Modify ⤷Object ⤷Clip	X18

```
Command: xclip
Select objects: [pick]
Select objects: [Enter]
ON/OFF/Clipdepth/Delete/generate Polyline/<New boundary>: [Enter]
Specify clipping boundary:
Select polyline/Polygonal/<Rectangular>: [Enter]
First corner: [pick]
Other corner: [pick]
```

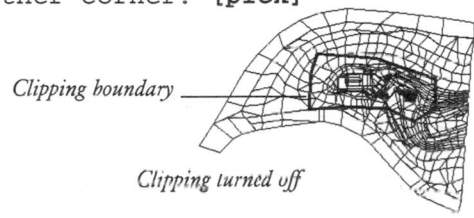

Clipping boundary

Clipping turned off

Clipping turned on

COMMAND LINE OPTIONS

Select objects Selects the xref or block, *not* the clipping polyline.
ON Turns on clipped display.
OFF Turns off clipped display; displays all of the xref or block.
Clipdepth Sets front and back clipping planes for 3D xrefs and blocks.
Delete Erases the clipping boundary.
generate Polyline
 Draws a polyline over top the clipping boundary.
New Boundary Places a new rectangular or irregular (polygon) clipping boundary; or creates an irregular clipping boundary from an existing polyline.

RELATED COMMANDS

XBind Bind parts of the externally referenced drawing to the current drawing.
Xref Displays an externally referenced drawing in the current drawing.

RELATED SYSTEM VARIABLE

XClipFrame Toggles the display of the clipping boundary.

TIPS

- While the old **XRefClip** command could not create an irregularly clipped xref, the new **XClip** command is able to create an arbitrary clipping boundary.

- **XClip** works for both blocks and xrefs.

 # XLine

Rel.13 Places an infinitely long construction line.

Command	Alias	Ctrl+	F-key	Alt+	Menu Bar	Tablet
xline	xl	...	...	DT	Draw	L10
					⌐Construction Line	

```
Command: xline
Hor/Ver/Ang/Bisect/Offset/<From point>: [pick]
Through point: [pick]
```

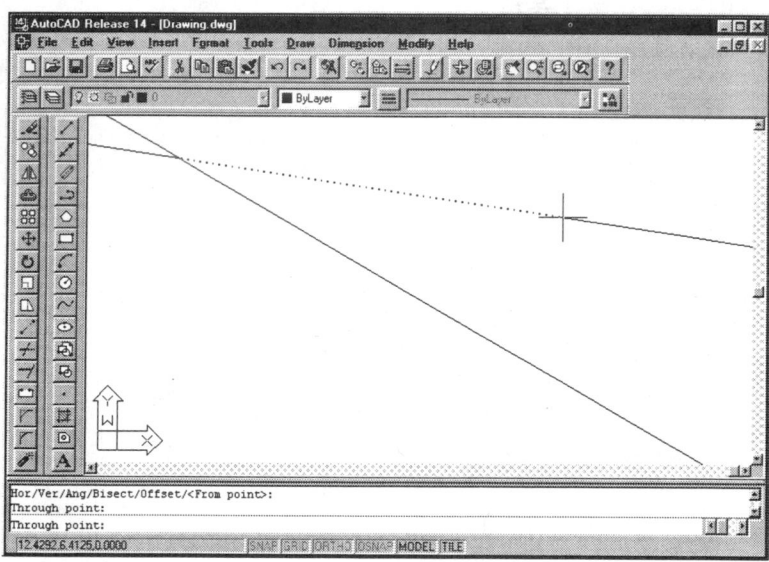

COMMAND LINE OPTIONS

Ang	Places the construction line at an angle.
Bisect	Bisects an angle with the construction line.
From point	Places the construction line through a point.
Hor	Places a horizontal construction line.
Offset	Places the construction line parallel to another object.
Ver	Places a vertical construction line.
[Enter]	Exits the **XLine** command.

RELATED COMMANDS

DdModify	Modifies characteristics of the xline and ray objects.
Ray	Places a semi-infinite construction line.

RELATED SYSTEM VARIABLE

OffsetDist	Current offset distance.

TIP

■ The ray and xline construction lines do not plot.

XRef

Rel.11 Attaches an externally referenced drawing to the current drawing (*short for eXternal REFerence*).

Command	Alias	Ctrl+	F-key	Alt+	Menu Bar	Tablet
xref	xr	...	...	IX	Insert ⟍External Reference	T4
-xref	-xr					

Command: **xref**
Displays dialog box:

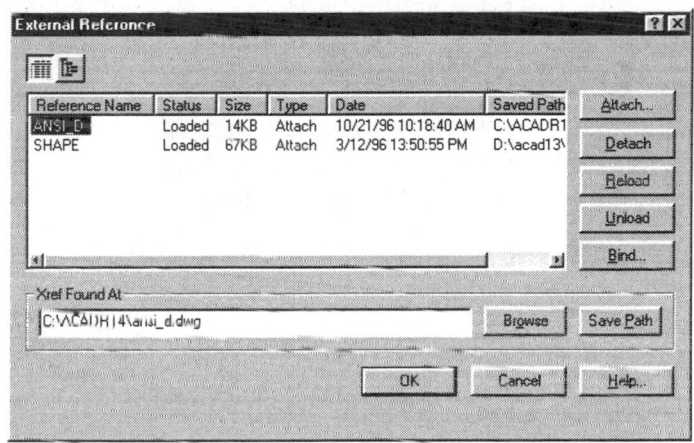

DIALOG BOX OPTIONS

Attach	Attaches a drawing as an external reference; displays the **Attach Xref** dialog box — see **XAttach** command.
Detach	Detaches an xref file.
Reload	Reloads and displays the most-recently saved version of the external reference.
Unload	Unloads the xref; does not remove it permanently; rather it does not display the xref.
Bind	Binds named objects — blocks, dimension styles, layer name, linetypes, and text styles — to the current drawing; displays the **Bind Xrefs** dialog box — see **XBind** command.
Xref Found At	Displays the path to the xref file.
Browse	Selects a path or filename; displays the **Select New Path** dialog box.
Save Path	Saves the path displayed by **Xref Found At**.

```
Command: -xref
?/Bind/Detach/Path/Reload/Overlay/<Attach>: [Enter]
```

COMMAND LINE OPTIONS

Attach	Attaches another drawing to the current drawing.
Bind	Makes the externally referenced drawing part of the current drawing.
Detach	Removes the externally referenced drawing.
Overlay	Overlays the externally referenced drawing.
Path	Respecifies the path to the externally referenced drawing.
Reload	Updates the externally referenced drawing.
?	Lists the names of externally referenced drawings.

RELATED TOOLBAR ICONS

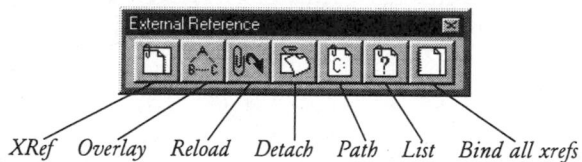

XRef   Overlay   Reload   Detach   Path   List   Bind all xrefs

RELATED COMMANDS

Insert	Adds another drawing to the current drawing.
XBind	Binds parts of the externally referenced drawing to the current drawing.
XClip	Lets you clip an area of an externally referenced drawing to attach to the current drawing.

RELATED SYSTEM VARIABLES

DemandLoad Specifies if and when AutoCAD demand loads a third-party application if a drawing contains custom objects created in that application:

DemandLoad	Meaning
0	Demand loading turned off.
1	Loads app when drawing contains proxy objects.
2	Loads app when the app's command is invoked.
3 (default)	Loads app when drawing contains proxy objects or when the app's command is invoked.

VisRetain Specifies the layer settings — on-off, freeze-thaw, color, and linetype — in xref drawings:

VisRetain	Meaning
0	Xref layer definition in the current drawing takes precedence.
1	Settings for xref-dependent layers take precedence over xref layer definition in the current drawing.

XLoadCtl	Controls the loading of xref drawings:

XLoadCtl	Meaning
0	Loads entire xref drawing.
1	Demand loading; xref is opened.
2	Demand loading; copy of the xref is opened

XLoadPath   Stores the path of temporary copies of demand-loaded xref drawings.

XRefCtl   Controls whether XLG external reference log files are written:

XRefCtl	Meaning
0	XLG file not written (*default*).
1	XLG log file written.

TIPS

- The **XRef** command lets you view other drawings at the same time as the currently loaded drawing; however, you cannot edit the externally referenced drawing.

- *Caution:* Nested xrefs cannot be unloaded.

'Zoom *or* **RtZoom**

V. 1.0 Displays a drawing larger or smaller in the current viewport.

Command	Alias	Ctrl+	F-key	Alt+	Menu Bar	Tablet
'zoom	z	...	...	VZ	View	J3 -
					Zoom	M11

rtzoom

Command: **zoom**
All/Center/Dynamic/Extents/Previous/Scale(X/XP)/Window/
<Realtime>: **[Enter]**
Press Esc or Enter to exit, or right-click to activate pop-up menu.

Command: **rtzoom**
Press Esc or Enter to exit, or right-click to activate pop-up menu.

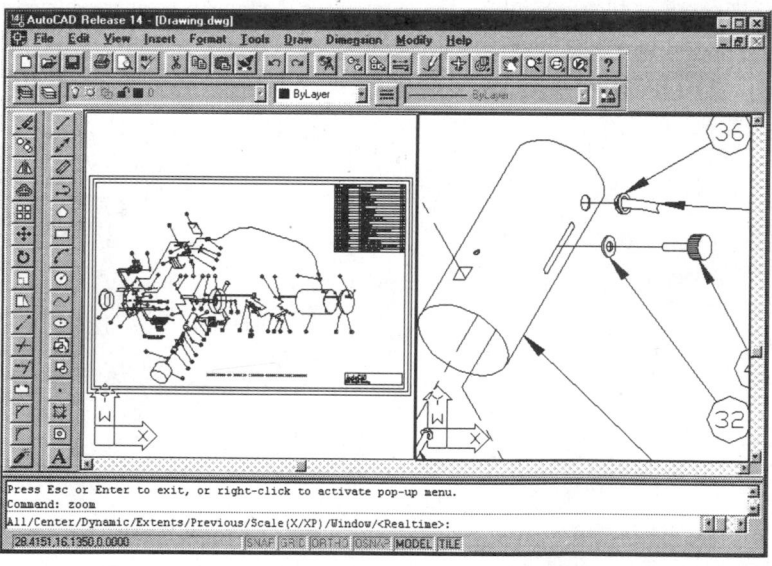

COMMAND LINE OPTIONS

All	Displays the drawing limits or extents, whichever is greater.

Center options:

Center point   Indicates the center point of the new view.
Magnification or Height
     Indicate sa magnification value or height of view.

Dynamic	Brings up the dynamic zoom view.
Extents	Displays the current drawing extents.

Left options:

Lower left corner point
     Indicates the lower-left corner of the new view.

Magnification or Height
Indicates a magnification value or height of view.

Previous Displays the previous view generated by **Pan**, **View**, or **Zoom**.
Realtime Starts real-time zoom.
Vmax Displays the current virtual screen limits (*short for Virtual MAXimum*).
Window Indicate the two corners of the new view.

Scale(X/XP) options:
X Display a new view as a factor of the current view.
XP Display a paper space view as a factor of model space.

[pick] Begins window option.
[Enter] *or* **[Esc]** Ends real-time zoom.

RIGHT-CLICK OPTIONS

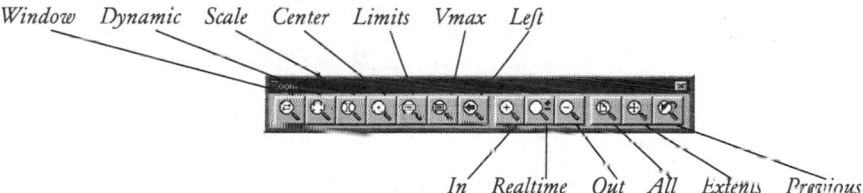

Exit real-time pan mode: — Exit
Real-time pan: — Pan
Real-time zoom: — Zoom
Zoom window: — Zoom Window
Previous view: — Zoom Previous
Zoom to drawing extents: — Zoom Extents

RELATED TOOLBAR ICONS

Window   Dynamic   Scale   Center   Limits   Vmax   Left

In   Realtime   Out   All   Extents   Previous

RELATED COMMANDS
DsViewer Displays **Aerial View** window.
Limits Specifies the limits of the drawing.
Pan Moves the view to a different location.
View Saves views by name.

RELATED SYSTEM VARIABLES
ViewCtr Coordinates of the current view's center point.
ViewSize Height of the current view.
VsMax Upper-right corner of the virtual screen.
VsMin Lower-left corner of the virtual screen.

TIPS
- A scale factor of 1 displays the entire drawing as defined by the limits.

- A zoom factor of 2 enlarges objects (*zooms in*), while 0.5 makes objects smaller (*zooms out*).

3D

Rel.11 Draws 3D primitives with polymeshes (*an external command in 3D.Lsp*).

Command	Alias	Ctrl+	F-key	Alt+	Menu Bar	Tablet
3d	...	...	...	DF3	Draw	N8
					↳Surfaces	
					↳3D Surfaces	

Command: **3d**
Box/Cone/DIsh/DOme/Mesh/Pyramid/Sphere/Torus/Wedge:
*See **Ai_Box** command for more details.*
*Selecting **Draw | Surfaces | 3D Surfaces** from the menu bar displays dialog box:*

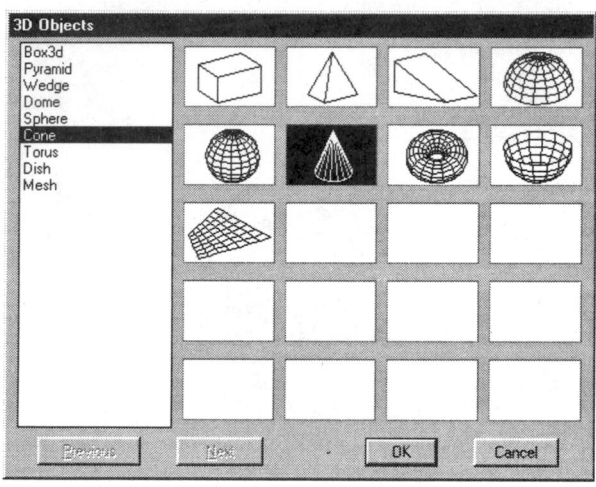

COMMAND LINE & DIALOG BOX OPTIONS

Box	Draws a 3D box or cube.
Cone	Draws cone shapes.
DIsh	Draws a dish — bottom-half of a sphere.
DoOme	Draws a dome — top-half of a sphere.
Mesh	Draws a 3D mesh.
Pyramid	Draws pyramid shapes.
Sphere	Draws a sphere.
Torus	Draw torus — 3D donut — shapes.
Wedge	Draws wedge shapes.

RELATED COMMANDS

Ai_Box	Draws a 3D surface box or cube.
Ai_Cone	Draws a 3D surface cone shape.
Ai_Dish	Draws a 3D surface dish.
Ai_Dome	Draws a 3D surface dome.
Ai_Mesh	Draws a 3D mesh.
Ai_Pyramid	Draws a 3D surface pyramid.
Ai_Sphere	Draws a 3D surface sphere.

Ai_Torus	Draw a 3D surface torus.
Ai_Wedge	Draws a 3D surface wedge.
Box	Draws a 3D solid box or cube.
Cone	Draws a 3D solid cone.
Cylinder	Draws a 3D solid cylinder.
Sphere	Draws a 3D solid sphere.
Torus	Draws a 3D solid torus.
Wedge	Draws a 3D solid wedge.

RELATED TOOLBAR ICONS

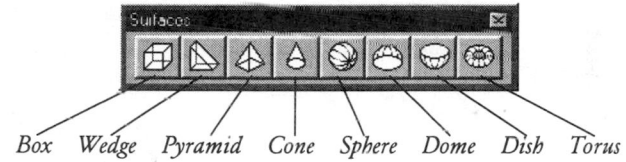

Box   Wedge   Pyramid   Cone   Sphere   Dome   Dish   Torus

TIPS

- The **3D** command creates 3D objects made of 3D meshes and *not* 3D solids.

- To draw a cylinder, apply thickness to a circle.

- You *cannot* perform Boolean operations on 3D surface models.

- To convert a 3D solid model to a 3D surface model, export the drawing with the **3dsOut** command, then import with the **3dsIn** command.

- Use the **Ucs** command to place 3D surface models in space; use the **VPoint** and **Dview** commands to view surface models from different 3D viewpoints.

- You can apply the **Hide, Shade,** and **Render** commands to 3D surface models.

3dArray

Rel.11 Creates 3D rectangular and polar arrays (*an external command in 3dArray.Lsp*).

Command	Alias	Ctrl+	F-key	Alt+	Menu Bar	Tablet
3darray	...	...	...	M33	Modify ↳3D Operation ↳3D Array	W20

```
Command: 3darray
Select objects: [pick]
Select objects: [Enter]
Rectangular or Polar array (R/P):
```

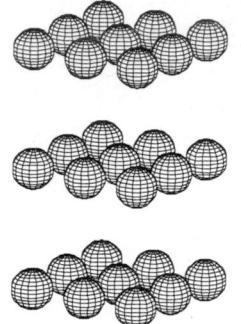

3D rectangular array   *3D Polar array.*

Rectangular array options:
```
Number of rows (---) <1>: [Enter]
Number of columns (|||) <1>: [Enter]
Number of levels (...) <1>: [Enter]
Distance between rows (---) <1>: [Enter]
Distance between columns (|||) <1>: [Enter]
Distance between levels (...) <1>: [Enter]
```

Polar array options:
```
Number of items: [type number]
Angle to fill <360>: [Enter]
Rotate objects as they are copied? <Y>: [Enter]
Center point of array: [pick]
Second point on axis of rotation: [pick]
```

COMMAND LINE OPTIONS

Rectangular array options:

R	Creates a rectangular 3D array.
Number of rows	Specifies the number of rows in x-direction.

Number of columns
Specifies the number of columns in y-direction.

Number of levels
Specifies the number of levels in z-direction.

Distance between rows
Specifies the distance between objects in the x-direction.

Distance between columns
Specifies the distance between objects in the y-direction.

Distance between levels
Specifies the distance between objects in the z-direction.

Polar array options:

P	Creates a polar array in 3D space.

Number of items
Specifies the number of objects to array.

Angle, to fill
Specifies the distance along the circumference that objects are arrayed (*default = 360 degrees*).

Rotate objects as they are copied?
Yes: objects are rotated so that they face the central axis (*default*).
No: objects are not rotated.

Center point of array
Specifies the x,y,z-coordinates for one end of the axis for the polar array.

Second point on axis of rotation
Specifies the x,y,z-coordinates for the other end of the array axis.

[Esc]	Interrupts drawing of array.

RELATED COMMANDS

Array	Creates rectangular or polar array in 2D space.
Copy	Creates one or more copies of the selected object.
MInsert	Creates a rectangular block-array of blocks.

 # 3dFace

V. 2.6 Draws a 3D face with three or four corners.

Command	Alias	Ctrl+	F-key	Alt+	Menu Bar	Tablet
3dface	3f	...	...	DFF	Draw	M8
					⌖Surfaces	
					⌖3D Face	

```
Command: 3dface
First point: [pick]
Second point: [pick]
Third point: [pick]
Fourth point: [pick]
```

COMMAND LINE OPTIONS

First point Picks the first corner of the face.
Second point Picks the second corner of the face.
Third point Picks the third corner of the face.
Fourth point Picks the fourth corner of the face; or
         press **[Enter]** to create a triangular face.
i Prefix for corner coordinates to make edge invisible.

RELATED COMMANDS

3D Draws 3D objects: box, cone, dome, dish, pyramid, sphere, torus, and wedge.
Edge Changes the visibility of the edges of 3D faces.
EdgeSurf Draws 3D surfaces made of 3D meshes.
PEdit Edits 3D meshes.
PFace Draws generalized 3D meshes.

RELATED SYSTEM VARIABLE

SplFrame Controls the visibility of edges.

TIPS

- A 3D face is the same as a 2D solid, except that each corner can have a different z-coordinate.

- Unlike the **Solid** command, corner coordinates are entered in natural order.

- The **i** (*short for invisible*) suffix must be entered before object snap modes, point filters, and corner coordinates.

- Invisible 3D faces (where all four edges are invisible) do not appear in wireframe views; however, they hide objects behind them in hidden-line mode and are rendered in shaded views.

- 3D faces cannot be extruded.

# 3dMesh

Rel.10 Draws an open 3D rectangular mesh made of 3D faces.

Command	Alias	Ctrl+	F-key	Alt+	Menu Bar	Tablet
3dmesh	. . .	. . .	. . .	DFM	Draw	. . .
					⇘Surfaces	
					⇘3D Mesh	

```
Command: 3dmesh
Mesh M size:
Mesh N size:
Vertex (0, 0):
Vertex (0, 1):
```
...et cetera.

COMMAND LINE OPTIONS

Mesh M size	Specifies the m-direction mesh size (*between 2 and 256*).
Mesh N size	Specifies the m-direction mesh size (*between 2 and 256*).
Vertex (m,n)	Enter a 2D or 3D coordinate for each vertex.

RELATED COMMANDS

3D	Draws a variety of 3D objects.
Explode	Explodes a 3D mesh into individual 3D faces.
PEdit	Edits a 3D mesh.
PFace	Draws a generalized 3D face.
Xplode	Explodes a group of 3D meshes.

RELATED SYSTEM VARIABLES

SurfU	Surface density in m-direction (*default = 6*).
SurfV	Surface density in n-direction (*default = 6*).

TIPS

- It is more convenient to use the **EdgeSurf**, **RevSurf**, **RuleSurf**, and **TabSurf** commands than the **3dMesh** command.

- The range of values for the m- and n-mesh size is 2 to 256.

- The number of vertices = **m x n**.

- The first vertex is at (0,0). The vertices can be any distance from each other.

- The coordinates for each vertex in row **m** must be entered before starting on vertices in row **m+1**.

- Use the **PEdit** command to close the mesh, since it is always created open.

3dPoly

Rel.10 Draws 3D polylines (*short for 3D POLYline*).

Command	Alias	Ctrl+	F-key	Alt+	Menu Bar	Tablet
3dpoly	...	...	...	D3	Draw	O10
					↳3D Polyline	

```
Command: 3dpoly
From point: [pick]
Close/Undo/<Endpoint of line>: [pick]
Close/Undo/<Endpoint of line>: [pick]
Close/Undo/<Endpoint of line>: [Enter]
```

COMMAND LINE OPTIONS

From point	Indicates the starting point of the 3D polyline.
Close	Joins the last endpoint with the start point.
Undo	Erases the last-drawn segment.
Endpoint of line	
	Indicates the endpoint of the current segment.
[Enter]	Ends the **3dPoly** command.

RELATED COMMANDS

Explode	Reduces a 3D polyline into lines and arcs.
PEdit	Edits 3D polylines.
PLine	Draws 2D polylines.

TIPS

- Since 3D polylines are made of straight lines, use the **PEdit** command to spline the polyline as a curve.

- 3D polylines do not support linetypes and widths.

3dsin

Rel.13 Imports a 3DS file created by 3D Studio (*short for 3D Studio IN; an external command in Render.Arx*).

Command	Alias	Ctrl+	F-key	Alt+	Menu Bar	Tablet
3dsin	...	...	...	I3	Insert ↳3D Studio	...

Command: **3dsin**
Displays **3D Studio File Import** *dialog box.*
After selecting a 3DS file, displays dialog box:

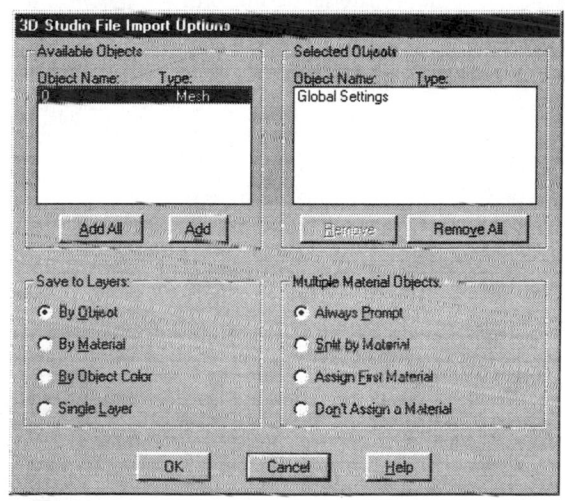

DIALOG BOX OPTIONS

Available and Selected Objects options:

Object Name	Names the object.
Type	Specifies the type of object.
Add	Adds object to Selected Objects list.
Add All	Adds all objects to Selected Objects list.
Remove	Removes object from Selected Objects list.
Remove All	Removes all objects from Selected Objects list.

Save to Layers options:

By Object	Places each object on its own layer.
By Material	Places objects on layers named after materials.
By Object Color	
	Places objects on layers named "Color*nn*."
Single Layer	Places all objects on layer "AvLayer."

Multiple Material Objects options:

Always Prompt Prompts you for each material.

Split by Material
> Splits objects with more than one material into multiple objects, each with one material.

Assign First Material
> Assigns first material to entire object.

Don't Assign to a Material
> Loses all 3D Studio material definitions.

RELATED COMMAND
3dsOut Exports drawing as a 3DS file.

RELATED FILES
*.3DS 3D Studio files.
*.TGA Converted bitmap and animation files.

TIPS
- You are limited to selecting a maximum of 70 3D Studio objects.

- Conflicting object names are truncated and given a sequence number.

- The **By Object** option gives the AutoCAD layer the name of the object.

- The **By Object Color** option places all objects on layer "ColorNone" when no colors are defined in the 3DS file.

- 3D Studio assigns materials to faces, elements, and objects; AutoCAD only assigns materials to object, color, and layer.

- 3D Studio bitmaps are converted to TGA (Targa format) bitmaps.

- Only the first frame of an animation file (CEL, CLI, FLC, and IFL) is converted to a Targa bitmap file.

- Converted TGA files are saved to the 3DS file's subdirectory.

- 3D Studio ambient lights loose their color.

- 3D Studio "omni lights" become point lights in AutoCAD.

- 3D Studio cameras become a named view in AutoCAD.

3dsOut

Rel.13 Exports the AutoCAD drawing as a 3DS file for 3D Studio (*short for 3D Studio OUT; an external command in Render.Arx*).

Command	Alias	Ctrl+	F-key	Alt+	Menu Bar	Tablet
3dsout	...	...	...	FE	File	...
				⇩3DS	⇩Export	
					⇩3D Studio	

Command: **3dsout**
Select objects: **[pick]**
Select objects: **[Enter]**
*Displays **3D Studio File Export** dialog box.*
After specifying a 3DS filename, displays dialog box:

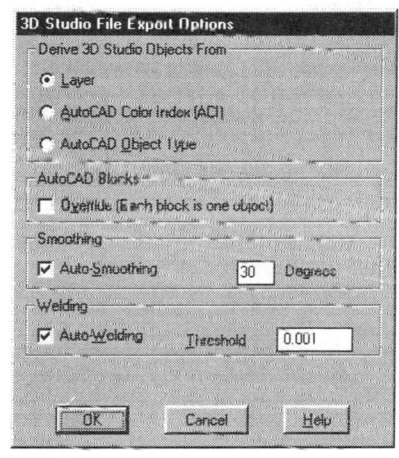

*After selecting options, **3dsOut** exports selected objects:*
Generating objects
Writing preamble
Converting and writing material definitions
Collecting geometry
Converting object *n*
Unifying normals
Assigning smoothing
3D Studio file output completed

COMMAND LINE OPTION

Select objects Selects objects to export; note that **3dsOut** exports only objects with a surface.

DIALOG BOX OPTIONS

Derive 3D Studio Objects From options:

Layer	All objects on an AutoCAD layer become a single 3D Studio object (*default*).
ACI	All objects of an ACI color become a single 3D Studio object.
Object Type	All objects on an AutoCAD object type become a single 3D Studio object.

AutoCAD Blocks option:

Override	Each AutoCAD block becomes a single 3D Studio object; overrides the **Derive 3D Studio Objects From** options.

Smoothing options:

Auto-Smoothing

> *Yes*: Creates a 3D Studio smoothing group (*default*).
> *No*: No smoothing assigned to new 3D Studio objects.

Degrees	Face normals are smoothed when the angle between two face normals is equal to or less than this value (*default = 30 degrees*).

Welding options:

Auto-Welding	*Yes*: Creates a 3D Studio welded vertex (*default*). *No*: Vertices remain unwelded upon export.
Threshold	Two vertices are welded into a single vertex when their interdistance is less than or equal to this value (*default = 0.001*).

RELATED AUTOCAD COMMAND

3dsIn	Imports 3DS file to the drawing.

RELATED FILE

*.3DS	3D studio files.

TIPS

- AutoCAD objects with 0 thickness are not exported, with the exception of circles, polygons, and polyface meshes.
- Solids and 3D faces must have at least three vertices.
- 3D solids and bodies are converted to meshes.
- AutoCAD blocks are exploded unless **Override** is turned on.
- The weld threshold distance ranges from 0.00 000 001 to 99,999,999.
- AutoCAD named views become 3D Studio cameras.
- AutoCAD point lights become 3D Studio "omni lights."

Bonus CAD Tools

AutoCAD Release 14 includes 44 bonus commands available from the **Bonus** menu item. In addition, 11 commands are only available by typing at the 'Command' prompt or are meant for use in AutoLISP routines.

BONUS DRAWING TOOLS

Command	Meaning
AscPoint	Reads coordinate points from an ASCII file.
RevCloud	Draws a revision cloud.

BONUS EDITING TOOLS

Command	Meaning
ExChProp	Extends the **DdChProp** command.
ExTrim	Extended **Trim** command.
MoCoRo	Moves, copies, rotates, and scales in one command.
MpEdit	**PEdit** applied to more than one polyline.
MStretch	**Stretch** applied to more than one object.
WipeOut	Solid fills an area in the background color.
Xplode	Extended version of the **Explode** command.

BONUS LAYER TOOLS

Command	Meaning
LayCur	Changes the layer of selected objects to the current layer.
LayFrz	Freezes the layer of the selected object.
LayIso	Freezes all layers, *except* of the selected object.
LayLck	Locks the layer of the selected object.
LayMch	Changes the layer of the selected objects to the layer of destination objects.
LayOff	Turns off the layer of the selected object.
LayOn	Turns on *all* layers.
LayThw	Thaws *all* layers.
LayUlk	Unlocks the selected layer.
LMan	Exports and imports layer settings to LAY file.

BONUS TEXT TOOLS

Command	Meaning
ArcText	Places text along an arc.
ChT	Globally changes text properties.
Find	Finds and replaces text in the drawing.
TextFit	Fits text between two points.
TextMask	Masks drawing objects underneath text.
TxtExp	Explodes text into lines and arcs.

BONUS DIMENSION TOOLS

Command	Meaning
DimEx	Exports dimension styles to a .DIM file.
DimIm	Imports dimension styles to a .DIM file.
QLAttach	Attaches text to a leader.
QLAttachSet	Attaches text to the most like leaders.
QLDetachSet	Detaches annotation text from a group of leaders.
QLeader	Creates leaders via dialog box.

BONUS BLOCK TOOLS

Command	Meaning
BExtend	Extends objects to a block or xref.
BlkLst	Lists the definition of a user-selected block.
BlkTbl	Lists the block table in the drawing.
Block?	Lists all objects in a block.
BTrim	Trims objects to a block or xref.
ClipIt	Cookie cutter for blocks, xrefs, and images.
Count	Counts all blocks in a drawing.
CrossRef	Cross-references a block with named objects.
NCopy	Copies objects from blocks and xrefs.
XList	Lists data about blocks and xrefs.

BONUS ATTRIBUTE TOOLS

Command	Meaning
AttLst	Lists all attributes in a block insertion
Burst	Explodes attribute values into text.
CAttL	Lists all constant attributes of a selected block.
GAttE	Global attribute editor.

BONUS CUSTOMIZING TOOLS

Command	Meaning
AliasEdit	Edits the Acad.Pgp file.
BonusPopup	Displays any menu item as a popup menu.
CmdStat	Keeps track of commands used.
ConvertPLines	Converts "old" polylines to Lwpolyline format.
GetSel	Creates selection set of objects on a layer.
Pack	Packs up a drawing and support files for transport.
Ssx	Creates a selection set.
SysVDlg	Dialog box for changing system variables.
XData	Attaches extended entity data to an object.
XdList	Lists extended entity data attached to an object.

 # AliasEdit

Rel.14   Edits command aliases in Acad.Pgp (*an external command in Alias.Exe*).

Command	Alias	Ctrl+	F-key	Alt+	Menu Bar	Tablet
aliasedit	...	...	...	BTA	Bonus	...
					ⓑTools	
					ⓑCommand Alias Editor	

Command: **aliasedit**
Displays tabbed dialog box:

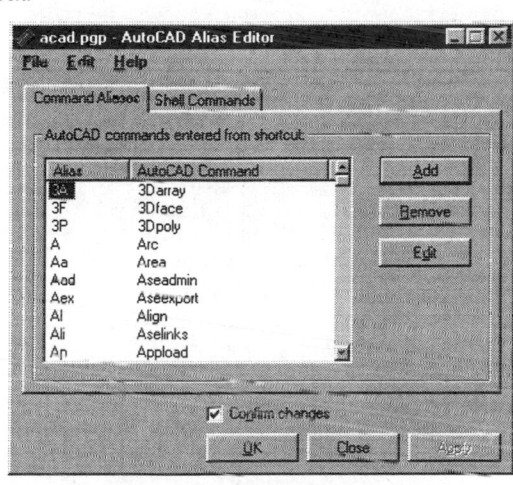

MENU OPTIONS

File menu:

New	Clears the display for creating a new set of aliases.
Open	Opens a PGP file.
Save	Saves settings to a PGP file.
Import	Imports another alias file into the current file; no dubplicate aliases are imported.
Export	Exports the current alias settings to an ASCII TXT text file or PGP file.
Print Setup	Sets options for the current printer.
Print	Prints the alias settings.
Exit	Exits the program.

Edit menu:

Add	Adds a alias or shell command; displays the **New Command Alias** dialog box.
Remove	Removes the currently selected alias.
Edit	Edits a alias or shell command; displays the **Edit Command Alias** dialog box.

Help menu:

Contents	Brings up the help file.
Search	Brings up the help file with the **Search** tab.
About	Displays copyright screen.

DIALOG BOX OPTIONS
Command Aliases tab:

Add	Adds a new command alias to the Acad.Pgp file; displays **New Command Alias** dialog box.
Remove	Removes an command alias from the Acad.Pgp file.
Edit	Edits the selected alias; displays **Edit Command Alias** dialog box.

Confirm Changes

Yes: Prompts for confirmation when an alias is created or modified; displays dialog box:

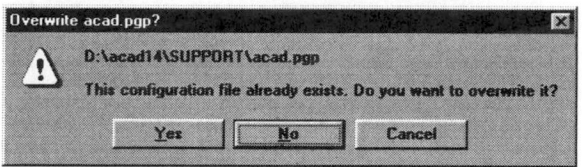

No: Does not prompt for confirmation.

OK	Applies changes and closes the dialog box.
Close	Closes the dialog box.
Apply	Applies changes without closing the dialog box.

New Command Alias dialog box:

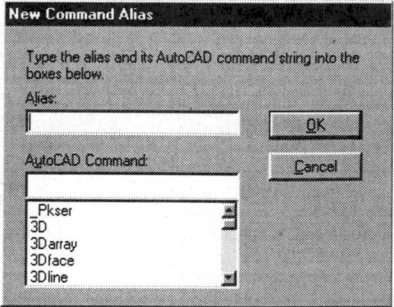

Alias   Specifies the alias name for the selcted command or system variable.

AutoCAD Command

Selects a command or system variable name from the list.

Edit Command Alias dialog box:

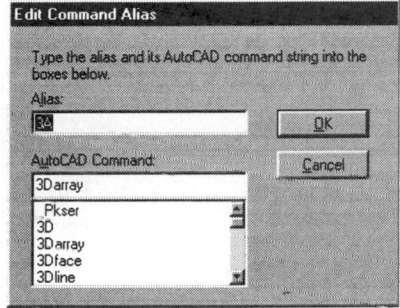

Alias   Specifies the alias name for the selcted command or system variable.
AutoCAD Command
                Selects a command or system variable name from the list.

Shell Commands tab:

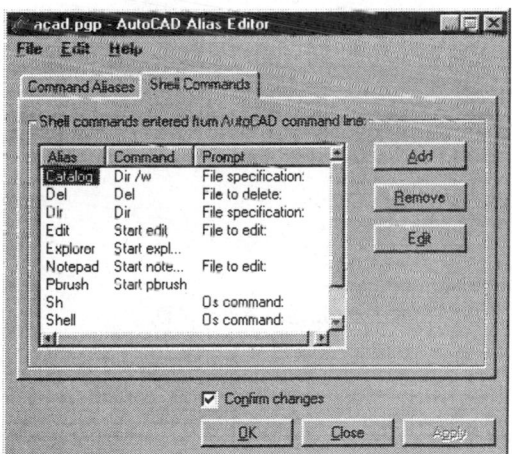

Add   Adds a new shell command; displays **New Shell Command** dialog box.
Remove   Removes a shell command from the Acad.pgp file.
Edit   Edits the selected shell command; displays Edit Shell Command dialog box.
Confirm Changes
                Yes: Prompts for confirmation when an shell command is created or
                modified; displays dialog box:

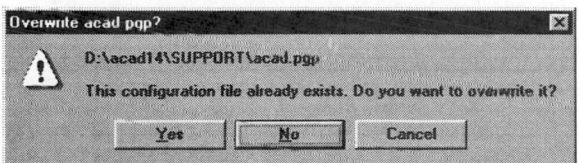

                No: Does not prompt for confirmation.

New Shell Command dialog box:

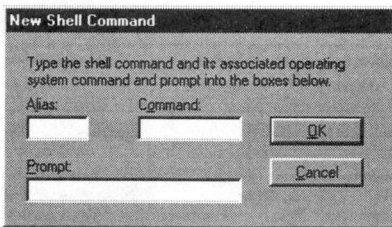

Alias	Specifies the alias for the shell command.
Command	Specifies the DOS command sequence.
Prompt	Specifies the user prompt.

Edit Shell Command dialog box:

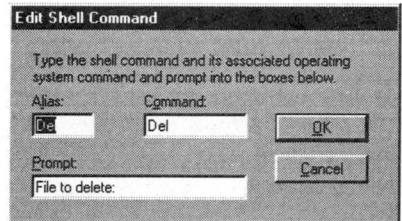

Alias	Edits the alias for the shell command.
Command	Edits the DOS command sequence.
Prompt	Edits the user prompt.

RELATED COMMANDS

Reinit	Reloads the Acad.Pgp file into AutoCAD.
Shell	Runs another program outside of AutoCAD.

RELATED FILE

Acad.Pgp	Store alias and shell command definitions.

TIPS

■ An *alias* is a keyboard shortcut for AutoCAD commands, such as **L** for the **Line** command.

■ Aliases cannot be created for commands in AutoLISP, ADS, and ObjectARx routines; the program must contain its own aliases, such as **XP** for the **Xplode** command.

■ A *shell* command executes a program external to AutoCAD.

■ **AliasEdit** is itself external to AtoCAD via the Alias.Exe command. It prompts:

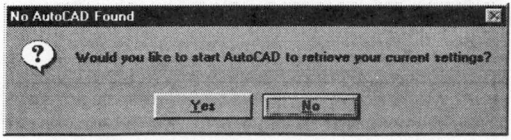

 # ArcText

Rel.14 Places text along an arc (*an external command in ArcText.Arx*).

Command	Alias	Ctrl+	F-key	Alt+	Menu Bar	Tablet
arctext	...	...	...	BEA	Bonus ↳Text ↳Arc Aligned Text	...

atext

Command: **arctext** *or* **atext**
Select an arc or an ArcAlignedText: **[pick]**
Displays dialog box:

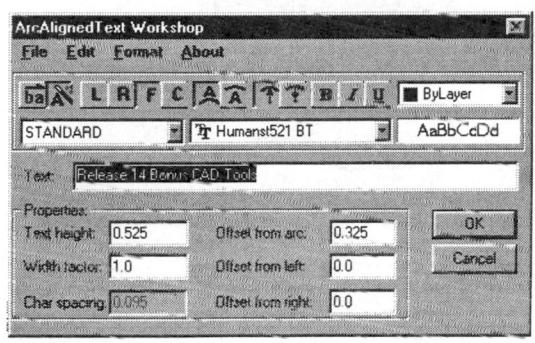

COMMAND LINE OPTIONS

Select an arc Select an arc; displays **ArcAlignedText Workshop** dialog box without text.
Select an ArcAlignedText
Select arced text; displays **ArcAlignedText Workshop** dialog box with text.

DIALOG BOX OPTIONS

File menu:
Update to AutoCAD
Applies text to arc and dismisses dialog box; equivalent to clicking **OK**.
Exit to AutoCAD
Cancels the command; equivalent to clicking **Cancel**.

Edit menu:
Undo	Undo changes to text in the **Text** box.
Redo	Undo the undo.
Cut	Cut selected text to the Windows Clipboard.
Copy	Copy selected text to the Clipboard.
Paste	Paste text from the Clipboard.
Select All	Select all text in **Text** box.
Clear	Erase all text.

Reverse Text   Mirrors text.

Alignment   Justifies the text left, right, fit (*default*), or centered.

Position   Places text on the convex (*outside; default*) or concave (*inside*) side of the arc; see figure below.

Direction   Places text outward from center (*default*) or inward from center.

Typeface   Changes text to display in **boldface**, *italic*, or <u>underlined</u>.

RELATED COMMANDS

Arc   Draws an arc.

MText   Places paragraph text in a straight line.

TIPS

■ For the **ArcText** command to work, you need to first draw an arc with the **Arc** command.

■ For help with the dialog box's many buttons, pause the cursor over buttons for tool tips.

AscPoint

Imports coordinate data from an ASCII file and generates (*short for ASCii POINT; an external command in AscPoint.Lsp*).

Command	Alias	Ctrl+	F-key	Alt+	Menu Bar	Tablet
ascpoint	...	...	...	...	...	...

```
Command: ascpoint
File to read: [type filename]
Comma/Space delimited <Comma>: [Enter]
Generate Copies/Lines/Nodes/3Dpoly/<Pline>: [Enter]
```

COMMAND LINE OPTIONS

File to read Indicates the filename to import; must be in ASCII format.
Comma Specifies that the file format in comma delimited.
Space delimited Specifies that the file format in space delimited.
Generate Copies
Places a copy of an existing object in the drawing at each coordinate point.
Lines Draws line segments from coordinate to coordinate.
Nodes Draws a point at each coordinate point.
3Dpoly Draws a continuous 3D polyline from coordinate to coordinate.
PLine Draws a continuous 2D polyline from coordinate to coordinate; z-coordinates are ignored.

RELATED COMMANDS

DxbIn Imports a DXF file, which can contain coordinate data.
DxfIn Imports a DXF file, which can contain coordinate data.

TIPS

■ The **AscPoint** command can read 2D and/or 3D coordinates.

■ Space delimited format has one coordinate pair (or triplet) per line, with each coordinate separated by one or more spaces, such as the following 3D data:

```
1.2  3.4  5.6
2.3  4.5  7.8
```

■ Comma delimited format has one coordinate pair (or triplet) per line, with each component separated by a comma, such as the following 3D data:

```
1.2,3.4,5.6
2.3,4.5,7.8
```

AttLst

Rel.14 Lists the attributes stored in a block (*short for ATTribute LiST; an external command in Blk_Lst.Lsp*).

Command	Alias	Ctrl+	F-key	Alt+	Menu Bar	Tablet
attlst	...	...	...	...	...	...

Command: **attlst**
Select object: **[pick]**

Sample response:
```
(7.07288 2.80533 0.0) "SNAME": "Splotlight"
(7.74907 2.69533 0.0) "INTENSITY": "1"
(7.74907 2.68033 0.0) "COLOR": "1,1,1"
(7.74907 2.66533 0.0) "ZSIZE": "0"
(7.74907 2.65033 0.0) "BIASMIN": "-1"
(7.74907 2.63533 0.0) "BIASMAX": "-1"
(7.74907 2.62033 0.0) "CONEAN": "10.0"
(7.74907 2.60533 0.0) "CONEDE": "0.0"
(7.74907 2.59033 0.0) "BEAMDI": "0.0"
(7.74907 2.57533 0.0) "LFXYZ": "0,0,0"
Block SH_SPOT has 0 constant attributes.
Block SH_SPOT has 10 variable attributes.
```

COMMAND LINE OPTION
Select object   Select one block.

RELATED COMMANDS
AttDef   Defines attributes.
Block   Creates a block.
BlkLst   Lists the definition of a block.
BlkTbl   Lists the block table to show all block definitions in the current drawing.
CAttL   Lists the constant and variable attributes of a block.

TIPS
■ The **Blk_Lst.Lsp** AutoLISP program is automatically loaded the first time this command is used.

■ This command lists all attributes stored in the block. Constant attributes are read from the block definition; variable attributes are read from the inserted block.

BExtend

Rel.14 Extends objects to a block or xref (*short for Block EXTEND; an external command in TrExBlk.Lsp*).

Command	Alias	Ctrl+	F-key	Alt+	Menu Bar	Tablet
bextend	...	...	...	BMN	Bonus	...
					⤷Modify	
					⤷Extend to Block Entities	

```
Command: bextend
Select edges for extend: [pick]
<Select object to extend>/Project/Edge/Undo: [pick]
```

COMMAND LINE OPTIONS
Select edges for extend
> Selects the object that will form the boundary.

Select objects to extend
> Selects the objects to extend.

Undo Undoes the most recent extend operation.

Project options:
None Extends objects to boundary.
Ucs Specifies that the boundary is the x,y-plane of current UCS.
View Specifies that the boundary is the current view plane.

Edge options:
Extend Extends to implied boundary.
No extend Extends only to actual boundaries.

RELATED COMMANDS
Extend The standard extend-object command.
Insert Inserts a block into the drawing.
XAttach Loads an externally referenced drawing.

TIP
■ The **BExtend** command operates exactly like the **Extend** command, except that it allows the use of a block or externally referenced drawing as the boundary edge.

BlkLst

Rel.14 Lists the definition of a block (*short for BLocK LiST; an external command in Blk_Lst.Lsp*).

Command	Alias	Ctrl+	F-key	Alt+	Menu Bar	Tablet
blklst	...	...	...	...	...	...

```
Command: blklst
Block name: [type name]
```

Sample response:
```
"ATTDEF"
"ATTDEF"
"ATTDEF"
"ATTDEF"
"LINE"
"LINE"
"LINE"
"LINE"
"LINE"
```

COMMAND LINE OPTION

Block name   Type the name of a block.

RELATED COMMANDS

AttDef   Defines attributes.
AttLst   Lists all attributes of a block insertion.
Block   Creates a block.
BlkTbl   Lists the block table to show all block definitions in the current drawing.
CAttL   Lists the constant and variable attributes of a block.

TIPS

■ The **Blk_Lst.Lsp** AutoLISP program is automatically loaded the first time this command is used.

■ This command lists the definition of the block you name.

BlkTbl

<u>Rel.14</u> Lists the block table in the current drawing (*short for BLocK TaBLe; an external command in Blk_Lst.Lsp*).

Command	Alias	Ctrl+	F-key	Alt+	Menu Bar	Tablet
blktbl	. . .	. . .	. . .	. . .	. . .	. . .

Command: **blktbl**

Sample response in dotted pair notation, shown formatted:

```
(
  (0 . "BLOCK")
  (2 . "SH_SPOT")
  (70 . 2)
  (10 0.0 0.0 0.0)
  (-2 . <Entity name: 20e0548>)
)
```

COMMAND LINE OPTION

Block name   Type the name of a block.

RELATED COMMANDS

AttDef	Defines attributes.
AttLst	Lists all attributes of a block insertion.
Block	Creates a block.
BlkLst	Lists the definition of a block.
CAttL	Lists the constant and variable attributes of a block.

TIPS

■ The **Blk_Lst.Lsp** AutoLISP program is automatically loaded the first time this command is used.

■ This command lists the block table, which defines all blocks in the current drawing in dotted pair format.

Block?

<u>Rel.14</u> Lists all objects contained in a block (*an external command in BlockQ.Lsp*).

Command	Alias	Ctrl+	F-key	Alt+	Menu Bar	Tablet
block?	...	...	...	...	...	...

```
Command: block?
Block name/<Return to select>: [Enter]
Pick a block: [pick]
An entity type/<Return for all>: [Enter]
```

Sample response:
```
(                              (100 . "AcDbText")
                               (10 0.0 -0.1 0.0)
  (0 . "BLOCK")                (40 . 0.2)
  (2 . "SH_SPOT")              (1 . "")
  (70 . 2)                     (50 . 0.0)
  (10 0.0 0.0 0.0)             (41 . 1.0)
  (-2 . <Entity name:          (51 . 0.0)
20e0548>)                      (7 . "ASHADE")
)                              (71 . 0)
(                              (72 . 1)
  (-1 . <Entity name:          (11 0.0 -0.1 0.0)
20e0548>)                      (210 0.0 0.0 1.0)
  (0 . "ATTDEF")               (100 . "AcDbAttributeDefinition")
  (5 . "29")                   (3 . "Light Name")
  (100 . "AcDbEntity")         (2 . "SNAME")
  (67 . 0)                     (70 . 0)
  (8 . "ASHADE")               (73 . 0)
  (62 . 1)                     (74 . 0)
  (6 . "CONTINUOUS")         )
```

COMMAND LINE OPTION

Block name   Type the name of a block.
Return to select Press **[Enter]** to pick a block in the drawing.
Pick a block   Picks the block to list.
An entity type Searches for a specific object, such as a line or text.
Return for all Press **[Enter]** to list all objects in the block.

RELATED COMMANDS

AttDef	Defines attributes.
AttLst	Lists all attributes of a block insertion.
Block	Creates a block.
BlkLst	Lists the definition of a block.
CAttL	Lists the constant and variable attributes of a block.
Count	Counts all occurrences of blocks in the drawing.
CrossRef	Searches for named objects in blocks.

This command lists all of the objects contained in a block.

BonusPopup

Allows you to decide which menu pops up at the cursor (*an external command in Popup.Arx*).

Command	Alias	Ctrl+	F-key	Alt+	Menu Bar	Tablet
bonuspopup	...	...	...	BTU	Bonus	...
					⇔Tools	
					⇔Popup Menu	

Command: **bonuspopup**
Ctrl right mouse click to use, or Alt right mouse click to configure.
Command: **[Alt]+[left button]**
Displays popup menu:

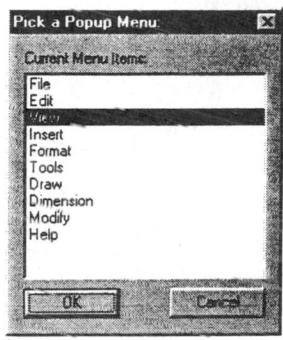

DIALOG BOX OPTION
Current Menu Items
>   Lists the names of all menu items; select one and click **OK**.

Command: **[Alt]+[right button]**
Displays popup menu:

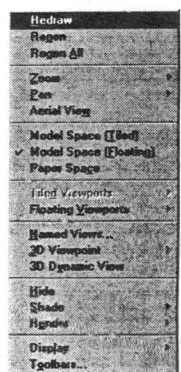

RELATED COMMANDS
Menu	Loads a menu file, replacing the current menu bar and toolbars.
MenuLoad	Loads and unloads partial menu files.

Using the popup menu.

The popup menu displays any one of the items on the menu bar. The default menu is **View**. Here is how to change it to any other menu item:

Step 1: LOAD POPUP.ARX

The popup menu program normally loads automatically into AutoCAD. If the following steps do not work, you need to load the Popup.Arx program on your own. You can do that in any of three ways:

1. Drag the PopUp.Arx file from Windows Explorer or File Manager into AutoCAD. AutoCAD loads the program and reports:

   ```
   (ARXLOAD "D:/ACAD14/BONUS/CADTOOLS/POPUP.ARX")
   "D:/ACAD14/BONUS/CADTOOLS/POPUP.ARX"
   ```

2. Use the **AppLoad** command to load the PopUp.Arx program via dialog box.

3. Use the Arx command to load the program, as follows:

   ```
   Command: arx
   ?/Load/Unload/Commands/Options: l
   ```

AutoCAD displays the **Select ARX File** dialog box. Click on PopUp.Arx and click **Open**.

Step 2: PRESS [ALT]+[RIGHT]

To choose a menu to display in the popup menu:

1. Hold down the **[Alt]** key and press the right mouse button. PopUp displays a list of the current menu items.

2. Select one to appear as the cursor menu.

Step 3: PRESS [CTRL]+[RIGHT]

To bring up the popup menu:

1. Hold down the **[Ctrl]** key and press the right mouse button. **BonusPopUp** displays the menu item.

2. Move the cursor and click on an item.

BTrim

Rel.14 Trims objects to a block (*short for Block TRIM; an external command in TrExBlk.Lsp*).

Command	Alias	Ctrl+	F-key	Alt+	Menu Bar	Tablet
btrim	...	...	...	BMR	Bonus ⤷Modify ⤷Trim to Block Entities	...

Command: **btrim**
Select cutting edges: **[pick]**
<Select object to trim>/Project/Edge/Undo: **[pick]**

COMMAND LINE OPTIONS

Select cutting edges
 Picks the object that forms the trim boundary.
Select object to trim
 Picks the object to be trimmed; pick object at the end you want trimmed.
Undo Untrims the last trim action.

Edge options:
Extend Extends cutting edge to trim object.
No extend Only trims at actual cutting edge.

Project options:
None Uses only objects as cutting edge.
Ucs Trims at x,y-plane of current UCS.
View Trims at current view plane.

RELATED COMMANDS

Trim The standard trim-object command.
XAttach Loads an externally referenced drawing.

TIP

- The **BTrim** command operates just like the **Trim** command, except that it allows the use of a block or externally referenced drawing as the cutting edge.

Burst

Rel.14 Explodes an attribute and keeps the value as text (*an external command in Burst.Lsp*).

Command	Alias	Ctrl+	F-key	Alt+	Menu Bar	Tablet
burst	...	...	...	BEP	Bonus	...
					⌁Text	
					⌁Explode Attributes to Text	

```
Command: burst
Select objects: [pick]
Select objects: [Enter]
```

Original block (left), exploded block with attribute tag (center), and burst block with attribute value (right).

COMMAND LINE OPTION
Select objects   Selects a block or attribute text.

RELATED COMMANDS
AttDef   Creates an attribute definition.
Explode   Explodes an attribute to its original tag.

TIP
■ When the **Explode** command explodes an attribute to its *tag*, the *value* is lost. When the **Burst** command explodes an attribute, it retains the *value*.

CAttL

Rel.14 Lists all constant attributes in a block (*short for Constant ATTribute List; an external command in Blk_Lst.Lsp*).

Command	Alias	Ctrl+	F-key	Alt+	Menu Bar	Tablet
cattl	...	...	...	...	...	...

Command: **cattl**
Block name: **[type name]**
Displays constant attribute data.

When block contains no constant attributes, CAttL reports:
Block name has 0 constant attributes.

COMMAND LINE OPTION
Block name   Type the name of a block.

RELATED COMMANDS
AttDef   Defines attributes.
AttLst   Lists all attributes of a block insertion.
Block   Creates a block.
BlkLst   Lists the definition of a block.
BlkTbl   Lists the block table to show all block definitions in the current drawing.

TIPS
■ The **Blk_Lst.Lsp** AutoLISP program is automatically loaded the first time this command is used.

■ This command lists the constant attributes of a block.

ChT

Rel.14 Globally changes text properties (*short for CHange Text; an external command in ChText.Lsp*).

Command	Alias	Ctrl+	F-key	Alt+	Menu Bar	Tablet
cht	...	...	...	BEC	Bonus	...
					↳Text	
					↳Change Text	

```
Command: cht
Select text to change.
Select objects: [pick]
Verifying the selected entities...
x text entities found.
CHText: Height/Justification/Location/Rotation/Style/Text/
Undo/Width:
```

COMMAND LINE OPTIONS

Select objects	Selects the text objects to change.
Height	Changes the height of text.
Justification	Changes the justification.
Location	Changes the insertion point.
Rotation	Changes the rotation angle of the text string.
Style	Changes the style name.
Text	Changes the wording of the text.
Width	Changes the width factor.

RELATED COMMANDS

DdModify	Changes one line of text at a time.
MText	Places paragraph text.

TIPS

- The **ChT** command is a text property modifier that operates in a global manner on all text objects you select.

- When you select more than one text object with heights that differ, **ChT** displays the range, such as:

```
Height — Min: 0.01  Max: 2.00  Ave: 0.56
```

ClipIt

Rel.14 Defines clipping boundaries for blocks, xrefs, and images using arcs, circles, or polylines (*an external command in ClipIt.Lsp*).

Command	Alias	Ctrl+	F-key	Alt+	Menu Bar	Tablet
clipit	...	...	...	BML	Bonus ⤷Modify ⤷Extended Clip	...

```
Command: clipit
Pick a POLYLINE/CIRCLE/ARC for clipping edge...
Select objects: [pick]
Pick an IMAGE, a WIPEOUT, or an XREF/BLOCK to clip...
Select objects: [pick]
Enter max error distance for resolution of arcs <0.0100>: [Enter]
```

Original block (left); circle boundary applied (center); clipped block (right).

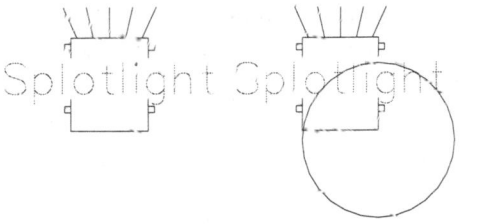

COMMAND LINE OPTIONS
Pick a Polyline/Circle/Arc for clipping edge
Selects a polyline, circle, or arc as the clipping boundary.
Pick an IMAGE, a WIPEOUT, or an XREF/BLOCK to clip
Selects a externally referenced image, wiped out area, xref drawing, or block.
Enter max error distance for resolution of arcs
Specifies the resolution of arced clipping boundary.

RELATED COMMANDS
Arc	Draws an arc.
Circle	Draws a circle
PLine	Draws a polyline.
ImageClip	Clips an image.
WipeOut	Wipes out an area.
XClip	Clips a block or an xref.

TIPS
- **ClipIt** approximates curved boundaries of arcs, circles, and polyline arcs with a series of short straight-line segments.

- If **ClipIt** is applied to the same block, xref, or image with a different boundary, the clipping boundary is recalculated.

CmdStat

<u>**Rel.14**</u> Keeps track of commands used in current editing session (*short for CoMmanD STATus; an external command in CmdCount.Arx*).

Command	Alias	Ctrl+	F-key	Alt+	Menu Bar	Tablet
cmdstat	...	...	...	...	...	...

```
Command: cmdstat
Cumulative/<Session>: [Enter]
```

Sample response:
```
Current Session Command Usage Statistics
Command                     Count       Elapsed Time
--------------------------- -------     ----------

ARX                            1        0:00:01.98
CMDSTAT                        1        0:00:00.00
```

COMMAND LINE OPTIONS
Cumulative Keeps track of command usage until turned off.
Session Keeps track of commands during the current editing session only.

RELATED COMMANDS
LogFileOn Records the Text window to a LOG file on disk.
LogFileOff Stops recording Text window.

TIP
■ This command keeps track of the following data: (1) the commands used; (2) the number of times the command is used; and (3) the total time a command is active.

■ The **CmdCount.Arx** must be manually loaded with the **AppLoad** or **Arx** commands.

■ This command begins to track command usage immediately upon being loaded.

ConvertPLines

Rel.14 Converts "old" polylines to Relase 14's lightweight polyline format (*an external command in PlConvrt.Arx*).

Command	Alias	Ctrl+	F-key	Alt+	Menu Bar	Tablet
convertplines	...	...	...	BTC	Bonus ↳Tools ↳Pline Converter	...

```
Command: convertplines
Type "YES" <all caps> to proceed: YES
***Warning: This will convert all polylines to lightweight
unconditionally. It removes all xdata on existing polylines
and may cause third-party applications reliant on this data
to fail.
```

COMMAND LINE OPTION

Type "YES"   Converts all polylines in the drawing to R14's Lwpolyline format.
[Enter]   Exits command without conversion.

RELATED COMMANDS

Convert   Converts hatch patterns and polylines found in drawings prior to R14.
PLine   Draws polylines.

TIPS

■ The **ConvertPLines** command converts polylines in drawings created prior to Release 14 to the new Lwpolyline object.

■ The advantage of the new Lwpolyline format is that the "lightweight" polyline takes up less space in the drawing file and redraws faster.

■ The disadvantage to the conversion is that it erases any xdata that might be attached.

■ Use the **XDList** command to check for xdata attached to polylines.

Count

Rel.14 Counts the number of insertions of each block (*an external command in Count.Lsp*).

Command	Alias	Ctrl+	F-key	Alt+	Menu Bar	Tablet
count	...	...	...	...	...	...

```
Command: count
Press ENTER to select entire drawing or, Select objects: [Enter]
Counting block insertions...Block Count
```

Sample response:
```
COMPUTER ....... 1
WORKSTATION ...... 2
CHAIR ...... 3
```

COMMAND LINE OPTIONS
Press ENTER to select entire drawing
         Selects all blocks in the current drawing.
Select objects Selects individual blocks.

RELATED COMMANDS
AttDef	Defines attributes.
AttLst	Lists all attributes of a block insertion.
Block	Creates a block.
Block?	Lists all objects contained in a block
BlkLst	Lists the definition of a block.
CAttL	Lists the constant attributes of a block.
Count	Counts all occurrences of blocks in the drawing.
CrossRef	Searches for named objects in blocks.

TIP
- This command counts the number of insertions of each block in the entire drawing.

CrossRef

Searches block definitions for references to a specified layer, linetype, style, dimstyle, mlinestyle, or block, and reports the names of all blocks that contain at least one reference to the specified object (*an external command in Count.Lsp*).

Command	Alias	Ctrl+	F-key	Alt+	Menu Bar	Tablet
crossref	...	...	...	...	...	...

```
Command: crossref
Cross reference Block/LType/Style/Dimstyle/Mlinestyle/<Layer>: [Enter]
Name of Layer to cross reference: [type name]
```

Sample output:

```
Cross reference Block/LType/Style/Dimstyle/Mlinestyle/<Layer>: b
Name of BLOCK to cross reference: sh_spot
Scanning blocks for references to block SH_SPOT.
Scanning block: SH_SPOT
No nested references to block SH_SPOT found.
```

```
Command: crossref
Cross reference Block/LType/Style/Dimstyle/Mlinestyle/<Layer>:
Name of LAYER to cross reference: ashade
Scanning blocks for references to layer ASHADE.
Layer ASHADE is referenced in definition of block SH_SPOT
Scanning block:
Done, layer ASHADE is referenced in 1 block definition(s).
```

COMMAND LINE OPTIONS

Block	Specifies block name.
LType	Specifies linetype name.
Style	Specifies text style name.
Dimstyle	Specifies dimension style name.
Mlinestyle	Specifies multiline style name.
Layer	Specifies layer name (*default*).

Name of layer to cross reference
Specifies the name of the selected named object to reference.

RELATED COMMAND

List   Lists selected objects in the drawing.

TIP

- The **CrossRef** command looks for references to a specified layer, linetype, text style, dimension style, multiline style, or block in all blocks.

- This command reports the names of blocks that contain at least one reference to the specified named object.

DimEx

Rel.14 Exports a dimension style to a .DIM file on disk (*short for DIMension style EXport; an external command in DimSIO.Arx*).

Command	Alias	Ctrl+	F-key	Alt+	Menu Bar	Tablet
dimex	...	...	...	BTE	Bonus	...
					⤷Tools	
					⤷Dimstyle Export	

Command: **dimex**
Displays dialog box:

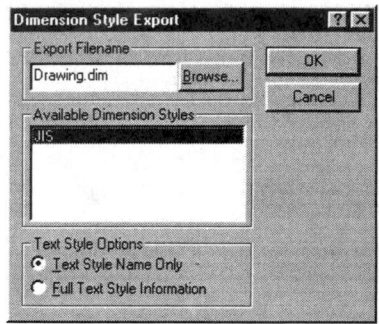

Dimension styles were successfully exported.

DIALOG BOX OPTIONS
Export Filename options:
Filename   Specifies the name for the file; .DIM extension is automatic.
Browse   Selects a filename; displays the **Open** dialog box.

Available Dimension Styles
    Lists the names of all named dimension styles; select only one for export.

Text Style Options options:
Text Style Name Only
    Includes only the name of the text style used by the dimension style.
Full Text Style Information
    Includes all information about the text style.

RELATED COMMANDS
DimIm   Imports a dimension style from file.
DDim   Set dimension settings and creates dimension styles.

TIPS
■ When the drawing contains more than one named dimension style, you must choose one to export.

The dimstyles are exported to a file with the .DIM extension, a plain ASCII file, which lists all dimstyles and their settings.

Dimim

Rel.14 Imports a dimension style from a .DIM file into the current drawing
(short for DIMension style Import; an external command in DimSIO.Arx).

Command	Alias	Ctrl+	F-key	Alt+	Menu Bar	Tablet
dimim	...	...	...	BTI	Bonus	...
					⤷Tools	
					⤷Dimstyle Import	

Command: **dimim**
Displays dialog box:

Dimension styles were successfully imported.

DIALOG BOX OPTIONS

Import Filename options:
Filename   Specifies the name for the file; .DIM extension is automatic.
Browse   Selects a filename; displays the **Open** dialog box.

Import Options options:
Keep Existing Style
Creates a new dimension style in the drawing, perserving the existing style(s).
Overwrite Existing Style
Replaces the existing dimension style.

RELATED COMMANDS

DimEx   Exports a dimension style to file on disk.
DDim   Set dimension settings and creates dimension styles.

TIP

■ The dimstyles are imported from a file with the .DIM extension (a plain ASCII file), which
lists all dimstyles and their settings. A portion of the output:

```
                                                     ——————————DIM file header
          DIMENSION_STYLE_NAME JIS
          DIMTOL 0
          DIMLIM 0
          DIMTIH 0
          ...
          DIMTXSTY STANDARD ——————————————— Text style data
          DIMTXT_FULLINFO 0
          END_DIMTXT
          DIMSCALE 1
          ...
          DIMCLRT 0            ——————————————————DIM file footer
          END_OF_STYLE JIS
```

ExChProp

Rel.13 Extends the **DdChProp** command's dialog box for polylines and text (*short for EXtended CHange PROPerties; formerly the DdChProp2 command; an external command in ExChProp.Lsp*).

Command	Alias	Ctrl+	F-key	Alt+	Menu Bar	Tablet
exchprop	...	...	...	BME	Bonus	...
					⌐Modify	
					⌐Extended Change Properties	

```
Command: exchprop
Select objects: [pick]
Select objects: [Enter]
```
Displays dialog box:

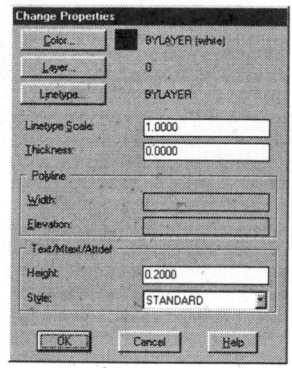

DIALOG BOX OPTIONS

Color   Changes the color of the selected objects.
Layer   Changes the layer.
Linetype   Changes the linetype.
Linetype Scale   Changes the linetype scale.
Thickness   Changes the thickness.

Polyline options:
Width   Changes the width of all segments of the selected polylines.
Elevation   Changes the elevation of the polylines.

Text/MText/Attdef options:
Height   Changes the height of the selected text.
Style   Changes the style name of the text.

RELATED COMMANDS

DdChProp   The predecessor to the **ExChProp** command.
DdModify   Changes all aspects of a single object.
PLine   Draws an polyline.
DText   Places one or more lines of text.
MText   Places paragraph text.

ExTrim

Rel.14 Trims all objects crossing a cutting edge (*short for EXtended TRIM; an external command in ExTrim.Lsp*).

Command	Alias	Ctrl+	F-key	Alt+	Menu Bar	Tablet
extrim	...	...	...	BMT	Bonus	...
					⇘Modify	
					⇘Cookie Cutter Trim	

Command: **extrim**
Pick a Polyline, Line, Circle, or Arc for cutting edge: **[pick]**
Pick the side to trim on: **[pick]**

*Drawing before (left) and after (right) applying **ExTrim** to a circle.*

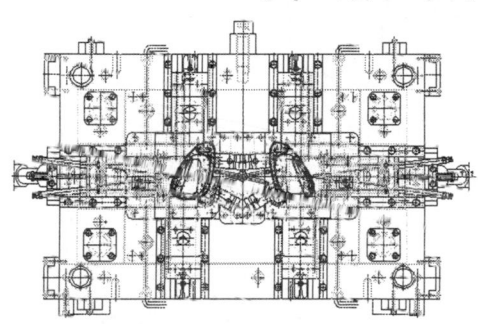 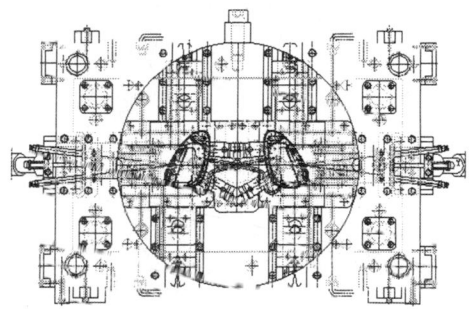

COMMAND LINE OPTIONS

Pick a ... for cutting edge
> Selects an arc, circle, line, or polyline as the trim line.

Pick the side to trim on
> Selects the side to trim objects crossing the cutting line.

RELATED COMMAND

Trim   Trims one object at a time.

TIPS

■ **ExTrim** trims all objects that cross the cutting edge, even a complex polyline.

■ The **ExTrim** command may not work with objects with a linetype other than Continuous.

■ When **ExTrim** cannot trim an object, it reports the following error messages: "Object does not intersect an edge." and "Cannot TRIM this object."

 # Find

Rel.14   Finds and replaces text in the drawing (*an external command in Find.Lsp*).

Command	Alias	Ctrl+	F-key	Alt+	Menu Bar	Tablet
find	...	...	...	BER	Bonus	...
					⤷Text	
					⤷Find and Replace Text	

Command: **find**
Displays dialog box:

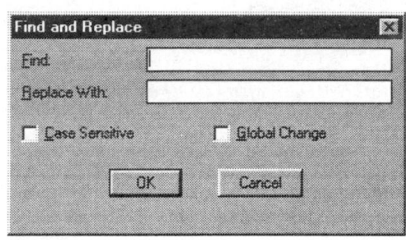

Select objects: **[pick]**
Select objects: **[Enter]**
Changing text (100%)

DIALOG BOX OPTIONS

Find   Type the text to find.
Replace With Type the text to replace with.
Case Sensitive *Yes*: Find and replace are sensitive to upper and lower case.
                  No: Find and replace are not case-sensitive; matches either case.
Global Change *Yes*: Replaces all text.
                  No: Allows user control over replacement; displays dialog box:

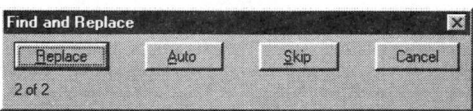

Find and Replace options:

Replace   Replaces this instance of text.
Auto   Automatically replace text.
Skip   Does not replace this instance of text.

RELATED COMMANDS

DText   Places text in the drawing.
DdEdit   Edits text.
MText   Allows search and replace in one paragraph block.
Spell   Checks for recognizable words.

TIPS

■ This command works only with text created with **Text** and **DText** commands; it does *not* work for mtext and attribute text.

■ When performing a search and replace, it is best to *not* use **Global Change**.

 # GAttE

Rel. 14 Globally changes an attribute value in all blocks (*short for Global ATTribute Editor; an external command in GAttE.Lsp*).

Command	Alias	Ctrl+	F-key	Alt+	Menu Bar	Tablet
gatte	...	...	...	BEG	Bonus	...
					⤷Text	
					⤷Global Attribte Edit	

```
Command: gatte
Block name/<select block or attribute>: [pick block]
Block: SH_SPOT    Attribute tag: SNAME
New Text: [type new value for tag]
Number of inserts in drawing = x
Process all of them? <Yes>/No: [Enter]
Please wait...
x attributes changed.
```

COMMAND LINE OPTIONS

Block name   Name of the block containing the attributes you want changed.
Select block   Selects the block — useful when you don't know the block's name.
New Text   Type the new text for the attribute values.

RELATED COMMANDS

AttDef   Defines an attribute.
AttEdit   Edits attributes.

TIPS

■ The **GAttE** command globally edits the value of a tag in all blocks of the same name. After you type in a new value for the attribute, **GAttE** changes the value in *all* blocks in the drawing.

■ GAttE does not change attributes on frozen layers.

GetSel

Rel.14 Creates a selection set of objects on layers (*short for GET SELection; an external command in GetSel.Lsp*).

Command	Alias	Ctrl+	F-key	Alt+	Menu Bar	Tablet
getsel	...	...	...	BTG	Bonus	...
					⃫Tools	
					⃫Get Selection Set	

```
Command: getsel
Select Object on layer to Select from <*>: [pick]
Select type of entity you want <*>: [pick]
Collecting all x items on layer x...
One x item has been placed in the active selection set.
```

COMMAND LINE OPTIONS
Select Object on layer to Select from
> [pick]: Selects the layer from the picked object.
> [Enter]: Selects all layers.

Select type of entity you want
> [pick]: Selects the object.
> [Enter]: Selects all objects.

RELATED COMMAND
Select   Creates a selection set with more options than the **GetSel** command.

TIPS
- The **GetSel** command is like the **Select** command, except that it is limited to selecting layers and objects.

- At both prompts, you can pick an object or press **[Enter]** to select all layers and all objects, respectively.

- The result of the **GetSel** command is a selection set consisting of selected objects that reside only on selected layers.

- In any command you use after **GetSel**, type "P" (short for **Previous**) at the 'Select objects' prompt to access the selection set created by **GetSel**.

 # LayCur

Rel.14 Changes the layer of selected objects to the current layer *(short for LAYer CURrent; an external command in BnsLayer.Lsp).*

Command	Alias	Ctrl+	F-key	Alt+	Menu Bar	Tablet
laycur	...	...	...	BLC	Bonus	...
					ⓑLayer	
					ⓑChange to Current Layer	

```
Command: laycur
Select objects to be CHANGED to the current layer:
Select objects: [pick]
```

COMMAND LINE OPTION

Select objects   Selects the objects to be moved to the current layer.

RELATED COMMANDS

Layer	Displays the **Layer & Linetype** dialog box.
LayIso	Freezes all layers, expect the layer of the selected object.
LayFrz	Freezes the layer of the selected object.
LayMch	Matches the layer of the selected object.
LayOff	Turns off the layer of the selected object.
LayLck	Locks the layer of the selected object.
LayOn	Turns on all layers.
LayThw	Thaws all layers.
LayUlk	Unlocks the layer of the selected object.

TIP

■ This command changes the layer name of the selected objects to the current layer.

 # LayFrz

Rel.14 Freezes the layer of the selected object (*short for LAYer FReeZe; an external command in BnsLayer.Lsp*).

Command	Alias	Ctrl+	F-key	Alt+	Menu Bar	Tablet
layfrz	...	...	...	BLF	Bonus	...
					⬦Layer	
					⬦Layer Freeze	

```
Command: layfrz
Options/Undo/<Pick an object on the layer to be FROZEN>: o
Entity level nesting/No nesting/<Block level nesting>: e
Options/Undo/<Pick an object on the layer to be FROZEN>: [pick]
Layer x has been frozen.
Options/Undo/<Pick an object on the layer to be FROZEN>: [Enter]
```

COMMAND LINE OPTIONS

Pick an object Picks an object, then freezes the layer that the object is on.
Undo   Undoes the previous selection.

Options options:
Entity level nesting
        Freezes the layers of objects, including those nested in block or xref.
No nesting   Freezes the layers of objects selected, including the insertion layer of a block
        or xref.
Block level nesting
        Freezes the layers of objects selected and combines the above two options.

RELATED COMMANDS

Layer	Displays the **Layer & Linetype** dialog box.
LayCur	Changes the layer of selected objects to the current layer
LayIso	Freezes all layers, expect the layer of the selected object.
LayFrz	Freezes the layer of the selected object.
LayMch	Matches the layer of the selected object.
LayOff	Turns off the layer of the selected object.
LayLck	Locks the layer of the selected object.
LayOn	Turns on all layers.
LayThw	Thaws all layers.
LayUlk	Unlocks the layer of the selected object.

TIPS

■ This routine freezes the layer containing the object you picked. To thaw the layer, use the **LayThw** command, which thaws all layers, or use the **Layer** command to selectively thaw layers.

■ When you pick the current layer, **LayFrz** reports, "Cannot freeze layer x. It is the CURRENT layer."

LayIso

Rel.14 Freezes all layers except the layer of the selected object (*short for LAYer ISOlate; an external command in BnsLayer.Lsp*).

Command	Alias	Ctrl+	F-key	Alt+	Menu Bar	Tablet
layiso	. . .	. . .	. . .	BLI	Bonus	. . .
					⤷Layer	
					⤷Layer Isolate	

```
Command: layfrz
Pick an object on the layer to be ISOLATED: [pick]
Layer x has been isolated
```

COMMAND LINE OPTION

Pick an object When you choose an object, this command freezes all layers except the one that the object is on.

RELATED COMMANDS

Layer	Displays the **Layer & Linetype** dialog box.
LayCur	Changes the layer of selected objects to the current layer.
LayFrz	Freezes the layer of the selected object.
LayMch	Matches the layer of the selected object.
LayOff	Turns off the layer of the selected object.
LayLck	Locks the layer of the selected object.
LayOn	Turns on all layers.
LayThw	Thaws all layers.
LayUlk	Unlocks the layer of the selected object.

TIP

- This routine freezes all layers, except the one containing the object you picked. To thaw, use the **LayThw** command, which thaws all layers, or use the **Layer** command to selectively thaw layers.

 # LayLck

Rel.14   Locks the layer of the selected object (*short for LAYer LoCK; an external command in BnsLayer.Lsp*).

Command	Alias	Ctrl+	F-key	Alt+	Menu Bar	Tablet
laylck	...	...	...	BLK	Bonus	...
					⤷Layer	
					⤷Layer Lock	

```
Command: laylck
Pick an object on the layer to be LOCKED: [pick]
Layer x has been locked.
```

COMMAND LINE OPTION

Pick an object When you choose an object, this command locks the layer of the object.

RELATED COMMANDS

Layer	Displays the **Layer & Linetype** dialog box.
LayCur	Changes the layer of selected objects to the current layer
LayIso	Freezes all layers, expect the layer of the selected object.
LayFrz	Freezes the layer of the selected object.
LayMch	Matches the layer of the selected object.
LayOff	Turns off the layer of the selected object.
LayOn	Turns on all layers.
LayThw	Thaws all layers.
LayUlk	Unlocks the layer of the selected object.

TIPS

- This routine locks the layer containing the object you picked. To unlock the layer, use the **LayUlk** command, or use the **Layer** command to selectively thaw layers.

- A locked layer is visible but cannot be edited.

LayMch

Rel.14 Changes the layer name of the selected objects to match the destination layer (*short for LAYer MatCH; an external command in BnsLayer.Lsp*).

Command	Alias	Ctrl+	F-key	Alt+	Menu Bar	Tablet
laymch	...	...	...	BLM	Bonus	...
					⮡Layer	
					⮡Layer Match	

```
Command: laymch
Select objects to be changed:
Select objects: [pick]
Type Name/Select entity on destination layer: [pick]
```

COMMAND LINE OPTIONS

Select objects Selects the objects to be moved to another layer.
Type Name Types the name of the layer.
Select entity on destination layer
Picks the layer based on the object you pick.

RELATED COMMANDS

Layer	Displays the **Layer & Linetype** dialog box.
LayCur	Changes the layer of selected objects to the current layer
LayIso	Freezes all layers, expect the one of the selected object.
LayFrz	Freezes the layer of the selected object.
LayOff	Turns off the layer of the selected object.
LayLck	Locks the layer of the selected object.
LayOn	Turns on all layers.
LayThw	Thaws all layers.
LayUlk	Unlocks the layer of the selected object.

TIPS

■ This command changes the layer name of the selected objects to match the destination layer.

■ At the 'Type Name' prompt, you can type T to type the name of the destination layer, or pick an object on the destination layer.

 # LayOff

Rel.14 Turns off the layer of the selected object (*short for LAYer OFF; an external command in BnsLayer.Lsp*).

Command	Alias	Ctrl+	F-key	Alt+	Menu Bar	Tablet
layoff	...	...	...	BLF	Bonus	...
					⅏Layer	
					⅏Layer Off	

```
Command: layfrz
Pick an object on the layer to be turned OFF: [pick]
Layer x has been turned off.
```

COMMAND LINE OPTION

Pick an object When you selet an object, this command turns off the layer of that object.

RELATED COMMANDS

Layer	Displays the **Layer & Linetype** dialog box.
LayCur	Changes the layer of selected objects to the current layer
LayIso	Freezes all layers, except the one of the selected object.
LayFrz	Freezes the layer of the selected object.
LayMch	Matches the layer of the selected object.
LayLck	Locks the layer of the selected object.
LayOn	Turns on all layers.
LayThw	Thaws all layers.
LayUlk	Unlocks the layer of the selected object.

TIPS

- This routine turns off the layer containing the object you picked. To thaw the layer, use the **LayOn** command, which turns on all layers, or use the **Layer** command to selectively turn on layers.

- Objects are invisible on a layer that is turned off and they not plot. This is exactly like a frozen layer, except that a frozen layer is not regenerated and is thus more efficient.

- When you pick the current layer, **LayOff** asks, "Really want layer *x* (the CURRENT layer) off? <N>: ."

LayOn

Rel.14 Turns on all layers (*short for LAYer ON; an external command in BnsLayer.Lsp*).

Command	Alias	Ctrl+	F-key	Alt+	Menu Bar	Tablet
layon	...	...	...	BLO	Bonus	...
					⇘Layer	
					⇘Turn All Layers On	

```
Command: layon
All layers turned ON.
```

COMMAND LINE OPTIONS
None.

RELATED COMMANDS

Layer	Displays the **Layer & Linetype** dialog box.
LayCur	Changes the layer of selected objects to the current layer
LayIso	Freezes all layers, except the one of the selected object.
LayFrz	Freezes the layer of the selected object.
LayMch	Matches the layer of the selected object.
LayOff	Turns off the layer of the selected object.
LayLck	Locks the layer of the selected object.
LayThw	Thaws all layers.
LayUlk	Unlocks the layer of the selected object.

TIPS
■ This commands turns *on* all layers in the drawing.

LayThw

Rel.14 Thaws all frozen layers (*short for LAYer THaW; an external command in BnsLayer.Lsp*).

Command	Alias	Ctrl+	F-key	Alt+	Menu Bar	Tablet
laythw	...	...	...	BLT	Bonus	...
					⌐Layer	
					⌐Thaw All Layers	

```
Command: laythw
All layers THAWED.
```

COMMAND LINE OPTIONS
None.

RELATED COMMANDS
Layer	Displays the **Layer & Linetype** dialog box.
LayCur	Changes the layer of selected objects to the current layer
LayIso	Freezes all layers, except the one of the selected object.
LayFrz	Freezes the layer of the selected object.
LayMch	Matches the layer of the selected object.
LayOff	Turns off the layer of the selected object.
LayLck	Locks the layer of the selected object.
LayOn	Turns on all layers.
LayUlk	Unlocks the layer of the selected object.

TIPS
- The **LayThw** command thaws *all* frozen layers.

- It is not possible to pick an object to thaw its layer since objects on frozen layers are invisible.

 # LayUlk

Rel.14 Unlocks the layer of the selected object (*short for LAYer UnLocK; an external command in BnsLayer.Lsp*).

Command	Alias	Ctrl+	F-key	Alt+	Menu Bar	Tablet
layulk	...	...	...	BLU	Bonus	...
					⬐Layer	
					⬐Layer Unlock	

```
Command: layulk
Pick an object on the layer to be UNLOCKED: [pick]
Layer x has been unlocked.
```

COMMAND LINE OPTION

Pick an object When you select an object, this command unlocks the layer of that object.

RELATED COMMANDS

Layer	Displays the **Layer & Linetype** dialog box.
LayCur	Changes the layer of selected objects to the current layer
LayIso	Freezes all layers, except the one of the selected object.
LayFrz	Freezes the layer of the selected object.
LayMch	Matches the layer of the selected object.
LayOff	Turns off the layer of the selected object.
LayLck	Locks the layer of the selected object.
LayOn	Turns on all layers.
LayThw	Thaws all layers.

TIPS

- This command is the opposite of the **LayLck** command: it unlocks the layer containing the object you picked.

- Locked layers are visible but cannot be edited.

 # LMan

Rel.14 Saves the settings of layers; allows the export and import of layer tables
(*short for Layer MANager; an external command in LMan.Lsp*).

Command	Alias	Ctrl+	F-key	Alt+	Menu Bar	Tablet
lman	...	...	...	BLL	Bonus	...
					⇘Layers	
					⇘Layer Manager	

Command: **lman**
Displays dialog box:

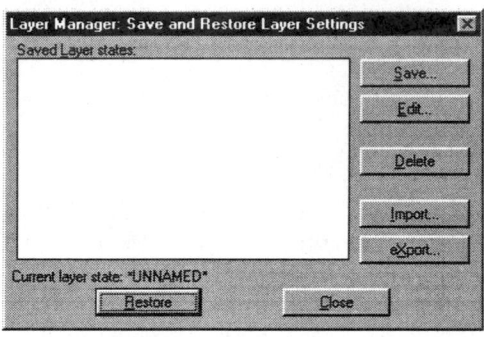

DIALOG BOX OPTIONS

Save   Saves the state of the current layer settings; specifies a new name for a new
            state:

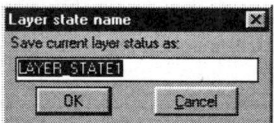

Edit   Allows changes to layer states; displays the **Layer & Linetype** dialog box.
Delete   Deletes a layer state; displays dialog box:

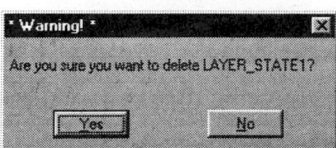

Import   Imports a .LAY file; displays the **Import File** dialog box.
Export   Exports the current layer settings to a .LAY file; displays the **Export File**
            dialog box.
Restore   Restores the layer settings for the selected layer state.

RELATED COMMAND

Layer   Creates and edits layers.

RELATED FILE

*.LAY   Stores the layer settings in an ASCII file format.

TIPS

■ The **LMan** command lets you save layers in two ways: (1) save layer states, where LMan memorizes the status of all layers, such as frozen, locked, on, and current; and (2) save the layer names and states to a LAY file on disk.

■ You can restore the layer states within the same drawing, or import the LAY file into other drawings.

■ The layer manager is an excellent way to create layer standards for different projects and clients.

■ The **Export** function saves the drawing's layers in dotted pair format:

```
"0"
(1000 . "{LAYER_STATE1")
(1070 . 0)
(1070 . 7)
(1000 . "CONTINUOUS")
(1000 . "LAYER_STATE1}")
"DEFPOINTS"
(1000 . "{LAYER_STATE1")
(1070 . 0)
(1070 . 7)
(1000 . "CONTINUOUS")
(1000 . "LAYER_STATE1}")
```

MoCoRo

Rel.14 Moves, copies, scales, and rotates selected objects (*short for MOve COpy ROtate; an external command in MoCoRo.Arx*).

Command	Alias	Ctrl+	F-key	Alt+	Menu Bar	Tablet
mocoro	...	...	...	BMO	Bonus	...
					⤷Modify	
					⤷Move Copy Rotate	

```
Command: mocoro
Select objects: [pick]
Base point: [pick]
Move/Copy/Rotate/Scale/Base pt/Undo/<eXit>:
```

COMMAND LINE OPTIONS

Select objects Select one or more objects to transform.
Move Moves the objects.
Copy Copies the objects.
Rotate Rotates the objects.
Scale Scales the objects.
Base pt Indicates the base point from which the transform takes place.
Undo Undoes the last transform.
eXit Exits the command (*default*).

RELATED COMMANDS

Align Moves, rotates, and scales objects in 2D and 3D space.
Move Moves one or more objects.
Copy Copies one or more objects.
Rotate Rotates one or more objects.
Scale Scales one or more objects.

TIPS

■ The **MoCoRo** command is like the **Align** command, except that the **Align** command is more complicated to use.

■ Starting with a base point, you can move, copy, rotate, and scale the selected objects.

■ The command keeps repeating its options until you type **X** for exit.

MPEdit

Rel.14 Edits more than one polyline at the same time (*short for Multiple Polyline EDITor; an external command in MPEdit.Lsp*).

Command	Alias	Ctrl+	F-key	Alt+	Menu Bar	Tablet
mpedit	...	...	...	BMP	Bonus ⤷Modify ⤷Multiple Pedit	...

```
Command: mpedit
Select objects: [pick]
Select objects: [Enter]
Convert Lines and Arcs to polylines? <Yes>: [Enter]
Open/Close/Width/Fit/Spline/Decurve/Ltype gen/eXit <X>:
```

COMMAND LINE OPTIONS

Select objects Select polylines, lines, and arcs; removes all other objects from selection set.

Convert Lines and Arcs to polylines?

        Yes: Converts lines to polylines; converts arcs to polyarcs.

        No: Removes lines and arcs from the selection set.

Open Opens all closed polylines.

Close Closes all open polylines.

Width Changes the width of all segments of all polylines.

Fit Applies curve fitted to all polylines.

Spline Applies a spline to all polylines.

Decurve Removes the curve and spline from all polylines.

Ltype gen *On*: Linetypes are generated through all the vertices of all polylines.

        Off: Linetypes are generated from vertex to vertex.

eXit Exits the **MPedit** command.

RELATED COMMANDS

PLine Draws a 2D polyline.

PEdit Edits one polyline at a time.

3dPoly Draws a 3D polyline.

TIPS

- This command lets you select more than one polyline, then perform a **PEdit**-like operation.

- Missing are the **PEdit** command's **Join** and **Edit** vertex options.

MStretch

Rel.14 Stretches more than one object at a time (*short for Multiple STRETCH; an external command in MStretch.Lsp*).

Command	Alias	Ctrl+	F-key	Alt+	Menu Bar	Tablet
mstretch	...	...	...	BMM	Bonus ↳Modify ↳Multiple Entity Stretch	...

```
Command: mstretch
Define crossing windows or crossing polygons...
CP(crossing polygon)/<Crossing First point>: [pick]
Other corner: [pick]
CP/Undo/<Crossing First point>: [Enter]
Done defining windows for stretch...
Remove objects/<Base point>: [pick]
Second base point: [pick]
```

COMMAND LINE OPTIONS

CP Defines selection set by crossing polygon.

Crossing First point
Defines selection set by crossing window.

Undo Undoes the last selection.

Remove objects Removes objects from the selection set.

Base point Specifies the base point to start stretching from.

Second base point
Specifies the point to stretch to.

RELATED COMMAND

Stretch Stretches (or shrinks) one object at a time.

TIP

- Unlike the **Stretch** command, **MStretch** lets you stretch one or more object at a time.

NCopy

Rel.14 Copies objects nested in a block or an externally referenced file (*short for Nested COPY; an external command in TrExBlk.Lsp*).

Command	Alias	Ctrl+	F-key	Alt+	Menu Bar	Tablet
ncopy	...	...	...	BMC	Bonus	...
					⤷Modify	
					⤷Copy Nested Entities	

```
Command: ncopy
Select nested objects to copy: [pick]
<Base point or displacement>/Multiple: [pick]
Second point of displacement: [pick]
```

COMMAND LINE OPTIONS

Select nested objects to copy
>Selects nested objects.

Base point or displacement
>Picks the starting point for the copy operation.

Multiple Specifies that the copy operation repeat.

Second point of displacement
>Picks the destination for the copy operation.

RELATED COMMANDS

Block Creates blocks and nested blocks.

Copy The original copying command.

TIPS

- The **NCopy** command operates just like the **Copy** command, except that it copies the objects nested in a block or an externally referenced file.

- The **NCopy** command lets you copy objects from an xref into the current drawing.

Pack

Rel.14 Copies the drawing and all support files to a subdirectory (*an external command in Packngo.Arx*).

Command	Alias	Ctrl+	F-key	Alt+	Menu Bar	Tablet
pack	...	...	...	BTP	Bonus ☛Tools ☛Pack'n Go	...

Command: **pack**
Displays dialog box:

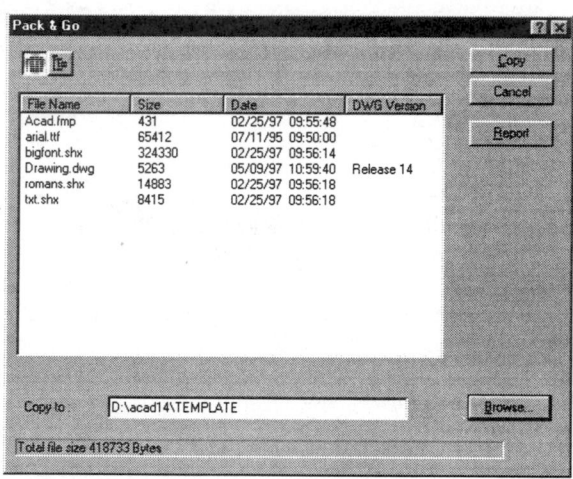

DIALOG BOX OPTIONS

Copy   Copies the drawing and its support file to the specified subdirectory.
Cancel   Dismisses the dialog box.
Report   Creates a report about the drawing and its support files.
Copy to   Names the destination subdirectory.
Browse   Selects subdirectory, hard drive, or network drive; displays dialog box:

RELATED COMMANDS

None.

TIPS

- When you need to send a drawing to a client, the **Pack** command ensures all required support files go along.

- The **Pack N Go** dialog box lists the names of all support files required by the current drawing. When you click **Copy**, it copies all the files to a subdirectory or another drive. Once in the subdirectory, you can use PkZip to compress the files for a floppy or copy them to a Zip file for transport to your client.

- Clicking the **Report** button displays a report about the support files:

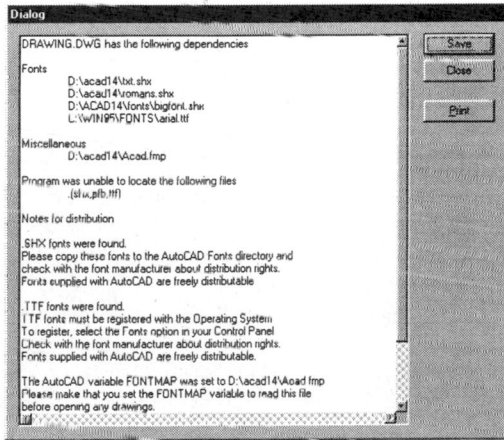

- The report is stored as file *drawingname*.Txt in the destination subdirectory.

- The tree view shows the relationship between files:

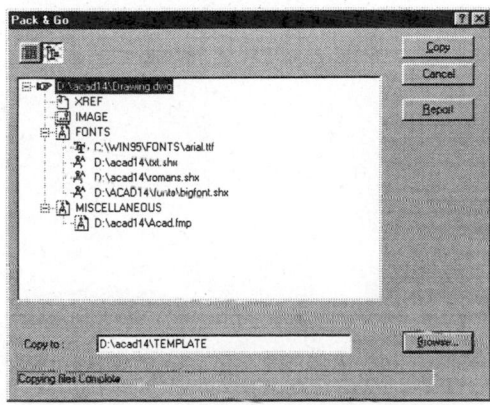

QLAttach

Rel.14 Moves the leader endpoint to another annotation (*short for Quick Leader ATTACH; an external command in LeaderEx.Arx*).

Command	Alias	Ctrl+	F-key	Alt+	Menu Bar	Tablet
qlattach	qat	...	...	BDLA	Bonus	...
					⤷Draw	
					⤷Leader Tools	
					⤷Attach Leader to Annotation	

```
Command: qlattach
Select Leader: [pick]
Select Annotation: [pick]
```

COMMAND LINE OPTIONS

Select Leader   Select a leader.
Select Annotation
        Select text, tolerance symbol, or block.

RELATED COMMANDS

DdEdit	Edits leader text.
DDim	Sets dimension variables, including leaders.
Leader	Draws leaders without dialog boxes.
QLAttachSet	Globally attaches leaders to annotations.
QLDetachSet	Detaches leaders from annotations.
QLeader	The leader command with dialog boxes.

TIP

- The **QLAttach** command moves the end of a leader line to the insertion point of mtext, tolerance symbol, or block.

QLAttachSet

Rel.14 Globally attaches leaders to likely annotation (*short for Quick Leader ATTACH SET; an external command in LeaderEx.Arx*).

Command	Alias	Ctrl+	F-key	Alt+	Menu Bar	Tablet
qlattachset	qall	...	...	BDLG	Bonus	...
					⮑Draw	
					⮑Leader Tools	
					⮑Global Attach Leader to Annotation	

```
Command: qlattachset
Select objects: [pick]
Select objects: [Enter]
Number of Leaders = x
Number with annotation attached = x.
```

COMMAND LINE OPTION
Select objects   Select one or more leaders and annotations — text, tolerance symbol, or block.

RELATED COMMANDS
DdEdit   Edits leader text.
DDim   Sets dimension variables, including leaders.
Leader   Draws leaders without dialog boxes.
QLAttach   Attaches a leader to an annotation.
QLDetachSet   Detaches leaders from annotations.
QLeader   The leader command with dialog boxes.

TIP
■ The **QLAttachAll** command attempts to automatically attach all selected leaders with their likely annotations.

The Illustrated AutoCAD Quick Reference   ■   **569**

QLDetachSet

Rel.14 Detaches selected leaders from their annotations (*short for Quick Leader DETACH SET; an external command in LeaderEx.Arx*).

Command	Alias	Ctrl+	F-key	Alt+	Menu Bar	Tablet
qldetachset	qdt	...	...	BDLD	Bonus	...
					⤷Draw	
					⤷Leader Tools	
					⤷Detach Leader from Annotation	

```
Command: qldetachset
Select objects: [pick]
Select objects: [Enter]
Number of Leaders = x
Number with annotation detached = x.
```

COMMAND LINE OPTION

Select objects   Select one or more leaders and attached annotations.

RELATED COMMANDS

DdEdit	Edits leader text.
DDim	Sets dimension variables, including leaders.
Leader	Draws leaders without dialog boxes.
QLAttach	Attaches a leader to an annotation.
QLAttachSet	Globally attaches leaders to annotations.
QLeader	The leader command with dialog boxes.

TIP

■ The **QLDetachSet** command detaches annotation from the selected leader lines.

QLeader

Rel.14 Creates leaders with dialog boxes (*short for Quick Leader; an external command in LeaderEx.Arx*).

Command	Alias	Ctrl+	F-key	Alt+	Menu Bar	Tablet
qleader	ql	...	...	BDLQ	Bonus	...
					↳Draw	
					↳Leader Tools	
					↳Quick Leader	

Command: **qleader**
First Leader point or press Enter to set Options: **[Enter]**
Displays dialog box.

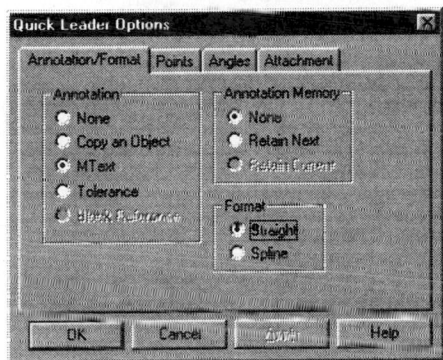

First Leader point or press Enter to set Options: **[pick]**
Next Leader point: **[pick]**
Next Leader point: **[Enter]**
Enter Leader text: **[type text]**
Enter Leader text: **[Enter]**

COMMAND LINE OPTIONS

First Leader point
> Picks the location for the leader's arrowhead; press **[Enter]** to display tabbed dialog box.

Next Leader point
> Picks the vertices of the leader; press **[Enter]** to end the leader line.

Enter Leader text
> Type text for leader annotation; press **[Enter]** twice to end.

DIALOG BOX OPTIONS

Annotation/Format tab:

Annotation options:

None   Attaches no annotation.
Copy an Object Attaches any object in the drawing as an annotation.
MText   Prompts you to type text for the annotation.
Tolerance   Prompts you to select tolerance symbols for the annotation.

Block Reference
>Prompts you to select a block for the annotation.

Annotation Memory options:
None   Does not retain annoation for next leader.
Retain Next Remembers the current annotation for the next leader.
Retain Current Uses the last annotation for the current leader.

Format options:
Straight   Draws the leader with straight lines.
Spline   Draws the leader as a spline curve.

Points tab:

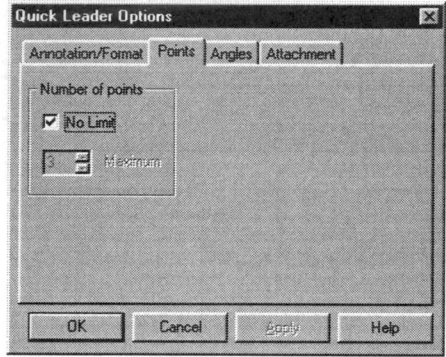

Number of points options:
No limit   The **QLeader** command keeps prompting for leader vertex points until you press the **[Enter]** key.
Maximum   The **QLeader** command stops prompting for leader vertex points (*default = 3*).

Angles tab:

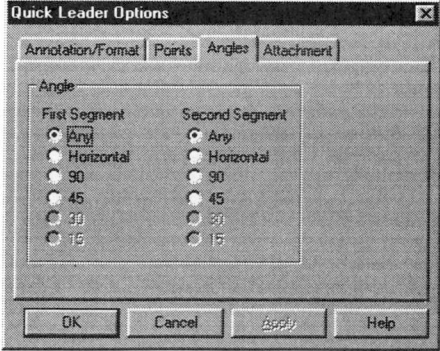

Angle options:

First Segment Selects from **Any** angle (user-specified), **Horizontal** (0 degrees), **90**, **45**, **30**, or **15**-degree leader line, first segment.

Second Segment Selects from **Any** angle (user-specified), **Horizontal**, **90**, **45**, **30**, or **15**-degree leader line, second segment.

Attachment tab:

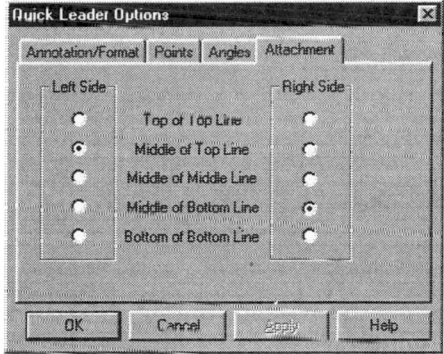

Left Side Positions the annotation at one of five different locations relative to the last leader segment, when the annotation is located to the left of the leader.

Right Side Positions the annotation at one of five different locations relative to the last leader segment, when the annotation is located to the right of the leader.

RELATED COMMANDS

DdEdit	Edits leader text.
DDim	Sets dimension variables, including leaders.
Leader	Draws leaders without dialog boxes.
QLAttach	Attaches a leader to an annotation.
QLAttachSet	Globally attaches leaders to annotations.
QLDetachSet	Detaches leaders from annotations.

TIPS

- The **QLeader** command draws leaders, just like the **Leader** command in Release 13 and 14. The difference is it brings up a quadruple-tab dialog box for setting the leader options.

- Some options have interesting possibilities, such as using any object in the drawing in place of the leader text.

RevCloud

Rel.14 Semiautomatically draws a revision cloud (*short for REVision CLOUD; an external command in RevCloud.Lsp*).

Command	Alias	Ctrl+	F-key	Alt+	Menu Bar	Tablet
revcloud	...	...	...	BDR	Bonus	...
					⇘Draw	
					⇘Revision Cloud	

```
Command: revcloud
Length of cloud bulge <1">:  [Enter]
Pick cloud start point: [pick]
Guide cursor along cloud path... [move cursor]
Ending cloud...
```

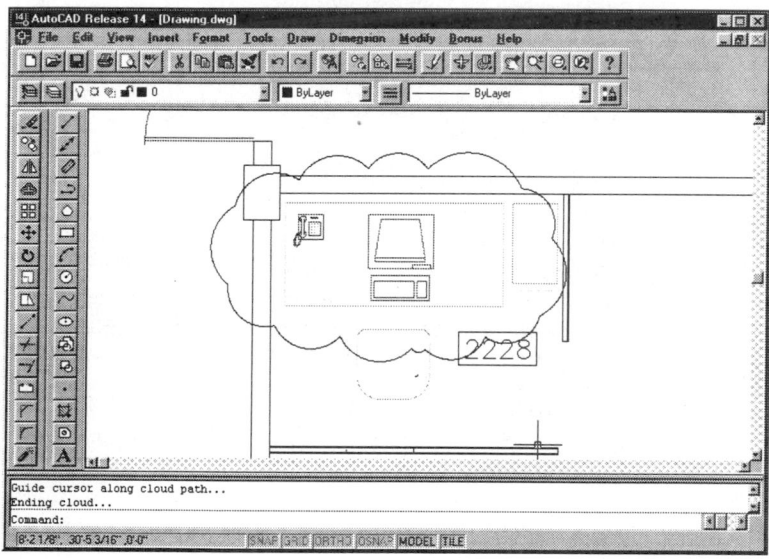

COMMAND LINE OPTIONS
Length of cloud bulge
> Specifies the distance between cloud vertices (*default = 1"*).

Pick cloud start point
> Picks the starting point for the cloud.

Guide cursor along cloud path...
> As you move the cursor, **RevCloud** automatically draws the cloud.

RELATED COMMANDS
None.

TIPS
- In addition to moving the cursor, you can pick points along the path.

- **RevCloud** automatically closes the cloud when it is near the starting point.

Ssx

Rel.14 Creates a selection set *(short for Selection Set eXtended; an external command in Ssx.Lsp)*.

Command	Alias	Ctrl+	F-key	Alt+	Menu Bar	Tablet
ssx	...	...	...	...	...	...

```
Command: ssx
Select object/<None>: [pick]
Block name/Color/Entity/Flag/LAyer/LType/Pick/Style/Thickness/Vector:
```

Sample output:
```
Select object/<None>: [pick]
Filter: ((0 . "LEADER") (8 . "OBJECT") (210 0.0 0.0 1.0))
>>Block name/Color/Entity/Flag/LAyer/LType/Pick/Style/Thickness/
  Vector: c
>>Color number to add/?/<RETURN to remove>: [Enter]
Filter: ((0 . "LEADER") (8 . "OBJECT") (210 0.0 0.0 1.0))
>>Block name/Color/Entity/Flag/LAyer/LType/Pick/Style/Thickness/
  Vector: [Enter]
1 found.
```

COMMAND LINE OPTIONS

Select object	Selects an object that forms the template for the selection set.
None	Selects no object.
Block name	Adds or removes a block name.
Color	Adds or removes a color.
Entity	Adds or removes an object type.
Flag	Turns on and off the **Entities Follow** flag.
LAyer	Adds or removes a layer name.
LType	Adds or removes a linetype name.
Pick	Picks one or more objects.
Style	Adds or removes a text style name.
Thickness	Adds or removes the thickness.
Vector	Adds or removes the extrusion vector.

RELATED COMMANDS

GetSel	Creates a selection set on a layer.
Select	Creates a selection set.

TIPS

- Like the **Select** and **GetSel** commands, **Ssx** creates a selection set that is accessed in the following commands by responding "P" (short for **Previous**) to the 'Select objects' prompt.

- Use the 'Select object' prompt in the **Ssx** command to create a selection set identical to the selected object.

SysVDlg

Rel.14   System variable and shell command editor (*short for SYStem Variable DiaLoG; an external command in SysVDlg.Arx*).

Command	Alias	Ctrl+	F-key	Alt+	Menu Bar	Tablet
sysvdlg	sd	...	...	BTV	Bonus	...
					⤷Tools	
					⤷System Variable Editor	

Command: **sysvdlg**
Displays tabbed dialog box:

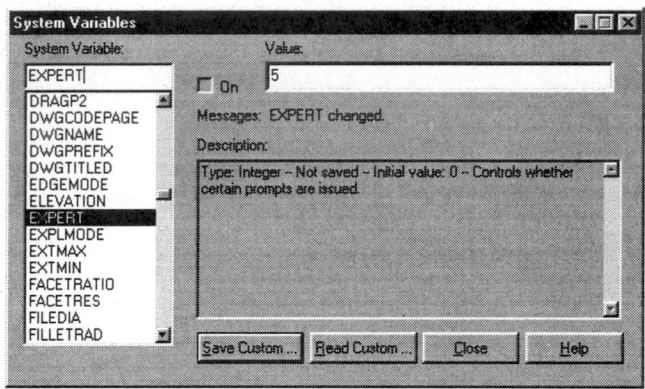

DIALOG BOX OPTIONS
System Variable Displays the names of system variables in Release 14.
Value   Allows editing of the system variable value.
                  Caution: System variables change immediately, not after dialog is dismissed.
On   Toggles binary system variables on and off.
Description   Describes the selected system variable.
Save Custom   Saves current settings to an SVF file.
Read Custom   Reads system variables settings from an SVF file.

RELATED COMMANDS
Script   Reads the SVF file as a script file.
SysVar   Edits system variables at the command line.

RELATED FILE
*.SVF   Contains the settings of system variables exported by **SysVDlg**.

TIPS
■ *Caution*: Reading an SVF file overwrites all system variable settings.

■ File **Defaults.Svf** contains the "factory default" system variable settings found in Acad.Dwg.

■ You can read the SVF file into any version of AutoCAD as a script: (1) change the .SVF extension to .SCR; and (2) use the **Script** command to read in the file.

# TextFit

Rel.14 Fits text between two points (*an external command in TextFit.Lsp*).

Command	Alias	Ctrl+	F-key	Alt+	Menu Bar	Tablet
textfit	...	...	...	BEF	Bonus	...
					⮡Text	
					⮡Text Fit	

```
Command: textfit
Select Text to stretch/shrink: [pick]
Enter new starting point: [pick]
Enter new ending point: [pick]
```

COMMAND LINE OPTIONS

Select Text to stretch/shrink
> Picks the text to be fitted.

Enter new starting point
> Indicates the new starting point for the text.

Enter new ending point
> Indicates the new ending point.

RELATED COMMANDS

ArcText	Places text along an arc.
ChT	Globally changes most properties of text.
DdEdit	Edits text.
DdModify	Changes all aspects of a single text object.
Find	Finds and replaces non-MText text.
TextFit	Fits text between two points.
TextMask	Masks area under text.
TxtExp	Explodes text into lines and arcs.

TIPS

- The **TextFit** command changes the width factor; the text height remains the same.

- When text is center-justified, this routine may not work correctly; you may need to move it into place.

TextMask

Rel.14 Masks the area under selected text (*an external command in TextMask.Lsp*).

Command	Alias	Ctrl+	F-key	Alt+	Menu Bar	Tablet
TextMask	...	...	...	BEM	Bonus	...
					⬐Text	
					⬐Text Mask	

Command: **textmask**
Enter offset factor relative to text height <0.35>: **[Enter]**
Select text to Mask
Select objects: **[pick]**

COMMAND LINE OPTIONS

Enter offset factor relative to text height
　　　Specifies a percentage distance around the text to be masked (*default = 0.35*).
Select objects　Selects text object to be masked.

RELATED COMMANDS

ArcText	Places text along an arc.
ChT	Globally changes most properties of text.
DdEdit	Edits text.
DdModify	Changes all aspects of a single text object.
Find	Find and replace non-MText text.
TextFit	Fits text between two points.
TxtExp	Explodes text into lines and arcs.

TxtExp

Rel.14 Explodes text into lines and arcs (*short for TEXT EXPlode; an external command in TxtExp.Lsp*).

Command	Alias	Ctrl+	F-key	Alt+	Menu Bar	Tablet
txtexp	...	...	...	BEX	Bonus ↳Text ↳Explode Text	...

```
Command: txtexp
Select text to be EXPLODED: [pick]
```

COMMAND LINE OPTION

Select text Selects the text, that is to be exploded into lines and arcs.

RELATED COMMANDS

ArcText Places text along an arc.
ChT Globally changes most properties of text.
DdEdit Edits text.
DdModify Changes all aspects of a single text object.
Find Finds and replaces non-mtext text.
TextFit Fits text between two points.
TextMask Masks area under text.

TIPS

- The **TxtExp** command explodes text – created by the **Text** and **DText** commands – and paragraph text – created by the **MText** and **Leader** commands – into simple lines and arcs.
- To explode attribute text, use the **Burst** command first to convert the attribute value to text, then use the **TxtExp** command.

 # WipeOut

Rel.14 Wipes out an area with the background color (*an external command in WipeOut.Arx*).

Command	Alias	Ctrl+	F-key	Alt+	Menu Bar	Tablet
wipeout	...	...	...	BDW	Bonus	...
					⤷Draw	
					⤷Wipeout	

```
Command: wipeout
Frame/New <New>: [Enter]
Select a polyline: [pick]
Erase polyline? Yes/No <No>: [Enter]
```

COMMAND LINE OPTIONS

Frame Toggles the display of the polyline boundary of an existing wipeout.
New Creates a new wipeout area.
Select a polyline
  Selects the polyline that will be filled with the background color.
Erase polyline *Yes*: Erases the polyline when the command is finished.
  No: Leaves the polyline in place; default.

RELATED COMMANDS

DrawOrder Changes the display order of objects.
BHatch Places solid-filled hatch pattern.
PLine Draws a polyline.

TIPS

- Here's how the **Wipeout** command works: it uses the solid hatch pattern to fill a closed polyline with the background color, then moves the fill to the top of the drawing order. This makes it appear as if the area has been wiped out.

- The **Frame** option toggles the display of the wipeout frame, after the wipeout area has been created *and* you answered "No" to the 'Erase polyline?' prompt.

- The **New** option requires that you draw a polyline first; it defines the wipeout frame.

XData

Rel.13 Attaches extended entity data to an object (*short for eXtended DATA; an external command in XData.Lsp*).

Command	Alias	Ctrl+	F-key	Alt+	Menu Bar	Tablet
xdata	...	...	...	BTX	Bonus	...
					⌂Tools	
					⌂XData Attachment	

```
Command: xdata
Select object: [pick]
Application name: [type name]
x new application.
3Real/DIR/DISP/DIST/Hand/Int/LAyer/LOng/Pos/Real/SCale/STr/<eXit>:
```

COMMAND LINE OPTIONS

Select object   Select one object in the drawing.

Application name

Type a name for the application.

3Real   Type three real numbers, such as 1.2,3.4,5.6 (*group code 1010*).

DIR   Type a 3D WCS space direction, such as 1,2,3 (*group code 1013*).

DISP   Type a 3D WCS space displacement, such as 4,5,6 (*group code 1012*).

DIST   Type a distance, such as 7 (*group code 1041*).

Hand   Type an object handle, such as 8A0 (*group code 1005*).

Int   Type a 16-bit integer, such as 9876 (*group code 1070*).

LAyer   Type a layer name, such as DOOR (*group code 1003*).

LOng   Type a 32-bit signed long integer, such as 1876543 (*group code 1071*).

Pos   Type a 3D WCS space position, such as 7,8,9 (*group code 1011*).

Real   Type a real number, such as 3.141 (*group code 1040*).

SCale   Type a scale factor, such as 1.5 (*group code 1042*).

STr   Type any ASCII string up to 255 characters long, such as "This is sample xdata" (*group code 1000*).

eXit   Exits the command.

RELATED COMMAND

XDList   Lists xdata contained in an object.

XDList

Rel.14 Lists extended entity data stored in an object (*short for eXtended Data LIST; an external command in XList.Lsp*).

Command	Alias	Ctrl+	F-key	Alt+	Menu Bar	Tablet
xdlist	...	...	,...	BTD	Bonus	...
					↳Tools	
					↳List Entity Xdata	

```
Command: xdlist
Select object: [pick]
Application name <*>: [Enter]
```

Sample output:
```
* Registered Application Name: ASDF
* Code 1002, Starting or ending brace: {
* Code 1000, ASCII string: This is a sample of extended entity data.
* Code 1042, Scale factor: 1.0000
* Code 1040, Real number: 12.3000
* Code 1011, 3D World space position: (-2.7000 7.5000 -2.0000)
* Code 1071, 32-bit signed long integer: 1234
* Code 1003, Layer name: TABLE
* Code 1070, 16-bit integer: 1234
* Code 1005, Database handle: 0
* Code 1041, Distance: 2.0000
* Code 1012, 3D World space displacement: (-5.0000 8.0000 -2.0000)
* Code 1013, 3D World space direction: (-3.2000 7.4000 -2.0000)
* Code 1010, 3 real numbers: (1.0000 2.0000 3.0000)
* Code 1002, Starting or ending brace: }
Object has 16186 bytes of Xdata space available.
```

COMMAND LINE OPTIONS
Select object Selects one object in the drawing.
Application name
   Specifies an application name or press **[Enter]** for all applications.

RELATED COMMAND
XData Attaches xdata to an object.

TIP
■ When the object contains no xdata, the **XdList** command responds, "No Xdata associated with Application Name(s)."

 # XList

Rel.14 Lists nested blocks and xrefs (*an external command in XList.Lsp*).

Command	Alias	Ctrl+	F-key	Alt+	Menu Bar	Tablet
xlist	...	...	...	BTL	Bonus	...
					↳Tools	
					↳List Xref/Block Entities	
-xlist						

Command: **xlist**
Select nested block or xref to list: **[pick]**
Displays dialog box:

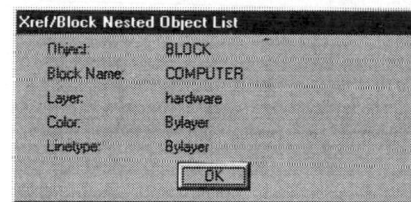

DIALOG BOX OPTIONS
None.

Command: **-xlist**
Select nested xref or block object to list: **[pick]**
      Object: LINE
      Layer: ASHADE
      Color: White
      Linetype: CONTINUOUS0

COMMAND LINE OPTION
Select nested block or xref to list
      Selects a block or externally referenced drawing.

RELATED COMMANDS
Block   Creates blocks and nested blocks.
XAttach   Attaches an externally referenced drawing.

TIPS
- The **XList** command displays information about nested blocks.

- Example of a block nested in another block: You create a block called "Workstation" that contains two other blocks, "Monitor" and "Keyboard." When you pick the keyboard with the **XList** command, it displays information about the Keyboard block.

Xplode

Rel.12 Reduces complex objects to their primitive constituent parts; provides greater user control than the Explode command (*short for eXplode; an external command in Xplode.Lsp*).

Command	Alias	Ctrl+	F-key	Alt+	Menu Bar	Tablet
xplode	xp	...	...	BMX	Bonus Modify Extended Explode	W20

```
Command: xplode
Select objects: [pick]
Select objects: [Enter]
Xplode Individually/<Globally>: [Enter]
All/Color/LAyer/LType/Inherit from parent block/<Explode>:
```

COMMAND OPTIONS

Select objects	Selects one or more associative dimensions, polylines, polymeshes, and/or block insertions.
Individually	Explodes one object at a time.
Globally	Applies explode to all selected objects.
All	Prompts for changes *after* exploding.
Color	Specifies color after explosion.
LAyer	Specifies layer after explosion.
LType	Specifies linetype after explosion.
Inherit	Sets color, linetype, and layer to that of the original block.
Explode	Mimics the **Explode** command.

RELATED AUTOCAD COMMANDS

Explode	Original explode command.
TxtExp	Explodes text into lines and arcs.
U	Undoes the effects of the **Xplode** command.

TIPS

- BYLAYER means that exploded objects inherit color (or linetype) from the original object.

- BYBLOCK means that exploded objects inherit color (or linetype) from the original object.

- By default, exploded objects inherit the current layer, not the original's layer.

System Variables

AutoCAD stores information about the current state of itself, the drawing and the operating system in 282 *system variables*. The variables help programmers — who often work with menu macros and AutoLISP — determine the state of the AutoCAD system.

The following pages list all documented system variables, plus several more not documented by Autodesk. The listing uses the following conventions:

Symbol	Meaning
Bold Italicized	Undocumented system variable.
~~Italicized~~	System variable removed from Release 14.
📷	Not available at the 'Command' prompt; accessed via the SetVar command.
00	System variable is new to Release 14.
Default	Default values as set in the Acad.Dwg prototype drawing.
R/O	Read-only; cannot be changed by the user or by programming.
Loc	Location where the system variable is stored:

Location	Meaning
ACAD	AutoCAD.
DWG	Current drawing.
REG	Windows registration file.
...	Not saved.

TIPS

■ TheSetVar command lets you change the value of all variables, except those marked read-only. You get a list of system variables at the 'Command' prompt with the ? option of the SetVar command:

```
Command: setvar
Variable name or ?: ?
Variable(s) to list <*>: [Enter]
```

■ The bonus commandSysVDlg lets you set the value of variables via a dialog box.

■ When a system variable is stored in the Windows registration file, the variable affects all drawings.

■ When a system variable is stored in the drawing, the variable affects only the current drawing.

■ When a system variable is not stored, the variable is set when AutoCAD loads. The value of the variable is either: (1) read from the operating system; or (2) set to the default value.

Variable	Default	R/O	Loc	Meaning
_PkSer	117-999999	R/O	ACAD	*Software package serial number.*
_Server	0	R/O	REG	*Network authorization code.*

A

Variable	Default	R/O	Loc	Meaning
AcadPrefix	""	R/O	...	Path spec'd by ACAD environment var.
AcadVer	"14"	R/O	...	AutoCAD version number.
AcisSaveVer	16	R/O	...	⓪ ACIS version number.
AFlags	0	...	...	Attribute display code:
				0 No mode specified.
				1 Invisible.
				2 Constant.
				4 Verify.
				128 Preset.
AngBase	0	...	DWG	Direction of zero degrees relative to UCS
AngDir	0	...	DWG	Rotation of angles:
				0 Clockwise
				1 Counterclockwise
ApBox	1	...	REG	⓪ AutoSnap aperture box cursor:
				0 Off.
				1 On.
Aperture	10	...	REG	▦ Object snap aperture in pixels:
				1 Minimum size
				10 Default size
				50 Maximum size
Area	0.0000	R/O	...	▦ Area measured by **Area**, **List**, or **Dblist**.
AttDia	0	...	DWG	Attribute entry interface:
				0 Command-line prompts.
				1 Dialog box.
AttMode	1	...	DWG	Display of attributes:
				0 Off.
				1 Normal.
				2 On.
AttReq	1	...	DWG	Attribute values during insertion are:
				0 Default values.
				1 Prompt for values.
AuditCtl	0	...	REG	Determines creation of ADT audit log file:
				0 File not created.
				1 ADT file created.
AUnits	0	...	DWG	Mode of angular units:
				0 Decimal degrees.
				1 Degrees-minutes-seconds.
				2 Grads.
				3 Radians.
				4 Surveyor's units.

Variable	Default	R/O	Loc	Meaning
AUPrec	0	...	DWG	Decimals places displayed by angles.
AutoSnap	7	...	DWG	04 Controls AutoSnap display:
				0 Turns off all AutoSnap features.
				1 Turns on marker.
				2 Turns on SnapTip.
				4 Turns on magnetic cursor.
AuxStat	*0*	...	DWG	*-32768 Minimum value.*
				32767 Maximum value.
AxisMode	*0*	...	DWG	*Obsolete system variable.*
AxisUnit	*0.0000*	...	DWG	*Obsolete system variable.*

B

Variable	Default	R/O	Loc	Meaning
BackZ	0.0000	R/O	DWG	Back clipping plane offset.
BlipMode	1	...	DWG	▥ Display of blip marks:
				0 Off.
				1 On.

C

Variable	Default	R/O	Loc	Meaning
CDate	19560915.15560660	R/O	...	Current date and time; format: YyyyMmDd.HhMmSsDd
CeColor	"BYLAYER"	...	DWG	Current object color.
CeLTscale	1.0000	...	DWG	Global linetype scale.
CeLType	"BYLAYER"	...	DWG	Current layer linetype.
ChamferA	0.5000	...	DWG	First chamfer distance.
ChamferB	0.5000	...	DWG	Second chamfer distance.
ChamferC	1.0000	...	DWG	Chamfer length.
ChamferD	0	...	DWG	Chamfer angle.
ChamMode	0	...		Chamfer input mode:
				0 Chamfer by two lengths.
				1 Chamfer by length and angle.
CircleRad	0.0000	...	...	Most-recent circle radius.
CLayer	"0"	...	DWG	Current layer name.
CmdActive	1	R/O	...	Type of current command:
				1 Regular command.
				2 Transparent command.
				4 Script file.
				8 Dialog box.
				16 DDE command active 04 .

Variable	Default	R/O	Loc	Meaning
CmdDia	1	...	REG	Plot command interface: 0 Command line prompt. 1 Dialog box.
CmdEcho	1	...	...	AutoLISP command display: 0 No command echoing. 1 Command echoing.
CmdNames	"SETVAR"	R/O	...	Current command.
CMLJust	0	...	REG	Multiline justification mode: 0 Top. 1 Middle. 2 Bottom.
CMLScale	1.0000	...	REG	Scales width of multiline: <0 Flips offsets of multiline. 0 Collapses to single line. 1 Default. 2 Doubles multiline width.
CMLStyle	"STANDARD"	REG	...	Current multiline style name.
Coords	1	...	DWG	Coordinate display style: 0 Updated by screen picks. 1 Continuous display. 2 Polar display upon request.
CursorSize	5	...	REG	00 Cursor size, in pixels: 1 Minimum size. 5 Default size. 100 Full screen.
CVPort	2	...	DWG	Current viewport number: 2 Minimum (*default*)

D

Variable	Default	R/O	Loc	Meaning
Date	2448860.54043252	R/O	...	Current date in Julian format.
DBGListAll	*0*	...	...	*Toggle.*
DBMod	0	R/O	...	Drawing modified in these areas: 0 No modification made. 1 Object database. 2 Symbol table. 4 Database variable. 8 Window. 16 View.
DctCust	""	...	REG	Name of custom spelling dictionary.

Variable	Default	R/O	Loc	Meaning
DctMain	"enu"	...	REG	Code for spelling dictionary:

   ca Catalan.
   cs Czech.
   da Danish.
   de German; sharp 's'.
   ded German; double 's'.
   ena English; Australian.
   ens English; British 'ise'.
   enu English; American.
   enz English; British 'ize'.
   es Spanish; unaccented capitals.
   esa Spanish; accented capitals.
   fi Finish
   fr French; unaccented capitals.
   fra French; accented capitals.
   it Italian
   nl Dutch; primary.
   nls Dutch; secondary.
   no Norwegian; Bokmal.
   non Norwegian; Nynorsk.
   pt Portuguese; Iberian.
   ptb Portuguese; Brazilian.
   ru Russian; infrequent 'io'.
   rui Russian; frequent 'io'.
   sv Swedish.

Variable	Default	R/O	Loc	Meaning
DelObj	1	...	DWG	Toggle source objects deletion:

   0 Objects deleted.
   1 Objects retained.

Variable	Default	R/O	Loc	Meaning
DemandLoad	3	...	REG	**00** AutoCAD loads app when drawing contains proxy objects:

   0 Demand loading turned off.
   1 Load app when drawing opened.
   2 Load app at first command.
   3 Load app when drawing opened or at first command.

Variable	Default	R/O	Loc	Meaning
DiaStat	1	R/O	...	User exited dialog box by clicking on:

   0 **Cancel** button.
   1 **OK** button.

DIMENSION VARIABLES

Variable	Default	R/O	Loc	Meaning
DimADec	-1	...	DWG	**00** Angular dimension precision:

   -1 Use **DimDec** setting (*default*).
   0 Zero decimal places (*minimum*).
   8 Eight decimal places (*maximum*).

Variable	Default	R/O	Loc	Meaning
DimAlt	0	...	DWG	Alternate units selected.
DimAltD	2	...	DWG	Alternate unit decimal places.

Variable	Default	R/O	Loc	Meaning
DimAltF	25.4000	...	DWG	Alternate unit scale factor.
DimAltTD	2	...	DWG	Tolerance alternate unit decimal places.
DimAltTZ	0	...	DWG	Alternate tolerance units zeros:
				0 Zeros not suppressed.
				1 Zeros suppressed.
DimAltU	2	...	DWG	Alternate units:
				1 Scientific.
				2 Decimal.
				3 Engineering.
				4 Architectural; stacked.
				5 Fractional; stacked.
				6 Architectural **00**.
				7 Fractional **00**.
				8 Windows desktop units setting **00**.
DimAltZ	0		DWG	Zero suppression for alternate units:
				0 Suppress zero ft and zero in.
				1 Include zero ft and zero in.
				2 Include zero ft; suppress zero in **00**.
				3 Suppress zero ft; include zero in **00**.
				4 Suppress leading zero in dec dim **00**.
				8 Suppress trailing zero in dec dim **00**.
				12 Suppress leading and trailing zeroes **00**.
DimAPost	""	...	DWG	Suffix for alternate text.
DimAso	1	...	DWG	Create associative dimensions.
DimASz	0.1800	...	DWG	Arrow size.
DimAUnit	0	...	DWG	Angular dimension format:
				0 Decimal degrees.
				1 Degrees.Minutes.Seconds.
				2 Grad.
				3 Radian.
				4 Surveyor units.
DimBlk	""	R/O	DWG	Arrowhead block name.
				. (*Period*) None.
DimBlk1	""	R/O	DWG	First arrowhead block name.
DimBlk2	""	R/O	DWG	Second arrowhead block name.
DimCen	0.0900	...	DWG	Center mark size:
				<0 Draws center lines.
				0 No center mark or lines drawn.
				>0 Draws center marks.
DimClrD	0	...	DWG	Dimension line color:
				0 BYBLOCK (*default*)
				1 Red.
				...

Variable	Default	R/O	Loc	Meaning
				255 Dark gray.
				256 BYLAYER.
DimClrE	0	...	DWG	Extension line and leader color.
DimClrT	0	...	DWG	Dimension text color.
DimDec	4	...	DWG	Primary tolerance decimal places.
DimDLE	0.0000	...	DWG	Dimension line extension.
DimDLI	0.3800	...	DWG	Dimension line continuation increment.
DimExe	0.1800	...	DWG	Extension above dimension line.
DimExO	0.0625	...	DWG	Extension line origin offset.
DimFit	3	...	DWG	Placement of text and arrowheads between extension lines:
				0 Both text and arrows, if possible.
				1 Text has priority over arrowheads.
				2 Whichever fits between ext lines.
				3 Whatever fits.
				4 Place text at end of leader line.
				5 Place text without leader line **09**.
DimGap	0.0900	...	DWG	Gap from dimension line to text.
DimJust	0	...	DWG	Horizontal text positioning:
				0 Center justify.
				1 Next to first extension line.
				2 Next to second extension line.
				3 Above first extension line.
				4 Above second extension line.
DimLFac	1.0000	...	DWG	Linear unit scale factor.
DimLim	0	...	DWG	Generate dimension limits.
DimPost	""	...	DWG	Default suffix for dimension text:
				"" No suffix.
				<>mm Millimeter suffix.
				<>Å Angstrom suffix.
DimRnd	0.0000	...	DWG	Rounding value.
DimSAh	0	...	DWG	Separate arrowhead blocks.
DimScale	1.0000	...	DWG	Overall scale factor:
				0 Value is computed from the scale between current modelspace viewport and paperspace.
				>0 Scales text and arrowheads.
DimSD1	Off	...	DWG	Suppress first dimension line.
DimSD2	Off	...	DWG	Suppress second dimension line.
DimSE1	0	...	DWG	Suppress the first extension line.
DimSE2	0	...	DWG	Suppress the second extension line.

Variable	Default	R/O	Loc	Meaning
DimSho	1	...	DWG	Update dimensions while dragging.
DimSOXD	0	...	DWG	Suppress outside extension dimension.
DimStyle	"STANDARD"	R/O	DWG	Current dimension style.
DimTAD	0	...	DWG	Vertical position of dimension text: 0 Centered between extension lines. 1 Above dimension line, except when dimension line is not horizontal and **DimTIH** = 1. 2 On side of dimension line farthest from the defpoints. 3 Conform to JIS.
DimTDec	4	...	DWG	Primary tolerance decimal places.
DimTFac	1.0000	...	DWG	Tolerance text height scaling factor.
DimTIH	1	...	DWG	Text inside extensions is horizontal.
DimTIX	0	...	DWG	Place text inside extensions.
DimTM	0.0000	...	DWG	Minus tolerance.
DimTOFL	0	...	DWG	Force line inside extension lines.
DimTOH	1	...	DWG	Text outside extensions is horizontal.
DimTol	0	...	DWG	Generate dimension tolerances.
DimTolJ	1	...	DWG	Tolerance vertical justification: 0 Bottom. 1 Middle. 2 Top.
DimTP	0.0000	...	DWG	Plus tolerance.
DimTSz	0.0000	...	DWG	Size of oblique tick strokes: 0 Arrowheads. >0 Oblique strokes.
DimTVP	0.0000	...	DWG	Text vertical position when **DimTAD** =0: 1 Turns **DimTAD** on. >-0.7 *or* <0.7 Dimension line is split for text.
DimTxSty	"STANDARD"	...	DWG	Dimension text style.
DimTxt	0.1800	...	DWG	Text height.
DimTZin	0	...	DWG	Tolerance zero suppression: 0 Suppress zero ft and zero in. 1 Include zero ft and zero in. 2 Include zero ft; suppress zero in 00. 3 Suppress zero ft; include zero in 00. 4 Suppress leading zero in dec dim 00. 8 Suppress trailing zero in dec dim 00. 12 Suppress leading and trailing zeroes 00.

Variable	Default	R/O	Loc	Meaning
DimUnit	2	...	DWG	Dimension unit format: 1 Scientific. 2 Decimal. 3 Engineering. 4 Architectural; stacked. 5 Fractional; stacked. 6 Architectural **00**. 7 Fractional **00**. 8 Windows desktop units setting **00**.
DimUPT	Off	...	DWG	User-positioned text: 0 Cursor positions dimension line 1 Cursor also positions text
DimZIN	0	...	DWG	Suppression of zero in feet-inches units: 1 Scientific. 2 Decimal. 3 Engineering. 4 Architectural; stacked. 5 Fractional; stacked. 6 Architectural **00**. 7 Fractional **00**. 8 Windows desktop units setting **00**.
DispSilh	0	...	DWG	Silhouette display of 3D solids: 0 Off. 1 On.
Distance	0.0000	R/O	...	Distance measured by **Dist** command.
~~Dither~~				*Removed from Release 14.*
DonutId	0.5000	...	...	Inside radius of donut.
DonutOd	1.0000	...	...	Outside radius of donut.
DragMode	2	...	DWG	⌨ Drag mode: 0 No drag. 1 On if requested. 2 Automatic.
DragP1	10	...	REG	Regen drag display.
DragP2	25	...	REG	Fast drag display.
DwgCodePage	"ANSI_1252"	DWG	...	Drawing code page.
DwgName	"Drawing.dwg"	R/O	...	Current drawing filename.
DwgPrefix	"d:\"	R/O	...	Drawing's drive and subdirectory.
DwgTitled	0	R/O	...	Drawing has filename: 0 "Drawing.Dwg". 1 User-assigned name.
~~DwgWrite~~				*Removed from Release 14.*

Variable	Default	R/O	Loc	Meaning
E				
EdgeMode	0	...	...	Toggle edge mode for **Trim** and **Extend** commands: 0 No extension. 1 Extends cutting edge.
Elevation	0.0000	...	DWG	Current elevation, relative to current UCS.
ErrNo	*0*	...	...	*Error number from AutoLISP,ADS,Arx*
~~*ExtDir*~~				*Removed from Release 14.*
Expert	0	...	...	Suppresses the displays of prompts: 0 Normal prompts 1 "About to regen, proceed?" and "Really want to turn the current layer off?" 2 "Block already defined. Redefine it?" and"A block with this name already exists. Overwrite it?" 3 **Linetype** command messages. 4 **UCS Save** and **VPorts Save**. 5 **DimStyle Save** and **DimOverride**.
ExplMode	1	...	DWG	Toggle whether **Explode** and **Xplode** commands explode non-uniformly scaled blocks: 0 Does not explode. 1 Does explode.
ExtMax	-1.0000E+20,	R/O	DWG	Upper-right coordinate of drawing extents. -1.0000E+20, -1.0000E+20
ExtMin	1.0000E+20,	R/O	DWG	Lower-left coordinate of drawing extents. 1.0000E+20, 1.0000E+20
F				
FaceTRres	0.5000	...	DWG	Adjusts smoothness of shaded and hidden-line objects: 0.01 Minimum value. 0.05 Default value. 10.0 Maximum value.
~~*FfLimit*~~	...	...	...	*Removed from Release 14.*
FileDia	1	...	REG	User interface: 0 Command-line prompts. 1 Dialog boxes, when available.
FilletRad	0.5000	...	DWG	Current fillet radius.
FillMode	1	...	DWG	Fill of solid objects: 0 Off. 1 On.

Variable	Default	R/O	Loc	Meaning
Flatland	*0*	R/O	...	*Obsolete system variable.*
FontAlt	"arial.ttf"	...	REG	Name for substituted font.
FontMap	"Acad.fmp"	...	REG	Name of font mapping file.
Force_Paging	*0*	...	...	*0 Minimum (default).*
				1,410,065,408 Maximum.
FrontZ	0.0000	R/O	DWG	Front clipping plane offset.

G

Variable	Default	R/O	Loc	Meaning
GlobCheck	*0*	...	...	*Reports statistics on dialog boxes:*
				0 Turn off.
				1 Warns if larger than 640x400.
				2 Also reports size in pixels.
				3 Additional info.
GridMode	0	...	DWG	Display of grid:
				0 Off.
				1 On.
GridUnit	0.0000,0.0000	...	DWG	X,y-spacing of grid.
GripBlock	0	...	...	Display of grips in blocks:
				0 At insertion point.
				1 At all objects within block.
GripColor	5	...	REG	Color of unselected grips:
				1 Minimum color number; red.
				5 Default color; blue.
				255 Maximum color number.
GripHot	1	...	REG	Color of selected grips:
				1 Default color, red.
				255 Maximum color number.
Grips	1	...	REG	Display of grips:
				0 Off.
				1 On
GripSize	3	...	REG	Size of grip box, in pixels:
				1 Minimum size.
				3 Default size.
				255 Maximum size.

H

Variable	Default	R/O	Loc	Meaning
Handles	1	R/O	...	Obsolete system variable.
Highlight	1	...	...	Object selection highlighting:
				0 Disabled.
				1 Enabled.
HPAng	0	...	...	Current hatch pattern angle.
HPBound	1	...	DWG	Object created by **BHatch** and **Boundary** commands:
				0 Polyline.
				1 Region.

Variable	Default	R/O	Loc	Meaning
HPDouble	0	...	...	Double hatching: 0 Disabled. 1 Enabled.
HPName	"ANSI31"	...	...	Current hatch pattern name "" No default. . (*Period*) Set no default.
HPScale	1.0000	...	...	Current hatch pattern scale factor; cannot be zero.
HPSpace	1.0000	...	...	Current spacing of user-defined hatching; cannot be zero.

I

Variable	Default	R/O	Loc	Meaning
IndexCtl	0	...	DWG	**00** Creates layer and spatial indices: 0 No indices created. 1 Layer index created. 2 Spatial index created. 3 Both indices created.
InetLocation	"www.autodesk.com"	...	DWG	**00** Default browser URL.
InsBase	0.0000,0.0000,0.0000	...	DWG	Insertion base point relative to the current UCS for **Insert** and **DdInsert**.
InsName	""	...	...	Current block name: . (*Period*) Set to no default. "" No default.
ISaveBak	1	...	REG	Controls whether BAK file is created: 0 No BAK file created. 1 BAK backup file created.
ISavePercent	50	...	REG	Percentage of waste in DWG file before cleanup occurs: 0 Every save is a full save.
IsoLines	4	...	DWG	Isolines on 3D solids: 0 No isolines; minimum. 4 Default. 16 Good-looking. 2,047 Maximum.

L

Variable	Default	R/O	Loc	Meaning
LastAngle	0	R/O	...	Ending angle of last-drawn arc.
LastPoint	0.0000,0.0000,0.0000	...	DWG	Last-entered point.
LastPrompt	""	r/o	...	**00** Last string on the command line; includes user input.
LazyLoad	0	...	...	🖳 *Toggle 0 or 1.*
LensLength	50.0000	R/O	DWG	Perspective view lens length, in mm.

Variable	Default	R/O	Loc	Meaning
LimCheck	0	...	DWG	Drawing limits checking: 0 Disabled. 1 Enabled.
LimMax	12.0000,9.0000	...	DWG	Upper right drawing limits.
LimMin	0.0000,0.0000	...	DWG	Lower left drawing limits.
ListInit	1	...	REG	✇ AutoLISP functions and variables are: 0 Preserved from drawing to drawing. 1 Valid in current drawing only.
Locale	"en"	R/O		ISO language code.
LogFileMode	0	...	REG	✇ Text window written to log file: 0 No. 1 Yes.
LogFileName	"d:\acad14\acad.log"	...	REG	✇ Filename and path for log file.
LogInName	" "	R/O	DWG	User's login name; max = 30 chars.
LongFName				*Removed from Release 14.*
LTScale	1.0000	...	DWG	⌨ Current linetype scale factor; cannot be zero.
LUnits	2	...	...	Linear units mode: 1 Scientific. 2 Decimal. 3 Engineering. 4 Architectural. 5 Fractional.
LUPrec	4	...	DWG	Decimal places of linear units.

M

Variable	Default	R/O	Loc	Meaning
MacroTrace	*0*	...	...	*Diesel debug mode:* *0 Off.* *1 On.*
MaxActVP	48	...	...	Maximum viewports to regenerate: 0 Minimum. 48 Default. 32767 Maximum
MaxObjMem	2,147,483,647	...	...	Maximum number of objects in memory; object pager is turned off when value = 0, <0, or 2,147,483,647.
MaxSort	200	...	REG	Maximum names sorted alphabetically.
MeasureInit	0	...	REG	✇ Drawing units: 0 English. 1 Metric.
Measurement	0	...	DWG	✇ Drawing units (overrides **MeasureInit**): 0 English. 1 Metric.

Variable	Default	R/O	Loc	Meaning
MenuCtl	1	...	...	Submenu display:
				0 Only with menu picks.
				1 Also with keyboard entry.
MenuEcho	0	...		Menu and prompt echoing:
				0 All prompts displayed.
				1 Suppress menu echoing.
				2 Suppress system prompts.
				4 Disable ^P toggle.
				8 Display all input-output strings.
MenuName	"acad"	R/O	...	Current menu filename.
MirrText	1	...	DWG	Text handling during **Mirror** command:
				0 Mirror text.
				1 Retain text orientation.
ModeMacro	""	...	...	Invoke Diesel programming language.
MTextEd	"internal"	...	REG	Name of the **MText** editor:
				. (*Period*) Use default editor.

N

Variable	Default	R/O	Loc	Meaning
NodeName	*"AC$"*	*R/O*	*REG*	*Name of network node; range is 1 to 3 chars.*

O

Variable	Default	R/O	Loc	Meaning
OffsetDist	1.0000	...	...	Current offset distance:
				<0 Offsets through a specified point.
				>0 Default offset distance.
OleHide	1	...	REG	Display and plotting of OLE objects:
				0 Visible.
				1 Visible in paper space only.
				2 Visible in model space only.
				3 Not visible.
OrthoMode	0	...	DWG	Orthographic mode:
				0 Off.
				1 On.
OSMode	0	...	DWG	Current object snap mode:
				0 NONe.
				1 ENDpoint.
				2 MIDpoint.
				4 CENter.
				8 NODe.
				16 QUAdrant.
				32 INTersection.
				64 INSertion.
				128 PERpendicular.
				256 TANgent.
				512 NEARest.
				1024 QUIck.
				2048 APPint.

Variable	Default	R/O	Loc	Meaning
OSnapCoord	2	...	REG	⬤⬤ Keyboard overrides object snap: 0 Object snap override keyboard. 1 Keyboard overrides object snap. 2 Keyboard overrides object snap, except in script.

P

Variable	Default	R/O	Loc	Meaning
PDMode	0	...	DWG	Point display mode: 0 Dot. 1 No display. 2 +-symbol. 3 x-symbol. 4 Short line. 32 Circle. 64 Square.
PDSize	0.0000	...	DWG	Point display size, in pixels: >0 Absolute size. 0 5% of drawing area height. >0 Percentage of viewport size.
PEllipse	0	...	DWG	Toggle **Ellipse** creation: 0 True ellipse. 1 Polyline arcs.
Perimeter	0.0000	R/O	...	Perimeter calculated by **Area** command.
PFaceVMax	4	R/O	...	Maximum vertices per 3D face.
PHandle	*0*	...	...	*2,803,348,672 Maximum*
PickAdd	1	...	REG	Effect of **[Shift]** key on selection set: 0 Adds to selection set. 1 Removes from selection set.
PickAuto	1	...	REG	Selection set mode: 0 Single pick mode. 1 Automatic windowing and crossing.
PickBox	3	...	REG	Object selection pickbox size, in pixels.
PickDrag	0	...	REG	Selection window mode: 0 Pick two corners. 1 Pick 1 corner; drag to 2nd corner.
PickFirst	1	...	REG	Command-selection mode: 0 Enter command first. 1 Select objects first.

For PDMode, the point symbols are illustrated with numbers: 0 1 2 3 4 / 32 33 34 35 36 / 64 65 66 67 68 / 96 97 98 99 100

Variable	Default	R/O	Loc	Meaning
PickStyle	1	...	DWG	Included groups and associative hatches in selection: 0 Neither included. 1 Include groups. 2 Include associative hatches. 3 Include both.
Platform	"Microsoft Windows Version 4.0 (x86)"	R/O	Acad	AutoCAD platform name.
PLineGen	0	...	DWG	Polyline linetype generation: 0 From vertex to vertex. 1 From end to end.
PLineType	1	...	REG	◑ Automatic conversion and creation of 2D polylines by **PLine**: 0 Not converted; old-format polylines created. 1 Not converted; optimized polylines created. 2 Polylines in older drawings are converted on open; **PLine** creates optimized polylines with Lwpolyline object.
PLineWid	0.0000	...	DWG	Current polyline width.
PlotId	""	...	REG	Current plotter.
PlotRotMode	1	...	DWG	Orientation of plots: 0 Lowerleft = 0,0. 1 Lowerleft plotter area = lowerleft of media.
Plotter	1	...	REG	Current plotter configuration number: 0 No plotter configured. 29 Maximum configurations.
PolySides	4	...	...	Current number of polygon sides: 3 Minimum sides. 4 Default. 1024 Maximum sides.
Popups	1	R/O	...	Display driver support of AUI: 0 Not available. 1 Available.
ProjectName	""	...	DWG	◑ Project name of the current drawing.
ProjMode	1	...	REG	Projection mode for **Trim** and **Extend** commands: 0 No projection. 1 Project to x,y-plane of current UCS. 2 Project to view plane.
ProxyGraphics	1	...	REG	◑ Proxy image saved in the drawing: 0 Not saved; displays bounding box. 1 Image saved with drawing.

Variable	Default	R/o	Loc	Meaning
ProxyNotice	1	...	DWG	○○ Display warning message: 0 No. 1 Yes.
ProxyShow	1	...	REG	○○ Display of proxy objects: 0 Not displayed. 1 All displayed. 2 Bounding box displayed.
PSLTScale	1	...	DWG	Paper space linetype scaling: 0 Use model space scale factor. 1 Use viewport scale factor.
PSProlog	""	...	REG	PostScript prologue filename
PSQuality	75	...	DWG	Resolution of PostScript display, in pixels: <0 Display as outlines; no fill. 0 Not displayed. >0 Display filled.

Q

Variable	Default	R/o	Loc	Meaning
QAFlags	*1*	*...*	*...*	*Quality assurance flags.*
QTextMode	0	...	DWG	Quick text mode: 0 Off. 1 On.

R

Variable	Default	R/o	Loc	Meaning
RasterPreview	1	...	DWG	Preview image: 0 None saved. 1 Saved in BMP format.
RegenMode	1	...	DWG	Regeneration mode: 0 Regen with each new view. 1 Regen only when required.
Re-Init	0	...	...	Reinitialize I/O devices: 1 Digitizer port. 2 Plotter port. 4 Digitizer. 8 Plotter. 16 Reload PGP file.
~~RIAspect~~				*Removed from Release 14.*
~~RIBackG~~				*Removed from Release 14.*
~~RIEdge~~				*Removed from Release 14.*
~~RIGamut~~				*Removed from Release 14.*
~~RIGrey~~				*Removed from Release 14.*
~~RIThresh~~				*Removed from Release 14.*
RTDisplay	1	...	REG	○○ Realtime zoom and pan display: 0 Raster image content. 1 Raster image outline only.

Variable	Default	R/O	Loc	Meaning
S				
SaveFile	"auto.sv$"	R/O	REG	Automatic save filename
SaveName	""	R/O	...	Drawing save-as filename
SaveTime	0	...	REG	Automatic save interval, in minutes: 　0　Disable auto save.
ScreenBoxes	0	R/O	REG	Maximum number of menu items 　0　Screen menu turned off
ScreenMode	0	R/O	REG	State of AutoCAD display screen: 　0　Text screen 　1　Graphics screen 　2　Dual-screen display
ScreenSize	575.0000,423.0000	R/O	...	Current viewport size, in pixels.
ShadEdge	3	...	DWG	**Shade** style: 　0　Shade faces; 256-color shading. 　1　Shade faces; edges background color. 　2　Hidden-line removal. 　3　16-color shading.
ShadeDif	70	...	DWG	Percent of diffuse to ambient light: 　　0　Minimum. 　70　Default. 100　Maximum
ShpName	""	...	...	Current shape name: 　.　(*Period*) Set to no default. 　""　No default.
SketchInc	0.1000	...	DWG	Sketch command's recording increment.
SKPoly	0	...	DWG	Sketch line mode: 　0　Record as lines. 　1　Record as polylines.
SnapAng	0	...	DWG	Current rotation angle for snap and grid.
SnapBase	0.0000,0.0000	...	DWG	Current origin for snap and grid.
SnapIsoPair	0	...	DWG	Current isometric drawing plane: 　0　Left isoplane. 　1　Top isoplane. 　2　Right isoplane.
SnapMode	0	...	DWG	Snap mode: 　0　Off. 　1　On.
SnapStyl	0	...	DWG	Snap style: 　0　Normal. 　1　Isometric.
SnapUnit	1.0000,1.0000	...	DWG	X,y-spacing for snap

Variable	Default	R/O	Loc	Meaning
SortEnts	96	...	REG	Object display sort order: 0 Off. 1 Object selection. 2 Object snap. 4 Redraw. 8 Slide generation. 16 Regeneration. 32 Plot. 64 PostScript output.
SplFrame	0	...	DWG	Polyline and mesh display: 0 Polyline control frame not displayed; display polygon fit mesh; 3D faces invisible edges not displayed 1 Polyline control frame displayed; display polygon defining mesh; 3D faces invisible edges displayed
SplineSegs	8	...	DWG	Number of line segments that define a splined polyline.
SplineType	6	...	DWG	Spline curve type: 5 Quadratic Bezier spline. 6 Cubic Bezier spline.
SurfTab1	6	...	DWG	Density of surfaces and meshes: 2 Minimum. 6 Default. 32766 Maximum.
SurfTab2	6	...	DWG	Density of surfaces and meshes: 2 Minimum. 6 Default. 32766 Maximum.
SurfType	6	...	DWG	Pedit surface smoothing: 5 Quadratic Bezier spline. 6 Cubic Bezier spline. 8 Bezier surface.
SurfU	6	...	DWG	Surface density in m-direction: 2 Minimum. 6 Default. 200 Maximum.
SurfV	6	...	DWG	Surface density in n-direction: 2 Minimum. 6 Default. 200 Maximum.
SysCodePage	"ansi_1252"	R/O	DWG	System code page.

Variable	Default	R/O	Loc	Meaning
T				
TabMode	0	...	...	Tablet mode: 0 Off. 1 On.
Target	0.0000,0.0000,0.0000	R/O	DWG	Target in current viewport.
TDCreate	2448860.54014699	R/O	DWG	Time and date drawing created.
TDInDwg	0.00040625	R/O	DWG	Duration drawing loaded.
TDUpdate	2448860.54014699	R/O	DWG	Time and date of last update.
TDUsrTimer	0.00040694	R/O	DWG	Time elapsed by user-timer.
TempPrefix	"d:\win\temp"	R/O	...	Path for temporary files.
TextEval	0	...	...	Interpretation of text input: 0 Literal text. 1 Read (and ! as AutoLISP code.
TextFill	0	...	DWG	Toggle fill of TrueType fonts: 0 Outline text. 1 Filled text.
TextQlty	50	...	DWG	Resolution of TrueType fonts: 0 Minimum resolution. 50 Default. 100 Maximum resolution.
TextSize	0.2000	...	DWG	Current height of text.
TextStyle	"STANDARD"	...	DWG	Current name of text style.
Thickness	0.0000	...	DWG	Current object thickness.
TileMode	1	...	DWG	Viewport mode: 0 Display tiled viewports. 1 Display overlapping viewports.
ToolTips	1	...	REG	Display tooltips: 0 Off. 1 On.
TraceWid	0.0500	...	DWG	Current width of traces.
TreeDepth	3020	...	DWG	Maximum branch depth in *xxyy* format: *xx* Model-space nodes. *yy* Paper-space nodes. >0 3D drawing. <0 2D drawing.
TreeMax	10000000	...	REG	Limits memory consumption during drawing regeneration,
TrimMode	1			Trim toggle for **Chamfer** and **Fillet** commands: 0 Leave selected edges in place. 1 Trim selected edges.

Variable	Default	R/O	Loc	Meaning
U				
UcsFollow	0	...	DWG	New UCS views: 0 No change. 1 Automatic display of plan view.
UcsIcon	1	...	DWG	▦ Display of UCS icon: 0 Off. 1 On. 2 Display at UCS origin, if possible.
UcsName	""	R/O	DWG	Name of current UCS view: "" Current UCS is unnamed.
UcsOrg	0.0000,0.0000,0.0000	R/O	DWG	Origin of current UCS relative to WCS.
UcsXDir	1.0000,0.0000,0.0000	R/O	DWG	X-direction of current UCS relative to WCS.
UcsYDir	0.0000,1.0000,0.0000	R/O	DWG	Y-direction of current UCS relative to WCS.
UndoCtl	5	R/O	...	State of undo: 0 Undo disabled. 1 Undo enabled. 2 Undo limited to one command. 4 Auto-group mode. 8 Group currently active.
UndoMarks	0	R/O	...	Current number of undo marks
UnitMode	0	...	DWG	Units display: 0 As set by **Units** command. 1 As entered by user.
UserI1–I5	0	...	...	Five user-definable integer variables
UserR1–R5	0.0000	...	...	Five user-definable real variables
UserS1–S5	""	...	...	Five user-definable string variables
V				
ViewCtr	6.2433,4.5000,0.0000	R/O	DWG	X,y-coordinate of center of current view.
ViewDir	0.0000,0.0000,1.0000	R/O	DWG	Current view direction relative to UCS.
ViewMode	0	R/O	DWG	Current view mode: 0 Normal view. 1 Perspective mode on. 2 Front clipping on. 4 Back clipping on. 8 UCS-follow on. 16 Front clip not at eye.
ViewSize	9.0000	R/O	DWG	Height of current view.
ViewTwist	0	R/O	DWG	Twist angle of current view.

Variable	Default	R/O	Loc	Meaning
VisRetain	0	...	DWG	Determines xref drawing's layer settings — on-off, freeze-thaw, color, and linetype: 0 Xref layer settings in the current drawing takes precedence for xref-dependent layers. 1 Settings for xref-dependent layers take precedence over the xref layer definition in the current drawing.
VSMax	37.4600,27.00,0.00	R/O	DWG	Upper-right corner of virtual screen.
VSMin	-24.9734,-18.00,0.00	R/O	DWG	Lower-left corner of virtual screen.
W				
WorldUcs	1	R/O	...	Matching of WCS with UCS: 0 Current UCS is not WCS. 1 UCS is WCS.
WorldView	1	...	DWG	Display during **DView** and **VPoint** commands: 0 Display UCS. 1 Display WCS.
X				
XClipFrame	0	...	DWG	○○ Visibility of xref clipping boundary: 0 Not visible. 1 Visible.
XLoadCtl	1	...	REG	○○ Controls demand loading: 0 Demand loading turned off; entire drawing is loaded. 1 Demand loading turned on; xref file opened. 2 Demand loading turned on; a *copy* of the xref file is opened.
XLoadPath	""	...	REG	○○ Path for loading xref file.
XRefCtl	0	...	REG	Determines creation of XLG xref log files: 0 File not written. 1 XLG file written.

Obsolete Commands

The following commands have been removed from AutoCAD:

Command	Introduced	Removed	Replacement	Reaction
3Dline	R9	R11	Line	"Line"
AmeLite	R11	R12	Region	"Unknown command"
AscText	R11	R13	MText	"Unknown command"
Ase...	R12	R13	ASE...	"Unknown command"
(Most R12 ASE commands were combined into fewer ASE commands.)				
AseUnload	R12	R14	Arx Unload	"Unknown command"
Axis	v1.4	R12	*none*	"Discontinued command"
DdEModes	R9	R14	Object Properties	"Discontinued command"
DL, DLine	R11	R13	MLine	"Unknown commnad"
EndRep	v1.0	v2.5	Minsert	"Discontinued command"
EndSv	v2.0	v2.5	End	"End"
Files	v1.4	R14	*Explorer*	"Discontinued command"
FilmRoll	v2.6	R13	*none*	"Unknown command"
FlatLand	R10	R11	*none*	"Cannot set Flatland to that value"
GifIn	R12	R14	ImageAttach	"No longer supported"
IgesIn, IgesOut	v2.5	R13	*none*	"Discontinued command"
MakePreview	R13	R14	*none*	"Discontinued command"
PcxIn	R12	R14	ImageAttach	"No longer supported"
PrPlot	v2.1	R12	Plot	"Discontinued command."
QPlot	v1.1	v2.0	Saveimg	"Unknown command"
RConfig	R12	R14	*none*	"Unknown command"
RenderUnload	R12	R14	Arx Unload	"Unknown command"
Repeat	v1.0	v2.5	Minsert	"Discontinued command"
SaveAsR12	R13	R14	SaveAs	"Save As Release 12 Drawing"
Snapshot	v2.0	v2.1	Saveimg	"Unknown command"
Sol...	R11	R13	*(AME commands lost their SOL-prefix.)*	
TiffIn	R12	R14	ImageAttach	"No longer supported"
VlConv	R13	R14	*none*	"Unknown command"

TIPS

■ Support for the RND (short for render) file format, used by AutoCAD and AutoShade, was dropped in Release 13.

■ The "Release 11" hidden-line removal algorithm was dropped in Release 13.

■ The **DdLModes** and **DdLType** commands will be removed in Release 15.

Index

Legend:

00   Indicates that the command name is new to AutoCAD Release 14.
~~VlConv~~   Indicates the command was discontinued from AutoCAD Release 14.

AutoCAD 14

Selection Sets
[pick] select one object.
ALL select ALL objects.
AU AUtomatic: **[pick]** or BOX (*default*).
BOX BOX (left to right: Crossing;
right to left: Window).
C Crossing.
CP Crossing Polygon.
F Fence.
G Group.
L Last.
M Multiple (no highlight).
P Previous.
SI SIngle selection.
U Undo (remove from selection).
W Window.
WP Window Polygon.

Selection modes:
A Add to selection set (*default*).
R Remove from selection set.

Insert Command Options
~ Force display of dialogue box.
* Explode block upon insertion.
= Rename block upon insertion

Color Numbers and Names
0 ... Background color.
1 R Red.
2 Y Yellow.
3 G Green.
4 C Cyan.
5 B Blue.
6 M Magenta.
7 W White.
250 - 255 ... Shades of grey.
BYLAYER ... Default color.
BYBLOCK ...

Hatch Command Options
N Normal hatching.
O Outer hatching.
I Ignore hatching.
U User-defined hatching.

Special Text Characters
For Text and DText commands:
%%c Center symbol.
%%d Degree symbol.
%%o Overline.
%%% Percent symbol.
%%p Plus-minus symbol.
%%u Underline.
%%nnn ASCII character *nnn*.

In Mtext:
\~ nonbreaking space.
**** backslash.
\{ opening brace.
\} closing brace.
\C*n* set Color *n*.
\F*x*; change to Font filename *x*.
\H*n*; change text Height to *n* units.
\L underLine.
\l turn off underLine.
\M+*n* Multibyte shape number *n*.
\O Overline.
\o turn off Overline.
\P end of Paragraph.
\Q*n*; change obliQuing angle to *n*.
\S*n*^*m* Stack character *n* over *m*.
\T*n*; change Tracking to *n*.
\U+*n* place Unicode character *n*.
\W*n*; change Width factor to *n*.

Filter Modes
Logical operators:
* Equal to any value.
= Equal.
!= Not equal.
< Less than.
> Greater than.
<= Less than or equal.
>= Greater than or equal.

Grouping operators:
**BEGIN Begin group.
AND intersection.
OR union.
NOT exclude.
XOR eXclusive or.
**END End of group.